Readings
in American
Government

TENTH EDITION

Mary P. Nichols

David K. Nichols
Baylor University

Kevin J. Burns
Christendom College

Kendall Hunt
publishing company

MARY P. NICHOLS is Professor Emerita of Political Science at Baylor University.

DAVID K. NICHOLS teaches in American politics in the department of political science at Baylor University.

KEVIN J. BURNS teaches American politics and political theory at Christendom College.

Cover image © Shutterstock, Inc.

www.kendallhunt.com
Sent all inquiries to:
4050 Westmark Drive
Dubuque, IA 52004-1840

Contents

Chapter I

The Founding and the Principles of Government

The Declaration of Independence states the principles of equality and freedom which provide the basis for an American public philosophy. American politics has revolved around interpretation and applications of those principles. Abraham Lincoln provides a classic statement of the meaning of the Declaration when he argues against the institution of slavery. The equality of rights proclaimed by the Declaration, he argues, was meant to function as a goal or standard for Americans to revere and to seek to approximate in their politics.

The equal rights that legitimate governments protect, according to the Declaration, include the rights to life, liberty, and the pursuit of happiness. Men are equal in their possession of freedom. But when equality is interpreted to mean an equal right to rule, or democratic government, a conflict between equality and freedom might result. The Lincoln-Douglas exchange reveals the danger in deriving an unqualified majority rule from the principle of equality. Douglas, supporting state sovereignty on the question of slavery, argues that slavery should be permitted in a state if a majority of its people desire it. In contrast to Douglas, Lincoln maintains that no majority can legislate slavery because that institution deprives men of their inalienable rights. There are some things that are not open to majority decision. It is necessary to limit majority rule by the ends of government stated in the Declaration.

Martin Diamond argues that the Declaration actually leaves open the possibility that other forms of government besides democracy may be legitimate. The principle of equality in the Declaration, according to Diamond, demands only that governments protect the inalienable rights of men and that they be based on the consent of the governed. Majority rule is only one way to achieve the legitimate end of government. While the Declaration established both the legitimate end and foundation of government, it is the Constitution, Diamond argues, that institutes a democracy, although one that tries to check majority rule in order to safeguard the end of government—security of rights.

The Founders, then, tried to establish a government that would combine the ends given in the Declaration with majority rule. Alternate means to these ends, the Virginia and the New Jersey Plans, were presented at the Constitutional Convention. The Virginia Plan assumes that only a

1

strong national government would protect liberty, while the New Jersey Plan reflects a concern that a strong national government operating over a large territory would eventually destroy liberty and prevent the people from governing themselves. This small republic argument is stated by the Anti-Federalist Centinel: a republic is possible only in a small territory, since only a despotism could hold a large country together. Madison, one of the authors of the Virginia Plan, gives his answer to the partisans of the small republic in his account to Jefferson of what happened at the Convention. He says that those who oppose a strong national government fearing that its distance from the people would lead to tyranny forget that majorities too can be tyrannical. They trust majorities, says Madison, because they assume that the local population is homogeneous in character, with no conflicts of interest among the parts.

Indeed, for Madison, the way to prevent majority tyranny is to establish a large republic with a flourishing commerce. Since commerce over a large territory produces many different interests, especially those based on different kinds of property, no one interest could form a majority of the whole. Majorities would be composed of a large number of smaller groups which would have to moderate their demands in order to form majorities. A tyrannical majority would therefore be less likely. Separation of powers, checks and balances, and bicameralism are institutional arrangements that work together with the extended sphere of the large republic to protect liberty. As in the formation of majorities by coalition, interest will counteract interest, in a system that necessitates compromise and mutual accommodation.

John Adams, like Madison, sought to prevent despotism and preserve liberty by the working of self-interest. And in this regard, bicameralism is a crucial part of Adam's theory of government. For Adams, however, the Senate was to represent the wealthy class of citizens, and the House to represent the poor; and since the concurrence of both was necessary to pass laws, neither class could oppress the other. Adams is perhaps too optimistic about the ability of such simple means to achieve the desired end of accommodating rich and poor to each other, and he fails to see, as did Madison, that the people of a large commercial republic would form groups not so much on the basis of the amount of property as on the kind of property they own. Indeed, Madison thought that the large commercial republic would overcome divisions between rich and poor—precisely what Adams sought to institutionalize. Because Madison understood that the two houses of Congress would not represent different classes, he sought to ensure their dissimilarity by institutional means.

Hamilton too is well aware of the benefits of economic self-interest, but attempts to elevate its operation in government above the mean or petty. At the Constitutional Convention he proposed life tenure for Senators in order to give the office sufficient power and prestige to interest the best citizens. He doubted that a shorter term "would induce the sacrifices of private affairs, which an acceptance of public trust would require, so as to ensure the services of the best citizens." He had written earlier that the best legislator would consider it "not more the duty, than the privilege of his office, to do good to mankind; from this commanding eminence, he would look down on any mean or interested pursuit." Intrigue for personal aggrandizement, Hamilton thought, would be inconsistent with the legislator's "dignity of pride" and "delicacy of honor."

Hamilton's argument for a standing army suggests that in a commercial republic men are preoccupied by their private affairs, pursuing their own economic gain. It is for this reason we cannot rely on a militia, whose members would not wish to leave their occupations and families in peacetime. But why would such private men be capable of patriotic pride in the American republic? Would such men be the material out of which Hamilton could forge America's strength? Must not there be something more than commercialism to make Hamilton's splendid commercial republic? Tocqueville explains how men in times of equality have a passion for physical well-being, or a desire to satisfy even the least wants of the body. Men continually seek greater wealth and fear economic ruin. In contrast to Hamilton, Tocqueville thought that commercial activity in times of equality produces only mediocrity.

Furthermore, although the commercial man Tocqueville describes would be a good member of the groups of which Madison hoped majorities would be formed, he might not be a good citizen of a republican or self-governing community. The Anti-Federalists, somewhat more than the Federalists, were concerned with the good character of the citizenry. When the Centinel asks how the happiness of the community can come from "jarring adverse interests," he is not asking about the efficacy of coalition majorities and checks and balances, but about the quality of life in a republic where such expedients set the tone of life. The alternative he suggests is not the aristocratic society described by Tocqueville, where only a few can attain a lofty greatness, nor Hamilton's complex, industrious society infused with pride. Rather, Centinel longs for a simple society of citizens whose liberties are preserved by their own participation in a government close to them and simple enough for them to understand. Checks and balances are not needed to prevent majority tyranny, for the people are virtuous and there are no great disparities in wealth.

The Anti-Federalists and Hamilton both have reservations against the low character of the commercial republic. Hamilton attempted to elevate the commercial spirit to great heights, and endow Americans with strength of character and breadth of vision. The Anti-Federalists, in contrast, emphasized simple or unchecked democracy, virtue in the citizens, and public spiritedness as the best means to preserve republican liberty. These reservations against the commercial republic have continued to this day in various forms, for each represent legitimate, if conflicting, aspirations. Indeed, the American regime itself is constituted by a tension or dialogue between the commercial republic and the reservations against it.

Jefferson shares with the Anti-Federalists a concern with republican liberty. He desired to divide the country into wards or "small republics" where every citizen transacted in person the public business. Because each man participated in political affairs, he would be ready to fight for his liberties and serve in the militia of his ward.

One does not have to go as far as organizing the country into wards, however, to obtain some of the benefits that the Anti-Federalists saw attached to small republics. American federalism itself institutionalizes local self-government and thus necessitates the involvement of the people in governing themselves. Federalism is a way of combining some of the advantages of a small republic with those of a national commercial republic. Federalist 39 and *McCulloch v. Maryland* present the argument for a strong national government that nevertheless maintains a sphere for independent state action.

Tocqueville shows why the community and local government that the Anti-Federalists desired is all the more important where the principle of equality prevails. Equal social conditions, Tocqueville argues, isolate or alienate men, whereas local governments serve to bring men together into communities, converting self-interested individuals into citizens who consider the interests of others as well as their own.

Robert Putnam observes a decline in Americans' participation in organizations such as bowling leagues. He sees this as a sign of the alienating effects of liberal individualism as described by Tocqueville. Without the lessons in social organization learned through participation in such groups, Putnam fears that democracy cannot function. But how can participation be encouraged?

William A. Schambra argues that we need to create a contemporary vision for government and society based upon the idea of a "new citizenship." The goal of this new citizenship according to Schambra is "the reconstruction of civil society, the return of America to the self-governing republic described by Alexis de Tocqueville and envisioned by the Founding Fathers." This "new citizenship" stands in contrast to the idea of national community created by progressive thinkers such as Herbert Croly and Walter Lippman, and championed by politicians from Theodore Roosevelt to Lyndon Johnson, Jimmy Carter, and Bill Clinton. This Progressive idea sought to attain at the national level the kind of community Anti-Federalists desired, with its public spirited sacrifice and egalitarianism. By combining the Anti-Federalist view of community with the nationalism of the Federalists, the progressives sought an easy resolution of these two strands of American political thought. But Schambra points out that the idea of national community is not only based on unreasonable expectations of human nature, but also undermines the local governments and civic associations, where public spiritedness is actually nurtured. It is not enough, Schambra concludes, for conservatives to preach against the evils of an ever-expanding national government based upon the national community ideal, they must also develop a positive message of citizenship that shows that they too "care enough about the whole."

1

Thomas Jefferson

The Declaration of Independence (1776)

When in the Course of human events, it becomes necessary for one people to dissolve the political bands which have connected them with another, and to assume among the powers of the earth, the separate and equal station to which the Laws of Nature and of Nature's God entitle them, a decent respect to the opinions of mankind requires that they should declare the causes which impel them to the separation. We hold these truths to be self-evident, that all men are created equal, that they are endowed by their Creator with certain unalienable Rights, that among these are Life, Liberty and the pursuit of Happiness. That to secure these rights, Governments are instituted among Men, deriving their just powers from the consent of the governed, That whenever any Form of Government becomes destructive to these ends it is the Right of the People to alter or to abolish it, and to institute new Government, laying its foundation on such principles and organizing its powers in such form, as to them shall seem most likely to effect their Safety and Happiness. Prudence, indeed, will dictate that Governments long established should not be changed for light and transient causes; and accordingly all experience hath shewn, that mankind are more disposed to suffer, while evils are sufferable, than to right themselves by abolishing the forms to which they are accustomed. But when a long train of abuses and usurpations, pursuing invariably the same Object evinces a design to reduce them under absolute Despotism, it is their right, it is their duty, to throw off such Government, and to provide new Guards for their future security. Such has been the patient sufferance of these Colonies; and such is now the necessity which constrains them to alter their former Systems of Government. The history of the present King of Great Britain is a history of repeated injuries and usurpations, all having in direct object the establishment of an absolute Tyranny over these States. To prove this, let Facts be

The text reprinted here is from *The Papers of Thomas Jefferson*, edited by Julian P. Boyd (Princeton: Princeton University Press, 1950–). This is the text of the parchment copy of the Declaration (now in the National Archives) which was signed on August 2, 1776. It is generally accepted as the most authentic of various copies.

submitted to a candid world. He has refused his Assent to Laws, the most wholesome and necessary for the public good. He has forbidden his Governors to pass Laws of immediate and pressing importance, unless suspended in their operation till his Assent should be obtained; and when so suspended, he has utterly neglected to attend to them. He has refused to pass other Laws for the accommodation of large districts of people, unless those people would relinquish the right of Representation in the Legislature, a right inestimable to them and formidable to tyrants only. He has called together legislative bodies at places unusual, uncomfortable, and distant from the depository of their public Records, for the sole purpose of fatiguing them into compliance with his measures. He has dissolved Representative Houses repeatedly, for opposing with manly firmness his invasions on the rights of the people. He has refused for a long time, after dissolutions, to cause others to be elected; whereby the Legislative powers, incapable of Annihilation, have returned to the People at large for their exercise; the State remaining in the mean time exposed to all the dangers of invasion from without, and convulsions within. He has endeavoured to prevent the population of these States; for that purpose obstructing the Laws for Naturalization of Foreigners; refusing to pass others to encourage their migrations hither, and raising the conditions of new Appropriations of Lands. He has obstructed the Administration of Justice, by refusing his Assent to Laws for establishing Judiciary powers. He has made Judges dependent on his Will alone, for the tenure of their offices, and the amount and payment of their salaries. He has erected a multitude of New Offices, and sent hither swarms of Officers to harrass our people, and eat out their substance. He has kept among us, in times of peace, standing Armies without the Consent of our legislatures. He has affected to render the Military independent of and superior to the Civil power. He has combined with others to subject us to a jurisdiction foreign to our constitution, and unacknowledged by our laws; giving his Assent to their Acts of pretended Legislation: For Quartering large bodies of armed troops among us: For protecting them, by a mock Trial, from punishment for any Murders which they should commit on the Inhabitants of these States: For cutting off our Trade with all parts of the world: For imposing Taxes on us without our Consent: For depriving us in many cases of the benefits of Trial by Jury: For transporting us beyond Seas to be tried for pretended offences: For abolishing the free System of English Laws in a neighbouring Province, establishing therein an Arbitrary government, and enlarging its Boundaries so as to render it at once an example and fit instrument for introducing the same absolute rule into these Colonies: For taking away our Charters, abolishing our most valuable Laws, and altering fundamentally the Forms of our Governments: For suspending our own Legislatures, and declaring themselves invested with power to legislate for us in all cases whatsoever. He has abdicated Government here, by declaring us out of his Protection and waging

War against us. He has plundered our seas, ravaged our Coasts, burnt our towns, and destroyed the Lives of our people. He is at this time transporting large Armies of foreign Mercenaries to compleat the works of death, desolation and tyranny, already begun with circumstances of Cruelty & perfidy scarcely paralleled in the most barbarous ages, and totally unworthy the Head of a civilized nation. He has constrained our fellow Citizens taken Captive on the high Seas to bear Arms against their Country, to become the executioners of their friends and Brethren, or to fall themselves by their Hands. He has excited domestic insurrections amongst us, and has endeavoured to bring on the inhabitants of our frontiers, the merciless Indian Savages, whose known rule of warfare, is an undistinguished destruction of all ages, sexes and conditions. In every stage of these Oppressions We have Petitioned for Redress in the most humble terms: Our repeated Petitions have been answered only by repeated injury. A Prince, whose character is thus marked by every act which may define a Tyrant, is unfit to be the ruler of a free people. Nor have We been wanting in attentions to our Brittish brethren. We have warned them from time to time of attempts by their legislature to extend an unwarrantable jurisdiction over us. We have reminded them of the circumstances of our emigration and settlement here. We have appealed to their native justice and magnanimity, and we have conjured them by the ties of our common kindred to disavow these usurpations, which, would inevitably interrupt our connections and correspondence. They too have been deaf to the voice of Justice and of consanguinity. We must, therefore, acquiesce in the necessity, which denounces our Separation, and hold them, as we hold the rest of mankind, Enemies in War, in Peace Friends.

We, therefore, the Representatives of the United States of America, in General Congress, Assembled, appealing to the Supreme Judge of the world for the rectitude of our intentions, do, in the Name, and by Authority of the good People of these Colonies, solemnly publish and declare, That these United Colonies are, and of Right ought to be Free and Independent States; that they are Absolved from all Allegiance to the British Crown, and that all political connection between them and the State of Great Britain, is and ought to be totally dissolved; and that as Free and Independent States, they have full Power to levy War, conclude Peace, contract Alliances, establish Commerce, and to do all other Acts and Things which Independent States may of right do. And for the support of this Declaration, with a firm reliance on the protection of divine Providence, we mutually pledge to each other our Lives, our Fortunes and our sacred Honor.

2

Abraham Lincoln

The Meaning of the Declaration of Independence (1857)

. . . Chief Justice Taney, in his opinion in the Dred Scott case, admits that the language of the Declaration is broad enough to include the whole human family, but he and Judge Douglas argue that the authors of that instrument did not intend to include negroes, by the fact that they did not at once, actually place them on an equality with the whites. Now this grave argument comes to just nothing at all, by the other fact, that they did not at once, *or ever afterwards,* actually place all white people on an equality with one or another. And this is the staple argument of both the Chief Justice and the Senator, for doing this obvious violence to the plain unmistakable language of the Declaration. I think the authors of that notable instrument intended to include all men, but they did not intend to declare all men equal in all respects. They did not mean to say all were equal in color, size, intellect, moral developments, or social capacity. They defined with tolerable distinctness, in what respects they did consider all men created equal—equal in "certain inalienable rights, among which are life, liberty, and the pursuit of happiness." This they said, and this meant. They did not mean to assert the obvious untruth, that all were then actually enjoying that equality, nor yet, that they were about to confer it immediately upon them. In fact they had no power to confer such a boon. They meant simply to declare the *right,* so that the *enforcement* of it might follow as fast as circumstances should permit. They meant to set up a standard maxim for free society, which should be familiar to all, and revered by all; constantly looked to, constantly labored for, and even though never perfectly attained, constantly approximated, and thereby constantly spreading and deepening its influence, and augmenting the happiness and value of life to all people of all colors everywhere. The assertion that "all men are created equal" was of no practical use in effecting our separation from Great Britain; and it was placed in the Declaration, not for that, but for future use. Its authors

From Speech at Springfield, Illinois, June 26, 1857, in *The Collected Works of Abraham Lincoln*, Vol. II, Rutgers University Press, 1953.

meant it to be, thank God, it is now proving itself, a stumbling block to those who in after times might seek to turn a free people back into the hateful paths of despotism. They knew the proneness of prosperity to breed tyrants, and they meant when such should re-appear in this fair land and commence their vocation they should find left for them at least one hard nut to crack.

I have now briefly expressed my view of the *meaning and objects* of that part of the Declaration of Independence which declares that "all men are created equal."

Now let us hear Judge Douglas' view of the same subject, as I find it in the printed report of his late speech. Here it is:

"No man can vindicate the character, motives and conduct of the signers of the Declaration of Independence, except upon the hypothesis that they referred to the white race alone, and not to the African, when they declared all men to have been created equal—that they were speaking of British subjects on this continent being equal to British subjects born and residing in Great Britain—that they were entitled to the same inalienable rights, and among them were enumerated life, liberty, and the pursuit of happiness. The Declaration was adopted for the purpose of justifying the colonists in the eyes of the civilized world in withdrawing their allegiance from the British crown, and dissolving their connection with the mother country."

My good friends, read that carefully over some leisure hour, and ponder well upon it—see what a mere wreck—mangled ruin—it makes of our once glorious Declaration.

"They were speaking of British subjects on this continent being equal to British subjects born and residing in Great Britain!" Why, according to this, not only negroes but white people outside of Great Britain and America are not spoken of in that instrument. The English, Irish, and Scotch, along with white Americans, were included to be sure, but the French, Germans, and other white people of the world are all gone to pot along with the Judge's inferior races.

I had thought the Declaration promised something better than the condition of British subjects; but no, it only meant that we should be *equal* to them in their own oppressed and *unequal* condition. According to that, it gave no promise that having kicked off the King and Lords of Great Britain, we should not at once be saddled with a King and Lords of our own.

I had thought the Declaration contemplated the progressive improvement in the condition of all men everywhere; but no, it merely "was adopted for the purpose of justifying the colonists in the eyes of the civilized world in withdrawing their allegiance from the British crown, and dissolving their connection with the mother country." Why, that object having been effected some eighty years ago, the Declaration is of no practical use now—mere rubbish—old wadding left to rot on the battle-field after the victory is won.

I understand you are preparing to celebrate the "Fourth," tomorrow week. What for? The doings of that day had no reference to the present; and quite half of you are not even descendants of those who were referred to at that day. But I suppose you will celebrate; and will even go so far as to read the Declaration. Suppose after you read it once in the old fashioned way, you read it once more with Judge Douglas' version. It will then run thus: "We hold these truths to be self-evident that all British subjects who were on this continent eighty-one years ago, were created equal to all British subjects born and *then* residing in Great Britain."

And now I appeal to all—to Democrats as well as others,—are you really willing that the Declaration shall be thus frittered away?—thus left no more at most, than an interesting memorial of the dead past? thus shorn of its vitality, and practical value; and left without the *germ* or even the *suggestion* of the individual rights of man in it? . . .

3

Stephen A. Douglas and Abraham Lincoln

Exchange on State Sovereignty and the Problem of Majority Rule (1858)

SENATOR DOUGLAS' SPEECH

LADIES AND GENTLEMEN: It is now nearly four months since the canvass between Mr. Lincoln and myself commenced. On the 16th of June the Republican Convention assembled at Springfield and nominated Mr. Lincoln as their candidate for the U.S. Senate, and he, on that occasion, delivered a speech in which he laid down what he understood to be the Republican creed and the platform on which he proposed to stand during the contest. The principal points in that speech of Mr. Lincoln's were: First, that this government could not endure permanently divided into free and slave States, as our fathers made it; that they must all become free or all become

From the Lincoln-Douglas Debates, Oct. 15, 1858, in *The Collected Works of Abraham Lincoln*, Vol. III, Rutgers University Press, 1953.

slave; all become one thing or all become the other, otherwise this Union could not continue to exist. I give you his opinions almost in the identical language he used. His second proposition was a crusade against the Supreme Court of the United States because of the Dred Scott decision; urging as an especial reason for his opposition to that decision that it deprived the negroes of the rights and benefits of that clause in the Constitution of the United States which guarantees to the citizens of each State, all the rights, privileges, and immunities of the citizens of the several States. . . . In that Chicago speech [of July 11] he even went further than he had before, and uttered sentiments in regard to the negro being on an equality with the white man. (That's so.) He adopted in support of this position the argument which Lovejoy and Codding, and other Abolition lecturers had made familiar in the northern and central portions of the State, to wit: that the Declaration of Independence having declared all men free and equal, by Divine law, also that negro equality was an inalienable right, of which they could not be deprived. He insisted, in that speech, that the Declaration of Independence included the negro in the clause asserting that all men were created equal, and went so far as to say that if one man was allowed to take the position, that it did not include the negro, others might take the position that it did not include other men. He said that all these distinctions between this man and that man, this race and the other race, must be discarded, and we must all stand by the Declaration of Independence, declaring that all men were created equal. . . .

I took up Mr. Lincoln's . . . propositions in my several speeches, analyzed them, and pointed out what I believed to be the radical errors contained in them. First, in regard to his doctrine that this government was in violation of the law of God which says, that a house divided against itself cannot stand, I repudiated it as a slander upon the immortal framers of our constitution. I then said, have often repeated, and now again assert, that in my opinion this government can endure forever, (good) divided into free and slave States as our fathers made it,—each State having the right to prohibit, abolish or sustain slavery just as it pleases. ("Good," "right," and cheers.) This government was made upon the great basis of the sovereignty of the States, the right of each State to regulate its own domestic institutions to suit itself, and that right was conferred with understanding and expectation that inasmuch as each locality had separate interests, each locality must have different and distinct local and domestic institutions, corresponding to its wants and interests. Our fathers knew when they made the government, that the laws and institutions which were well adapted to the green mountains of Vermont, were unsuited to the rice plantations of South Carolina. They knew then, as well as we know now, that the laws and institutions which would be well adapted to the beautiful prairies of Illinois would not be suited to the mining regions of California. They knew that in a Republic as broad as this, having such a variety of soil, climate and interest, there must necessarily be a corresponding variety of local laws—the policy and institutions of each State adapted to its condition and wants. For this reason this Union was established on the right of each State to do as it pleased on the question of slavery, and every other question; and the various States were not allowed to complain of, much less interfere, with the policy of their neighbors. ("That's good doctrine," "that's the doctrine," and cheers.)

Suppose the doctrine advocated by Mr. Lincoln and the abolitionists of this day had prevailed when the Constitution was made, what would have been the result? Imagine for a moment that Mr. Lincoln had been a member of the convention that framed the Constitution of the United States, and that when its members were about to sign that wonderful document, he had arisen in that convention as he did at Springfield this summer, and addressing himself to the President, had said "a house divided against itself cannot stand: (laughter) this government divided into free and slave States cannot endure, they must all be free or all be slave, they must all be one thing or all be the other, otherwise, it is a violation of the law of God, and cannot continue to exist;"—suppose Mr. Lincoln had convinced that body of sages, that that doctrine was sound. What would have been the result? Remember that the Union was then composed of thirteen States, twelve of which were slaveholding and one free. Do you think that the one free State would have outvoted the twelve slaveholding States, and thus have secured the abolition of slavery? (No, no.) On the other hand, would not the twelve slaveholding States have outvoted the one free State, and thus have fastened slavery, by a Constitutional provision, on every foot of the American Republic forever? You see that if this abolition doctrine of Mr. Lincoln had prevailed when the government was made, it would have established slavery as a permanent institution, in all the States whether they wanted it or not, and the question for us to determine in Illinois now as one of the free States is, whether or not we are willing, having become the majority section, to enforce a doctrine on the minority, which we would have resisted with our heart's blood had it been attempted on us when we were in a minority. ("We never will," "good, good," and cheers.) How has the South lost her power as the majority section in this Union, and how have the free States gained it, except under the operation of that principle which declares the right of the people of each State and each territory to form and regulate their domestic institutions in their own way. It was under that principle that slavery was abolished in New Hampshire, Rhode Island, Connecticut, New York, New Jersey, and Pennsylvania; it was under that principle that one half of the slaveholding States became free; it was under that principle that the number of free States increased until from being one out of twelve States, we have grown to be the majority of States of the whole Union, with the power to control the House of Representatives and Senate, and the power, consequently, to elect a President by Northern votes without the aid of a Southern State. Having obtained this power under the operation of that great principle, are you now prepared to abandon the principle and declare that merely because we have the power you will wage a war against the Southern States and their institutions until you force them to abolish slavery everywhere. (No, never, and great applause.) . . .

I hold that there is no power on earth, under our system of government, which has the right to force a constitution upon an unwilling people. (That's so.) Suppose there had been a majority of ten to one in favor of slavery in Kansas, and suppose there had been an abolition President, and an abolition administration, and by some means the abolitionists succeeded in forcing an abolition constitution on those slaveholding people, would the people of the South have submitted to that act for one instant. (No, no.) Well, if you of the South would not have submitted to it a day, how can you, as fair, honorable, and honest men insist on putting a slave constitution on a people who desire a free State. ("That's so," and cheers.) Your safety and ours depend upon both of us acting in good faith, and living up to that great principle which asserts the right of every people to form and regulate their domestic institutions to suit themselves, subject only to the Constitution of the United States. ("That's the doctrine," and immense applause.) . . .

I hold that it is a violation of the fundamental principles of this government to throw the weight of federal power into the scale, either in favor of the free or the slave States. Equality among all the States of this Union is a fundamental principle in our political system. We have no more right to throw the weight of the federal government into the scale in favor of the slaveholding than the free States, and last of all should our friends in the South consent for a moment that Congress should withhold its powers either way when they know that there is a majority against them in both Houses of Congress. . . .

The whole South are rallying to the support of the doctrine that if the people of a Territory want slavery they have a right to have it, and if they do not want it that no power on earth can force it upon them. I hold that there is no principle on earth more sacred to all the friends of freedom than that which says that no institution, no law, no constitution, should be forced on an unwilling people contrary to their wishes. . . . I say to you that there is but one hope, one safety for this country, and that is to stand immovably by that principle which declares the right of each State and each territory to decide these questions for themselves. (Hear him, hear him.) This government was founded on that principle, and must be administered in the same sense in which it was founded.

But the Abolition party really think that under the Declaration of independence the negro is equal to the white man, and that negro equality is an inalienable right conferred by the Almighty, and hence, that all human laws in violation of it are null and void. With such men it is no use for me to argue. I hold that the signers of the Declaration of Independence had no reference to negroes at all when they declared all men to be created equal. They did not mean negro, nor the savage Indians, nor the Fejee Islanders, nor any other barbarous race. They were speaking of white men. ("It's so," "it's so," and cheers.) They alluded to men of European birth and European descent—to white men, and to none others, when they declared that doctrine. ("That's the truth.") I hold that this government was established on the white basis. It was established by white men for the benefit of white men and their posterity forever, and should be administered by white men, and none others. But it does not follow, by any means, that merely because the negro is not a citizen, and merely because he is not our equal, that, therefore, he should be a slave. On the contrary, it does follow, that we ought to extend to the negro race, and to all other dependent races all the rights, all the privileges, and all the immunities which they can exercise consistently with the safety of society. Humanity requires that we should give them all these privileges; christianity commands that we should extend those privileges to them. The question then arises what are those privileges, and what is the nature and extent of them. My answer is that that is a question which each State must answer for itself. We in Illinois have decided it for ourselves. We tried slavery, kept it up for twelve years, and finding that it was not profitable we abolished it for that reason, and became a free State. We adopted in its stead the policy that a negro in this State shall not be a slave and shall not be a citizen. We have a right to adopt that policy. For my part I think it is a wise and sound policy for us. You in Missouri must judge for yourselves whether it is a wise policy for you. If you choose to follow our example, very good; if you reject it, still well, it is your business, not ours. So with Kentucky. Let Kentucky adopt a policy to suit herself. If we do not like it we will keep away from it, and if she does not like ours let her stay at home, mind her own business and let us alone. If the people of all the States will act on that great principle, and each State mind its own business, attend to its own affairs, take care of its own negroes and not meddle with its neighbors, then there will be peace between the North and the South, and East and the West, throughout the whole Union. (Cheers.) Why can we not thus have peace? Why should we thus allow a sectional party to agitate this country, to array the North against the South, and convert us into enemies instead of friends, merely that a few ambitious men may ride into power on a sectional hobby? How long is it since these ambitious Northern men wished for a sectional organization? Did any one of them dream of a sectional party as long as the North was the weaker section and the South the stronger? Then all were opposed to sectional parties; but the moment the North obtained the majority in the House and Senate by the admission of California, and could elect a President without the aid of Southern votes, that moment ambitious Northern men formed a scheme to excite the North against the South, and make the people be governed in their votes by geographical lines, thinking that the North, being the stronger section, would outvote the South, and consequently they, the leaders, would ride into office on a sectional hobby. I am told that my hour is out. It was very short.

Mr. Lincoln's Reply

. . . I have stated upon former occasions, and I may as well state again, what I understand to be the real issue in this controversy between Judge Douglas and myself. On the point of my wanting to make war between the free and the slave States, there has been no issue between us. So, too, when he assumes that I am in favor of introducing a perfect social and political equality between the white and black races. These are false issues, upon which Judge Douglas has tried to force the controversy. There is no foundation in truth for the charge that I maintain either of these propositions. The real issue in this controversy—the one pressing upon every mind—is the sentiment on the part of one class that looks upon the institution of slavery *as a wrong,* and of another class that *does not* look upon it as a wrong. The sentiment that contemplates the institution of slavery in this country as a wrong is the sentiment of the Republican party. It is the sentiment around which all their actions—all their arguments circle—from which all their propositions radiate. They look upon it as being a moral, social and political wrong; and while they contemplate it as such, they nevertheless have due regard for its actual existence among us, and the difficulties of getting rid of it in any satisfactory way and to all the constitutional obligations thrown about it. Yet having a due regard for these, they desire a policy in regard to it that looks to its not creating any more danger. They insist that it should as far as may be, *be treated* as a wrong, and one of the methods of treating it as a wrong is to *make provision that it shall grow no larger.* (Loud applause.) They also desire a policy that looks to a peaceful end of slavery at sometime, as being wrong. These are the views they entertain in regard to it as I understand them; and all their sentiments—all their arguments and propositions are brought within this range. I have said and I repeat it here, that if there be a man amongst us who does not think that the institution of slavery is wrong in any one of the aspects of which I have spoken, he is misplaced and ought not to be with us. And if there be a man amongst us who is so impatient of it as a wrong as to disregard its actual presence among us and the difficulty of getting rid of it suddenly in a satisfactory way, and to disregard the constitutional obligations thrown about it, that man is misplaced if he is on our platform. We disclaim sympathy with him in practical action. He is not placed properly with us.

On this subject of treating it as a wrong, and limiting its spread, let me say a word. Has any thing ever threatened the existence of this Union save and except this very institution of Slavery? What is it that we hold most dear amongst us? Our own liberty and prosperity. What has ever threatened our liberty and prosperity save and except this institution of Slavery? If this is true, how do you propose to improve the condition of things by enlarging Slavery—by spreading it out and making it bigger? You may have a wen or a cancer upon your person and not be able to cut it out lest you bleed to death; but surely it is no way to cure it, to engraft it and spread it over your whole body. That is no proper way of treating what you regard a wrong. You see this peaceful way of dealing with it as a wrong—restricting the spread of it, and not allowing it to go into new countries where it has not already existed. That is the peaceful way, the old-fashioned way, the way in which the fathers themselves set us the example.

On the other hand, I have said there is a sentiment which treats it as *not* being wrong. That is the Democratic sentiment of this day. I do not mean to say that every man who stands within that range positively asserts that it is right. That class will include all who positively assert that it is right, and all who like Judge Douglas treat it as indifferent and do not say it is either right or wrong. These two classes of men fall within the general class of those who do not look upon it as a wrong. And if there be among you anybody who supposes that he as a Democrat, can consider himself "as much opposed to slavery as anybody," I would like to reason with him. You never treat it as a wrong. What other thing that you consider as a wrong, do you deal with as you deal with that? Perhaps you *say* it is wrong, *but your leader never does, and you quarrel with anybody who says it is wrong*. Although you pretend to say so yourself you can find no fit place to deal with it as a wrong. You must not say anything about it in the free States, *because it is not here*. You must not say anything about it in the slave States, *because it is there*. You must not say anything about it in the pulpit, because that is religion and has nothing to do with it. You must not say anything about it in politics, *because that will disturb the security of "my place."* (Shouts of laughter and cheers.) There is no place to talk about it as being a wrong, although you say yourself it *is* a wrong. But finally you will screw yourself up to the belief that if the people of the slave States should adopt a system of gradual emancipation on the slavery question, you would be in favor of it. You would be in favor of it. You say that is getting it in the right place, and you would be glad to see it succeed. But you are deceiving yourself. You all know that Frank Blair and Gratz Brown, down there in St. Louis, undertook to introduce that system in Missouri. They fought as valiantly as they could for the system of gradual emancipation which you pretend you would be glad to see succeed. Now I will bring you to the test. After a hard fight they were beaten, and when the news came over here you threw up your hats *and hurrahed for Democracy*. (Great applause and laughter.) More than that, take all the argument made in favor of the system you have proposed, and it carefully excludes the idea that there is anything wrong in the institution of slavery. The arguments to sustain that policy carefully excluded it. Even here to-day you heard Judge Douglas quarrel with me because I uttered a wish that it might sometime come to an end. Although Henry Clay could say he wished every slave in the United States was in the country of his ancestors, I am denounced by those pretending to respect Henry Clay for uttering a wish that it might sometime, in some peaceful way, come to an end. The Democratic policy in regard to that institution will not tolerate the merest breath, the slightest hint, of the least degree of wrong about it. Try it by some of Judge Douglas' arguments. He says he "don't care whether it is voted up or voted down" in the Territories. I do not care myself in dealing with that expression, whether it is intended to be expressive of his individual sentiments on the subject, or only of the national policy he desires to have established. It is alike valuable for my purpose. Any man can say that who does not see anything wrong in slavery, but no man can logically say it who does see a wrong in it; because no man can logically say he don't care whether a wrong is voted up or voted down. He may say he don't care whether an indifferent thing is voted up or down, but he must logically have a choice between a right thing and a wrong thing. He contends that whatever community wants slaves has a right to have them. So they have if it is not a wrong. But if it is a wrong, he cannot say people have a right to do wrong. He says that upon the score of equality, slaves should be allowed to go in a new Territory, like other property. This is strictly logical if there is no difference between it and other property. If it and other property are equal, his argument is entirely logical. But if you insist that one is wrong and the other right, there is no use to institute a comparison between right and wrong. You may turn over everything in the Democratic policy from beginning to end, whether in the shape it takes on the statute book, in the shape it takes in the Dred Scott decision, in the shape it takes in conversation or the shape it takes in short maxim-like arguments—it everywhere carefully excludes the idea that there is anything wrong in it. . . .

4

Martin Diamond

The Revolution of Sober Expectations (1975)

. . . What wants understanding is precisely how our institutions of government sprang from the principle of the Declaration of Independence. How and to what extent were they generated by the Declaration of Independence? And what more had to be added actually to frame those institutions? . . .

We must read the Declaration closely to free ourselves from two centuries of obscuring usage. We have transformed the Declaration in our minds by reading the phrase "consent of the governed" as meaning rule by majorities, that is, democratic government. Indeed we think of the Declaration as our great democratic document, as the clarion call to and the guide to our democratic nature. But the Declaration does *not* say that consent is the means by which government is to operate. Rather, it says that consent is necessary only to institute the government, that is, to establish it.

The people need not, then, *establish* a government which *operates* by means of their consent. In fact, the Declaration says that they may organize government on "such principles" as they choose, and they may choose "any form of government" they deem appropriate to secure their rights. That is, the Declaration was not prescribing any particular form of government at all, but rather was following John Locke's contract theory, which taught the right of the people, in seeking to secure their liberties, to establish *any* form of government. And by any form of government the Declaration emphatically includes—as any literate eighteenth century reader would have understood—not only the democratic form of government but also aristocratic and monarchical government as well. That is why, for example, the Declaration has to submit facts to a "candid world" to prove the British king guilty of a "long train of abuses." Tom Paine, by way of contrast, could dispose of King George more simply. Paine

From Diamond, "The Revolution of Sober Expectations," in *America's Continuing Revolution: An Act of Conservation*, published by American Enterprise Institute, 1975. Reprinted by permission.

deemed George III unfit to rule simply because he was a *king* and kingly rule was illegitimate as such. The fact that George was a "Royal Brute" was only frosting on the cake; for Paine his being royal was sufficient warrant for deposing him. But the Declaration, on the contrary, is obliged to prove that George was indeed a brute. That is, the Declaration holds George III "unfit to be the ruler of a free people" not because he was a king, but because he was a *tyrannical* king. Had the British monarchy continued to secure to the colonists their rights, as it had prior to the long train of abuses, the colonists would not have been entitled to rebel. It was only the fact, according to the Declaration, that George had become a tyrannical king that supplied the warrant for revolution.

Thus the Declaration, strictly speaking, is neutral on the question of forms of government: *any* form is legitimate provided it secures equal freedom and is instituted by popular consent. . . .

It is to the constitution that we must ultimately turn as the completion of the American Revolution. As to those democratic institutions, the Declaration says no more than this: If you choose the democratic form of government, rather than the aristocratic or monarchic or any mixture thereof, it must be a democratic government which secures to all people their unalienable rights. But how to do that? The Declaration is silent. . . .

What was truly revolutionary in the American Revolution and its Declaration of Independence was that liberty, civil liberty—the doctrine of certain unalienable rights—was made the end of government. Not, as had been the case for millennia, whatever end power haphazardly imposed upon government; nor any longer the familiar variety of ends—not virtue, not piety, not privilege or wealth, not merely protection, and not empire and dominion; but now deliberately the principle of liberty. . . .

While modern followers of Edmund Burke may warn of the dangers of devotion to abstract principles, they cannot blink aside the revolutionary American devotion to precisely such an abstract principle. The American truth was undeniably as abstract as, say, Robespierre's tyrannizing truth or Lenin's tyrannizing truth. And yet there is indeed something moderate and nonutopian in the American devotion to liberty which warrants Burkean celebration. Whence then the difference? Wherein was the American Revolution one of sober expectations while the Jacobin and Leninist were revolutions of unbridled expectations? The answer lies not in degrees of devotion to abstractness, but in the substantive nature of the principle each was abstractly devoted to. It is one thing to be abstractly devoted to the Reign of Virtue or to unlimited equality in all respects or to mass fraternity or to classless society or to the transformation of the human condition itself, and quite another to be devoted to the abstract principle of civil liberty. Civil liberty as a goal constrains its followers to moderation, legality, and rootedness in regular institutions. Moreover, moderate civil liberty does not require terror and tyranny for its fulfillment.

Liberty is an abstract principle capable of achievement; Jacobin or Leninist equality or mass fraternity are not. Moderate civil liberty is a possible dream, utopian equality and fraternity are impossible dreams. And the recent popular song to the contrary notwithstanding, the political pursuit of impossible dreams leads to terror and tyranny in the vain effort to actualize what cannot be. . . .

[S]obriety also lies in the Founding Fathers' coolheaded and cautious acceptance of democracy. Perhaps not a single American voice was raised in unqualified, doctrinaire praise of democracy. On the contrary, there was universal recognition of the problematic character of democracy, a concern for its weaknesses and a fear of its dangers. The debate in American life during the founding decade gradually became a debate over how to create a decent democratic regime. Contrary to our too complacent modern perspective regarding democracy, which assumes that a government cannot be decent unless democratic, our Founding Fathers more skeptically, sensibly, and soberly, were concerned how to make this new government *decent even though democratic*. All the American revolutionaries, whether they were partisans of the theory that democratic republics had to be small or agrarian or only loosely confederated in order to remain free, or whether they retained the traditional idea that democracy had to be counterbalanced by nobility or wealth, or whether they subscribed to the large-republic theory implicit in the new Constitution—all the American revolutionaries knew that democracy was a problem in need of constant solution, in constant need of moderation, in constant need of institutions and measures to mitigate its defects and guard against its dangers. . . .

The half-revolution begun in 1776 reached its completion only when the peculiar American posture toward democracy received its definitive form in the framing and ratification of the Constitution a decade later. . . . [I]n contemplating that convention we would find the answer to our earlier question: how did our institutions spring from the Declaration and what had to be added to bring those institutions into being? They sprang on the one hand from the love of free government inspired by the *noble sentiments* of Jefferson's Declaration, and on the other hand from the theoretic *wisdom* of James Madison whose sober clarity regarding democracy gave the shape and thrust to our unique democratic form of government and way of life. . . .

5

Centinel

The Small Republic Argument (1787)

. . . The late Convention have submitted to your consideration a plan of a new federal government. The subject is highly interesting to your future welfare. Whether it be calculated to promote the great ends of civil society, viz., the happiness and prosperity of the community, it behoves you well to consider, uninfluenced by the authority of names. Instead of that frenzy of enthusiasm, that has actuated the citizens of Philadelphia, in their approbation of the proposed plan, before it was possible that it could be the result of a rational investigation into its principles, it ought to be dispassionately and deliberately examined on its own intrinsic merit, the only criterion of your patronage. If ever free and unbiased discussion was proper or necessary, it is on such an occasion. All the blessings of liberty and the dearest privileges of freemen are now at stake and dependent on your present conduct. . . .

The late revolution having effaced in a great measure all former habits, and the present institutions are so recent, that there exists not that great reluctance to innovation, so remarkable in old communities, and which accords with reason, for the most comprehensive mind cannot foresee the full operation of material changes on civil polity. . . .

I am fearful that the principles of government inculcated in Mr. Adams' treatise, and enforced in the numerous essays and paragraphs in the newspapers, have misled some well designing members of the late Convention. . . . He asserts that the administrators of every government, will ever be actuated by views of private interest and ambition, to the prejudice of the public good; that therefore the only effectual method to secure the rights of the people and promote their welfare, is to create an opposition of interests. . . .

Suppose a government could be formed and supported on such principles, would it answer the great purposes of civil society? If the administrators

From "Centinel I" (believed to have been written by Samual Bryan), in *Pennsylvania and the Federal Constitution 1787–1788*, ed. John Bach McMaster and Frederick D. Stone, The Historical Society of Pennsylvania, 1888.

of every government are actuated by views of private interest and ambition, how is the welfare and happiness of the community to be the result of such jarring adverse interests?

Therefore, as different orders in government will not produce the good of the whole, we must recur to other principles. I believe it will be found that the form of government, which holds those entrusted with power in the greatest responsibility to their constituents, the best calculated for freemen. A republican, or free government, can only exist where the body of the people are virtuous, and where property is pretty equally divided. In such a government the people are the sovereign and their sense or opinion is the criterion of every public measure; for when this ceases to be the case, the nature of the government is changed, and an aristocracy, monarchy or despotism will rise on its ruin. The highest responsibility is to be attained in a simple structure of government, for the great body of the people never steadily attend to the operations of government, and for want of due information are liable to be imposed on. If you complicate the plan by various orders, the people will be perplexed and divided in their sentiments about the source of abuses or misconduct; some will impute it to the senate, others to the house of representatives, and so on, that the interposition of the people may be rendered imperfect or perhaps wholly abortive. But if, imitating the constitution of Pennsylvania, you vest all the legislative power in one body of men (separating the executive and judicial) elected for a short period, and necessarily excluded by rotation from permanency, and guarded from precipitancy and surprise by delays imposed on its proceedings, you will create the most perfect responsibility; for then, whenever the people feel a grievance, they cannot mistake the authors, and will apply the remedy with certainty and effect, discarding them at the next election. This tie of responsibility will obviate all the dangers apprehended from a single legislature, and will the best secure the rights of the people. . . .

[I]f the United States are to be melted down into one empire, it becomes you to consider whether such a government, however constructed, would be eligible in so extended a territory; and whether it would be practicable, consistent with freedom? It is the opinion of the greatest writers, that a very extensive country cannot be governed on democratical principles, on any other plan than a confederation of a number of small republics, possessing all the powers of internal government, but united in the management of their foreign and general concerns.

It would not be difficult to prove, that anything short of despotism could not bind so great a country under one government; and that whatever plan you might, at the first setting out, establish, it would issue in a despotism.

If one general government could be instituted and maintained on principles of freedom, it would not be so competent to attend to the various local concerns and wants, of every particular district, as well as the peculiar governments, who are nearer the scene, and possessed of superior means of information; besides, if the business of the *whole* union is to be managed by one government, there would not be time. Do we not already see, that the inhabitants in a number of larger States, who are remote from the seat of government, are loudly complaining of the inconveniences and disadvantages they are subjected to on this account, and that, to enjoy the comforts of local government, they are separating into smaller divisions? . . .

6

Selections from the Records of the Federal Convention of 1787

A. THE VIRGINIA PLAN

Mr. Randolph (then) opened the main business. He expressed his regret, that it should fall to him, rather than those, who were of longer standing in life and political experience, to open the great subject of their mission. But, as the convention had originated from Virginia, and his colleagues supposed, that some proposition was expected from them, they had imposed this task on him.

He then commented on the difficulty of the crisis, and the necessity of preventing the fulfillment of the prophecies of the American downfall. . . .

In speaking of the defects of the confederation he professed a high respect for its authors, and considered them as having done all that patriots could do, in the then infancy of the science, of constitutions, & of confederacies,— when the inefficiency of requisitions was unknown—no commercial discord had arisen among any states—no rebellion had appeared as in Mass.—foreign debts had not become urgent—the havoc of paper money had not been foreseen—treaties had not been violated—and perhaps nothing better could be obtained from the jealousy of the states with regard to their sovereignty.

From *Records of the Federal Convention of 1787*, ed. Max Farrand.

He then proceeded to enumerate the defects: 1. that the confederation produced no security against foreign invasion; congress not being permitted to prevent a war nor to support it by their own authority—Of this he cited many examples; most of which tended to show, that they could not cause infractions of treaties or of the law of nations, to be punished: that particular states might by their conduct provoke war without control; and that neither militia nor draughts being fit for defense on such occasions, enlistments only could be successful, and these could not be executed without money.

2. that the federal government could not check the quarrels between states, nor a rebellion in any not having constitutional power nor did it have means to interpose according to the exigency.

3. that there were many advantages, which the U.S. might acquire, which were not attainable under the confederation—such as a productive impost—counteraction of the commercial regulations of other nations—pushing of commerce. . . .

4. that the federal government could not defend itself against the encroachments from the states.

5. that it was not even paramount to the state constitutions, ratified as it was in many of the states.

6. He next reviewed the danger of our situation, appealed to the sense of the best friends of the U.S.—the prospect of anarchy from the laxity of government everywhere; and to other considerations.

7. He then proceeded to the remedy; the basis of which he said, must be the republican principle.

He proposed as conformable to his ideas the following resolutions, which he explained one by one.

Resolutions proposed by Mr. Randolph in Convention. May 29, 1787.

1. Resolved that the articles of Confederation ought to be so corrected & enlarged as to accomplish the objects proposed by their institution; namely, "common defense, security of liberty and general welfare."

2. Resd. therefore that the rights of suffrage in the National Legislature ought to be proportioned to the quotas of contribution, or to the number of free inhabitants, as the one or the other rule may seem best in different cases.

3. Resd. that the National Legislature ought to consist of two branches.

4. Resd. that the members of the first branch of the National Legislature ought to be elected by the people of the several States every _____ for the term of _____; to be of the age of _____ years at least, to receive liberal stipends by which they may be compensated for the devotion

of their time to public service; to be ineligible to any office established by a particular State, or under the authority of the United States, except those peculiarly belonging to the functions of the first branch, during the term of service, and for the space of _____ after its expiration; to be incapable of re-election for the space of _____ after the expiration of their term of service, and to be subject to recall.

5. Resd. that the members of the second branch of the National Legislature ought to be elected by those of the first, out of a proper number of persons nominated by the individual Legislatures, to be of the age of _____ years at least; to hold their offices for a term sufficient to ensure their independency, to receive liberal stipends, by which they may be compensated for the devotion of their time to public service; and to be ineligible to any office established by a particular State, or under the authority of the United States, except those peculiarly belonging to the functions of the second branch, during the term of service, and for the space of _____ after the expiration thereof.

6. Resd. that each branch ought to possess the right of originating Acts; that the National Legislature ought to be impowered to enjoy the Legislative Rights vested in Congress by the Confederation & moreover to legislate in all cases to which the separate States are incompetent, or in which the harmony of the United States may be interrupted by the exercise of individual Legislation; to negative all laws passed by the several States, contravening in the opinion of the National Legislature the articles of Union; and to call forth the force of the Union against any member of the Union failing to fulfill its duty under the articles thereof.

7. Resd. that a National Executive be instituted; to be chosen by the National Legislature for the term of _____ years, to receive punctually at stated times, a fixed compensation for the services rendered, in which no increase or diminution shall be made so as to affect the Magistracy, existing at the time of increase or diminution, and to be ineligible a second time; and that besides a general authority to execute the National laws, it ought to enjoy the Executive rights vested in Congress by the Confederation.

8. Resd. that the Executive and a convenient number of the National Judiciary, ought to compose a council of revision with authority to examine every act of the National Legislature before it shall operate, & every act of a particular Legislature before a Negative thereon shall be final; and that the dissent of the said Council shall amount to a rejection, unless the Act of the National Legislature be again passed, or that of a particular Legislature be again negatived by _____ of the members of each branch.

9. Resd. that a National Judiciary be established. . . .

10. Resd. that a Republican Government & the territory of each State, except in the instance of a voluntary junction of Government & territory, ought to be guaranteed by the United States to each State. . . .

11. Resd. that the Legislative Executive & Judiciary powers within the several States ought to be bound by oath to support the articles of Union.

12. Resd. that the amendments which shall be offered to the Confederation, by the Convention ought at a proper time, or times, after the approbation of Congress to be submitted to an assembly or assemblies of Representatives, recommended by the several Legislatures to be expressly chosen by the people, to consider & decide thereon.

B. THE NEW JERSEY PLAN

Mr. Patterson, laid before the Convention the plan which he said several of the deputations wished to be substituted in place of that proposed by Mr. Randolph. . . .

The propositions from N. Jersey moved by Mr. Patterson were in the words following.

1. Resd. that the articles of Confederation ought to be so revised, corrected & enlarged, as to render the federal Constitution adequate to the exigencies of Government, & the preservation of the Union.

2. Resd. that in addition to the powers vested in the U. States in Congress, by the present existing articles of Confederation, they be authorized to pass acts for raising a revenue by levying a duty or duties on all goods or merchandizes of foreign growth or manufacture, imported into any part of the U. States, by stamps on paper, vellum or parchment and by a postage on all letters or packages passing through the general post-office, to be applied to such federal purposes as they shall deem proper & expedient; to make rules & regulations for the collection thereof; and the same from time to time, to alter & amend in such manner as they shall think proper: to pass Acts for the regulation of trade & commerce as well with foreign nations as with each other provided that all punishments, fines, forfeitures & penalties to be incurred for contravening such acts rules and regulations shall be adjudged by the Common law Judiciaries of the State in which any offense contrary to the true intent & meaning of such Acts rules & regulations shall have been committed or perpetrated, with liberty of commencing in the first instance all suits & prosecutions for that purpose in the superior common law Judiciary in such State, subject nevertheless, for the correction of all errors, both in law & fact in rendering judgment, to an appeal to the Judiciary of the U. States. . . .

3. Resd. that the U. States in Congress be authorized to elect a federal Executive to consist of _____ persons, to continue in office for the term of _____ years, to receive punctually at stated times a fixed compensation for their services, in which no increase or diminution shall be made so as to affect the persons composing the Executive at the time of such

increase or diminution, to be paid out of the federal treasury; to be incapable of holding any other office or appointment during their time of service and for _____ years thereafter; to be ineligible a second time, & removable by Congress on application by a majority of the Executives of the several States; that the Executives besides their general authority to execute the federal acts ought to appoint all federal officers not otherwise provided for, & to direct all military operations; provided that none of the persons composing the federal Executive shall on any occasion take command of any troops, so as personally to conduct any enterprise as General, or in other capacity.

4. Resd. that a federal Judiciary be established. . . .

5. Resd. that all Acts of the U. States in Congress made by virtue & in pursuance of the powers hereby & by the articles of confederation vested in them, and all Treaties made & ratified under the authority of the U. States shall be the supreme law of the respective States so far forth as those Acts or Treaties shall relate to the said States or their Citizens, and that the Judiciary of the several States shall be bound thereby in their decisions, any thing in the respective laws of the Individual States to the contrary notwithstanding; and that if any State, or any body of men in any State, shall oppose or prevent the carrying into execution such acts or treaties, the federal Executive shall be authorized to call forth the power of the Confederated States, or so much thereof as may be necessary to enforce and compel an obedience to such Acts, or an observance of such Treaties. . . .

C. Alexander Hamilton: Proposal for a New Government

The extent of the Country to be governed, discouraged him. The expense of a general Govt. was also formidable; unless there were such a diminution of expense on the side of the State Govts. as the case would admit. If they were extinguished, he was persuaded that great economy might be obtained by substituting a general Govt. He did not mean however to shock the public opinion by proposing such a measure. On the other hand he saw no *other* necessity for declining it. They are not necessary for any of the great purposes of commerce, revenue, or agriculture. Subordinate authorities he was aware would be necessary. There must be district tribunals: corporations for local purposes. But cui bono, the vast & expensive apparatus now appertaining to the States. The only difficulty of a serious nature which occurred to him, was that of drawing representatives from the extremes to the center of the community. What inducements can be offered that will suffice? The moderate wages for the 1st. branch, would only be a bait to little demagogues. Three dollars or thereabouts he supposed would be the utmost. The Senate he feared from a similar cause, would be filled by certain undertakers who wish for particular offices under the Govt. This view of the subject almost led him to despair that a Republican Govt. could be established over so great an extent. He was sensible at the same time that it would be unwise to propose one of any other form. In his private opinion he had no scruple in declaring, supported as he was by the opinions of so many of the wise & good, that the British Govt. was the best in the world: and that he doubted much whether any thing short of it would do in America. He hoped gentlemen of different opinions would bear with him in this, and begged them to recollect the change of opinion on this subject which had taken place and was still going on. It was once thought that the power of Congress was amply sufficient to secure the end of their institution. The error was now seen by every one. The members most tenacious of republicanism, he observed, were as loud as any in declaiming against the vices of democracy. This progress of the public mind led him to anticipate the time, when others as well as himself would join in the praise bestowed by Mr. Neckar on the British Constitution, namely, that it is the only Govt. in the world "which unites public strength with individual security."—In every community where industry is encouraged, there will be a division of it into the few & the many. Hence separate interests will arise. There will be debtors & creditors &c. Give all power to the many, they will oppress the few. Give all power to the few they will oppress the many. Both therefore ought to have power, that each may defend itself against the other. To the want of this check we owe our paper money—installment laws &c. To the proper adjustment of it the British owe the excellence of their Constitution. Their house of Lords is a most noble institution. Having nothing to hope for by a change, and a sufficient interest by means of their property, in being faithful to the national interest, they form a permanent barrier against every pernicious innovation, whether attempted on the part of the Crown or of the Commons. No temporary Senate will have firmness enough to answer the purpose. . . Gentlemen differ in their opinions concerning the necessary checks, from the different estimates they form of the human passions. They suppose seven years a sufficient period to give the Senate an adequate firmness, from not duly considering the amazing violence & turbulence of the democratic spirit. When a great object of Govt. is pursued, which seizes the popular passions, they spread like wild fire, and become irresistable. He appealed to the gentlemen from the N. England States whether experience had not there verified the remark. As to the Executive, it seemed to be admitted that no good one could be established on republican principles. Was not this giving up the merits of the question; for can there be a good govt. without a good Executive. The English model was the only good one on this subject. The hereditary interest of the King was so interwoven with that of the nation, and his personal emoluments so great, that he was placed above the danger of being corrupted from abroad—and at the same time was both sufficiently independent and sufficiently controlled, to answer the purpose of the institution at home. One of the weak sides of Republics was their being liable to foreign influence & corruption. Men of little character, acquiring great power become easily the tools of intermedling neighbors. Sweden was a striking instance. The French & English had each their parties during the late Revolution which was effected by the predominant influence of the former. What is the inference from all these observations? That we ought to go as far in order to attain stability and permanency, as republican principles will admit. Let one branch of the Legislature hold their places for life or at least during good-behavior. Let the Executive also be for life. He appealed to the feelings of the members present whether a term of seven years, would induce the sacrifices of private affairs which an acceptance of public trust would require, so as to ensure the services of the best citizens. On this plan we should have in the Senate a permanent will, a weighty interest, which would answer essential purposes. But is this a Republican Govt. it will be asked? Yes, if all the Magistrates are appointed, and vacancies are filled, by the people, or a process of election originating with the people. He was sensible that an Executive constituted as he proposed would have in fact but little of the power and independence that might be necessary. On the other plan of appointing him for 7 years, he thought the Executive ought to have but little power. He would be ambitious, with the means of making creatures; and as the object of his ambition would be to *prolong* his power, it is probable that in case of a war, he would avail himself of the emergency, to evade or refuse a degradation from his place. An Executive for life has not this motive for forgetting his fidelity, and will therefore be a safer depositary of power. It will be objected probably, that such an executive will be an *elective Monarch*, and will give birth to the tumults which characterize that form of Govt. He would reply that *Monarch* is an indefinite term. It marks not either the degree or duration of power. If this Executive Magistrate would be a monarch for life—the other proposed by the Report from the Committee of the whole, would be a monarch for seven years. The circumstance of being elective was also applicable to both. It had been observed by judicious writers that elective monarchies would be the best if they could be guarded against the *tumults* excited by the ambition and intrigues of competitors. . . .

7

James Madison

The Work of the Constitutional Convention (1787)

To Thomas Jefferson

Dear Sir:

You will herewith receive the result of the convention, which continued its session till the 17th of September. . . .

It appeared to be the sincere and unanimous wish of the convention to cherish and preserve the union of the states. No proposition was made, no suggestion was thrown out, in favor of a partition of the empire into two or more confederacies.

It was generally agreed that the objects of the Union could not be secured by any system founded on the principle of a confederation of sovereign states. A *voluntary* observance of the federal law by all the members could never be hoped for. A *compulsive* one could evidently never be reduced to practice, and if it could, involved equal calamities to the innocent & the guilty, the necessity of a military force both obnoxious & dangerous, and in general a scene resembling much more a civil war than the administration of a regular government.

Hence was embraced the alternative of a government which instead of operating, on the states, should operate without their intervention on the individuals composing them; and hence the change in the principle and proportion of representation.

This ground-work being laid, the great objects which presented themselves were (1) to unite a proper energy in the Executive, and a proper stability in the Legislative departments, with the essential characters of Republican Government. (2) to draw a line of demarkation which would give to the General Government every power requisite for general purposes, and leave to the States every power which might be most beneficially administered by them. (3) to provide for the different interests of different parts of the Union. (4) to adjust the clashing pretensions of the large and small States. Each

From *The Writings of James Madison*, Oct. 24, 1787, Vol. V, G. P. Putnam's Sons, 1904.

of these objects was pregnant with difficulties. The whole of them together formed a task more difficult than can be well conceived by those who were not concerned in the execution of it. Adding to these considerations the natural diversity of human opinions on all new and complicated subjects, it is impossible to consider the degree of concord which ultimately prevailed as less than a miracle.

The first of these objects, as respects the Executive, was peculiarly embarrassing. On the question whether it should consist of a single person, or a plurality of co-ordinate members, on the mode of appointment, on the duration in office, on the degree of power, on the re-eligibility, tedious and reiterated discussions took place. The plurality of co-ordinate members had finally but few advocates. Governor Randolph was at the head of them. The modes of appointment proposed were various, as by the people at large—by electors chosen by the people—by the Executives of the States—by the Congress, some preferring a joint ballot of the two Houses—some a separate concurrent ballot, allowing to each a negative on the other house—some, a nomination of several candidates by one House, out of whom a choice should be made by the other. Several other modifications were started. The expedient at length adopted seemed to give pretty general satisfaction to the members. As to the duration in office, a few would have preferred a tenure during good behavior—a considerable number would have done so in case an easy & effectual removal by impeachment could be settled. It was much agitated whether a long term, seven years for example, with a subsequent & perpetual ineligibility, or a short term with a capacity to be re-elected, should be fixed. In favor of the first opinion were urged the danger of a gradual degeneracy of re-elections from time to time, into first a life and then a hereditary tenure, and the favorable effect of an incapacity to be reappointed on the independent exercise of the Executive authority. On the other side it was contended that the prospect of necessary degradation would discourage the most dignified characters from aspiring to the office, would take away the principal motive to the faithful discharge of its duties—the hope of being rewarded with a reappointment would stimulate ambition to violent efforts for holding over the Constitutional term—and instead of producing an independent administration, and a firmer defense of the constitutional rights of the department, would render the officer more indifferent to the importance of a place which he would soon be obliged to quit forever, and more ready to yield to the encroachments of the Legislature of which he might again be a member. The questions concerning the degree of power turned chiefly on the appointment to offices, and the control on the Legislature. An absolute appointment to all offices—to some offices—to no offices, formed the scale of opinions on the first point. On the second, some contended for an absolute negative, as the only possible mean of reducing to practice the theory of a free Government which forbids a mixture of the Legislative & Executive powers. Others would be content with a revisionary power, to be overruled by three fourths of both Houses. It was warmly urged that the judiciary department should be associated in the revision. The idea of some was that a separate revision should be given to the two departments—that if either objected two thirds, if both, three fourths, should be necessary to overrule.

In forming the Senate, the great anchor of the Government, the questions as they came within the first object, turned mostly on the mode of appointment, and the duration of it. The different modes proposed were (1) by the House of Representatives, (2) by the Executive. (3) by electors chosen by the people for the purpose. (4) by the State Legislature. On the point of duration, the propositions descended from good behavior to four years, through the intermediate terms of nine, seven, six, & five years. The election of the other branch was first determined to be triennial, and afterwards reduced to biennial.

The second object, the due partition of power between the General & local Governments, was perhaps of all, the most nice and difficult. A few contended for an entire abolition of the States; some for indefinite power of Legislation in the Congress, with a negative on the laws of the States; some for such a power without a negative; some for a limited power of legislation, with such a negative; the majority finally for a limited power without the negative. The question with regard to the negative underwent repeated discussions, and was finally rejected by a bare majority. As I formerly intimated to you my opinion in favor of this ingredient, I will take this occasion of explaining myself on the subject. Such a check on the States appears to me necessary (1) to prevent encroachments on the General authority, (2) to prevent instability and injustice in the legislation of the States.

1. Without such a check in the whole over the parts, our system involves the evil of imperia in imperio. If a complete supremacy somewhere is not necessary in every Society, a controlling power at least is so, by which the general authority may be defended against encroachments of the subordinate authorities, and by which the latter may be restrained from encroachments on each other. If the supremacy of the British Parliament is not necessary as has been contended, for the harmony of that Empire; it is evident I think that without the royal negative or some equivalent control, the unity of the system would be destroyed. The want of some such provision seems to have been mortal to the ancient Confederacies, and to be the disease of the modern. Of the Lycian confederacy little is known. That of the Amphyctions is well known to have been rendered of little use whilst it lasted, and in the end to have been destroyed, by the predominance of the local over the federal authority. . . . The case of the United Netherlands is in point. The authority of a Stadtholder, the influence of a Standing Army, the common interest in the conquered possessions, the pressure of surrounding danger, the guarantee of foreign powers, are not sufficient

to secure the authority and interest of the generality against the anti-federal tendency of the provincial sovereignties. . . . Still more to the purpose is our own experience both during the war and since the peace. Encroachments of the States on the general authority, sacrifices of national to local interests, interferences of the measures of different States, form a great part of the history of our political system. It may be said that the new Constitution is founded on different principles, and will have a different operation. I admit the difference to be material. It presents the aspect rather of a feudal system of republics, if such a phrase may be used, than of a Confederacy of independent States. And what has been the progress and event of the feudal Constitutions? In all of them a continual struggle between the head and the inferior members, until a final victory has been gained in some instances by one, in others, by the other of them. In one respect indeed there is a remarkable variance between the two cases. In the feudal system the sovereign, though limited, was independent; and having no particular sympathy of interests with the Great Barons, his ambition had as full play as theirs in the mutual projects of usurpation. In the American Constitution the general authority will be derived entirely from the subordinate authorities. The Senate will represent the States in their political capacity; the other House will represent the people of the States in their individual capacity. The former will be accountable to their constituents at moderate, the latter at short periods. The President also derives his appointment from the States, and is periodically accountable to them. This dependence of the General on the local authorities, seems effectually to guard the latter against any dangerous encroachments of the former; whilst the latter, within their respective limits, will be continually sensible of the abridgement of their power, and be stimulated by ambition to resume the surrendered portion of it. We find the representatives of Counties and Corporations in the Legislatures of the States, much more disposed to sacrifice the aggregate interest, and even authority, to the local views of their constituents, than the latter to the former. I mean not by these remarks to insinuate that an esprit de corps will not exist in the National Government or that opportunities may not occur of extending its jurisdiction in some points. I mean only that the danger of encroachments is much greater from the other side, and that the impossibility of dividing powers of legislation, in such a manner, as to be free from different constructions by different interests, or even from ambiguity in the judgment of the impartial, requires some such expedient as I contend for. Many illustrations might be given of this impossibility. . . . The line of distinction between the power of regulating trade and that of drawing revenue from it, which was once considered the barrier of our liberties, was found on fair discussion, to be absolutely undefinable. . . . Even the boundaries between the Executive, Legislative, & Judiciary powers, though in general so strongly marked in themselves, consist in many instances of mere shades of difference. It may be said that the Judicial authority, under our new system will keep the States within their proper limits, and supply the place of a negative on their laws. The answer is, that it is more convenient to prevent the passage of a law than to declare it void after it is passed; that this will be particularly the case, where the law aggrieves individuals, who may be unable to support an appeal against a State to the supreme Judiciary; that a State which would violate the Legislative rights of the Union, would not be very ready to obey a Judicial decree in support of them, and that a recurrence to force, which, in the event of disobedience would be necessary, is an evil which the new Constitution meant to exclude as far as possible.

2. A constitutional negative on the laws of the States seems equally necessary to secure individuals against encroachments on their rights. The mutability of the laws of the States is found to be a serious evil. The injustice of them has been so frequent and so flagrant as to alarm the most steadfast friends of Republicanism. I am persuaded I do not err in saying that the evils issuing from these sources contributed more to that uneasiness which produced the Convention, and prepared the Public mind for a general reform, than those which accrued to our national character and interest from the inadequacy of the Confederation to its immediate objects. A reform therefore which does not make provision for private rights, must be materially defective. The restraints against paper emissions, and violations of contracts are not sufficient. Supposing them to be effectual as far as they go, they are short of the mark. Injustice may be effected by such an infinitude of legislative expedients, that where the disposition exists it can only be controlled by some provision which reaches all cases whatsoever. The partial provision made, supposes the disposition which will evade it. It may be asked how private rights will be more secure under the Guardianship of the General Government than under the State Governments, since they are both founded on the republican principle which refers the ultimate decision to the will of the majority, and are distinguished rather by the extent within which they will operate, than by any material difference in their structure. A full discussion of this question would, if I mistake not, unfold the true Principles of Republican Government, and prove in contradiction to the concurrent opinions of the theoretical writers that this form of Government, in order to effect its purposes, must operate not within a small but an extensive sphere. I will state some of the ideas which have occurred to me on the subject. Those who contend for a simple Democracy, or a pure republic, actuated by the sense of the majority, and operating within narrow limits, assume or suppose a case which is altogether fictitious. They found their reasoning on the idea, that the people composing the Society, enjoy not only an equality of political rights; but that they have all precisely the same interests, and the same feelings in every respect. Were this in reality the case, their reasoning would be conclusive. The interest of the majority would be that of the minority also; the decisions could only turn on mere opinion concerning the good of the whole, of which the major voice would be the safest criterion; and within a small sphere, this

voice could be most easily collected, and the public affairs most accurately managed. We know however that no society ever did or can consist of so homogeneous a mass of Citizens. In the savage state indeed, an approach is made towards it; but in that state little or no Government is necessary. In all civilized societies, distinctions are various and unavoidable. A distinction of property results from that very protection which a free Government gives to unequal faculties of acquiring it. There will be rich and poor; creditors and debtors; a landed interest, a monied interest, a mercantile interest, a manufacturing interest. These classes may again be subdivided according to the different productions of different situations & soils, & according to different branches of commerce and of manufactures. In addition to these natural distinctions, artificial ones will be founded, on accidental differences in political, religious, or other opinions, or an attachment to the persons of leading individuals. However erroneous or ridiculous these grounds of dissention and faction may appear to the enlightened Statesman or the benevolent philosopher, the bulk of mankind who are neither Statesmen nor Philosophers, will continue to view them in a different light. It remains then to be enquired whether a majority having any common interest, or feeling any common passion, will find sufficient motives to restrain them from oppressing the minority. An individual is never allowed to be a judge or even a witness in his own cause. If two individuals are under the bias of interest or enmity against a third, the rights of the latter could never be safely referred to the majority of the three. Will two thousand individuals be less apt to oppress one thousand, or two hundred thousand one hundred thousand? Three motives only can restrain in such cases: (1) a prudent regard to private or partial good, as essentially involved in the general and permanent good of the Whole. This ought no doubt to be sufficient of itself. Experience however shows that it has little effect on individuals, and perhaps still less on a collection of individuals, and least of all on a majority with the public authority in their hands. If the former are ready to forget that honesty is the best policy; the last do more. They often proceed on the converse of the maxim, that whatever is politic is honest. (2) respect for character. This motive is not found sufficient to restrain individuals from injustice. And loses its efficacy in proportion to the number which is to divide the pain or the blame. Besides as it has reference to public opinion, which is that of the majority, the standard is fixed by those whose conduct is to be measured by it. (3) Religion. The inefficacy of this restraint on individuals is well known. The conduct of every popular Assembly, acting on oath, the strongest of religious ties, shows that individuals join without remorse in acts against which their consciences would revolt, if proposed to them separately in their closets. When indeed Religion is kindled into enthusiasm, its force like that of other passions is increased by the sympathy of a multitude. But enthusiasm is only a temporary state of Religion, and whilst it lasts will hardly be seen with pleasure at the helm. Even in its coolest state, it has been much oftener a motive to oppression than a restraint from it. If then there must be different interests and parties in society; and a majority when united by a common interest or passion cannot be restrained from oppressing the minority, what remedy can be found in a republican Government, where the majority must ultimately decide, but that of giving such an extent to its sphere, that no common interest or passion will be likely to unite a majority of the whole number in an unjust pursuit. In a large Society, the people are broken into so many interests and parties, that a common sentiment is less likely to be felt, and the requisite concert less likely to be formed, by a majority of the whole. The same security seems requisite for the civil as for the religious rights of individuals. If the same sect form a majority and have the power, other sects will be sure to be depressed. Divide et impera, the reprobated axiom of tyranny, is under certain qualifications, the only policy, by which a republic can be administered on just principles. It must be observed however that this doctrine can only hold within a sphere of a mean extent. As in too small a sphere oppressive combinations may be too easily formed against the weaker party; so in too extensive a one, a defensive concert may be rendered too difficult against the oppression of those entrusted with the administration. The great desideratum in Government is, so to modify the sovereignty as that it may be sufficiently neutral between different parts of the Society to control one part from invading the rights of another, and at the same time sufficiently controlled itself, from setting up an interest adverse to that of the entire Society. In absolute monarchies, the Prince may be tolerably neutral towards different classes of his subjects but may sacrifice the happiness of all to his personal ambition or avarice. In small republics, the sovereign will is controlled from such a sacrifice of the entire Society, but is not sufficiently neutral towards the parts composing it. In the extended Republic of the United States, the General Government would hold a pretty even balance between the parties of particular States, and be at the same time sufficiently restrained by its dependence on the community, from betraying its general interests.

Begging pardon for this immoderate digression I return to the third object above mentioned, the adjustments of the different interests of different parts of the Continent. Some contended for an unlimited power over trade including exports as well as imports, and over slaves as well as other imports; some for such a power, provided the concurrence of two thirds of both Houses were required; Some for such a qualification of the power, with an exemption of exports and slaves, others for an exemption of exports only. The result is seen in the Constitution. S. Carolina & Georgia were inflexible on the point of the slaves.

The remaining object created more embarrassment, and a greater alarm for the issue of the Convention than all the rest put together. The little States insisted on retaining their equality in both branches, unless a complete abolition of the State Governments should take place; and made an equality in the Senate a sine qua non. The large States on the other hand urged that as the new Government was to be drawn principally from the people immediately and was to operate directly on them, not on the States; and consequently as the States would lose that importance which is now proportioned to the importance of their voluntary compliances with the requisitions of Congress, it was necessary that the representation in both Houses should be in proportion to their size. It ended in the compromise which you will see, but very much to the dissatisfaction of several members from the large States. . . .

8

James Madison

Federalist 10 (1787)

Among the numerous advantages promised by a well-constructed Union, none deserves to be more accurately developed than its tendency to break and control the violence of faction. The friend of popular governments never finds himself so much alarmed for their character and fate as when he contemplates their propensity to this dangerous vice. He will not fail, therefore, to set a due value on any plan which, without violating the principles to which he is attached, provides a proper cure for it. The instability, injustice, and confusion introduced into the public councils have, in truth, been the mortal diseases under which popular governments have everywhere perished, as they continue to be the favorite and fruitful topics from which the adversaries to liberty derive their most specious declamations. The valuable improvements made by the American constitutions on the popular models, both ancient and modern, cannot certainly be too much admired; but it would be an unwarrantable partiality to contend that they have as effectually obviated the danger on this side, as was wished and expected. Complaints are everywhere heard from our most considerate and virtuous citizens; equally the friends of public and private faith and of public and personal liberty, that our governments are too unstable, that the public good is

From *The Federalist.*

disregarded in the conflicts or rival parties, and that measures are too often decided, not according to the rules of justice and the rights of the minor party, but by the superior force of an interested and overbearing majority. However anxiously we may wish that these complaints had no foundation, the evidence of known facts will not permit us to deny that they are in some degree true. It will be found, indeed, on a candid review of our situation, that some of the distresses under which we labor have been erroneously charged on the operation of our governments; but it will be found, at the same time, that other causes will not alone account for many of our heaviest misfortunes; and, particularly, for that prevailing and increasing distrust of public engagements and alarm for private rights which are echoed from one end of the continent to the other. These must be chiefly, if not wholly, effects of the unsteadiness and injustice with which a factious spirit has tainted our public administration.

By a faction I understand a number of citizens, whether amounting to a majority or minority of the whole, who are united and actuated by some common impulse of passion, or of interest, adverse to the rights of other citizens, or to the permanent and aggregate interests of the community.

There are two methods of curing the mischiefs of faction: the one, by removing its causes; the other, by controlling its effects.

There are again two methods of removing the causes of faction: the one, by destroying the liberty which is essential to its existence; the other, by giving to every citizen the same opinions, the same passions, and the same interests.

It could never be more truly said than of the first remedy that it was worse than the disease. Liberty is to faction what air is to fire, an aliment without which it instantly expires. But it could not be a less folly to abolish liberty, which is essential to political life, because it nourishes faction than it would be to wish the annihilation of air, which is essential to animal life, because it imparts to fire its destructive agency.

The second expedient is as impracticable as the first would be unwise. As long as the reason of man continues fallible, and he is at liberty to exercise it, different opinions will be formed. As long as the connection subsists between his reason and his self-love, his opinions and his passions will have a reciprocal influence on each other; and the former will be objects to which the latter will attach themselves. The diversity in the faculties of men, from which the rights of property originate, is not less an insuperable obstacle to a uniformity of interests. The protection of these faculties is the first object of government. From the protection of different and unequal faculties of acquiring property, the possession of different degrees and kinds of property immediately results; and from the influence of these on the sentiments and views of the respective proprietors ensues a division of the society into different interests and parties.

The latent causes of faction are thus sown in the nature of man; and we see them everywhere brought into different degrees of activity, according to the different circumstances of civil society. A zeal for different opinions concerning religion, concerning government, and many other points, as well of speculation as of practice; an attachment to different leaders ambitiously contending for pre-eminence and power; or to persons of other descriptions whose fortunes have been interesting to the human passions, have, in turn, divided mankind into parties, inflamed them with mutual animosity, and rendered them much more disposed to vex and oppress each other than to co-operate for their common good. So strong is this propensity of mankind to fall into mutual animosities that where no substantial occasion presents itself the most frivolous and fanciful distinctions have been sufficient to kindle their unfriendly passions and excite their most violent conflicts. But the most common and durable source of factions has been the various and unequal distribution of property. Those who hold and those who are without property have ever formed distinct interests in society. Those who are creditors, and those who are debtors, fall under a like discrimination. A landed interest, a manufacturing interest, a mercantile interest, a moneyed interest, with many lesser interests, grow up of necessity in civilized nations, and divide them into different classes, actuated by different sentiments and views. The regulation of these various and interfering interests forms the principal task of modern legislation and involves the spirit of party and faction in the necessary and ordinary operations of government.

No man is allowed to be a judge in his own cause, because his interest would certainly bias his judgment, and, not improbably, corrupt his integrity. With equal, nay with greater reason, a body of men are unfit to be both judges and parties at the same time; yet what are many of the most important acts of legislation but so many judicial determinations, not indeed concerning the rights of single persons, but concerning the rights of large bodies of citizens? And what are the different classes of legislators but advocates and parties to the causes which they determine? Is a law proposed concerning private debts? It is a question to which the creditors are parties on one side and the debtors on the other. Justice ought to hold the balance between them. Yet the parties are, and must be, themselves the judges; and the most numerous party, or in other words, the most powerful faction must be expected to prevail. Shall domestic manufacturers be encouraged, and in what degree, by restrictions on foreign manufacturers? are questions which would be differently decided by the landed and the manufacturing classes, and probably by neither with a sole regard to justice and the public good. The apportionment of taxes on the various descriptions of property is an act which seems to require the most exact impartiality; yet there is, perhaps, no legislative act in which greater opportunity and temptation are given to a predominant party to trample on the rules of justice. Every shilling with which they overburden the inferior number is a shilling saved to their own pockets.

It is in vain to say that enlightened statesmen will be able to adjust these clashing interests and render them all subservient to the public good. Enlightened statesmen will not always be at the helm. Nor, in many cases, can such an adjustment be made at all without taking into view indirect and remote considerations, which will rarely prevail over the immediate interest which one party may find in disregarding the rights of another or the good of the whole.

The inference to which we are brought is that the *causes* of faction cannot be removed and that relief is only to be sought in the means of controlling its *effects*.

If a faction consists of less than a majority, relief is supplied by the republican principle, which enables the majority to defeat its sinister views by regular vote. It may clog the administration, it may convulse the society; but it will be unable to execute and mask its violence under the forms of the Constitution. When a majority is included in a faction, the form of popular government, on the other hand, enables it to sacrifice to its ruling passion or interest both the public good and the rights of other citizens. To secure the public good and private rights against the danger of such a faction, and at the same time to preserve the spirit and the form of popular government, is then the great object to which our inquiries are directed. Let me add that it is the great desideratum by which alone this form of government can be rescued from the opprobrium under which it has so long labored and be recommended to the esteem and adoption of mankind.

By what means is this object attainable? Evidently by one of two only. Either the existence of the same passion or interest in a majority at the same time must be prevented, or the majority, having such coexistent passion or interest, must be rendered, by their number and local situation, unable to concert and carry into effect schemes of oppression. If the impulse and the opportunity be suffered to coincide, we well know that neither moral nor religious motives can be relied on as an adequate control. They are not found to be such on the injustice and violence of individuals, and lose their efficacy in proportion to the number combined together, that is, in proportion as their efficacy becomes needful.

From this view of the subject it may be concluded that a pure democracy, by which I mean a society consisting of a small number of citizens, who assemble and administer the government in person, can admit of no cure for the mischiefs of faction. A common passion or interest will, in almost every case, be felt by a majority of the whole; a communication and concert results from the form of government itself; and there is nothing to check the inducements to sacrifice the weaker party or an obnoxious individual. Hence it is that such democracies have ever been spectacles of turbulence and contention; have ever been found incompatible with personal security or the rights of property; and have in general been as short in their lives as they have been violent in their deaths. Theoretic politicians, who have patronized this species of government, have erroneously supposed that by reducing mankind to a perfect equality in their political rights, they would at the same time be perfectly equalized and assimilated in their possessions, their opinions, and their passions.

A republic, by which I mean a government in which the scheme of representation takes place, opens a different prospect and promises the cure for which we are seeking. Let us examine the points in which it varies from pure democracy, and we shall comprehend both the nature of the cure and the efficacy which it must derive from the Union.

The two great points of difference between a democracy and a republic are: first, the delegation of the government, in the latter, to a small number of citizens elected by the rest; secondly, the greater number of citizens and greater sphere of country over which the latter may be extended.

The effect of the first difference is, on the one hand, to refine and enlarge the public views by passing them through the medium of a chosen body of citizens, whose wisdom may best discern the true interest of their country and whose patriotism and love of justice will be least likely to sacrifice it to temporary or partial considerations. Under such a regulation it may well happen that the public voice, pronounced by the representatives of the people, will be more consonant to the public good than if pronounced by the people themselves, convened for the purpose. On the other hand, the effect may be inverted. Men of factious tempers, of local prejudices, or of sinister designs, may, by intrigue, by corruption, or by other means, first obtain the suffrages, and then betray the interests of the people. The question resulting is, whether small or extensive republics are most favorable to the election of proper guardians of the public weal; and it is clearly decided in favor of the latter by two obvious considerations.

In the first place it is to be remarked that however small the republic may be the representatives must be raised to a certain number in order to guard against the cabals of a few; and that however large it may be they must be limited to a certain number in order to guard against the confusion of a multitude. Hence, the number of representatives in the two cases not being in proportion to that of the constituents, and being proportionally greatest in the small republic, it follows that if the proportion of fit characters be not less in the large than in the small republic, the former will present a greater option, and consequently a greater probability of a fit choice.

In the next place, as each representative will be chosen by a greater number of citizens in the large than in the small republic, it will be more difficult for unworthy candidates to practice with success the vicious arts by which elections are too often carried; and the suffrages of the people being more free, will be more likely to center on men who possess the most attractive merit and the most diffusive and established characters.

It must be confessed that in this, as in most other cases, there is a mean, on both sides of which inconveniencies will be found to lie. By enlarging too much the number of electors, you render the representative too little acquainted with all their local circumstances and lesser interest; as by reducing it too much, you render him unduly attached to these, and too little fit to comprehend and pursue great and national objects. The federal Constitution forms a happy combination in this respect; the great and aggregate interests being referred to the national, the local and particular to the State legislatures.

The other point of difference is the greater number of citizens and extent of territory which may be brought within the compass of republican than of democratic government; and it is this circumstance principally which renders factious combinations less to be dreaded in the former than in the latter. The smaller the society, the fewer probably will be the distinct parties and interests composing it; the fewer the distinct parties and interests, the more frequently will a majority be found of the same party; and the smaller the number of individuals composing a majority, and the smaller the compass within which they are placed, the more easily will they concert and execute their plans of oppression. Extend the sphere and you take in a greater variety of parties and interests; you make it less probable that a majority of the whole will have a common motive to invade the rights of other citizens; or if such a common motive exists, it will be more difficult for all who feel it to discover their own strength and to act in unison with each other. Besides other impediments, it may be remarked that, where there is a consciousness of unjust or dishonorable purposes, communication is always checked by distrust in proportion to the number whose concurrence is necessary.

Hence, it clearly appears that the same advantage which a republic has over a democracy in controlling the effects of faction is enjoyed by a large over a small republic—is enjoyed by the Union over the States composing it. Does this advantage consist in the substitution of representatives whose enlightened views and virtuous sentiments render them superior to local prejudices and to schemes of injustice? It will not be denied that the representation of the Union will be most likely to possess these requisite endowments. Does it consist in the greater security afforded by a greater variety of parties, against the event of any one party being able to outnumber and oppress the rest? In an equal degree does the increased variety of parties comprised within the Union increase this security. Does it, in fine, consist in the greater obstacles opposed to the concert and accomplishment of the secret wishes of an unjust and interested majority? Here again the extent of the Union gives it the most palpable advantage.

The influence of factious leaders may kindle a flame within their particular States but will be unable to spread a general conflagration through the other States. A religious sect may degenerate into a political faction in a part of the

Confederacy; but the variety of sects dispersed over the entire face of it must secure the national councils against any danger from that source. A rage for paper money, for an abolition of debts, for an equal division of property, or for any other improper or wicked project, will be less apt to pervade the whole body of the Union than a particular member of it, in the same proportion as such a malady is more likely to taint a particular county or district than an entire State.

In the extent and proper structure of the Union, therefore, we behold a republican remedy for the diseases most incident to republican government. And according to the degree of pleasure and pride we feel in being republicans ought to be our zeal in cherishing the spirit and supporting the character of federalists.

9

James Madison

Federalist 51 (1788)

To what expedient, then, shall we finally resort, for maintaining in practice the necessary partition of power among the several departments as laid down in the Constitution? The only answer that can be given is that as all these exterior provisions are found to be inadequate the defect must be supplied, by so contriving the interior structure of the government as that its several constituent parts may, by their mutual relations, be the means of keeping each other in their proper places. Without presuming to undertake a full development of this important idea I will hazard a few general observations which may perhaps place it in a clearer light, and enable us to form a more correct judgment of the principles and structure of the government planned by the convention.

In order to lay a due foundation for that separate and distinct exercise of the different powers of government, which to a certain extent is admitted on all hands to be essential to the preservation of liberty, it is evident that each department should have a will of its own; and consequently should be so constituted that the members of each should have as little

From *The Federalist*.

agency as possible in the appointment of the members of the others. Were this principle rigorously adhered to, it would require that all the appointments for the supreme executive, legislative, and judiciary magistracies should be drawn from the same fountain of authority, the people, through channels having no communication whatever with one another. Perhaps such a plan of constructing the several departments would be less difficult in practice than it may in contemplation appear. Some difficulties, however, and some additional expense would attend the execution of it. Some deviations, therefore, from the principle must be admitted. In the constitution of the judiciary department in particular, it might be inexpedient to insist rigorously on the principle: first, because peculiar qualifications being essential in the members, the primary consideration ought to be to select that mode of choice which best secures these qualifications; second, because the permanent tenure by which the appointments are held in that department must soon destroy all sense of dependence on the authority conferring them.

It is equally evident that the members of each department should be as little dependent as possible on those of the others for the emoluments annexed to their offices. Were the executive magistrate, or the judges, not independent of the legislature in this particular, their independence in every other would be merely nominal.

But the great security against a gradual concentration of the several powers in the same department consists in giving to those who administer each department the necessary constitutional means and personal motives to resist encroachments of the others. The provision for defense must in this, as in all other cases, be made commensurate to the danger of attack. Ambition must be made to counteract ambition. The interest of the man must be connected with the constitutional rights of the place. It may be a reflection on human nature that such devices should be necessary to control the abuses of government. But what is government itself but the greatest of all reflections on human nature? If men were angels, no government would be necessary. If angels were to govern men, neither external nor internal controls on government would be necessary. In framing a government which is to be administered by men over men, the great difficulty lies in this: you must first enable the government to control the governed; and in the next place oblige it to control itself. A dependence on the people is, no doubt, the primary control on the government; but experience has taught mankind the necessity of auxiliary precautions.

This policy of supplying, by opposite and rival interests, the defect of better motives, might be traced through the whole system of human affairs, private as well as public. We see it particularly displayed in all the subordinate distributions of power, where the constant aim is to divide and arrange the several offices in such a manner as that each may be a check on the other—that the private interest of every individual may be a sentinel over the public rights.

These inventions of prudence cannot be less requisite in the distribution of the supreme powers of the State.

But it is not possible to give to each department an equal power of self-defense. In republican government, the legislative authority necessarily predominates. The remedy for this inconveniency is to divide the legislature into different branches; and to render them, by different modes of election and different principles of action, as little connected with each other as the nature of their common functions and their common dependence on the society will admit. It may even be necessary to guard against dangerous encroachments by still further precautions. As the weight of the legislative authority requires that it should be thus divided, the weakness of the executive may require, on the other hand, that it should be fortified. An absolute negative on the legislature appears, at first view, to be the natural defense with which the executive magistrate should be armed. But perhaps it would be neither altogether safe nor alone sufficient. On ordinary occasions it might not be exerted with the requisite firmness, and on extraordinary occasions it might be perfidiously abused. May not this defect of an absolute negative be supplied by some qualified connection between this weaker department and the weaker branch of the stronger department, by which the latter may be led to support the constitutional rights of the former, without being too much detached from the rights of its own department?

If the principles on which these observations are founded be just, as I persuade myself they are, and they be applied as a criterion to the several State constitutions, and to the federal Constitution, it will be found that if the latter does not perfectly correspond with them, the former are infinitely less able to bear such a test.

There are, moreover, two considerations particularly applicable to the federal system of America, which place that system in a very interesting point of view.

First. In a single republic, all the power surrendered by the people is submitted to the administration of a single government; and the usurpations are guarded against by a division of the government into distinct and separate departments. In the compound republic of America, the power surrendered by the people is first divided between two distinct governments, and then the portion allotted to each subdivided among distinct and separate departments. Hence a double security arises to the rights of the people. The different governments will control each other, at the same time that each will be controlled by itself.

Second. It is of great importance in a republic not only to guard the society against the oppression of its rulers, but to guard one part of the society against the injustice of the other part. Different interests necessarily exist in different classes of citizens. If a majority be united by a common interest, the rights of the minority will be insecure. There are but two methods of providing against this evil: the one by creating a will in the community independent of the majority—that is, of the society itself; the other, by comprehending in the society so many separate descriptions of citizens as will render an unjust combination of a majority of the whole very improbable, if not impracticable. The first method prevails in all governments possessing an hereditary or self-appointed authority. This, at best, is but a precarious security; because a power independent of the society may as well espouse the unjust views of the major as the rightful interests of the minor party, and may possibly be turned against both parties. The second method will be exemplified in the federal republic of the United States. Whilst all authority in it will be derived from and dependent on the society, the society itself will be broken into so many parts, interests, and classes of citizens, that the rights of individuals, or of the minority, will be in little danger from interested combinations of the majority. In a free government the security for civil rights must be the same as that for religious rights. It consists in the one case in the multiplicity of interests, and in the other in the multiplicity of sects. The degree of security in both cases will depend on the number of interests and sects; and this may be presumed to depend on the extent of country and number of people comprehended under the same government. This view of the subject must particularly recommend a proper federal system to all the sincere and considerate friends of republican government, since it shows that in exact proportion as the territory of the Union may be formed into more circumscribed Confederacies, or States, oppressive combinations of a majority will be facilitated; the best security, under the republican forms, for the rights of every class of citizen, will be diminished; and consequently the stability and independence of some member of the government, the only other security, must be proportionally increased. Justice is the end of government. It is the end of civil society. It ever has been and ever will be pursued until it be obtained, or until liberty be lost in the pursuit. In a society under the forms of which the stronger faction can readily unite and oppress the weaker, anarchy may as truly be said to reign as in a state of nature, where the weaker individual is not secured against the violence of the stronger; and as, in the latter state, even the stronger individuals are prompted, by the uncertainty of their condition, to submit to a government which may protect the weak as well as themselves; so, in the former state, will the more powerful factions or parties be gradually induced, by a like motive, to wish for a government which will protect all parties, the weaker as well as the more powerful. It can be little doubted that if the State of Rhode Island was separated from the Confederacy and left to itself, the insecurity of rights under the popular form of government within such narrow limits would be displayed by such reiterated oppressions of factious majorities that some power altogether independent of the people would soon be called for by the voice of the very factions whose misrule had proved the necessity of it. In the extended republic of the United States, and among the great variety of interests, parties, and sects which it embraces, a coalition of a majority of the whole society could seldom take place on any other principles than those of justice and the general good; whilst there being thus less danger to a minor from the will of a major party, there must be less pretext, also, to provide for the security of the former, by introducing into the government a will not dependent on the latter, or, in other words, a will independent of the society itself. It is no less certain than it is important, notwithstanding the contrary opinions which have been entertained, that the larger the society, provided it lie within a practicable sphere, the more duly capable it will be of self-government. And happily for the *republican cause*, the practicable sphere may be carried to a very great extent by a judicious modification and mixture of the *federal principle*.

10

John Adams

The Role of the Rich and the Poor in the Legislature (1787)

. . . There can be no free government without a democratical branch in the constitution. . . .

The rich, the well-born, and the able, acquire an influence among the people that will soon be too much for simple honesty and plain sense, in a house of representatives. The most illustrious of them must, therefore, be separated from the mass, and placed by themselves in a senate; this is, to all honest and useful intents, an ostracism. A member of a senate, of immense wealth, the most respected birth, and transcendent abilities, has no influence in the nation, in comparison of what he would have in a single representative assembly. When a senate exists, the most powerful man in the state may be safely admitted into the house of representatives, because the people have it in their power to remove him into the senate as soon as his influence becomes dangerous. The senate becomes the great object of ambition; and the richest and the most sagacious wish to merit an advancement to it by services to the public in the house. When he has obtained the object of his wishes, you may still hope for the benefits of his exertions, without dreading his passions; for the executive power being in other hands, he has lost much

From A *Defense of the Constitutions of the Government of the United States,* in *The Life and Work of John Adams,* Vol. IV and Vol. VI, Little, Brown, and Co., 1851.

of his influence with the people, and can govern very few votes more than his own among the senators. . . .

⁓⁓ ⁓⁓

Marchamont Nedham lays it down as a fundamental principle and an undeniable rule, "that the people, (that is, such as shall be successively chosen to represent the people), are the best keepers of their own liberties, and that for many reasons. First, because they never think of usurping over other men's rights, but mind which way to preserve their own." . . .

Would Mr. Nedham be responsible that, if all were to be decided by a vote of the majority, the eight or nine millions who have no property, would not think of usurping over the rights of the one or two millions who have? Property is surely a right of mankind as really as liberty. Perhaps, at first, prejudice, habit, shame or fear, principle or religion, would restrain the poor from attacking the rich, and the idle from usurping on the industrious; but the time would not be long before courage and enterprise would come, and pretexts be invented by degrees, to countenance the majority in dividing all the property among them, or at least, in sharing it equally with its present possessors. Debts would be abolished first; taxes laid heavy on the rich, and not at all on the others; and at last a downright equal division of every thing be demanded, and voted. What would be the consequence of this? The idle, the vicious, the intemperate, would rush into the utmost extravagance of debauchery, sell and spend all their share, and then demand a new division of those who purchased from them. The moment the idea is admitted into society, that property is not as sacred as the laws of God, and that there is not a force of law and public justice to protect it, anarchy and tyranny commence. . . .

Though we allow benevolence and generous affections to exist in the human breast, yet every moral theorist will admit the selfish passions in the generality of men to be the strongest. There are few who love the public better than themselves, though all may have some affection for the public. . . .

The only remedy is to take away the power, controlling the selfish avidity of the governor, by the senate and house; of the senate, by the governor and house; and of the house, by the governor and senate. Of all possible forms of government, a sovereignty in one assembly, successively chosen by the people, is perhaps the best calculated to facilitate the gratification of self-love, and the pursuit of the private interest of a few individuals; a few eminent conspicuous characters will be continued in their seats in the sovereign assembly, from one election to another, whatever changes are made in the seats around them, by superior art, address, and opulence, by more splendid birth, reputations, and connections, they will be able to intrigue with the people and their leaders, out of doors, until they worm out most of their opposers, and introduce their friends; to this end, they will bestow all offices, contracts, privileges in commerce, and other emoluments, on the latter and their connections, and throw every vexation and disappointment in the way of the former, until they establish such a system of hopes and fears throughout the state, as shall enable them to carry a majority in every fresh election of the house. The judges will be appointed by them and their party, and of consequence, will be obsequious enough to their inclinations. . . .

It is agreed that "the end of all government is the good and ease of the people, in a secure enjoyment of their rights, without oppression;" but it must be remembered, that the rich are *people* as well as the poor; that they have rights as well as others; that they have as clear and as *sacred* a right to their large property as others have to theirs which is smaller; that oppression to them is as possible and as wicked as to others; that stealing, robbing, cheating, are the same crimes and sins, whether committed against them or others. The rich, therefore, ought to have an effectual barrier in the constitution against being robbed, plundered, and murdered, as well as the poor; and this can never be without an independent senate. The poor should have a bulwark against the same dangers and oppressions; and this can never be without a house of representatives of the people. But neither the rich nor the poor can be defended by their respective guardians in the constitution, without an executive power, vested with a negative, equal to either, to hold the balance even between them, and decide when they cannot agree. If it is asked, When will this negative be used? it may be answered, Perhaps never. The known existence of it will prevent all occasion to exercise it; but if it has not a being, the want of it will be felt every day. . . .

11

Alexander Hamilton

On the Character of the Legislator (1778)

. . . The station of a member of Congress is the most illustrious and important of any I am able to conceive. He is to be regarded not only as a legislator, but as the founder of an empire. A man of virtue and ability, dignified with so precious a trust, would rejoice that fortune had given him birth at a time, and placed him in circumstances so favourable for promoting human happiness.

From Hamilton, "Publius Letter, III." Nov. 16, 1779, in *The Papers of Alexander Hamilton*, Vol. I, Columbia University Press, 1969.

He would esteem it not more the duty, than the privilege and ornament of his office, to do good to mankind; from this commanding eminence, he would look down with contempt upon every mean or interested pursuit.

To form useful alliances abroad—to establish a wise government at home—to improve the internal resources, and finances of the nation would be the generous objects of his care. He would not allow his attention to be diverted from these to intrigue for personal connections, to confirm his own influence; nor would be able to reconcile it, either to the delicacy of his honour, or to the dignity of his pride, to confound in the same person the representative of the Commonwealth, and the little member of a trading company. Anxious for the permanent power and prosperity of the State, he would labour to perpetuate the union and harmony of the several parts. He would not meanly court a temporary importance, by patronizing the narrow views of local interest, or by encouraging dissensions either among the people or in Congress. In council, or debate, he would discover the candor of a statesman, zealous for truth, and the integrity of a patriot studious of the public welfare; not the cavilling petulance of an attorney, contending for the triumph of an opinion, nor the perverse duplicity of a partisan, devoted to the service of a cabal. Despising the affectation of superior wisdom, he would prove the extent of his capacity, by foreseeing evils, and contriving expedients to prevent or remedy them. He would not expose the weak sides of the State, to find an opportunity of displaying his own discernment, by magnifying the follies and mistakes of others. In his transactions with individuals, whether foreigners or countrymen, his conduct would be guided by the sincerity of a man, and the politeness of a gentleman, not by the temporising flexibility of a courtier, nor the fawning complaisance of a sycophant. . . .

12

Alexander Hamilton

The Military in a Commercial Republic (1787)

. . . [Opponents of the Constitution would like standing armies to be prohibited.] From a close examination it will appear that restraints upon the

From Federalist 8 and 24, in *The Federalist*.

discretion of the legislature in respect to military establishments in time of peace, would be improper to be imposed, and if imposed, from the necessities of society, would be unlikely to be observed.

Though a wide ocean separates the United States from Europe, yet there are various considerations that warn us against an excess of confidence or security. On one side of us, and stretching far into our rear, are growing settlements subject to the dominion of Britain. On the other side, and extending to meet the British settlements, are colonies and establishments subject to the dominion of Spain. This situation and the vicinity of the West India Islands, belonging to these two powers, create between them, in respect to their American possessions and in relation to us, a common interest. . . .

Previous to the Revolution, and ever since the peace, there has been a constant necessity for keeping small garrisons on our Western frontier. No person can doubt that these will continue to be indispensable, if it should only be against the ravages and depredations of the Indians. These garrisons must either be furnished by occasional detachments from the militia, or by permanent corps in the pay of the government. The first is impracticable; and if practicable, would be pernicious. The militia would not long, if at all, submit to be dragged from their occupations and families to perform that most disagreeable duty in times of profound peace. And if they could be prevailed upon or compelled to do it, the increased expense of a frequent rotation of service, and the loss of labor and disconcertion of the industrious pursuits of individuals, would form conclusive objections to the scheme. It would be as burdensome and injurious to the public as ruinous to private citizens. The latter resource of permanent corps in the pay of the government amounts to a standing army in time of peace; a small one, indeed, but not the less real for being small. Here is a simple view of the subject, that shows us at once the impropriety of a constitutional interdiction of such establishments, and the necessity of leaving the matter to the discretion and prudence of the legislature. . . .

. . . The industrious habits of the people of the present day, absorbed in the pursuits of gain, and devoted to the improvements of agriculture and commerce, are incompatible with the condition of a nation of soldiers, which was the true condition of the people of those republics. The means of revenue, which have been so greatly multiplied by the increase of gold and silver and of the arts of industry, and the science of finance, which is the offspring of modern times, concurring with the habits of nations, have produced an entire revolution in the system of war, and have rendered disciplined armies, distinct from the body of the citizens, the inseparable companions of frequent hostility. . . .

13

Alexis de Tocqueville

Equality and Commerce (1840)

In America the passion for physical well-being is not always exclusive, but it is general; and if all do not feel it in the same manner, yet it is felt by all. Carefully to satisfy all, even the least wants of the body, and to provide the little conveniences of life is uppermost in every mind. . . .

When riches are hereditarily fixed in families, there are a great number of men who enjoy the comforts of life without feeling an exclusive taste for those comforts. The heart of man is not so much caught by the undisturbed possession of anything valuable as by the desire, as yet imperfectly satisfied, of possessing it and by the incessant dread of losing it. In aristocratic communities the wealthy, never having experienced a condition different from their own, entertain no fear of changing it; the existence of such conditions hardly occurs to them. The comforts of life are not to them the end of life, but simply a way of living; they regard them as existence itself, enjoyed but scarcely thought of. As the natural and instinctive taste that all men feel for being well off is thus satisfied without trouble and without apprehension, their faculties are turned elsewhere and cling to more arduous and lofty undertakings, which excite and engross their minds.

Hence it is that in the midst of physical gratifications the members of an aristocracy often display a haughty contempt of these very enjoyments and exhibit singular powers of endurance under the privation of them. All the revolutions which have ever shaken or destroyed aristocracies have shown how easily men accustomed to superfluous luxuries can do without the necessaries of life; whereas men who have toiled to acquire a competency can hardly live after they have lost it.

If I turn my observation from the upper to the lower classes, I find analogous effects produced by opposite causes. Among a nation where aristocracy predominates in society and keeps it stationary, the people in the end get as much accustomed to poverty as the rich to their opulence. The latter bestow

From *Democracy in America* by Alexis de Tocqueville, translated by Henry Reeve, 1862, with minor changes.

no anxiety on their physical comforts because they enjoy them without an effort; the former do not think of things which they despair of obtaining and which they hardly know enough of to desire. In communities of this kind the imagination of the poor is driven to seek another world; the miseries of real life enclose it, but it escapes from their control and flies to seek its pleasures far beyond.

When, on the contrary, the distinctions of ranks are confounded together and privileges are destroyed, when hereditary property is subdivided and education and freedom widely diffused, the desire of acquiring the comforts of the world haunts the imagination of the poor, and the dread of losing them that of the rich. Many scanty fortunes spring up; those who possess them have a sufficient share of physical gratifications to conceive a taste for these pleasures, not enough to satisfy it. They never procure them without exertion, and they never indulge in them without apprehension. They are therefore always straining to pursue or to retain gratifications so delightful, so imperfect, so fugitive.

If I were to inquire what passion is most natural to men who are stimulated and circumscribed by the obscurity of their birth or the mediocrity of their fortune, I could discover none more peculiarly appropriate to their condition than this love of physical prosperity. The passion for physical comforts is essentially a passion of the middle classes; with those classes it grows and spreads, with them it preponderates. From them it mounts into the higher orders of society and descends into the mass of the people.

I never met in America with any citizen so poor as not to cast a glance of hope and envy on the enjoyments of the rich or whose imagination did not possess itself by anticipation of those good things that fate still obstinately withheld from him.

On the other hand, I never perceived among the wealthier inhabitants of the United States that proud contempt of physical gratifications which is sometimes to be met with even in the most opulent and dissolute aristocracies. Most of these wealthy persons were once poor; they have felt the sting of want; they were long a prey to adverse fortunes; and now that the victory is won, the passions which accompanied the contest have survived it; their minds are, as it were, intoxicated by the small enjoyments which they have pursued for forty years. . . .

. . . It commonly happens that in the ages of privilege the practice of almost all the arts becomes a privilege, and that every profession is a separate walk, upon which it is not allowable for everyone to enter. Even when productive industry is free, the fixed character that belongs to aristocratic nations gradually segregates all the persons who practice the same art till they form a distinct class, always composed of the same families, whose members are all known to each other and among whom a public opinion of their own and a species of corporate pride soon spring up. In a class or guild of this kind each artisan has not only his fortune to make, but his reputation to preserve. He is not exclusively swayed by his own interest or even by that of his customer, but by that of the body to which he belongs; and the interest of that body is that each artisan should produce the best possible workmanship. In aristocratic ages the object of the arts is therefore to manufacture as well as possible, not with the greatest dispatch or at the lowest cost.

When, on the contrary, every profession is open to all, when a multitude of persons are constantly embracing and abandoning it, and when its several members are strangers to each other, indifferent, and from their numbers hardly seen among themselves, the social tie is destroyed, and each workman, standing alone, endeavors simply to gain the greatest quantity of money at the least possible cost. The will of the customer is then his only limit. But at the same time a corresponding revolution takes place in the customer also. In countries in which riches as well as power are concentrated and retained in the hands of a few, the use of the greater part of this world's goods belongs to a small number of individuals, who are always the same. Necessity, public opinion, or moderate desires exclude all others from the enjoyment of them. As this aristocratic class remains fixed at the pinnacle of greatness on which it stands, without diminution or increase, it is always acted upon by the same wants and affected by them in the same manner. The men of whom it is composed naturally derive from their superior and hereditary position a taste for what is extremely well made and lasting. This affects the general way of thinking of the nation in relation to the arts. It often occurs among such a people that even the peasant will rather go without the objects he covets than procure them in a state of imperfection. In aristocracies, then, the handicraftsmen work for only a limited number of very fastidious customers; the profit they hope to make depends principally on the perfection of their workmanship.

Such is no longer the case when, all privileges being abolished, ranks are intermingled and men are forever rising or sinking upon the ladder of society. Among a democratic people a number of citizens always exists whose patrimony is divided and decreasing. They have contracted, under more prosperous circumstances, certain wants, which remain after the means of satisfying such wants are gone; and they are anxiously looking out for some surreptitious method of providing for them. On the other hand, there is always in democracies a large number of men whose fortune is on the increase, but whose desires grow much faster than their fortunes, and who gloat upon the gifts of wealth in anticipation, long before they have means to command them. Such men are eager to find some short cut to these gratifications, already almost within their reach. From the combination of these two causes the result is that in democracies there is always a multitude of persons whose wants are above their means and who are very willing to take up with imperfect satisfaction rather than abandon the object of their desires.

The artisan readily understands these passions, for he himself partakes in them. In an aristocracy he would seek to sell his workmanship at a high price to the few; he now conceives that the more expeditious way of getting rich is to sell them at a low price to all. But there are only two ways of lowering the price of commodities. The first is to discover some better, shorter, and more ingenious method of producing them; the second is to manufacture a larger quantity of goods, nearly similar, but of less value. Among a democratic population all the intellectual faculties of the workman are directed to these two objects: he strives to invent methods that may enable him not only to work better, but more quickly and more cheaply; or if he cannot succeed in that, to diminish the intrinsic quality of the thing he makes, without rendering it wholly unfit for the use for which it is intended. When none but the wealthy had watches, they were almost all very good ones; few are now made that are worth much, but everybody has one in his pocket. Thus the democratic principle not only tends to direct the human mind to the useful arts, but it induces the artisan to produce with great rapidity a quantity of imperfect commodities, and the consumer to content himself with these commodities. . . .

The handicraftsmen of democratic ages not only endeavor to bring their useful productions within the reach of the whole community, but they strive to give to all their commodities attractive qualities that they do not in reality possess. In the confusion of all ranks everyone hopes to appear what he is not, and makes great exertions to succeed in this object. This sentiment, indeed, which is but too natural to the heart of man, does not originate in the democratic principle; but that principle applies it to material objects. To mimic virtue is of every age, but the hypocrisy of luxury belongs more particularly to the ages of democracy.

To satisfy these new cravings of human vanity the arts have recourse to every species of imposture. . . .

When I arrived for the first time at New York, by that part of the Atlantic Ocean which is called the Narrows, I was surprised to perceive along the shore, at some distance from the city, a considerable number of little palaces of white marble, several of which were built after the models of ancient architecture. When I went the next day to inspect more closely the building which had particularly attracted my notice, I found that its walls were of whitewashed brick, and its columns of painted wood. All the edifices that I had admired the night before were of the same kind.

The social condition and the institutions of democracy impart, moreover, certain peculiar tendencies to all the imitative arts, which it is easy to point out. They frequently withdraw them from the delineation of the soul to fix them exclusively on that of the body, and they substitute the representation of motion and sensation for that of sentiment and thought; in a word, they put the Real in the place of the Ideal.

I doubt whether Raphael studied the minute intricacies of the mechanism of the human body as thoroughly as the draftsmen of our own time. He did not attach the same importance to rigorous accuracy on this point as they do because he aspired to surpass nature. He sought to make of man something which should be superior to man and to embellish beauty's self. David and his scholars were, on the contrary, as good anatomists as they were good painters. They wonderfully depicted the models that they had before their eyes, but they rarely imagined anything beyond them; they followed nature with fidelity, while Raphael sought for something better than nature. They have left us an exact portraiture of man, but he discloses in his works a glimpse of the Divinity.

This remark as to the manner of treating a subject is no less applicable to the choice of it. The painters of the Middle Ages generally sought far above themselves, and away from their own time, for mighty subjects, which left to their imagination an unbounded range. Our painters frequently employ their talents in the exact imitation of the details of private life, which they have always before their eyes; and they are forever copying trivial objects, the originals of which are only too abundant in nature. . . .

. . . In Europe we are wont to look upon a restless disposition, an unbounded desire of riches, and an excessive love of independence as propensities very formidable to society. Yet these are the very elements that ensure a long and peaceful duration to the republics of America. Without these unquiet passions the population would collect in certain spots and would soon be subject to wants like those of the Old World, which it is difficult to satisfy; for such is the present good fortune of the New World that the vices of its inhabitants are scarcely less favorable to society than their virtues. These circumstances exercise a great influence on the estimation in which human actions are held in the two hemispheres. The Americans frequently term what we should call cupidity a laudable industry; and they blame as faintheartedness what we consider to be the virtue of moderate desires.

In France simple tastes, orderly manners, domestic affections, and the attachment that men feel to the place of their birth are looked upon as great guarantees of the tranquility and happiness of the state. But in America nothing seems to be more prejudicial to society than these virtues. The French Canadians, who have faithfully preserved the traditions of their pristine manners, are already embarrassed for room in their small territory; and this little community, which has so recently begun to exist, will shortly be a prey to the calamities incident to old nations. In Canada the most enlightened, patriotic, and humane inhabitants make extraordinary efforts to render the people dissatisfied with those simple enjoyments which still content them. There the seductions of wealth are vaunted with as much zeal as the charms of a moderate but limited income in the Old World; and more exertions are made to excite the passions of the citizens there than to calm them elsewhere. If we listen to their eulogies, we shall hear that nothing is more praiseworthy than to exchange the pure and homely pleasures which even the poor man tastes in his own country for the dull delights of prosperity under a foreign sky; to leave the patrimonial hearth and the turf beneath which his forefathers sleep—in short, to abandon the living and the dead, in quest of fortune. . . .

In America too much knowledge cannot be diffused; for all knowledge, while it may serve him who possesses it, turns also to the advantage of those who are without it. New wants are not to be feared, since they can be satisfied without difficulty. . . .

The American republics of the present day are like companies of [merchants], formed to explore in common the wastelands of the New World and busied in a flourishing trade. The passions that agitate the Americans most deeply are not their political, but their commercial passions; or, to speak more correctly, they introduce the habits they contract in business into their political life. They love order, without which affairs do not prosper; and they set an especial value upon regular conduct, which is the foundation of a solid business. They prefer the good sense which amasses large fortunes to that enterprising spirit which frequently dissipates them; general ideas alarm their minds, which are accustomed to positive calculations; and they hold practice in more honor than theory. . . .

In certain remote corners of the Old World you may still sometimes stumble upon a small district that seems to have been forgotten amid the general tumult, and to have remained stationary while everything around it was in motion. The inhabitants are, for the most part, extremely ignorant and poor; they take no part in the business of the country and are frequently oppressed by the government, yet their countenances are generally placid and their spirits light.

In America I saw the freest and most enlightened men placed in the happiest circumstances that the world affords; it seemed to me as if a cloud habitually hung upon their brow, and I thought them serious and almost sad, even in their pleasures.

The chief reason of this contrast is that the former do not think of the ills they endure, while the latter are forever brooding over advantages they do not possess. It is strange to see with what feverish ardor the Americans pursue their own welfare, and to watch the vague dread that constantly torments them lest they should not have chosen the shortest path which may lead to it.

A native of the United States clings to this world's goods as if he were certain never to die; and he is so hasty in grasping at all within his reach that one would suppose he was constantly afraid of not living long enough to enjoy them. He clutches everything, he holds nothing fast, but soon loosens his grasp to pursue fresh gratifications.

In the United States a man builds a house to spend his latter years in it, and he sells it before the roof is on; he plants a garden and lets it just as the trees are coming into bearing; he brings a field into tillage and leaves other men to gather the crops; he embraces a profession and gives it up; he settles in a place, which he soon afterwards leaves to carry his changeable longings elsewhere. If his private affairs leave him any leisure, he instantly plunges into the vortex of politics; and if at the end of a year of unremitting labor he finds he has a few days' vacation, his eager curiosity whirls him over the vast extent of the United States, and he will travel fifteen hundred miles in a few days to shake off his happiness. Death at length overtakes him, but it is before he is weary of his bootless chase of that complete felicity which is forever on the wing.

At first sight there is something surprising in this strange unrest of so many happy men, restless in the midst of abundance. The spectacle itself, however, is as old as the world; the novelty is to see a whole people furnish an exemplification of it.

Their taste for physical gratifications must be regarded as the original source of that secret disquietude which the actions of the Americans betray and of that inconstancy of which they afford fresh examples every day. He who has set his heart exclusively upon the pursuit of worldly welfare is always in a hurry, for he has but a limited time at his disposal to reach, to grasp, and to enjoy it. The recollection of the brevity of life is a constant spur to him. Besides the good things that he possesses, he every instant fancies a thousand others that death will prevent him from trying if he does not try them soon. This thought fills him with anxiety, fear, and regret and keeps his mind in ceaseless trepidation, which leads him perpetually to change his plans and his abode.

If in addition to the taste for physical well-being a social condition be superadded in which the laws and customs make no condition permanent, here is a great additional stimulant to this restlessness of temper. Men will then be seen continually to change their track for fear of missing the shortest cut to happiness.

It may readily be conceived that if men passionately bent upon physical gratifications desire eagerly, they are also easily discouraged; as their ultimate object is to enjoy, the means to reach that object must be prompt and easy

or the trouble of acquiring the gratification would be greater than the gratification itself. Their prevailing frame of mind, then, is at once ardent and
relaxed, violent and enervated. Death is often less dreaded than persever-
ance in continuous efforts to one end. . . .

. . . We must first understand what the purport of society and the aim of government is held to be. If you wish to give a certain elevation to the human
mind and teach it to regard the things of this world with generous feelings, to
inspire men with a scorn of mere temporal advantage, to give birth to living
convictions and keep alive the spirit of honorable devotedness; if you hold it
to be a good thing to refine the habits, embellish the manners, to cultivate
the arts of a nation, and to promote the love of poetry, of beauty, and of
renown; if you would constitute a people not unfitted to act with power upon
all other nations, nor unprepared for those high enterprises which, whatever
be the results of its efforts, will leave a name forever famous in time; if you
believe such to be the principal object of society, you must avoid the government of democracy, which would be a very uncertain guide to the end you
have in view.

But if you hold it to be expedient to divert the moral and intellectual
activity of man to the production of comfort and the acquirement of the
necessities of life; if a clear understanding be more profitable to man than
genius; if your object be not to stimulate the virtues of heroism, but to create the habits of peace; if you had rather witness vices than crimes, and are
content to meet with fewer noble deeds, provided offenses be diminished in
the same proportion; if, instead of living in the midst of a brilliant state of
society, you are contented to have prosperity around you; if, in short, you
are of the opinion that the principal object of a government is not to confer
the greatest possible share of power and glory upon the body of the nation,
but to ensure the greatest degree of enjoyment and the least degree of misery
to each of the individuals who compose it—if such be your desires, you can
have no surer means of satisfying them, than by equalizing the conditions of
men and establishing democratic institutions. . . .

14

Thomas Jefferson

On Citizenship (1824, 1816, 1814)

. . . My own State . . . is now proposing to call a convention for amendment. Among other improvements, I hope they will adopt the subdivision of our counties into wards. The former may be estimated at an average of twenty-four miles square; the latter should be about six miles square each, and would answer to the hundreds of your Saxon Alfred. In each of these might be: 1st. an elementary school; 2nd. a company of militia with its officers; 3rd. a justice of the peace and constable; 4th. each ward should take care of their own poor; 5th. their own roads; 6th. their own police; 7th. elect within themselves one or more jurors to attend the courts of justice; and, 8th. give in at their Folkhouse their votes for all functionaries reserved to their election. Each ward would thus be a small republic within itself, and every man in the State would thus become an acting member of the common government, transacting in person a great portion of its rights and duties, subordinate indeed, yet important, and entirely within his competence. The wit of man cannot devise a more solid basis for a free, durable, and well administered republic.

. . . If it is believed that these elementary schools will be better managed by the governor and council, the commissioners of the literary fund, or any other general authority of the government, than by the parents within each ward, it is a belief against all experience. Try the principle one step further and amend the bill so as to commit to the governor and council the management of all our farms, our mills, and merchants' stores. No, my friend, the way to have good and safe government is not to trust it all to one but to divide it among the many, distributing to everyone exactly the functions he is competent to. Let the national government be entrusted with the defense of the nation and its foreign and federal relations; the State governments with the civil rights, laws, police, and administration of what concerns the

From *The Writings of Thomas Jefferson*, Vol. VII and VI, Taylor and Maury, 1854.

State generally; the counties with the local concerns of the counties, and each ward direct the interests within itself. It is by dividing and subdividing these republics from the great national one down through all its subordinations until it ends in the administration of every man's farm by himself, by placing under everyone what his own eye may superintend, that all will be done for the best. What has destroyed liberty and the rights of man in every government which has ever existed under the sun? The generalizing and concentrating all cares and powers into one body, no matter whether of the autocrats of Russia or France, or of the aristocrats of a Venetian senate. And I do believe that if the Almighty has not decreed that man shall never be free (and it is a blasphemy to believe it), that the secret will be found to be in the making himself the depository of the powers respecting himself, so far as he is competent to them, and delegating only what is beyond his competence by a synthetical process to higher and higher orders of functionaries, so as to trust fewer and fewer powers in proportion as the trustees become more and more oligarchical. The elementary republics of the wards, the county republics, the State republics, and the republic of the Union would form a gradation of authorities, standing each on the basis of law, holding every one its delegated share of powers, and constituting truly a system of fundamental balances and checks for the government. Where every man is a sharer in the direction of his ward-republic, or of some of the higher ones, and feels that he is a participator in the government of affairs, not merely at an election one day in the year but every day; when there shall not be a man in the State who will not be a member of some one of its councils, great or small, he will let the heart be torn out of his body sooner than his power be wrested from him by a Caesar or a Bonaparte. How powerfully did we feel the energy of this organization in the case of embargo? . . .

. . . [W]e have no paupers. . . . The great mass of our population is of laborers; our rich, who can live without labor, either manual or professional, being few, and of moderate wealth. Most of the laboring class possess property, cultivate their own lands, have families, and from the demand for their labor are enabled to exact from the rich and the competent such prices as enable them to be fed abundantly, clothed above mere decency, to labor moderately and raise their families. They are not driven to the ultimate resources of dexterity and skill, because their wares will sell although not quite so nice as those of England. The wealthy, on the other hand, and those at their ease, know nothing of what the Europeans call luxury. They have only somewhat more of the comforts and decencies of life than those who furnish them. Can any condition of society be more desirable than this? . . . In England, happiness is the lot of the aristocracy only; and the proportion they bear to the laborers and paupers, you know better than

I do. Were I to guess that they are four in every hundred, then the happiness of the nation would be to its misery as one in twenty-five. In the United States it is as eight millions to zero, or as all to none. But it is said they possess the means of defense, and that we do not. How so? Are we not men? Yes; but our men are so happy at home that they will not hire themselves to be shot at for a shilling a day. Hence we can have no standing armies for defense, because we have no paupers to furnish the materials. The Greeks and Romans had no standing armies, yet they defended themselves. The Greeks by their laws, and the Romans by the spirit of their people, took care to put into the hands of their rulers no such engine of oppression as a standing army. Their system was to make every man a soldier, and oblige him to repair to the standard of his country whenever that was reared. This made them invincible; and the same remedy will make us so. In the beginning of our government we were willing to introduce the least coercion possible on the will of the citizen. Hence a system of military duty was established too indulgent to his indolence. This is the first opportunity we have had of trying it, and it has completely failed; an issue foreseen by many, and for which remedies have been proposed. That of classing the militia according to age, and allotting each age to the particular kind of service to which it was competent, was proposed to Congress in 1805, and subsequently; and, on the last trial, was lost, I believe, by a single vote only.

Had it prevailed, what has now happened would not have happened. Instead of burning our Capitol, we should have possessed theirs in Montreal and Quebec. We must now adopt it, and all will be safe.

15

James Madison

Federalist 39 (1788)

. . . The first question that offers itself is whether the general form and aspect of the government be strictly republican. It is evident that no other form would be reconcilable with the genius of the people of America; with the fundamental principles of the Revolution; or with that honorable

From *The Federalist*.

determination which animates every votary of freedom to rest all our political experiments on the capacity of mankind for self-government. If the plan of the convention, therefore, be found to depart from the republican character, its advocates must abandon it as no longer defensible. . . .

If we resort for a criterion to the different principles on which different forms of government are established, we may define a republic to be, or at least may bestow that name on, a government which derives all its powers directly or indirectly from the great body of the people, and is administered by persons holding their offices during pleasure for a limited period, or during good behavior. It is *essential* to such a government that it be derived from the great body of the society, not from an inconsiderable proportion or a favored class of it; otherwise a handful of tyrannical nobles, exercising their oppressions by a delegation of their powers, might aspire to the rank of republicans and claim for their government the honorable title of republic. It is *sufficient* for such a government that the persons administering it be appointed, either directly or indirectly, by the people; and that they hold their appointments by either of the tenures just specified; otherwise every government in the United States, as well as every other popular government that has been or can be well organized or well executed, would be degraded from the republican character. . . .

On comparing the Constitution planned by the convention with the standard here fixed, we perceived at once that it is, in the most rigid sense, comformable to it. The House of Representatives, like that of one branch at least of all the State legislatures, is elected immediately by the great body of the people. The Senate, like the present Congress and the Senate of Maryland, derives its appointment indirectly from the people. The President is indirectly derived from the choice of the people, according to the example in most of the States. Even the judges, with all other officers of the Union, will, as in the several States, be the choice, though a remote choice, of the people themselves. The duration of the appointments is equally conformable to the republican standard and to the model of State constitutions.

Could any further proof be required of the republican complexion of this system, the most decisive one might be found in its absolute prohibition of titles of nobility, both under the federal and the State governments; and in its express guaranty of the republican form to each of the latter.

"But it was not sufficient," say the adversaries of the proposed Constitution, "for the convention to adhere to the republican form. They ought with equal care to have preserved the *federal* form, which regards the Union as a *Confederacy* of sovereign states; instead of which they have framed a national government, which regards the Union as a *consolidation* of the States." And it is asked by what authority this bold and radical innovation was undertaken. The handle which has been made of this objection requires that it should be examined with some precision.

Without inquiring into the accuracy of the distinction on which the objection is founded, it will be necessary to a just estimate of its force, first, to ascertain the real character of the government in question; secondly, to inquire how far the convention were authorized to propose such a government; and thirdly, how far the duty they owed to their country could supply any defect of regular authority.

First.—In order to ascertain the real character of the government, it may be considered in relation to the foundation on which it is to be established; to the sources from which its ordinary powers are to be drawn; to the operation of those powers; to the extent of them; and to the authority by which future changes in the government are to be introduced.

On examining the first relation, it appears, on one hand, that the Constitution is to be founded on the assent and ratification of the people of America, given by deputies elected for the special purpose; but, on the other, that this assent and ratification is to be given by the people, not as individuals composing one entire nation, but as composing the distinct and independent States to which they respectively belong.

It is to be the assent and ratification of the several States, derived from the supreme authority in each State—the authority of the people themselves. The act, therefore, establishing the Constitution will not be a *national* but a *federal act*.

That it will be a federal and not a national act, as these terms are understood by the objectors—the act of the people, as forming so many independent States, not as forming one aggregate nation—is obvious from this single consideration: that it is to result neither from the decision of a *majority* of the people of the Union, nor from that of a *majority* of the States. It must result from the *unanimous* assent of the several States that are parties to it, differing not otherwise from their ordinary assent than in its being expressed, not by the legislative authority, but by that of the people themselves. Were the people regarded in this transaction as forming one nation, the will of the majority of the whole people of the United States would bind the minority, in the same manner as the majority in each State must bind the minority; and the will of the majority must be determined either by a comparison of the individual votes, or by considering the will of the majority of the States as evidence of the will of a majority of the people of the United States. Neither of these rules has been adopted. Each State, in ratifying the Constitution, is considered as a sovereign body independent of all others, and only to be bound by its own voluntary act. In this relation, then, the new Constitution will, if established, be a *federal* and not a *national* constitution.

The next relation is to the sources from which the ordinary powers of government are to be derived. The House of Representatives will derive its powers from the people of America; and the people will be represented in the same proportion and on the same principle as they are in the legislature of a particular State. So far the government is *national*, not *federal*. The Senate, on the other hand, will derive its powers from the States as political and coequal societies; and these will be represented on the principle of equality in the Senate, as they now are in the existing Congress. So far the government is *federal,* not national. The executive power will be derived from a very compound source. The immediate election of the President is to be made by the States in their political characters. The votes allotted to them are in a compound ratio, which considers them partly as distinct and coequal societies, partly as unequal members of the same society. The eventual election, again, is to be made by that branch of the legislature which consists of the national representatives; but in this particular act they are to be thrown into the form of individual delegations from so many distinct and co-equal bodies politic. From this aspect of the government it appears to be of a mixed character, presenting at least as many *federal* as *national* features.

The difference between a federal and national government, as it relates to the *operation of the government,* is by the adversaries of the plan of the convention supposed to consist in this, that in the former the powers operate on the political bodies composing the confederacy in their political capacities; in the latter, on the individual citizens composing the nation in their individual capacities. On trying the Constitution by this criterion, it falls under the *national* not the *federal* character; though perhaps not so completely as has been understood. In several cases, and particularly in the trial of controversies to which States may be parties, they must be viewed and proceeded against in their collective and political capacities only. But the operation of the government on the people in their individual capacities, in its ordinary and most essential proceedings, will, in the sense of its opponents, on the whole, designate it, in this relation, a *national* government.

But if the government be national with regard to the *operation* of its powers, it changes its aspect again when we contemplate it in relation to the extent of its powers. The idea of a national government involves in it not only an authority over the individual citizens, but an indefinite supremacy over all persons and things, so far as they are objects of lawful government. Among a people consolidated into one nation, this supremacy is completely vested in the national legislature. Among communities united for particular purposes, it is vested partly in the general and partly in the municipal legislatures. In the former case, all local authorities are subordinate to the supreme; and may be controlled, directed, or abolished by it at pleasure. In the latter, the local or municipal authorities form distinct and independent portions of the supremacy, no more subject, within their respective spheres, to the general authority than the general authority is subject to them, within its own sphere. In this relation, then, the proposed government cannot be deemed a *national* one; since its jurisdiction extends to certain enumerated objects only, and leaves to the several States a residuary and inviolable sovereignty over all other objects. It is true that in controversies relating to the boundary between the two jurisdictions, the tribunal which is ultimately to decide is to be established under the general government. But this does not change the principle of the case. The decision is to be impartially made, according to the rules of the Constitution; and all the usual and most effectual precautions are taken to secure this impartiality. Some such tribunal is clearly essential to prevent an appeal to the sword and a dissolution of the compact; and that it ought to be established under the general rather than under the local governments, or, to speak more properly, that it could be safely established under the first alone, is a position not likely to be combated.

If we try the Constitution by its last relation to the authority by which amendments are to be made, we find it neither wholly *national* nor wholly *federal*. Were it wholly national, the supreme and ultimate authority would reside in the *majority* of the people of the Union; and this authority would be competent at all times, like that of a majority of every national society to alter or abolish its established government. Were it wholly federal, on the other hand, the concurrence of each State in the Union would be essential to every alteration that would be binding on all. The mode provided by the plan of the convention is not founded on either of these principles. In requiring more than a majority, and particularly in computing the proportion by *States*, not by *citizens*, it departs from the national and advances towards the *federal* character; in rendering the concurrence of less than the whole number of States sufficient, it loses again the *federal* and partakes of the *national* character.

The proposed Constitution, therefore, even when tested by the rules laid down by its antagonists, is, in strictness, neither a national nor a federal Constitution, but a composition of both. In its foundation it is federal, not national; in the sources from which the ordinary powers of the government are drawn, it is partly federal and partly national; in the operation of these powers, it is national, not federal; in the extent of them, again, it is federal, not national; and, finally in the authoritative mode of introducing amendments, it is neither wholly federal nor wholly national.

16

McCulloch v. Maryland (1819)

Mr. Chief Justice Marshall delivered the opinion of the Court.*

In the case now to be determined, the defendant, a sovereign state, denies the obligation of a law enacted by the legislature of the Union, and

From *McCulloch v. Maryland*, 4 Wheat. 316 (1819).

---

*Citations omitted throughout the Supreme Court cases in this volume.

the plaintiff, on his part, contests the validity of an act which has been passed by the legislature of that state. The constitution of our country, in its most interesting and vital parts, is to be considered; the conflicting powers of the government of the Union and of its members, as marked in that constitution, are to be discussed; and an opinion given, which may essentially influence the great operations of the government. . . . On the Supreme Court of the United States has the constitution of our country devolved this important duty.

The first question made in the cause is, has Congress power to incorporate a bank?

It has been truly said that this can scarcely be considered as an open question, entirely unprejudiced by the former proceedings of the nation respecting it. The principle now contested was introduced at a very early period of our history, has been recognized by many successive legislatures, and has been acted upon by the judicial department, in cases of peculiar delicacy, as a law of undoubted obligation.

It will not be denied that a bold and daring usurpation might be resisted, after an acquiescence still longer and more complete than this. But it is conceived that a doubtful question . . . if not put at rest by the practice of the government, ought to receive a considerable impression from that practice. An exposition of the constitution, deliberately established by legislative acts, on the faith of which an immense property has been advanced, ought not to be lightly disregarded.

The power now contested was exercised by the first Congress elected under the present constitution. The bill for incorporating the bank of the United States did not steal upon an unsuspecting legislature, and pass unobserved. . . . After being resisted, first in the fair and open field of debate, and afterwards in the executive cabinet, with as much persevering talent as any measure has ever experienced, and being supported by arguments which convinced minds as pure and as intelligent as this country can boast, it became a law. . . . It would require no ordinary share of intrepidity to assert that a measure adopted under these circumstances was a bold and plain usurpation, to which the constitution gave no countenance. . . .

The government of the Union, then (whatever may be the influence of this fact on the case), is, emphatically, and truly, a government of the people. In form and in substance it emanates from them. Its powers are granted by them, and are to be exercised directly on them, and for their benefit.

This government is acknowledged by all to be one of enumerated powers. . . . But the question respecting the extent of the powers actually granted, is perpetually arising, and will probably continue to arise, as long as our system shall exist.

In discussing these questions, the conflicting powers of the general and state governments must be brought into view, and the supremacy of their respective laws, when they are in opposition, must be settled.

If any one proposition could command the universal assent of mankind, we might expect it would be this—that the government of the Union, though limited in its powers, is supreme within its sphere of action. This would seem to result necessarily from its nature. It is the government of all; its powers are delegated by all; it represents all, and acts for all. Though any one state may be willing to control its operations, no state is willing to allow others to control them. The nation, on those subjects on which it can act, must necessarily bind its component parts. But this question is not left to mere reason; the people have, in express terms, decided it by saying, "this constitution, and the laws of the United States, which shall be made in pursuance thereof," "shall be the supreme law of the land," and by requiring that the members of the state legislatures, and the officers of the executive and judicial departments of the states shall take the oath of fidelity to it.

The government of the United States, then, though limited in its powers, is supreme; and its laws when made in pursuance of the constitution, form the supreme law of the land, "anything in the constitution or laws of any state to the contrary notwithstanding."

Among the enumerated powers, we do not find that of establishing a bank or creating a corporation. But there is no phrase in the instrument which, like the articles of confederation, excludes incidental or implied powers; and which requires that everything granted shall be expressly and minutely described. . . . A constitution, to contain an accurate detail of all the subdivisions of which its great powers will admit, and of all the means by which they may be carried into execution, would partake of a prolixity of a legal code, and could scarcely be embraced by the human mind. It would probably never be understood by the public. Its nature, therefore, requires, that only its great outlines should be marked, its important objects designated, and the minor ingredients which compose those objects be deduced from the nature of the objects themselves. . . . In considering this question, then, we must never forget that it is a constitution we are expounding.

Although, among the enumerated powers of government, we do not find the word "bank" or "incorporation," we find the great powers to lay and collect taxes; to borrow money; to regulate commerce; to declare and conduct a war; and to raise and support armies and navies. The sword and the purse, all the external relations, and no inconsiderable portion of the industry of the nation, are entrusted to its government. It can never be pretended that these vast powers draw after them others of inferior importance, merely because they are inferior. Such an idea can never be advanced. But it may with great reason be contended, that a government, entrusted with such ample powers, on the due execution of which the happiness and prosperity of the nation so vitally depends, must also be entrusted with ample means for their execution. The power being given, it is the interest of the nation to facilitate its execution. It can never be their interest, and cannot be presumed to have been their intention, to clog and embarrass its execution by withholding the most appropriate means. Throughout this vast republic, from the St. Croix to the Gulf of Mexico, from the Atlantic to the Pacific, revenue is to be collected and expended, armies are to be marched and supported. The exigencies of the nation may require that the treasure raised in the north shall be transported to the south, that raised in the east conveyed to the west, or that this order should be reversed. Is that construction of the constitution to be preferred which would render these operations difficult, hazardous, and expensive? . . . [The Constitution] does not profess to enumerate the means by which the powers it confers may be executed; nor does it prohibit the creation of a corporation, if the existence of such a being be essential to the beneficial exercise of those powers. It is, then, the subject of fair inquiry, how far such means may be employed. . . .

The power of creating a corporation, though appertaining to sovereignty, is not, like the power of making war, or levying taxes, or of regulating commerce, a great substantive and independent power, which cannot be implied as incidental to other powers, or used as a means of executing them. It is never the end for which other powers are exercised, but a means by which other objects are accomplished. . . .

But the constitution of the United States has not left the right of Congress to employ the necessary means for the execution of the powers conferred on the government to general reasoning. To its enumeration of powers is added that of making "all laws which shall be necessary and proper, for carrying into execution the foregoing powers, and all other powers vested by this constitution, in the government of the United States, or in any department thereof."

The counsel for the State of Maryland have urged various arguments, to prove that this clause, though in terms a grant of power, is not so in effect; but is really restrictive of the general right, which might otherwise be implied of selecting means for executing the enumerated powers. . . .

[T]he argument on which most reliance is placed, is drawn from the peculiar language of this clause. Congress is not empowered by it to make all laws, which may have relation to the powers conferred on the government, but such only as may be "necessary and proper" for carrying them into execution. The word "necessary" is considered as controlling the whole sentence, and as limiting the right to pass laws for the execution of the granted powers, to such as are indispensable, and without which the power would be nugatory. That it excludes the choice of means, and leaves to Congress, in each case, that only which is most direct and simple.

Is it true that this is the sense in which the word "necessary" is always used? Does it always import an absolute physical necessity, so strong that one thing, to which another may be termed necessary, cannot exist without that other? We think it does not. . . . To employ the means necessary to an end, is generally understood as employing any means calculated to produce the end, and not as being confined to those single means, without which the end would be entirely unattainable. . . . Almost all compositions contain words, which, taken in their rigorous sense, would convey a meaning different from that which is obviously intended. It is essential to just construction, that many words which import something excessive should be understood in a more mitigated sense—in that sense which common usage justifies. The word "necessary" is of this description. . . . It admits of all degree of comparison; and is often connected with other words, which increase or diminish the impression the mind receives of the urgency it imports. A thing may be necessary, very necessary, absolutely or indispensably necessary. To no mind would the same idea be conveyed by these several phrases. This comment on the word is well illustrated by the passage cited at the bar, from the 10th section of the 1st article of the constitution. It is, we think, impossible to compare the sentence which prohibits a state from laying "imposts or duties on imports or exports, except what may be absolutely necessary for executing its inspection laws," with that which authorizes Congress "to make all laws which shall be necessary and proper for carrying into execution" the powers of the general government, without feeling a conviction that the convention understood itself to change materially the meaning of the word "necessary," by prefixing the word "absolutely." This word, then, like others, is used in various senses; and, in its construction, the subject, the context, the intention of the person using them, are all to be taken into view.

Let this be done in the case under consideration. The subject is the execution of those great powers on which the welfare of a nation essentially depends. It must have been the intention of those who gave these powers, to insure, as far as human prudence could insure, their beneficial execution. . . . This provision is made in a constitution intended to endure for ages to come, and consequently, to be adapted to the various crises of human affairs. To have prescribed the means by which government should, in all future time, execute its powers, would have been to change entirely the character of the instrument, and give it the properties of a legal code. It would have been an unwise attempt to provide, by immutable rules, for exigencies which, if foreseen at all, must have been seen dimly, and which can be best provided for as they occur. To have declared that the best means shall not be used, but those alone without which the power given would be nugatory, would have been to deprive the legislature of the capacity to avail itself of experience, to exercise its reason, and to accommodate its legislation to circumstances. If we apply this principle of construction to any of the powers of the government, we shall find it so pernicious in its operation that we shall be compelled to discard it. . . .

Take, for example, the power "to establish post-offices and post-roads." This power is executed by the single act of making the establishment. But, from this has been inferred the power and duty of carrying the mail along the post-road, from one post-office to another. And, from this implied power, has again been inferred the right to punish those who steal letters from the post-office, or rob the mail. It may be said, with some plausibility, that the right to carry the mail, and to punish those who rob it, is not indispensably necessary to the establishment of a post-office and post-road. This right is indeed essential to the beneficial exercise of the power, but not indispensably necessary to its existence. . . .

This clause, as construed by the state of Maryland, would abridge, and almost annihilate this useful and necessary right of the legislature to select its means. That this could not be intended is, we should think, had it not been already controverted, too apparent for controversy. We think so for the following reasons:

1st. The clause is placed among the powers of Congress, not among the limitations on those powers.

2nd. Its terms purport to enlarge, not to diminish the powers vested in the government. It purports to be an additional power, not a restriction on those already granted. . . .

If no other motive for its insertion can be suggested, a sufficient one is found in the desire to remove all doubts respecting the right to legislate on that vast mass of incidental powers which must be involved in the constitution, if that instrument is not a splendid bauble.

We admit, as all must admit, that the powers of the government are limited, and that its limits are not to be transcended. But we think the sound construction of the constitution must allow to the national legislature that discretion, with respect to the means by which the powers it confers are to be carried into execution, which will enable that body to perform the high duties assigned to it, in the manner most beneficial to the people. Let the end be legitimate, let it be within the scope of the constitution, and all means which are appropriate, which are plainly adapted to that end, which are not prohibited, but consist with the letter and spirit of the constitution, are constitutional. . . .

It being the opinion of the court that the act incorporating the bank is constitutional, and that the power of establishing a branch in the state of Maryland might be properly exercised by the bank itself, we proceed to inquire:

2. Whether the state of Maryland may, without violating the constitution, tax that branch? . . .

[The] great principle is, that the constitution, and the laws made in pursuance thereof are supreme; that they control the constitution and laws of the respective states, and cannot be controlled by them. From this, which may be almost termed an axiom, other propositions are deduced as corollaries, on the truth or error of which, and on their application to this case, the cause has been supposed to depend. These are, 1st. that a power to create implies a power to preserve. 2d. That a power to destroy, if wielded by a different hand, is hostile to, and incompatible with these powers to create and to preserve. 3d. That where this repugnancy exists, that authority which is supreme must control, not yield to that over which it is supreme. . . .

That the power of taxing [the bank] by the states may be exercised so as to destroy it, is too obvious to be denied. . . .

All subjects over which the sovereign power of a state extends, are objects of taxation; but those over which it does not extend, are, upon the soundest principles, exempt from taxation. This proposition may almost be pronounced self-evident.

The sovereignty of a state extends to everything which exists by its own authority, or is introduced by its permission; but does it extend to those means which are employed by Congress to carry into execution—powers conferred on that body by the people of the United States? We think it demonstrable that it does not. Those powers are not given by the people of a single state. They are given by the people of the United States, to a government whose laws, made in pursuance of the constitution, are declared to be supreme. . . .

If we measure the power of taxation residing in a state, by the extent of sovereignty which the people of a single state possess, and can confer on its government, we have an intelligible standard, applicable to every case to which the power may be applied. We have a principle which leaves the power of taxing the people and property of a state unimpaired; which leaves to a state the command of all its resources, and which places beyond its reach, all those powers which are conferred by the people of the United States on the government of the Union, and all those means which are given for the purpose of carrying those powers into execution. We have a principle which is safe for the states, and safe for the Union. We are relieved, as we ought to be, from clashing sovereignty; from interfering powers; from a repugnancy between a right in one government to pull down what there is an acknowledged right in another to build up; from the incompatibility of a right in one government to destroy what there is a right in another to preserve. We are not driven to the perplexing inquiry, so unfit for the judicial department, what degree of taxation is the legitimate use, and what degree may amount to the abuse of the power. . . .

We are unanimously of opinion that the law passed by the legislature of Maryland, imposing a tax on the Bank of the United States, is unconstitutional and void. . . .

17

Alexis de Tocqueville

The Purposes Served by Local Self-Government (1840)

. . . Egotism is a vice as old as the world, which does not belong to one form of society more than to another; individualism is of democratic origin, and it threatens to spread in the same ratio as the equality of conditions.

Among aristocratic nations, as families remain for centuries in the same condition, often on the same spot, all generations become, as it were, contemporaneous. A man almost always knows his forefathers and respects them; he thinks he already sees his remote descendants and he loves them. He willingly imposes duties on himself towards the former and the latter, and he will frequently sacrifice his personal gratifications to those who went before and to those who will come after him. Aristocratic institutions have, moreover, the effect of closely binding every man to several of his fellow citizens. As the classes of an aristocratic people are strongly marked and permanent, each of them is regarded by its own members as a sort of lesser country, more tangible and more cherished than the country at large. As in aristocratic communities all the citizens occupy fixed positions, one above another, the result is that each of them always sees a man above himself whose patronage is necessary to him, and below himself another man whose co-operation he may claim. Men living in aristocratic ages are therefore almost always closely attached to something placed out of their own sphere, and they are often disposed to forget themselves. It is true that in those ages the notion of human fellowship is faint and that men seldom think of sacrificing themselves for mankind; but they often sacrifice themselves for other men. In democratic ages, on the contrary, when the duties of each individual to the race are much more clear, devoted service to any one man becomes more rare; the bond of human affection is extended, but it is relaxed.

Among democratic nations new families are constantly springing up, others are constantly falling away, and all that remain change their

From *Democracy in America* by Alexis de Tocqueville, translated by Henry Reeve, 1862, with minor changes.

condition; the woof of time is every instant broken and the track of generations effaced. Those who went before are soon forgotten; of those who will come after, no one has any idea: the interest of man is confined to those in close propinquity to himself. As each class approximates to other classes and mingles with them, its members become indifferent and as strangers to one other. Aristocracy had made a chain of all the members of the community, from the peasant to the king; democracy breaks that chain and severs every link of it. . . .

Thus not only does democracy make every man forget his ancestors, but it hides his descendants and separates his contemporaries from him; it throws him back forever upon himself alone and threatens in the end to confine him entirely within the solitude of his own heart. . . .

Despotism, which is of a very timorous nature, is never more secure of continuance than when it can keep men asunder; and all its influence is commonly exerted for that purpose. . . .

Thus the vices which despotism engenders are precisely those which equality fosters. These two things mutually and perniciously complete and assist each other. Equality places men side by side, unconnected by any common tie; despotism raises barriers to keep them asunder. . . .

It is easy to see that in those same ages men stand most in need of freedom. When the members of a community are forced to attend to public affairs, they are necessarily drawn from the circle of their own interests and snatched at times from self-observation. As soon as a man begins to treat of public affairs in public, he begins to perceive that he is not so independent of his fellow men as he had at first imagined, and that in order to obtain their support he must often lend them his cooperation.

When the public is supreme, there is no man who does not feel the value of public goodwill or who does not endeavor to court it by drawing to himself the esteem and affection of those among whom he is to live. Many of the passions which congeal and keep asunder human hearts are then obliged to retire and hide below the surface. Pride must be dissembled; disdain dares not break out; egotism fears its own self. Under a free government, as most public offices are elective, the men whose elevated minds or aspiring hopes are too closely circumscribed in private life constantly feel that they cannot do without the population which surrounds them. Men learn at such times to think of their fellow men from ambitious motives; and they frequently find it, in a manner, their interest to forget themselves. . . .

The desire of being elected may lead some men for a time to violent hostility; but this same desire leads all men in the long run to support each other; and if it happens that an election accidentally severs two friends, the electoral system brings a multitude of citizens permanently together who would otherwise always have remained unknown to each other. . . .

The Americans have combated by free institutions the tendency of equality to keep men asunder, and they have subdued it. The legislators of America did not suppose that a general representation of the whole nation would suffice to ward off a disorder at once so natural to the frame of democratic society and so fatal; they also thought that it would be well to infuse political life into each portion of the territory in order to multiply to an infinite extent opportunities of acting in concert for all the members of the community and to make them constantly feel their mutual dependence on each other. The plan was a wise one. The general affairs of a country only engage the attention of leading politicians, who assemble from time to time in the same places; and as they often lose sight of each other afterwards, no lasting ties are established between them. But if the object be to have the local affairs of a district conducted by the men who reside there, the same persons are always in contact, and they are, in a manner, forced to be acquainted and to adapt themselves to one another.

It is difficult to draw a man out of his own circle to interest him in the destiny of the state, because he does not clearly understand what influence the destiny of the state can have upon his own lot. But if it is proposed to make a road cross the end of his estate, he will see at a glance that there is a connection between this small public affair and his greatest private affairs; and he will discover, without its being shown to him, the close tie that unites private to general interest. Thus far more may be done by entrusting to the citizens the administration of minor affairs than by surrendering to them the control of important ones, towards interesting them in the public welfare and convincing them that they constantly stand in need one of the other in order to provide for it. A brilliant achievement may win for you the favor of a people at one stroke; but to earn the love and respect of the population that surrounds you, a long succession of little services rendered and of obscure good deeds, a constant habit of kindness, and an established reputation for disinterestedness will be required. Local freedom, then, which leads a great number of citizens to value the affection of their neighbors and of their kindred, perpetually brings men together and forces them to help one another in spite of the propensiries that sever them. . . .

18

Robert D. Putnam

Bowling Alone: America's Declining Social Capital (1995)

Many students of the new democracies that have emerged over the past decade and a half have emphasized the importance of a strong and active civil society to the consolidation of democracy. Especially with regard to the postcommunist countries, scholars and democratic activists alike have lamented the absence or obliteration of traditions of independent civic engagement and a widespread tendency toward passive reliance on the state. To those concerned with the weakness of civil societies in the developing or postcommunist world, the advanced Western democracies and above all the United States have typically been taken as models to be emulated. There is striking evidence, however, that the vibrancy of American civil society has notably declined over the past several decades.

Ever since the publication of Alexis de Tocqueville's *Democracy in America*, the United States has played a central role in systematic studies of the links between democracy and civil society. Although this is in part because trends in American life are often regarded as harbingers of social modernization, it is also because America has traditionally been considered unusually "civic" (a reputation that, as we shall later see, has not been entirely unjustified).

When Tocqueville visited the United States in the 1830s, it was the Americans' propensity for civic association that most impressed him as the key to their unprecedented ability to make democracy work. "Americans of all ages, all stations in life, and all types of disposition," he observed, "are forever forming associations. There are not only commercial and industrial associations in which all take part, but others of a thousand different types—religious, moral, serious, futile, very general and very limited, immensely

Putnam, Robert D. Bowling Alone: America's Declining Social Capital. Journal of Democracy 6:1 (1995), 65–78. Copyright © 1995 The National Endowment for Democracy and the Johns Hopkins University Press. Its argument was amplified and to some extent modified in Robert D. Putnam's book, *Bowling Alone: The Collapse and Revival of American Community* (Simon & Schuster, 2000) Reprinted with permission of the Johns Hopkins University Press.

large and very minute. . . . Nothing, in my view, deserves more attention than the intellectual and moral associations in America."

Recently, American social scientists of a neo-Tocquevillean bent have unearthed a wide range of empirical evidence that the quality of public life and the performance of social institutions (and not only in America) are indeed powerfully influenced by norms and networks of civic engagement. Researchers in such fields as education, urban poverty, unemployment, the control of crime and drug abuse, and even health have discovered that successful outcomes are more likely in civically engaged communities. Similarly, research on the varying economic attainments of different ethnic groups in the United States has demonstrated the importance of social bonds within each group. These results are consistent with research in a wide range of settings that demonstrates the vital importance of social networks for job placement and many other economic outcomes.

Meanwhile, a seemingly unrelated body of research on the sociology of economic development has also focused attention on the role of social networks. Some of this work is situated in the developing countries, and some of it elucidates the peculiarly successful "network capitalism" of East Asia. Even in less exotic Western economies, however, researchers have discovered highly efficient, highly flexible "industrial districts" based on networks of collaboration among workers and small entrepreneurs. Far from being paleoindustrial anachronisms, these dense interpersonal and interorganizational networks undergird ultramodern industries, from the high tech of Silicon Valley to the high fashion of Benetton.

The norms and networks of civic engagement also powerfully affect the performance of representative government. That, at least, was the central conclusion of my own 20-year, quasi-experimental study of subnational governments in different regions of Italy. Although all these regional governments seemed identical on paper, their levels of effectiveness varied dramatically. Systematic inquiry showed that the quality of governance was determined by longstanding traditions of civic engagement (or its absence). Voter turnout, newspaper readership, membership in choral societies and football clubs—these were the hallmarks of a successful region. In fact, historical analysis suggested that these networks of organized reciprocity and civic solidarity, far from being an epiphenomenon of socioeconomic modernization, were a precondition for it.

No doubt the mechanisms through which civic engagement and social connectedness produce such results—better schools, faster economic development, lower crime, and more effective government—are multiple and complex. While these briefly recounted findings require further confirmation and perhaps qualification, the parallels across hundreds of empirical studies in a dozen disparate disciplines and subfields are striking. Social scientists in several fields have recently suggested a common framework for understanding these phenomena, a framework that rests on the concept of *social capital*. By analogy with notions of physical capital and human capital—tools and training that enhance individual productivity—"social capital" refers to features of social organization such as networks, norms, and social trust that facilitate coordination and cooperation for mutual benefit.

For a variety of reasons, life is easier in a community blessed with a substantial stock of social capital. In the first place, networks of civic engagement foster sturdy norms of generalized reciprocity and encourage the emergence of social trust. Such networks facilitate coordination and communication, amplify reputations, and thus allow dilemmas of collective action to be resolved. When economic and political negotiation is embedded in dense networks of social interaction, incentives for opportunism are reduced. At the same time, networks of civic engagement embody past success at collaboration, which can serve as a cultural template for future collaboration. Finally, dense networks of interaction probably broaden the participants' sense of self, developing the "I" into the "we," or (in the language of rational-choice theorists) enhancing the participants' "taste" for collective benefits.

I do not intend here to survey (much less contribute to) the development of the theory of social capital. Instead, I use the central premise of that rapidly growing body of work—that social connections and civic engagement pervasively influence our public life, as well as our private prospects—as the starting point for an empirical survey of trends in social capital in contemporary America. I concentrate here entirely on the American case, although the developments I portray may in some measure characterize many contemporary societies.

Whatever Happened to Civic Engagement?

We begin with familiar evidence on changing patterns of political participation, not least because it is immediately relevant to issues of democracy in the narrow sense. Consider the well-known decline in turnout in national elections over the last three decades. From a relative high point in the early 1960s, voter turnout had by 1990 declined by nearly a quarter; tens of millions of Americans had forsaken their parents' habitual readiness to engage in the simplest act of citizenship. Broadly similar trends also characterize participation in state and local elections.

It is not just the voting booth that has been increasingly deserted by Americans. A series of identical questions posed by the Roper Organization to national samples ten times each year over the last two decades reveals that since 1973 the number of Americans who report that "in the past year" they have "attended a public meeting on town or school affairs" has fallen by more than a third (from 22 percent in 1973 to 13 percent in 1993). Similar (or even greater) relative declines are evident in responses to questions about attending a political rally or speech, serving on a committee of some local organization, and working for a political party. By almost every measure, Americans' direct engagement in politics and government has fallen steadily and sharply over the last generation, despite the fact that average levels of education—the best individual-level predictor of political participation—have risen sharply throughout this period. Every year over the last decade or two, millions more have withdrawn from the affairs of their communities.

Not coincidentally, Americans have also disengaged psychologically from politics and government over this era. The proportion of Americans who reply that they "trust the government in Washington" only "some of the time" or "almost never" has risen steadily from 30 percent in 1966 to 75 percent in 1992.

These trends are well known, of course, and taken by themselves would seem amenable to a strictly political explanation. Perhaps the long litany of political tragedies and scandals since the 1960s (assassinations, Vietnam, Watergate, Irangate, and so on) has triggered an understandable disgust for politics and government among Americans, and that in turn has motivated their withdrawal. I do not doubt that this common interpretation has some merit, but its limitations become plain when we examine trends in civic engagement of a wider sort.

Our survey of organizational membership among Americans can usefully begin with a glance at the aggregate results of the General Social Survey, a scientifically conducted, national-sample survey that has been repeated 14 times over the last two decades. Church-related groups constitute the most common type of organization joined by Americans; they are especially popular with women. Other types of organizations frequently joined by women include school-service groups (mostly parent-teacher associations), sports groups, professional societies, and literary societies. Among men, sports clubs, labor unions, professional societies, fraternal groups, veterans' groups, and service clubs are all relatively popular.

Religious affiliation is by far the most common associational membership among Americans. Indeed, by many measures America continues to be (even more than in Tocqueville's time) an astonishingly "churched" society. For example, the United States has more houses of worship per capita than any other nation on Earth. Yet religious sentiment in America seems to be becoming somewhat less tied to institutions and more self-defined.

How have these complex crosscurrents played out over the last three or four decades in terms of Americans' engagement with organized religion? The general pattern is clear: The 1960s witnessed a significant drop in reported weekly churchgoing—from roughly 48 percent in the late 1950s to roughly 41 percent in the early 1970s. Since then, it has stagnated or (according to some surveys) declined still further. Meanwhile, data from the General Social Survey show a modest decline in membership in all "church-related groups" over the last 20 years. It would seem, then, that net participation by Americans, both in religious services and in church-related groups, has declined modestly (by perhaps a sixth) since the 1960s.

For many years, labor unions provided one of the most common organizational affiliations among American workers. . . .

The parent-teacher association (PTA) has been an especially important form of civic engagement in twentieth-century America because parental involvement in the educational process represents a particularly productive form of social capital. It is, therefore, dismaying to discover that participation in parent-teacher organizations has dropped drastically over the last generation, from more than 12 million in 1964 to barely 5 million in 1982 before recovering to approximately 7 million now.

Next, we turn to evidence on membership in (and volunteering for) civic and fraternal organizations. These data show some striking patterns. First, membership in traditional women's groups has declined more or less steadily since the mid-1960s. For example, membership in the national Federation of Women's Clubs is down by more than half (59 percent) since 1964, while membership in the League of Women Voters (LWV) is off 42 percent since 1969.

Similar reductions are apparent in the numbers of volunteers for mainline civic organizations, such as the Boy Scouts (off by 26 percent since 1970) and the Red Cross (off by 61 percent since 1970). But what about the possibility that volunteers have simply switched their loyalties to other organizations? Evidence on "regular" (as opposed to occasional or "drop-by") volunteering is available from the Labor Department's Current Population Surveys of 1974 and 1989. These estimates suggest that serious volunteering declined by roughly one-sixth over these 15 years, from 24 percent of adults in 1974 to 20 percent in 1989. The multitudes of Red Cross aides and Boy Scout troop leaders now missing in action have apparently not been offset by equal numbers of new recruits elsewhere.

Fraternal organizations have also witnessed a substantial drop in membership during the 1980s and 1990s. Membership is down significantly in such groups as the Lions (off 12 percent since 1983), the Elks (off 18 percent since 1979), the Shriners (off 27 percent since 1979), the Jaycees (off 44 percent since 1979), and the Masons (down 39 percent since 1959). In sum, after expanding steadily throughout most of this century, many major civic organizations have experienced a sudden, substantial, and nearly simultaneous decline in membership over the last decade or two.

The most whimsical yet discomfiting bit of evidence of social disengagement in contemporary America that I have discovered is this: more Americans are bowling today than ever before, but bowling in organized leagues has plummeted in the last decade or so. Between 1980 and 1993 the total number of bowlers in America increased by 10 percent, while league bowling decreased by 40 percent. (Lest this be thought a wholly trivial example, I should note that nearly 80 million Americans went bowling at least once during 1993, *nearly a third more than voted in the 1994 congressional elections* and roughly the same number as claim to attend church regularly. Even after the 1980s' plunge in league bowling, nearly 3 percent of American adults regularly bowl in leagues.) The rise of solo bowling threatens the livelihood of bowling-lane proprietors because those who bowl as members of leagues consume three times as much beer and pizza as solo bowlers, and the money in bowling is in the beer and pizza, not the balls and shoes. The broader social significance, however, lies in the social interaction and even occasionally civic conversations over beer and pizza that solo bowlers forgo. Whether or not bowling beats balloting in the eyes of most Americans, bowling teams illustrate yet another vanishing form of social capital.

COUNTERTRENDS

At this point, however, we must confront a serious counterargument. Perhaps the traditional forms of civic organization whose decay we have been tracing have been replaced by vibrant new organizations. For example, national environmental organizations (like the Sierra Club) and feminist groups (like the National Organization for Women) grew rapidly during the 1970s and 1980s and now count hundreds of thousands of dues-paying members. An even more dramatic example is the American Association of Retired Persons (AARP), which grew exponentially from 400,000 card-carrying members in 1960 to 33 million in 1993, becoming (after the Catholic Church) the largest private organization in the world. The national administrators of these organizations are among the most feared lobbyists in Washington, in large part because of their massive mailing lists of presumably loyal members.

These new mass-membership organizations are plainly of great political importance. From the point of view of social connectedness, however, they are sufficiently different from classic "secondary associations" that we need to invent a new label—perhaps "tertiary associations." For the vast majority of their members, the only act of membership consists in writing a check for dues or perhaps occasionally reading a newsletter. Few ever attend any meetings of such organizations, and most are unlikely ever (knowingly) to encounter any other member. The bond between any two members of the Sierra Club is less like the bond between any two members of a gardening club and more like the bond between any two Red Sox fans (or perhaps any two devoted Honda owners): they root for the same team and they share some of the same interests, but they are unaware of each other's existence. Their ties, in short, are to common symbols, common leaders, and perhaps common ideals, but not to one another. The theory of social capital argues that associational membership should, for example, increase social trust, but this prediction is much less straightforward with regard to membership in tertiary associations. . . .

Some able researchers have argued that the last few decades have witnessed a rapid expansion in "support groups" of various sorts. Robert Wuthnow reports that fully 40 percent of all Americans claim to be "currently involved in [a] small group that meets regularly and provides support or caring for those who participate in it." Many of these groups are religiously affiliated, but many others are not. For example, nearly 5 percent of Wuthnow's national sample claim to participate regularly in a "self-help" group, such as Alcoholics Anonymous, and nearly as many say they belong to book-discussion groups and hobby clubs.

The groups described by Wuthnow's respondents unquestionably represent an important form of social capital, and they need to be accounted for in any serious reckoning of trends in social connectedness. On the other hand, they do not typically play the same role as traditional civic associations. As Wuthnow emphasizes,

> Small groups may not be fostering community as effectively as many of their proponents would like. Some small groups merely provide occasions for individuals to focus on themselves in the presence of others. The social contract binding members together asserts only the weakest of obligations. Come if you have time. Talk if you feel like it. Respect everyone's opinion. Never criticize. Leave quietly if you become dissatisfied. . . . We can imagine that [these small groups] really substitute for families, neighborhoods, and broader community attachments that may demand lifelong commitments, when, in fact, they do not.

. . . Within all educational categories, total associational membership declined significantly between 1967 and 1993. Among the college-educated, the average number of group memberships per person fell from 2.8 to 2.0 (a 26-percent decline); among high-school graduates, the number fell from 1.8 to 1.2 (32 percent); and among those with fewer than 12 years of education, the number fell from 1.4 to 1.1 (25 percent). In other words, at *all* educational (and hence social) levels of American society, and counting *all* sorts of group memberships, *the average number of associational memberships has fallen by about a fourth over the last quarter-century*. Without controls for educational levels, the trend is not nearly so clear, but the central point is this: *more Americans than ever before are in social circumstances that foster associational involvement (higher education, middle age, and so on), but nevertheless aggregate associational membership appears to be stagnant or declining*. . . . In short, the available survey evidence confirms our earlier conclusion: American social capital in the form of civic associations has significantly eroded over the last generation.

Good Neighborliness and Social Trust

. . . [T]he most fundamental form of social capital is the family, and the massive evidence of the loosening of bonds within the family (both extended and nuclear) is well known. This trend, of course, is quite consistent with—and may help to explain—our theme of social decapitalization.

A second aspect of informal social capital on which we happen to have reasonably reliable time-series data involves neighborliness. In each General

Social Survey since 1974 respondents have been asked, "How often do you spend a social evening with a neighbor?" The proportion of Americans who socialize with their neighbors more than once a year has slowly but steadily declined over the last two decades, from 72 percent in 1974 to 61 percent in 1993. (On the other hand, socializing with "friends who do not live in your neighborhood" appears to be on the increase, a trend that may reflect the growth of workplace-based social connections.)

Americans are also less trusting. The proportion of Americans saying that most people can be trusted fell by more than a third between 1960, when 58 percent chose that alternative, and 1993, when only 37 percent did. The same trend is apparent in all educational groups; indeed, because social trust is also correlated with education and because educational levels have risen sharply, the overall decrease in social trust is even more apparent is we control for education. . . .

WHY IS U.S. SOCIAL CAPITAL ERODING?

As we have seen, something has happened in America in the last two or three decades to diminish civic engagement and social connectedness. What could that "something" be? Here are several possible explanations, along with some initial evidence on each.

The movement of women into the labor force. Over these same two or three decades, many millions of American women have moved out of the home into paid employment. This is the primary, though not the sole, reason why the weekly working hours of the average American have increased significantly during these years. It seems highly plausible that this social revolution should have reduced the time and energy available for building social capital. For certain organizations, such as the PTA, the League of Women Voters, the Federation of Women's Clubs, and the Red Cross, this is almost certainly an important part of the story. The sharpest decline in women's civic participation seems to have come in the 1970s; membership in such "women's" organizations as these has been virtually halved since the late 1960s. By contrast, most of the decline in participation in men's organizations occurred about ten years later; the total decline to date has been approximately 25 percent for the typical organization. On the other hand, the survey data imply that the aggregate declines for men are virtually as great as those for women. It is logically possible, of course, that the male declines might represent the knock-on effect of women's liberation, as dishwashing crowded out the lodge, but time-budget studies suggest that most husbands of working wives have assumed only a minor part of the housework. In short, something besides the women's revolution seems to lie behind the erosion of social capital.

Mobility. The "re-potting" hypothesis. Numerous studies of organizational involvement have shown that residential stability and such related phenomena as homeownership are clearly associated with greater civic engagement. Mobility, like frequent re-potting of plants, tends to disrupt root systems, and it takes time for an uprooted individual to put down new roots. It seems plausible that the automobile, suburbanization, and the movement to the Sun Belt have reduced the social rootedness of the average American, but one fundamental difficulty with this hypothesis is apparent: the best evidence shows that residential stability and homeownership in America have risen modestly since 1965, and are surely higher now than during the 1950s, when civic engagement and social connectedness by our measures was definitely higher.

Other demographic transformations. A range of additional changes have transformed the American family since the 1960s—fewer marriages, more divorces, fewer children, lower real wages, and so on. Each of these changes might account for some of the slackening of civic engagement, since married, middle-class parents are generally more socially involved than other people. Moreover, the changes in scale that have swept over the American economy in these years—illustrated by the replacement of the corner grocery by the supermarket and now perhaps of the supermarket by electronic shopping at home, or the replacement of community-based enterprises by outposts of distant multinational firms—may perhaps have undermined the material and even physical basis for civic engagement.

The technological transformation of leisure. There is reason to believe that deep-seated technological trends are radically "privatizing" or "individualizing" our use of leisure time and thus disrupting many opportunities for social-capital formation. The most obvious and probably the most powerful instrument of this revolution is television. Time-budget studies in the 1960s showed that the growth in time spent watching television dwarfed all other changes in the way Americans passed their days and nights. Television has made our communities (or, rather, what we experience as our communities) wider and shallower. In the language of economics, electronic technology enables individual tastes to be satisfied more fully, but at the cost of the positive social externalities associated with more primitive forms of entertainment. The same logic applies to the replacement of vaudeville by the movies and now of movies by the VCR. The new "virtual reality" helmets that we will soon don to be entertained in total isolation are merely the latest extension of this trend. Is technology thus driving a wedge between our individual interests and our collective interests? It is a question that seems worth exploring more systematically.

WHAT IS TO BE DONE?

The last refuge of a social-scientific scoundrel is to call for more research. Nevertheless, I cannot forbear from suggesting some further lines of inquiry.

- We must sort out the dimensions of social capital, which clearly is not a unidimensional concept, despite language (even in this essay) that implies the contrary. What types of organizations and networks most effectively embody—or generate—social capital, in the sense of mutual reciprocity, the resolution of dilemmas of collective action, and the broadening of social identities? In this essay I have emphasized the density of associational life. In earlier work I stressed the structure of networks, arguing that "horizontal" ties represented more productive social capital than vertical ties.

- Another set of important issues involves macrosociological crosscurrents that might intersect with the trends described here. What will be the impact, for example, of electronic networks on social capital? My hunch is that meeting in an electronic forum is not the equivalent of meeting in a bowling alley—or even in a saloon—but hard empirical research is needed. . . .

- Finally, and perhaps most urgently, we need to explore creatively how public policy impinges on (or might impinge on) social-capital formation. In some well-known instances, public policy has destroyed highly effective social networks and norms. American slum-clearance policy of the 1950s and 1960s, for example, renovated physical capital, but at a very high cost to existing social capital. The consolidation of country post offices and small school districts has promised administrative and financial efficiencies, but full-cost accounting for the effects of these policies on social capital might produce a more negative verdict. On the other hand, such past initiatives as the county agricultural-agent system, community colleges, and tax deductions for charitable contributions illustrate that government can encourage social-capital formation. Even a recent proposal in San Luis Obispo, California, to require that all new houses have front porches illustrates the power of government to influence where and how networks are formed.

The concept of "civil society" has played a central role in the recent global debate about the preconditions for democracy and democratization. In the newer democracies this phrase has properly focused attention on the need to foster a vibrant civic life in soils traditionally inhospitable to self-government. In the established democracies, ironically, growing numbers of citizens are questioning the effectiveness of their public institutions at the very moment when liberal democracy has swept the battlefield, both ideologically and geopolitically. In America, at least, there is reason to suspect that this democratic disarray may be linked to a broad and continuing erosion of civic engagement that began a quarter-century ago. High on our scholarly agenda should be the question of whether a comparable erosion of social capital may be under way in other advanced democracies, perhaps in different institutional and behavioral guises. High on America's agenda should be the question of how to reverse these adverse trends in social connectedness, thus restoring civic engagement and civic trust.

19

William A. Schambra

By the People: The Old Values of the New Citizenship (1994)

. . . That the institutions and values of civil society are deeply imperiled and desperately in need of resuscitation today is a conviction widely shared across the political spectrum. . . .

The consequences of civil society's decline are evident throughout our daily life, in soaring rates of crime, divorce, illegitimacy, neighborhood deterioration, welfare dependency, chemical addiction, suicide, and virtually every other indicator of pathology. While these symptoms are most vividly on display in the inner city, they are rapidly taking root in suburban culture as well.

In his classic, *The Quest for Community*, Robert Nisbet describes the powerful forces of modernity complicit in this civic and moral unraveling, with assaults on civil society coming both from below and from above. From below, the authority of family, church, neighborhood, and school is quietly eroded by the proliferation of individual rights, especially the right of self-expression— that is, expression of self with utter disregard for civil society. From above, civil institutions are pressured to surrender authority and function to the professional elites of the centralized, bureaucratic state. Today's Boy Scout troops, for instance, may as well turn themselves over to the federal courts for management, given the relentless legal assault on their morally rigorous organizational principles by champions of the rights of "alternative lifestyles." Caught in a pincers movement between individual rights and the central state, Nisbet notes, the intermediate associations of civil society languish.

However, it would be an error to suppose that the erosion of civil society is somehow a natural or inevitable consequence of modern progress. Rather,

From Schambra, "By the People," *Policy Review*, published by the Heritage Foundation, Summer, 1994. Reprinted by permission.

the central project of the modern progressive liberal state is to eradicate civil society, and to transfer its functions to government. It is doing so, ironically, in the name of restoring community—now understood as *national* community.

THE NATIONAL COMMUNITY

The idea of national community sprang from the minds of Herbert Croly, Walter Lippmann, John Dewey, and others at the turn of the century, and was introduced into American politics by Theodore Roosevelt's enunciation of a "new nationalism" in 1910. It is progressive liberalism's grand intellectual attempt to reconcile the centralized, bureaucratic, therapeutic state with the idea of public-spirited citizenship and community.

According to the progressive vision, various forces of modernity—industrialization, urbanization, advanced communications and transportation—had forever shattered the boundaries of America's traditional, self-contained, village-centered way of life. But those same forces—when gathered into the guiding hand of the centralized bureaucratic state—now permitted a degree of rationalized, efficient management of human affairs unimaginable in the earlier epoch of diverse local communities. In Dewey's famous formulation, it was now possible and necessary to convert the "Great Society created by steam and electricity" into the "Great Community."

Humanizing and softening the harsh, mechanistic aspects of this new national leviathan was the president, standing at the center and articulating a vision of grand, national purpose—which in turn bestowed legitimacy upon the new national state. That vision would summon citizens out of merely self-interested, materialistic pursuits, into public-spirited, civic-minded devotion to a common national idea and a unifying national state. (If this sounds far-fetched, recall Walter Mondale's insistence in the 1984 campaign that the president's preeminent task was to "make us a community and keep us a community.")

If the devotion to national purpose and state should falter, the president could reach into his quiver of national "wars" and "crises," which would serve to remind Americans of the need to pull together as one in the face of perilous conditions or threats to national integrity. Thus would Lyndon Johnson describe his program as a "war on poverty" precisely because the "military image" would "sound a call to arms which will stir people . . . to lend their talents to a massive effort to eradicate the evil." Thus would Jimmy Carter declare the "energy crisis" to be the "moral equivalent of war," which would "give us all a sense of unity and purpose again."

According to the progressives, this new idea of national community—coherent, efficient, rational, yet infused with the warm glow of purpose and belonging—was vastly preferable to the chaotic jumble of divergent civic institutions and local loyalties, which the state would now proceed to eliminate or absorb.

The theme of national community—an old chestnut of Democratic presidential candidates throughout this century—has already found an honored place in Clinton rhetoric. The "New Covenant" speech at Georgetown University in October, 1991, laying out the larger message of the Clinton campaign, was tellingly sub-titled "Responsibility and Rebuilding the American Community." Clinton complained that "there's a hole in our politics where a sense of common purpose used to be," and called for a "New Covenant" to "restore a sense of community to this great nation." Again and again, he has returned to this vision of a renewed national family or community, sharply posing its demands for national service and public-mindedness to the "gilded age" of the 1980s, when "greed, selfishness, irresponsibility, excess, and neglect" prevailed.

In light of this larger project, one appreciates all the more Clinton's deft deployment of Oprah-style media forms to cultivate a warm, caring, nurturing, "feel your pain," family atmosphere among a sprawling population of 250 million. That there suddenly should be a great national "crisis" in health care requiring—what else?—a massive extension of government power is a page right out of liberalism's dog-eared playbook.

Moreover, the national community ideal offers a facile, rhetorical bridge over the chasm between "new Democrat" supporters who genuinely yearn for a revitalization of civic life, and "old Democrats" who prefer the further expansion of government's reach. It permits Clinton to speak the language of civic revival, while pursuing the policy of government revival.

If the national community idea is a dead end, however, how are we to go about resuscitating civil society? . . .

FALSE STARTS

Unhappily, the past three Republican administrations have left a dismal record in this regard. . . .

After boldly calling for "an end of giantism, for a return to the human scale . . . the scale of the local fraternal lodge, the church organization, the block club, the farm bureau," President Reagan could manage little more than the "Task Force on Private Sector Initiatives." Filled with liberal foundation officers and well-intentioned but naive corporate CEOs, the task force quickly bogged down in pointless debates about whether or not corporations should be expected to foot the bill for welfare state programs, As Reagan's ACTION director Tom Pauken put it, task force members seemed to believe the mission was to "change one set of bureaucrats for another and say we've accomplished something just because they're off the federal payroll." A genuine return to local citizen democracy was never on the agenda.

Likewise, after grandly proclaiming his vision of America as a "nation of communities, of thousands of ethnic, religious, social, business, labor union, neighborhood, regional, and other organizations, all of them varied, voluntary, and unique," President Bush could only come up with the "points of light" initiative, which passed out hundreds of daily awards to worthy volunteer groups, but otherwise had nothing to say about the broader transformation of public policy toward a genuine, community-oriented basis.

THE LIMITS OF PUBLIC POLICY

These false starts toward civic revival should lead us to be considerably more modest in our expectations of policy. To be sure, there are some policies that could help promote localism and civic renewal—such as offering unrestricted education vouchers, restoring family income by increasing the tax deduction for children, and toughening laws concerning child support and divorce. But most useful measures in the public policy realm involve shrinking that realm itself, by diminishing the reach of the therapeutic state and its debilitating effects on private institutions.

Even when public policy approaches the civic realm with the best of intentions, it more often than not only makes things worse. . . . Again and again—whether it's child care, foster care, adoption, homes for unwed mothers, resettlement of refugees, or disaster relief—the appearance of even well-intentioned federal assistance inevitably signals the retreat of civic institutions, and the worsening of problems they previously ameliorated.

Too often in the past, conservatives have made this essential point about the limits of public policy, concluding that "it's up to civil society" to address our social problems—and then walked away. . . .

For conservatives, "it's up to civil society" should not be the conclusion of inquiry, but the beginning. Indeed, the central questions for conservatism at this moment in its history should be: How can we *recreate* civil society where it has collapsed, retreated, or never formed? And most important, how can we do so on the terms of civil society itself—that is, relying chiefly on resources available within the private sector, rather than on the problematic instrument of public policy?

If excessive conservative optimism about the resilience of civil society is one way to evade this question, excessive pessimism is another, more popular way. Many conservatives understand civic devastation to be vast—and irreparable. A minor industry has sprung up around detailing the decline and seemingly permanent disappearance of our most important civic institutions. Some conservatives go so far as to suggest that we should in essence dig moats around the remaining Midwestern towns and Southern villages where community virtues still prevail, and let the rest of the nation stew in modernity's corrosive juices.

Leaving aside other problems with this approach, let's just say that there is little reason to be so pessimistic. After all, Tocqueville was one of the first to ponder the destruction modern forces would visit on traditional institutions—over a century and a half ago. Indeed, his purpose in writing *Democracy in America* was to warn about the impending storm of modernity—to tell us that the old, established institutions of civil society would soon be borne away by the cyclonic winds of modern individualism and the centralized state.

A GENIUS FOR ASSOCIATION

In America, however, he witnessed the remarkable spectacle of unrelated individuals—as he put it, "people having different languages, beliefs, opinions . . . without roots, without memories, without prejudices, without routines, without common ideas"—coming together to create wholly new forms of civil institutions, in the very teeth of the modern storm. The impulse toward association—the yearning for genuine citizenship within civil society—is not so easy to destroy, he seemed to suggest. . . .

The American genius for association is evident throughout American history. . . . Even in the midst of the community-eroding forces of modernity, other powerful impulses are compelling heretofore isolated individuals to reengage with or recreate civic institutions. Parenthood is one such potent motivation.

Time and again, individuals who have abandoned themselves to disorganized lives or passive dependence on the state are suddenly galvanized into civic activity when they become parents, and realize that their children face an identically bleak future unless they take dramatic action. The sight of their children walking to school through the litter of IV needles and the clusters of drug dealers, or the thought of their daughter growing up permanently locked in welfare dependency, is simply unbearable. They may put up with any amount of abuse in their own lives, but as parents their cry becomes "not with my children, you don't."

The central goal for such parents is the recreation of a safe, orderly, structured, neighborhood environment for their children—one in which they are physically safe, emotionally and spiritually nurtured, and intellectually and morally instructed. Parents seek to reestablish the web of institutional supports that express, reinforce, and pass on to their children the wisdom and moral discipline necessary for a fruitful life, with family, church, school, and neighborhood all reflecting certain common ethical themes. . . .

This yearning for community applies equally to the urban and suburban middle class. Many professional couples for the first time are being spurred by parenthood to begin working within churches, neighborhoods, Little League teams, and a host of other groups and institutions.

In a recent *New York Times* interview, sociologist Wade Clark Roof suggested this was true of baby boomer parents in particular: "In an era of enormous fragmentation, parents are expressing concern about the moral and religious socialization of their children." And so they are turning toward church and community to create an orderly moral universe. As Irving Kristol notes, in the face of "the single most important question that adults face"—how shall we raise our children?—modern parents suddenly drop the trendy project of personal liberation, and begin to focus instead on the restoration of social order.

Kristol predicts that the growing urgency of this question for millions of new parents will help fuel a major religious revival across the land. Without a doubt, churches, synagogues, and other religious institutions will play a central role in civic regeneration—particularly in the inner city. Over the years he has worked with neighborhood groups, Bob Woodson has found that at the heart of the most successful—those that genuinely change individual lives, as well as material surroundings—is an explicit call for personal spiritual transformation.

In many inner-city neighborhoods, the church is one of the only institutions of civil society left. Many congregations are taking the lead in securing better housing and improved city services, providing drug and alcohol rehabilitation, job training, and family support, and opening small business opportunities—often inspired and sustained by an unwavering spiritual commitment. . . .

While such efforts must proceed largely without "benefit" of public policy, a certain degree of political involvement will nonetheless be thrust upon "new citizenship" efforts. For bureaucratic elites will need to be evicted from regions of civil society over which they currently exercise dominion, and their furious counterassaults repelled.

Certainly the struggle over education reform at the state level suggests the outlines of a new, grassroots political activism that will emerge as the new citizenship expands. Newly energized parents are striving to reclaim authority over schools from entrenched education bureaucracies. Their primary goal is to reestablish the schools as stable, structured, demanding learning environments, reflecting—rather than subverting—the moral commitments of the family. . . .

Similar battles against government elites are underway elsewhere: Families in public housing trying to rebuild community life are confronting legal obstacles to fighting crime and becoming economically self-sufficient; entrepreneurs struggle to establish small businesses in the face of oppressive regulation. . . .

The feisty populism of the new citizenship will not be welcomed by all those traditionally found under the conservative tent. Certainly the substance, to say nothing of the style, of the new citizenship will be somewhat off-putting to the old-line, country-club Republicans, who came to dominate the upper reaches of the last administration, and who winced at the Houston Convention's foray into "family values." For them, talk about fullscale assaults on ruling cultural elites will be vaguely menacing, and earnest discussion of restoring the spiritual and moral vitality of the inner city will seem, well, vulgar. . . .

OUT OF THE IVORY TOWER

. . . Conservative commitment to civic revival will thus clearly demand far more attention to and personal involvement with *doing*, with actual experience in deploying the instruments of civil society to promote that revival. Consequently, more of us must be prepared to support those conservative activists already working at the grassroots level to restore civic vitality— through encouragement of tenant management of public housing, neighborhood economic development, private schools for inner-city children, and church-based moral reconstruction. . . .

Perhaps the most widespread form and clearest practical example of conservative civic activism today, however, is the so-called "private voucher movement." In a number of cities across the nation, philanthropic foundations and corporations have finally despaired of reforming public education from within. At the same time, many inner city parents gaze longingly at nearby church-based schools, which promise instruction in morality and character as well as academics, but whose modest tuitions put them just out of reach. Private voucher systems broker the needs and desires of all these parties: Low-income parents are given vouchers to redeem at any school of their choice, religious or nonsectarian, by reform-minded philanthropists, while value-generating educational institutions receive much-needed financial support. . . .

While these groups and movements are promoting the reconstruction of civil society, they are contributing to another sort of reconstruction as well—that of American conservatism. The public image of conservatism still remains firmly fixed where it was some 15 years ago, when Jeane Kirkpatrick explained that she was not (at the time) a Republican, because Republicans simply did not seem to "*care enough* about the whole."

When conservatives respond to pressing human needs in the inner city with arid discourses on the virtues of the free market, or cuts in the capital gains tax, or vague assurances that "it's up to civil society," we are doing little to dispel our own negative image. Small wonder that liberals still find it so easy to persuade the American people that conservatives, in President Clinton's words, represent only "greed, selfishness, irresponsibility, excess and neglect."

But if conservatives will squarely back the spontaneous uprisings of citizens around the nation against the tyrannies of the therapeutic state— if conservatives place at the center of their agenda a commitment to the reconstruction of civil society, whose institutions and values are of most benefit to the least well off—then finally we may lay to rest the charge that we do not care enough about the whole. That the task of civic reconstruction promises to be complex and difficult—that it demands so much more of us than merely dashing off charity or IRS checks to perpetuate the same failed public policies—might at last begin to change public views about who is genuinely compassionate, and who merely hides behind compassion while continuing to line their own pockets.

In short, the new citizenship implies a new conservatism—a conservatism that should be able to construct for itself a broad-based and enduring majority among the citizens of the United States.

Chapter II

Political Parties and Elections

Alexis de Tocqueville claims that parties are "a necessary evil in free governments," but not all parties are the same. He distinguishes between great parties based on principles and an idea of the public good and small parties that are motivated more by self-interest. Each party presents its own particular danger. "Society is convulsed by great parties, by minor ones it is agitated; it is torn by the former, by the latter it is degraded. . . ." Writing in the 1830s Tocqueville claims that there are no longer great parties in the United States. It is a nation in which "opinion is divided into a thousand minute shades of difference upon questions of very little moment. . . ."

James Ceaser argues that the development of such parties was consistent with the spirit of the Constitution. Martin Van Buren institutionalized "small parties" in order to moderate the ambition of presidential candidates who might otherwise be tempted to tear the nation apart in their pursuit of the office of the presidency. By placing the nomination of presidential candidates in the hands of local party leaders, candidates would have to address the multiplicity of local interests rather than broad questions of principle. Such broad-based consensus parties would help to moderate popular election campaigns and to restrain the President once in office.

Ceaser goes on to explain that contemporary reforms of political parties and the electoral process are rooted in the Progressive rejection of consensus politics and of institutions designed to moderate or restrain public opinion. The Progressive conception of politics viewed elections as plebiscite in which voters choose between different political principles formulated by party leaders. The Progressives wanted "great parties" because they would counter the corrupting influences of self-interest. But Ceaser questions whether parties that substitute principles for interests will be either healthy or viable. He fears that a politics based exclusively on principles will be potentially demagogic and dangerously divisive.

The system of Presidential selection created by the Constitution was originally non-partisan, but the operation of the electoral college described by Alexander Hamilton is very different than the Presidential selection process we see today. Hamilton thought the electoral college would allow for

95

both popular opinion and the deliberate choice of a select body of citizens to operate in the election of the President. Popular opinion would determine the choice of electors, but electors operating in "circumstances favorable to deliberation" would choose the President.

The electoral college never operated in the way Hamilton envisioned. The selection of George Washington was a foregone conclusion. By the time the election of 1796 occurred, the rise of political parties transformed independent electors into delegates pledged to vote for the nominee of their party. Martin Diamond argues, however, that even though the electoral college does not operate in the way intended by the framers, it nonetheless promotes Constitutional principles. Electors may not exercise independent judgment, but the building of electoral majorities on a state by state basis creates a complex majority. Presidential candidates must build a coalition of competing interests in a variety of states rather than appeal to a simple national majority based upon the lowest common denominator of national public opinion. A national direct popular election, according to Diamond, would undermine interest based politics and encourage the development of more principled, but less stable and more dangerous political parties.

There are costs associated with a system based on interest group politics. First, as Lord Bryce argues, such a system does not encourage the selection of great statesmen. Second, interest based politics may create the potential for corruption. Campaign finance laws passed in the early 1970s sought to minimize corruption and the appearance of corruption in the electoral process. The case of *Buckley v. Valeo* illustrates that the state's interest in restricting campaign finance practices may come into conflict with the Constitutional protection of free speech. The case also raises the question of whether equal political influence can or should be guaranteed by the government. As Chief Justice Warren Burger points out in his dissent, limitations on contributions and federal campaign financing may not equalize influence but will likely provide incumbents with an increased advantage. The attempt to limit the influence of private contributors may ultimately help to insulate incumbents from effective electoral challenges.

In *Citizens United v. Federal Election Commission* (2010), the Court declared unconstitutional a federal law that prohibited corporations from using their funds to advocate for or against a candidate, and from making electioneering statements within a certain time frame before an election. The Court rejected the notion that the First Amendment applies differently to corporations. In effect, the Court argued that Congress has unjustifiably censored speech based solely on the identity of the speaker, while the alternative outlet Congress allowed—the Political Action Committee (PAC)—comes with such onerous regulations that they may have a chilling effect on free speech.

Finally, it is important to recognize that parties and elections are driven by more than rules and laws. They also are shaped by ideas. In a 1977 speech on "The New Republican Party," Reagan showed how principle might unite economic and social conservatives, while Barack Obama emphasized in his Second Inaugural how by working together Americans could advance their principles of liberty and equality for themselves and their posterity. Donald Trump's Inaugural tries to rally the people against the elites who have ruled in their own interests rather than those of the people as a whole. Addressing Ceaser's criticism of presidential rhetoric, Mark A. Scully provides examples of how constructive and unifying popular presidential leadership can be when presidents use common and overarching ideas to forge consensus between different party groups. He concludes that although Trump effectively exploited the tensions within both the Democratic and Republican coalitions, it is unclear that he created a unifying rhetoric that can provide the basis for a new and lasting coalition. It is possible to win an election by exploiting the belief that elites of both parties have failed to represent the interests of working class Americans. The test will be whether Trump, or anyone else, can offer a set of principles that can hold together the diverse and often conflicting interests of a successful majority party.

20

Alexis de Tocqueville

On Great and Small Parties (1835)

A great distinction must be made between parties. Some countries are so large that the different populations which inhabit them have contradictory interests, although they are the subjects of the same Government, and they may thence be in a perpetual state of opposition. In this case the different fractions of the people may more properly be considered as distinct nations than as mere parties; and if a civil war breaks out, the struggle is carried on by rival peoples rather than by factions in the State.

But when the citizens entertain different opinions upon subjects which affect the whole country alike, such, for instance, as the principles upon which the government is to be conducted, then distinctions arise which may correctly be styled parties. Parties are a necessary evil in free govern-

From *Democracy in America* by Alexis de Tocqueville, translated by Henry Reeve, 1862, with minor changes.

ments; but they have not at all times the same character and the same propensities. . . .

The political parties which I style great are those which cling to principles more than to their consequences; to general, and not to especial cases; to ideas, and not to men. These parties are usually distinguished by a nobler character, by more generous passions, more genuine convictions, and a more bold and open conduct than the others. In them private interest, which always plays the chief part in political passions, is more studiously veiled under the pretext of the public good; and it may even be sometimes concealed from the eyes of the very persons whom it excites and impels.

Minor parties are, on the other hand, generally deficient in political faith. As they are not sustained or dignified by a lofty purpose, they ostensibly display the egotism of their character in their actions. They glow with a factitious zeal; their language is vehement, but their conduct is timid and irresolute. The means they employ are as wretched as the end at which they aim. . . . Society is convulsed by great parties, by minor ones it is agitated; it is torn by the former, by the latter it is degraded; and if these sometimes save it by a salutary perturbation, those invariably disturb it to no good end.

America has already lost the great parties which once divided the nation; and if her happiness is considerably increased, her morality has suffered by their extinction. When the War of Independence was terminated, and the foundations of the new Government were to be laid down, the nation was divided between two opinions—two opinions which are as old as the world, and which are perpetually to be met with under all the forms and all the names which have ever obtained in free communities—the one tending to limit, the other to extend indefinitely, the power of the people. The conflict of these two opinions never assumed that degree of violence in America which it has frequently displayed elsewhere. Both parties of the Americans were, in fact, agreed upon the most essential points; and neither of them had to destroy a traditional constitution, or to overthrow the structure of society, in order to ensure its own triumph. In neither of them, consequently, were a great number of private interests affected by success or by defeat; but moral principles of a high order, such as the love of equality and of independence, were concerned in the struggle, and they sufficed to kindle violent passions.

The party which desired to limit the power of the people endeavored to apply its doctrines more especially to the Constitution of the Union, whence it derived its name of Federal. The other party, which affected to be more exclusively attached to the cause of liberty, took that of Republican. America is a land of democracy, and the Federalists were always in a minority. . . .

The means by which the Federalists had maintained their position were artificial, and their resources were temporary. . . . When the Republicans attained to that lofty station, their opponents were overwhelmed by utter defeat. . . . From that moment the Republican or Democratic party has proceeded from conquest to conquest, until it has acquired absolute supremacy in the country. The Federalists, perceiving that they were vanquished without resource, and isolated in the midst of the nation, fell into two divisions, of which one joined the victorious Republicans, and the other abandoned its rallying-point and its name. Many years have already elapsed since they ceased to exist as a party.

Great political parties are not, then, to be met with in the United States at the present time. Parties, indeed, may be found which threaten the future tranquillity [sic] of the Union; but there are none which seem to contest the present form of Government or the present course of society. The parties by which the Union is menaced do not rest upon abstract principles, but upon temporal interests. These interests, disseminated in the provinces of so vast an empire, may be said to constitute rival nations rather than parties. Thus, upon a recent occasion, the North contended for the system of commercial prohibition, and the South took up arms in favor of free trade, simply because the North is a manufacturing and the South an agricultural district; and that the restrictive system which was profitable to the one was prejudicial to the other.

In the absence of great parties, the United States abound with lesser controversies; and public opinion is divided into a thousand minute shades of difference upon questions of very little moment. . . . In the United States there is no religious animosity, because all religion is respected, and no sect is predominant; there is no jealousy of rank, because the people is everything, and none can contest its authority; lastly, there is no public indigence to supply the means of agitation, because the physical position of the country opens so wide a field to industry that man is able to accomplish the most surprising undertakings with his own native resources. . . .

All the domestic controversies of the Americans at first appear to a stranger to be so incomprehensible and so puerile that he is at a loss whether to pity a people which takes such arrant trifles in good earnest, or to envy the happiness which enables it to discuss them. But when he comes to study the secret propensities which govern the factions of America, he easily perceives that the greater part of them are more or less connected with one or the other of those two divisions which have always existed in free communities. The deeper we penetrate into the working of these parties, the more do we perceive that the object of the one is to limit, and that of the other to extend, the popular authority. I do not assert that the ostensible end, or even that the secret aim, of American parties is to promote the rule of aristocracy or democracy in the country; but I affirm that aristocratic or democratic passions may easily be detected at the bottom of all parties, and that, although they escape a superficial observation, they are the main point and the very soul of every faction in the United States.

To quote a recent example. When the President attacked the Bank, the country was excited and parties were formed; the well-informed classes rallied round the Bank, the common people round the President. But it must not be imagined that the people had formed a rational opinion upon a question which offers so many difficulties to the most experienced statesmen. The Bank is a great establishment which enjoys an independent existence, and the people, accustomed to make and unmake whatsoever it pleases, is startled to meet with this obstacle to its authority. In the midst of the perpetual fluctuation of society the community is irritated by so permanent an institution, and is led to attack it in order to see whether it can be shaken and controlled, like all the other institutions of the country.

21

James W. Ceaser

Political Parties and Constitutional Principles

In 1844, the first message ever sent by telegraph—from Baltimore, Maryland to Washington, D.C.—slowly ticked out the news that James K. Polk had been nominated by the Democratic party as its candidate for the presidency. On receiving this news, Democrats in Washington ran jubilantly through the streets shouting, "Hurrah for Polk," only pausing now and then to inquire of each other, "Who is James Polk?" Today, by contrast, when a presidential candidate is nominated, few find cause for celebration merely because their party has chosen a nominee. Americans today are much more likely to take interest in the individuals who are running for office. The party label is important, but no longer decisive.

This change is one example of the diminished hold of political parties over the American electorate. This decline is evident in a number of areas. A century ago, the press routinely branded the few voters who considered themselves independents as "oddballs"; today, almost 40 percent of the voters call themselves "independents" without feeling the least sense of inferiority. A century ago, party organizations chose the party's nominees for all elective offices through a system of party conventions; today, most candidates are nominated in primary elections in which the individual candidates present themselves directly to the voters. (In presidential nominating contests, party conventions still make the final choice, but most of the delegates are chosen in primaries.) A century ago, the nation's major newspapers were all associated with one or the other of the political parties and presented highly partisan accounts of events; today, candidates for federal offices contact the voters largely through the newspapers and television, which provide news on a nonpartisan basis and which feature paid advertisements that focus more on the candidates' individual qualities than on their party identification.

Less than two decades ago, many were predicting an imminent collapse of our traditional party system. No such thing has occurred, and as we shall see, in certain respects political parties have even gained ground. The current situation, accordingly, cannot be summed up by a single slogan. American parties have declined in strength relative to the position they once held, and electoral competition today focuses much more on the individual candidates rather than the party labels. But the major parties are still alive, and almost all office holders are elected under their labels.

Does it matter if parties decline? Some think it a positive development, arguing that electoral procedures have become more democratic, while others see it as a loss for our system that has made effective governance all the more difficult. . . .

THE FOUNDERS AND FEARS OF FACTIONAL PARTIES

Eighteenth century British politician and philosopher Edmund Burke considered a party to be a group united by common political interests in service to the national interest. According to Burke, the aggregation of people in support of common political interests promoted the public good and corrected the factious nature of unaffiliated or independent politicians. The founders initially held a different view about parties, regarding them as organizations that inflated the tendency for faction by multiplying the selfish or uninformed interests of individuals. Hence, during the drafting and ratification of the Constitution, parties were discouraged as dangerous and prone to promoting majority tyranny. . . .

The founders opposed national political parties, preferring instead a nonpartisan system in which candidates would compete for office on the basis of their individual qualifications and political beliefs. The founders wanted no formal associational links between candidates for the presidency, the House, and the Senate; no permanent national political organization of citizens for nominating candidates; and no labels dividing the population into opposing camps.

Nominating candidates is one of the most important functions performed by political parties; and the founders—at least in the case of the presidency—established a formal constitutional alternative to party nominations. The original plan for the electoral college was to select the president in a nonpartisan fashion by elevating individuals of outstanding national reputation.

The nonpartisan character of the founders' intentions becomes even more strikingly evident when one considers that the vice president was selected not as a candidate on a ticket with the president but as the runner-up in the total of electoral votes. This arrangement, defensible in a system without parties, is untenable in a system with them. In 2016, for example, it would have produced Donald J. Trump as president with Hillary Rodham Clinton as vice-president. In fact, a result no less strange occurred in 1796 when John Adams, a Federalist, was elected president and Thomas Jefferson, the opposition leader, became vice president. By 1804, the Twelfth Amendment was adopted, which implicitly acknowledged the existence of political parties and provided for separate balloting by the electors for president and vice president.

Why did the founders oppose party competition? Their hostility to parties was based first on their fear that parties tended to be factious in nature, promoting particular goals over the public good. Madison in *Federalist* 10 barely distinguishes between a faction and a party. He observed that this perceived tendency of "the spirit of party and faction" to promote polices "adverse to the rights of other citizens, or to the permanent and aggregate interests of the community" presented a threat to democratic regimes. In addition to promoting policies adverse to the public good, the founders thought that parties would stir up unnecessary and dangerous divisions, "agitating the community," as George Washington argued in his Farewell Address of 1796, "with ill-founded jealousies and false alarm." The proper way to express conflict was through elections of individual officers and not through party organization. In fact, something of the same mistrust of parties exists today, as indicated by the appeals of leaders, often in moments of crisis, to put "petty" partisan concerns aside and consider the true national interest.

Second, the founders worried that permanent national parties would conflict with the intended roles of the presidency and the Congress. A president elected as the head of a party might have to defer to partisan demands rather than exercise personal judgment and might lose the intangible claim of being "president of all the people." As President Taft once explained, "It seems to me impossible to be a strict party man and serve the whole country impartially." In the case of Congress, the founders feared that parties would prevent deliberation. Representatives would meet in party caucus, decide on a party position, and then vote automatically as a bloc in formal congressional sessions. Congress would cease to be a forum for serious debate and would instead merely register predetermined party positions.

Finally, some founders feared that powerful parties would introduce too popular an influence on the political system, undermining its representative character. Parties are instruments for bringing representative institutions closer to the people by linking elements of the public with the elected officials. Certain founders saw dangers in this link, especially if it resulted in elections that would bind both the president and Congress to a party program backed by a national majority. Elections, as the founders understood them, should not closely tie down the decisions of the government, but should instead indicate in a general way what the public wants.

Even though the founders opposed political parties, they never considered introducing a constitutional ban against them. . . . What the founders hoped was that national parties could be avoided because the government could function without them and because most people would believe that parties were dangerous. Plainly, the founders' expectation that the United States would be a nonpartisan regime proved incorrect. Yet we should not conclude that the emergence of parties totally transformed the political system. Parties have clearly modified the original constitutional design, but they have just as clearly been shaped by it. They never assumed the rigid form that founders feared. In fact, many scholars believe that the way in which parties eventually developed served to promote many of the founders' most important goals.

Martin Van Buren and the Case for Party Competition

The transformation from the founders' nonpartisan system to a system of party competition occurred in two phases: during the Jeffersonian era, when parties formed temporarily but were not widely regarded as permanent or legitimate institutions; and during the Jacksonian era, when parties were reestablished and eventually accepted as legitimate and normal components of the political system.

In the first phase, political leaders made use of political parties but never really embraced the concept of permanent party competition. After the crucial election of 1800, in which Jefferson's party won control of the presidency and both houses of Congress, the Federalist party went into a rapid decline, and by 1816 it had dwindled to a tiny regional party that could no longer offer candidates for the presidency. Thereafter, in the period known as the "era of good feelings" (1817–1824), the political system had effectively returned to a nonpartisan—though Jeffersonian—footing, and most of the leading politicians of the period were as firm in their denunciation of the evils of party competition as the founders had been in the early 1790s.

The task of reestablishing parties and transforming the public's perception of them was undertaken by Martin Van Buren in the 1820s. Van Buren, then a senator from New York, proposed viewing parties in a way different from the founders—"in a sincerer and wiser spirit [that] recognizes their necessity and gives them the credit they deserve."

As the focal point for his analysis of parties, Van Buren looked at the presidential election of 1824, a nonpartisan contest between four major candidates, none of whom could win an electoral majority. According to Van Buren, the experience of 1824 pointed to three problems with the existing nonpartisan system. First, without party nominations to mark the beginning of the race, the activity of governing was distracted and agitated by an open campaign begun some two years in advance of the election. Second, with nothing to restrain or moderate the positions of the candidates, the campaign itself featured dangerous appeals stimulating sectional animosities and popular appetites for charismatic leaders. Finally, with so many contenders allowed to enter the race, the possibility that any candidate would capture a national majority was small, and the incentive for the candidates was therefore to establish a firm base of support in a particular region or with a particular constituency. As suggested by the controversial selection of John Quincy Adams for president by the House of Representatives in 1824, which Jackson claimed had robbed him of the office, no one was satisfied with a system that allowed the House to decide the presidential contest.

Van Buren also thought that the era of nonpartisan politics led to a breakdown in coordination between the presidency and Congress. Without parties, there was no common program or coordination between the two institutions and no mechanism for helping to push through a legislative agenda. The policymaking process tended to lose focus, and the government lacked the necessary energy to follow a coherent line.

All these problems led Van Buren to the conclusion that if parties were not reestablished, the stability of the political system itself would be threatened. Van Buren accordingly set forth the basic case for party competition that remains today the classic defense of reasonably strong political parties. It consisted of four points.

First, party competition would prevent the election from being decided by the House, because the nominees of a major party would have the broad support of a large segment of the people, enabling them to win a majority in the electoral college. (With minor parties, it is still possible for the election to go to the House, but since 1824 this has not happened.)

Second, party competition limits the appeals of candidates to the safer issues backed by the broad parties and their general principles. Narrow demagogic appeals or sectional pleas would be avoided. The parties in effect would be placed "above" the individual candidacies, forcing presidential aspirants to adopt a general set of party principles rather than appeal to momentary issues of the candidate's own devising. . . .

Third, under party competition, voters can more easily grasp what elections are all about, because parties, more than individual candidates, have a long history and set of principles that most voters come to know and understand. . . .

Fourth, party competition would provide a greater degree of coordination between the president and Congress than that provided in a nonpartisan system. Van Buren's intention was not that parties would override the Constitutional separation of powers, but that they would help smooth the relationship between the executive and the legislative branches, at least when both were controlled by the same party. . . .

The advent of party competition altered American politics. Parties assumed control of the conduct of political campaigns. They recruited and nominated candidates, created strong partisan feelings in the electorate, and exercised control over the dissemination of news by the creation of party-run newspapers. Party competition also stimulated political interest within the electorate and contributed to the extension of the suffrage, as the parties vied to mobilize new segments of the public. Finally, parties changed the governing process by introducing a new, extra-Constitutional institution that helped bridge the separation of powers and tie national politics to state politics.

While these changes were significant, they were not revolutionary. They took their place within the basic constitutional structure, modifying it but not overturning it. In fact, as different as the "form" of partisan competition was from the founders' goal of nonpartisanship, the effects of partisan competition frequently were in line with the founders' objectives. Van Buren, like the founders, sought stable competition in an electoral process that regulated the ambitions of politicians and promoted moderate majorities; and while Van Buren clearly favored a democratic system of choosing the president, democracy was not the only objective he valued. Like the founders, he thought that the electoral system should operate to prevent dangerous divisions and promote candidates having the support of broad coalitions. While the electoral process, in Van Buren's view, was responsible for expressing divisions, electoral choice should be structured to express them in a responsible way. One of Van Buren's main arguments, in fact, was that the nonpartisan electoral system that had emerged in the 1820s did not promote the founders' own goal of political stability.

Because of the many similarities between the goals of the founders and those of Martin Van Buren, many later analysts of American politics have tended to see the party system as virtually a part of the basic constitutional design. The main feature of Van Buren's model of parties—governing with the aid of broad and moderate majorities—promoted the Madisonian goal of safe majority coalitions. Yet parties on occasions, as in 1800, 1856–1860, and 1932–1936, have also served as vehicles for national majorities that have reinterpreted the American constitutional order in ways that their opponents have viewed as dangerous and extreme. Parties, in other words, have performed the dual function—at different moments—of maintaining continuity and promoting change. As agents of change that emerge in part from the mass public, parties have added a distinctly new element to the original political system as conceived by the founders.

PROGRESSIVES AND THE ATTACK ON PARTIES

All in all, Van Buren had accomplished a remarkable feat of constitution making. But the results were not without defects, which became more apparent as time went on. After the Civil War, critics began to attack the party system on interrelated grounds: that the major parties no longer stood for any important principles, and that they stayed in existence only for the corrupt purpose of securing public service jobs for their members.

Critics may have exaggerated the absence of party principles during the late nineteenth century, but there can be no disputing the importance for the parties of what one analyst called "the hunting for office." Party patronage, simply defined, is a system in which the victorious party distributes jobs in the public service to faithful party workers. Personal qualifications for these jobs are sometimes ignored, and continuity in administrative service often takes a backseat to responsiveness to the party majority. . . .

Patronage became so widespread after the Civil War that a group of intellectuals, journalists, and working politicians—known as "reformers"—insisted that the parties had lost their rightful character. Instead of being organizations devoted to principle, which incidentally awarded jobs to their adherents, they had become organizations of office seekers which incidentally proclaimed a concern with principles. Patronage undermined the efficiency of the public service by driving away anyone who wanted a serious career, and it degraded the entire system of politics by giving effective control of the nomination of candidates to political organizations that were unconcerned with matters of policy and principle. As a cure, reformers proposed placing government jobs beyond the reach of partisan politics by making all hiring decisions subject to merit standards. . . .

The attack on parties assumed more far-reaching proportions during the "progressive era" (1908-1916). The Progressives rejected the reformers' view that parties could be saved merely by changing the rules for employment in the public service. The abuses and deficiencies of the parties, the progressives believed, were too deep-seated to be cured by such mild reform. The parties were corrupt, wedded to old and outmoded ideas, parochial, and unable to offer new ideas to solve the problems of a rapidly industrializing national economy. There was no way to proceed other than by attacking and destroying the existing party organizations.

Some Progressives also had in mind the positive goal of instituting a more popular or democratic method of selecting candidates. The existing system of nominations by the party organizations, they argued, took from the people their right to a free choice of public officials. The Progressives' ideal was a rational and public-spirited electorate that would select candidates without the interference of party bosses and without any old-fashioned attachment to party labels. Exactly how this would work in practice, however, was a matter of dispute between two strains of progressive thought.

One group favored the gradual elimination of parties and the establishment of a democratic, nonpartisan system. Adherents of this group led the movement for a legal ban on party activity from local elections. For higher offices they favored primaries open to all voters. This group extended its attack upon parties to an attack on representative institutions, advocating in the name of democracy the referendum, the recall, and direct popular election of judges. This "populist" understanding of nonpartisanship obviously rested on a different view than the founders' nonpartisan system.

A second group of Progressives had a different conception of the role of parties, though the difference has turned out to be much greater in theory than in practice. Like the first group, these Progressives advocated primaries as a way of destroying traditional parties. But instead of a nonpartisan system, this group favored rebuilding new and more powerful parties that would be democratic and operate as cohesive units at the governing level. Some Progressives went so far as to claim that the doctrine of separation of powers was outmoded. What the nation needed were strong national parties that would allow the majority party to govern without the impediments of checks and balances. The check on power should come from democratic elections, not separate institutions contending with each other. Early in his academic career, Woodrow Wilson, in his book *Congressional Government*, suggested the person and duties of the presidency could be folded into the Congress in a parliamentary style of government. Advocates of this doctrine of "pure" party government, modeled after the British parliamentary system, never succeeded in winning much popular support for their views.

Both strains of progressivism agreed on the need for a more democratic electoral process. The nineteenth-century system had favored nominations made by party leaders, after which the voters would choose from among the party nominees at the general election. The standard of legitimacy for electoral politics had been that of *interparty* democracy. The Progressives considered this insufficient and, where they still tolerated parties, called for the additional criterion of *intraparty* democracy—democracy within the parties—enforced through state-run primaries, in which individual leaders competed for nominations.

Instead of putting the party "above" the presidential aspirant as a means of limiting the appeals of candidates to safe principles, as Van Buren had wanted, the Progressives favored placing the individual candidate "above" the party and having the party take shape around the principles of the nominees. Only in this way could the stimulus of new programs and new ideas that the country needed be attained. Woodrow Wilson best encapsulated this formula: "No leaders, no principles; no principles, no parties." The Progressives went a long way toward establishing the idea of presidents as popular leaders who commanded their parties and the nation through their ability to shape public opinion.

Progressive thought on political parties left a confused legacy. By all accounts the progressives succeeded in giving traditional parties a bad name, though they never managed to destroy them. The Progressives criticized parties—and not without justification—for being closed, selfish, boss-ridden, and obsolete in their principles. They went on to deplore what many considered to be the virtues of traditional partisanship—the spirit of compromise within party counsels, the warm enthusiasm of voters for party traditions, and the willingness of elected officials to accept some party discipline from traditional organizations. But having attacked parties for all their supposed faults, the Progressives were divided on what should take their place. Where they favored strong parties—as many did—they failed to establish any method for securing them, leaving the nation instead with a set of norms and laws that in fact have weakened the parties.

Modern Reforms (1968—)

The Progressives had a great impact on the legal status of parties. They transformed the method of nominations for senators and House members, though they did not completely eliminate the party organizations' influence. In the case of the nomination of the president, the Progressives had less success. After failing in 1913 to pass federal legislation establishing national presidential primaries, they turned to the states and persuaded many of them to adopt primary elections to select delegates to the national conventions (or at least to register the voters' presidential preferences). Yet most delegates continued to be selected in party-run caucuses in which the organizational regulars dominated. Thus, as late as 1968, aspirants for the presidency did not necessarily have to enter primaries to win the nomination, although participation in some primaries was the usual practice.

The modern reform movement arose in reaction to this one remaining vestige of "traditional" organizational control. The immediate impetus came in 1968, when Hubert Humphrey was nominated at the riot-torn Democratic convention in Chicago. Humphrey had not entered any primaries, and his nomination was likened by many in Chicago to the kind of corruption and back-room management that the Progressives had deplored. Large public protests took place during the convention, fueled by the supporters of the candidates who opposed the Vietnam war. . . . The disappointed followers of these reform candidates insisted on wholesale changes in the presidential nomination process that would eliminate the influence of party organizations and increase the power of the rank and file voter. To accomplish this goal, reformers alternatively proposed a national primary, more state primaries, and "open" caucus procedures in those states still using party-run selection processes.

Like the Progressives, these new reformers held ambivalent views about parties. Some opposed parties altogether, preferring a democratic form of nonpartisan politics that focused on competition between individual leaders. Others wanted to strengthen the parties and place them on a new footing, although they could not say exactly how and were convinced that all the prerogatives of the existing party organizations must first be destroyed.

The most important structural change of the reform era has been the decline in the number of party-run selection procedures in favor of primaries. In 2016, thirty-nine states held presidential primaries for at least one party and selected about eighty percent of the delegates. In presidential nominations, parties have tended to become merely labels under which individual aspirants compete for public support, often from independents and members of the other party. Nevertheless, because the electorate voting in each party's primaries is different, the parties still retain very different characters.

Beginning in 1980, many party leaders, especially in the Democratic party where the reforms had gone furthest, attempted to restore some prerogatives to the party organizations. They were concerned about the absence of party professionals at the conventions, which had led to chaotic platform fights and weakened any sense of collective responsibility between the presidential candidate and the other major party leaders. Also, as the grassroots party activists that participated in nominating conventions became more radical, delegates were selected who were at odds with the larger American electorate. Party leaders in this movement called for a renewed look at the role of the party organizations and a greater say for party officials in the selection of the presidential candidates.

So far, the postreform movement has had a limited, but by no means negligible, impact on the party system. More attention has been paid in recent years to upgrading the technical capacities of both national political parties. And in 1984 the national Democratic party added 561 new delegates ("superdelegates") drawn from among party leaders and elected officials (members of Congress, chairs of state parties, and mayors of large cities). These delegates were chosen outside of the primary process and were not officially bound to any candidate. Although this contingent made up only 14 percent of all the delegates to the 1984 Democratic party convention, it marked a first step in an effort to "reform the reforms" and return more power to party organizations and elected officials.

22

Alexander Hamilton

The Electoral College (1788)

The mode of appointment of the Chief Magistrate of the United States is almost the only part of the system, of any consequence, which has escaped without severe censure, or which has received the slightest mark of approbation from its opponents. The most plausible of these, who has appeared in print, has even deigned to admit that the election of the President is pretty well guarded. I venture somewhat further, and hesitate not to affirm that if the manner of it be not perfect, it is at least excellent. It unites in an eminent degree all the advantages the union of which was to be wished for.

It was desirable that the sense of the people should operate in the choice of the person to whom so important a trust was to be confided. This end will be answered by committing the right of making it, not to any preestablished body, but to men chosen by the people for the special purpose, and at the particular conjuncture.

It was equally desirable, that the immediate election should be made by men most capable of analyzing the qualities adapted to the station, and acting under circumstances favorable to deliberation, and to a judicious combination of all the reasons and inducements which were proper to govern their choice. A small number of persons, selected by their fellow-citizens from the general mass, will be most likely to possess the information and discernment requisite to such complicated investigations.

It was also peculiarly desirable to afford as little opportunity as possible to tumult and disorder. This evil was not least to be dreaded in the election of a magistrate, who was to have so important an agency in the administration of the government as the President of the United States. But the precautions which have been so happily concerted in the system under consideration, promise an effectual security against this mischief. The choice of *several*, to form an intermediate body of electors, will be much less apt to convulse the community with any extraordinary or violent movements, than the choice of *one* who was himself to be the final object of the public wishes. And as the electors, chosen in each State, are to assemble and vote

From Federalist 68, in *The Federalist*.

in the State in which they are chosen, this detached and divided situation will expose them much less to heats and ferments, which might be communicated from them to the people, than if they were all to be convened at one time, in one place.

Nothing was more to be desired than that every practicable obstacle should be opposed to cabal, intrigue, and corruption. . . . They have not made the appointment of the President to depend on any preexisting bodies of men, who might be tampered with beforehand to prostitute their votes; but they have referred it in the first instance to an immediate act of the people of America, to be exerted in the choice of persons for the temporary and sole purpose of making the appointment. And they have excluded from eligibility to this trust, all those who from situation might be suspected of too great devotion to the President in office. No senator, representative, or other person holding a place of trust or profit under the United States, can be of the numbers of the electors. Thus without corrupting the body of the people, the immediate agents in the election will at least enter upon the task free from any sinister bias. Their transient existence, and their detached situation, already taken notice of, afford a satisfactory prospect of their continuing so, to the conclusion of it. The business of corruption, when it is to embrace so considerable a number of men, requires time as well as means. Nor would it be found easy suddenly to embark them, dispersed as they would be over thirteen States, in any combinations founded upon motives, which though they could not properly be denominated corrupt, might yet be of a nature to mislead them from their duty.

Another and no less important desideratum was, that the Executive should be independent for his continuance in the office on all but the people themselves. He might otherwise be tempted to sacrifice his duty to his complaisance for those whose favor was necessary to the duration of his official consequence. This advantage will also be secured, by making his reelection to depend on a special body of representatives, deputed by the society for the single purpose of making the important choice. . . .

The process of election affords a moral certainty, that the office of President will never fall to the lot of any man who is not in an eminent degree endowed with the requisite qualifications. Talents for low intrigue, and the little arts of popularity, may alone suffice to elevate a man to the first honors in a single State; but it will require other talents, and a different kind of merit, to establish him in the esteem and confidence of the whole Union, or of so considerable a portion of it as would be necessary to make him a successful candidate for the distinguished office of President of the United States. It will not be too strong to say, that there will be a constant probability of seeing the station filled by characters preeminent for ability and virtue. And this will be thought no inconsiderable recommendation of the Constitution, by those who are able to estimate the share which the executive in every government must necessarily have in its good or ill administration. Though we cannot acquiesce in the political heresy of the poet who says:

> "For forms of government let fools contest—
> That which is best administered is best."

—yet we may safely pronounce, that the true test of a good government is its aptitude and tendency to produce a good administration. . . .

23

Martin Diamond

The Electoral College and the American Idea of Democracy (1977)

In 1967, a distinguished commission of the American Bar Association recommended that the Electoral College be scrapped and replaced by a nationwide popular vote for the President, with provision for a runoff election between the top two candidates in the event no candidate received at least 40 percent of the popular vote. This recommendation was passed by the House in 1969, came close to passage in the Senate in 1970, and is now once again upon us. It is this proposal that has just been endorsed by President Carter and that is being pressed upon Congress under the leadership of Senator Bayh.

The theme of this attack upon the Electoral College is well-summarized in a much-quoted sentence from the 1969 ABA Report: "The electoral college method of electing a President of the United States is archaic, undemocratic, complex, ambiguous, indirect, and dangerous." . . .

Not only is [the Electoral College] not at all archaic, [however,] but one might say that it is the very model of up-to-date constitutional flexibility. Perhaps no other feature of the Constitution has had a greater capacity for dynamic historical adaptiveness. The electors became nullities; presidential elections became dramatic national contests; the federal elements in

From Diamond, "The Electoral College and the American Idea of Democracy," published by American Enterprise Institute, 1977. Reprinted by permission.

the process became strengthened by the general-ticket practice (that is, winner-take-all); modern mass political parties developed; campaigning moved from rather rigid sectionalism to the complexities of a modern technological society—and all this occurred tranquilly and legitimately within the original constitutional framework (as modified by the Twelfth Amendment).

The Electoral College thus has experienced an immense historical evolution. But the remarkable fact is that while it now operates in historically transformed ways, in ways not at all as the Framers intended, it nonetheless still operates largely to the ends that they intended. What more could one ask of a constitutional provision?

To appreciate why the original electoral provisions proved so adaptable, we have to recollect what the original intention was. . . .

The device of independent electors as a substitute for direct popular election was hit upon for three reasons, none of which supports the thesis that the intention was fundamentally undemocratic. First, and above all, the electors were not devised as an undemocratic substitute for the popular will, but rather as a nationalizing substitute for the state legislatures. In short, the Electoral College, like so much else in the Constitution, was the product of the give-and-take and the compromises between the large and the small states, or, more precisely, between the confederalists—those who sought to retain much of the Articles of Confederation—and those who advocated a large, primarily national, republic. . . .

[T]he confederalists fought hard to have the President selected by the state legislatures or by some means that retained the primacy of the states as states. It was to fend off this confederalizing threat that the leading Framers, Madison, James Wilson, and Gouverneur Morris, hit upon the Electoral College device. . . .

Second, the system of electors also had to be devised because most of the delegates to the Convention feared, not democracy itself, but only that a straightforward national election was "impracticable" in a country as large as the United States, given the poor internal communications it then had. Many reasonably feared that, in these circumstances, the people simply could not have the national information about available candidates to make any real choice, let alone an intelligent one. And small-state partisans feared that, given this lack of information, ordinary voters would vote for favorite sons, with the result that large-state candidates would always win the presidential pluralities. How seriously concerned the Framers were with this "communications gap" is shown by the famous faulty mechanism in the original provisions (the one that made possible the Jefferson-Burr deadlock in 1801). Each elector was originally to cast two votes, but without specifying which was for President and which for Vice-President. The Constitution required that at least one of these two votes be for a non-home-state candidate, the intention being to force the people and their electors to cast at least one electoral vote for a truly "continental" figure. Clearly, then, what the Framers were seeking was not an undemocratic way to substitute elite electors for the popular will; rather, as they claimed, they were trying to find a practicable way to extract from the popular will a nonparochial choice for the President.

The third reason for the electoral scheme likewise had nothing to do with frustrating democracy, but rather with the wide variety of suffrage practices in the states. Madison dealt with this problem at the Constitutional Convention on July 19, 1787. While election by "the people was in his opinion the fittest in itself," there was a serious circumstantial difficulty. "The right of suffrage was much more diffusive in the Northern than the Southern states; and the latter could have no influence in the election on the score of the Negroes. The substitution of electors obviated this difficulty." That is, the electoral system would take care of the discrepancies between state voting population and total population of the states until, as Madison hoped and expected, slavery would be eliminated and suffrage discrepancies gradually disappeared. . . .

These were the main reasons, then, why the leading Framers settled for the electoral system instead of a national popular election, and none may fairly be characterized as undemocratic. . . .

[T]he chief contemporary attack on the Electoral College has little to do with the autonomous elector or, as is said, the "faithless elector." The autonomous elector could be amended out of existence (and without doing violence to the constitutional intention of the Electoral College), but this would not lessen the contemporary hostility to it as undemocratic. . . .

The gravamen of the "undemocratic" indictment of the Electoral College rests on the possibility that, because votes are aggregated within the states by the general-ticket system, in which the winner takes all, a loser in the national popular vote may nonetheless become President by winning a majority of the electoral votes of the states. . . . [I]t suffices to reformulate the issue and get it on its proper footing.

In fact, presidential elections are already just about as democratic as they can be. We already have one-man, one-vote—but *in the states*. Elections are as freely and democratically contested as elections can be—*but in the states*. Victory always goes democratically to the winner of the raw popular vote—*but in the states*. The label given to the proposed reform, "direct popular election," is a misnomer; the elections have already become as directly popular as they can be—*but in the states*. Despite all their democratic rhetoric, the reformers do not propose to make our presidential elections more directly democratic, they only propose to make them more directly *national*, by entirely removing the states from the electoral process. Democracy thus is not the question regarding the Electoral College, federalism is: should our presidential elections remain in part *federally* democratic, or should we make them completely *nationally* democratic?

Whatever we decide, then, democracy itself is not at stake in our decision, only the prudential question of how to channel and organize the popular will. That makes everything easier. When the question is only whether the federally democratic aspect of the Electoral College should be abandoned in order to prevent the remotely possible election of a President who had not won the national popular vote, it does not seem so hard to opt for retaining some federalism in this homogenizing, centralizing age. When federalism has already been weakened, perhaps inevitably in modern circumstances, why further weaken the federal elements in our political system by destroying the informal federal element that has historically evolved in our system of presidential elections? The crucial general-ticket system, adopted in the 1830s for reasons pertinent then, has become in our time a constitutionally unplanned but vital support for federalism. Also called the "unit rule" system, it provides that the state's entire electoral vote goes to the winner of the popular vote in the state. Resting entirely on the voluntary legislative action of each state, this informal historical development, combined with the formal constitutional provision, has generated a federal element in the Electoral College which sends a federalizing impulse throughout our whole political process. It makes the states as states dramatically and pervasively important in the whole presidential selection process, from the earliest strategies in the nominating campaign through the convention and final election. Defederalize the presidential election—which is what direct popular election boils down to—and a contrary nationalizing impulse will gradually work its way throughout the political process. The nominating process naturally takes its cues from the electing process; were the President to be elected in a single national election, the same cuing process would continue, but in reverse. . . .

Our consciences will be further eased when we note that the abhorrence of the federal aspect of the Electoral College—which causes the potential discrepancy between electoral and popular votes—cannot logically be limited to the Electoral College. It rests upon premises that necessitate abhorrence of any and all *district* forms of election. What is complained about in the Electoral College is endemic to all districted electoral systems, whether composed of states, or congressional districts, or parliamentary constituencies. If population is not exactly evenly distributed in all the districts (and it never can be), both in sheer numbers and in their political predispositions, then the possibility cannot be removed that the winner of a majority of the districts may not also be the winner of the raw popular vote. . . .

[T]he national popular-vote/district-vote discrepancy . . . can and does occur here regarding control of both the House and the Senate. Why is it not a loaded pistol to our democratic heads when control over our lawmaking bodies can fall, and has fallen, into the hands of the party that lost in the national popular vote? . . .

The House has largely escaped the "undemocratic" charge (especially now, after major reapportionment) despite the fact that its districted basis likewise creates a potential discrepancy between winning a majority of seats and winning the national popular vote for Congress. By the populistic reasoning and rhetoric that attacks the Electoral College, the House also fails the standard of national majoritarianism. But we quite ungrudgingly see the wisdom in departing from that standard in order to secure the many advantages of local districting. To indicate only a few: First, there is democratic responsiveness to local needs, interests, and opinions in general. Americans have always believed that there is more to democracy itself than merely maximizing national majoritarianism; our idea of democracy includes responsiveness to *local* majorities as well. Further, because of our multiplicity of interests, ethnic groups, religions, and races, we have always believed in local democratic responsiveness to geographically based minorities whose interests may otherwise be utterly neglected; such minorities secure vigorous direct representation, for example, only because of the districted basis of the House of Representatives. The state-by-state responsiveness of the Electoral College is an equally legitimate form of districted, local democratic responsiveness. There is also the security to liberty that results from the districted decentralization of the political basis of the legislature; and we cherish also the multiplication of opportunities for voluntary political participation that likewise results from that districted decentralization. Finally, we cherish the guarantee that districting provides, that power in the legislature will be nationally distributed, rather than concentrated in regional majorities, as would be possible in a nondistricted election of the House. . . .

This kind of complex reasoning is the hallmark of the American idea of democracy: a taking into account of local as well as national democratic considerations and, even more importantly, blending democratic considerations with all the other things that contribute to political well-being. . . .

[I]n the next place, t]o judge fairly the charge of ambiguity . . . the Electoral College must be compared in this regard with other electoral systems and, especially, with the 40 percent plus/runoff system proposed by President Carter and Senator Bayh as its replacement. . . .

The American electorate has a fundamental tendency to divide closely, with "photo finish" elections being almost the rule rather than the exception. The Electoral College almost always announces these close election outcomes with useful amplification. In purely numerical popular votes, an election outcome might be uncertain and vulnerable to challenge; but the Electoral College replaces the numerical uncertainty with an unambiguously visible constitutional majority that sustains the legitimacy of the electoral result. If this magnifying lens is removed, the "squeaker" aspect of our presidential elections will become more visible and, probably, much more troubling. For example, the problem of error and fraud, no doubt endemic in some degree to all electoral systems, could very well be aggravated under the proposed national system, because every single precinct polling place could come under bitter scrutiny as relevant to a close and disputed national outcome. In contrast, under the Electoral College, ambiguity of outcome sufficient even to warrant challenge is infrequent and is always limited to but a few states. . . .

Not only is it extremely unlikely that the proposed replacement could match this record of unambiguity, but the 40 percent plus plurality provision could very well introduce a different and graver kind of ambiguity into our political system. This would not be uncertainty as to who is the winner, but a profounder uncertainty as to whether the winner is truly the choice of the American people. . . .

The Electoral College strongly encourages the two-party system by almost always narrowing the election to a race between the two major-party candidates. Obviously, when there are only two serious competitors, the winner usually has a majority or large plurality of the total vote cast. But, as we shall shortly see, the new system would encourage minor and maverick candidacies. This multiplication of competitors would likely reduce the winning margin to the bare 40 percent plurality requirement of the new system. If so, we would have traded in a majority—or high plurality—presidency for one in which nearly 60 percent of the people might often have voted against the incumbent. How ironic it would be if a reform demanded in the name of democracy and majority rule resulted in a permanent minority presidency! . . .

[A]ll the dangers critics claim to see in the Electoral College are entirely matters of speculation. Some have never actually occurred, and others have not occurred for nearly a century. . . .

[But t]hree dangers seem seriously to threaten under the proposed reform: weakening the two-party system, weakening party politics generally, and further imperializing the presidency.

Many have warned that the 40 percent plus/runoff system would encourage minor parties and in time undermine the two-party system. The encouragement consists in the runoff provision of the proposed reform, that is, in the possibility that minor parties will get enough votes in the first election to force a runoff. Supporters of the proposed change deny this likelihood. For example, the ABA Report argues that a third party is unlikely to get the 20 percent of the popular vote necessary to force a runoff. Perhaps so, and this has been very reassuring to supporters of the reform. But why does it have to be just "a" third party? Why cannot the runoff be forced by the combined votes of a half dozen or more minor parties that enter the first election? Indeed, they are all there waiting in the wings. The most powerful single constraint on minor-party presidential candidacies has always been the "don't throw your vote away" fear that caused their support to melt as election day approached. Norman Thomas, who knew this better than anyone, was certain that a national popular election of the kind now proposed would have immensely improved the Socialist electoral results. Now this is not to say that the Electoral College alone is what prevents ideological parties like that of the Socialists from winning elections in America. Obviously, other and more powerful factors ultimately determine that. But what the electoral machinery can determine is whether such parties remain electorally irrelevant, minuscule failures, or whether they can achieve sufficient electoral success to fragment the present two-party system. . . .

Moreover, not only ideological parties would be encouraged by the proposed change, but also minor parties and minor candidacies of all sorts. Sectional third parties would not be weakened by the 40 percent plus/runoff arrangement; they would retain their sectional appeal and pick up additional votes all over the country. The threat that dissident wings might bolt from one of the two major parties would instantly become more credible and thereby more disruptive within them; sooner or later the habit of bolting would probably take hold. Would there not also be an inducement to militant wings of ethnic, racial, and religious groups to abandon the major party framework and go it alone? And, as the recent proliferation of primary candidacies suggests, would-be "charismatics" might frequently take their case to the general electorate, given the inducements of the proposed new machinery. . . .

If runoffs become the rule as is likely, [t]here would be two winners in [the first election]; we would have created a valuable new electoral prize—a second place finish in the preliminary election. This would be a boon to the strong minor candidacies; needing now only to seem a "viable" alternative for second place, they could more easily make a plausible case to potential supporters. But, more important, there would be something to win for nearly everyone in the first, or preliminary, election. Minor party votes now shrink away as the election nears and practically disappear on election day. As is well known, this is because minor-party supporters desert their preferred candidates to vote for the "lesser evil" of the major candidates. But the proposed reform would remove the reason to do so. On the contrary, as in multiparty parliamentary systems, the voter could vote with his heart because that would in fact also be the calculating thing to do. There would be plenty of time to vote for the lesser evil in the eventual runoff election. The trial heat would be the time to help the preferred minor party show its strength. Even a modest showing would enable the minor party to participate in the frenetic bargaining inevitably incident to runoff elections. And even a modest showing would establish a claim to the newly available public financing that would simultaneously be an inducement to run and a means to strengthen one's candidacy. . . .

Most Americans agree that the two-party system is a valuable way of channelling democracy because that mode of democratic decision produces valuable qualities of moderation, consensus, and stability. It follows then that the proposed reform threatens a serious injury to the American political system.

Not only might the change weaken the two-party system, but it might well also have an enfeebling effect on party politics generally. The regular party politicians, which is to say, the state and local politicians, would become less important to presidential candidates. This tendency is already evident in the effect the presidential primaries are having; regular party machinery is becoming less important in the nominating process, and the individual apparatus of the candidates more important. The defederalizing of the presidential election seems likely to strengthen this tendency. No longer needing to carry states, the presidential candidates would find the regular politicians, who are most valuable for tipping the balance in a state, of diminishing importance for their free-wheeling search for popular votes. They probably would rely more and more on direct-mail and media experts, and on purely personal coteries, in conducting campaigns that would rely primarily on the mass media. The consequence would seem to be to disengage the presidential campaign from the party machinery and from the states and to isolate the presidency from their moderating effect. If "merchandising" the President has become an increasingly dangerous tendency, nationalizing and plebiscitizing the presidency would seem calculated only to intensify the danger.

This raises, finally, the question of the effect of the proposed reform on the presidency as an institution, that is, on the "imperial presidency." . . . The presidency has always derived great moral authority and political power from the claim that the President is the only representative of all the people. Why increase the force of that claim by magnifying the national and plebiscitary foundations of the presidency? . . .

24

James Bryce

Why Great Men Are Not Chosen Presidents (1888)

Europeans often ask, and Americans do not always explain, how it happens that this great office, the greatest in the world, unless we except the Papacy, to which any man can rise by his own merits, is not more frequently filled by great and striking men? In America, which is beyond all other countries the

From *The American Commonwealth*, Vol. 1, Chapter 3.

country of a "career open to talents," a country, moreover, in which political life is unusually keen and political ambition widely diffused, it might be expected that the highest place would always be won by a man of brilliant gifts. But since the heroes of the Revolution died out with Jefferson and Adams and Madison some sixty years ago, no person except General Grant has reached the chair whose name would have been remembered had he not been President, and no President except Abraham Lincoln has displayed rare or striking qualities in the chair. Who now knows or cares to know anything about the personality of James K. Polk or Franklin Pierce? The only thing remarkable about them is that being so commonplace they should have climbed so high.

Several reasons may be suggested for the fact, which Americans are themselves the first to admit.

One is that the proportion of first-rate ability drawn into politics is smaller in America than in most European countries. This is a phenomenon whose causes must be elucidated later: in the meantime it is enough to say that in France and Italy, where half-revolutionary conditions have made public life exciting and accessible; in Germany, where an admirably-organized civil service cultivates and develops statecraft with unusual success; in England, where many persons of wealth and leisure seek to enter the political arena, while burning questions touch the interests of all classes and make men eager observers of the combatants, the total quantity of talent devoted to parliamentary or administrative work is far larger, relatively to the population, than in America, where much of the best ability, both for thought and for action, for planning and for executing, rushes into a field which is comparatively narrow in Europe, the business of developing the material resources of the country.

Another is that the methods and habits of Congress, and indeed of political life generally, seem to give fewer opportunities for personal distinction, fewer modes in which a man may commend himself to his countrymen by eminent capacity in thought, in speech, or in administration, than is the case in the free countries of Europe.

A third reason is that eminent men make more enemies, and give those enemies more assailable points, than obscure men do. They are therefore in so far less desirable candidates. It is true that the eminent man has also made more friends, that his name is more widely known, and may be greeted with louder cheers. Other things being equal, the famous man is preferable. But other things never are equal. The famous man has probably attacked some leaders in his own party, has supplanted others, has expressed his dislike to the crotchet of some active section, has perhaps committed errors which are capable of being magnified into offences. No man stands long before the public and bears a part in great affairs without giving openings to censorious criticism. Fiercer far than the light which beats upon a throne is the light which beats upon a presidential candidate, searching out all the recesses of his past life. Hence, when the choice lies between a brilliant man and a safe man, the safe man is preferred. Party feeling, strong enough to carry in on its back a man without conspicuous positive merits, is not always strong enough to procure forgiveness for a man with positive faults.

A European finds that this phenomenon needs in its turn to be explained, for in the free countries of Europe brilliancy, be it eloquence in speech, or some striking achievement in war or administration, or the power through whatever means of somehow impressing the popular imagination, is what makes a leader triumphant. Why should it be otherwise in America? Because in America party loyalty and party organization have been hitherto so perfect that any one put forward by the party will get the full party vote if his character is good and his "record," as they call it, unstained. The safe candidate may not draw in quite so many votes from the moderate men of the other side as the brilliant one would, but he will not lose nearly so many from his own ranks. Even those who admit his mediocrity will vote straight when the moment for voting comes. Besides, the ordinary American voter does not object to mediocrity. He has a lower conception of the qualities requisite to make a statesman than those who direct public opinion in Europe have. He likes his candidate to be sensible, vigorous, and, above all, what he calls "magnetic," and does not value, because he sees no need for, originality or profundity, a fine culture or a wide knowledge. Candidates are selected to be run for nomination by knots of persons who, however expert as party tacticians, are usually commonplace men; and the choice between those selected for nomination is made by a very large body, an assembly of over eight hundred delegates from the local party organizations over the country, who are certainly no better than ordinary citizens. How this process works will be seen more fully when I come to speak of those Nominating Conventions which are so notable a feature in American politics.

It must also be remembered that the merits of a President are one thing and those of a candidate another thing. An eminent American is reported to have said to friends who wished to put him forward, "Gentlemen, let there be no mistake. I should make a good President, but a very bad candidate." Now to a party it is more important that its nominee should be a good candidate than that he should turn out a good President. A nearer danger is a greater danger. As Saladin says in *The Talisman*, "A wild cat in a chamber is more dangerous than a lion in a distant desert." It will be a misfortune to the party, as well as to the country, if the candidate elected should prove a bad President. But it is a greater misfortune to the party that it should be beaten in the impending election, for the evil of losing national patronage will have come four years sooner. "B" (so reason the leaders), "who is one of our possible candidates, may be an abler man than A, who is the other. But we have a better chance of winning with A than with B, while X, the candidate of our opponents, is anyhow no better than A. We must therefore run A." This reasoning is all the more forcible because the previous career of the possible candidates has generally made it easier to say who will succeed as a candidate than who will succeed as a President; and because the wire-pullers with whom the choice rests are better judges of the former question than of the latter.

After all, too, and this is a point much less obvious to Europeans than to Americans, a President need not be a man of brilliant intellectual gifts. Englishmen, imagining him as something like their prime minister, assume that he ought to be a dazzling orator, able to sway legislatures or multitudes, possessed also of the constructive powers that can devise a great policy or frame a comprehensive piece of legislation. They forget that the President does not sit in Congress, that he ought not to address meetings, except on ornamental and (usually) non-political occasions, that he cannot submit bills nor otherwise influence the action of the legislature. His main duties are to be prompt and firm in securing the due execution of the laws and maintaining the public peace, careful and upright in the choice of the executive officials of the country. Eloquence, whose value is apt to be overrated in all free countries, imagination, profundity of thought or extent of knowledge, are all in so far a gain to him that they make him a bigger man, and help him to gain a greater influence over the nation, an influence which, if he be a true patriot he may use for its good. But they are not necessary for the due discharge in ordinary times of the duties of his post. A man may lack them and yet make an excellent President. . . .

So far we have been considering personal merits. But in the selection of a candidate many considerations have to be regarded besides personal merits, whether they be the merits of a candidate, or of a possible President. The chief of these considerations is the amount of support which can be secured from different States or from different regions, or, as the Americans say, "sections," of the Union. State feeling and sectional feeling are powerful factors in a presidential election. The Northwest, including the States from Ohio to Dakota, is now the most populous region of the Union, and therefore counts for most in an election. It naturally conceives that its interests will be best protected by one who knows them from birth and residence. Hence *prima facie* a North-western man makes the best candidate. A large State casts a heavier vote in the election; and every State is of course more likely to be carried by one of its own children than by a stranger, because his fellow-citizens, while they feel honoured by the choice, gain also a substantial advantage, having a better prospect of such favours as the administration can bestow. Hence, *coeteris paribus,* a man from a large State is preferable as a candidate. . . . The problem is further complicated by the fact that some States are already safe for one or other party, while others are doubtful. The North-western and New England States are most of them certain to go Republican: the Southern States are (at present) all of them certain to go Democratic. It is more important to gratify a doubtful State than one you have got already; and hence, *coeteris paribus,* a candidate from a doubtful State, such as New York or Indiana, is to be preferred. . . .

"What shall we do with our ex-Presidents?" is a question often put in America, but never yet answered. The position of a past chief magistrate is not a happy one. He has been a species of sovereign at home. He is received—General Grant was—with almost royal honours abroad. His private income may be insufficient to enable him to live in ease, yet he cannot without loss of dignity, the country's dignity as well as his own, go back to practice at the bar or become partner in a mercantile firm. If he tries to enter the Senate, it may happen that there is no seat vacant for his own State, or that the majority in the State legislature is against him. It has been suggested that he might be given a seat in that chamber as an extra member; but to this plan there is the objection that it would give to the State from which he comes a third senator, and thus put other States at a disadvantage. In any case, however, it would seem only right to bestow such a pension as would relieve him from the necessity of re-entering business or a profession.

We may now answer the question from which we started. Great men are not chosen Presidents, firstly, because great men are rare in politics; secondly, because the method of choice does not bring them to the top; thirdly, because they are not, in quiet times, absolutely needed. I may observe that the Presidents, regarded historically, fall into three periods, the second inferior to the first, the third rather better than the second.

Down till the election of Andrew Jackson in 1828, all the Presidents had been statesmen in the European sense of the word, men of education, of administrative experience, of a certain largeness of view and dignity of character. All except the first two had served in the great office of secretary of state; all were well known to the nation from the part they had played. In the second period, from Jackson till the outbreak of the Civil War in 1861, the Presidents were either mere politicians, such as Van Buren, Polk, or Buchanan, or else successful soldiers, such as Harrison or Taylor, whom their party found useful as figure-heads. They were intellectual pygmies beside the real leaders of that generation—Clay, Calhoun, and Webster. A new series begins with Lincoln in 1861. He and General Grant his successor, who cover sixteen years between them, belong to the history of the world. The other less distinguished Presidents of this period contrast favourably with the Polks and Pierces of the days before the war, but they are not, like the early Presidents, the first men of the country. If we compare the eighteen Presidents who have been elected to office since 1789 with the nineteen English prime ministers of the same hundred years, there are but six of the latter, and at least eight of the former whom history calls personally insignificant, while only Washington, Jefferson, Lincoln, and Grant can claim to belong to a front rank represented in the English list by seven or possibly eight names. It would seem that the natural selection of the English parliamentary system, even as modified by the aristocratic habits of that country, has more tendency to bring the highest gifts to the highest place than the more artificial selection of America.

25

Buckley v. Valeo (1976)

Per Curiam.*

These appeals present constitutional challenges to the key provisions of the Federal Election Campaign Act of 1971, as amended in 1974. . . . The Act, summarized in broad terms, contains the following provisions: (a) individual political contributions are limited to $1,000 to any single candidate per election, with an overall annual limitation of $25,000 by any contributor; independent expenditures by individuals and groups "relative to a clearly identified candidate" are limited to $1,000 a year; campaign spending by candidates for various federal offices and spending for national conventions by political parties are subject to prescribed limits; (b) contributions and expenditures above certain threshold levels must be reported and publicly disclosed; (c) a system for public funding of Presidential campaign activities is established by Subtitle H of the Internal Revenue Code. . . .

The Act's contribution and expenditure limitations operate in an area of the most fundamental First Amendment activities. Discussion of public issues and debate on the qualifications of candidates are integral to the operation of the system of government established by our Constitution. . . . In a republic where the people are sovereign, the ability of the citizenry to make informed choices among candidates for office is essential. . . .

The interests served by the Act include restricting the voices of people and interest groups who have money to spend and reducing the overall scope of federal election campaigns. Although the Act does not focus on the ideas expressed by persons or groups subjected to its regulations, it is aimed in part

From *Buckley v. Valeo*, 424 U.S. 1 (1976).

---

*Only Justices Brennan, Stewart, and Powell joined all portions of the per curiam opinion. Included among the plaintiffs were a candidate for the Presidency of the United States, a United States Senator who is a candidate for reelection, a potential contributor, the Committee for a Constitutional Presidency—McCarthy '76, the Conservative Party of the State of New York, the Mississippi Republican Party, the Libertarian Party, the New York Civil Liberties Union, Inc., the American Conservative Union, the Conservative Victory Fund, and Human Events, Inc.

at equalizing the relative ability of all voters to affect electoral outcomes by placing a ceiling on expenditures for political expression by citizens and groups. . . .

A restriction on the amount of money a person or group can spend on political communication during a campaign necessarily reduces the quantity of expression by restricting the number of issues discussed, the depth of their exploration, and the size of the audience reached. This is because virtually every means of communicating ideas in today's mass society requires the expenditure of money. . . .

By contrast with a limitation upon expenditures for political expression, a limitation upon the amount that any one person or group may contribute to a candidate or political committee entails only a marginal restriction upon the contributor's ability to engage in free communication. A contribution serves as a general expression of support for the candidate and his views, but does not communicate the underlying basis for the support. The quantity of communication by the contributor does not increase perceptibly with the size of his contribution, since the expression rests solely on the undifferentiated, symbolic act of contributing. . . . While contributions may result in political expression if spent by a candidate or an association to present views to the voters, the transformation of contributions into political debate involves speech by someone other than the contributor.

Given the important role of contributions in financing political campaigns, contribution restrictions could have a severe impact on political dialogue if the limitations prevented candidates and political committees from amassing the resources necessary for effective advocacy. There is no indication, however, that the contribution limitations imposed by the Act would have any dramatic adverse effect on the funding of campaigns and political associations. The overall effect of the Act's contribution ceilings is merely to require candidates and political committees to raise funds from a greater number of persons and to compel people who would otherwise contribute amounts greater than the statutory limits to expend such funds on direct political expression, rather than to reduce the total amount of money potentially available to promote political expression.

The Act's contribution and expenditure limitations also impinge on protected associational freedoms. . . . [T]he Act's contribution limitations permit associations . . . to aggregate large sums of money to promote effective advocacy. By contrast, the Act's $1,000 limitation on independent expenditures "relative to a clearly identified candidate" precludes most associations from effectively amplifying the voice of their adherents, the original basis for the recognition of First Amendment protection of the freedom of association. . . .

In sum, although the Act's contribution and expenditure limitations both implicate fundamental First Amendment interests, its expenditure ceilings impose significantly more severe restrictions on protected freedoms of political expression and association than do its limitations on financial contributions. . . .

It is unnecessary to look beyond the Act's primary purpose—to limit the actuality and appearance of corruption resulting from large individual financial contributions—in order to find a constitutionally sufficient justification for the $1,000 contribution limitation. . . . To the extent that large contributions are given to secure political quid pro quos from current and potential officeholders, the integrity of our system of representative democracy is undermined. . . .

Of almost equal concern as the danger of actual quid pro quo arrangements is the impact of the appearance of corruption stemming from public awareness of the opportunities for abuse inherent in a regime of large individual financial contributions. . . . Congress could legitimately conclude that the avoidance of the appearance of improper influence "is also critical [if] confidence in the system of representative Government is not to be eroded to a disastrous extent." . . .

[However, w]e find that the governmental interest in preventing corruption and the appearance of corruption is inadequate to justify 608(e) (1)'s ceiling on independent expenditures.

The parties defending § 608(e) (1) contend that it is necessary to prevent would-be contributors from avoiding the contribution limitations by the simple expedient of paying directly for media advertisements or for other portions of the candidate's campaign activities. . . . Yet such controlled or coordinated expenditures are treated as contributions rather than expenditures under the Act. . . . Unlike contributions, such independent expenditures may well provide little assistance to the candidate's campaign and indeed may prove counterproductive. The absence of prearrangement and coordination of an expenditure with the candidate or his agent not only undermines the value of the expenditure to the candidate, but also alleviates the danger that expenditures will be given as a quid pro quo for improper commitments from the candidate. . . .

It is argued, however, that the ancillary governmental interest in equalizing the relative ability of individuals and groups to influence the outcome of elections serves to justify [this limitation]. But the concept that government may restrict the speech of some elements of our society in order to enhance the relative voice of others is wholly foreign to the First Amendment, which was designed "to secure 'the widest possible dissemination of information from diverse and antagonistic sources,' " and " 'to assure unfettered interchange of ideas for the bringing about of political and social changes desired by the people.' " *New York Times v. Sullivan*. The First Amendment's protection against governmental abridgment of free expression cannot properly be made to depend on a person's financial ability to engage in public discussion. . . .

The Act also sets limits on expenditures by a candidate "from his personal funds, or the personal funds of his immediate family, in connection with his campaigns during any calander year." . . .

[These ceilings also impose] a substantial restraint on the ability of persons to engage in protected First Amendment expression. The candidate, no less than any other person, has a First Amendment right to engage in the discussion of public issues and vigorously and tirelessly to advocate his own election and the election of other candidates. . . .

The primary governmental interest served by the Act—the prevention of actual and apparent corruption of the political process—does not support the limitation on the candidate's expenditure of his own personal funds. . . . [T]he use of personal funds reduces the candidate's dependence on outside contributions and thereby counteracts the coercive pressures and attendant risks of abuse to which the Act's contribution limitations are directed.

The ancillary interest in equalizing the relative financial resources of candidates competing for elective office, therefore, provides the sole relevant rationale for Section 608(a)'s expenditure ceiling. . . . [T]he First Amendment simply cannot tolerate § 608(a)'s restriction upon the freedom of a candidate to speak without legislative limit on behalf of his own candidacy. . . .

Section 608(c) of the Act places limitations on overall campaign expenditures by candidates seeking nomination for election and election to federal office. . . .

No governmental interest that has been suggested is sufficient to justify the restriction on the quantity of political expression imposed by § 608(c)'s campaign expenditure limitations. . . . The interest in alleviating the corrupting influence of large contributions is served by the Act's contribution limitations and disclosure provisions rather than by § 608(c)'s campaign expenditure ceilings.

The interest in equalizing the financial resources of candidates competing for federal office is no more convincing a justification for restricting the scope of federal election campaigns. Given the limitation on the size of outside contributions, the financial resources available to a candidate's campaign, like the number of volunteers recruited, will normally vary with the size and intensity of the candidate's support. There is nothing invidious, improper, or unhealthy in permitting such funds to be spent to carry the candidate's message to the electorate. . . .

In sum, the [contribution limits] are constitutionally valid. These limitations along with the disclosure provisions, constitute the Act's primary weapons against the reality or appearance of improper influence stemming from the dependence of candidates on large campaign contributions. The contribution ceilings thus serve the basic governmental interest in safeguarding the integrity of the electoral process without directly impinging upon the rights of individual citizens and candidates to engage in political debate and discussion. By contrast, the First Amendment requires the invalidation of the Act's independent expenditure ceiling, its limitation on a candidate's expenditures from his own personal funds, and its ceilings on overall campaign expenditures. These provisions place substantial and direct restrictions on the ability of candidates, citizens, and associations to engage in protected political expression, restrictions that the First Amendment cannot tolerate. . . .

[The disclosure requirements of the Act] are attacked as overbroad—both in their application to minor-party and independent candidates and in their extension to contributions as small as $10 or $100. . . .

The governmental interests sought to be vindicated by the disclosure requirements . . . fall into three categories. First, disclosure provides the electorate with information "as to where political campaign money comes from and how it is spent by the candidate" in order to aid the voters in evaluating those who seek Federal office. . . .

Second, disclosure requirements deter actual corruption and avoid the appearance of corruption by exposing large contributions and expenditures to the light of publicity. . . . A public armed with information about a candidate's most generous supporters is better able to detect any postelection special favors that may be given in return. . . .

Third, and not least significant, record-keeping, reporting and disclosure requirements are an essential means of gathering the data necessary to detect violations of the contribution limitations described above.

The disclosure requirements, as a general matter, directly serve substantial governmental interests. In determining whether these interests are sufficient to justify the requirements we must look to the extent of the burden that they place on individual rights.

It is undoubtedly true that public disclosure of contributions to candidates and political parties will deter some individuals who otherwise might contribute. In some instances, disclosure may even expose contributors to harassment or retaliation. . . .

[A]ppellants primarily rely on "the clearly articulated fears of individuals, well experienced in the political process." At best they offer the testimony of several minor-party officials that one or two persons refused to make contributions because of the possibility of disclosure. On this record, the substantial public interest in disclosure identified by the legislative history of this Act outweighs the harm generally alleged. . . .

[The Court next considers public financing of Presidential campaigns.] A series of statutes for the public financing of Presidential election campaigns produced [this] scheme. . . .

A major party is defined as a party whose candidate for President in the most recent election received 25% or more of the popular vote. A minor party is defined as a party whose candidate received at least 5% but less than 25%

of the vote at the most recent election. . . . Major parties are entitled to $2,000,000 to defray their national committee Presidential nominating convention expenses [and] must limit total expenditures to that amount. . . . A minor party receives a portion of the major-party entitlement determined by the ratio of the votes received by the party's candidate in the last election to the average of the votes received by the major-parties' candidates. . . . No financing is provided for [the conventions of] new parties. . . .

For expenses in the general election campaign, § 9004(a)(1) entitles each major-party candidate to $20,000,000. To be eligible for funds the candidate must pledge not to incur expenses in excess of the entitlement under § 9004(a)(1) and not to accept private contributions except to the extent that the fund is insufficient to provide the full entitlement. Minor-party candidates are also entitled to funding, again based on the ratio of the vote received by the party's candidate in the preceding election to the average of the major-party candidates. Minor-party candidates must certify that they will not incur campaign expenses in excess of the major-party entitlement and that they will accept private contributions only to the extent needed to make up the difference between that amount and the public funding grant. New-party candidates receive no money prior to the general election, but any candidate receiving 5% or more of the popular vote in the election is entitled to post-election payments according to the formula applicable to minor-party candidates. . . .

Appellants argue that as constructed public financing invidiously discriminates [against minor party candidates]. . . .

In several situations concerning the electoral process, the principle has been developed that restrictions on access to the electoral process must survive exacting scrutiny. The restriction can be sustained only if it furthers a "vital" governmental interest, that is "achieved by a means that does not unfairly or unnecessarily burden either a minority party's or an individual candidate's equally important interest in the continued availability of political opportunity." . . . [T]he inability, if any, of minority-party candidates to wage effective campaigns will derive not from lack of public funding but from their inability to raise private contributions. . . . Congress enacted [this legislation] in furtherance of sufficiently important governmental interests and has not unfairly or unnecessarily burdened the political opportunity of any party or candidate.

It cannot be gainsaid that public financing as a means of eliminating the improper influence of large private contributions furthers a significant governmental interest. . . . Congress' interest in not funding hopeless candidacies with large sums of public money necessarily justifies the withholding of public assistance from candidates without significant public support. . . .

Mr. Chief Justice Burger, concurring in part and dissenting in part.

. . . Disclosure is, in principle, the salutary and constitutional remedy for most of the ills Congress was seeking to alleviate. I therefore agree fully with the broad proposition that public disclosure of contributions by individuals and by entities—particularly corporations and labor unions—is an effective means of revealing the type of political support that is sometimes coupled with expectations of special favors or rewards. . . .

The Court's theory, however, goes beyond permissible limits. Under the Court's view, disclosure serves broad informational purposes, enabling the public to be fully informed on matters of acute public interest. Forced disclosure of one aspect of a citizen's political activity, under this analysis, serves the public right-to-know. This open-ended approach is the only plausible justification for the otherwise irrationally low ceilings of $10 and $100 for anonymous contributions. The burdens of these low ceilings seem to me obvious, and the Court does not try to question this. With commendable candor, the Court acknowledges:

> "It is undoubtedly true that public disclosure of contributions to candidates and political parties will deter some individuals who otherwise might contribute."

Examples come readily to mind. Rank-and-file union members or rising junior executives may now think twice before making even modest contributions to a candidate who is disfavored by the union or management hierarchy. Similarly, potential contributors may well decline to take the obvious risks entailed in making a reportable contribution to the opponent of a well-entrenched incumbent. . . .

The public right-to-know ought not be absolute when its exercise reveals private political convictions. Secrecy, like privacy, is not *per se* criminal. On the contrary, secrecy and privacy as to political preferences and convictions are fundamental in a free society. . . .

Finally, no legitimate public interest has been shown in forcing the disclosure of modest contributions that are the prime support of new, unpopular or unfashionable political causes. There is no realistic possibility that such modest donations will have a corrupting influence especially on parties that enjoy only "minor" status. Major parties would not notice them; minor parties need them. . . .

I would therefore hold unconstitutional the provisions requiring reporting of contributions of $10 or more and to make a public record of the name, address, and occupation of a contributor of $100 or more.

I agree fully with that part of the Court's opinion that holds unconstitutional the limitations the Act puts on campaign expenditures which "place substantial and direct restrictions on the ability of candidates, citizens, and associations to engage in protected political expression, restrictions that the First Amendment cannot tolerate." Yet when it approves similarly stringent limitations on contributions, the Court ignores the reasons it finds so persuasive in the context of expenditures. For me contributions and expenditures are two sides of the same First Amendment coin. . . .

Limiting contributions, as a practical matter, will limit expenditures and will put an effective ceiling on the amount of political activity and debate that the Government will permit to take place. . . .

I dissent from Part III sustaining the constitutionality of the public financing provisions of the Act. . . .

The Court chooses to treat this novel public financing of political activity as simply another congressional appropriation whose validity is "necessary and proper" to Congress' power to regulate and reform elections and primaries. . . .

Senator Howard Baker remarked during the debate on this legislation:

> "I think there is something politically incestuous about the Government financing and, I believe, inevitably then regulating, the day to day procedures by which the Government is selected. I think it is extraordinarily important that the Government not control the machinery by which the public expresses the range of its desires, demands, and dissent."

[I]n my view, the inappropriateness of subsidizing, from general revenues, the actual political dialog of the people—the process which begets the Government itself—is as basic to our national tradition as the separation of church and state . . . or the separation of civilian and military authority, neither of which is explicit in the Constitution but which have developed through case by case adjudication of express provisions of the Constitution.

Recent history shows dangerous examples of systems with a close, "incestuous" relationship between "government" and "politics." . . . [T]he Court points to no basis for predicting that the historical pattern of "varying measures of control and surveillance," which usually accompany grants from Government will not also follow in this case. . . .

[T]he scheme approved by the Court today invidiously discriminates against minor parties. . . . [T]he present system could preclude or severely hamper access to funds before a given election by a group or an individual who might, at the time of the election, reflect the views of a major segment or even a majority of the electorate. . . .

I would also find unconstitutional the system of "matching grants" which makes a candidate's ability to amass private funds the sole criterion for eligibility for public funds. Such an arrangement can put at serious disadvantage a candidate with a potentially large, widely diffused—but poor—constituency. The ability of a candidate's supporters to help pay for his campaign cannot be equated with their willingness to cast a ballot for him. . . .

Moreover, the Act—or so much as the Court leaves standing—creates significant inequities. A candidate with substantial personal resources is now given by the Court a clear advantage over his less affluent opponents, who are constrained by law in fundraising, because the Court holds that the "First Amendment cannot tolerate" any restrictions on spending. Minority parties, whose situation is difficult enough under an Act that excludes them from public funding, are prevented from accepting large single-donor contributions. . . .

26

Citizens United v. Federal Election Commission (2010)

Justice Kennedy delivered the opinion of the Court.

Federal law prohibits corporations and unions from using their general treasury funds to make independent expenditures for speech defined as an "electioneering communication" or for speech expressly advocating the election or defeat of a candidate. Limits on electioneering communications were upheld in *McConnell v. Federal Election Commission* (2003). The holding of *McConnell* rested to a large extent on an earlier case, *Austin v. Michigan Chamber of Commerce* (1990). *Austin* had held that political speech may be banned based on the speaker's corporate identity.

In this case we are asked to reconsider *Austin* and, in effect, *McConnell*. It has been noted that "*Austin* was a significant departure from ancient First Amendment principles." We agree with that conclusion and hold that stare decisis does not compel the continued acceptance of *Austin*. The Government may regulate corporate political speech through disclaimer and disclosure requirements, but it may not suppress that speech altogether. We turn to the case now before us.

Citizens United is a nonprofit corporation. . . .

Citizens United has an annual budget of about $12 million. Most of its funds are from donations by individuals; but, in addition, it accepts a small portion of its funds from for-profit corporations.

In January 2008, Citizens United released a film entitled *Hillary: The Movie*. We refer to the film as *Hillary*. It is a 90-minute documentary about then-Senator Hillary Clinton, who was a candidate in the Democratic Party's 2008 Presidential primary elections. *Hillary* mentions Senator Clinton by name and depicts interviews with political commentators and other persons, most of them quite critical of Senator Clinton. *Hillary* was released in theaters and on DVD, but Citizens United wanted to increase distribution by making it available through video-on-demand.

. . . In December 2007, a cable company offered, for a payment of $1.2 million, to make *Hillary* available on a video-on-demand channel called

From *Citizens United v. Federal Election Commission*, 558 U.S. 310 (2010).

"Elections '08." Some video-on-demand services require viewers to pay a small fee to view a selected program, but here the proposal was to make *Hillary* available to viewers free of charge.

To implement the proposal, Citizens United was prepared to pay for the video-on-demand; and to promote the film, it produced two 10-second ads and one 30-second ad for *Hillary*. Each ad includes a short (and, in our view, pejorative) statement about Senator Clinton, followed by the name of the movie and the movie's Website address. Citizens United desired to promote the video-on-demand offering by running advertisements on broadcast and cable television. . . .

Corporations and unions are barred from using their general treasury funds for express advocacy or electioneering communications. They may establish, however, a "separate segregated fund" (known as a political action committee, or PAC) for these purposes. The moneys received by the segregated fund are limited to donations from stockholders and employees of the corporation or, in the case of unions, members of the union.

Citizens United wanted to make *Hillary* available through video-on-demand within 30 days of the 2008 primary elections. It feared, however, that both the film and the ads would be covered by [the Bipartisan Campaign Reform Act] §441b's ban on corporate-funded independent expenditures, thus subjecting the corporation to civil and criminal penalties under §437g. In December 2007, Citizens United sought declaratory and injunctive relief against the FEC. It argued that (1) §441b is unconstitutional as applied to *Hillary*; and (2) BCRA's disclaimer and disclosure requirements, BCRA §§201 and 311, are unconstitutional as applied to *Hillary* and to the three ads for the movie. . . .

The First Amendment provides that "Congress shall make no law . . . abridging the freedom of speech." Laws enacted to control or suppress speech may operate at different points in the speech process. . . .

The law before us is an outright ban, backed by criminal sanctions. Section 441b makes it a felony for all corporations—including nonprofit advocacy corporations—either to expressly advocate the election or defeat of candidates or to broadcast electioneering communications within 30 days of a primary election and 60 days of a general election. Thus, the following acts would all be felonies under §441b: The Sierra Club runs an ad, within the crucial phase of 60 days before the general election, that exhorts the public to disapprove of a Congressman who favors logging in national forests; the National Rifle Association publishes a book urging the public to vote for the challenger because the incumbent U. S. Senator supports a handgun ban; and the American Civil Liberties Union creates a Web site telling the public to vote for a Presidential candidate in light of that candidate's defense of free speech. These prohibitions are classic examples of censorship.

Section 441b is a ban on corporate speech notwithstanding the fact that a PAC created by a corporation can still speak. A PAC is a separate association from the corporation. So the PAC exemption from §441b's expenditure ban, does not allow corporations to speak. Even if a PAC could somehow allow a corporation to speak—and it does not—the option to form PACs does not alleviate the First Amendment problems with §441b. PACs are burdensome alternatives; they are expensive to administer and subject to extensive regulations. . . .

. . . [For example,] PACs must file detailed monthly reports with the FEC, which are due at different times depending on the type of election that is about to occur:

> " 'These reports must contain information regarding the amount of cash on hand; the total amount of receipts, detailed by 10 different categories; the identification of each political committee and candidate's authorized or affiliated committee making contributions, and any persons making loans, providing rebates, refunds, dividends, or interest or any other offset to operating expenditures in an aggregate amount over $200; the total amount of all disbursements, detailed by 12 different categories; the names of all authorized or affiliated committees to whom expenditures aggregating over $200 have been made; persons to whom loan repayments or refunds have been made; the total sum of all contributions, operating expenses, outstanding debts and obligations, and the settlement terms of the retirement of any debt or obligation.' "

PACs have to comply with these regulations just to speak. This might explain why fewer than 2,000 of the millions of corporations in this country have PACs. PACs, furthermore, must exist before they can speak. Given the onerous restrictions, a corporation may not be able to establish a PAC in time to make its views known regarding candidates and issues in a current campaign.

Section 441b's prohibition on corporate independent expenditures is thus a ban on speech. . . . Were the Court to uphold these restrictions, the Government could repress speech by silencing certain voices at any of the various points in the speech process. If §441b applied to individuals, no one would believe that it is merely a time, place, or manner restriction on speech. Its purpose and effect are to silence entities whose voices the Government deems to be suspect. . . .

The Court has recognized that First Amendment protection extends to corporations. This protection has been extended by explicit holdings to the context of political speech. Under the rationale of these precedents, political speech does not lose First Amendment protection "simply because its source is a corporation." The Court has thus rejected the argument that political speech of corporations or other associations should be treated differently under the First Amendment simply because such associations are not "natural persons."

At least since the latter part of the 19th century, the laws of some States and of the United States imposed a ban on corporate direct contributions to candidates. Yet not until 1947 did Congress first prohibit independent expenditures by corporations and labor unions in §304 of the Labor Management Relations Act 1947. In passing this Act Congress overrode the veto of President Truman, who warned that the expenditure ban was a "dangerous intrusion on free speech." . . .

In *Buckley*, the Court addressed various challenges to the Federal Election Campaign Act of 1971 (FECA) as amended in 1974. These amendments created 18 U. S. C. §608(e), an independent expenditure ban separate from §610 that applied to individuals as well as corporations and labor unions. . . .

The *Buckley* Court explained that the potential for quid pro quo corruption distinguished direct contributions to candidates from independent expenditures. The Court emphasized that "the independent expenditure ceiling . . . fails to serve any substantial governmental interest in stemming the reality or appearance of corruption in the electoral process," because "[t]he absence of prearrangement and coordination . . . alleviates the danger that expenditures will be given as a quid pro quo for improper commitments from the candidate." *Buckley* invalidated §608(e)'s restrictions on independent expenditures, with only one Justice dissenting. . . .

Less than two years after *Buckley*, [*First National Bank of Boston v.*] *Bellotti* reaffirmed the First Amendment principle that the Government cannot restrict political speech based on the speaker's corporate identity. *Bellotti* could not have been clearer when it struck down a state-law prohibition on corporate independent expenditures related to referenda issues. . . .

Thus the law stood until *Austin*. *Austin* "uph[eld] a direct restriction on the independent expenditure of funds for political speech for the first time in [this Court's] history." . . . There, the Michigan Chamber of Commerce sought to use general treasury funds to run a newspaper ad supporting a specific candidate. Michigan law, however, prohibited corporate independent expenditures that supported or opposed any candidate for state office. A violation of the law was punishable as a felony. The Court sustained the speech prohibition.

To bypass *Buckley* and *Bellotti*, the *Austin* Court identified a new governmental interest in limiting political speech: an anti-distortion interest. *Austin* found a compelling governmental interest in preventing "the corrosive and distorting effects of immense aggregations of wealth that are accumulated with the help of the corporate form and that have little or no correlation to the public's support for the corporation's political ideas."

The Court is thus confronted with conflicting lines of precedent: a pre-*Austin* line that forbids restrictions on political speech based on the speaker's corporate identity and a post-*Austin* line that permits them. No case before *Austin* had held that Congress could prohibit independent expenditures for political speech based on the speaker's corporate identity. . . .

If the First Amendment has any force, it prohibits Congress from fining or jailing citizens, or associations of citizens, for simply engaging in political speech. If the anti-distortion rationale were to be accepted, however, it would permit Government to ban political speech simply because the speaker is an association that has taken on the corporate form. The Government contends that *Austin* permits it to ban corporate expenditures for almost all forms of communication stemming from a corporation. If *Austin* were correct, the Government could prohibit a corporation from expressing political views in media beyond those presented here, such as by printing books. The Government responds "that the FEC has never applied this statute to a book," and if it did, "there would be quite [a] good challenge [to the law as applied in this case]." This troubling assertion of brooding governmental power cannot be reconciled with the confidence and stability in civic discourse that the First Amendment must secure. . . .

Austin's anti-distortion rationale would produce the dangerous, and unacceptable, consequence that Congress could ban political speech of media corporations. Media corporations are now exempt from §441b's ban on corporate expenditures. Yet media corporations accumulate wealth with the help of the corporate form, the largest media corporations have "immense aggregations of wealth," and the views expressed by media corporations often "have little or no correlation to the public's support" for those views. Thus, under the Government's reasoning, wealthy media corporations could have their voices diminished to put them on par with other media entities. There is no precedent for permitting this under the First Amendment.

The media exemption discloses further difficulties with the law now under consideration. There is no precedent supporting laws that attempt to distinguish between corporations which are deemed to be exempt as media corporations and those which are not. "We have consistently rejected the proposition that the institutional press has any constitutional privilege beyond that of other speakers." With the advent of the Internet and the decline of print and broadcast media, moreover, the line between the media and others who wish to comment on political and social issues becomes far more blurred.

The law's exception for media corporations is, on its own terms, all but an admission of the invalidity of the anti-distortion rationale. . . . The exemption applies to media corporations owned or controlled by corporations that have diverse and substantial investments and participate in endeavors other than news. So even assuming the most doubtful proposition that a news organization has a right to speak when others do not, the exemption would allow a conglomerate that owns both a media business and an unrelated business to influence or control the media in order to advance its overall business interest. At the same time, some other corporation, with an identical business interest but no media outlet in its ownership structure, would be forbidden to speak or inform the public about the same issue. This differential treatment cannot be squared with the First Amendment.

There is simply no support for the view that the First Amendment, as originally understood, would permit the suppression of political speech by media corporations. . . .

When Government seeks to use its full power, including the criminal law, to command where a person may get his or her information or what distrusted source he or she may not hear, it uses censorship to control thought. This is unlawful. The First Amendment confirms the freedom to think for ourselves. . . .

What we have said also shows the invalidity of other arguments made by the Government. For the most part relinquishing the anti-distortion rationale, the Government falls back on the argument that corporate political speech can be banned in order to prevent corruption or its appearance. In *Buckley*, the Court found this interest "sufficiently important" to allow limits on contributions but did not extend that reasoning to expenditure limits. When *Buckley* examined an expenditure ban, it found "that the governmental interest in preventing corruption and the appearance of corruption [was] inadequate to justify [the ban] on independent expenditures." . . .

We must give weight to attempts by Congress to seek to dispel either the appearance or the reality of these influences. The remedies enacted by law, however, must comply with the First Amendment; and, it is our law and our tradition that more speech, not less, is the governing rule. An outright ban on corporate political speech during the critical preelection period is not a permissible remedy. . . .

When word concerning the plot of the movie *Mr. Smith Goes to Washington* reached the circles of Government, some officials sought, by persuasion, to discourage its distribution. Under *Austin*, though, officials could have done more than discourage its distribution—they could have banned the film. After all, it, like *Hillary*, was speech funded by a corporation that was critical of Members of Congress. *Mr. Smith Goes to Washington* may be fiction and caricature; but fiction and caricature can be a powerful force.

Modern day movies, television comedies, or skits on Youtube.com might portray public officials or public policies in unflattering ways. Yet if a covered transmission during the blackout period creates the background for candidate endorsement or opposition, a felony occurs solely because a corporation, other than an exempt media corporation, has made the "purchase, payment, distribution, loan, advance, deposit, or gift of money or anything of value" in order to engage in political speech. Speech would be suppressed in the realm where its necessity is most evident: in the public dialogue preceding a real election. Governments are often hostile to speech, but under our law and our tradition it seems stranger than fiction for our Government to make this political speech a crime. Yet this is the statute's purpose and design.

Some members of the public might consider *Hillary* to be insightful and instructive; some might find it to be neither high art nor a fair discussion on how to set the Nation's course; still others simply might suspend judgment on these points but decide to think more about issues and candidates. Those choices and assessments, however, are not for the Government to make. "The First Amendment underwrites the freedom to experiment and to create in the realm of thought and speech. Citizens must be free to use new forms, and new forums, for the expression of ideas. The civic discourse belongs to the people, and the Government may not prescribe the means used to conduct it."

The judgment of the District Court is reversed with respect to the constitutionality of 2 U. S. C. §441b's restrictions on corporate independent expenditures. . . .

It is so ordered.

Justice Stevens, with whom Justice Ginsburg , Justice Breyer, and Justice Sotomayor join, concurring in part and dissenting in part.

The real issue in this case concerns how, not if, the appellant may finance its electioneering. Citizens United is a wealthy nonprofit corporation that runs a political action committee (PAC) with millions of dollars in assets. Under the Bipartisan Campaign Reform Act of 2002 (BCRA), it could have used those assets to televise and promote *Hillary: The Movie* wherever and whenever it wanted to. It also could have spent unrestricted sums to broadcast *Hillary* at any time other than the 30 days before the last primary election. Neither Citizens United's nor any other corporation's speech has been "banned." All that the parties dispute is whether Citizens United had a right to use the funds in its general treasury to pay for broadcasts during the 30-day period. The notion that the First Amendment dictates an affirmative answer to that question is, in my judgment, profoundly misguided. Even more misguided is the notion that the Court must rewrite the law relating to campaign expenditures by for-profit corporations and unions to decide this case.

The basic premise underlying the Court's ruling is its iteration, and constant reiteration, of the proposition that the First Amendment bars regulatory distinctions based on a speaker's identity, including its "identity" as a corporation. While that glittering generality has rhetorical appeal, it is not a correct statement of the law. . . . The conceit that corporations must be treated identically to natural persons in the political sphere is not only inaccurate but also inadequate to justify the Court's disposition of this case.

In the context of election to public office, the distinction between corporate and human speakers is significant. Although they make enormous contributions to our society, corporations are not actually members of it.

They cannot vote or run for office. Because they may be managed and controlled by nonresidents, their interests may conflict in fundamental respects
with the interests of eligible voters. The financial resources, legal structure,
and instrumental orientation of corporations raise legitimate concerns about
their role in the electoral process. Our lawmakers have a compelling constitutional basis, if not also a democratic duty, to take measures designed
to guard against the potentially deleterious effects of corporate spending in
local and national races.

The majority's approach to corporate electioneering marks a dramatic break
from our past. Congress has placed special limitations on campaign spending by
corporations ever since the passage of the Tillman Act in 1907. . . .

I would affirm the judgment of the District Court.

27

Ronald Reagan

The New Republican Party (1977)

. . . Three weeks ago here in our nation's capital I told a group of conservative
scholars that we are currently in the midst of a re-ordering of the political
realities that have shaped our time. We know today that the principles and
values that lie at the heart of conservatism are shared by the majority.

Despite what some in the press may say, we who are proud to call ourselves "conservative" are not a minority of a minority party; we are part of
the great majority of Americans of both major parties and of most of the
independents as well. . . .

Yes, conservatism can and does mean different things to those who call
themselves conservatives.

You know, as I do, that most commentators make a distinction between
[what] they call "social" conservatism and "economic" conservatism. The

Delivered on February 6, 1977 at the 4th Annual Convention of the Conservative
Political Action Conference. The speech can be found at http://www.conservative.org/
pressroom/reagan/reagaon1977.asp

so-called social issues—law and order, abortion, busing, quota systems—are usually associated with blue-collar, ethnic and religious groups themselves traditionally associated with the Democratic Party. The economic issues— inflation, deficit spending and big government—are usually associated with Republican Party members and independents who concentrate their attention on economic matters.

Now I am willing to accept this view of two major kinds of conservatism— or, better still, two different conservative constituencies. But at the same time let me say that the old lines that once clearly divided these two kinds of conservatism are disappearing.

In fact, the time has come to see if it is possible to present a program of action based on political principle that can attract those interested in the so-called "social" issues and those interested in "economic" issues. In short, isn't it possible to combine the two major segments of contemporary American conservatism into one politically effective whole? . . .

. . . What I envision is not simply a melding together of the two branches of American conservatism into a temporary uneasy alliance, but the creation of a new, lasting majority.

This will mean compromise. But not a compromise of basic principle. What will emerge will be something new: something open and vital and dynamic, something the great conservative majority will recognize as its own, because at the heart of this undertaking is principled politics.

I have always been puzzled by the inability of some political and media types to understand exactly what is meant by adherence to political principle. All too often in the press and the television evening news it is treated as a call for "ideological purity." Whatever ideology may mean—and it seems to mean a variety of things, depending upon who is using it—it always conjures up in my mind a picture of a rigid, irrational clinging to abstract theory in the face of reality. We have to recognize that in this country "ideology" is a scare word. And for good reason. Marxist-Leninism is, to give but one example, an ideology. All the facts of the real world have to be fitted to the Procrustean bed of Marx and Lenin. If the facts don't happen to fit the ideology, the facts are chopped off and discarded.

I consider this to be the complete opposite to principled conservatism. If there is any political viewpoint in this world which is free from slavish adherence to abstraction, it is American conservatism.

When a conservative states that the free market is the best mechanism ever devised by the mind of man to meet material needs, he is merely stating what a careful examination of the real world has told him is the truth.

When a conservative says that totalitarian Communism is an absolute enemy of human freedom he is not theorizing—he is reporting the ugly reality captured so unforgettably in the writings of Alexander Solzhenitsyn.

When a conservative says it is bad for the government to spend more than it takes in, he is simply showing the same common sense that tells him to come in out of the rain. . . .

Conservatism is the antithesis of the kind of ideological fanaticism that has brought so much horror and destruction to the world. The common sense and common decency of ordinary men and women, working out their own lives in their own way—this is the heart of American conservatism today. Conservative wisdom and principles are derived from willingness to learn, not just from what is going on now, but from what has happened before. . . .

Let us lay to rest, once and for all, the myth of a small group of ideological purists trying to capture a majority. Replace it with the reality of a majority trying to assert its rights against the tyranny of powerful academics, fashionable left-revolutionaries, some economic illiterates who happen to hold elective office and the social engineers who dominate the dialogue and set the format in political and social affairs. If there is any ideological fanaticism in American political life, it is to be found among the enemies of freedom on the left or right—those who would sacrifice principle to theory, those who worship only the god of political, social and economic abstractions, ignoring the realities of everyday life. They are not conservatives.

Our first job is to get this message across to those who share most of our principles. If we allow ourselves to be portrayed as ideological shock troops without correcting this error we are doing ourselves and our cause a disservice. Wherever and whenever we can, we should gently but firmly correct our political and media friends who have been perpetuating the myth of conservatism as a narrow ideology. Whatever the word may have meant in the past, today conservatism means principles evolving from experience and a belief in change when necessary, but not just for the sake of change.

Once we have established this, the next question is: What will be the political vehicle by which the majority can assert its rights?

I have to say I cannot agree with some of my friends—perhaps including some of you here tonight—who have answered that question by saying this nation needs a new political party.

I respect that view and I know that those who have reached it have done so after long hours of study. But I believe that political success of the principles we believe in can best be achieved in the Republican Party. I believe the Republican Party can hold and should provide the political mechanism through which the goals of the majority of Americans can be achieved. For one thing, the biggest single grouping of conservatives is to be found in that party. It makes more sense to build on that grouping than to break it up and start over. Rather than a third party, we can have a new first party made up of people who share our principles. I have said before that if a formal change in name proves desirable, then so be it. But tonight, for purpose of discussion, I'm going to refer to it simply as the New Republican Party.

And let me say so there can be no mistakes as to what I mean: The New Republican Party I envision will not be, and cannot, be one limited to the country club-big business image that, for reasons both fair and unfair, it is burdened with today. The New Republican Party I am speaking about is going to have room for the man and the woman in the factories, for the farmer, for the cop on the beat and the millions of Americans who may never have thought of joining our party before, but whose interests coincide with those represented by principled Republicanism. If we are to attract more working men and women of this country, we will do so not by simply "making room" for them, but by making certain they have a say in what goes on in the party. The Democratic Party turned its back on the majority of social conservatives during the 1960s. The New Republican Party of the late '70s and '80s must welcome them, seek them out, enlist them, not only as rank-and-file members but as leaders and as candidates.

The time has come for Republicans to say to black voters: "Look, we offer principles that black Americans can, and do, support." We believe in jobs, real jobs; we believe in education that is really education; we believe in treating all Americans as individuals and not as stereotypes or voting blocs— and we believe that the long-range interest of black Americans lies in looking at what each major party has to offer, and then deciding on the merits. The Democratic Party takes the black vote for granted. Well, it's time black America and the New Republican Party move toward each other and create a situation in which no black vote can be taken for granted. . . .

I need not remind you that you can have the soundest principles in the world, but if you don't have candidates who can communicate those principles, candidates who are articulate as well as principled, you are going to lose election after election. I refuse to believe that the good Lord divided this world into Republicans who defend basic values and Democrats who win elections. We have to find tough, bright young men and women who are sick and tired of cliches and the pomposity and the mind-numbing economic idiocy of the liberals in Washington.

It is at this point, however, that we come across a question that is really the essential one: What will be the basis of this New Republican Party? To what set of values and principles can our candidates appeal? Where can Americans who want to know where we stand look for guidance? . . .

The New Republican Party can and should use the Republican platform of 1976 as the major source from which a Declaration of Principles can be created and offered to the American people.

Tonight I want to offer to you my own version of what such a declaration might look like. I make no claim to originality. This declaration

I propose is relatively short, taken, for most part, word for word from the Republican platform. It concerns itself with basic principles, not with specific solutions.

We, the members of the New Republican Party, believe that the preservation and enhancement of the values that strengthen and protect individual freedom, family life, communities and neighborhoods and the liberty of our beloved nation should be at the heart of any legislative or political program presented to the American people. Toward that end, we, therefore, commit ourselves to the following propositions and offer them to each American believing that the New Republican Party, based on such principles, will serve the interest of all the American people.

We believe that liberty can be measured by how much freedom Americans have to make their own decisions, even their own mistakes. Government must step in when one's liberties impinge on one's neighbor's. Government must protect constitutional rights, deal with other governments, protect citizens from aggressors, assure equal opportunity, and be compassionate in caring for those citizens who are unable to care for themselves.

Our federal system of local-state-national government is designed to sort out on what level these actions should be taken. Those concerns of a national character—such as air and water pollution that do not respect state boundaries, or the national transportation system, or efforts to safeguard your civil liberties—must, of course, be handled on the national level.

As a general rule, however, we believe that government action should be taken first by the government that resides as close to you as possible.

We also believe that Americans, often acting through voluntary organizations, should have the opportunity to solve many of the social problems of their communities. This spirit of freely helping others is uniquely American and should be encouraged in every way by government.

Families must continue to be the foundation of our nation.

Families—not government programs—are the best way to make sure our children are properly nurtured, our elderly are cared for, our cultural and spiritual heritages are perpetuated, our laws are observed and our values are preserved.

Thus it is imperative that our government's programs, actions, officials and social welfare institutions never be allowed to jeopardize the family. We fear the government may be powerful enough to destroy our families; we know that it is not powerful enough to replace them. The New Republican Party must be committed to working always in the interest of the American family.

Every dollar spent by government is a dollar earned by individuals. Government must always ask: Are your dollars being wisely spent? Can we afford it? Is it not better for the country to leave your dollars in your pocket?

Elected officials, their appointees, and government workers are expected to perform their public acts with honesty, openness, diligence, and special integrity.

Government must work for the goal of justice and the elimination of unfair practices, but no government has yet designed a more productive economic system or one which benefits as many people as the American market system.

The beauty of our land is our legacy to our children. It must be protected by us so that they can pass it on intact to their children.

The United States must always stand for peace and liberty in the world and the rights of the individual. We must form sturdy partnerships with our allies for the preservation of freedom. We must be ever willing to negotiate differences, but equally mindful that there are American ideals that cannot be compromised. Given that there are other nations with potentially hostile design, we recognize that we can reach our goals only while maintaining a superior national defense, second to none. . . .

And just to set the record straight, let me say this about our friends who are now Republicans but who do not identify themselves as conservatives: I want the record to show that I do not view the new revitalized Republican Party as one based on a principle of exclusion. After all, you do not get to be a majority party by searching for groups you won't associate or work with. If we truly believe in our principles, we should sit down and talk. Talk with anyone, anywhere, at any time if it means talking about the principles for the Republican Party. Conservatism is not a narrow ideology, nor is it the exclusive property of conservative activists. . . .

Our party must be the party of the individual. It must not sell out the individual to cater to the group. No greater challenge faces our society today than ensuring that each one of us can maintain his dignity and his identity in an increasingly complex, centralized society.

Extreme taxation, excessive controls, oppressive government competition with business, galloping inflation, frustrated minorities and forgotten Americans are not the products of free enterprise. They are the residue of centralized bureaucracy, of government by a self-anointed elite.

Our party must be based on the kind of leadership that grows and takes its strength from the people. Any organization is in actuality only the lengthened shadow of its members. A political party is a mechanical structure created to further a cause. The cause, not the mechanism, brings and holds the members together. And our cause must be to rediscover, reassert and reapply America's spiritual heritage to our national affairs.

Then with God's help we shall indeed be as a city upon a hill with the eyes of all people upon us.

28

Barack Obama

Second Inaugural Address (2013)

Each time we gather to inaugurate a president, we bear witness to the enduring strength of our Constitution. We affirm the promise of our democracy.
We recall that what binds this nation together is not the colors of our skin
or the tenets of our faith or the origins of our names. What makes us exceptional—what makes us American—is our allegiance to an idea, articulated in
a declaration made more than two centuries ago:

> "We hold these truths to be self-evident, that all men are created equal, that they are en-
> dowed by their Creator with certain unalienable rights, that among these are Life, Liberty,
> and the pursuit of Happiness."

Today we continue a never-ending journey, to bridge the meaning of
those words with the realities of our time. For history tells us that while these
truths may be self-evident, they have never been self-executing; that while
freedom is a gift from God, it must be secured by His people here on Earth. . . .
[The patriots of 1776] gave to us a Republic, a government of, and by, and for
the people, entrusting each generation to keep safe our founding creed.

For more than two hundred years, we have.

Through blood drawn by lash and blood drawn by sword, we learned
that no union founded on the principles of liberty and equality could survive
half-slave and half-free. We made ourselves anew, and vowed to move forward together.

Together, we determined that a modern economy requires railroads and
highways to speed travel and commerce; schools and colleges to train our
workers.

Together, we discovered that a free market only thrives when there are
rules to ensure competition and fair play.

Together, we resolved that a great nation must care for the vulnerable,
and protect its people from life's worst hazards and misfortune.

Delivered on January 21, 2013. The speech can be found at http://www.whitehouse
.gov/the-press-office/2013/01/21/inaugural-address-president-barack-obama

Through it all, we have never relinquished our skepticism of central authority, nor have we succumbed to the fiction that all society's ills can be cured through government alone. Our celebration of initiative and enterprise; our insistence on hard work and personal responsibility, these are constants in our character.

But we have always understood that when times change, so must we; that fidelity to our founding principles requires new responses to new challenges; that preserving our individual freedoms ultimately requires collective action. For the American people can no more meet the demands of today's world by acting alone than American soldiers could have met the forces of fascism or communism with muskets and militias. No single person can train all the math and science teachers we'll need to equip our children for the future, or build the roads and networks and research labs that will bring new jobs and businesses to our shores. Now, more than ever, we must do these things together, as one nation, and one people.

This generation of Americans has been tested by crises that steeled our resolve and proved our resilience. A decade of war is now ending. An economic recovery has begun. America's possibilities are limitless, for we possess all the qualities that this world without boundaries demands: youth and drive; diversity and openness; an endless capacity for risk and a gift for reinvention. My fellow Americans, we are made for this moment, and we will seize it—so long as we seize it together.

For we, the people, understand that our country cannot succeed when a shrinking few do very well and a growing many barely make it. We believe that America's prosperity must rest upon the broad shoulders of a rising middle class. We know that America thrives when every person can find independence and pride in their work; when the wages of honest labor liberate families from the brink of hardship. . . .

We, the people, still believe that every citizen deserves a basic measure of security and dignity. We must make the hard choices to reduce the cost of health care and the size of our deficit. But we reject the belief that America must choose between caring for the generation that built this country and investing in the generation that will build its future. . . . The commitments we make to each other—through Medicare, and Medicaid, and Social Security—these things do not sap our initiative; they strengthen us. They do not make us a nation of takers; they free us to take the risks that make this country great.

We, the people, still believe that our obligations as Americans are not just to ourselves, but to all posterity. We will respond to the threat of climate change, knowing that the failure to do so would betray our children and future generations. Some may still deny the overwhelming judgment of science, but none can avoid the devastating impact of raging fires, and crippling drought, and more powerful storms. The path towards sustainable energy sources will be long and sometimes difficult. But America cannot resist this transition; we must lead it. We cannot cede to other nations the technology that will power new jobs and new industries—we must claim its promise. That's how we will maintain our economic vitality and our national treasure—our forests and waterways; our croplands and snowcapped peaks. That is how we will preserve our planet, commanded to our care by God. . . .

We, the people, still believe that enduring security and lasting peace do not require perpetual war. . . .

We will defend our people and uphold our values through strength of arms and rule of law. We will show the courage to try and resolve our differences with other nations peacefully—not because we are naïve about the dangers we face, but because engagement can more durably lift suspicion and fear. . . . We will support democracy from Asia to Africa; from the Americas to the Middle East, because our interests and our conscience compel us to act on behalf of those who long for freedom. And we must be a source of hope to the poor, the sick, the marginalized, the victims of prejudice—not out of mere charity, but because peace in our time requires the constant advance of those principles that our common creed describes: tolerance and opportunity; human dignity and justice.

We, the people, declare today that the most evident of truths—that all of us are created equal—is the star that guides us still; just as it guided our forebears through Seneca Falls, and Selma, and Stonewall; just as it guided all those men and women, sung and unsung, who left footprints along this great Mall, to hear a preacher say that we cannot walk alone; to hear a King proclaim that our individual freedom is inextricably bound to the freedom of every soul on Earth.

It is now our generation's task to carry on what those pioneers began. For our journey is not complete until our wives, our mothers, and daughters can earn a living equal to their efforts. Our journey is not complete until our gay brothers and sisters are treated like anyone else under the law—for if we are truly created equal, then surely the love we commit to one another must be equal as well. Our journey is not complete until no citizen is forced to wait for hours to exercise the right to vote. Our journey is not complete until we find a better way to welcome the striving, hopeful immigrants who still see America as a land of opportunity . . .

That is our generation's task—to make these words, these rights, these values—of Life, and Liberty, and the Pursuit of Happiness—real for every American. Being true to our founding documents does not require us to agree on every contour of life; it does not mean we all define liberty in exactly the same way, or follow the same precise path to happiness. Progress does not compel us to settle centuries-long debates about the role of government for all time—but it does require us to act in our time.

For now decisions are upon us, and we cannot afford delay. We cannot mistake absolutism for principle, or substitute spectacle for politics, or treat name-calling as reasoned debate. We must act, we must act knowing that our work will be imperfect. We must act, knowing that today's victories will be only partial, and that it will be up to those who stand here in four years, and forty years, and four hundred years hence to advance the timeless spirit once conferred to us in a spare Philadelphia hall.

My fellow Americans, the oath I have sworn before you today, like the one recited by others who serve in this Capitol, was an oath to God and country, not party or faction—and we must faithfully execute that pledge during the duration of our service. . . .

Let each of us now embrace, with solemn duty and awesome joy, what is our lasting birthright. With common effort and common purpose, with passion and dedication, let us answer the call of history, and carry into an uncertain future that precious light of freedom.

29

Donald Trump

Inaugural Address (2017)

Chief Justice Roberts, President Carter, President Clinton, President Bush, President Obama, fellow Americans, and people of the world: thank you.

We, the citizens of America, are now joined in a great national effort to rebuild our country and to restore its promise for all of our people.

Together, we will determine the course of America and the world for years to come.

We will face challenges. We will confront hardships. But we will get the job done.

Every four years, we gather on these steps to carry out the orderly and peaceful transfer of power, and we are grateful to President Obama and First Lady Michelle Obama for their gracious aid throughout this transition. They have been magnificent.

Today's ceremony, however, has very special meaning. Because today we are not merely transferring power from one Administration to another, or from one party to another—but we are transferring power from Washington, D.C. and giving it back to you, the American People.

For too long, a small group in our nation's Capital has reaped the rewards of government while the people have borne the cost.

Washington flourished—but the people did not share in its wealth.

Politicians prospered—but the jobs left, and the factories closed.

The establishment protected itself, but not the citizens of our country.

Their victories have not been your victories; their triumphs have not been your triumphs; and while they celebrated in our nation's Capital, there was little to celebrate for struggling families all across our land.

That all changes—starting right here, and right now, because this moment is your moment: it belongs to you.

It belongs to everyone gathered here today and everyone watching all across America.

This is your day. This is your celebration.

And this, the United States of America, is your country.

What truly matters is not which party controls our government, but whether our government is controlled by the people.

January 20th 2017, will be remembered as the day the people became the rulers of this nation again.

The forgotten men and women of our country will be forgotten no longer.

Everyone is listening to you now.

You came by the tens of millions to become part of a historic movement the likes of which the world has never seen before.

At the center of this movement is a crucial conviction: that a nation exists to serve its citizens.

Americans want great schools for their children, safe neighborhoods for their families, and good jobs for themselves.

These are the just and reasonable demands of a righteous public.

But for too many of our citizens, a different reality exists: Mothers and children trapped in poverty in our inner cities; rusted-out factories scattered like tombstones across the landscape of our nation; an education system, flush with cash, but which leaves our young and beautiful students deprived of knowledge; and the crime and gangs and drugs that have stolen too many lives and robbed our country of so much unrealized potential.

This American carnage stops right here and stops right now.

We are one nation—and their pain is our pain. Their dreams are our dreams; and their success will be our success. We share one heart, one home, and one glorious destiny.

The oath of office I take today is an oath of allegiance to all Americans.

For many decades, we've enriched foreign industry at the expense of American industry; subsidized the armies of other countries while allowing for the very sad depletion of our military; we've defended other nation's borders while refusing to defend our own; and spent trillions of dollars overseas while America's infrastructure has fallen into disrepair and decay.

We've made other countries rich while the wealth, strength, and confidence of our country has disappeared over the horizon.

One by one, the factories shuttered and left our shores, with not even a thought about the millions upon millions of American workers left behind.

The wealth of our middle class has been ripped from their homes and then redistributed across the entire world.

But that is the past. And now we are looking only to the future.

We assembled here today are issuing a new decree to be heard in every city, in every foreign capital, and in every hall of power.

From this day forward, a new vision will govern our land.

From this moment on, it's going to be America First.

Every decision on trade, on taxes, on immigration, on foreign affairs, will be made to benefit American workers and American families.

We must protect our borders from the ravages of other countries making our products, stealing our companies, and destroying our jobs. Protection will lead to great prosperity and strength.

I will fight for you with every breath in my body—and I will never, ever let you down.

America will start winning again, winning like never before.

We will bring back our jobs. We will bring back our borders. We will bring back our wealth. And we will bring back our dreams.

We will build new roads, and highways, and bridges, and airports, and tunnels, and railways all across our wonderful nation.

We will get our people off of welfare and back to work—rebuilding our country with American hands and American labor.

We will follow two simple rules: Buy American and Hire American.

We will seek friendship and goodwill with the nations of the world—but we do so with the understanding that it is the right of all nations to put their own interests first.

We do not seek to impose our way of life on anyone, but rather to let it shine as an example for everyone to follow.

We will reinforce old alliances and form new ones—and unite the civilized world against Radical Islamic Terrorism, which we will eradicate completely from the face of the Earth.

At the bedrock of our politics will be a total allegiance to the United States of America, and through our loyalty to our country, we will rediscover our loyalty to each other.

When you open your heart to patriotism, there is no room for prejudice.

The Bible tells us, "how good and pleasant it is when God's people live together in unity."

We must speak our minds openly, debate our disagreements honestly, but always pursue solidarity.

When America is united, America is totally unstoppable.

There should be no fear—we are protected, and we will always be protected.

We will be protected by the great men and women of our military and law enforcement and, most importantly, we are protected by God.

Finally, we must think big and dream even bigger.

In America, we understand that a nation is only living as long as it is striving.

We will no longer accept politicians who are all talk and no action—constantly complaining but never doing anything about it.

The time for empty talk is over.

Now arrives the hour of action.

Do not let anyone tell you it cannot be done. No challenge can match the heart and fight and spirit of America.

We will not fail. Our country will thrive and prosper again.

We stand at the birth of a new millennium, ready to unlock the mysteries of space, to free the Earth from the miseries of disease, and to harness the energies, industries and technologies of tomorrow.

A new national pride will stir our souls, lift our sights, and heal our divisions.

It is time to remember that old wisdom our soldiers will never forget: that whether we are black or brown or white, we all bleed the same red blood of patriots, we all enjoy the same glorious freedoms, and we all salute the same great American Flag.

And whether a child is born in the urban sprawl of Detroit or the windswept plains of Nebraska, they look up at the same night sky, they fill their heart with the same dreams, and they are infused with the breath of life by the same almighty Creator.

So to all Americans, in every city near and far, small and large, from mountain to mountain, and from ocean to ocean, hear these words:

You will never be ignored again.

Your voice, your hopes, and your dreams, will define our American destiny. And your courage and goodness and love will forever guide us along the way.

Together, We Will Make America Strong Again.

We Will Make America Wealthy Again.

We Will Make America Proud Again.

We Will Make America Safe Again.

And, Yes, Together, We Will Make America Great Again. Thank you, God Bless You, And God Bless America.

30

Mark A. Scully

Presidential Leadership and Party Unity: How Parties Organize Factions, and Presidents Organize Parties (2019)

Many see in American political parties fiercely divided organizations. Indeed, our parties are as competitive as they have ever been in our nation's history. To make matters worse, the American constitutional system exacerbates party conflict by dividing the instruments of government in such a way that both parties often hold power simultaneously: one party may control the presidency while the other holds majorities in Congress. Rarely in American history has one party ever truly held the reins of government. The 2016 election began our current season of anxieties about party conflict. At almost any point during that election season, more than half of Americans viewed both candidates unfavorably. Things did not improve after the election. In 2018 Democrats took the majority in the House of Representatives, and they used House committees to launch investigations into allegations against Trump, including the collusion between his campaign with Russia and obstruction of Special Counsel Robert Muller's probe, which was also investigating possible Russian collusion. Meanwhile, the White House and its advocates retorted that their partisan foes are leading a "witch hunt."

Despite the frenzied impression created by the day-to-day news or social media, I believe we can see in the broad arc of American history that the anxiety about conflict between parties is misplaced. In fact, that anxiety obscures a very important role parties play in *diminishing* political conflict in the United States. American political parties are extremely important institutions in fostering consensus and cooperation, thus unifying the American public. Sharp conflict *between* parties reflects the success of parties in unifying disparate preferences *within* their organizations. That is, parties perform the valuable function of tamping down small-scale and local conflict in order to refocus their partisans' attention on widely-shared goals in order to gain a majority.

Parties possess a number of mechanisms to organize their conflict. One of the most important figures in this process is the president. Given the tremendous energy around presidential elections, his nearly ubiquitous name recognition, and his command of public attention, he plays a crucial role in unifying the party. By articulating basic political principles, values, or aspirations, presidents provide a coherent message that different party groups can unite behind. In so doing, the president can help the party act less like a hodgepodge of narrow interest groups and more like a broad and inclusive organization united by a vision for the common good.

To see more clearly the president's potential as a party unifier, we must delve deeper into the idea that sharper conflict between parties reflects reduced conflict within parties. What is the political party? One way to think of the party is as a network of different people who are highly engaged in political activity. That includes individuals that work for the Republican or Democratic parties, professional or amateur activists that work regularly with party officials or politicians, or citizens with greater-than-average levels of involvement participation or activism. Taken individually, these groups often have very little in common. Their supporters belong to different demographic groups coming from different geographical areas. Often they passionately care about one or a few interrelated issues, but outside of that they can be ambivalent about each other's interests. A Wall Street trader has very different priorities from a small-business owner on Main Street; a social activist from San Francisco tends to look at policies differently than a union worker in El Paso. They are allies within their respective partisan networks, but they likely care very little for the priorities of the other. Indeed, in some cases they may be in direct opposition. The citizens those groups represent often are vastly different people with very little shared life experience. Viewed from this perspective, parties as networks are broad groupings of people who are loosely connected, but deeply intertwined in America's social and political milieu.

Seeing parties as networks helps highlight the unique challenges of party politicians that rely on these networks for electoral support. Some political scientists have described these party networks as "intense policy demanders"—groups that demand that their first priority also be the party's first priority. Parties so understood are in fact loose collections of groups each scrambling to make the party agenda look more like their own agenda. When groups in the network feel that the party no longer supports their priorities they can respond in different ways. During elections, they may vote for the other party or, almost as bad, they may not vote at all. After an election, they may threaten to withhold campaign contributions or signal to their loyal followers their dissatisfaction with party politicians. Individual members in these party networks can offer broad and far-reaching financial and electoral support, but, for the same reason, they can seriously hurt politicians' chances of winning.

Presidents are more sensitive to intra-party quarrelling than any other elected officials. The president is the only figure in American politics with a national constituency, and as such, he is the only figure who relies on the support of the entire national party. Congressmen can turn to the groups within the party network that are most relevant to their constituencies. The smaller the area a member of Congress represents, the fewer conflicts within his or her district. A southern Republican can ignore the Chamber of Congress as long as he listens to the Moral Majority; a rural Democrat likely worries more about his relationship with unions or the NRA than he does with PETA. In contrast, since the president must cobble together a national majority, he has less freedom to pick and choose the groups within his party network to favor. If a president expects his party to stand with him, therefore, he must remain solicitous of the many priorities and preferences of the groups within his party. Often, a president feels the need to maintain the support of a variety of groups, each of which seeks different or even contradictory goals, but must also recognize that he lacks the political power to satisfy each of these groups equally.

At this point it is useful to recall the work of a group of presidential scholars writing about forty years ago, whose work is featured in this volume, and who first introduced the idea that major changes were afoot in the presidency and political parties. In particular in "The Rise of the Rhetorical Presidency," James W. Ceaser, Glen E. Thurow, Jeffrey K. Tulis, and Joseph M. Bessette argued that factions were tearing apart the consensus in both parties, and that these changes were aided by the increasing role of presidential public rhetoric. Intra-party divisions often create problems that presidents attempt to solve by means of irresponsible rhetoric. They may know that they cannot deliver for every faction, but use rhetoric to compensate for the limits on their power by promising party groups everything they want. This leads to a troubling problem of demagoguery. The gap between speech and action ultimately contributes to voters viewing politicians as cynical and dishonest.

In light of modern partisan divisions and increasingly heated rhetoric, this warning about modern politics seems particularly appropriate. Nevertheless, we should not forget that there are important counter examples of the unifying power of rhetoric. That is, examples of presidents who manage their party networks with principled leadership instead of demagoguery. Principled leadership attempts to create unity by articulating the basic principles that can unite the diverse interests and factions within a party. More than that, presidents try to encourage members to see their specific goals in light of those principles. They try to help groups care deeply about the principles uniting the party—and in so doing care less about the narrower policy preferences that might divide groups into factions. Ultimately, the goal of this style of leadership is to help party members redefine "winning" in a political sense. Getting one's preferred policies is ideal, but impossible to achieve universally. Instead, rhetoric can help members of the party recognize that specific policies actually embody broad values and goals. More practical would be to help everyone in the party to support it even if it is not *their* preferred policy. They begin to identify their own success with the success of a team that is defined by their shared principles and aspirations.

Consider, for instance, President Reagan, who articulated a conservative vision of Republicanism that reverberated in the party system for decades. He was explicit about his desire to find a principled consensus to help hold together a fractious Republican party. In 1977 he addressed the Conservative Political Action Conference with a speech entitled "The New Republican Party." In it, he identified the conflicting groups within the party that we group together as social conservatives and economic conservatives. He presented a vision of conservative principles, which he hoped would unite the party and overcome weaknesses that arose from the party acting like a "temporary uneasy alliance." Reagan explained that he desired to articulate conservative principles that the different "conservative constituencies" could "recognize as [their] own." That is, in essence, the point of principled presidential rhetoric. Thus, by articulating a "principled conservatism" around which the entire party could rally, he hoped to strengthen the Republican Party, taking a network of loosely aligned "intense policy demanders" who cooperated solely out of a desire to promote their narrow self-interest and transforming it into a "politically effective whole."

To accomplish this goal, Reagan spoke about restoring self-rule to the American people, encouraging the public to reclaim power which had been lost as elites of both parties continually promoted massive expansions of governmental power. For Reagan, restoring self-rule meant allowing individual men and women—in addition to non-governmental institutions such as families, churches, and businesses—to make decisions without government oversight. The power of this message was its simplicity. For instance, Reagan argued that limitations on government power were needed to allow Americans the freedom to "make their own decisions," even if that meant not protecting them from the consequences of "their own mistakes." The idea of self-rule as the freedom to make mistakes resonated with both the social and economic constituencies in Republican conservatism.

Social conservatives, who cared deeply about issues like abortion, prayer in school, or school busing, likely heard in this proposition a promise of freedom for families, neighborhoods, and local communities to make moral judgements and hold each other and themselves accountable for moral decisions without the federal government second guessing them. Reagan bolstered this message by saying that government action should first be taken "as close to you as possible" or that "voluntary organizations should have the opportunity to solve many of the social problems of their communities."

Similarly, he insisted that "families—not government programs—are the best way to make sure our children are properly nurtured, our elderly are cared for, our cultural and spiritual heritages are perpetuated." In all these examples, social conservatives would likely find inspiration. When Reagan talked about restoring individual and communal freedom, he had in mind restoring a local or familial autonomy to reverse what they saw as an assault on traditional morality.

But in the same basic message—that individuals should be allowed to make mistakes and not be shielded from the consequences—Reagan touched upon important themes for economic conservatism as well. Namely, Reagan's message asserts that the federal government cannot and should not coercively redistribute wealth to provide a social safety net. His reference to voluntarism or social action beginning "as close to you as possible" tenders the possibility that charitable and philanthropic organizations can ease the state's burden to provide a social safety net. Were government to share its responsibilities with these organization, it could reduce its tax rates and regulations. This is a small, but useful example of how appealing principled rhetoric can be for presidents facing the strategic dilemma that rests at the heart of American political parties. Self-government and individual responsibility are broad and vague themes that provide a number of conservative groups with the opportunity to see the common aspirations that narrow self-interest might otherwise obscure.

President Obama was less explicit about his desire to articulate a principled consensus, but nonetheless his rhetorical leadership of the party bears some resemblances to Reagan's in this regard. Like Reagan, Obama led a party whose members often competed for control of the policy agenda. The Democratic coalition increasingly represented two distinct positions, each with somewhat different constituencies. It maintained its New Deal era brand of economic liberalism, which appealed to people in the lower half of America's income scale. In the cities, this often translated into strong support among urban minority communities (though surely Democratic support for Civil Rights in the '60s is part of the reason for minority support of the Democrats). In suburban or rural areas, this economic message often reverberated with America's blue-collar and wage workers. However, Democrats had also developed a brand as the socially liberal party. In many ways, this new brand was about loosening the strictures of sexual morality. The abortion issue first initiated this movement, and it grew dramatically to include the panoply of issues associated with the LGBTQ movement. Though sexual freedom remained central, this brand really came to emphasize autonomy in lifestyle: urban gentrification, the go-green movement, and multi-cultural or identity politics. These "lifestyle liberals" occupy the same space as economic liberals, but in many ways live in two different cities with directly contradictory goals; for example, urban gentrification or environmental regulations may disproportionately benefit lifestyle liberals to the detriment of lower-income Americans. Since lifestyle liberals are wealthier, they may also disagree with economic liberals on tax or regulatory policy. Finally, lifestyle liberals may push for social change farther and faster than the more traditional economic liberals would prefer.

Like Reagan, Obama appears to see the promise of principled rhetoric to help ameliorate potential tension. As we can see from his second inaugural address, the power of this rhetoric is its simplicity. Consider the potential for conflict over climate change policy in the Democratic Party. Though it is a highly important issue for lifestyle liberals, it brings with it rising consumer prices and threatens many carbon-producing industries. Both threaten economic liberals' livelihood more than the livelihood of lifestyle liberals. However, Obama minimized these conflicts by explaining the controversial policy with language that was likely to resonate most among the more morally and religiously traditional economic liberals. Thus, he argued that "green" energy is "how we will preserve [the] planet [which is] commanded to our care by God." The biblical rationale provided economic liberals reason to see their own values and aspirations in a policy that they may otherwise see as a threat to their own preferences.

Sexual morality is another potential flashpoint between more morally traditional economic liberals and the socially and culturally progressive lifestyle liberals. Obama approached this issue in the same way as climate change: by explaining it in terms that are likely to resonate with the values of the group least likely to support it. Obama simply linked together the histories of the major social movements: "Seneca Falls, Selma, and Stonewall." By comparing the Stonewall Riots—that raised the public profile of homosexual activism—to Martin Luther King's March to Selma Alabama and the Seneca Falls convention on women's rights, Obama lent credibility to the contemporary movement on behalf of the interests of gays and lesbians. Same-sex marriage became more than a policy preference. Instead, it was part of the larger Democratic aspiration to stand up for cultural minorities. That is far more consistent with the traditional brand of economic liberalism (which includes the New Deal and the Civil Rights movement of the Great Society) than the new brand of moral and sexual autonomy of lifestyle liberalism. Obama, therefore, appealed to the language of economic liberalism to justify a policy preference of lifestyle liberalism. He emphasized the common values and principles embodied in a policy that might only tangibly benefit one member of the party network. In so doing, he reminded the whole party network that they can find the similar aspirations in one another's preferred policies.

While presidents can and often do turn to principled rhetoric to manage their party networks, it is not a foregone conclusion that all presidents will do so, or that when they do, they will be successful. President Trump, for instance, has not shown in his major speeches an attempt to use principled speech to moderate and integrate groups and factions within the Republican Party. He is a controversial leader precisely because he tends to unite partisan groups by vilifying others. Trump's victory is very closely connected to the party dynamics at work during Obama's presidency. To understand Trump's rise it is important to see the ways that the Democratic coalition frayed at the conclusion of Obama's term.

The unabated ascendency of lifestyle liberalism appears to have jeopardized the Democratic Party's cohesion in 2016 and allowed Trump to coopt the message of economic liberalism. First, consider the impressive dominance of lifestyle liberals in the Democratic Party. Obama's evolution on the constellation of issues important to lifestyle liberals is one measure of that dominance. At the end of his first term, Obama was still concerned about the rifts that open support for same-sex marriage could cause in his party. By the end of his second, Obama's administration was aggressively challenging male-female gender normativity by requiring public schools across the nation to allow self-identifying transgender people to use whatever bathroom they preferred. The dramatic change clearly reflects the new reality that lifestyle liberals aggressively advanced their priorities in the Democratic network. Indeed, the country as a whole became far less traditional. Thirty-seven states—almost three quarters of the fifty states—legalized same-sex marriage before the Supreme Court ultimately declared it a constitutional right. Traditional morality retreated, and Obama's Democrats led the charge. This is important context for understanding Donald Trump's place as leader of the Republican coalition.

First, this shift in the Democrat's balance of power created an opportunity for Trump to pilfer weaker partisans in the economic liberal wing of the Democratic Party. Indeed, Trump's victory hinged upon breaking through the "blue wall" and capturing rust-belt states like Wisconsin, Michigan, Ohio, and Pennsylvania. These states are not states known for their innovative, "global city" urban centers where lifestyle liberalism thrives. Their reputation comes from their once proud manufacturing prowess. These economic liberals felt little loyalty to the Democratic brand that Obama cultivated and Hillary Clinton continued. This created an opportunity for Trump to champion the traditional Democratic brand of economic nationalism and manufacturing renewal. It is possible that Trump's message resonated in these former Democratic strongholds more strongly precisely because of the increasing profile of lifestyle liberalism during the Obama administration.

Changes in the Republican Party also helped foster Trump's success. The same demise of traditional sexual morality that catapulted lifestyle liberals also weakened the grip of social conservatives on the Republican Party. That left Trump free to draw new cultural battle lines—ones that would complement his message of economic nationalism. Hence, anger over immigration and frustration with government and corporate elitism became the two pillars of Trump's new cultural platform. In this way, Trump's economic and cultural messages fused into one behind the "America First" banner. Trade restrictions would restore American jobs *and* stop corporate elites and their government stooges from lining their pockets at the expense of American wage growth. Immigration enforcement would bolster American jobs *and* defy politically correct multiculturalism. In sum, therefore, Trump dramatically changed the direction of the Republican Party. He adopted a message of economic nationalism to lure former Democratic voters at a time when their connection to the Democratic Party was most tenuous, and transformed Republican's social message at a time when social conservatives were weakest.

Trump's method of leading this coalition has relied less on the unity created by common principles—the approach we saw from Reagan and Obama above—and more on the kind of unity created by identifying a common enemy. Economic liberals found Trump's Republican Party appealing precisely because he was willing to denounce the out-of-touch elite within both parties. He was more anti-Washington than anti-Democrat. The fact that some Republican insiders declared themselves "never-Trumpers" tended to bolster his credibility with voters that may have previously aligned with the Democrats. Trump continues to harp on this same message, which brought him so much success in his campaign. In his inaugural address, Trump decried "a small group in our Nation's Capital" that "reaped the rewards of Government while the people have borne the cost. Washington flourished, but the people did not share in its wealth. Politicians prospered, but the jobs left, and the factories closed. The establishment protected itself, but not the citizens of our country." While elements of this may resonate with Republicans and conservatives of all stripes, Trump's open-ended indictment of "the establishment" surely includes both Republicans and Democrats.

Another telling example is Trump's speech before the Conservative Political Action Committee, in which he proclaimed that "[t]he forgotten men and women of America will be forgotten no longer. That is the heart of this new movement and the future of the Republican Party. . . . We will not answer to donors or lobbyists or special interests, but we will serve the citizens of the United States of America, believe me." Of course the context here matters. He is talking to conservative activists who have long been members of the Republican Party about their own failures as leaders of the *old* Republican Party: it was too elitist, responding to the desires of lobbyists and special interests. The future of the Republican Party depends on Trump's own brand of anti-elite leadership.

Of course, these are Trump's scripted speeches, and therefore are more refined. On Twitter he tended to lay bare the criticism of fellow Republicans that sometimes are in the sub-text of his scripted speeches. For instance,

Trump attacked a favorite of the Republican establishment and former Republican speaker of the House Paul Ryan: "Paul Ryan almost killed the Republican Party. Weak, ineffective & stupid are not exactly the qualities that Republicans, or the CITIZENS of our Country, were looking for." The message in all three examples is the same: antipathy toward government elites *of both parties* is the essential reason Trump give as a basis for voters to support him.

Trump's victory undoubtedly signaled an expansion of Republican influence into once strong Democratic geography. In that sense, he expanded the Republican coalition to the benefit of the entire party. The obvious question outstanding is whether Republicans can hold their newly acquired territory in the next presidential election. Republicans lost the House in the 2018 midterm election, and many blamed Trump's unite-by-dividing rhetorical strategy. While the president's party typically loses seats in the first mid-term election of the president's term, there are a few indications that Republicans will struggle as a party in 2020. One portent is that, as of the writing of this essay, several Republicans in the House and Senate have chosen to retire rather than seek reelection. Higher than normal retirement rates usually indicates that incumbents expect to lose the next election. Principled rhetoric is by no means a panacea for party harmony—if it were, Obama's Democrats would not have struggled to keep economic liberals within the fold. Nevertheless, its potential strength is finding a common conviction that is stronger than the self-interested forces that pull parties apart. Trump may succeed by virtue of his forceful and polarizing personality. Nevertheless, Republicans will be seeking common goals and aspirations strong enough to hold together the diverse and factional preferences that go hand-in-hand with American political parties.

Chapter III

Congress and the Separation of Powers

Is Congress as originally conceived by the Constitution or as it has developed over time capable of performing its law-making and representative functions? How does the Congress fit into the larger framework of the separation of powers?

The authors of *The Federalist* thought that the Senate and the House would be different in character because of their different structures. The more numerous members of the House, with short two year terms, would be more dependent on their constituents and therefore more attentive to their constituents' interests. On the other hand, Senators, with six year terms, would have more freedom than members of the House to promote the long-term interests of the nation. Characterized by knowledge, foresight, and stability, the Senate would provide a unifying sense of national character, helping to connect the particular laws to the principles and purposes of the nation. Given this complex character of Congress, legislation would emerge, in the best case, as a compromise among the particular interests of the parts, in light of a long-range conception of the good of the whole.

From *The Federalist*'s description of Congressmen, particularly Senators, it is clear that members were expected to rely on their own individual judgment rather than merely reflect the immediate interests and opinions of their constituents. Furthermore, *The Federalist* seems aware of a possible conflict between the good of the parts, which the members of Congress represent, and the good of the whole nation. Nonetheless, there is no recommendation that one good be pursued to the exclusion of the other.

Woodrow Wilson proposed major reforms of American government in an attempt to eliminate self-interested politics from the system established by the Founders. Political leaders, he thought, should aim at the common good rather than private or particular goods. To promote this goal, Wilson called for the establishment of Cabinet or parliamentary government as well as the development of ideological political parties. Ideological parties would offer the electorate a choice between coherent programs based on different views of the public good. The leaders in a parliamentary system would have the power to enact the program chosen by the voters. Thus, parliamentary

government would overcome the deadlock caused by the separation of powers and the decentralized Congressional committee system.

Morris Fiorina contends that the self-interest of individual members is
far more important than particular institutional arrangements in determining
the behavior of Congress. The desire for re-election leads members to ignore
national policy issues in favor of pork barrel legislation and constituent services. Taking a stand on policy creates enemies as well as friends, whereas
pork and constituent services are pure profit in terms of voter support. Members of Congress spend little time deliberating about issues because it is not
in their self-interest to do so.

William F. Connelly, however, argues that Congress and Congressmen continue to operate as the Founders intended and that is for the good.
Connelly shows that the Founders intended to create a tension between
pluralist coalition building and coherent principled policy-making, between
representation of individual constituencies and representation of the national
interest, between the Congressman's self-interest and the interest of his or her
constituency, and between principles and self-interest more broadly understood. Congressional critics and Congressional reformers have often failed to
appreciate the complex character of Congress and have consequently misdi-
agnosed its problems and promoted inappropriate prescriptions for reform.
Connelly explains that recent critics of hyperpartisanship in Congress fail to
appreciate that partisanship is inherent in the constitutional functioning of
the institution. Partisanship reflects genuine differences over the direction
of public policy, differences that should be given their due in a democracy.
Moreover, he argues that complaints of gridlock are also overstated. Partisanship is not always an obstacle to legislation and may in fact help to improve it.

Joseph M. Bessette argues that Fiorina underestimates the role of deliberation in Congress. According to Bessette at least some members see the
possibility that they can best represent their own interests and those of their
constituents by engaging their colleagues in a search for common ground.
Congress has succeeded in developing national policies because leaders have
understood the value of genuine deliberation.

Nonetheless we continue to see many proposals for reform of Congress.
One popular proposal in the 1990s was that of term limits. By limiting the
number of terms members of Congress could serve it was thought that the
hold of special interests would be broken and we could return to an ideal
of citizen legislators. Although this proposal failed to gain sufficient support at the national level, several states tried to impose term limits on their
Congressional delegations by limiting access to the ballot by incumbents.
Although conservative dissenters in U.S. Term Limits, Inc. v. Thornton
found this to be a legitimate exercise of the powers of the states in our federal system, the majority of the Court determined that the qualifications for
members were established by the Constitution, and that the states had no

authority to alter or amend the Constitutional requirements for national office.

In the 1970s reformers wished to reassert the power of Congress in foreign policy. The authors of the War Powers Act wanted to insure that the collective judgment of Congress and the President would apply to the use of the armed forces of the United States. But the War Powers Act was clearly based on the premise that even in foreign policy Congress should establish policy. The President is to carry out Congressional policy, not to act independently. Independent executive action was thought to be inconsistent with the rule of law and the primacy of Congress in the law-making process.

The Act has proved ineffective in restraining Presidential initiatives involving the armed forces, in part because of the Supreme Court's decision in the case of *INS v. Chadha* (1983). One of the provisions of the War Powers Act stated that Congress could at any time by concurrent resolution order the immediate withdrawal of troops from hostilities. In *Chadha*, however, the Court declared that Congress would violate the Constitutional separation of powers if it unilaterally vetoed an executive action or decision. Both the majority opinion by Chief Justice Warren Burger and the concurring opinion by Justice Lewis Powell point to the limits of Congressional power as defined by the Constitution. Justice Burger defends the Constitutional role of the President in the legislative process and Justice Powell explains the Constitutional restrictions on the right of the legislature to alter the legal status of particular individuals.

Congressional reform may be desirable, but As Joseph Wysocki explains, the state of contemporary Congressional rhetoric makes sensible reform difficult to achieve. Many scholars have noted the rise of a rhetorical presidency where the increasing reliance on popular rhetoric undermines the constitutional authority of the office of the presidency. Wysocki shows that there has been a similar evolution in Congressional rhetoric. Whereas some previous reform efforts were marked by a rhetoric of institutional responsibility, more recent efforts have used popular rhetoric to score political points rather than engage in serious discussion of Constitutional framework by which reform efforts should be guided.

31

Alexander Hamilton and James Madison

On Congress (1788)

A representative of the United States must be of the age of twenty-five years; must have been seven years a citizen of the United States; must, at the time of his election, be an inhabitant of the State he is to represent; and, during the time of his service, must be in no office under the United States. Under these reasonable limitations, the door of this part of the federal government is open to merit of every description, whether native or adoptive, whether young or old, and without regard to poverty or wealth, or to any particular profession or religious faith. . . .

As it is essential to liberty that the government in general should have a common interest with the people, so it is particularly essential that the branch of it under consideration should have an immediate dependence on, and an intimate sympathy with, the people. Frequent elections are unquestionably the only policy by which this dependence and sympathy can be effectually secured. . . .

[It has been objected that] the House of Representatives is not sufficiently numerous for the reception of all the different classes of citizens in order to combine the interests and feelings of every part of the community, and to produce a true sympathy between the representative body and its constituents. . . .

The idea of an actual representation of all classes of the people by persons of each class is altogether visionary. Unless it were expressly provided in the Constitution that each different occupation should send one or more members, the thing would never take place in practice. Mechanics and manufacturers will always be inclined, with few exceptions, to give their votes to merchants in preference to persons of their own professions or trades. Those discerning citizens are well aware that the mechanic and manufacturing arts furnish the materials of mercantile enterprise and industry. Many of them, indeed, are immediately connected with the operations of commerce. They know that the merchant is their natural patron and friend; and they are aware

From Federalists 35, 52, 55, 57, 62, and 63, in *The Federalist.*

that however great the confidence they may justly feel in their own good sense, their interests can be more effectually promoted by the merchant than by themselves. They are sensible that their habits in life have not been such as to give them those acquired endowments, without which in a deliberative assembly the greatest natural abilities are for the most part useless; and that the influence and weight and superior acquirements of the merchants render them more equal to a contest with any spirit which might happen to infuse itself into the public councils, unfriendly to the manufacturing and trading interests. These considerations and many others that might be mentioned prove, and experience confirms it, that artisans and manufacturers will commonly be disposed to bestow their votes upon merchants and those whom they recommend. We must therefore consider merchants as the natural representatives of all these classes of the community.

With regard to the learned professions, little need be observed; they truly form no distinct interest in society, and according to their situation and talents, will be indiscriminately the objects of the confidence and choice of each other and of other parts of the community.

Nothing remains but the landed interest; and this in a political view, and particularly in relation to taxes, I take to be perfectly united from the wealthiest landlord to the poorest tenant. No tax can be laid on land which will not affect the proprietor of millions of acres as well as the proprietor of a single acre. Every landholder will therefore have a common interest to keep the taxes on land as low as possible; and common interest may always be reckoned upon as the surest bond of sympathy. But if we even could suppose a distinction of interest between the opulent landholder and the middling farmer, what reason is there to conclude that the first would stand a better chance of being deputed to the national legislature than the last? . . .

It is said to be necessary that all classes of citizens should have some of their own number in the representative body in order that their feelings and interests may be the better understood and attended to. But we have seen that this will never happen under any arrangement that leaves the votes of the people free. Where this is the case, the representative body, with too few exceptions to have any influence on the spirit of the government, will be composed of landholders, merchants, and men of the learned professions. But where is the danger that the interests and feelings of the different classes of citizens will not be understood or attended to by these three descriptions of men? Will not the landholder know and feel whatever will promote or injure the interest of landed property? And will he not, from his own interest in that species of property, be sufficiently prone to resist every attempt to prejudice or encumber it? Will not the merchant understand and be disposed to cultivate, as far as may be proper, the interests of the mechanic and manufacturing arts to which his commerce is so nearly allied? Will not the man of the learned profession, who will feel a neutrality to the rivalships between the different branches of industry, be likely to prove an impartial arbiter between them, ready to promote either, so far as it shall appear to him conducive to the general interests of the society? . . .

[Furthermore,] a certain number [of members of the House] at least seems to be necessary to secure the benefits of free consultation and discussion, and to guard against too easy a combination for improper purposes; as, on the other hand, the number ought at most to be kept within a certain limit, in order to avoid the confusion and intemperance of a multitude. In all very numerous assemblies, of whatever character composed, passion never fails to wrest the sceptre from reason. . . .

The number of which this branch of the legislature is to consist, at the outset of the government, will be sixty-five. Within three years a census is to be taken, when the number may be augmented to one for every thirty thousand inhabitants; and within every successive period of ten years the census is to be renewed, and augmentations may continue to be made under the above limitation. It will not be thought an extravagant conjecture that the first census will, at the rate of one for every thirty thousand, raise the number of representatives to at least one hundred. . . . At the expiration of twenty-five years, according to the computed rate of increase, the number of representatives will amount to two hundred; and of fifty years, to four hundred. This is a number which, I presume, will put an end to all fears arising from the smallness of the body. . . .

[Moreover, the members of the House] will enter into the public service under circumstances which cannot fail to produce a temporary affection at least to their constituents. . . .

[T]hose ties which bind the representative to his constituents are strengthened by motives of a more selfish nature. His pride and vanity attach him to a form of government which favors his pretensions and gives him a share in its honors and distinctions. . . .

All these securities, however, would be found very insufficient without the restraint of frequent elections. Hence . . . the House of Representatives is so constituted as to support in the members an habitual recollection of their dependence on the people. Before the sentiments impressed on their minds by the mode of their elevation can be effaced by the exercise of power, they will be compelled to anticipate the moment when their power is to cease, when their exercise of it is to be reviewed, and when they must descend to the level from which they were raised; there forever to remain unless a faithful discharge of their trust shall have established their title to a renewal of it. . . .

Such will be the relation between the House of Representatives and their constituents. Duty, gratitude, interest, ambition itself, are the chords by which they will be bound to fidelity and sympathy with the great mass of the people. . . .

I must be permitted to add [one observation on the constitution of the House of Representatives.] It is, that in all legislative assemblies the greater the number composing them may be, the fewer will be the men who will in fact direct their proceedings. In the first place, the more numerous an assembly may be, of whatever characters composed, the greater is known to be the ascendancy of passion over reason. In the next place, the larger the number, the greater will be the proportion of members of limited information and of weak capacities. Now, it is precisely on characters of this description that the eloquence and address of the few are known to act with all their force. In the ancient republics, where the whole body of the people assembled in person, a single orator, or an artful statesman, was generally seen to rule with as complete a sway as if a sceptre had been placed in his single hand. On the same principle, the more multitudinous a representative assembly may be rendered, the more it will partake of the infirmities incident to collective meetings of the people. Ignorance will be the dupe of cunning, and passion the slave of sophistry and declamation. The people can never err more than in supposing that by multiplying their representatives beyond a certain limit, they strengthen the barrier against the government of a few. Experience will forever admonish them that, on the contrary, *after securing a sufficient number for the purposes of safety, of local information, and of diffusive sympathy with the whole society,* they will counteract their own views by every addition to their representatives. The countenance of the government may become more democratic, but the soul that animates it will be more oligarchic. The machine will be enlarged, but the fewer, and often the more secret, will be the springs by which its motions are directed. . . .

I. The qualifications proposed for senators, as distinguished from those of representatives, consist in a more advanced age and a longer period of citizenship. A senator must be thirty years of age at least; as a representative must be twenty-five. And the former must have been a citizen nine years; as seven years are required for the latter. The propriety of these distinctions is explained by the nature of the senatorial trust, which, requiring greater extent of information and stability of character, requires at the same time that the senator should have reached a period of life most likely to supply these advantages; and which, participating immediately in transactions with foreign nations, ought to be exercised by none who are not thoroughly weaned from the prepossessions and habits incident to foreign birth and education. The term of nine years appears to be a prudent mediocrity between a total exclusion of adopted citizens, whose merits and talents may claim a share in the public confidence, and an indiscriminate and hasty admission of them, which might create a channel for foreign influence on the national councils.

II. It is equally unnecessary to dilate on the appointment of senators by the State legislatures. Among the various modes which might have been devised for constituting this branch of the government, that which has been proposed by the convention is probably the most congenial with the public opinion. It is recommended by the double advantage of favoring a select appointment, and of giving to the State governments such an agency in the formation of the federal government as must secure the authority of the former, and may form a convenient link between the two systems.

III. The equality of representation in the Senate is another point, which, being evidently the result of compromise between the opposite pretensions of the large and the small States, does not call for much discussion. If indeed it be right, that among a people thoroughly incorporated into one nation, every district ought to have a *proportional* share in the government, and that among independent and sovereign States, bound together by a simple league, the parties, however unequal in size, ought to have an equal share in the common councils, it does not appear to be without some reason that in a compound republic, partaking both of the national and federal character, the government ought to be founded on a mixture of the principles of proportional and equal representation. . . .

IV. The number of senators, and the duration of their appointment, come next to be considered. In order to form an accurate judgment on both these points, it will be proper to inquire into the purposes which are to be answered by a senate; and in order to ascertain these, it will be necessary to review the inconveniences which a republic must suffer from the want of such an institution.

First. It is a misfortune incident to republican government, though in a less degree than to other governments, that those who administer it may forget their obligations to their constituents, and prove unfaithful to their important trust. In this point of view, a senate, as a second branch of the legislative assembly, distinct from, and dividing the power with, a first, must be in all cases a salutary check on the government. It doubles the security to the people, by requiring the concurrence of two distinct bodies in schemes of usurpation or perfidy, where the ambition or corruption of one would otherwise be sufficient. . . . I will barely remark, that as the improbability of sinister combinations will be in proportion to the dissimilarity in the genius of the two bodies, it must be politic to distinguish them from each other by every circumstance which will consist with a due harmony in all proper measures, and with the genuine principles of republican government.

Secondly. The necessity of a senate is not less indicated by the propensity of all single and numerous assemblies to yield to the impulse of sudden and violent passions, and to be seduced by factious leaders into intemperate and pernicious resolutions. . . . All that need be remarked is, that a body which is to correct this infirmity ought itself to be free from it, and consequently ought to be less numerous. It ought, moreover, to possess great firmness, and consequently ought to hold its authority by a tenure of considerable duration.

Thirdly. Another defect to be supplied by a senate lies in a want of due acquaintance with the objects and principles of legislation. It is not possible that an assembly of men called for the most part from pursuits of a private nature, continued in appointment for a short time, and led by no permanent motive to devote the intervals of public occupation to a study of the laws, the affairs, and the comprehensive interests of their country, should, if left wholly to themselves, escape a variety of important errors in the exercise of their legislative trust. It may be affirmed, on the best grounds, that no small share of the present embarrassments of America is to be charged on the blunders of our governments; and that these have proceeded from the heads rather than the hearts of most of the authors of them. What indeed are all the repealing, explaining, and amending laws, which fill and disgrace our voluminous codes, but so many monuments of deficient wisdom; so many impeachments exhibited by each succeeding against each preceding session; so many admonitions to the people, of the value of those aids which may be expected from a well-constituted senate? . . .

Fourthly. The mutability in the public councils arising from a rapid succession of new members, however qualified they may be, points out, in the strongest manner, the necessity of some stable institution in the government. Every new election in the States is found to change one half of the representatives. From this change of men must proceed a change of opinions; and from a change of opinions, a change of measures. But a continual change even of good measures is inconsistent with every rule of prudence and every prospect of success. . . .

In the first place, it forfeits the respect and confidence of other nations, and all the advantages connected with national character. An individual who is observed to be inconstant to his plans, or perhaps to carry on his affairs without any plan at all, is marked at once, by all prudent people, as a speedy victim to his own unsteadiness and folly. His more friendly neighbors may pity him, but all will decline to connect their fortunes with his; and not a few will seize the opportunity of making their fortunes out of his. . . .

The internal effects of a mutable policy are still more calamitous. It poisons the blessing of liberty itself. It will be of little avail to the people, that the laws are made by men of their own choice, if the laws be so voluminous that they cannot be read, or so incoherent that they cannot be understood; if they be repealed or revised before they are promulgated, or undergo such incessant changes that no man, who knows what the law is to-day, can guess what it will be to-morrow. Law is defined to be a rule of action; but how can that be a rule, which is little known, and less fixed?

Another effect of public instability is the unreasonable advantage it gives to the sagacious, the enterprising, and the moneyed few over the industrious and uninformed mass of the people. Every new regulation concerning commerce or revenue, or in any manner affecting the value of the different species of property, presents a new harvest to those who watch the change, and can trace its consequences; a harvest, reared not by themselves, but by the toils and cares of the great body of their fellow-citizens. . . .

In another point of view, great injury results from an unstable government. The want of confidence in the public councils damps every useful undertaking, the success and profit of which may depend on a continuance of existing arrangements. What prudent merchant will hazard his fortunes in any new branch of commerce when he knows not but that his plans may be rendered unlawful before they can be executed? What farmer or manufacturer will lay himself out for the encouragement given to any particular cultivation or establishment, when he can have no assurance that his preparatory labors and advances will not render him a victim to an inconstant government? In a word, no great improvement or laudable enterprise can go forward which requires the auspices of a steady system of national policy.

But the most deplorable effect of all is that diminution of attachment and reverence which steals into the hearts of the people, towards a political system which betrays so many marks of infirmity, and disappoints so many of their flattering hopes. No government, any more than an individual, will long be respected without being truly respectable; nor be truly respectable, without possessing a certain portion of order and stability.

[A fifth] desideratum, illustrating the utility of a senate, is the want of a due sense of national character. Without a select and stable member of the government, the esteem of foreign powers will not only be forfeited by an unenlightened and variable policy, proceeding from the causes already mentioned, but the national councils will not possess that sensibility to the opinion of the world, which is perhaps not less necessary in order to merit, than it is to obtain, its respect and confidence.

An attention to the judgment of other nations is important to every government for two reasons: the one is, that, independently of the merits of any particular plan or measure, it is desirable, on various accounts, that it should appear to other nations as the offspring of a wise and honorable policy; the second is, that in doubtful cases, particularly where the national councils may be warped by some strong passion or momentary interest, the presumed or known opinion of the impartial world may be the best guide that can be followed. What has not America lost by her want of character with foreign nations; and how many errors and follies would she not have avoided, if the justice and propriety of her measures had, in every instance, been previously tried by the light in which they would probably appear to the unbiased part of mankind?

Yet however requisite a sense of national character may be, it is evident that it can never be sufficiently possessed by a numerous and changeable body. It can only be found in a number so small that a sensible degree of the praise and blame of public measures may be the portion of each individual; or in an assembly so durably invested with public trust, that the pride and consequence of its members may be sensibly incorporated with the reputation and prosperity of the community. . . .

I add, as a *sixth* defect, the want, in some important cases, of a due responsibility in the government to the people, arising from that frequency of elections which in other cases produces this responsibility. This remark will, perhaps, appear not only new, but paradoxical. . . .

Responsibility, in order to be reasonable, must be limited to objects within the power of the responsible party, and in order to be effectual, must relate to operations of that power, of which a ready and proper judgment can be formed by the constituents. The objects of government may be divided into two general classes: the one depending on measures which have singly an immediate and sensible operation; the other depending on a succession of well-chosen and well-connected measures, which have a gradual and perhaps unobserved operation.

The importance of the latter description to the collective and permanent welfare of every country, needs no explanation. And yet it is evident that an assembly elected for so short a term as to be unable to provide more than one or two links in a chain of measures, on which the general welfare may essentially depend, ought not to be answerable for the final result, any more than a steward or tenant, engaged for one year, could be justly made to answer for places or improvements which could not be accomplished in less than half a dozen years. Nor is it possible for the people to estimate the *share* of influence which their annual assemblies may respectively have on events resulting from the mixed transactions of several years. It is sufficiently difficult to preserve a personal responsibility in the members of a *numerous* body, for such acts of the body as have an immediate, detached, and palpable operation on its constituents.

The proper remedy for this defect must be an additional body in the legislative department, which, having sufficient permanency to provide for such objects as require a continued attention, and a train of measures, may be justly and effectually answerable for the attainment of those objects.

Thus far I have considered the circumstances which point out the necessity of a well-constructed Senate only as they relate to the representatives of the people. To a people as little blinded by prejudice or corrupted by flattery as those whom I address, I shall not scruple to add, that such an institution may be sometimes necessary as a defence to the people against their own temporary errors and delusions. As the cool and deliberate sense of the community ought, in all governments, and actually will in all free governments ultimately prevail over the views of its rulers; so there are particular moments in public affairs when the people, stimulated by some irregular passion, or some illicit advantage, or misled by the artful misrepresentations of interested men, may call for measures which they themselves will afterwards be the most ready to lament and condemn. In these critical moments, how salutary will be the interference of some temperate and respectable body of citizens, in order to check the misguided career, and to suspend the blow meditated by the people against themselves, until reason, justice, and truth can regain their authority over the public mind? . . .

32

Woodrow Wilson

The Need for Cabinet Government in the United States (1879)

. . . At its highest development, *representative* government is that form which best enables a free people to govern themselves. The main object of a representative assembly, therefore, should be the discussion of public business. They should legislate as if in the presence of the whole country, because they come under the closest scrutiny and fullest criticism of all the representatives of the country speaking in open and free debate. . . .

Nothing can be more obvious than the fact that the very life of free, popular institutions is dependent upon their breathing the bracing air of thorough, exhaustive, and open discussions, or that select Congressional committees, whose proceedings must from their very nature be secret, are, as means of legislation, dangerous and unwholesome. . . .

Our Government is practically carried on by irresponsible committees. Too few Americans take the trouble to inform themselves as to the methods of Congressional management; and, as a consequence, not many have perceived that almost *absolute* power has fallen into the hands of men whose irresponsibility prevents the regulation of their conduct by the people from whom they derive their authority. . . .

From Wilson, "Cabinet Government in the United States," *International Review*, VII (August 1879).

[Almost] every bill introduced [in the house] must be referred, without debate, to the proper Standing Committee, with whom rests the privilege of embodying it, or any part of it, in their reports, or of rejecting it altogether. The House very seldom takes any direct action upon any measures introduced by individual members; its votes and discussions are almost entirely confined to committee reports and committee dictation. The whole attitude of business depends upon . . . Standing Committees. . . .

This is certainly a phase of representative government peculiar to ourselves. And yet its development was most natural and apparently necessary. It is hardly possible for a body of several hundred men, without official or authoritative leaders, to determine upon any line of action without interminable wrangling and delays injurious to the interests under their care. Left to their own resources, they would be as helpless as any other mass meeting. Without leaders having authority to guide their deliberations and give a definite direction to the movement of legislation; and, moreover, with none of that sense of responsibility which constantly rests upon those whose duty it is to work out to a successful issue the policies which they themselves originate, yet with full power to dictate policies which others must carry into execution,—a recognition of the need of some sort of leadership, and of a division of labor, led to the formation of these Standing Committees, to which are intrusted the shaping of the national policy in the several departments of administration, as well as the prerogatives of the initiative in legislation and leadership in debate. When theoretically viewed, this is an ingenious and apparently harmless device, but one which, in practice, subverts that most fundamental of all the principles of a free State,—the right of the people to a potential voice in their own government. Great measures of legislation are discussed and determined, not conspicuously in public session of the people's representatives, but in the unapproachable privacy of committee rooms.

But what less imperfect means of representative government can we find without stepping beyond the bounds of a true republicanism? . . .

What . . . is Cabinet government? What is the change proposed? Simply to give to the heads of the Executive departments—the members of the Cabinet—seats in Congress, with the privilege of the initiative in legislation and some part of the unbounded privileges now commanded by the Standing Committees. But the advocates of such a change—and they are now not a few—deceive themselves when they maintain that it would not necessarily involve the principle of ministerial responsibility,—that is, the resignation of the Cabinet upon the defeat of any important part of their plans. For, if Cabinet officers sit in Congress as official representatives of the Executive, this principle of responsibility must of necessity come sooner or later to be recognized. Experience would soon demonstrate the practical impossibility of their holding their seats, and continuing to represent the Administration, after they had found themselves unable to gain the consent of a majority to their policy. Their functions would be peculiar. They would constitute a link between the legislative and executive branches of the general Government, and, as representatives of the Executive, must hold the right of the initiative in legislation. Otherwise their position would be an anomalous one, indeed. There would be little danger and evident propriety in extending to them the first right of introducing measures relative to the administration of the several departments; and they could possess such a right without denying the fullest privileges to other members. But, whether granted this initiative or not, the head of each department would undoubtedly find it necessary to take a decided and open stand for or against every measure bearing upon the affairs of his department, by whomsoever introduced. No highspirited man would long remain in an office in the business of which he was not permitted to pursue a policy which tallied with his own principles and convictions. If defeated by both Houses, he would naturally resign; and not many years would pass before resignation upon defeat would have become an established precedent,—and resignation upon defeat is the essence of responsible government. . . .

But, to give to the President the right to choose whomsoever he pleases as his constitutional advisers, after having constituted Cabinet officers *ex officio* members of Congress, would be to empower him to appoint a limited number of representatives, and would thus be plainly at variance with republican principles. The highest order of responsible government could, then, be established in the United States only by laying upon the President the necessity of selecting his Cabinet from among the number of representatives already chosen by the people. . . .

33

Morris P. Fiorina

The Rise of the Washington Establishment (1989)

I assume that most people most of the time act in their own self-interest. This is not to say that human beings seek only to amass tangible wealth but rather to say that human beings seek to achieve their own ends—tangible and intangible—rather than the ends of their fellow men. I do not condemn such behavior

From Morris P. Florina, *Congress: Keystone of the Washington Establishment.* Copyright © 1977, 1989 by Yale University. All rights reserved. Reprinted with permission of Yale University Press.

nor do I condone it (although I rather sympathize with Thoreau's comment that "if I knew for a certainty that a man was coming to my house with the conscious design of doing me good, I should run for my life"). I only claim that political and economic theories which presume self-interested behavior will prove to be more widely applicable than those which build on more altruistic assumptions.

What does the axiom imply when used in the specific context of this book, a context peopled by congressmen, bureaucrats, and voters? I assume that the primary goal of the typical congressman is reelection. Over and above the salary plus "perks" and outside money, the office of congressman carries with it prestige, excitement, and power. It is a seat in the cockpit of government. But in order to retain the status, excitement, and power (not to mention more tangible things) of office, the congressman must win reelection every two years. Even those congressmen genuinely concerned with good public policy must achieve reelection in order to continue their work. Whether narrowly self-serving or more publicly oriented, the individual congressman finds reelection to be at least a necessary condition for the achievement of his goals.

Moreover, there is a kind of natural selection process at work in the electoral arena. On average, those congressmen who are not primarily interested in reelection will not achieve reelection as often as those who are interested. We, the people, help to weed out congressmen whose primary motivation is not reelection. We admire politicians who courageously adopt the aloof role of the disinterested statesman, but we vote for those politicians who follow our wishes and do us favors.

What about the bureaucrats? A specification of their goals is somewhat more controversial—those who speak of appointed officials as public servants obviously take a more benign view than those who speak of them as bureaucrats. The literature provides ample justification for asserting that most bureaucrats wish to protect and nurture their agencies. The typical bureaucrat can be expected to seek to expand his agency in terms of personnel, budget, and mission. One's status in Washington (again, not to mention more tangible things) is roughly proportional to the importance of the operation one oversees. And the sheer size of the operation is taken to be a measure of importance. As with congressmen, the specified goals apply even to those bureaucrats who genuinely believe in their agency's mission. If they believe in the efficacy of their programs, they naturally wish to expand them and add new ones. All of this requires more money and more people. The genuinely committed bureaucrat is just as likely to seek to expand his agency as the proverbial empire-builder.

And what of the third element in the equation, us? What do we, the voters who support the Washington system, strive for? Each of us wishes to receive a maximum of benefits from government for the minimum cost. This goal suggests maximum government efficiency, on the one hand, but it also suggests mutual exploitation on the other. Each of us favors an arrangement in which our fellow citizens pay for our benefits.

With these brief descriptions of the cast of characters in hand, let us proceed.

What should we expect from a legislative body composed of individuals whose first priority is their continued tenure in office? We should expect, first, that the normal activities of its members are those calculated to enhance their chances of reelection. And we should expect, second, that the members would devise and maintain institutional arrangements which facilitate their electoral activities.

For most of the twentieth century, congressmen have engaged in a mix of three kinds of activities: lawmaking, pork barreling, and casework. Congress is first and foremost a lawmaking body, at least according to constitutional theory. In every postwar session Congress "considers" thousands of bills and resolutions, many hundreds of which are brought to a record vote (over 500 in each chamber in the 93d Congress). Naturally the critical consideration in taking a position for the record is the maximization of approval in the home district. If the district is unaffected by and unconcerned with the matter at hand, the congressman may then take into account the general welfare of the country. (This sounds cynical, but remember that "profiles in courage" are sufficiently rare that their occurrence inspires books and articles.) Abetted by political scientists of the pluralist school, politicians have propounded an ideology which maintains that the good of the country on any given issue is simply what is best for a majority of congressional districts. This ideology provides a philosophical justification for what congressmen do while acting in their own self-interest.

A second activity favored by congressmen consists of efforts to bring home the bacon to their districts. Many popular articles have been written about the pork barrel, a term originally applied to rivers and harbors legislation but now generalized to cover all manner of federal largesse. Congressmen consider new dams, federal buildings, sewage treatment plants, urban renewal projects, etc. as sweet plums to be plucked. Federal projects are highly visible, their economic impact is easily detected by constituents, and sometimes they even produce something of value to the district. The average constituent may have some trouble translating his congressman's vote on some civil rights issue into a change in his personal welfare. But the workers hired and supplies purchased in connection with a big federal project provide benefits that are widely appreciated. The historical importance congressmen attach to the pork barrel is reflected in the rules of the House. That body accords certain classes of legislation "privileged" status: they may come directly to the floor without passing through the Rules Committee, a traditional graveyard for legislation. What kinds of legislation are privileged? Taxing and spending bills, for one: the government's power to raise and spend money must be kept relatively unfettered. But in addition, the omnibus rivers and harbors bills of the Public Works

Committee and public lands bills from the Interior Committee share privileged status. The House will allow a civil rights or defense procurement or environmental bill to languish in the Rules Committee, but it takes special precautions to insure that nothing slows down the approval of dams and irrigation projects.

A third major activity takes up perhaps as much time as the other two combined. Traditionally, constituents appeal to their Congressman for myriad favors and services. Sometimes only information is needed, but often constituents request that their congressman intervene in the internal workings of federal agencies to affect a decision in a favorable way, to reverse an adverse decision, or simply to speed up the glacial bureaucratic process. On the basis of extensive personal interviews with congressmen, Charles Clapp writes:

> Denied a favorable ruling by the bureaucracy on a matter of direct concern to him, puzzled or irked by delays in obtaining a decision, confused by the administrative maze through which he is directed to proceed, or ignorant of whom to write, a constituent may turn to his congressman for help. These letters offer great potential for political benefit to the congressman since they affect the constituent personally. If the legislator can be of assistance, he may gain a firm ally; if he is indifferent, he may even lose votes.

Actually congressmen are in an almost unique position in our system, a position shared only with high-level members of the executive branch. Congressmen possess the power to expedite and influence bureaucratic decisions. This capability flows directly from congressional control over what bureaucrats value most: higher budgets and new program authorizations. In a very real sense each congressman is a monopoly supplier of bureaucratic unsticking services for his district.

Every year the federal budget passes through the appropriations committees of Congress. Generally these committees make perfunctory cuts. . . . Deep and serious cuts are made occasionally, and the threat of such cuts keeps most agencies attentive to congressional wishes. . . . Moreover, the bureaucracy must keep coming back to Congress to have its old programs reauthorized and new ones added. Again, most such decisions are perfunctory, but exceptions are sufficiently frequent that bureaucrats do not forget the basis of their agencies' existence. . . . The bureaucracy needs congressional approval in order to survive, let alone expand. Thus, when a congressman calls about some minor bureaucratic decision or regulation, the bureaucracy considers his accommodation a small price to pay for the goodwill its cooperation will produce, particularly if he has any connection to the substantive committee or the appropriations subcommittee to which it reports.

From the standpoint of capturing voters, the congressman's lawmaking activities differ in two important respects from his pork-barrel and casework activities. First, programmatic actions are inherently controversial. Unless his district is homogeneous, a congressman will find his district divided on many major issues. Thus when he casts a vote, introduces a piece of non-trivial legislation, or makes a speech with policy content he will displease some elements of his district. Some constituents may applaud the congressman's civil rights record, but others believe integration is going too fast. Some support foreign aid, while others believe it's money poured down a rathole. Some advocate economic equality, others stew over welfare cheaters. On such policy matters the congressman can expect to make friends as well as enemies. Presumably he will behave so as to maximize the excess of the former over the latter, but nevertheless a policy stand will generally make some enemies.

In contrast, the pork barrel and casework are relatively less controversial. New federal projects bring jobs, shiny new facilities, and general economic prosperity, or so people believe. Snipping ribbons at the dedication of a new post office or dam is a much more pleasant pursuit than disposing of a constitutional amendment on abortion. Republicans and Democrats, conservatives and liberals, all generally prefer a richer district to a poorer one. Of course, in recent years the river damming and stream-bed straightening activities of the Army Corps of Engineers have aroused some opposition among environmentalists. Congressmen happily reacted by absorbing the opposition and adding environmentalism to the pork barrel: water treatment plants are currently a hot congressional item.

Casework is even less controversial. Some poor, aggrieved constituent becomes enmeshed in the tentacles of an evil bureaucracy and calls upon Congressman St. George to do battle with the dragon. . . .

In sum, when considering the benefits of his programmatic activities, the congressman must tote up gains and losses to arrive at a net profit. Pork barreling and casework, however, are basically pure profit.

A second way in which programmatic activities differ from casework and the pork barrel is the difficulty of assigning responsibility to the former as compared with the latter. No congressman can seriously claim that he is responsible for the 1964 Civil Rights Act, the ABM, or the 1972 Revenue Sharing Act. Most constituents do have some vague notion that their congressman is only one of hundreds and their senator one of an even hundred. Even committee chairmen have a difficult time claiming credit for a piece of major legislation, let alone a rank-and-file congressman. Ah, but casework, and the pork barrel. In dealing with the bureaucracy, the congressman is not merely one vote of 435. Rather, he is a nonpartisan power, someone whose phone calls snap an office to attention. He is not kept on hold. The constituent who receives aid believes that his congressman and his congressman alone got results. Similarly, congressmen find it easy to claim credit for federal projects awarded their districts. The congressman may have instigated the proposal for the project in the first place, issued regular progress reports, and ultimately announced the award through his office. Maybe he can't claim credit for the 1965 Voting Rights Act, but he can take credit for Littletown's spanking new sewage treatment plant.

Overall then, programmatic activities are dangerous (controversial), on the one hand, and programmatic accomplishments are difficult to claim credit for, on the other. While less exciting, casework and pork barreling are both safe and profitable. For a reelection-oriented congressman the choice is obvious.

The key to the rise of the Washington establishment (and the vanishing marginals) is the following observation: *the growth of an activist federal government has stimulated a change in the mix of congressional activities*. Specifically, a lesser proportion of congressional effort is now going into programmatic activities and a greater proportion into pork-barrel and casework activities. As a result, today's congressmen make relatively fewer enemies and relatively more friends among the people of their districts.

To elaborate, a basic fact of life in twentieth-century America is the growth of the federal role and its attendant bureaucracy. . . .

As the years have passed, more and more citizens and groups have found themselves dealing with the federal bureaucracy. They may be seeking positive actions—eligibility for various benefits and awards of government grants. Or they may be seeking relief from the costs imposed by bureaucratic regulations—on working conditions, racial and sexual quotas, market restrictions, and numerous other subjects. While not malevolent, bureaucracies make mistakes, both of commissions and omission, and normal attempts at redress often meet with unresponsiveness and inflexibility and sometimes seeming incorrigibility. Whatever the problem, the citizen's congressman is a source of succor. The greater the scope of government activity, the greater the demand for his services. . . .

I seriously doubt that congressmen resist their gradual transformation from national legislators to errand boy-ombudsmen. As we have noted, casework is all profit. Congressmen have buried proposals to relieve the casework burden by establishing a national ombudsman or Congressman Reuss's proposed Administrative Counsel of the Congress. One of the congressmen interviewed by Clapp stated:

> Before I came to Washington I used to think that it might be nice if the individual states had administrative arms here that would take care of necessary liaison between citizens and the national government. But a congressman running for reelection is interested in building fences by providing personal services. The system is set to reelect incumbents regardless of party, and incumbents wouldn't dream of giving any of this service function away to any subagency. As an elected member I feel the same way.

In fact, it is probable that at least some congressmen deliberately stimulate the demand for their bureaucratic fixit services. (See the exhibit at the end of this chapter). Recall that the new Republican in district A travels about his district saying:

> I'm your man in Washington. What are your problems? How can I help you?

And in district B, did the demand for the congressman's services rise so much between 1962 and 1964 that a "regiment" of constituency staff became necessary? Or, having access to the regiment, did the new Democrat stimulate the demand to which he would apply his regiment?

In addition to greatly increased casework, let us not forget that the growth of the federal role has also greatly expanded the federal pork barrel. The creative pork barreler need not limit himself to dams and post offices— rather old-fashioned interests. Today, creative congressmen can cadge LEAA money for the local police, urban renewal and housing money for local politicians, educational program grants for the local education bureaucracy. And there are sewage treatment plants, worker training and retraining programs, health services, and programs for the elderly. The pork barrel is full to overflowing. The conscientious congressman can stimulate applications for federal assistance (the sheer number of programs makes it difficult for local officials to stay current with the possibilities), put in a good word during consideration, and announce favorable decisions amid great fanfare.

In sum, everyday decisions by a large and growing federal bureaucracy bestow significant tangible benefits and impose significant tangible costs. Congressmen can affect these decisions. Ergo, the more decisions the bureaucracy has the opportunity to make, the more opportunities there are for the congressman to build up credits.

The nature of the Washington system is now quite clear. Congressmen (typically the majority Democrats) earn electoral credits by establishing various federal programs (the minority Republicans typically earn credits by fighting the good fight). The legislation is drafted in very general terms, so some agency, existing or newly established, must translate a vague policy mandate into a functioning program, a process that necessitates the promulgation of numerous rules and regulations and, incidentally, the trampling of numerous toes. At the next stage, aggrieved and/or hopeful constituents petition their congressman to intervene in the complex (or at least obscure) decision processes of the bureaucracy. The cycle closes when the congressman lends a sympathetic ear, piously denounces the evils of bureaucracy, intervenes in the latter's decisions, and rides a grateful electorate to ever more impressive electoral showings. Congressmen take credit coming and going. They are the alpha and the omega.

The popular frustration with the permanent government in Washington is partly justified, but to a considerable degree it is misplaced resentment. *Congress is the linchpin of the Washington establishment.* . . . Congress does not just react to big government—it creates it. All of Washington prospers. More and more bureaucrats promulgate more and more regulations and dispense more and more money. Fewer and fewer congressmen suffer electoral defeat. Elements of the electorate benefit from government programs, and all of the electorate is eligible for ombudsman services. But the general, long-term welfare of the United States is no more than an incidental by-product of the system.

34

William F. Connelly, Jr.

Congress Is Not the Broken Branch (2013)

Today we are, according to some political scientists and journalists, in the midst of a "second civil war," characterized by "off center," "freak show," "fight club" politics, complete with a contentious "broken branch" Congress where "it's even worse than it looks"—all titles of recent books!

In *The Broken Branch* Tom Mann and Norm Ornstein insist Congress is broken because congressional politics is characterized by corrosive partisanship, a permanent campaign, confrontation rather than compromise, gridlock more than legislative productivity, and inadequate legislative oversight. Partisan polarization and invective drown out serious and thoughtful deliberation, they insist, while campaigning trumps governing. The Senate has become more like the House and the executive has eclipsed the legislature; Congress is no longer the "First Branch," as Mann and Ornstein maintain the Founders intended; Congress has ceded too much authority to the president.

Others similarly maintain that hyperpartisanship has intensified our differences, producing stalemate; polarization coupled with gridlock is alienating the public. We are losing the capacity to compromise, indispensable for progress, critics insist, thus we are left with polarization and paralysis. Confrontation trumps compromise; ideology precludes pragmatic consensus building, engendering animosity rather than solutions.

The critics surely identify serious problems, but is it really the case that the Constitution and the politics it engenders are inadequate to the challenges of today? And have we not heard this before? These problems have been with us since the founding of the American Republic. So, too, have the criticisms they articulate.

WERE THE FOUNDERS ANTI-PARTY?

Some today insist the Founders did not expect political parties to form, that parties only arose later in American history. Yet in a 1792 essay titled "A Candid State of Parties" Madison argues that partisan division is

Courtesy of William F. Connelly, Jr.

"natural to most political societies," and will endure as long as freedom is protected. Madison notes in *Federalist 10*:

> Liberty is to faction what air is to fire, an aliment without which it instantly expires. But it could not be less folly to abolish liberty, which is essential to political life, because it nourishes faction, than it would be to wish the annihilation of air, which is essential to animal life, because it imparts to fire its destructive agency.

Madison notes that the "principle task of modern legislation" is the regulation of "various and interfering interests," which "involves the spirit of party and faction in the necessary and ordinary operations of government." He thus understood that in a free society, politics, including the "spirit of party," is ubiquitous. Since the "latent causes of faction" and "the spirit of party" are natural to man, Madison sought to control the effects of factions, rather than remove their causes. Madison did not think it possible to take factionalism or partisanship out of politics; therefore, he sought instead to multiply factions and *control their effects* by means of republican institutions governed by constitutional structure. The separation of powers, bicameralism and federalism mitigate the dangers of partisan factionalism, often pitting *intraparty* factions against one another as much as *interparty* factions.

The Founders' practice of their principles in the first decade of the new Republic, moreover, hardly suggests that they were anti-party. We have come to think of the Founders as statesmen, and James Madison, in particular, as a soft-spoken gentleman inclined toward the politics of compromise and reconciliation presumably embodied in Madisonian pluralism. Yet these statesmen were also politicians and ardent partisans. Madison was a particularly effective congressional party strategist, dubbed "Jemmy the Knife" by friend and foe alike. The 1790s have been termed as "a decade long shouting match" unparalleled in American history. Partisans were quick to label their opponents "Jacobins" or "Monarchists" as they tussled over contentious issues. Party spirit dominated the early Republic.

Temperamentally, Madison may have been a balancer and reconciler, "the master committeeman" interested in promoting comity and civility. Yet Madison did not try to take the "spirit of party" out of politics; nor did he share Jefferson's pretense to rising above party. Madison understood clearly that the spirit of party and faction was fated to be a constant in free governments, even if factionalism did not always take the form of two ideologically distinct party coalitions. Partisan and personal differences in the 1790s were sharp, significant, and often rooted in competing constitutional interpretations—just like today!

Arguably, the two increasingly polarized parties evolving in the 1790s even perpetuated a "permanent campaign" premised on a fundamental tension built into our Constitution rooted in two central principles: the separation of powers and federalism—legislative vs. executive authority, state vs. national power—bones of contention in the 1790s and today.

In many ways, the 1790s were like today. Just as Federalist majorities eventually gave way to Jefferson's "Second Revolution" Republicans, so, too, the "permanent majority" House Democrats' succumbed to the "House Republican Revolution" in 1994, with House Republicans, in turn, losing their own extended majority to the Democrats in the bitter partisan warfare leading up to the 2006 election, only to regain their House majority in 2010.

By 1800, America had two clear ideologically polarized political parties. Jeffersonian Republicans offered a choice rather than an echo of the Federalists, thus Jefferson's election in 1800 came to be called the "Second Revolution." This "revolution" was at least as great a challenge to the existing order as would be Newt Gingrich's so-called "House Republican Revolution" in 1994 or Democrats' return to power in 2006 and 2008. Congressional party leaders then and now questioned the constitutional legitimacy of their partisan opponents as they gazed across the vast "empty center" dividing their two parties. Yet one lesson all congressional leaders learn in their time: majorities fall, but Congress and the Constitution stand. If the dangers of partisanship, polarization, and paralysis were as disastrous as the critics of our government contend, we could not have managed to muddle through the past two centuries, perhaps especially the last two decades.

In Praise of Deadlock?

In his delightful book *In Praise of Deadlock: How Partisan Struggle Makes Better Laws*, Lee Rawls dares to defend both partisanship and gridlock; he even defends the oft-maligned Senate filibuster. Rawls argues the filibuster promotes *both* gridlock and *bi*partisanship because the filibuster forces negotiations, thus requiring bipartisanship. Rawls doubts whether partisanship truly diminishes our capacity to address critical policy challenges. Studies have shown that increased polarization does not necessarily hinder legislative productivity; partisanship can lead to hard bargaining rather than gridlock.

Indeed, much of the energy in American politics originates from party competition. In *Democracy in America* in the 1830s Alexis de Tocqueville also recognized the energy inherent in democracy: "What strikes one most on arrival in the United States is the kind of tumultuous agitation in which one finds political society." Tocqueville adds: "The political activity prevailing in the United States is harder to conceive than the freedom and equality found there. The continual feverish activity of the legislatures is only an episode and an extension of a movement that is universal." Tocqueville sees this energy in American politics, together with the mutability of our laws, as both *virtue and defect*.

The mutability of laws Tocqueville ties to the frequency of elections. "When elections quickly follow one another, they keep society in feverish activity, with endless mutability in public affairs . . . for democracy has a taste amounting to passion for variety. A strange mutability in . . . legislation is the result." Tocqueville understood that the passion for legislative productivity is rooted in democracy. Consider the possibility that the disdain for purported gridlock today reflects democracy's passion for change, the impatience and avidity of a democratic people—us.

Madison also warned "[t]he facility and excess of lawmaking seem to be diseases to which our governments are most liable." Madison sought to control this "excess of lawmaking" with his constitutional structure, including, the separation of powers and bicameralism. Hence, gridlock can be a form of governing. Preventing legislation may also demonstrate effective governance. At times, the status quo may be preferable to legislative change. Who has not agreed with this observation at one time or another? For example, Republicans on the 2010 health care reform or the Pelosi-lead Democrats on Bush's Social Security initiative in 2005–2006. Limited government, as opposed to activist government, may at times be desirable.

FREE AND EFFECTIVE GOVERNMENT

Moreover, contrary to the conventional wisdom, the separation of powers is *not* reducible to the checks and balances inevitably resulting in partisan stalemate and gridlock. We can blame Woodrow Wilson, and before him, the Whigs, for this common contemporary *mis*understanding. Rather, the Founders sought to create limited, yet effective government by means of a functional separation of powers with each branch independent and powerful within its sphere.

To replace the ineffective government of the Articles of Confederation, the Founders designed the constitutional separation of powers to promote stability *and* energy—to impede change *and* advance innovation. A modern example can be seen in the way the landmark 1997 budget accord followed upon the 1995–1996 government showdown/shutdown. Gridlock gave way to governing. In fact, the former may have been the predicate for the latter. A similar, albeit temporary and incremental, compromise resolution followed the "fiscal cliff" standoff in early 2013.

Congress brings energy to the legislative process precisely because power is fragmented and decentralized. Congress unleashes the entrepreneurial ambitions of individual members; separation of powers, federalism, and bicameralism—all constitutional principles governing Congress—provide opportunities for change as much as obstacles to change. Multiple veto points may in fact be multiple access points in our complex legislative process.

Competition and not just compromise may be good and may facilitate good government. Institutional and partisan conflict may be necessary and healthy. Confrontation—including partisan confrontation—is a *natural* part of the legislative process; airing disagreement is one purpose of democratic lawmaking. Disagreement may be a necessary predicate to accommodation, as seen, for example, in the way the 1997 budget accord followed the1994–95 budget showdown/shutdown. Competition is a natural part of the legislative and electoral processes, consequently, a can't-we-all-get-along civility may be contrary to the nature of Madison's Congress. Partisanship can be beneficial by rousing us from our slumber, overcoming the blight of apathy and alienation; political parties inspire debate and increase voter turnout. Indeed, heightened partisanship has had precisely this effect on voter turnout in recent years. Partisanship is potentially constructive and constitutionally permissible; it is a normal, natural, and necessary part of our political system.

A Constitutional Politics of Pluralism and Partisanship

During the 1950s, political scientists—in their APSA Report: *Toward a More Responsible Two Party System*—lamented the excessively local, parochial, and pluralistic character of our politics. Our parties were said to be tweedle-dee and twiddle-dum. The APSA called for a more *disciplined* and *responsible* two-party system providing a *choice* not an *echo*. *Perhaps we should be careful what we wish for?* Today we have choice parties and political scientists complain. A politics of consensus and compromise can sometimes hinder needed change; consensus can be a cover for domination by an established status quo. Nostalgia for the partisan tranquility of the 1950s may, for example, overlook failures during that decade to address needed change in civil rights.

The compromising pluralism of the 1950s and the confrontational partisanship of today may both be normal and permissible. The potential for both pluralist incrementalism and conditional party government may be contained in our constitutional order. American politics arguably oscillates between an all-politics-is-local pluralism and an all-politics-is-national approximation of party government. Former House Speakers Tip O'Neill and Newt Gingrich may both be right; thus, all politics is local, except when it is national.

Our politics oscillates across the decades, as witness the disaggregation of the 1950s and the polarization of today. Our politics oscillates even within presidential terms. For example, the bipartisanship of George W. Bush's first term, as seen in passage of No Child Left Behind, contrasts with the bitter partisanship during his second term. To some extent, American politics alternates within congressional terms, with the first year of a new Congress producing more policy, while the second year gives way to politics as the next election approaches. Alternation may be encouraged by bicameralism, which incorporates the proclivity of the House for conflict and the Senate for consensus. So too does American politics fluctuate with the issues; for example, partisan warfare in the 2008 election year gave way repeatedly to bipartisan cooperation on Capitol Hill to deal with the looming economic and financial crises (e.g. TARP).

Pluralism and party government are paradigms or perspectives—models if you will—within political science. Each captures only *part* of the complexity of our constitutional system arguably, thus neither is ever the dominant paradigm in political science. Unlike economics, there is no dominant paradigm in political science. In fact, there may be a reason rooted in the Constitution for the oscillating of our politics between these competing perspectives within political science.

Innovation and stalemate are both built into our constitutional routines, with alternating and overlapping patterns of activity and impasse in congressional policymaking. Neither mode is exclusively "natural" to Congress; both are "historically characteristic" of Congress; both are grounded in the overall constitutional design. Congressional politics may be a pendulum swing between "pluralism" and "party government," encompassing compromise and confrontation, bipartisanship and partisanship—like two halves of a whole. The ebb and flow of partisanship is a natural part of our constitutional system, and in and of itself provides evidence of the dynamic, rather than static, character of the separation of powers. The separation of powers promotes both energy and stability, innovation and deliberation because the separation of powers both humbles and empowers Democrats and Republicans, majority and minority parties, presidents and Congress, though at different times and on different issues.

The decision by Democrats to advance comprehensive, nonincremental health care reform in 2009–2010 may by its very nature have been partisan since it raised fundamental questions about the role of government. During the House debate Democrats, according to the *Washington Post*, "cast the vote as a long-overdue opportunity to provide affordable health coverage to tens of millions of people and as the final pillar of economic security, alongside Social Security and Medicare. Republicans cast it as the ultimate government overreach, an assault on American liberty that would drive the nation deeper into debt." Comprehensive reform augmenting the role of government inevitably may promote polarizing partisanship. In order to avoid partisan confrontation, should Democrats have curbed their ambition? Few Democrats would suggest so. We can agree or disagree with "Obamacare," yet it is a huge legislative achievement. Those who favor Obamacare should not lament the resulting increased partisan polarization caused by the clash between the two parties—each of whom on principle stand for two very, very different "narratives."

The same might be said—on the other side of the partisan divided—about dramatic attempts to re-limit government contrary to already settled consensus.

House Budget Committee Chair Paul Ryan's proposal to replace traditional Medicare with a system of vouchers is a prime example. The principled differences between the two parties matter; again, sometimes partisan warfare serves a larger purpose.

Yet it is not just attempts at comprehensive reform that invite partisan polarization. James Q. Wilson once observed that at one time government was about a few things, whereas today it is about everything. Arguably, big government gives you big politics. The long-term growth of government, in general, may be feeding the "scourge" of partisanship.

Is Partisanship Politics as Usual?

Madison clearly understood: "In every political society, parties are unavoidable," in fact, he concluded parties "must always be expected in a government as free as ours" since "no free Country has ever been without parties, which are a natural offspring of Freedom." Madison recognized that American politics and partisanship are rooted in constitutionalism and the Constitution. Mere partisanship is possible precisely because of limited constitutional government. The Constitution governs parties more than parties govern the Constitution. Political parties can be more partial and more partisan precisely because parties do not govern; rather, the Constitution governs. Our constitutional concrete is sufficient to withstand partisan warfare today, just as it did in the 1790s.

Madison did not want to take the politics out of politics, because doing so would run contrary to the Constitution and our liberal experiment embodied in the Constitution. Freedom of speech, freedom of the press, freedom of association, and the right to petition government all invite the formation and exercise of factions, parties, and a partisan press.

Partisanship is also rooted in the Constitution in another fundamental way. Throughout our history, beginning in the 1790s, partisanship has been premised on the fault lines of constitutional debate. Differences over constitutional interpretation continue to provide fodder for our political, including partisan, debates. In fact, American politics may consist of an ongoing and ever deepening debate between the principles of the Federalists and Anti-Federalists. Contentious partisanship has its roots in the Constitution.

Ultimately, the "broken branch" is not broken. We are not on the verge of a second civil war. Since we never form a government, as Lloyd Cutler notes, the permanent campaign is permanent, and strict partisan accountability is impossible. Both parties are to blame. While the party wars may seem never ending, in fact our politics is marked by intermittent compromise and confrontation. Just as the waxing and waning of legislative and executive power is a normal feature of Madison's constitutional system, so, too, is the ebb and flow of partisanship to be expected. The separation of powers is dynamic, not static.

Rather than criticize the Constitution and call for fundamental constitutional reform—with all its potential unintended consequences—perhaps we should try instead to understand the Constitution with its latent potential for both partisanship and bipartisanship, conflict and compromise, limited and effective government, stability and energy.

35

Joseph M. Bessette

Deliberation Defended (1994)

The deliberation that lies at the core of the kind of democracy established by the American constitutional system can be defined most simply as *reasoning on the merits of public policy*. As commonly and traditionally understood, deliberation is a reasoning process in which the participants seriously consider substantive information and arguments and seek to decide individually and to persuade each other as to what constitutes good public policy. Thus, deliberation includes a variety of activities often called "problem solving" or "analytic": the investigation and identification of social, economic, or governmental problems; the evaluation of current policies or programs; the consideration of various and competing proposals; and the formulation of legislative or administrative remedies. In any genuine deliberative process the participants must be open to the facts, arguments, and proposals that come to their attention and must share a general willingness to learn from their colleagues and others.

So defined, the proximate aim of a deliberative process is the conferral of some public good or benefit. Such a benefit need not necessarily be national in scope (such as a healthy economy or a sound national defense); it may instead be a locally oriented good (such as a flood control project or a new highway), a good directed toward a broad class of citizens (as with civil rights laws or labor legislation), or even transnational in its reach (such as foreign aid). Thus, the existence of deliberation does not turn on the distinction between local and national interests. An over-riding desire to serve one's local constituents does not in itself close a legislator to the persuasive effects of information and arguments, although such a legislator will respond to different kinds of appeals than one who seeks to promote national interests. This is true even if the desire to confer local benefits results directly from self-interested calculations, such as the representative's desire to be reelected; for the legislator who seeks singlemindedly to be reelected may well find that in some situations this goal requires him to give real consideration to the merits of legislative proposals designed to benefit his constituents. . . .

Although legislators may deliberate about local, or partial, interests as well as those of a national dimension, there remains a relationship between the likelihood and nature of deliberation in Congress and the scope of the public benefits that legislators seek to confer. Consider, for example, legislators who deliberate about how to promote the well-being of specific interests. If such legislators see their job essentially in terms of doing good for external groups, they will be inclined to accept the groups' determination as to how this should be done; for who knows the groups' interests better than they do. The narrower and more specific the group (wheat farmers, auto workers, coal miners, etc.) the less difference of opinion or conflict there will be and therefore the less need for such a legislator to consider different arguments or to reason about alternative proposals. However, as the scope of the legislator's concerns widens, to encompass more or broader interests, the more difficult it will become to defer to the interests themselves for guidance. A variety of differing and often conflicting opinions will highlight the complexity of the issues at stake and place a greater obligation on the lawmaker to exercise some independent judgment. For the legislator who seeks to promote the national interests, personal deliberation will be essential; insofar as other legislators share the same goal, collective deliberation will be pervasive.

Personal deliberation by individual legislators does not require that others in the lawmaking body share the same goals. A member of the House, for example, could deliberate in a serious way about how the federal government could solve a transportation problem within his or her district even if no other House members shared the same concern. Collective deliberation, however, necessarily requires some sharing of goals, purposes, or values. If legislators are to reason together about the merits of public policy, there must be some common ground for the arguments and appeals essential to deliberation. Whether the shared goal is quite specific and well defined (e.g., a national health insurance plan along the British model) or much broader and even somewhat vague (e.g., a healthy economy or a sound national defense), it will provide the basis for legislators, who may have little else in common, to share information and to reason and argue together about public policy.

Although the geographically based representation of the American system of government has a tendency to elevate localized interests and needs over broad programmatic concerns, district and state representation also provides a solid basis for the sharing of goals within Congress. Similar kinds of constituencies are likely to have common interests and needs and therefore similar desires or expectations for national policy. Inner-city residents throughout the nation are likely to have similar desires regarding social welfare policy. Farmers from the Midwest, South, and West are likely to agree on the need for price supports. Blue-collar workers in threatened industries across the country are likely to desire high tariffs or other protectionist measures. Those elected to Congress to represent these kinds of constituents will soon discover that many of their colleagues represent similar electorates and thus share many of the same policy goals. In some cases such like-minded legislators institutionalize and promote their shared policy interests through an informal caucus which helps them to share information and ideas and to coordinate policy efforts.

In describing what deliberation is, it is important to clarify what it is not; for policy deliberation is not just any kind of reasoning involved in the policy process. . . . [P]olicy deliberation necessarily involves reasoning about the substantive benefits of public policy, reasoning about some *public* good—some good external to the decisionmakers themselves. "Reasoning on the merits" of public policy means reasoning about how public policy can benefit the broader society or some significant portion thereof. Thus, there is a sharp analytical distinction between deliberation and merely self-interested calculations (however complex the relationship between these two in practice). Similarly, deliberation does not include reasoning about legislative tactics, such as drafting a bill to facilitate its referral to a sympathetic committee or determining how to use the rules of the House or Senate to greatest advantage during the legislative process.

Although a deliberative process is per se rational or analytical, the values or dispositions that the participants bring to bear on the determination of good public policy may reflect a host of diverse influences: general upbringing, parental values, personal experiences, the views of friends and acquaintances, influential teachers, partisan attachments, social class, economic status, etc. Thus, it is not surprising that different individuals often reach opposed conclusions about the merits of policy proposals even when exposed to the same information and arguments. Such disagreement is not in itself evidence of the absence of deliberation.

Deliberation, as defined here, may take a variety of forms. It may be a largely consensual process in which like-minded individuals work together to fashion the details of a policy they all desire; or it may involve deep-seated conflicts over fundamental issues or principles. It may result in unanimity of view, where no votes are necessary; or it may reveal sharp disagreements that require formal voting to determine the majority view. It may range from private reflection in the quiet of an office or study to an emotionally charged exchange on the floor of the House or Senate. It may take the form of open and public discussions preserved in official records or of private exchanges hidden from public view. It may involve direct discussions among elected officials themselves or, perhaps more frequently, conversations among their staff. It may be limited to those who hold formal positions in the government, either elective or appointive; or it may include the ideas and opinions of interest groups, trade associations, national organizations, or the scholarly community. . . .

[B]argaining and reelection theories are the two great pillars that support the widespread contemporary view that Congress is not a deliberative institution (at least in any fundamental sense) and, by implication, that American democracy is not a deliberative democracy. . . .

We must be careful how we frame the issue. . . .

[T]he issue here is not whether the members of Congress pursue reelection but rather whether the reelection incentive squeezes out deliberative activities in a way that undermines, or even destroys, Congress's character as a deliberative institution. This could occur in two ways. First, reelection-oriented activities could so consume the time and resources of the member that nothing is left for serious reasoning about public policy. Second, the reelection incentive could intrude upon formal legislative activities in such a way as to distort otherwise deliberative behavior. For example, the committee member who single-mindedly plays to the cameras during some hearing on a controversial matter because it is good politics has allowed his private interests to overcome his deliberative responsibilities.

While it is certainly possible for the reelection incentive to undermine deliberation in these two ways, it is not necessary. The fact that the members of Congress do certain things to promote their reelection is hardly proof that they do not do other things to reach reasoned judgments about the merits of public policy. Indeed, those who designed the American Congress saw no necessary incompatibility between the reelection incentive and deliberation. The framers believed not only that the legislator's desire to return to Congress would not disable him from engaging in genuine deliberation about national laws, but also that the reelection incentive was the vital link between deliberations in Congress and popular interests and attitudes. Indeed, to argue that the system of public accountability in the modern Congress makes genuine deliberation impossible is virtually the equivalent of saying that deliberation and democracy, as presently constituted in the United States, are incompatible.

It follows, then, that in assessing Congress as a deliberative institution the issue is not so much whether the reelection incentive is a powerful motive in influencing congressional behavior, but rather whether and to what degree legislators in the U.S. Congress embrace and act upon the independent desire to promote good public policy, the end for which deliberation is the means. How much evidence do we have that the ambitious and reelection-seeking members of Congress actually care about and work to promote good public policy? . . .

. . . A theory of legislative behavior that posits only the low motive of reelection cannot even provide the vocabulary to describe and explain serious lawmaking. . . . [H]ow can the reelection incentive explain why any legislator would choose substance over symbols, hard work over posturing, or responsibility over popularity? And, most incongruous of all, why would any legislator moved primarily by the reelection incentive ever take any political risks for the sake of substantive policy goals?

Conversely, a full understanding and appreciation of the high art of lawmaking allows the low arts of mere self-seeking to reveal themselves fully for what they are. Could it even be said that it is only some sense of what constitutes serious lawmaking that makes it possible to understand fully the nature of the lower self-seeking arts (what Hamilton called "the little arts of popularity")? Consider "posturing," for example. . . . Lawmakers and those who observe and study lawmakers have little difficulty identifying posturing when they see it; but surely this is because in the back of their minds they possess a rather clear picture or model of what posturing is not: reasoned argument and effort at genuine persuasion. Posturing can be understood fully only in contrast to this thing which it is not, in contrast to something higher than itself.

What, then, are the principal characteristics of those who engage in serious lawmaking in the United States Congress? . . .

- Serious lawmakers are not satisfied simply to serve in Congress and enjoy its many perks. They want to make a difference, to accomplish something of importance, to make the nation (and perhaps the world) a better place through their governing activities. They believe that there is a public interest, that it is knowable, and that their efforts in Congress can help to achieve it.
- By virtue of their office (membership in the House or Senate, committee and subcommittee chairmanships, leadership positions, etc.) they feel a sense of responsibility to something beyond their personal advantage, a duty to larger ends. It is the accomplishment of these larger ends that is the source of their deepest political satisfaction.
- They seek to earn the respect of their colleagues and of those outside Congress through their deliberative efforts and their substantive achievements. They want to be known as effective legislators. The respect they so earn from their colleagues is a principal source of their power in Congress.
- They develop substantive expertise in the areas under their jurisdiction through careful and thorough analysis, engaging in the hard work necessary to master a subject. Open to facts and arguments, they are willing to learn from others.
- They seek to influence others on legislative matters principally through reasoned persuasion. Although they recognize that raw political bargaining may be necessary to build majorities, their decided preference is to influence through facts and arguments, not through bargains.

- They try to protect the opportunities for responsible lawmaking from the consequences of unrestrained publicity seeking. They have little respect for "legislators" who seek only popularity and reelection.
- Although they wish and seek reelection to Congress, they are, nonetheless, willing to take some political risks for the sake of good public policy.

It would be an understatement to say that these kinds of characteristics are not well accounted for by the reigning self-interest theories of Congress or of American government more generally. Moreover, the point here is not that the 535 members of the House and Senate fall neatly into two categories: the merely ambitious who pursue only narrow self-interest and the high-minded who strive for the public good. Rather these represent something like the extremes of a continuum, from the low to the high, between which the various members of Congress can be found. . . . [S]ome members of the U.S. Congress, perhaps especially the leaders within the institution, look more like the serious lawmaker described by these characteristics than like the mere self-seeker we have come to view as the norm. If, as those who created the U.S. Congress believed, the serious lawmaker is nothing less than essential to the success of American democracy, then we ought to have a very great interest indeed in assessing the status and activities of such legislators in the contemporary Congress: How many members of the institution behave like serious lawmakers and has this changed over time? What electoral conditions promote the election of the serious-minded, public-spirited legislator as opposed to the mere self-seeking politician? How much influence do serious lawmakers have in the two branches? What are the forces that affect their lawmaking behavior? And what procedural or structural reforms, if any, would enhance the prospects of serious lawmaking in Congress? . . .

In addition to the evidence that serious lawmakers are more prevalent within Congress than modern theories acknowledge, there is also reason for believing that they have a greater impact on policymaking than their mere numbers (and relative proportion of the membership) might suggest. One reason is that because the serious lawmaker undertakes the kind of substantive legislative work that does not interest the mere self-seeker, he will *ipso facto* influence the details of policy in a way that the self-seeker rarely will. After all, the legislator dominated by the reelection incentive has "only a modest interest in what goes into bills or what their passage accomplishes." He knows that "in a large class of undertakings the electoral payment is for positions rather than for effects." The second reason is that the serious lawmaker may be more prevalent among institutional leaders than among the membership generally. In part this is because the members of Congress may select as their leaders those with a reputation for legislative skill and seriousness of purpose. In addition, for formal leadership positions within committees and subcommittees, where selection is virtually automatic, the office itself may foster a sense of responsibility to ends larger than mere private advantage.

This latter point is one of the conclusions of Martha Derthick and Paul Quirk in their study of the deregulation movement of the Carter and Reagan years. . . . [A]s they say about congressional leaders in particular:

> To the extent that a congressman finds or places himself in [a position of leadership on an issue] . . ., two related conditions follow, both of them likely to affect his response: his actions will be more consequential to the outcome; and because they will be more consequential, they will also be more widely observed. Leaders on an issue will be more prone to act on their conception of the public interest, because it is more irresponsible for those in a position of power to do otherwise.

It follows that even a handful of serious, responsible lawmakers in key positions within Congress may have a more consequential effect on the substance of public policy than a much larger number of mere self-seeking politicians who can pursue and achieve private advantage through non-legislative means.

36

U.S. Term Limits, Inc. v. Thornton (1995)

Justice Stevens delivered the opinion of the Court.

. . . Today's cases present a challenge to an amendment to the Arkansas State Constitution that prohibits the name of an otherwise eligible candidate for Congress from appearing on the general election ballot if that candidate has already served three terms in the House of Representatives or two terms in the Senate. The Arkansas Supreme Court held that the amendment violates the Federal Constitution. We agree with that holding. Such a state imposed restriction is contrary to the "fundamental principle of our representative democracy," embodied in the Constitution, that "the people should choose whom they please to govern them." *Powell v. McCormack.* Allowing individual States to adopt their own qualifications for congressional service would be inconsistent with the Framers' vision of a uniform National Legislature

From *U.S. Term Limits, Inc. v. Thornton,* 514 U.S. 779 (1995).

representing the people of the United States. If the qualifications set forth in the text of the Constitution are to be changed, that text must be amended.

[T]he constitutionality of Amendment 73 depends critically on the resolution of two distinct issues. The first is whether the Constitution forbids States from adding to or altering the qualifications specifically enumerated in the Constitution. The second is, if the Constitution does so forbid, whether the fact that Amendment 73 is formulated as a ballot access restriction rather than as an outright disqualification is of constitutional significance. Our resolution of these issues draws upon our prior resolution of a related but distinct issue: whether Congress has the power to add to or alter the qualifications of its Members.

. . . In November 1966, Adam Clayton Powell, Jr., was elected from a District in New York to serve in the United States House of Representatives for the 90th Congress. Allegations that he had engaged in serious misconduct while serving as a committee chairman during the 89th Congress led to the appointment of a Select Committee to determine his eligibility to take his seat. That Committee found that Powell met the age, citizenship, and residency requirements set forth in Art. I, §2, cl. 2. The Committee also found, however, that Powell had wrongfully diverted House funds for the use of others and himself and had made false reports on expenditures of foreign currency. Based on those findings, the House after debate adopted House Resolution 278, excluding Powell from membership in the House, and declared his seat vacant. Powell and several voters of the District from which he had been elected filed suit seeking a declaratory judgment that the House Resolution was invalid because Art. I, §2, cl. 2, sets forth the exclusive qualifications for House membership. We ultimately accepted that contention, concluding that the House of Representatives has no "authority to *exclude* any person, duly elected by his constituents, who meets all the requirements for membership expressly prescribed in the Constitution." . . .

. . . Our conclusion that States lack the power to impose qualifications vindicates the same "fundamental principle of our representative democracy" that we recognized in *Powell,* namely that "the people should choose whom they please to govern them."

As we noted earlier, the *Powell* Court recognized that an egalitarian ideal—that election to the National Legislature should be open to all people of merit—provided a critical foundation for the Constitutional structure. This egalitarian theme echoes throughout the constitutional debates. In The Federalist No. 57, for example, Madison wrote:

> "Who are to be the objects of popular choice? Every citizen whose merit may recommend him to the esteem and confidence of his country. No qualification of wealth, of birth, of religious faith, or of civil profession is permitted to fetter the judgment or disappoint the inclination of the people."

. . . And Timothy Pickering noted that, "while several of the state constitutions prescribe certain degrees of property as indispensable qualifications for offices, this which is proposed for the U. S. throws the door wide open for the entrance of *every man* who enjoys the confidence of his fellow citizens." Additional qualifications pose the same obstacle to open elections whatever their source. The egalitarian ideal, so valued by the Framers, is thus compromised to the same degree by additional qualifications imposed by States as by those imposed by Congress.

Similarly, we believe that state imposed qualifications, as much as congressionally imposed qualifications, would undermine the second critical idea recognized in *Powell:* that an aspect of sovereignty is the right of the people to vote for whom they wish. Again, the source of the qualification is of little moment in assessing the qualification's restrictive impact.

Finally, state imposed restrictions, unlike the congressionally imposed restrictions at issue in *Powell,* violate a third idea central to this basic principle: that the right to choose representatives belongs not to the States, but to the people. From the start, the Framers recognized that the "great and radical vice" of the Articles of Confederation was "the principle of LEGISLATION for STATES or GOVERNMENTS, in their CORPORATE or COLLECTIVE CAPACITIES, and as contradistinguished from the INDIVIDUALS of whom they consist." Thus the Framers, in perhaps their most important contribution, conceived of a Federal Government directly responsible to the people, possessed of direct power over the people, and chosen directly, not by States, but by the people. The Framers implemented this ideal most clearly in the provision, extant from the beginning of the Republic, that calls for the Members of the House of Representatives to be "chosen every second Year by the People of the several States." Art. I, §2, cl. 1. Following the adoption of the 17th Amendment in 1913, this ideal was extended to elections for the Senate. The Congress of the United States, therefore, is not a confederation of nations in which separate sovereigns are represented by appointed delegates, but is instead a body composed of representatives of the people. . . .

Petitioners argue that, even if States may not add qualifications, Amendment 73 is constitutional because it is not such a qualification, and because Amendment 73 is a permissible exercise of state power to regulate the "Times, Places and Manner of Holding Elections." We reject these contentions.

. . . As we have often noted, "[c]onstitutional rights would be of little value if they could be . . . indirectly denied." *Harman v. Forssenius.* The Constitution "nullifies sophisticated as well as simple minded modes" of infringing on Constitutional protections. . . . Indeed, it cannot be seriously contended that the intent behind Amendment 73 is other than to prevent the election of incumbents. The preamble of Amendment 73 states explicitly:

"[T]he people of Arkansas . . . herein limit the terms of elected officials." Sections 1 and 2 create absolute limits on the number of terms that may be served. There is no hint that §3 was intended to have any other purpose.

. . . Moreover, petitioners' broad construction of the Elections Clause is fundamentally inconsistent with the Framers' view of that Clause. The Framers intended the Elections Clause to grant States authority to create procedural regulations, not to provide States with license to exclude classes of candidates from federal office. During the Convention debates, for example, Madison illustrated the procedural focus of the Elections Clause by noting that it covered "[w]hether the electors should vote by ballot or vivâ voce, should assemble at this place or that place; should be divided into districts or all meet at one place, sh[oul]d all vote for all the representatives; or all in a district vote for a number allotted to the district." . . . Hamilton made a similar point in The Federalist No. 60, in which he defended the Constitution's grant to Congress of the power to override state regulations. Hamilton expressly distinguished the broad power to set qualifications from the limited authority under the Elections Clause, noting that

> "there is no method of securing to the rich the preference apprehended but by prescribing qualifications of property either for those who may elect or be elected. But this forms no part of the power to be conferred upon the national government. Its authority would be expressly restricted to the regulation of the *times*, the *places*, and the *manner* of elections."

As Hamilton's statement suggests, the Framers understood the Elections Clause as a grant of authority to issue procedural regulations, and not as a source of power to dictate electoral outcomes, to favor or disfavor a class of candidates, or to evade important constitutional restraints.

. . . We do not understand the dissent to contest our primary thesis, namely that if the qualifications for Congress are fixed in the Constitution, then a State passed measure with the avowed purpose of imposing indirectly such an additional qualification violates the Constitution. The dissent, instead, raises two objections, challenging the assertion that the Arkansas amendment has the likely effect of creating a qualification, and suggesting that the true intent of Amendment 73 was not to evade the Qualifications Clause but rather to simply "level the playing field". Neither of these objections has merit.

As to the first, it is simply irrelevant to our holding today. . . . [W]e hold that a state amendment is unconstitutional when it has the likely effect of handicapping a class of candidates and has the sole purpose of creating additional qualifications indirectly. Thus, the dissent's discussion of the evidence concerning the possibility that a popular incumbent will win a write in election is simply beside the point.

As to the second argument, we find wholly unpersuasive the dissent's suggestion that Amendment 73 was designed merely to "level the playing field." As we have noted, it is obvious that the sole purpose of Amendment 73 was to limit the terms of elected officials, both State and federal, and that Amendment 73, therefore, may not stand. . . .

We are . . . firmly convinced that allowing the several States to adopt term limits for congressional service would effect a fundamental change in the constitutional framework. Any such change must come not by legislation adopted either by Congress or by an individual State, but rather—as have other important changes in the electoral process—through the Amendment procedures set forth in Article V. The Framers decided that the qualifications for service in the Congress of the United States be fixed in the Constitution and be uniform throughout the Nation. That decision reflects the Framers' understanding that Members of Congress are chosen by separate constituencies, but that they become, when elected, servants of the people of the United States. They are not merely delegates appointed by separate, sovereign States; they occupy offices that are integral and essential components of a single National Government. In the absence of a properly passed constitutional amendment, allowing individual States to craft their own qualifications for Congress would thus erode the structure envisioned by the Framers, a structure that was designed, in the words of the Preamble to our Constitution, to form a "more perfect Union."

Justice Thomas with whom the Chief Justice, O'Connor and Scalia join, dissenting.

Nothing in the Constitution deprives the people of each State of the power to prescribe eligibility requirements for the candidates who seek to represent them in Congress. The Constitution is simply silent on this question. And where the Constitution is silent, it raises no bar to action by the States or the people.

Because the majority fundamentally misunderstands the notion of "reserved" powers, I start with some first principles. Contrary to the majority's suggestion, the people of the States need not point to any affirmative grant of power in the Constitution in order to prescribe qualifications for their representatives in Congress, or to authorize their elected state legislators to do so.

Our system of government rests on one overriding principle: all power stems from the consent of the people. To phrase the principle in this way, however, is to be imprecise about something important to the notion of "reserved" powers. The ultimate source of the Constitution's authority is the consent of the people of each individual State, not the consent of the undifferentiated people of the Nation as a whole.

The ratification procedure erected by Article VII makes this point clear. The Constitution took effect once it had been ratified by the people gathered in convention in nine different States. But the Constitution went into effect only "between the States so ratifying the same," it did not bind the people of North Carolina until they had accepted it. In Madison's words, the popular consent upon which the Constitution's authority rests was "given by the people, not as individuals composing one entire nation, but as composing the distinct and independent States to which they respectively belong."

When they adopted the Federal Constitution, of course, the people of each State surrendered some of their authority to the United States. . . . Because the people of the several States are the only true source of power, however, the Federal Government enjoys no authority beyond what the Constitution confers: the Federal Government's powers are limited and enumerated. . . .

In each State, the remainder of the people's powers—"[t]he powers not delegated to the United States by the Constitution, nor prohibited by it to the States," Amdt.10—are either delegated to the state government or retained by the people. . . . As far as the Federal Constitution is concerned, then, the States can exercise all powers that the Constitution does not withhold from them. The Federal Government and the States thus face different default rules: where the Constitution is silent about the exercise of a particular power—that is, where the Constitution does not speak either expressly or by necessary implication—the Federal Government lacks that power and the States enjoy it. . . .

To be sure, when the Tenth Amendment uses the phrase "the people," it does not specify whether it is referring to the people of each State or the people of the Nation as a whole. But the latter interpretation would make the Amendment pointless. . . . [I]t would make no sense to speak of powers as being reserved to the undifferentiated people of the Nation as a whole, because the Constitution does not contemplate that those people will either exercise power or delegate it. The Constitution simply does not recognize any mechanism for action by the undifferentiated people of the Nation. Thus, the amendment provision of Article V calls for amendments to be ratified not by a convention of the national people, but by conventions of the people in each State. . . . Even the selection of the President—surely the most national of national figures—is accomplished by an electoral college made up of delegates chosen by the various States. . . .

In short, the notion of popular sovereignty that undergirds the Constitution does not erase state boundaries, but rather tracks them. . . . As Chief Justice Marshall put it, "[n]o political dreamer was ever wild enough to think of breaking down the lines which separate the States, and of compounding the American people into one common mass." *McCulloch v. Maryland*

Any ambiguity in the Tenth Amendment's use of the phrase "the people" is cleared up by the body of the Constitution itself. Article I begins by providing that the Congress of the United States enjoys "[a]ll legislative

Powers herein granted," §1, and goes on to give a careful enumeration of Congress' powers, §8. It then concludes by enumerating certain powers that are *prohibited* to the States. The import of this structure is the same as the import of the Tenth Amendment: if we are to invalidate Arkansas' Amendment 73, we must point to something in the Federal Constitution that deprives the people of Arkansas of the power to enact such measures.

The majority disagrees that it bears this burden. But its arguments are unpersuasive.

. . . The majority's essential logic is that the state governments could not "reserve" any powers that they did not control at the time the Constitution was drafted. But it was not the state governments that were doing the reserving. The Constitution derives its authority instead from the consent of *the people* of the States. Given the fundamental principle that all governmental powers stem from the people of the States, it would simply be incoherent to assert that the people of the States could not reserve any powers that they had not previously controlled.

. . . I take it to be established, then, that the people of Arkansas do enjoy "reserved" powers over the selection of their representatives in Congress. Purporting to exercise those reserved powers, they have agreed among themselves that the candidates covered by §3 of Amendment 73—those whom they have already elected to three or more terms in the House of Representatives or to two or more terms in the Senate—should not be eligible to appear on the ballot for reelection, but should nonetheless be returned to Congress if enough voters are sufficiently enthusiastic about their candidacy to write in their names. Whatever one might think of the wisdom of this arrangement, we may not override the decision of the people of Arkansas unless something in the Federal Constitution deprives them of the power to enact such measures.

The majority settles on "the Qualifications Clauses" as the constitutional provisions that Amendment 73 violates. Because I do not read those provisions to impose any unstated prohibitions on the States, it is unnecessary for me to decide whether the majority is correct to identify Arkansas' ballot access restriction with laws fixing true term limits or otherwise prescribing "qualifications" for congressional office. . . .

In addition to its arguments about democratic principles, the majority asserts that more specific historical evidence supports its view that the Framers did not intend to permit supplementation of the Qualifications Clauses. But when one focuses on the distinction between congressional power to add qualifications for congressional office and the power of the people or their state legislatures to add such qualifications, one realizes that this assertion has little basis.

In particular, the detail with which the majority recites the historical evidence set forth in *Powell v. McCormack* should not obscure the fact that this evidence has no bearing on the question now before the Court. As the majority ultimately concedes, it does not establish "the Framers' intent that the qualifications in the Constitution be fixed and exclusive," it shows only that the Framers did not intend Congress to be able to enact qualifications laws. . . .

. . . No matter how narrowly construed . . . today's decision reads the Qualifications Clauses to impose substantial implicit prohibitions on the States and the people of the States. I would not draw such an expansive negative inference from the fact that the Constitution requires Members of Congress to be a certain age, to be inhabitants of the States that they represent, and to have been United States citizens for a specified period. Rather, I would read the Qualifications Clauses to do no more than what they say.

37

War Powers Resolution (1973)

Resolved by the Senate and House of Representatives of the United States of America in Congress assembled, That:

Section 1. This joint resolution may be cited as the "War Powers Resolution."

Sec. 2. (a) It is the purpose of this joint resolution to fulfill the intent of the framers of the Constitution of the United States and insure that the collective judgment of both the Congress and the President will apply to the introduction of United States Armed Forces into hostilities, or into situations where imminent involvement in hostilities is clearly indicated by the circumstances, and to the continued use of such forces in hostilities or in such situations.

(b) Under article 1, section 8, of the Constitution, it is specifically provided that the Congress shall have the power to make all laws necessary and proper for carrying into execution, not only its own powers but also all other powers vested by the Constitution in the Government of the United States, or in any department or officer thereof.

(c) The constitutional powers of the President as Commander-in-Chief to introduce United States Armed Forces into hostilities, or into

From War Powers Resolution, 87 Stat. 555 (1973).

situations where imminent involvement in hostilities is clearly indicated by the circumstances, are exercised only pursuant to (1) a declaration of war, (2) specific statutory authorization, or (3) a national emergency created by attack upon the United States, its territories or possessions, or its armed forces.

Sec. 3. The President in every possible instance shall consult with Congress before introducing United States Armed Forces into hostilities or into situations where imminent involvement in hostilities is clearly indicated by the circumstances, and after every such introduction shall consult regularly with the Congress until United States Armed Forces are no longer engaged in hostilities or have been removed from such situations.

Sec. 4. (a) In the absence of a declaration of war, in any case in which United States Armed Forces are introduced—

(1) into hostilities or into situations where imminent involvement in hostilities is clearly indicated by the circumstances;

(2) into the territory, airspace or waters of a foreign nation, while equipped for combat, except for deployments which relate solely to supply, replacement, repair, or training of such forces; or

(3) in numbers which substantially enlarge United States Armed Forces equipped for combat already located in a foreign nation; the President shall submit within 48 hours to the Speaker of the House of Representatives and to the President pro tempore of the Senate a report, in writing, setting forth—

(A) the circumstances necessitating the introduction of United States Armed Forces;

(B) the constitutional and legislative authority under which such introduction took place; and

(C) the estimated scope and duration of the hostilities or involvement.

(b) The President shall provide such other information as the Congress may request in the fulfillment of its constitutional responsibilities with respect to committing the Nation to war and to the use of United States Armed Forces abroad. . . .

Sec. 5. (a) Each report submitted pursuant to section 4(a) (1) shall be . . . referred to the Committee on Foreign Affairs of the House of Representatives and to the Committee on Foreign Relations of the Senate for appropriate action. If, when the report is transmitted, the Congress has adjourned sine die or has adjourned for any period in excess of three calendar days, the Speaker of the House of Representatives and the President pro tempore of the Senate, if they deem it advisable (or if petitioned by at least 30 percent of the membership of their respective Houses) shall jointly request the President to convene Congress in order that it may consider the report and take appropriate action pursuant to this section.

(b) Within sixty calendar days after a report is submitted or is required to be submitted pursuant to section 4 (a) (1), whichever is earlier, the President shall terminate any use of United States Armed Forces with respect to which such report was submitted (or required to be submitted), unless the Congress (1) has declared war or has enacted a specific authorization for such use of United States Armed Forces, (2) has extended by law such sixty-day period, or (3) is physically unable to meet as a result of an armed attack upon the United States. Such sixty-day period shall be extended for not more than an additional thirty days if the President determines and certifies to the Congress in writing that unavoidable military necessity respecting the safety of United States Armed Forces requires the continued use of such armed forces in the course of bringing about a prompt removal of such forces.

(c) Notwithstanding subsection (b), at any time that United States Armed Forces are engaged in hostilities outside the territory of the United States, its possessions and territories without a declaration of war or specific statutory authorization, such forces shall be removed by the President if the Congress so directs by concurrent resolution. . . .

Sec. 8. . . . (d) Nothing in this joint resolution—

(1) is intended to alter the constitutional authority of the Congress or of the President, or the provisions of existing treaties; or

(2) shall be construed as granting any authority to the President with respect to the introduction of United States Armed Forces into hostilities or into situations wherein involvement in hostilities is clearly indicated by the circumstances which authority he would not have had in the absence of this joint resolution. . . .

[Passed over presidential veto Nov. 7, 1973.]

38

INS v. Chadha (1983)

Chief Justice Burger delivered the opinion of the Court.

Chadha is an East Indian who was born in Kenya and holds a British passport. He was lawfully admitted to the United States in 1966 on a non-immigrant student visa. His visa expired on June 30, 1972. On October 11, 1973, the District Director of the Immigration and Naturalization Service ordered Chadha to show cause why he should not be deported for having "remained in the United States for a longer time than permitted." Pursuant to § 242(b) of the Immigration and Nationality Act, a deportation hearing was held before an Immigration Judge on January 11, 1974. Chadha conceded that he was deportable for overstaying his visa, and the hearing was adjourned to enable him to file an application for suspension of deportation under § 244(a)(1) of the Act. Section 244(a)(1), at the time in question, provided:

> As hereinafter prescribed in this section, the Attorney General may, in his discretion, suspend deportation and adjust the status to that of an alien lawfully admitted for permanent residence, in the case of an alien who applies to the Attorney General for suspension of deportation and is deportable under any law of the United States . . .; has been physically present in the United States for a continuous period of not less than seven years immediately preceding the date of such application, and proves that during all of such period he was and is a person of good moral character; and is a person whose deportation would, in the opinion of the Attorney General, result in extreme hardship to the alien or to his spouse, parent, or child, who is a citizen of the United States or an alien lawfully admitted for permanent residence.

After Chadha submitted his application for suspension of deportation, the deportation hearing was resumed on February 7, 1974. On the basis of evidence adduced at the hearing, affidavits submitted with the application, and the results of a character investigation conducted by the INS, the Immigration Judge, on June 25, 1974, ordered that Chadha's deportation be suspended. The Immigration Judge found that Chadha met the requirements of § 244(a)(1): he had resided continuously in the United States for over seven years, was of good moral character, and would suffer "extreme hardship" if deported.

From *INS v. Chadha*, 462 U.S. 919 (1983).

Pursuant to § 244(c)(1) of the Act, the Immigration Judge suspended Chadha's deportation and a report of the suspension was transmitted to Congress. Section 244(c)(1) provides:

> . . . If the deportation of any alien is suspended under the provisions of this subsection, a complete and detailed statement of the facts and pertinent provisions of law in the case shall be reported to the Congress with the reasons for such suspension. Such reports shall be submitted on the first day of each calendar month in which Congress is in session.

Once the Attorney General's recommendation for suspension of Chadha's deportation was conveyed to Congress, Congress had the power under § 244(c)(2) of the Act, to veto the Attorney General's determination that Chadha should not be deported. Section 244(c)(2) provides:

> . . . if during the session of the Congress at which a case [that recommends suspending the deportation of an alien] is reported, or prior to the close of the session of the Congress next following the session at which a case is reported, either the Senate or the House of Representatives passes a resolution stating in substance that it does not favor the suspension of such deportation, the Attorney General shall thereupon deport such alien or authorize the alien's voluntary departure at his own expense under the order of deportation in the manner provided by law. If, within the time above specified, neither the Senate nor the House of Representatives shall pass such a resolution, the Attorney General shall cancel deportation proceedings.

. . . On December 12, 1975, Representative Eilberg, Chairman of the Judiciary Subcommittee on Immigration, Citizenship, and International Law, introduced a resolution opposing "the granting of permanent residence in the United States to [six] aliens," including Chadha. . . . So far as the record before us shows, the House consideration of the resolution was based on Representative Eilberg's statement from the floor that

> [i]t was the feeling of the committee, after reviewing 340 cases, that the aliens contained in the resolution [Chadha and five others] did not meet these statutory requirements, particularly as it relates to hardship; and it is the opinion of the committee that their deportation should not be suspended.

The resolution was passed without debate or recorded vote. Since the House action was pursuant to § 244(c)(2), the resolution was not treated as an Art. I legislative act; it was not submitted to the Senate or presented to the President for his action.

After the House veto of the Attorney General's decision to allow Chadha to remain in the United States, the Immigration Judge reopened the deportation proceedings to implement the House order deporting Chadha. Chadha . . . filed a petition for review of the deportation order in the United States Court of Appeals for the Ninth Circuit. . . .

After full briefing and oral argument, the Court of Appeals held that the House was without constitutional authority to order Chadha's deportation. . . . The essence of its holding was that § 244(c)(2) violates the constitutional doctrine of separation of powers. . . .

We turn now to the question whether action of one House of Congress under § 244(c)(2) violates strictures of the Constitution. We begin, of course, with the presumption that the challenged statute is valid. Its wisdom is not the concern of the courts; if a challenged action does not violate the Constitution, it must be sustained. . . .

By the same token, the fact that a given law or procedure is efficient, convenient, and useful in facilitating functions of government, standing alone, will not save it if it is contrary to the Constitution. Convenience and efficiency are not the primary objectives—or the hallmarks—of democratic government, and our inquiry is sharpened, rather than blunted, by the fact that congressional veto provisions are appearing with increasing frequency in statutes which delegate authority to executive and independent agencies. . . .

Explicit and unambiguous provisions of the Constitution prescribe and define the respective functions of the Congress and of the Executive in the legislative process. Since the precise terms of those familiar provisions are critical to the resolution of these cases, we set them out verbatim. Article I provides:

> All legislative Powers herein granted shall be vested in a Congress of the United States, which shall consist of a Senate *and* House of Representatives. Art. I, § 1.
>
> Every Bill which shall have passed the House of Representatives *and* the Senate, *shall,* before it becomes a law, be presented to the President of the United States. . . . Art. I, 7, cl. 2.
>
> *Every* Order, Resolution, or Vote to which the Concurrence of the Senate and House of Representatives may be necessary (except on a question of Adjournment) *shall* be presented to the President of the United States; and before the Same shall take Effect, *shall* be approved by him, or being disapproved by him, *shall* be repassed by two thirds of the Senate and House of Representatives, according to the Rules and Limitations prescribed in the Case of a Bill. Art. I, § 7, cl. 3.

These provisions of Art. I are integral parts of the constitutional design for the separation of powers. . . .

The Presentment Clauses

The records of the Constitutional Convention reveal that the requirement that all legislation be presented to the President before becoming law was uniformly accepted by the Framers. Presentment to the President and the Presidential veto were considered so imperative that the draftsmen took special pains to assure that these requirements could not be circumvented. During the final debate on Art. I, § 7, cl. 2, James Madison expressed concern that it might easily be evaded by the simple expedient of calling a proposed law a "resolution" or "vote," rather than a "bill." As a consequence, Art. I, § 7, cl. 3, was added.

The decision to provide the President with a limited and qualified power to nullify proposed legislation by veto was based on the profound conviction of the Framers that the powers conferred on Congress were the powers to be most carefully circumscribed. It is beyond doubt that lawmaking was a power to be shared by both Houses and the President. . . .

The President's role in the lawmaking process also reflects the Framers' careful efforts to check whatever propensity a particular Congress might have to enact oppressive, improvident, or ill-considered measures. The President's veto role in the legislative process was described later during public debate on ratification:

> It establishes a salutary check upon the legislative body, calculated to guard the community against the effects of faction, precipitancy, or of any impulse unfriendly to the public good, which may happen to influence a majority of that body. . . . The primary inducement to conferring the power in question upon the Executive is to enable him to defend himself; the secondary one is to increase the chances in favor of the community against the passing of bad laws, through haste, inadvertence, or design.

The Court also has observed that the Presentment Clauses serve the important purpose of assuring that a "national" perspective is grafted on the legislative process:

> The President is a representative of the people just as the members of the Senate and of the House are, and it may be, at some times, on some subjects, that the President elected by all the people is rather more representative of them all than are the members of either body of the Legislature, whose constituencies are local and not countrywide. . . . *Myers v. United States* (1926).

BICAMERALISM

The bicameral requirement of Art. I, §§ 1, 7, was of scarcely less concern to the Framers than was the Presidential veto, and indeed the two concepts are interdependent. By providing that no law could take effect without the concurrence of the prescribed majority of the Members of both Houses, the Framers reemphasized their belief, already remarked upon in connection with the Presentment Clauses, that legislation should not be enacted unless it has been carefully and fully considered by the Nation's elected officials. In the Constitutional Convention debates on the need for a bicameral legislature, James Wilson, later to become a Justice of this Court, commented:

> Despotism comes on mankind in different shapes, sometimes in an Executive, sometimes in a military one. Is there danger of a Legislative despotism? Theory & practice both proclaim it. If the Legislative authority be not restrained, there can be neither liberty nor stability; and it can only be restrained by dividing it within itself, into distinct and independent branches.

In a single house there is no check but the inadequate one of the virtue & good sense of those who compose it.

. . . We see therefore that the Framers were acutely conscious that the bicameral requirement and the Presentment Clauses would serve essential constitutional functions. The President's participation in the legislative process was to protect the Executive Branch from Congress and to protect the whole people from improvident laws. The division of the Congress into two distinctive bodies assures that the legislative power would be exercised only after opportunity for full study and debate in separate settings. The President's unilateral veto power, in turn, was limited by the power of two-thirds of both Houses of Congress to overrule a veto, thereby precluding final arbitrary action of one person. It emerges clearly that the prescription for legislative action in Art. I, §§ 1, 7, represents the Framers' decision that the legislative power of the Federal Government be exercised in accord with a single, finely wrought and exhaustively considered, procedure.

The Constitution sought to divide the delegated powers of the new Federal Government into three defined categories, Legislative, Executive, and Judicial, to assure, as nearly as possible, that each branch of government would confine itself to its assigned responsibility. The hydraulic pressure inherent within each of the separate Branches to exceed the outer limits of its power, even to accomplish desirable objectives, must be resisted. . . .

Examination of the action taken here by one House pursuant to § 244(c)(2) reveals that it was essentially legislative in purpose and effect. In purporting to exercise power defined in Art. I, § 8, cl. 4, to "establish an uniform Rule of Naturalization," the House took action that had the purpose and effect of altering the legal rights, duties, and relations of persons, including the Attorney General, Executive Branch officials and Chadha, all outside the Legislative Branch. Section 244(c)(2) purports to authorize one House of Congress to require the Attorney General to deport an individual alien whose deportation otherwise would be canceled under § 244. The one-House veto operated in these cases to overrule the Attorney General and mandate Chadha's deportation; absent the House action, Chadha would remain in the United States. Congress has acted, and its action has altered Chadha's status.

The legislative character of the one-House veto in these cases is confirmed by the character of the congressional action it supplants. Neither the House of Representatives nor the Senate contends that, absent the veto provision in § 244(c)(2), either of them, or both of them acting together, could effectively require the Attorney General to deport an alien once the Attorney General, in the exercise of legislatively delegated authority, had determined the alien should remain in the United States. Without the challenged provision in § 244(c)(2), this could have been achieved, if at all, only by legislation requiring deportation. . . .

The nature of the decision implemented by the one-House veto in these cases further manifests its legislative character. After long experience with the clumsy, time-consuming private bill procedure, Congress made a deliberate choice to delegate to the Executive Branch, and specifically to the Attorney General, the authority to allow deportable aliens to remain in this country in certain specified circumstances. It is not disputed that this choice to delegate authority is precisely the kind of decision that can be implemented only in accordance with the procedures set out in Art. I. Disagreement with the Attorney General's decision on Chadha's deportation—that is, Congress' decision to deport Chadha—no less than Congress' original choice to delegate to the Attorney General the authority to make that decision, involves determinations of policy that Congress can implement in only one way; bicameral passage followed by presentment to the President. Congress must abide by its delegation of authority until that delegation is legislatively altered or revoked.

Finally, we see that, when the Framers intended to authorize either House of Congress to act alone and outside of its prescribed bicameral legislative role, they narrowly and precisely defined the procedure for such action. There are four provisions in the Constitution, explicit and unambiguous, by which one House may act alone with the unreviewable force of law, not subject to the President's veto:

(a) The House of Representatives alone was given the power to initiate impeachments. Art. I, § 2, cl. 5;

(b) The Senate alone was given the power to conduct trials following impeachment on charges initiated by the House, and to convict following trial. Art. I, § 3, cl. 6;

(c) The Senate alone was given final unreviewable power to approve or to disapprove Presidential appointments. Art. II, § 2, cl. 2;

(d) The Senate alone was given unreviewable power to ratify treaties negotiated by the President. Art. II, 2, cl. 2.

Clearly, when the Draftsmen sought to confer special powers on one House, independent of the other House, or of the President, they did so in explicit, unambiguous terms. . . . These exceptions are narrow, explicit, and separately justified; none of them authorize the action challenged here. On the contrary, they provide further support for the conclusion that congressional authority is not to be implied, and for the conclusion that the veto provided for in § 244(c)(2) is not authorized by the constitutional design of the powers of the Legislative Branch.

Since it is clear that the action by the House under § 244(c)(2) was not within any of the express constitutional exceptions authorizing one House to act alone, and equally clear that it was an exercise of legislative power, that action was subject to the standards prescribed in Art. I. The bicameral requirement, the Presentment Clauses, the President's veto, and Congress' power to override a veto were intended to erect enduring checks on each Branch and to protect the people from the improvident exercise of power by mandating certain prescribed steps. . . . To accomplish what has been attempted by one House of Congress in this case requires action in conformity with the express procedures of the Constitution's prescription for legislative action: passage by a majority of both Houses and presentment to the President. . . .

The choices we discern as having been made in the Constitutional Convention impose burdens on governmental processes that often seem clumsy, inefficient, even unworkable, but those hard choices were consciously made by men who had lived under a form of government that permitted arbitrary governmental acts to go unchecked. There is no support in the Constitution or decisions of this Court for the proposition that the cumbersomeness and delays often encountered in complying with explicit constitutional standards may be avoided, either by the Congress or by the President. With all the obvious flaws of delay, untidiness, and potential for abuse, we have not yet found a better way to preserve freedom than by making the exercise of power subject to the carefully crafted restraints spelled out in the Constitution.

We hold that the congressional veto provision in § 244(c)(2) is severable from the Act, and that it is unconstitutional. Accordingly, the judgment of the Court of Appeals is *Affirmed*.

Justice Powell, concurring in the judgment.

The Court's decision, based on the Presentment Clauses, Art. I, 7, cls. 2 and 3, apparently will invalidate every use of the legislative veto. The breadth of this holding gives one pause. Congress has included the veto in literally hundreds of statutes, dating back to the 1930's. Congress clearly views this procedure as essential to controlling the delegation of power to administrative agencies. One reasonably may disagree with Congress' assessment of the veto's utility, but the respect due its judgment as a coordinate branch of Government cautions that our holding should be no more extensive than necessary to decide these cases. In my view, the cases may be decided on a narrower ground. When Congress finds that a particular person does not satisfy the statutory criteria for permanent residence in this country, it has assumed a judicial function in violation of the principle of separation of powers. Accordingly, I concur only in the judgment. . . .

The impropriety of the House's assumption of this function is confirmed by the fact that its action raises the very danger the Framers sought to avoid—the exercise of unchecked power. . . . Unlike the judiciary or an administrative agency, Congress is not bound by established substantive rules. Nor is it subject to the procedural safeguards, such as the right to counsel and a hearing before an impartial tribunal, that are present when a court or an agency adjudicates individual rights. The only effective constraint on Congress' power is political, but Congress is most accountable politically when it prescribes rules of general applicability. When it decides rights of specific persons, those rights are subject to "the tyranny of a shifting majority." . . .

Justice White, dissenting.

Today the Court not only invalidates § 244(c)(2) of the Immigration and Nationality Act, but also sounds the death knell for nearly 200 other statutory provisions in which Congress has reserved a "legislative veto." For this reason, the Court's decision is of surpassing importance. And it is for this reason that the Court would have been well advised to decide the cases, if possible, on the narrower grounds of separation of powers, leaving for full consideration the constitutionality of other congressional review statutes operating on such varied matters as war powers and agency rulemaking, some of which concern the independent regulatory agencies.

The prominence of the legislative veto mechanism in our contemporary political system and its importance to Congress can hardly be overstated. It has become a central means by which Congress secures the accountability of executive and independent agencies. Without the legislative veto, Congress is faced with a Hobson's choice: either to refrain from delegating the necessary authority, leaving itself with a hopeless task of writing laws with the requisite specificity to cover endless special circumstances across the entire policy landscape, or, in the alternative, to abdicate its lawmaking function to the Executive Branch and independent agencies. To choose the former leaves major national problems unresolved; to opt for the latter risks unaccountable policymaking by those not elected to fill that role. Accordingly, over the past five decades, the legislative veto has been placed in nearly 200 statutes. The device is known in every field of governmental concern: reorganization, budgets, foreign affairs, war powers, and regulation of trade, safety, energy, the environment, and the economy. . . .

If Congress may delegate lawmaking power to independent and Executive agencies, it is most difficult to understand Art. I as prohibiting Congress from also reserving a check on legislative power for itself. Absent the veto, the agencies receiving delegations of legislative or quasi-legislative power may issue regulations having the force of law without bicameral approval and without the President's signature. It is thus not apparent why the reservation of a veto over the exercise of that legislative power must be subject to a more exacting test. In both cases, it is enough that the initial statutory authorizations comply with the Art. I requirement. . . .

I do not suggest that all legislative vetoes are necessarily consistent with separation of powers principles. A legislative check on an inherently executive function, for example, that of initiating prosecutions, poses an entirely different question. But the legislative veto device here—and in many other settings—is far from an instance of legislative tyranny over the Executive. It is a necessary check on the unavoidably expanding power of the agencies, both Executive and independent, as they engage in exercising authority delegated by Congress.

I regret that I am in disagreement with my colleagues on the fundamental questions that these cases present. But even more I regret the destructive scope of the Court's holding. It reflects a profoundly different conception of the Constitution than that held by the courts which sanctioned the modern administrative state. Today's decision strikes down in one fell swoop provisions in more laws enacted by Congress than the Court has cumulatively invalidated in its history . . .

I must dissent.

39

Joseph F. Wysocki

Congressional Crises: The Rhetoric of Reform (2019)

Although there has been much discussion of "the rise of the rhetorical presidency," there has been much less systematic inquiry into the changing rhetorical practices of Congress. This essay will ask whether such changes in congressional rhetoric affect its ability to carry out its constitutional function as our "deliberative" branch. For this purpose, we will examine the changes in Congress' rhetoric in its own attempts to reform itself.

Like the President, members of Congress, even when *formally* speaking to other members, have increasingly aimed their rhetoric at the public. In many of these cases, the public may even be the *primary* intended audience. This shift in audience has changed rhetorical behavior in a number of ways, but perhaps the most important change for our consideration is the change seen in "crisis" rhetoric.

Professor Tulis in *The Rhetorical Presidency* argued that as presidents increasingly "went public" the tendency to describe political issues as crises also increased. Unfortunately, in many cases, these attempts to energize the presidency through building public support for his policies led to the opposite effect. One need only remember the boy who cried wolf to understand why.

If this development is problematic for executive energy, it can be even more problematic for congressional deliberation. Responses to crises need to be quick and decisive. While such urgency can cause problems for all legislation, it is especially problematic for debates over institutional reform of Congress. This is because reform, in addition to addressing an institution's *symptoms*, seeks to address the underlying causes of the problem through reorienting its procedures and habits. In doing so, it seeks a long term solution to problems and prevention of future problems. Such work requires careful diagnosis and a deliberate response. Thus the quickness of response demanded once a situation is described as crisis is often at odds with the slow consideration necessary for reform.

On the other hand, it is also true that getting Congress, which was intentionally designed to be slow (because deliberative), to undertake the arduous task of reform might require some prodding. The urgency of crisis rhetoric can be useful here. Perhaps what is best for congressional reform then is a *restrained* crisis rhetoric. That is, rhetoric that emphasizes the seriousness of failing to address the current problems without using catastrophic language or blowing the consequences out of proportion. The floor debates in 1883 on civil service reform that resulted in the passage of the Pendleton Act and the 1910 effort to limit the power of the Speaker of the House, both of which occurred before the changes articulated in the "Rise of the Rhetorical Presidency", tended to use less crisis rhetoric and more restrained crisis rhetoric.

The debate on the Pendleton Act provides a particularly good example of this more restrained use of crisis rhetoric. Before its passage, almost all federal jobs, from cabinet members all the way down to postmen, were chosen by the "spoils system" where the primary qualification for positions was party loyalty rather technical competence. The Pendleton Act sought to begin professionalizing the civil service by: 1) creating a 3-person "nonpartisan" panel that would oversee merit-based exams for the civil service, 2) implementing civil service examination requirements, and 3) prohibiting "assessments," or forced contributions to political parties by civil servants. As the only reform that had the *assassination of a President* (by a dissatisfied job-seeker) as at least one of its causes, one might expect a liberal use of crisis rhetoric. Instead, members of Congress often used what one might call "anti-crisis" rhetoric. For example, the sponsor of the reform, Senator George H. Pendleton, stated in his opening speech that "I do not say that the civil service of the Government is *wholly* bad . . . but I do say that the civil service is inefficient; that it is expensive; that it is extravagant; that it is in *many cases* and in *some sense* corrupt." Another supporter of the reform added,

> I am not one of those reformers who are disposed to clamor and complain about everything . . . I say this bill is a step in the right direction, and although it may not come up

to that standard of radical reformation that some would have us inaugurate at a single step, I believe the principle of it . . . will tend very greatly to improve the civil service of the country.

Another supporter of the reform, Senator Joseph Roswell Hawley, tried to point out that while the current civil service had problems that needed addressing, he recognized that there would be evils, or weaknesses and corruptions, "no *matter what system* you may adopt." It therefore followed that he did *not* believe "that all the evils of the civil service will vanish the moment you shall have put an iron framework of some description upon the statute-book." Notice the restrained tone of these members who are actually in favor of reform.

On March 19th 1910, a coalition of Democrats and some Republicans (called "insurgents" by their opponents) offered a resolution that enlarged the House Rules Committee from 5 to 15 members, required that members of the Rules Committee be selected by special committees rather than by the Speaker, and made the Speaker ineligible for membership. This was done to break the control that Republican Speaker of the House Joseph Gurney Cannon exercised on the chamber through his three appointments (including himself) to the Rules Committee.

Due to the highly partisan and personal nature of this reform, the debate often became heated. Some reformers argued that their actions should be understood as resistance to a "tyrant". On the other hand, those who opposed the reform accused the reformers of encouraging "anarchy" in the House. Raising the stakes this high certainly qualifies as crisis rhetoric. However, the crisis rhetoric in this debate is tempered in two ways. First, unlike later debates, the crises articulated here were often limited in scope. For example, Congressman Henry Clayton, one of the leaders of the "revolt" states,

> Mr. Speaker, this is a *crisis in the legislative history* of our country. Those of us who favor the proposition . . . recognize that it may be denominated revolutionary. *So far as the parliamentary propositions are concerned*, I am willing to concede that it is revolutionary, but it is necessary to overcome this arbitrary *power of the Speaker*.

The crisis was not in the *country's* history, but only its *legislative* history. The problem was limited to the power of the Speaker. If this could be fixed, a crisis could be averted. Certainly, Clayton, along with others in revolt, believed that the current situation and its resolution had important implications for the nation as a whole. Yet, they tried to rhetorically limit the crisis to the issue at hand, rather than unnecessarily raising the stakes.

When the scope of the crisis rhetoric *did* become extravagant, a second type of restraint helped to moderate the overall tone of the debate. Unlike later debates, other members often pushed back and tried to deescalate the rhetoric. Perhaps the clearest example was when Mr. Miles Poindexter, a leader of the revolt, somewhat melodramatically cried, "Now is the day and hour of your salvation." The use of salvation raised the stakes of this reform to the level of an existential threat. Mr. Albert Douglas, an opponent of Mr. Poindexter's, responded, "I do not desire the gentleman from Washington to tell me the hour of my salvation. I think I will discover it for myself." There are a number of other similar examples of resisting overblown crisis rhetoric.

The next three reforms all occurred after the developments described in the "Rise of the Rhetorical Presidency." This led to a marked difference in the use of crisis rhetoric.

In 1946, Congress enacted the Legislative Reorganization Act. This was a comprehensive reform that sought to make both houses of Congress more efficient, responsive to the public, and competent to legislate on increasingly complex policy areas. Its main means of doing so were streamlining the committee structure, simplifying appropriations procedures, and improving congressional staffs and the Congressional Research Service (CRS).

Throughout this debate, which was arguably concerned with more mundane bureaucratic matters than the earlier two reforms, the articulated consequences of the crisis became far more extravagant. A leading proponent of the bill in the Senate introduced the legislation stating, "the fate of *representative government itself* is at stake," "the *fate of democracy* will depend upon whether we make the legislative arm of the Government efficient and responsive to the will of the people" and that something needed to be done in order to "save representative Government in America." Congressman Mike Monroney, a major advocate of the bill in the House, set the stage for debate observing, "Around the world the lights of democracy have gone out. They burn here alone, bright enough to rekindle the fires of freedom and democracy. If we fail, *we fail the world* which looks to us for leadership in this perilous hour." In sum, the crisis was not simply one of efficiency or responsibility in *Congress* but a crisis concerning the very idea of representative government, democracy, and the United States' role as a world leader. With examples like this from the floor leaders, other members followed suit.

Half a century after the revolt against Speaker Cannon, the House majority again enacted a substantial reorganization of the Rules Committee. Prior to 1961, the Rules Committee had twelve members, eight of whom belonged to the majority Democrats and four to the minority Republicans. However, due to the so-called "conservative coalition" between Republicans and Southern Democrats, votes on the committee were often split 6-6, with two Southern Democrats voting with the Republicans. In order to make the committee more responsible to the majority party, the House increased the number of the committee to fifteen members.

The crisis rhetoric used during the 1961 debate was even less restrained than in 1946. According to a number of proponents of the change, failure to add three members to the Rules Committee might very well lead to the Communists winning the Cold War. Such a disproportion between the actual proposed changes and predicted consequences of the reform's failure was unseen in any of the prior debates. One congressman cautioned that "the propaganda value of a negative vote on this resolution *cannot be over-estimated. A negative vote on the resolution will hand our enemies on a silver platter the priceless instrument which will be used in their attempts to destroy us.*" Another added, "as we sit here in this Chamber today the Russian Bear has its claws in the front door of our yard, and in the backyard there is a Red dragon as long as the back porch. So the challenge is ours. This is *no time for dissension* and lack of unity." Opponents of the change described it as launching a "stunning blow against the cornerstone of representative government," as creating a "clear and present danger," and as removing one of the "safeguards we have against *tyrannical* and punitive legislation." While the number of the members on the Rules Committee *could*, if traced through a number of steps, have had an impact on America's fate during the Cold War, the relationship between these two matters seems tenuous at best.

Finally, Congress enacted the Legislative Reorganization Act of 1970. The act was similar to the 1946 Act in its comprehensive scope and focus on the committee processes. However, there were a number of differences. It sought to reduce what some thought had become excessive control exercised by committee chairs that resulted from stripping party leadership of some of its powers after the revolt against Cannon. Additionally, it sought to increase transparency between party leadership and rank and file members of Congress as well as between Congress and the public through "anti-secrecy" measures. Finally, it made some attempts to protect the rights of the minority party.

The 1970 Legislative Reorganization Act saw two interesting occurrences in crisis rhetoric. The first was that the intensity of the crisis rhetoric was actually diminished significantly in comparison to both the 1946 and 1961 reforms. This was largely a credit to the moderate and prudent management of Congressman B. F. Sisk, the floor leader for the legislation. Sisk encouraged calm deliberation, allowed ample time for debate, and emphasized the importance of the current reforms without constantly preaching disaster. Such an example gives cause for hope. While developments of the rhetorical presidency *do* have a major influence on Congress, politicians still have the ability to make choices that resist these trends and avoid their dangers.

Unfortunately, the positive rhetorical contribution of Sisk's leadership may have been overshadowed by another development in crisis rhetoric. In all of the previous debates, the reform in question was viewed as a particular solution to a particular problem (even if the particular problem, as seen above, had wider implications). This was obviously more so in 1910 and

1961, which were revolts against a particular Rules Committee. However, even with the Pendleton Act and the 1946 reforms, there was a sense that after these reforms were passed, Congress would go back to its regular work. The crisis was over. In 1970, for the first time, there was a sense that institutional reform ought to become business as usual.

A number of reform leaders called for virtually perpetual reform. One member observed, "We can do a good deal this week, but there will always be more to do. . . . reform and modernization should be a continuing process, not something which only happens every 20 years." A number of other members echoed the desire to not wait so long in between reforms. One added, "The Legislative Reorganization Act of 1970 is only the beginning of a comprehensive effort to *free Congress of archaic, outmoded practices*. The act itself is a small beginning in the mammoth task of *overhauling* our legislative machinery." Another member argues for institutionalizing a mechanism for non-stop reform, arguing, "our final conclusion was that an agency of the Congress be created to concern itself *constantly* with Congress as an institution which would examine on a continuing basis, ways in which the Congress can be strengthened or constantly updated and/or improved."

If these members were questioned about their statements, they would have perhaps responded that having constant incremental change might avoid the need for radical overhauls in the future. This, they might argue, would *reduce* crises. However, if rhetoric emphasizes constant reform, this suggests that the system is always broken. Rather than "normalizing" crises the tendency will be to make crises the norm. Thus, although the 1970 Reorganization Act was secured by moderate rhetoric and measured debate, this approach now seems to be the exception rather than the rule. As illustrated above, reform efforts typically employed crisis rhetoric and the more recent reforms employed less restrained crisis rhetoric that warned of catastrophic consequences and urged immediate action. Multiplying the occasions for such rhetoric through adopting a culture of constant reform would likely further undercut deliberation.

Only one member during the entire debate pointed to the problem of making reform business as usual in Congress. Congressman Wayne Hays, who actually supported this reform, joked,

> There are certain areas in Washington where words and slogans become popular. We had the New Deal, the Fair Deal, the Square Deal, the Bull Moose, and right now it's reform. I told them [an audience in his home state] last night, publicly, I said if you wanted to pass a bill to legalize prostitution, *you call it a reform bill and you can get it through the House in 30 minutes*.

While joking, Hays seemed to be onto something. Once the language of reform is applied to every bill considered by Congress, it may become difficult for members to resist voting for the measure. Constant reform might lead to everything being considered crisis legislation that must be passed quickly. Unfortunately, since Congressman Hayes offered these remarks in a joking manner, the argument was not taken seriously.

In 1987 Professor Tulis warned in *The Rhetorical Presidency* that Congress would "respond in kind," to the changes he observed in presidential rhetoric. The examination above indicates that at least when it comes to crisis rhetoric, history has borne this out. This development has the potential to hurt Congress in two ways. The first is that it undermines deliberation. If the increase in crisis rhetoric seen here can be reasonably extended to debates on other legislative matters, then the tensions between the quick response required by crises and the deliberation necessary for better lawmaking will increasingly undermine Congress' institutional role in our constitutional system. In the particular case of institutional reform, deliberation is doubly undermined because reforms themselves often seek to *make* Congress more deliberative. It is easy to see the problems that result from Congress deliberating badly about how to make Congress more deliberative.

Second, although the executive branch is designed to be the primary "energetic" branch in our system of government, Congress also needs to be energetic at times. Congressional reform again provides a good example. Sometimes institutional problems really are serious and require the slow-moving Congress to *act*. Although it is true that crisis rhetoric can prompt quick action, it is also dangerous. The 1970 Legislative Reorganization Act shows us where crisis rhetoric eventually leads. Everything can become a crisis. When Congress, like the President, continuously "cries wolf" its calls to action are taken less seriously and become less effective. Perhaps this is why there has been no major successful congressional reform since 1970.

To return to the beginning of the essay, it is not certain that the rhetorical changes seen here are enough to label Congress "the broken branch" or that these changes alone have led to the decline of congressional deliberation—if such a categorical decline has actually occurred. However, the evidence presented here, showing that Congress has indeed followed the problematic rhetorical practices of the President, should lead us to examine congressional rhetoric more when attempting to diagnose Congress' problems and seeking solutions.

Chapter IV

The Presidency

Alexander Hamilton says that "Energy in the executive is a leading character in the definition of good government." Hamilton understands the potential conflict between an energetic government and republican principles, but he claims that an energetic executive is essential to the defense of the nation against foreign attacks and the steady administration of the laws. The ingredients that will produce an energetic executive are a unified presidential office, a term of sufficient duration, adequate financial support, and competent powers. These ingredients would insulate the President from an undue dependence on Congress and public opinion. He would have the independent resources necessary to the energetic execution of his office.

James W. Ceaser, Glen E. Thurow, Jeffrey K. Tulis, and Joseph M. Bessette claim that the greatest shortcoming of contemporary Presidents is their tendency to rely too much on popular persuasion and not enough on their Constitutional authority. Ceaser *et al.* argue that Presidents increasingly look not to their Constitutional office but to public opinion as a source of executive energy. They trace this development to the Progressives who saw public opinion as a more democratic and more powerful source of authority. But they think this is a dangerous trend. They contend that the reliance on popular opinion will undermine the exercise of Constitutionally created power, and will lead to an excessive reliance on popular rhetoric. The more rhetoric is seen as a source of authority, the more politicians will be tempted to make exaggerated claims in search of increased power.

In a 1960 campaign speech John F. Kennedy claims that his understanding of the Presidential office was far more important than his position on any particular policy issue. Kennedy accepts Hamilton's call for an energetic executive and criticizes those who wish to substitute rhetoric for more substantive results. But Kennedy is also willing to look to popular opinion and popular rhetoric as a source of presidential authority. He accepts Theodore Roosevelt's idea of the Presidency as a "bully pulpit." Kennedy wants the president "to summon his national constituency" and "alert the people to our dangers and our opportunities."

Early in his presidency George W. Bush showed how the bully pulpit could be used, not just for a call to action, but also as a tool to educate popular opinion on complex moral questions. In announcing his decision on federal funding for stem cell research, he tried to show the legitimate concerns that animated both sides of the debate, and his desire to take those competing goods into account in creating a policy that would seek common ground and allow for ongoing reflection about these difficult issues.

Bush, in this instance, was reflecting a view of Presidential rhetoric that can be traced to Abraham Lincoln. Lincoln saw the potential for ambitious men to subvert the Constitution in search of extraordinary powers and honors. Lincoln's solution, however, relied to a great extent on rhetoric. Lincoln did not wish to encourage the passionate rhetoric that would fan the flames of a mob, he looked instead to a cooler, more reasonable rhetoric that would support the Constitution and the laws. Only through the persuasive powers of rhetoric could the President maintain the institutions of government created by the Constitution.

Nonetheless some Presidents have claimed the right to exercise extra-legal authority, and the Court has on at least one occasion supported such claims. In *Curtiss-Wright Export Corporation v. United States* the Court distinguished the authority of the national government over domestic affairs, which is derived from the Constitution, and its authority over foreign affairs, which inheres in the concept of nationhood. The latter would exist whether or not the Constitution provided for it. Since the President represents the nation in foreign affairs, the Court's reasoning suggests that the President may exercise this virtually unlimited reservoir of extra-Constitutional authority.

Theodore Roosevelt's stewardship theory of the Presidency claimed such broad authority for the President in domestic as well as foreign affairs. Roosevelt argued that the President was free to act in the public interest as long he did not engage in an activity specifically prohibited by the Constitution. He thought such extraordinary powers were necessary in order to address the needs of modern American society. His successor, William Howard Taft, rejected this view, stating that the only legitimate powers of the Presidency are grounded in the authority of the Constitution. Unfortunately, whereas TR is widely seen as a successful, Taft's Presidency is typically viewed as a failure. The result has been that scholars have often concluded that Taft's reliance on formal Constitutional powers must give way to TR's more pragmatic approach if a modern President is to be successful.

Kevin Burns, however, argues that TR's view leaves us with no Constitutional way to restrain Presidential power. He shows us that Taft had a robust conception of Presidential power, although one that was ultimately subject to Constitutional restraint. The Supreme Court supported such restraint in *Youngstown Sheet and Tube v. Sawyer*. When President Harry Truman seized the steel mills during the Korean War, he claimed that such discretionary authority was implied in the executive power vested in him by the Constitution and by his constitutional duty to "take care that the laws be faithfully executed." But the Supreme Court found his action to be beyond his Constitutional and statutory authority. The Court ruled that his constitutional powers as commander-in-chief were broad, but did not extend beyond the battlefield to steel mills in Ohio; moreover, since Congress had specifically rejected the idea that a President could settle strikes by commandeering private property, the Court determined that Truman also lacked statutory power to seize the steel mills.

At the end of World War II the Court considered an even more troubling case of executive discretion. The immediate problem in the case of *Korematsu v. U.S.* is whether distinctions based on race can ever be legitimate. But Justices Robert Jackson and Felix Frankfurter take the opportunity offered by the case to elaborate their different views of the discretionary authority of the executive. Both admit that military necessity may occasionally take precedence over the protection of individual rights. But Justice Jackson says that even if such action is absolutely necessary, we should never call it Constitutional. To do so would be to establish a dangerous precedent that would undermine the protection of rights. Frankfurter disagrees. He finds it more dangerous to place the actions of the executive outside of the Constitution in any circumstance. Whether or not there is an emergency, Frankfurter wants to retain the possibility of Constitutional restraint. He concludes that the Constitution can and should be understood to include the possibility of effective action in an emergency.

Frankfurter's argument brings to mind Lincoln's defense of his suspension of the writ of habeas corpus. Lincoln claims that in times of emergency the government must deprive citizens of liberty without due process of law; indeed, in granting power to suspend the writ of habeas corpus, the Constitution itself recognizes the necessity for doing so. According to Lincoln the Presidential office established by the Constitution permits and even demands the exercise of discretion in extraordinary situations. Statesmanship is necessary for the preservation of the Constitution and the rule of law.

The potential for abuse of Presidential prerogative exists even outside the context of national emergencies. *Clinton v. Jones* points to both the difficulty and the necessity of distinguishing between the office of the Presidency and the person who occupies that office. A unanimous Court determined that whereas a President has absolute immunity from a civil suit arising from the performance of his duties, he remains subject to the reach of civil law in cases unrelated to official conduct. Jordan Cash addresses the role of Congress in preventing a particular President from abusing the powers of the office. Cash provides historical perspective on the recent conflicts between Donald Trump and Congress. He concludes that although Congress may use its oversight authority to contest what it sees as an abuse of power, its most important weapon is the ultimate threat of impeachment and removal.

Frederick Douglass's speech on the statesmanship of Lincoln provides a fitting conclusion to the discussion of the presidency. Douglass captures the essence of Lincoln's statesmanship: Lincoln's recognition of the need for compromise, his appreciation of the virtues and limits of law, and his sense of when to follow, when to lead, and when to ignore popular opinion. Douglass also recognizes that although Lincoln had different personal interests from his own, and represented different social interests, their common belief in certain fundamental principles provided a basis for mutual respect and political action.

40

Alexander Hamilton

On the Presidency (1788)

There is an idea, which is not without its advocates, that a vigorous Executive is inconsistent with the genius of republican government. The enlightened well-wishers to this species of government must at least hope that the supposition is destitute of foundation; since they can never admit its truth, without at the same time admitting the condemnation of their own principles. Energy in the Executive is a leading character in the definition of good government. It is essential to the protection of the community against foreign attacks; it is not less essential to the steady administration of the laws; to the protection of property against those irregular and high-handed combinations which sometimes interrupt the ordinary course of justice; to the security of liberty against the enterprises and assaults of ambition, of faction, and of anarchy. . . .

A feeble execution is but another phrase for a bad execution; and a government ill executed, whatever it may be in theory, must be, in practice, a bad government.

Taking it for granted, therefore, that all men of sense will agree in the necessity of an energetic Executive, it will only remain to inquire, what are the ingredients which constitute this energy? How far can they be combined with those other ingredients which constitute safety in the republican sense? And how far does this combination characterize the plan which has been reported by the convention?

The ingredients which constitute energy in the Executive are, first, unity; secondly, duration; thirdly, an adequate provision for its support; fourthly, competent powers.

The ingredients which constitute safety in the republican sense are, first, a due dependence on the people; secondly, a due responsibility. . . .

That unity is conducive to energy will not be disputed. Decision, activity, secrecy, and despatch will generally characterize the proceedings of one man in a much more eminent degree than the proceedings of any greater

From Federalists 70–73, in *The Federalist.*

number; and in proportion as the number is increased, these qualities will be diminished.

This unity may be destroyed in two ways: either by vesting the power in two or more magistrates of equal dignity and authority; or by vesting it ostensibly in one man, subject, in whole or in part, to the control and cooperation of others, in the capacity of counsellors to him. . . .

Wherever two or more persons are engaged in any common enterprise or pursuit, there is always danger of difference of opinion. If it be a public trust or office, in which they are clothed with equal dignity and authority, there is peculiar danger of personal emulation and even animosity. From either, and especially from all these causes, the most bitter dissensions are apt to spring. Whenever these happen, they lessen the respectability, weaken the authority, and distract the plans and operations of those whom they divide. If they should unfortunately assail the supreme executive magistracy of a country, consisting of a plurality of persons, they might impede or frustrate the most important measures of the government, in the most critical emergencies of the state. And what is still worse, they might split the community into the most violent and irreconcilable factions, adhering differently to the different individuals who composed the magistracy. . . .

Upon the principles of a free government, inconveniences from the source just mentioned must necessarily be submitted to in the formation of the legislature; but it is unnecessary, and therefore unwise, to introduce them into the constitution of the Executive. It is here too they may be most pernicious. In the legislature, promptitude of decision is oftener an evil than a benefit. The differences of opinion, and the jarrings of parties in that department of the government, though they may sometimes obstruct salutary plans, yet often promote deliberation and circumspection, and serve to check excesses in the majority. When a resolution too is once taken, the opposition must be at an end. That resolution is a law, and resistance to it punishable. But no favorable circumstances palliate or atone for the disadvantages of dissension in the executive department. Here, they are pure and unmixed. There is no point at which they cease to operate. They serve to embarrass and weaken the execution of the plan or measure to which they relate, from the first step to the final conclusion of it. They constantly counteract those qualities in the Executive which are the most necessary ingredients in its composition,—vigor and expedition, and this without any counterbalancing good. In the conduct of war, in which the energy of the Executive is the bulwark of the national security, every thing would be to be apprehended from its plurality. . . .

But one of the weightiest objections to a plurality in the Executive, and which lies as much against the last as the first plan, is, that it tends to conceal faults and destroy responsibility. Responsibility is of two kinds—to censure and to punishment. The first is the more important of the two, especially in an elective office. Man, in public trust, will much oftener act in such a manner as to render him unworthy of being any longer trusted, than in such a manner as to make him obnoxious to legal punishment. But the multiplication of the Executive adds to the difficulty of detection in either case. It often becomes impossible, amidst mutual accusations, to determine on whom the blame or the punishment of a pernicious measure, or series of pernicious measures, ought really to fall. . . .

Duration in office has been mentioned as the second requisite to the energy of the Executive authority. This has relation to two objects: to the personal firmness of the executive magistrate, in the employment of his constitutional powers; and to the stability of the system of administration which may have been adopted under his auspices. With regard to the first, it must be evident, that the longer the duration in office, the greater will be the probability of obtaining so important an advantage. It is a general principle of human nature, that a man will be interested in whatever he possesses, in proportion to the firmness or precariousness of the tenure by which he holds it; will be less attached to what he holds by a momentary or uncertain title, than to what he enjoys by a durable or certain title; and, of course, will be willing to risk more for the sake of the one, than for the sake of the other. This remark is not less applicable to a political privilege, or honor, or trust, than to any article of ordinary property. The inference from it is, that a man acting in the capacity of chief magistrate, under a consciousness that in a very short time he must lay down his office, will be apt to feel himself too little interested in it to hazard any material censure or perplexity, from the independent exertion of his powers, or from encountering the ill-humors, however transient, which may happen to prevail, either in a considerable part of the society itself, or even in a predominant faction in the legislative body. . . .

There are some who would be inclined to regard the servile pliancy of the Executive to a prevailing current, either in the community or in the legislature, as its best recommendation. But such men entertain very crude notions, as well of the purposes for which government was instituted, as of the true means by which the public happiness may be promoted. The republican principle demands that the deliberate sense of the community should govern the conduct of those to whom they intrust the management of their affairs; but it does not require an unqualified complaisance to every sudden breeze of passion, or to every transient impulse which the people may receive from the arts of men, who flatter their prejudices to betray their interest. It is a just observation, that the people commonly *intend* the PUBLIC GOOD. This often applies to their very errors. But their good sense would despise the adulator who should pretend that they always *reason right* about the *means* of promoting it. They know from experience that they sometimes err; and the wonder is that they so seldom err as they do, beset, as they continually are, by the wiles of parasites and sycophants, by the snares of the ambitious,

the avaricious, the desperate, by the artifices of men who possess their confidence more than they deserve it, and of those who seek to possess rather
than to deserve it. When occasions present themselves, in which the interests of the people are at variance with their inclinations, it is the duty of the
persons whom they have appointed to be the guardians of those interests, to
withstand the temporary delusion, in order to give them time and opportunity for more cool and sedate reflection. Instances might be cited in which
a conduct of this kind has saved the people from very fatal consequences of
their own mistakes, and has procured lasting monuments of their gratitude
to the men who had courage and magnanimity enough to serve them at the
peril of their displeasure.

But however inclined we might be to insist upon an unbounded complaisance in the Executive to the inclinations of the people, we can with
no propriety contend for a like complaisance to the humors of the legislature. The latter may sometimes stand in opposition to the former, and at
other times the people may be entirely neutral. In either supposition, it is
certainly desirable that the Executive should be in a situation to dare to act
his own opinion with vigor and decision. . . .

It cannot be affirmed, that a duration of four years, or any other limited
duration, would completely answer the end proposed; but it would contribute
towards it in a degree which would have a material influence upon the spirit
and character of the government. Between the commencement and termination of such a period, there would always be a considerable interval, in which
the prospect of annihilation would be sufficiently remote, not to have an
improper effect upon the conduct of a man imbued with a tolerable portion of
fortitude; and in which he might reasonably promise himself, that there would
be time enough before it arrived, to make the community sensible of the
propriety of the measures he might incline to pursue. Though it be probable
that, as he approached the moment when the public were, by a new election,
to signify their sense of his conduct, his confidence, and with it his firmness,
would decline; yet both the one and the other would derive support from the
opportunities which his previous continuance in the station had afforded him,
of establishing himself in the esteem and goodwill of his constituents. . . .

With a positive duration of considerable extent, I connect the circumstance of reeligibility. The first is necessary to give to the officer himself the
inclination and the resolution to act his part well, and to the community time
and leisure to observe the tendency of his measures, and thence to form an
experimental estimate of their merits. The last is necessary to enable the people,
when they see reason to approve of his conduct, to continue him in his station,
in order to prolong the utility of his talents and virtues, and to secure to the
government the advantage of permanency in a wise system of administration.

Nothing appears more plausible at first sight, nor more ill-founded upon
close inspection than a scheme which in relation to the present point has

had some respectable advocates,—I mean that of continuing the chief magistrate in office for a certain time, and then excluding him from it, either for a limited period or forever after. This exclusion, whether temporary or perpetual, would have nearly the same effects, and these effects would be for the most part rather pernicious than salutary.

One ill effect of the exclusion would be a diminution of the inducements to good behavior. There are few men who would not feel much less zeal in the discharge of a duty, when they were conscious that the advantages of the station with which it was connected must be relinquished at a determinate period, than when they were permitted to entertain a hope of *obtaining,* by *meriting,* a continuance of them. This position will not be disputed so long as it is admitted that the desire of reward is one of the strongest incentives of human conduct; or that the best security for the fidelity of mankind is to make their interest coincide with their duty. Even the love of fame, the ruling passion of the noblest minds, which would prompt a man to plan and undertake extensive and arduous enterprises for the public benefit, requiring considerable time to mature and perfect them, if he could flatter himself with the prospect of being allowed to finish what he had begun, would, on the contrary, deter him from the undertaking, when he foresaw that he must quit the scene before he could accomplish the work, and must commit that, together with his own reputation, to hands which might be unequal or unfriendly to the task. The most to be expected from the generality of men, in such a situation, is the negative merit of not doing harm, instead of the positive merit of doing good,

Another ill effect of the exclusion would be the temptation to sordid views, to peculation, and, in some instances, to usurpation. An avaricious man, who might happen to fill the office, looking forward to a time when he must at all events yield up the emoluments he enjoyed, would feel a propensity, not easy to be resisted by such a man, to make the best use of the opportunity he enjoyed while it lasted, and might not scruple to have recourse to the most corrupt expedients to make the harvest as abundant as it was transitory; though the same man, probably, with a different prospect before him, might content himself with the regular perquisites of his situation, and might even be unwilling to risk the consequences of an abuse of his opportunities. His avarice might be a guard upon his avarice. Add to this that the same man might be vain or ambitious, as well as avaricious. And if he could expect to prolong his honors by his good conduct, he might hesitate to sacrifice his appetite for them to his appetite for gain. But with the prospect before him of approaching an inevitable annihilation, his avarice would be likely to get the victory over his caution, his vanity, or his ambition.

An ambitious man, too, when he found himself seated on the summit of his country's honors, when he looked forward to the time at which he must descend from the exalted eminence forever, and reflected that no exertion of merit on his part could save him from the unwelcome reverse; such a man, in such a situation, would be much more violently tempted to embrace a favorable conjuncture for attempting the prolongation of his power, at every personal hazard, than if he had the probability of answering the same end by doing his duty.

Would it promote the peace of the community, or the stability of the government to have half a dozen men who had had credit enough to be raised to the seat of the supreme magistracy, wandering among the people like discontented ghosts, and sighing for a place which they were destined never more to possess?

A third ill effect of the exclusion would be, the depriving the community of the advantage of the experience gained by the chief magistrate in the exercise of his office. . . .

A fourth ill effect of the exclusion would be the banishing men from stations in which, in certain emergencies of the state, their presence might be of the greatest moment to the public interest or safety. . . .

The third ingredient towards constituting the vigor of the executive authority, is an adequate provision for its support. It is evident that, without proper attention to this article, the separation of the executive from the legislative department would be merely nominal and nugatory. The legislature, with a discretionary power over the salary and emoluments of the Chief Magistrate, could render him as obsequious to their will as they might think proper to make him. They might, in most cases, either reduce him by famine, or tempt him by largesses, to surrender at discretion his judgment to their inclinations. These expressions, taken in all the latitude of the terms, would no doubt convey more than is intended. There are men who could neither be distressed or won into a sacrifice of their duty, but this stern virtue is the growth of few soils; and in the main it will be found that a power over a man's support is a power over his will. If it were necessary to confirm so plain a truth by facts, examples would not be wanting. . . .

It is not easy, therefore, to commend too highly the judicious attention which has been paid to this subject in the proposed Constitution. It is there provided that "The President of the United States shall, at stated times, receive for his services a compensation *which shall neither be increased nor diminished during the period for which he shall have been elected.* . . ."

41

James W. Ceaser, Glen E. Thurow,
Jeffrey K. Tulis, Joseph M. Bessette

The Rise of the Rhetorical Presidency (1981)

Popular or mass rhetoric, which presidents once employed only rarely, now serves as one of their principal tools in attempting to govern the nation. Whatever doubts Americans may now entertain about the limitations of presidential leadership, they do not consider it unfitting or inappropriate for presidents to attempt to "move" the public by programmatic speeches that exhort and set forth grand and ennobling views.

It was not always so. Prior to this century, popular leadership through rhetoric was suspect. Presidents rarely spoke directly to the people, preferring communications between the branches of the government. Washington seldom delivered more than one major speech per year of his administration, and that one—the Annual Address—was almost mandated by the Constitution and was addressed to Congress. Jefferson even ceased delivering the address in person, a precedent that continued until Woodrow Wilson's appearance before Congress in 1913. The spirit of these early presidents' examples was followed throughout the nineteenth century. The relatively few popular speeches that were made differed in character from today's addresses. Most were patriotic orations, some raised constitutional issues, and several spoke to the conduct of war. Very few were domestic "policy speeches" of the sort so common today, and attempts to move the nation by means of an exalted picture of a perfect ideal were almost unknown. . . .

Today, a president has an assembly line of speechwriters efficiently producing words that enable him to say something on every conceivable occasion. Unless a president is deliberately "hiding" in the White House, a week scarcely goes by without at least one major news story devoted to coverage of a radio or TV speech, an address to Congress, a speech to a convention, a press conference, a news release, or some other presidential utterance. But more important even than the quantity of popular rhetoric is the fact that

From Ceaser, Thurow, Tulis, and Bessette, "The Rise of the Rhetorical Presidency," in *Presidential Studies Quarterly* (Spring, 1981). Reprinted by permission of *Presidential Studies Quarterly*.

presidential speech and action increasingly reflect the opinion that speaking is governing. Speeches are written to become the events to which people react no less than "real" events themselves. . . .

The excess of speech has perhaps fed a cynicism about it that is the opposite of [a] boundless faith in rhetoric. . . . Yet, despite this cynicism, it seems increasingly the case that for many who comment on and form opinions about the presidency, word rivals deed as the measure of presidential performance. The standard set for presidents has in large degree become an artifact of their own inflated rhetoric and one to which they frequently fall victim. While part of this difficulty can be blamed on the ineptness of certain presidents' rhetorical strategies, it is also the case that presidents operate in a context that gives them much less discretion over their rhetoric than one might think. The problem is thus not one simply of individual rhetorics, but is rather an institutional dilemma for the modern presidency. Beginning with the campaign, the candidates are obliged to demonstrate their leadership capacity through an ever growing number of rhetorical performances, with the potential impact of their words on future problems of governing often being the least of their concerns. The pressure to "say something" continues after the president has begun to govern. Presidents not only face the demand to explain what they have done and intend to do, but they also have come under increasing pressure to speak out on perceived crises and to minister to the moods and emotions of the populace. In the end, it may be the office of the presidency that is weakened by this form of leadership, puffed up by false expectations that bear little relationship to the practical tasks of governing and undermined by the resulting cynicism.

How did the rhetorical presidency come into existence? What are its strengths and weaknesses? Can presidents escape its burdens, and to what extent should they try to do so? These are some of the important questions that need addressing.

The rise of the rhetorical presidency has been primarily the result of three factors: (1) a modern doctrine of presidential leadership, (2) the modern mass media, and (3) the modern presidential campaign. Of these three, doctrine is probably the most important.

As strange as it may seem to us today, the framers of our Constitution looked with great suspicion on popular rhetoric. Their fear was that mass oratory, whether crudely demogogic or highly inspirational, would undermine the rational and enlightened self-interest of the citizenry which their system was designed to foster and on which it was thought to depend for its stability. The framers' well-known mistrust of "pure" democracy by an assembly—and by extension, of the kind of representative government that looked only to public opinion as its guide—was not based, as is generally supposed, on a simple doubt about the people's capacity go govern, but on a more complex case concerning the evils that would result from the interplay between the public and popular orators.

In democracies, they reasoned, political success and fame are won by those orators who most skillfully give expression to transient, often inchoate, public opinion. Governing by this means, if indeed it can be called governing, leads to constant instability as leaders compete with each other to tap the latest mood passing through the public. The paradox of government by mood is that it fosters neither democratic accountability nor statesmanly efficiency. Freed from the necessity to consult public opinion, understood as "the cool and deliberate sense of the community," popular orators would be so chained to public opinion, understood as "mood," that discretion and flexibility essential to statesmanship would be undermined.

The framers were not so impractical as to think that popular rhetoric could be entirely avoided in a republican system. But the government they designed was intended to minimize reliance on popular oratory and to establish institutions which could operate effectively without the immediate support of transient opinion. All of the powers of governing were to be given, not directly to the people, but to their representatives. These representatives would find themselves in a tripartite government in which the various tasks of governing would be clearly discernible and assigned, and in which they would be forced to deal with knowledgeable and determined men not easily impressed by facile oratory. As part of their solution, the framers were counting on the large size of the nation, which at the time erected a communication barrier that would mute the impact of national popular rhetoric, whether written or oral. Beyond this, the framers instituted a presidential selection system that was designed to preclude active campaigning by the candidates. As for the presidency itself, the framers discouraged any idea that the president should serve as a leader of the people who would stir mass opinion by rhetoric; their conception was rather that of a constitutional officer who would rely for his authority on the formal powers granted by the Constitution and on the informal authority that would flow from the office's strategic position.

These limitations on popular rhetoric did not mean, however, that presidents were expected to govern in silence. Ceremonial occasions presented a proper forum for reminding the public of the nation's basic principles; and communications to Congress, explicitly provided for by the Constitution, offered a mechanism by which the people also could be informed on matters of policy. Yet this intrabranch rhetoric, though public, was not meant to be popular. Addressed in the first instance to a body of informed representatives, it would possess a reasoned and deliberative character; and insofar as some in the public would read these speeches and state papers, they would implicitly be called on to raise their understanding to the level of characteristic deliberative speech.

Nineteenth century politics in America did not, of course, follow exactly the framer's model of an essentially nonrhetorical regime. . . . Yet the amount of nineteenth century presidential rhetoric that even loosely could be called popular is very little indeed, and the presidency remained, with some slight alterations, a constitutional office rather than the seat of popular leadership.

The Inaugural and the Annual Address (now called the State of the Union) were the principal speeches of a president given wide dissemination. The character of the Inaugural Address illustrates the general character of presidential popular speech during the period. Given on a formal occasion, it tended to follow a pattern which was set by Jefferson's First Inaugural Address in which he delivered an exposition of the principles of the Union and its republican character. . . .

Against this tradition Woodrow Wilson gave the Inaugural Address (and presidential speech generally) a new theme. Instead of showing how the policies of the incoming administration reflected the principles of our form of government, Wilson sought to articulate the unspoken desires of the people by holding out a vision of their fulfillment. Presidential speech, in Wilson's view, should articulate what is "in our hearts" and not necessarily what is in our Constitution. . . . Wilson articulated the doctrinal foundation of the rhetorical presidency and thereby provided an alternative theoretical model to that of the framers. . . .

The Wilsonian concept of the rhetorical presidency consists of two interfused elements. First, the president should employ oratory to create an active public opinion that, if necessary, will pressure Congress into accepting his program: "He [the president] has no means of compelling Congress except through public opinion." In advancing policy, deliberative, intra-branch rhetoric thus becomes secondary to popular rhetoric, and the president "speaks" to Congress not directly but through his popular addresses. Second, in order to reach and move the public, the character of the rhetoric must tap the public's feelings and articulate its wishes. Rhetoric does not instill old and established principles as much as it seeks to infuse a sense of vision into the president's particular legislative program.

> A nation is led by a man who . . . speaks, not the rumors of the street, but a new principle for a new age; a man in whose ears the voices of the nation do not sound like the accidental and discordant notes that come from the voice of a mob, but concurrent and concordant like the united voices of a chorus, whose many meanings, spoken by melodious tongues, unite in his understanding in a single meaning and reveal to him a single vision, so that he can speak what no man else knows, the common meaning of the common voice.

If the doctrine of the rhetorical presidency leaves us today with the occasional feeling that it is hollow or outworn, it is not because of a decline in its influence but because of the inevitable consequences of its ascendancy. . . .

The second factor that accounts for the rise of the rhetorical presidency is the modern mass media. The media did not create the rhetorical presidency—doctrine did—but it facilitated its development and has given to it some of its special characteristics. The mass media, meaning here primarily radio and television, must be understood first from the perspective of its technical capacities. It has given the president the means by which to communicate directly and instantaneously with a large national audience, thus tearing down the communications barrier on which the framers had relied to insulate representative institutions from direct contact with the populace. Besides increasing the size of the president's audience, the mass media have changed the mode by which he communicates with the public, replacing the written with the spoken word delivered in a dramatic visible performance. The written word formerly provided a partial screen or check against the most simplistic argumentations, as it allowed more control of the text by the reader and limited the audience to those with the most interest in politics. . . .

The influence of the mass media on presidential rhetoric is not limited to its technical capacities. The mass media have also created a new power center in American politics in the form of television news. If the technical aspect of the media has given the president an advantage or an opportunity, the existence of television news often serves as a rival or an impediment. Journalists are filters in the communication process, deciding what portions of the president's non-televised speeches they will show and how their arguments will be interpreted. When presidents speak in public today, their most important audience is not the one they are personally addressing, but rather the public as it is reached through the brief cuts aired on the news. Speeches accordingly tend to be written so that any segment can be taken to stand by itself—as a self-contained lead. Argument gives way to aphorism.

The direct impact of the news media's interpretation of the president's words is perhaps less important for presidential rhetoric than the indirect influence that derives from the character of news itself. Television news not only carries the messages of governing officials to the people; it also selects the issues that are presented to the government for "action" of some sort. "Real" expressions of mass opinion, which in the past were sporadic, are replaced by the news media's continuous "sophisticated" analyses that serve as a surrogate audience, speaking to the government and supposedly representing to it what the people are saying and thinking. Driven by its own inner dynamic to find and sustain exciting issues and to present them in dramatic terms, the news media create—or give the impression of creating—national moods and currents of opinion which appear to call for some form of action by the government and especially by the president.

The media and the modern presidency feed on each other. The media have found in the presidency a focal point on which to concentrate their peculiarly simplistic and dramatic interpretation of events; and the presidency has found a vehicle in the media that allows it to win public attention and with that attention the reality, but more often the pretense, of enhanced power. . . .

The modern presidential campaign is the third factor that accounts for the rise of the rhetorical presidency. The roots of the modern campaign go back to Wilson and the Progressives and to many of the same ideas that helped to create the rhetorical presidency. Prior to 1912, the parties were largely responsible for conducting the campaigns, and the candidates, with few exceptions, restricted their communications to letters of acceptance of the nomination. Wilson was the first victorious presidential candidate to have engaged in a full-scale speaking tour during the campaign. In his view, it was essential that the candidates replace the parties as the main rhetorical instruments of the campaign. This change would serve not only to down-grade the influence of traditional parties but also to prepare the people for the new kind of presidency that he hoped to establish. Indeed, with Wilson the distinction between campaigning and governing is blurred, as both involve the same essential function of persuading through popular oratory.

Although Wilson himself did not campaign extensively in the pre-convention period, he supported the idea of a preconvention campaign and pushed for nomination by national primaries. His ideal of a truly open presidential nomination campaign in which all candidates must take the "outside" route was not fully realized, however, until after the reforms that followed the 1968 election. Over the past three campaigns (1972, 1976 and 1980) we have seen the development of one of the most peculiarly irresponsible rhetorical processes ever devised. For a period of what is now well over a year, the various contenders have little else to offer except their rhetoric. Undisciplined by the responsibility of matching word to deed, they seek to create events out of their speeches, all the while oper-ating under the constant media-created pressure to say something new. As their goal is to win power, and as that goal, especially in the preconven-tion period, is remote, candidates can easily afford to disregard the impact of their speech on the demands of governing and instead craft their rheto-ric with a view merely to persuading. . . .

The presidential campaign is important for the kinds of inflated expec-tations it raises, but it is even more important for the effects it has on the process of governing. So formative has the campaign become of our tastes for oratory and of our conception of leadership that presidential speech and governing have come more and more to imitate the model of the campaign. . . .

The inflated expectations engendered by the rhetorical presidency have by now become a matter of serious concern among those who study the presi-dency. In response to this problem, a growing number of scholars have begun to argue that presidents should remove themselves from much day-to-day management of government and reserve themselves for crisis management. If this argument means only that presidents should not immerse themselves in details or spread themselves too thin, no one could quarrel with it. But if it means that the president should abandon the articulation of a broad legislative program or avoid general management of the bureaucracy at a time when the bureaucracy is becoming more and more unmanageable, then the argument is misguided. If the president does not give coherence to policy or enforce discipline on the Executive branch, who will? Certainly not Congress. The president remains our only national officer who, as Jefferson once said, "commands a view of the whole ground." A retrenched presidency that cedes much of its authority to others and merely reacts to crisis is hardly the answer to our difficulties. . . .

The roots of the rhetorical presidency extend so deeply into our political structure and national consciousness that talk of change may seem futile; and yet the evident failures of the current doctrine, together with the growing scholarly debate about the crisis of the presidency, suggest that the moment has arrived for a discussion of alternatives. It should not be forgotten that the foundations of the rhetorical presidency were deliberately laid by Woodrow Wilson and that other presidents might establish new doctrines. If a sensible reform of the institution is ever possible, the key will be found in reversing the order of President Carter's July 1979 formulation—that is, in restoring the president to his natural place as the head of government, and subordinating his awkward role of an itinerant leader of the people. But how could such change take place, and what would the contours of the office look like?

First, since the modern campaign is the source of so many of the problems of the presidency, it is evident that no reform of the office can hope to succeed without change in the selection process. The operative theoretical principle that must govern this change is that the selection process should be thought of not as an end in itself, but as a means of promoting, or at least not undermining, the character of the presidential office. Construed in practical terms, this principle translates into a call for electoral reform that would reduce the duration of the campaign, especially in the preconvention period. The elimination or dramatic reduction in the number of presidential primaries and the return of the power of selection to the parties would be helpful. This change would not eliminate the campaign, but it would reduce its public phase to a shorter period and thus focus public attention on the speechmaking that takes place after the nomination. . . .

Second, presidents should reduce the number of their speeches. As they speak less, there is at least the chance that their words will carry more weight; and if their words carry more weight, then perhaps more thought will be given to speech that can sensibly direct action. What applies to speeches applies equally to press conferences. Press conferences without cameras would probably allow for a more detailed exchange of information between the president and the press corps and avoid the pressures on the president (and the journalists) to make each news conference dramatic and newsworthy. Written messages might replace many presently oral performances, and personal television appearances would be reserved for truly important issues of public concern.

Third, it is obvious that a reduction in the quantity of rhetoric itself is not enough; its character must also change. To avoid inspirational rhetoric does not mean that the president must abandon firm principles, practical ideals or even a political party that connects this generation with the moorings of our political system. Indeed, such a rhetoric is perfectly consistent with the dignity of a head of state and the character of our political order. In respect to policy, however, presidents must recapture the capacity to address the nation's enlightened self-interest no less than its sense of idealism and the related capacity to approach Congress directly rather than through the people.

The gravest problem of the rhetorical presidency, however, goes deeper than any issue confined to presidential practice. It extends to the basic questions of how our nation can be governed. No one would deny that presidents need to hold up America's basic principles and on occasion mobilize the public to meet genuine challenges. Indeed, in a liberal system of government that frees men's acquisitive instincts and allows them to devote their energies to individual material improvement, there is room on occasion for presidents to lift up the public's vision to something beyond the clash of interests. But under the influence of the rhetorical presidency, we have seen an ever-increasing reliance on inspirational rhetoric to deal with the normal problems of politics. If there is a place for such rhetoric, it is necessary also to be aware of its danger and of the corresponding need to keep it within limits.

By itself, rhetoric does not possess the power to make citizens devote themselves selflessly to the common weal, particularly where the basic principles of society protect and encourage men's independent and private activities. The founders of our country created a complex representative governement designed to foster a knowledgeable concern for the common good in the concrete circumstances of political life that would be difficult, if not impossible, to elicit directly from a people led by orators. What the continued use of inspirational rhetoric fosters is not a simple credibility problem, but a deep tension between the publicly articulated understanding of the nature of our politics and the actual springs that move the system. No wonder, then, that some politicians, deceived by their own rhetoric, find it difficult to come to terms with the job of governing a nation of complex multiple interests. Far from reinforcing our country's principles and protecting its institutions, the rhetorical presidency leads us to neglect our principles for our hopes and to ignore the benefits and needs of our institutions for a fleeting sense of oneness with our leaders.

42

John F. Kennedy

Campaign Speech on the Presidency (1960)

The modern presidential campaign covers every issue in and out of the plat-form from cranberries to creation. But the public is rarely alerted to a candi-date's views about the central issue on which all the rest turn. That central issue—and the point of my comments this noon—is not the farm problem or defense or India. It is the Presidency itself. Of course a candidate's views on specific policies are important—but Theodore Roosevelt and William Howard Taft shared policy views with entirely different results in the White House. Of course it is important to elect a good man with good intentions—but Woodrow Wilson and Warren G. Harding were both good men of good intentions—so were Lincoln and Buchanan—but there is a Lincoln Room in the White House, and no Buchanan Room.

The history of this nation—its brightest and its bleakest pages—has been written largely in terms of the different views our Presidents have had of the Presidency itself. This history ought to tell us that the American peo-ple in 1960 have an imperative right to know what any man bidding for the Presidency thinks about the place he is bidding for—whether he is aware of and willing to use the powerful resources of that office—whether his model will be Taft or Roosevelt—Wilson or Harding.

Not since the days of Woodrow Wilson has any candidate spoken on the Presidency itself before the votes have been irrevocably cast. Let us hope that the 1960 campaign, in addition to discussing the familiar issues where our positions too often blur, will also talk about the Presidency itself—as an instrument for dealing with those issues—as an office with varying roles, powers, and limitations.

During the past eight years, we have seen one concept of the Presidency at work. Our needs and hopes have been eloquently stated—but the initia-tive and follow-through have too often been left to others. And too often his own objectives have been lost by the President's failure to override objec-tions from within his own party, in the Congress or even in his Cabinet.

Speech delivered to the National Press Club by John F. Kennedy on January 14, 1960.

The American people in 1952 and 1956 may well have preferred this detached, limited concept of the Presidency after twenty years of fastmoving, creative presidential rule. Perhaps historians will regard this as necessarily one of those frequent periods of consolidation, a time to draw breath, to recoup our national energy. To quote the State of the Union Message: "No Congress . . . on surveying the state of the nation, has met with a more pleasing prospect than that which appears at the present time." Unfortunately this is not Mr. Eisenhower's last message to the Congress, but Calvin Coolidge's. He followed to the White House Mr. Harding, whose "sponsor" declared very frankly that the times did not demand a first-rate President. If true, the times and the man met.

But the question is what do the times—and the people—demand for the next four years in the White House?

They demand a vigorous proponent of the national interest—not a passive broker for conflicting private interests. They demand a man capable of acting as the commander in chief of the grand alliance, not merely a bookkeeper who feels that his work is done when the numbers on the balance sheet come out even. They demand that he be the head of a responsible party, not rise so far above politics as to be invisible—a man who will formulate and fight for legislative policies, not be a casual bystander to the legislative process.

Today a restricted concept of the Presidency is not enough. For beneath today's surface gloss of peace and prosperity are increasingly dangerous, unsolved, long-postponed problems—problems that will inevitably explode to the surface during the next four years of the next Administration—the growing missile gap, the rise of Communist China, the despair of the underdeveloped nations, the explosive situations in Berlin and in the Formosa Straits, the deterioration of NATO, the lack of an arms control agreement, and all the domestic problems of our farms, cities, and schools.

This Administration has not faced up to these and other problems. Much has been said—but I am reminded of the old Chinese proverb: "There is a great deal of noise on the stairs but nobody comes into the room." The President's State of the Union Message reminded me of the exhortation from "King Lear" that goes: "I will do such things—what they are I know not . . . but they shall be the wonders of the earth. "

In the decade that lies ahead—in the challenging, revolutionary Sixties—the American Presidency will demand more than ringing manifestoes issued from the rear of the battle. It will demand that the President place himself in the very thick of the fight, that he care passionately about the fate of the people he leads, that he be willing to serve them at the risk of incurring their momentary displeasure.

Whatever the political affiliation of our next President, whatever his views may be on all the issues and problems that rush in upon us, he must above all be the Chief Executive in every sense of the word. He must be prepared to exercise the fullest powers of his office—all that are specified and some that are not. He must master complex problems as well as receive one-page memoranda. He must originate action as well as study groups. He must reopen the channels of communication between the world of thought and the seat of power.

Ulysses Grant considered the President "a purely administrative officer." If he administered the government departments efficiently, delegated his functions smoothly, and performed his ceremonies of state with decorum and grace, no more was to be expected of him. But that is not the place the Presidency was meant to have in American life. The President is alone, at the top—the loneliest job there is, as Harry Truman has said. If there is destructive dissension among the services, he alone can step in and straighten it out—instead of waiting for unanimity. If administrative agencies are not carrying out their mandate—if a brushfire threatens some part of the globe—he alone can act, without waiting for the Congress. If his farm program fails, he alone deserves the blame, not his Secretary of Agriculture.

"The President is at liberty, both in law and conscience, to be as big a man as he can." So wrote Professor Woodrow Wilson. But President Woodrow Wilson discovered that to be a big man in the White House inevitably brings cries of dictatorship. So did Lincoln and Jackson and the two Roosevelts. And so may the next occupant of that office, if he is the man the times demand. But how much better it would be, in the turbulent Sixties, to have a Roosevelt or a Wilson than to have another James Buchanan, cringing in the White House, afraid to move.

Nor can we afford a Chief Executive who is praised primarily for what he did not do, the disasters he prevented, the bills he vetoed—a President wishing his subordinates would produce more missiles or build more schools. We will need instead what the Constitution envisioned: a Chief Executive who is the vital center of action in our whole scheme of government.

This includes the legislative process as well. The President cannot afford—for the sake of the office as well as the nation—to be another Warren G. Harding, described by one backer as a man who "would, when elected, sign whatever bill the Senate sent him—and not send bills for the Senate to pass." Rather he must know when to lead the Congress, when to consult it and when he should act alone. Having served fourteen years in the Legislative Branch, I would not look with favor upon its domination by the Executive. Under our government of "power as the rival of power," to use Hamilton's phrase, Congress must not surrender its responsibilities. But neither should it dominate. However large its share in the formulation of domestic programs, it is the President alone who must make the major decisions of our foreign policy.

That is what the Constitution wisely commands. And even domestically, the President must initiate policies and devise laws to meet the needs of the nation. And he must be prepared to use all the resources of his office to insure the enactment of that legislation—even when conflict is the result. By the end of his term Theodore Roosevelt was not popular in the Congress—particularly when he criticized an amendment to the Treasury appropriation which forbade the use of Secret Service men to investigate congressmen! And the feeling was mutual, Roosevelt saying: "I do not much admire the Senate, because it is such a helpless body when efficient work is to be done." And Woodrow Wilson was even more bitter after his frustrating quarrels—asked if he might run for the Senate in 1920, he replied: "Outside of the United States, the Senate does not amount to a damn. And inside the United States, the Senate is mostly despised. They haven't had a thought down there in fifty years."

But, however bitter their farewells, the facts of the matter are that Roosevelt and Wilson did get things done—not only through their Executive powers but through the Congress as well. Calvin Coolidge, on the other hand, departed from Washington with cheers of Congress still ringing in his ears. But when his World Court bill was under fire on Capitol Hill he sent no messages, gave no encouragement to the bill's leaders and paid little or no attention to the whole proceeding—and the cause of world justice was set back. To be sure, Coolidge had held the usual White House breakfasts with congressional leaders—but they were aimed, as he himself said, at "good fellowship," not a discussion of "public business." And at his press conferences, according to press historians, where he preferred to talk about the local flower show and its exhibits, reporters who finally extracted from him a single sentence"I am against that bill"—would rush to file tongue-in-cheek dispatches, proclaiming that: "President Coolidge, in a fighting mood, today served notice on Congress that he intended to combat, with all the resources at his command, the pending bill. . . ."

But in the coming years, we will need a real fighting mood in the White House—a man who will not retreat in the face of pressure from his congressional leaders—who will not let down those supporting his views on the floor. Divided government over the past six years has only been further confused by this lack of legislative leadership. To restore it next year will help restore purpose to both the Presidency and the Congress.

The facts of the matter are that legislative leadership is not possible without party leadership, in the most political sense—and Mr. Eisenhower prefers to stay above politics (although a weekly news magazine last fall reported the startling news that "President Eisenhower is emerging as a major political figure"). When asked, early in his first term, how he liked the "game of politics," he replied with a frown that his questioner was using a derogatory phrase. "Being President," he said, "is a very great experience . . . but the word 'politics' . . . I have no great liking for that." But no President, it seems to me, can escape politics. He has not only been chosen by the nation—he has been chosen by his party. And if he insists that he is "President of all the people" and should, therefore, offend none of them—if he blurs the issues and differences between the parties—if he neglects the party machinery and avoids his party's leadership—then he has not only weakened the political party as an instrument of the democratic process—he has dealt a blow to the democratic process itself. I prefer the example of Abe Lincoln, who loved politics with the passion of a born practitioner. For example, he waited up all night in 1863 to get the crucial returns on the Ohio governorship. When the Unionist candidate was elected, Lincoln wired: "Glory to God in the highest! Ohio has saved the nation!"

But the White House is not only the center of political leadership. It must be the center of moral leadership—a "bully pulpit," as Theodore Roosevelt described it. For only the President represents the national interest. And upon him alone converge all the needs and aspirations of all parts of the country, all departments of the government, all nations of the world. It is not enough merely to represent prevailing sentiment—to follow McKinley's practice, as described by Joe Cannon, of "keeping his ear so close to the ground he got it full of grasshoppers." We will need in the Sixties a President who is willing and able to summon his national constituency to its finest hour—to alert the people to our dangers and our opportunities—to demand of them the sacrifices that will be necessary. Despite the increasing evidence of a lost national purpose and a soft national will, F.D.R.'s words in his first inaugural still ring true: "In every dark hour of our national life, a leadership of frankness and vigor has met with that understanding and support of the people themselves which is essential to victory."

Roosevelt fulfilled the role of moral leadership. So did Wilson and Lincoln, Truman and Jackson and Teddy Roosevelt. They led the people as well as the government—they fought for great ideals as well as bills. And the time has come to demand that kind of leadership again. And so, as this vital campaign begins, let us discuss the issues the next President will face—but let us also discuss the powers and tools with which he must face them. For he must endow that office with extraordinary strength and vision. He must act in the image of Abraham Lincoln summoning his wartime Cabinet to a meeting on the Emancipation Proclamation. That Cabinet had been carefully chosen to please and reflect many elements in the country. But "I have gathered you together," Lincoln said, "to hear what I have written down. I do not wish your advice about the main matter—that I have determined for myself." And later when he went to sign it after several hours of exhausting handshaking that had left his arm weak, he said to those present: "If my name goes down in history, it will be for this act. My whole soul is in it. If my hand trembles when I sign this proclamation, all who examine the document hereafter will say: 'He hesitated.' " But Lincoln's hand did not tremble. He did not hesitate. He did not equivocate. For he was the President of the United States. It is in this spirit that we must go forth in the coming months and years.

43

George W. Bush

On Stem Cell Research (2001)

Good evening. I appreciate you giving me a few minutes of your time tonight so I can discuss with you a complex and difficult issue, an issue that is one of the most profound of our time.

The issue of research involving stem cells derived from human embryos is increasingly the subject of a national debate and dinner table discussions. The issue is confronted every day in laboratories as scientists ponder the ethical ramifications of their work. It is agonized over by parents and many couples as they try to have children or to save children already born. The issue is debated within the church, with people of different faiths, even many of the same faith, coming to different conclusions.

Many people are finding that the more they know about stem cell research, the less certain they are about the right ethical and moral conclusions.

My administration must decide whether to allow federal funds, your tax dollars, to be used for scientific research on stem cells derived from human embryos.

A large number of these embryos already exist. They are the product of a process called in vitro fertilization which helps so many couples conceive children. When doctors match sperm and egg to create life outside the womb, they usually produce more embryos than are implanted in the mother. Once a couple successfully has children or if they are unsuccessful, the additional embryos remain frozen in laboratories. Some will not survive during long storage, others are destroyed. A number have been donated to science and used to create privately funded stem cell lines. And a few have been implanted in an adoptive mother and born and are today healthy children.

Based on preliminary work that has been privately funded, scientists believe further research using stem cells offers great promise that could help improve the lives of those who suffer from many terrible diseases, from juvenile diabetes to Alzheimer, from Parkinsons to spinal cord injuries.

George W. Bush, when President of the United States, delivered these remarks to the nation on August 9, 2001. The speech can be found at https://georgewbush-whitehouse.archives.gov/news/releases/2001/08/20010809-2.html.

And while scientists admit they are not yet certain, they believe stem cells derived from embryos have unique potential.

You should also know that stem cells can be derived from sources other than embryos: from adult cells, from umbilical cords that are discarded after babies are born, from human placentas. And many scientists feel research on these types of stem cells is also promising. Many patients suffering from a range of diseases are already being helped with treatments developed from adult stem cells.

However, most scientists, at least today, believe that research on embryonic stem cells offers the most promise because these cells have the potential to develop in all of the tissues in the body.

Scientists further believe that rapid progress in this research will come only with federal funds. Federal dollars help attract the best and brightest scientists. They ensure new discoveries are widely shared at the largest number of research facilities, and that the research is directed toward the greatest public good.

The United States has a long and proud record of leading the world toward advances in science and medicine that improve human life, and the United States has a long and proud record of upholding the highest standards of ethics as we expand the limits of science and knowledge.

Research on embryonic stem cells raises profound ethical questions, because extracting the stem cell destroys the embryo, and thus destroys its potential for life.

Like a snowflake, each of these embryos is unique, with the unique genetic potential of an individual human being.

As I thought through this issue I kept returning to two fundamental questions. First, are these frozen embryos human life and therefore something precious to be protected? And second, if they're going to be destroyed anyway, shouldn't they be used for a greater good, for research that has the potential to save and improve other lives?

I've asked those questions and others of scientists, scholars, bio-ethicists, religious leaders, doctors, researchers, members of Congress, my Cabinet and my friends. I have read heartfelt letters from many Americans. I have given this issue a great deal of thought, prayer, and considerable reflection, and I have found widespread disagreement.

On the first issue, are these embryos human life? Well, one researcher told me he believes this five-day-old cluster of cells is not an embryo, not yet an individual but a pre-embryo. He argued that it has the potential for life, but it is not a life because it cannot develop on its own.

An ethicist dismissed that as a callous attempt at rationalization. "Make no mistake," he told me, "that cluster of cells is the same way you and I, and all the rest of us, started our lives. One goes with a heavy heart if we use these," he said, "because we are dealing with the seeds of the next generation."

And to the other crucial question—If these are going to be destroyed anyway, why not use them for good purpose?—I also found different answers.

Many are these embryos are byproducts of a process that helps create life and we should allow couples to donate them to science so they can be used for good purpose instead of wasting their potential.

Others will argue there is no such thing as excess life and the fact that a living being is going to die does not justify experimenting on it or exploiting it as a natural resource.

At its core, this issue forces us to confront fundamental questions about the beginnings of life and the ends of science. It lives at a difficult moral intersection, juxtaposing the need to protect life in all its phases with the prospect of saving and improving life in all its stages.

As the discoveries of modern science create tremendous hope, they also lay vast ethical mine fields.

As the genius of science extends the horizons of what we can do, we increasingly confront complex questions about what we should do. We have arrived at that brave new world that seemed so distant in 1932 when Alduous Huxley wrote about human beings created in test tubes in what he called a hatchery.

In recent weeks, we learned that scientists have created human embryos in test tubes solely to experiment on them. This is deeply troubling and a warning sign that should prompt all of us to think through these issues very carefully.

Embryonic stem cell research is at the leading edge of a series of moral hazards. The initial stem cell researcher was at first reluctant to begin his research, fearing it might be used for human cloning. Scientists have already cloned a sheep. Researchers are telling us the next step could be to clone human beings to create individual designer stem cells, essentially to grow another you, to be available in case you need another heart or lung or liver.

I strongly oppose human cloning, as do most Americans. We recoil at the idea of growing human beings for spare body parts or creating life for our convenience.

And while we must devote enormous energy to conquering disease, it is equally important that we pay attention to the moral concerns raised by the new frontier of human embryo stem cell research. Even the most noble ends do not justify any means.

My position on these issues is shaped by deeply held beliefs. I'm a strong supporter of science and technology, and believe they have the potential for incredible good—to improve lives, to save life, to conquer disease. Research offers hope that millions of our loved ones may be cured of a disease and rid of their suffering. I have friends whose children suffer from juvenile diabetes. Nancy Reagan has written me about President Reagan's struggle with

Alzheimer's. My own family has confronted the tragedy of childhood leukemia. And like all Americans, I have great hope for cures.

I also believe human life is a sacred gift from our creator. I worry about a culture that devalues life, and believe as your president I have an important obligation to foster and encourage respect for life in America and throughout the world.

And while we're all hopeful about the potential of this research, no one can be certain that the science will live up to the hope it has generated.

Eight years ago, scientists believed fetal tissue research offered great hope for cures and treatments, yet the progress to date has not lived up to its initial expectations. Embryonic stem cell research offers both great promise and great peril, so I have decided we must proceed with great care.

As a result of private research, more than 60 genetically diverse stem cell lines already exist. They were created from embryos that have already been destroyed, and they have the ability to regenerate themselves indefinitely, creating ongoing opportunities for research.

I have concluded that we should allow federal funds to be used for research on these existing stem cell lines, where the life-and- death decision has already been made.

Leading scientists tell me research on these 60 lines has great promise that could lead to breakthrough therapies and cures. This allows us to explore the promise and potential of stem cell research without crossing a fundamental moral line by providing taxpayer funding that would sanction or encourage further destruction of human embryos that have at least the potential for life.

I also believe that great scientific progress can be made through aggressive federal funding of research on umbilical cord, placenta, adult and animal stem cells, which do not involve the same moral dilemma. This year your government will spend $250 million on this important research.

I will also name a president's council to monitor stem cell research, to recommend appropriate guidelines and regulations and to consider all of the medical and ethical ramifications of bio-medical innovation.

This council will consist of leading scientists, doctors, ethicists, lawyers, theologians and others, and will be chaired by Dr. Leon Kass, a leading bio-medical ethicist from the University of Chicago.

This council will keep us apprised of new developments and give our nation a forum to continue to discuss and evaluate these important issues.

As we go forward, I hope we will always be guided by both intellect and heart, by both our capabilities and our conscience.

I have made this decision with great care, and I pray it is the right one.

Thank you for listening. Good night, and God bless America.

44

Abraham Lincoln

The Perpetuation of Our Political Institutions (1838)

As a subject for the remarks of the evening, *the perpetuation of our political institutions*, is selected.

In the great journal of things happening under the sun, we, the American People, find our account running, under date of the nineteenth century of the Christian era. We find ourselves in the peaceful possession, of the fairest portion of the earth, as regards extent of territory, fertility of soil, and salubrity of climate. We find ourselves under the government of a system of political institutions, conducing more essentially to the ends of civil and religious liberty, than any of which the history of former times tells us. We, when mounting the stage of existence, found ourselves the legal inheritors of these fundamental blessings. We toiled not in the acquirement or establishment of them—they are a legacy bequeathed us, by a *once* hardy, brave, and patriotic, but *now* lamented and departed race of ancestors. Their's was the task (and nobly they performed it) to possess themselves, and through themselves, us, of this goodly land; and to uprear upon its hills and its valleys, a political edifice of liberty and equal rights; 'tis ours only, to transmit these, the former, unprofaned by the foot of an invader; the latter, undecayed by the lapse of time, and untorn by usurpation—to the latest generation that fate shall permit the world to know. This task of gratitude to our fathers, justice to ourselves, duty to posterity, and love for our species in general, all imperatively require us faithfully to perform.

How, then, shall we perform it? At what point shall we expect the approach of danger? By what means shall we fortify against it? Shall we expect some transatlantic military giant, to step the Ocean, and crush us at a blow? Never! All the armies of Europe, Asia and Africa combined, with all the treasure of the earth (our own excepted) in their military chest; with a Buonaparte for a commander, could not by force, take a drink from the Ohio, or make a track on the Blue Ridge, in a trial of a thousand years.

From *The Collected Works of Abraham Lincoln*, Vol. VI, Rutgers University Press, 1953.

At what point then is the approach of danger to be expected? I answer, if it ever reach us, it must spring up amongst us. It cannot come from abroad. If destruction be our lot, we must ourselves be its author and finisher. As a nation of freemen, we must live through all time, or die by suicide.

I hope I am over wary; but if I am not, there is, even now, something of ill-omen amongst us. I mean the increasing disregard for law which pervades the country; the growing disposition to substitute the wild and furious passions, in lieu of the sober judgment of Courts; and the worse than savage mobs, for the executive ministers of justice. This disposition is awfully fearful in any community; and that it now exists in ours, though grating to our feelings to admit, it would be a violation of truth, and an insult to our intelligence, to deny. Accounts of outrages committed by mobs, form the every-day news of the times. They have pervaded the country, from New England to Louisiana;—they are neither peculiar to the eternal snows of the former, nor the burning suns of the latter;—they are not the creature of climate—neither are they confined to the slaveholding, or the nonslaveholding States. Alike, they spring up among the pleasure hunting masters of Southern slaves, and the order loving citizens of the land of steady habits. Whatever, then, their cause may be, it is common to the whole country.

It would be tedious, as well as useless, to recount the horrors of all of them. Those happening in the State of Mississippi, and at St. Louis, are, perhaps, the most dangerous in example, and revolting to humanity. In the Mississippi case, they first commenced by hanging the regular gamblers: a set of men, certainly not following for a livelihood, a very useful, or very honest occupation, but one which, so far from being forbidden by the laws, was actually licensed by an act of the Legislature, passed but a single year before. Next, negroes, suspected of conspiring to raise an insurrection, were caught up and hanged in all parts of the State: then, white men, supposed to be leagued with the negroes; and finally, strangers, from neighboring States, going thither on business, were, in many instances, subjected to the same fate. Thus went on this process of hanging, from gamblers to negroes, from negroes to white citizens, and from these to strangers; till, dead men were seen literally dangling from the boughs of trees upon every road side; and in numbers almost sufficient, to rival the native Spanish moss of the country, as a drapery of the forest.

Turn, then, to that horror-striking scene at St. Louis. A single victim was only sacrificed there. His story is very short; and is, perhaps, the most highly tragic, of any thing of its length, that has ever been witnessed in real life. A mulatto man, by the name of McIntosh, was seized in the street, dragged to the suburbs of the city, chained to a tree, and actually burned to death; and all within a single hour from the time he had been a freeman, attending to his own business, and at peace with the world.

Such are the effects of mob law; and such are the scenes, becoming more and more frequent in this land so lately famed for love of law and order; and the stories of which, have even now grown too familiar, to attract anything more, than an idle remark.

But you are, perhaps, ready to ask, "What has this to do with the perpetuation of our political institutions?" I answer, it has much to do with it. Its direct consequences are, comparatively speaking, but a small evil; and much of its danger consists, in the proneness of our minds, to regard its direct, as its only consequences. Abstractly considered, the hanging of the gamblers at Vicksburg, was of but little consequence. They constitute a portion of population, that is worse than useless in any community; and their death, if no pernicious example be set by it, is never matter of reasonable regret with any one. If they were annually swept, from the stage of existence, by the plague or small pox, honest men would, perhaps, be much profited, by the operation. Similar too, is the correct reasoning, in regard to the burning of the negro at St. Louis. He had forfeited his life, by the perpetration of an outrageous murder, upon one of the most worthy and respectable citizens of the city; and had he not died as he did, he must have died by the sentence of the law, in a very short time afterwards. As to him alone, it was as well the way it was, as it could otherwise have been. But the example in either case, was fearful. When men take it in their heads today, to hang gamblers, or burn murderers, they should recollect, that, in the confusion usually attending such transactions, they will be as likely to hang or burn some one, who is neither a gambler nor a murderer as one who is; and that, acting upon the example they set, the mob of tomorrow, may, and probably will, hang or burn some of them, by the very same mistake. And not only so; the innocent, those who have ever set their faces against violations of law in every shape, alike with the guilty, fall victims to the ravages of mob law; and thus it goes on, step by step; till all the walls erected for the defence of the persons and property of individuals, are trodden down, and disregarded. But all this even, is not the full extent of the evil. By such examples, by instances of the perpetrators of such acts going unpunished, the lawless in spirit, are encouraged to become lawless in practice; and having been used to no restraint, but dread of punishment, they thus become, absolutely unrestrained. Having ever regarded Government as their deadliest bane, they make a jubilee of the suspension of its operations; and pray for nothing so much, as its total annihilation. While, on the other hand, good men, men who love tranquility, who desire to abide by the laws, and enjoy their benefits, who would gladly spill their blood in the defence of their country; seeing their property destroyed; their families insulted, and their lives endangered; their persons injured; and seeing nothing in prospect that forebodes a change for the better; become tired of, and disgusted with, a Government that offers them no protection; and are not much averse to a change in which they imagine they have nothing to lose. Thus, then, by the operation of this mobocratic spirit, which all must admit, is now abroad in the land, the strongest bulwark of any Government, and particularly of those constituted like ours, may effectually be broken down and destroyed—I mean the *attachment* of the People. Whenever this effect shall be produced among us; whenever the vicious portion of population shall be permitted to gather in bands of hundreds and thousands, and burn churches, ravage and rob provision stores, throw printing presses into rivers, shoot editors, and hang and burn obnoxious persons at pleasure, and with impunity; depend on it, this Government cannot last. By such things, the feelings of the best citizens will become more or less alienated from it; and thus it will be left without friends, or with too few, and those few too weak, to make their friendship effectual. At such a time and under such circumstances, men of sufficient talent and ambition will not be wanting to seize the opportunity, strike the blow, and overturn that fair fabric, which for the last half century, had been the fondest hope, of the lovers of freedom, throughout the world.

I know the American People are *much* attached to their Government;—I know they would suffer *much* for its sake;—I know they would endure evils long and patiently, before they would ever think of exchanging it for another. Yet, notwithstanding all this, if the laws be continually despised and disregarded, if their rights to be secure in their persons and property, are held by no better tenure than the caprice of a mob, the alienation of their affections from the Government is the natural consequence; and to that, sooner or later, it must come.

Here then, is one point at which danger may be expected.

The question recurs "how shall we fortify against it?" The answer is simple. Let every American, every lover of liberty, every well wisher to his posterity, swear by the blood of the Revolution, never to violate in the least particular, the laws of the country; and never to tolerate their violation by others. As the patriots of seventy-six did to the support of the Declaration of Independence, so to the support of the Constitution and Laws, let every American pledge his life, his property, and his sacred honor;—let every man remember that to violate the law, is to trample on the blood of his father, and to tear the charter of his own, and his children's liberty. Let reverence for the laws, be breathed by every American mother, to the lisping babe, that prattles on her lap—let it be taught in schools, in seminaries, and in colleges;—let it be written in Primers, spelling books, and in Almanacs;—let it be preached from the pulpit, proclaimed in legislative halls, and enforced in courts of justice. And, in short, let it become the *political religion* of the nation; and let the old and the young, the rich and the poor, the grave and the gay, of all sexes and tongues, and colors and conditions, sacrifice unceasingly upon its altars.

While ever a state of feeling, such as this, shall universally, or even, very generally prevail throughout the nation, vain will be every effort, and fruitless every attempt, to subvert our national freedom.

When I so pressingly urge a strict observance of all the laws, let me not be understood as saying there are no bad laws, nor that grievances may not arise, for the redress of which, no legal provisions have been made. I mean to say no such thing. But I do mean to say, that, although bad laws, if they exist, should be repealed as soon as possible, still while they continue in force, for the sake of example, they should be religiously observed. So also in unprovided cases. If such arise, let proper legal provisions be made for them with the least possible delay; but, till then, let them, if not too intolerable, be borne with.

There is no grievance that is a fit object of redress by mob law. In any case that arises, as for instance, the promulgation of abolitionism, one of two positions is necessarily true; that is, the thing is right within itself, and therefore deserves the protection of all law and all good citizens; or, it is wrong, and therefore proper to be prohibited by legal enactments; and in neither case, is the interposition of mob law, either necessary, justifiable, or excusable.

But, it may be asked, why suppose danger to our political institutions? Have we not preserved them for more than fifty years? And why may we not for fifty times as long?

We hope there is no *sufficient* reason. We hope all dangers may be overcome; but to conclude that no danger may ever arise, would itself be extremely dangerous. There are now, and will hereafter be, many causes, dangerous in their tendency, which have not existed heretofore; and which are not too insignificant to merit attention. That our government should have been maintained in its original form from its establishment until now, is not much to be wondered at. It had many props to support it through that period, which now are decayed, and crumbled away. Through that period, it was felt by all, to be an undecided experiment; now, it is understood to be a successful one. Then, all that sought celebrity and fame, and distinction, expected to find them in the success of that experiment. Their *all* was staked upon it:—their destiny was *inseparably* linked with it. Their ambition aspired to display before an admiring world, a practical demonstration of the truth of a proposition, which had hitherto been considered, at best no better, than problematical; namely, *the capability of a people to govern themselves*. If they succeeded, they were to be immortalized; their names were to be transferred to counties and cities, and rivers and mountains; and to be revered and sung, and toasted through all time. If they failed, they were to be called knaves and fools, and fanatics for a fleeting hour; then to sink and be forgotten. They succeeded. The experiment is successful; and thousands have won their deathless names in making it so. But the game is caught; and I believe it is true, that with the catching, end the pleasures of the chase. This field of glory is harvested, and the crop is already appropriated. But new reapers will arise, and *they*, too, will seek a field. It is to deny, what the history of the world tells us is true, to suppose that men of ambition and talents will not continue to spring up amongst us. And, when they do, they will as naturally seek the gratification of their ruling passion, as others have so done before them. The question then, is, can that gratification be found in supporting and maintaining an edifice that has been erected by others? Most certainly it cannot. Many great and good men sufficiently qualified for any task they should undertake, may ever be found, whose ambition would aspire to nothing beyond a seat in Congress, a gubernatorial or a presidential chair; *but such belong not to the family of the lion, or the tribe of the eagle*. What! think you these places would satisfy an Alexander, a Caesar, or a Napoleon? Never! Towering genius disdains a beaten path. It seeks regions hitherto unexplored. It sees *no distinction* in adding story to story, upon the monuments of fame, erected to the memory of others. It *denies* that it is glory enough to serve under any chief. It *scorns* to tread in the footsteps of *any* predecessor, however illustrious. It thirsts and burns for distinction; and, if possible, it will have it, whether at the expense of emancipating slaves, or enslaving freemen. Is it unreasonable then to expect, that some man possessed of the loftiest genius, coupled with ambition sufficient to push it to its utmost stretch, will at some time, spring up among us? And when such a one does, it will require the people to be united with each other, attached to the government and laws, and generally intelligent, to successfully frustrate his designs.

Distinction will be his paramount object; and although he would as willingly, perhaps more so, acquire it by doing good as harm; yet, that opportunity being past, and nothing left to be done in the way of building up, he would set boldly to the task of pulling down.

Here then, is a probable case, highly dangerous, and such a one as could not have well existed heretofore.

Another reason which *once was*; but which, to the same extent, is *now no more*, has done much in maintaining our institutions thus far. I mean the powerful influence which the interesting scenes of the revolution had upon the *passions* of the people as distinguished from their judgment. By this influence, the jealousy, envy, and avarice, incident to our nature, and so common to a state of peace, prosperity, and conscious strength, were, for the time, in a great measure smothered and rendered inactive; while the deep rooted principles of *hate*, and the powerful motive of *revenge*, instead of being turned against each other, were directed exclusively against the British nation. And thus, from the force of circumstances, the basest principles of our nature, were either made to lie dormant, or to become the active agents in the advancement of the noblest of causes—that of establishing and maintaining civil and religious liberty.

But this state of feeling *must fade, is fading, has faded*, with the circumstances that produced it.

I do not mean to say, that the scenes of the revolution *are now* or *ever will be* entirely forgotten; but that like every thing else, they must fade upon the memory of the world, and grow more and more dim by the lapse of time. In history, we hope, they will be read of, and recounted, so long as the Bible shall be read;—but even granting that they will, their influence *cannot be* what it heretofore has been. Even then, they *cannot be* so universally known, nor so vividly felt, as they were by the generation just gone to rest. At the close of that struggle, nearly every adult male had been a participator in some of its scenes. The consequence was, that of those scenes, in the form of a husband, a father, a son or a brother, a *living history* was to be found in every family—a history bearing the indubitable testimonies of its own authenticity, in the limbs mangled, in the scars of wounds received, in the midst of the very scenes related—a history, too, that could be read and understood alike by all, the wise and the ignorant, the learned and the unlearned. But *those* histories are gone. They *can* be read no more forever. They *were* a fortress of strength; but, what invading foemen could *never do*, the silent artillery of time *has done*; the levelling of its walls. They are gone. They *were* a forest of giant oaks; but the all-resistless hurricane has swept over them, and left only, here and there, a lonely trunk, despoiled of its verdure, shorn of its foliage; unshading and unshaded, to murmur in a few more gentle breezes, and to combat with its mutilated limbs, a few more ruder storms, then to sink, and be no more.

They *were* pillars of the temple of liberty; and now, that they have crumbled away, that temple must fall, unless we, their descendants, supply their places with other pillars, hewn from the solid quarry of sober reason. Passion has helped us; but can do so no more. It will in future be our enemy. Reason, cold, calculating, unimpassioned reason, must furnish all the materials for our future support and defence. Let those materials be molded into *general intelligence, sound morality* and, in particular, a *reverence for the constitution and laws*; and, that we improved to the last; that we remained free to the last; that we revered his name to the last; that, during his long sleep, we permitted no hostile foot to pass over or desecrate his resting place; shall be that which to learn and last trump shall awaken our WASHINGTON.

Upon these let the proud fabric of freedom rest, as the rock of its basis; and as truly as has been said of the only greater institution, *"the gates of hell shall not prevail against it."*

45

United States v. Curtiss-Wright Export Corporation (1936)

Justice Sutherland delivered the opinion of the Court.

On January 27, 1936, an indictment was returned in the court below, the first count of which charges that appellees, beginning with the 29th day of May, 1934, conspired to sell in the United States certain arms of war, namely, fifteen machine guns, to Bolivia, a country then engaged in armed conflict in the Chaco, in violation of the Joint Resolution of Congress approved May 28, 1934, and the provisions of a proclamation issued on the same day by the President of the United States pursuant to authority conferred by section 1 of the resolution. . . . The Joint Resolution follows:

> *Resolved by the Senate and House of Representatives of the United States of America in Congress assembled,* That if the President finds that the prohibition of the sale of arms and munitions of war in the United States to those countries now engaged in armed conflict in the Chaco may contribute to the reestablishment of peace between those countries, and if . . . he makes proclamation to that effect, it shall be unlawful to sell, except under such limitations and exceptions as the President prescribes, any arms or munitions of war in any place in the United States to the countries now engaged in that armed conflict, or to any person, company, or association acting in the interest of either country, until otherwise ordered by the President or by Congress. . . .

The President's proclamation, after reciting the terms of the joint Resolution, declares:

> Now, therefore, I, Franklin D. Roosevelt, President of the United States of America, acting under and by virtue of the authority conferred in me by the said joint resolution of Congress, do hereby declare and proclaim that I have found that the prohibition of the sale of arms and munitions of war in the United States to those countries now engaged in armed conflict in the Chaco may contribute to the reestablishment of peace between these countries . . . and I do hereby admonish all citizens of the United States and every person to abstain from every violation of the provisions of the joint resolution above set forth, hereby made applicable to Bolivia and Paraguay, and I do hereby warn them that all violations of such provisions will be rigorously prosecuted. . . .

From *United States v. Curtiss-Wright Export Corporation*, 299 U.S. 304 (1936).

On November 14, 1935, this proclamation was revoked [by the president]. . . .

Appellees severally demurred. . . [urging] that the Joint Resolution effects an invalid delegation of legislative power to the executive. . . .

It is contended that by the Joint Resolution the going into effect and continued operation of the resolution was conditioned (a) upon the President's judgment as to its beneficial effect upon the reestablishment of peace between the countries engaged in armed conflict in the Chaco; (b) upon the making of a proclamation, which was left to his unfettered discretion, thus constituting an attempted substitution of the President's will for that of Congress; (c) upon the making of a proclamation putting an end to the operation of the resolution, which again was left to the President's unfettered discretion; and (d) further, that the extent of its operation in particular cases was subject to limitation and exception by the President, controlled by no standard. In each of these particulars, appellees urge that Congress abdicated its essential functions and delegated them to the Executive.

Whether, if the Joint Resolution had related solely to internal affairs, it would be open to the challenge that it constituted an unlawful delegation of legislative power to the Executive, we find it unnecessary to determine. The whole aim of the resolution is to affect a situation entirely external to the United States, and falling within the category of foreign affairs. The determination which we are called to make, therefore, is whether the Joint Resolution, as applied to that situation, is vulnerable to attack under the rule that forbids a delegation of the lawmaking power. . . .

It will contribute to the elucidation of the question if we first consider the differences between the powers of the federal government in respect of foreign or external affairs and those in respect of domestic or internal affairs. That there are differences between them, and that these differences are fundamental, may not be doubted.

The two classes of powers are different, both in respect of their origin and their nature. The broad statement that the federal government can exercise no powers except those specifically enumerated in the Constitution, and such implied powers as are necessary and proper to carry into effect the enumerated powers, is categorically true only in respect of our internal affairs. In that field, the primary purpose of the Constitution was to carve from the general mass of legislative powers *then possessed by the states* such portions as it was thought desirable to vest in the federal government, leaving those not included in the enumeration still in the states. That this doctrine applies only to powers which the states had is self-evident. And since the states severally never possessed international powers, such powers could not have been carved from the mass of state powers but obviously were transmitted to the United States from some other source. During the Colonial period, those powers were possessed exclusively by and were entirely under the control of the Crown. By the Declaration of Independence, "the Representatives of the United States of America" declared the United (not the several) Colonies to be free and "independent states," and as such to have "full Power to levy War, conclude Peace, contract Alliances, establish Commerce and to do all other Acts and Things which Independent States may of right do."

As a result of the separation from Great Britain by the colonies, acting as a unit, the powers of external sovereignty passed from the Crown not to the colonies severally, but to the colonies in their collective and corporate capacity as the United States of America. . . .

The Union existed before the Constitution, which was ordained and established among other things to form "a more perfect Union." Prior to that event, it is clear that the Union, declared by the Articles of Confederation to be "perpetual," was the sole possessor of external sovereignty, and in the Union it remained without change save in so far as the Constitution in express terms qualified its exercise. The Framers' Convention was called and exerted its powers upon the irrefutable postulate that though the states were several their people in respect of foreign affairs were one. In that convention, the entire absence of state power to deal with those affairs was thus forcefully stated by Rufus King:

> The states were not "sovereigns" in the sense contended for by some. They did not possess the peculiar features of sovereignty,—they could not make war, nor peace, nor alliances, nor treaties. Considering them as political beings, they were dumb, for they could not speak to any foreign sovereign whatever. They were deaf, for they could not hear any propositions from such sovereign. They had not even the organs or faculties of defence or offence, for they could not of themselves raise troops, or equip vessels, for war.

It results that the investment of the federal government with the powers of external sovereignty did not depend upon the affirmative grants of the Constitution. The powers to declare and wage war, to conclude peace, to make treaties, to maintain diplomatic relations with other sovereignties, if they had never been mentioned in the Constitution, would have vested in the federal government as necessary concomitants of nationality. . . . The power to acquire territory by discovery and occupation, the power to make such international agreements as do not constitute treaties in the constitutional sense, none of which is expressly affirmed by the Constitution, nevertheless exist as inherently inseparable from the conception of nationality. This the court recognized, and in each of the cases cited found the warrant for its conclusions not in the provisions of the Constitution, but in the law of nations. . . .

Not only, as we have shown, is the federal power over external affairs in origin and essential character different from that over internal affairs, but participation in the exercise of the power is significantly limited. In this vast external realm, with its important, complicated, delicate and manifold problems, the President alone has the power to speak or listen as a representative of the nation. He *makes* treaties with the advice and consent of the Senate; but he alone negotiates. Into the field of negotiation the Senate cannot intrude; and Congress itself is powerless to invade it. As Marshall said in his great argument of March 7, 1800, in the House of Representatives, "The President is the sole organ of the nation in its external relations, and its sole representative with foreign nations." The Senate Committee on Foreign Relations at a very early day in our history (February 15, 1816), reported to the Senate, among other things, as follows:

> The President is the constitutional representative of the United States with regard to foreign nations. He manages our concerns with foreign nations and must necessarily be most competent to determine when, how, and upon what subjects negotiation may be urged with the greatest prospect of success. For his conduct he is responsible to the Constitution. The committee considers this responsibility the surest pledge for the faithful discharge of his duty. They think the interference of the Senate in the direction of foreign negotiations calculated to diminish that responsibility and thereby to impair the best security for the national safety. The nature of transactions with foreign nations, moveover, requires caution and unity of design, and their success frequently depends on secrecy and dispatch.

It is important to bear in mind that we are here dealing not alone with an authority vested in the President by an exertion of legislative power, but with such an authority plus the very delicate, plenary and exclusive power of the President as the sole organ of the federal government in the field of international relations—a power which does not require as a basis for its exercise an act of Congress, but which, of course, like every other governmental power, must be exercised in subordination to the applicable provisions of the Constitution. It is quite apparent that if, in the maintenance of our international relations, embarrassment—perhaps serious embarrassment—is to be avoided and success for our aims achieved, congressional legislation which is to be made effective through negotiation and inquiry within the international field must often accord to the President a degree of discretion and freedom from statutory restriction which would not be admissible were domestic affairs alone involved. Moreover, he, not Congress, has the better opportunity of knowing the conditions which prevail in foreign countries, and especially is this true in time of war. He has his confidential sources of information. He has his agents in the form of diplomatic, consular and other officials. Secrecy in respect of information gathered by them may be highly necessary, and the premature disclosure of it productive of harmful results. Indeed, so clearly is this true that the first President refused to accede to a request to lay before the House of Representatives the instructions, correspondence and documents relating to the negotiation of the Jay Treaty—a refusal the wisdom of which was recognized by the House itself and has never since been doubted. In his reply to the request, President Washington said:

> The nature of foreign negotiations requires caution, and their success must often depend on secrecy; and even when brought to a conclusion a full disclosure of all the measures, demands, or eventual concessions which may have been proposed or contemplated would be extremely impolitic; for this might have a pernicious influence on future negotiations, or produce immediate inconveniences, perhaps danger and mischief, in relation to other powers. The necessity of such caution and secrecy was one cogent reason for vesting the power of making treaties in the President, with the advice and consent of the Senate, the principle on which that body was formed confining it to a small number of members. To admit, then, a right in the House of Representatives to demand and to have as a matter of course all the papers respecting a negotiation with a foreign power would be to establish a dangerous precedent.

The marked difference between foreign affairs and domestic affairs in this respect is recognized by both houses of Congress in the very form of their requisitions for information from the executive departments. In the case of every department except the Department of State, the resolution *directs* the official to furnish the information. In the case of the State Department, dealing with foreign affairs, the President is *requested* to furnish the information "if not incompatible with the public interest." A statement that to furnish the information is not compatible with the public interest rarely, if ever, is questioned.

When the President is to be authorized by legislation to act in respect of a matter intended to affect a situation in foreign territory, the legislator properly bears in mind the important consideration that the form of the President's action—or, indeed, whether he shall act at all—may well depend, among other things, upon the nature of the confidential information which he has or may thereafter receive, or upon the effect which his action may have upon our foreign relations. This consideration, in connection with what we have already said on the subject, discloses the unwisdom of requiring Congress in this field of governmental power to lay down narrowly definite standards by which the President is to be governed. . . .

In the light of the foregoing observations, it is evident that this court should not be in haste to apply a general rule which will have the effect of condemning legislation like that under review as constituting an unlawful delegation of legislative power. The principles which justify such legislation find overwhelming support in the unbroken legislative practice which has prevailed almost from the inception of the national government to the present day. . . .

[For instance, t]he Act of June 4, 1794, authorized the President to lay, regulate and revoke embargoes. He was "authorized" whenever, in his opinion, the public safety shall so require, "to lay the embargo upon all ships and vessels in the ports of the United States, including those of foreign nations, under such regulations as the circumstances of the case may require, and to continue or revoke the same, whenever he shall think proper." A prior joint resolution of May 7, 1794, had conferred *unqualified* power on the President to grant clearances, notwithstanding an existing embargo, to ships or vessels belonging to citizens of the United States bound to any port beyond the Cape of Good Hope. . . .

Practically every volume of the United States Statutes contains one or more acts or joint resolutions of Congress authorizing action by the President in respect of subjects affecting foreign relations, which either leave the exercise of the power to his unrestricted judgment, or provide a standard far more general than that which has always been considered requisite with regard to domestic affairs. . . .

The result of holding that the joint resolution here under attack is void and unenforceable as constituting an unlawful delegation of legislative power would be to stamp this multitude of comparable acts and resolutions as likewise invalid. And while this court may not, and should not, hesitate to declare acts of Congress, however many times repeated, to be unconstitutional if beyond all rational doubt it finds them to be so, an impressive array of legislation . . . enacted by nearly every Congress from the beginning of our national existence to the present day, must be given unusual weight in the process of reaching a correct determination of the problem. A legislative practice such as we have here . . . goes a long way in the direction of proving the presence of unassailable ground for the constitutionality of the practice, to be found in the origin and history of the power involved, or in its nature, or in both combined. . . .

We deem it unnecessary to consider, *seriatim*, the several clauses which are said to evidence the unconstitutionality of the Joint Resolution as involving an unlawful delegation of legislative power. It is enough to summarize by saying that, both upon principle and in accordance with precedent, we conclude there is sufficient warrant for the broad discretion vested in the President. . . .

The judgment of the court below must be reversed. . . .

46

Theodore Roosevelt

The "Stewardship Theory" (1913)

The most important factor in getting the right spirit in my Administration, next to the insistence upon courage, honesty, and a genuine democracy of desire to serve the plain people, was my insistence upon the theory that the executive power was limited only by specific restrictions and prohibitions appearing in the Constitution or imposed by the Congress under its Constitutional powers. My view was that every executive officer, and above all every executive officer in high position, was a steward of the people bound actively and affirmatively to do all he could for the people, and not to content himself with the negative merit of keeping his talents undamaged in a napkin. I declined to adopt the view that what was imperatively necessary for the Nation could not be done by the President unless he could find some specific authorization to do it. My belief was that it was not only his right but his duty to do anything that the needs of the Nation demanded unless such action was forbidden by the Constitution or by the laws. Under this interpretation of executive power I did and caused to be done many things not previously done by the President and the heads of the departments. I did not usurp power, but I did greatly broaden the use of executive power. In other words, I acted for the public welfare, I acted for the common well-being of all our people, whenever and in whatever manner was necessary, unless prevented by direct constitutional or legislative prohibition. I did not care a rap for the mere form and show of power; I cared immensely for the use that could be made of the substance. . . .

As to all action of this kind there have long been two schools of political thought, upheld with equal sincerity. The division has not normally been along political, but temperamental, lines. The course I followed, of regarding the executive as subject only to the people, and, under the Constitution, bound to serve the people affirmatively in cases where the Constitution does not explicitly forbid him to render the service, was substantially the course followed by both Andrew Jackson and Abraham Lincoln. Other honorable and well-meaning Presidents, such as James Buchanan, took the opposite

From Theodore Roosevelt, *An Autobiography*. New York: Charles Scribner's Sons, 1913.

and, as it seems to me, narrowly legalistic view that the President is the servant of Congress rather than of the people, and can do nothing, no matter how necessary it be to act, unless the Constitution explicitly commands the action. Most able lawyers who are past middle age take this view, and so do large numbers of well-meaning, respectable citizens. My successor in office [William Howard Taft] took this, the Buchanan, view of the President's powers and duties. . . .

There are many worthy people who reprobate the Buchanan method as a matter of history, but who in actual life reprobate still more strongly the Jackson-Lincoln method when it is put into practice. These persons conscientiously believe that the President should solve every doubt in favor of inaction as against action, that he should construe strictly and narrowly the Constitutional grant of powers both to the National Government, and to the President within the National Government. In addition, however, to the men who conscientiously believe in this course from high, although as I hold misguided, motives, there are many men who affect to believe in it merely because it enables them to attack and to try to hamper, for partisan or personal reasons, an executive whom they dislike. There are other men in whom, especially when they are themselves in office, practical adherence to the Buchanan principle represents not well-thought-out devotion to an unwise course, but simple weakness of character and desire to avoid trouble and responsibility. Unfortunately, in practice it makes little difference which class of ideas actuates the President, who by his action sets a cramping precedent. Whether he is highminded and wrongheaded or merely infirm of purpose, whether he means well feebly or is bound by a mischievous misconception of the powers and duties of the National Government and of the President, the effect of his actions is the same. The President's duty is to act so that he himself and his subordinates shall be able to do efficient work for the people, and this efficient work he and they cannot do if Congress is permitted to undertake the task of making up his mind for him as to how he shall perform what is clearly his sole duty. . . .

The great Anthracite Strike of 1902 left an indelible impress upon the people of the United States. It showed clearly to all wise and far-seeing men that the labor problem in this country had entered upon a new phase. Industry had grown. Great financial corporations, doing a nation-wide and even a world-wide business, had taken the place of the smaller concerns of an earlier time. The old familiar, intimate relations between employer and employee were passing. . . .

[During the strike, the coal industry showed that it] . . . . did not see that both their interests and the interests of the workers must be accommodated, and if need be, subordinated, to the fundamental permanent interests of the whole community. No man and no group of men may so exercise their rights as to deprive the nation of the things which are necessary and vital to the common life. A strike which ties up the coal supplies of a whole section is a strike invested with a public interest.

So great was that public interest in the Coal Strike of 1902, so deeply and strongly did I feel the wave of indignation which swept over the whole country that had I not succeeded in my efforts to induce the operators to listen to reason, I should reluctantly but none the less decisively have taken a step which would have brought down upon my head the execrations of many of "the captains of industry," as well as of sundry "respectable" newspapers who dutifully take their cue from them. As a man should be judged by his intentions as well as by his actions, I will give here the story of the intervention that never happened.

While the coal operators were exulting over the fact that they had "turned down" the miners and the President, there arose in all parts of the country an outburst of wrath so universal that even so naturally conservative a man as Grover Cleveland wrote to me, expressing his sympathy with the course I was following, his indignation at the conduct of the operators, and his hope that I would devise some method of effective action. In my own mind I was already planning effective action; but it was of a very drastic character, and I did not wish to take it until the failure of all other expedients had rendered it necessary. Above all, I did not wish to talk about it until and unless I actually acted. I had definitely determined that somehow or other act I would, that somehow or other the coal famine should be broken. To accomplish this end it was necessary that the mines should be run, and, if I could get no voluntary agreement between the contending sides, that an Arbitration Commission should be appointed which would command such public confidence as to enable me, without too much difficulty, to enforce its terms upon both parties. . . .

Meanwhile the Governor of Pennsylvania had all the Pennsylvania militia in the anthracite region, although without any effect upon the resumption of mining. The method of action upon which I had determined in the last resort was to get the Governor of Pennsylvania to ask me to keep order. Then I would put in the army under the command of some first-rate general. I would instruct this general to keep absolute order, taking any steps whatever that was necessary to prevent interference by the strikers or their sympathizers with men who wanted to work. I would also instruct him to dispossess the operators and run the mines as a receiver until such time as the Commission might make its report, and until I, as President, might issue further orders in view of this report. I had to find a man who possessed the necessary good sense, judgment, and nerve to act in such event. He was ready to hand in the person of Major-General Schofield. I sent for him, telling him that if I had to make use of him it would be because the crisis was only less serious than that of the Civil War, that the action taken would be practically a war measure, and that if I sent him he must act in a purely military capacity under me as commander-in-chief, paying no heed to any authority, judicial or otherwise, except mine. He was a fine fellow—a most respectable-looking old boy, with side whiskers and a black skull-cap, without any of the outward aspect of the conventional military dictator; but in both nerve and judgment he was all right, and he answered quietly that if I gave the order he would take possession of the mines, and would guarantee to open them and to run them without permitting any interference either by the owners or the strikers or anybody else, so long as I told him to stay. I then saw Senator Quay, who, like every other responsible man in high position, was greatly wrought up over the condition of things. I told him that he need be under no alarm as to the problem not being solved, that I was going to make another effort to get the operators and miners to come together, but that I would solve the problem in any event and get coal; that, however, I did not wish to tell him anything of the details of my intention, but merely to have him arrange that whenever I gave the word the Governor of Pennsylvania should request me to intervene; that when this was done I would be responsible for all that followed, and would guarantee that the coal famine would end forthwith. The Senator made no inquiry or comment, and merely told me that he in his turn would guarantee that the Governor would request my intervention the minute I asked that the request be made.

These negotiations were concluded with the utmost secrecy, General Schofield being the only man who knew exactly what my plan was. . . . As I have above outlined, my efforts to bring about an agreement between the operators and miners were finally successful. I was glad not to have to take possession of the mines on my own initiative by means of General Schofield and the regulars. I was all ready to act, and would have done so without the slightest hesitation or a moment's delay if the negotiations had fallen through. And my action would have been entirely effective. But it is never well to take drastic action if the result can be achieved with equal efficiency in less drastic fashion; and, although this was a minor consideration, I was personally saved a good deal of future trouble by being able to avoid this drastic action. At the time I should have been almost unanimously supported. With the famine upon them the people would not have tolerated any conduct that would have thwarted what I was doing. Probably no man in Congress, and no man in the Pennsylvania State Legislature, would have raised his voice against me. Although there would have been plenty of muttering, nothing would have been done to interfere with the solution of the problem which I had devised, *until the solution was accomplished and the problem ceased to be a problem.* Once this was done, and when people were no longer afraid of a coal famine, and began to forget that they ever had been afraid of it, and to be indifferent as regards the consequences to those who put an end to it, then my enemies would have plucked up heart and begun a campaign against me. I doubt if they could have accomplished much anyway, for the only effective remedy against me would have been impeachment, and that they would not have ventured to try. . . .

47

William Howard Taft

Our Chief Magistrate and His Powers (1916)

The constitutional functions of the President seem very broad, and they are. When many speak of his great power, they have in mind that what the President does, goes, like kissing, by favor. I beg of you to believe that the Presidency offers but few opportunities for showing power of this sort. . . . The truth is that great as his powers are, when a President comes to exercise them, he is much more concerned with the limitations upon them than he is affected, like little Jack Horner, by a personal joy over the big personal things he can do. . . .

While the President's powers are broad, the lines of his jurisdiction are as fixed as a written constitution can properly make them. He has tremendous responsibilities. . . .

The widest power and the broadest duty which the President has is conferred and imposed by a clause in section three of article two, providing that "he shall take care that the laws be faithfully executed." This same duty is enforced by the provision that before he enter on the execution of his office, he shall take the following oath or affirmation:

I do solemnly swear or affirm that I will faithfully execute the office of President of the United States, and will to the best of my ability, preserve, protect and defend the Constitution of the United States.

In executing a statute of Congress, through the proper department and the proper subordinate officers, the President's course is as clear, or as doubtful, as the statute. In order that he or his subordinates shall enforce the statute, they must necessarily find out what it means, and on their interpretation of it enforce the law. Statutory construction is practically one of the greatest of executive powers. Some one has said, "Let me make the ballads of the country, and I care not who makes the laws." One might also say, paraphrasing this, "Let any one make the laws of the country, if I can construe them." Of course ultimately where a statute affects private right, it is likely to come before the courts in actual litigation and to put upon the courts the duty of its construction. But there are many statutes that do not affect private right in such a way that they come under the court's interpretation; and in such

From William Howard Taft, *Our Chief Magistrate and His Powers* (New York: Columbia University Press, 1916).

cases Executive interpretation is final. Even where it is not, it is very persuasive with courts who subsequently are obliged to adjudge the meaning of the
statute. . . .

The laws that the President must take care shall be faithfully executed
are not confined to acts of Congress. The treaties of the United States with
other countries are under the Constitution laws of the United States having
the same effect as Congressional enactments, in so far as they are intended to
operate in this way and are in form appropriate. . . .

Nor are the laws of the execution of which the President is to take care,
confined to express Congressional statutes and provisions having force of law
in treaties. The Supreme Court has declared that any obligation inferable
from the Constitution, or any duty of the President or the Attorney-General to be derived from the general code of his duties under the laws of the
United States is a law within the meaning of this phrase. This was decided
in an interesting case from California. Sarah Althea Hill, a resident in California, said she was married to Ex-Senator Sharon of Nevada, and Senator
Sharon said she was not. She brought suit . . . to secure a divorce, with ali-
mony, to be satisfied out of his very large estate. . . . In the Federal Court,
Mr. Justice Field rendered several decisions adverse to Miss Hill's claims.
Meantime, Senator Sharon had died and Miss Hill had married her counsel, Judge Terry. When Justice Field was delivering one of his judgments,
adverse to Mrs. Terry, Judge and Mrs. Terry were in the court-room, and
Mrs. Terry rose and denounced Judge Field and attempted to assault him. . . .
Judge and Mrs. Terry then and frequently thereafter threatened that when
the opportunity came they would kill Judge Field. . . . [N]otice of the threats
was brought to the attention of Attorney-General Miller. He deemed them
serious enough to direct the United States Marshal of California to assign
a deputy to accompany Justice Field when he was traveling upon the circuit the next year in California. After having held court at Los Angeles,
Mr. Justice Field was traveling to San Francisco to hold court there. He
got out of the train at Lathrop, a station near Fresno, to breakfast. At the
same time a train arrived from San Francisco upon which were Judge and
Mrs. Terry. Justice Field had entered the restaurant when the Terrys came
in and saw him. Mrs. Terry at once returned to her sleeping car to secure
a revolver which she had left in her satchel. Judge Terry advanced toward
Judge Field, and as the court found, attacked him from behind. Neagle, the
Deputy United States Marshal, who was protecting Judge Field, rose, called
to Terry that he was an officer, and demanded that he cease his attack. Terry,
as Neagle testified, made a movement as if to draw a weapon, and in defense
of Justice Field Neagle shot twice and killed Terry. Neagle was indicted in
the state court of California for murder for killing Terry. He applied to the
Circuit Court of the United States for a writ of habeas corpus. . . . The state
of California carried the case to the Supreme Court of the United States.

The question was whether in the absence of an express statute giving the President or the Attorney-General of the United States or the United States Marshal the duty and power to protect a United States Judge in the discharge of his duties such protection was an act in pursuance of a law of the United States. The Court [*In Re Neagle*] likened the word "law" to the term "laws" in the constitutional obligation of the President to take care that the laws of the United States be faithfully executed, and Mr. Justice Miller, speaking for the Court, held that the government of the United States, in view of the constitutional provision for the appointment of Judges and the establishment of a system of courts, was under an obligation to protect its Judges from assault by disappointed litigants when those Judges were in the discharge of their official duties, and that such an obligation constituted a law which it was the duty of the President to take care should be faithfully executed. He said, "It would be a great reproach to the system of government of the United States, declared to be within its sphere, sovereign and supreme, if there is to be found within the domain of its powers no means of protecting its Judges in the conscientious and faithful discharge of their duties from malice and hatred of those upon whom their judgments may operate unfavorably.". . . .

The President is the Commander-in-Chief of the army and navy, and the militia when called into the service of the United States. Under this, he can order the army and navy anywhere he will, if the appropriations furnish the means of transportation. . . .

As Commander-in-Chief and in taking care that the laws be faithfully executed. . . . [the president is charged with] maintaining what the Supreme Court had so often decided, that every foot of land within the jurisdiction of the United States, whether in a state or territory, or in the District of Columbia, is territory of the United States upon which the laws of the United States can be executed by the President with all the forces which he has at his lawful command; that there is a peace of the United States, a violation of which consists in forcible resistance to Federal laws. . . .

The true view of the Executive functions is, as I conceive it, that the President can exercise no power which cannot be fairly and reasonably traced to some specific grant of power or justly implied and included within such express grant as proper and necessary to its exercise. Such specific grant must be either in the Federal Constitution or in an act of Congress passed in pursuance thereof. There is no undefined residuum of power which he can exercise because it seems to him to be in the public interest, and there is nothing in the *Neagle* case and its definition of a law of the United States, or in other precedents, warranting such an inference. The grants of Executive power are necessarily in general terms in order not to embarrass the Executive within the field of action plainly marked for him, but his jurisdiction must be justified and vindicated by affirmative constitutional or statutory provision, or it does not exist. There have not been wanting, however, eminent men in high public office holding a different view and who have insisted upon the necessity for an undefined residuum of Executive power in the public interest. . . .

My judgment is that the view of . . . Mr. Roosevelt, ascribing an undefined residuum of power to the President is an unsafe doctrine and that it might lead under emergencies to results of an arbitrary character, doing irremediable injustice to private right. The mainspring of such a view is that the Executive is charged with responsibility for the welfare of all the people in a general way, that he is to play the part of a Universal Providence and set all things right, and that anything that in his judgment will help the people he ought to do, unless he is expressly forbidden not to do it. The wide field of action that this would give to the Executive one can hardly limit. It is enough to say that Mr. Roosevelt has expressly stated how far he thought this principle would justify him in going in respect to the coal famine and the Pennsylvania anthracite strike which he did so much useful work in settling. . . .

The Constitution does give the President wide discretion and great power, and it ought to do so. It calls from him activity and energy to see that within his proper sphere he does what his great responsibilities and opportunities require. He is no figurehead, and it is entirely proper that an energetic and active clear-sighted people, who, when they have work to do, wish it done well, should be willing to rely upon their judgment in selecting their Chief Agent, and having selected him, should entrust to him all the power needed to carry out their governmental purpose, great as it may be. . . .

48

Kevin J. Burns

The Presidency, Political Pragmatism, and Constitutional Principle (2019)

The competing views of presidential power presented by Theodore Roosevelt's *Autobiography* and William Howard Taft's *Our Chief Magistrate and His Powers* are often seen as key representatives of the "functionalist" and "formalist" understandings of the presidency. While Roosevelt tends to eschew careful consideration of the Constitution's limitations, seeing the president as the people's "steward" and insisting "I did not care a rap for the mere *form* and show of power; I cared immensely for the *use* that could be made of the substance," Taft expresses far more concern for constitutional forms, believing "the President can exercise no power which cannot be fairly and reasonably traced to some *specific grant* of power" (emphases added). But these well-known statements—which have often convinced scholars that TR was a strong modern president while Taft was a fastidious legalist unsuited to the presidency—may distract us from the complexities and implications of Roosevelt and Taft's claims. Taft, as I will argue, actually made a principled constitutional argument for a strong and energetic chief executive, a president who was both empowered and restrained by the fundamental law; and Roosevelt's pragmatic political case for presidential stewardship actually unmoored the president from the Constitution, destroying vital legal safeguards.

Admittedly, Roosevelt's argument for an energetic president may be quite appealing at first glance. He argued that the president ought to be a strong national leader, who had not only a right but a duty "to do anything that the needs of the Nation demanded" in order to protect and promote "the public welfare" and "the common well-being of all our people." The president, Roosevelt suggests, ought to view himself as the people's champion; he should use the tremendous powers and influences at his disposal to defend the "plain people" and promote their welfare. Like Andrew Jackson and Abraham Lincoln, TR argues, presidents must act boldly on behalf of the nation. The president may be a gargantuan force for good in the American regime.

Moreover, Roosevelt claimed that the president can take on this enlarged role as the people's "steward" without violating the Constitution or disrupting America's system of separation of powers. The chief executive should take affirmative and energetic action, rather than dithering and hesitating while worrying about "narrowly legalistic" constitutional niceties. Yet TR insists that he never "usurped power" but merely "broadened the use of executive power." The president had the power to serve the people in any way, so long as he did not violate any "specific restrictions and prohibitions" contained either in the Constitution or the laws enacted by Congress. For Roosevelt, the president's powers rely not on specific grants of power, but on omissions—he holds all powers not specifically denied to him.

A close look at this argument reveals serious flaws in TR's understanding of the presidency. Roosevelt insisted that he did not usurp power and claimed he obeyed the constitutional limitations on presidential power—he never violated the "specific restrictions" the Constitution imposes of the chief executive. Yet one would be hard pressed to find any specific restrictions on the president's powers in the Constitution. While it does ordain certain restrictions on presidential selection—the president must be 35 years old and a natural born citizen who has resided in the country for the fourteen years preceding his election—Article II contains not a single specific restriction on the president's actual powers. It is instructive to consider Roosevelt's threat to seize private coal mines and operate them under military rule. Apparently, Roosevelt believed the Constitution would permit such actions since it does not forbid them by explicitly stating "even in an emergency, the president shall not seize private coal mines, nor shall he operate them under the command of a man he himself refers to as a 'military dictator.'"

We might very well ask then: what are the limits on presidential power? Does Roosevelt recognize any? Roosevelt himself suggests that he recognized one key restraint: the president's powers were limited by the people's desires. Thus, although he actually admitted that he could have been impeached for seizing private property, TR believed he would have gotten away with it because "the people would not have tolerated" any attempts to thwart his actions. Elsewhere TR made this populist argument more explicitly, explaining "Whatever I did as president I was able to do only because I had the backing of the people. When on any point I did not have that backing . . . my power vanished." Popular will, the people's opinion of and response to a president's actions, determined the outside boundaries of executive power. Thus, Roosevelt does acknowledge limitations on executive power, but these limits are not *legal*—found in the Constitution or Bill of Rights—but *political*—arising from popular opinion.

If TR's theory is quite democratic, it is also quite dangerous, for it permits the president to ignore the Constitution so long as he maintains popular support for his actions. In 1902, Theodore Roosevelt threatened to use the powers of the presidency to seize coal mines, depriving their owners of property in order (he claimed) to protect the public. Forty years later, in the wake of the Japanese attack on Pearl Harbor, Franklin D. Roosevelt would rely on a similar claim to virtually unlimited presidential power to seize American citizens of Japanese descent and imprison them in detention camps, depriving American citizens of liberty, in order (he claimed) to protect the public. FDR's actions, we should remember, were popular with the people. Presidents like TR and FDR, who unmoor their office from its constitutional limitations, may be servants and "stewards" of the public. At the same time, there is a real risk that they may do harm both to the American people as a whole, by undermining constitutional safeguards, and to specific citizens (Japanese-Americans or coal magnates), by ignoring their rights to liberty and property.

Taft's constitutionalism provides a workable alternative to Roosevelt's "stewardship" theory. Taft understands that the Constitution may create a strong and energetic president, while still maintaining key limitations on his powers. He sees, as he puts it, that the "Constitution does give the President wide discretion and great power" while at the same time ensuring that "the lines of his jurisdiction are as fixed as a written constitution can properly make them." While Roosevelt rejected constitutional limitations because he feared they would unduly hamper the president, Taft recognized that the Constitution may create a president who is powerful enough to protect the people without becoming so powerful that he threatens their safety.

Taft, as we recall, insisted that the president's powers must find their source in the Constitution; all presidential powers must be "fairly and reasonably traced to some specific grant of power or justly implied and included within such express grant as proper and necessary to its exercise." While this argument may seem to impose rigid limitations on the president, Taft makes clear that the Constitution's text, through both specific and implied grants of power, actually guarantees the chief executive expansive powers.

As he argues, the president's greatest powers arise from two duties imposed on him: first, his oath to execute his office and defend the Constitution, and second, his duty to take care that the laws are faithfully executed. The Oath of Office and Take Care clauses, Taft insists, point to the president's "widest power and broadest duty," for by imposing such extensive duties on the president, the Constitution must also grant the president sufficient powers to carry out those duties. Taft essentially creates a Necessary and Proper clause for Article II, insisting that the Constitution guarantees the president sufficient discretion to do whatever he judges is "proper and necessary" to execute the laws, using all of the forces put at his disposal, including the army and navy.

Moreover, Taft believes that the president's duty to execute the law points beyond the mere enforcement of blackletter law. The president is required to enforce not only the statutes created by Congress, but also treaties and the Constitution itself. Most critical is Taft's argument that the president has a duty to use the means at his disposal to protect and maintain the "peace of the United States." This duty to enforce the peace requires the president to protect the workings of the federal government and to guard government officials as they carry out their functions. He must, for example, protect federal officials as they go about their duties and remove obstructions to the delivery of the federal mails—even though neither the Constitution nor federal statutes explicitly impose on the president a duty to use U.S. Marshalls to protect Supreme Court justices or to use the armed forces to break up violent strikes that prevent the Postal Service from operating. If Taft required presidential powers to be traced to specific or implied constitutional grants of power, nevertheless he also recognizes that the Constitution grants the president significant powers and implies a broad field of action for the president.

Roosevelt had embraced a view of the presidency that undermined constitutional limitations in order to free the president from rigid legal restraints on his powers. As TR explained, his theory avoided legalistic interpretations of the Constitution which would force the president to "solve every doubt in favor of inaction" and "construe strictly and narrowly the Constitutional grant of powers." Essentially, TR was afraid of a government that is so limited that it cannot act to serve the people. But in order to avoid this threat, Roosevelt did not argue simply for a powerful president, he argued for an all-powerful president, empowered to do whatever he believed was necessary to serve the nation and provide for its needs. Roosevelt favored strong executive action at the expense of law and constitutional government.

In contrast to Roosevelt, Taft sees that the grant of executive power flows through the Constitution and recognizes real limits on the president, limits that are inherent in constitutional government. He denies the existence of an extra-constitutional "undefined residuum of power" upon which the president can call to serve the public, rejecting TR's claim that the president has power to do anything the Constitution does not forbid. Executive powers, for Taft, must find their source in the Constitution's text and structure—not in vague appeals to the nation's needs or the people's wishes. But for all this, Taft recognized that while the Constitution did limit the president, it also empowered him. He showed that law could be a source of power as well as a restraint on the exercise of power; as a result, he saw that the Constitution—in both its empowering and limiting aspects—may be maintained without crippling the president's ability to act.

Roosevelt sought to unleash executive power from legal limitations, hopefully permitting the president to do great good, but opening the door to abuse. In contrast, Taft proposed a principled argument to explain that the Constitution empowers the president more than it limits him, but nevertheless does impose outside boundaries beyond which the president may not act. Roosevelt believed the president could use any powers at his disposal to attain any end result, so long as that end result was in the service of (what he believed to be) the public good. In contrast, Taft argues that the president may use any forces at his disposal to fulfill his duties under the Constitution, *not* as (TR thought) that the president may use his powers to advance his own understanding of the common good. Roosevelt's theory points to a president who may use unlimited means to reach unlimited "good" ends, while Taft presents a theory of unlimited executive means to attain limited constitutional ends. If Roosevelt's theory offered a high risk, high reward gamble on presidential decency, Taft's argument was far more moderate, but also far safer for the continuance of constitutional government and the rule of law.

49

Youngstown Sheet and Tube Co. v. Sawyer (1952)

Justice Black delivered the opinion of the Court.

We are asked to decide whether the President was acting within his constitutional power when he issued an order directing the Secretary of Commerce to take possession of and operate most of the Nation's steel mills. . . .

The President's power, if any, to issue the order must stem from an act of Congress or from the Constitution itself. There is no statute that expressly authorizes the President to take possession of property as he did here. Nor is there any act of Congress to which our attention has been directed from which such a power can fairly be implied. . . .

Moreover, the use of the seizure technique to solve labor disputes in order to prevent work stoppages was not only unauthorized by any congressional enactment; prior to this controversy, Congress has refused to adopt that method of settling labor disputes. When the Taft-Hartley Act was under consideration in 1947, Congress rejected an amendment which would have authorized such governmental seizures in cases of emergency. . . .

It is clear that if the President had authority to issue the order he did, it must be found in some provisions of the Constitution. And it is not claimed that express constitutional language grants this power to the President. The contention is that presidential power should be implied from the aggregate of his powers under the Constitution. Particular reliance is placed on provisions in Article II which say that "the executive Power shall be vested in a President . . ."; that "he shall take Care that the Laws be faithfully executed"; and that he "shall be Commander in Chief of the Army and Navy of the United States."

The order cannot properly be sustained as an exercise of the President's military power as Commander in Chief of the Armed Forces. The Government attempts to do so by citing a number of cases upholding broad powers in military commanders engaged in day-to-day fighting in a theater of war. Such cases need not concern us here. Even though "theater of war" be an expanding concept, we cannot with faithfulness to our constitutional system hold that the Commander in Chief of the Armed Forces has the ultimate power as such to take possession of private property in order to keep labor

From *Youngstown Sheet & Tube Co. v. Sawyer*, 343 U.S. 579 (1952).

disputes from stopping production. This is a job for the Nation's lawmakers, not for its military authorities.

Nor can the seizure order be sustained because of the several constitutional provisions that grant executive power to the President. In the framework of our Constitution, the President's power to see that the laws are faithfully executed refutes the idea that he is to be a lawmaker. The Constitution limits his functions in the law-making process to the recommending of laws he thinks wise and the vetoing of laws he thinks bad. And the Constitution is neither silent nor equivocal about who shall make laws which the President is to execute. . . .

The President's order does not direct that a congressional policy be executed in a manner prescribed by Congress—it directs that a presidential policy be executed in a manner prescribed by the President. The preamble of the order itself, like that of many statutes, sets out reasons why the President believes certain policies should be adopted, proclaims these policies as rules of conduct to be followed, and again, like a statute, authorizes a government official to promulgate additional rules and regulations consistent with the policy proclaimed and needed to carry that policy into execution. The power of Congress to adopt such public policies as those proclaimed by the order is beyond question. It can authorize the taking of private property for public use. It can make laws regulating the relationships between employers and employees, prescribing rules designed to settle labor disputes, and fixing wages and working conditions in certain fields of our economy. . . .

The Founders of this Nation entrusted the lawmaking power to the Congress alone in both good and bad times. It would do no good to recall the historical events, the fears of power and the hopes for freedom that lay behind their choice. Such a view would but confirm our holding that this seizure order cannot stand. . . .

Chief Justice Vinson, dissenting.

. . . Those who suggest that this is a case involving extraordinary powers should be mindful that these are extraordinary times. A world not yet recovered from the devastation of World War II has been forced to face the threat of another and more terrifying global conflict. . . .

The steel mills were seized for a public use. The power of eminent domain, invoked in this case, is an essential attribute of sovereignty and has long been recognized as a power of the Federal Government. . . .

Admitting that the Government could seize the mills, plaintiffs claim that the implied power of eminent domain can be exercised only under an Act of Congress; under no circumstances, they say, can that power be exercised by the President unless he can point to an express provision in enabling legislation. . . .

Under this view, the President is left powerless at the very moment when the need for action may be most pressing and when no one, other than he, is immediately capable of action. Under this view, he is left powerless because a power not expressly given to Congress is nevertheless found to rest exclusively with Congress. . . .

A review of executive action demonstrates that our Presidents have on many occasions exhibited the leadership contemplated by the Framers when they made the President Commander in Chief, and imposed upon him the trust to "take Care that the Laws be faithfully executed." With or without explicit statutory authorization, Presidents have at such times dealt with national emergencies by acting promptly and resolutely to enforce legislative programs, at least to save those programs until Congress could act. Congress and the courts have responded to such executive initiative with consistent approval. . . .

Jefferson's initiative in the Louisiana Purchase, the Monroe Doctrine, and Jackson's removal of Government deposits from the Bank of the United States further serve to demonstrate by deed what the Framers described by words when they vested the whole of the executive power in the President.

Without declaration of war, President Lincoln took energetic action with the outbreak of the Civil War. He summoned troops and paid them out of the Treasury without appropriation therefor. He proclaimed a naval blockade of the Confederacy and seized ships violating that blockade. Congress, far from denying the validity of these acts, gave them express approval. The most striking action of President Lincoln was the Emancipation Proclamation, issued in aid of the successful prosecution of the Civil War, but wholly without statutory authority.

In an action furnishing a most apt precedent for this case, President Lincoln directed the seizure of rail and telegraph lines leading to Washington without statutory authority. Many months later, Congress recognized and confirmed the power of the President to seize railroads and telegraph lines and provided criminal penalties for interference with Government operation. This Act did not confer on the President any additional powers of seizure. Congress plainly rejected the view that the President's acts had been without legal sanction until ratified by the legislature. Sponsors of the bill declared that its purpose was only to confirm the power which the President already possessed. Opponents insisted a statute authorizing seizure was unnecessary and might even be construed as limiting existing Presidential powers. . . .

[The Chief Justice then cites other examples of the exercise of emergency powers by American Presidents.]

Focusing now on the situation confronting the President on the night of April 8, 1952, we cannot but conclude that the President was performing his duty under the Constitution "to take care that the laws be faithfully executed"—a duty described by President Benjamin Harrison as "the central idea of the office."

The President reported to Congress the morning after the seizure that he acted because a work stoppage in steel production would immediately imperil the safety of the Nation by preventing execution of the legislative programs for procurement of military equipment. And, while a shutdown could be averted by granting the price concessions requested by plaintiffs, granting such concessions would disrupt the price stabilization program also enacted by Congress. Rather than fail to execute either legislative program, the President acted to execute both.

Much of the argument in this case has been directed at straw men. We do not now have before us the case of a President acting solely on the basis of his own notions of the public welfare. Nor is there any question of unlimited executive power in this case. The President himself closed the door to any such claim when he sent his Message to Congress stating his purpose to abide by any action of Congress, whether approving or disapproving his seizure action. Here, the President immediately made sure that Congress was fully informed of the temporary action he had taken only to preserve the legislative programs from destruction until Congress could act.

The absence of a specific statute authorizing seizure of the steel mills as a mode of executing the laws—both the military procurement program and the anti-inflation program—has not until today been thought to prevent the President from executing the laws. Unlike an administrative commission confined to the enforcement of the statute under which it was created, or the head of a department when administering a particular statute, the President is a constitutional officer charged with taking care that a "mass of legislation" be executed. Flexibility as to mode of execution to meet critical situations is a matter of practical necessity. . . .

50

Korematsu v. United States (1944)

Justice Black delivered the opinion of the Court.

The petitioner, an American citizen of Japanese descent, was convicted in the federal district court for remaining in San Leandro, California, a "Military Area," contrary to Civilian Exclusion Order No. 34 of

From *Korematsu v. United States*, 323 U.S. 214 (1944).

the Commanding General of the Western Command, U.S. Army, which directed that after May 9, 1942, all persons of Japanese ancestry should be excluded from that area. No question was raised as to petitioner's loyalty to the United States. The Circuit Court of Appeals affirmed, and the importance of the constitutional question involved caused us to grant certiorari.

It should be noted, to begin with, that all legal restrictions which curtail the civil rights of a single racial group are immediately suspect. That is not to say that all such restrictions are unconstitutional. It is to say that courts must subject them to the most rigid scrutiny. Pressing public necessity may sometimes justify the existence of such restrictions; racial antagonism never can.

In the instant case prosecution of the petitioner was begun by information charging violation of an Act of Congress, of March 21, 1942, which provides that "whoever shall enter, remain in, leave, or commit any act in any military area or military zone prescribed, under the authority of an Executive order of the President, by Secretary of War, or by any military commander designated by the Secretary of War, contrary to the restrictions applicable to any such area or zone or contrary to the order of the Secretary of War or any such military commander, shall . . . be guilty of a misdemeanor and upon conviction shall be liable to a fine of not to exceed $5,000 or to imprisonment for not more than one year, or both, for each offense."

Exclusion Order No. 34, which the petitioner knowingly and admittedly violated was one of a number of military orders and proclamations, all of which were substantially based upon Executive Order No. 9066. That order, issued after we were at war with Japan, declared that "the successful prosecution of the war requires every possible protection against espionage and against sabotage to national-defense material, national-defense premises, and national-defense utilities. . . .

One of the series of orders and proclamations, a curfew order, which like the exclusion order here was promulgated pursuant to Executive Order 9066, subjected all persons of Japanese ancestry in prescribed West Coast military areas to remain in their residences from 8 P.M. to 6 A.M.. As is the case with the exclusion order here, that prior curfew order was designed as a "protection against espionage and against sabotage." In *Kiyoshi Hirabayashi v. United States,* we sustained a conviction obtained for violation of the curfew order. The *Hirabayashi* conviction and this one thus rest on the same 1942 Congressional Act and the same basic executive and military orders, all of which orders were aimed at the twin dangers of espionage and sabotage. . . .

In the light of the principles we announced in the *Hirabayashi* case, we are unable to conclude that it was beyond the war power of Congress and the Executive to exclude those of Japanese ancestry from the West Coast war area at the time they did. True, exclusion from the area in which one's home is located is a far greater deprivation than constant confinement to the home from 8 P.M. to 6 A.M.. Nothing short of apprehension by the proper military authorities of the gravest imminent danger to the public safety can constitutionally justify either. But exclusion from a threatened area, no less than curfew, has a definite and close relationship to the prevention of espionage and sabotage. The military authorities, charged with the primary responsibility of defending our shores, concluded that curfew provided inadequate protection and ordered exclusion. They did so, as pointed out in our *Hirabayashi* opinion, in accordance with Congressional authority to the military to say who should, and who should not, remain in the threatened areas.

In this case the petitioner challenges the assumptions upon which we rested our conclusions in the *Hirabayashi* case. He also urges that by May 1942, when Order No. 34 was promulgated, all danger of Japanese invasion of the West Coast had disappeared. After careful consideration of these contentions we are compelled to reject them.

Here, as in the *Hirabayashi* case, "we cannot reject as unfounded the judgment of the military authorities and of Congress that there were disloyal members of that population, whose number and strength could not be precisely and quickly ascertained. We cannot say that the war-making branches of the Government did not have ground for believing that in a critical hour such persons could not readily be isolated and separately dealt with, and constituted a menace to the national defense and safety, which demanded that prompt and adequate measures be taken to guard against it."

Like curfew, exclusion of those of Japanese origin was deemed necessary because of the presence of an unascertained number of disloyal members of the group, most of whom we have no doubt were loyal to this country. It was because we could not reject the finding of the military authorities that it was impossible to bring about an immediate segregation of the disloyal from the loyal that we sustained the validity of the curfew order as applying to the whole group. In the instant case, temporary exclusion of the entire group was rested by the military on the same ground. The judgment that exclusion of the whole group was for the same reason a military imperative answers the contention that the exclusion was in the nature of group punishment based on antagonism to those of Japanese origin. That there were members of the group who retained loyalties to Japan has been confirmed by investigations made subsequent to the exclusion. Approximately five thousand American citizens of Japanese ancestry refused to swear unqualified allegiance to the United States and to renounce allegiance to the Japanese Emperor, and several thousand evacuees requested repatriation to Japan.

We uphold the exclusion order as of the time it was made and when the petitioner violated it. In doing so, we are not unmindful of the hardships imposed by it upon a large group of American citizens. But hardships are part of war. . . . Compulsory exclusion of large groups of citizens from their homes, except under circumstances of direct emergency and peril, is inconsistent with our basic governmental institutions. But when under conditions of modern warfare our shores are threatened by hostile forces, the power to protect must be commensurate with the threatened danger. . . .

It is said that we are dealing here with the case of imprisonment of a citizen in a concentration camp solely because of his ancestry, without evidence or inquiry concerning his loyalty and good disposition towards the United States. Our task would be simple, our duty clear, were this a case involving the imprisonment of a loyal citizen in a concentration camp because of racial prejudice. Regardless of the true nature of the assembly and relocation centers—and we deem it unjustifiable to call them concentration camps with all the ugly connotations that term implies—we are dealing specifically with nothing but an exclusion order. To cast this case into outlines of racial prejudice, without reference to the real military dangers which were presented, merely confuses the issue. Korematsu was not excluded from the Military Area because of hostility to him or his race. He was excluded because we are at war with the Japanese Empire, because the properly constituted military authorities feared an invasion of our West Coast and felt constrained to take proper security measures, because they decided that the military urgency of the situation demanded that all citizens of Japanese ancestry be segregated from the West Coast temporarily, and finally, because Congress, reposing its confidence in this time of war in our military leaders—as inevitably it must—determined that they should have the power to do just this. There was evidence of disloyalty on the part of some, the military authorities considered that the need for action was great, and time was short. We cannot—by availing ourselves of the calm perspective of hindsight—now say at that time these actions were unjustified.

Affirmed.

Justice Frankfurter, concurring.

. . . I join in the opinion of the Court, but should like to add a few words of my own.

The provisions of the Constitution which confer on the Congress and the President powers to enable this country to wage war are as much part of the Constitution as provisions looking to a nation at peace. And we have had recent occasion to quote approvingly the statement of former Chief Justice Hughes that the war power of the Government is "the power to wage war successfully." Therefore, the validity of action under the war power must be judged wholly in the context of war. That action is not to be stigmatized as lawless because like action in times of peace would be lawless. To talk about a military order that expresses an allowable judgment of war needs by those entrusted with the duty of conducting war as "an unconstitutional order" is to suffuse a part of the Constitution with an atmosphere of unconstitutionality. The respective spheres of action of military authorities and of judges are of course very different. But within their sphere, military authorities are no more outside the bounds of obedience to the Constitution than are judges within theirs. . . . To recognize that military orders are "reasonably expedient military precautions" in time of war and yet to deny them constitutional legitimacy makes of the Constitution an instrument for dialectic subtleties not reasonably to be attributed to the hardheaded Framers, of whom a majority had had actual participation in war. If a military order such as that under review does not transcend the means appropriate for conducting war, such action by the military is as constitutional as would be any authorized action by the Interstate Commerce Commission within the limits of the constitutional power to regulate commerce. And being an exercise of the war power explicitly granted by the Constitution for safeguarding the national life by prosecuting war effectively, I find nothing in the Constitution which denies to Congress the power to enforce such a valid military order by making its violation an offense triable in the civil courts. To find that the Constitution does not forbid the military measures now complained of does not carry with it approval of that which Congress and the Executive did. That is their business, not ours.

Justice Murphy, dissenting.

This exclusion of "all persons of Japanese ancestry, both alien and nonalien," from the Pacific Coast area on a plea of military necessity in the absence of martial law ought not to be approved. Such exclusion goes over "the very brink of constitutional power" and falls into the ugly abyss of racism.

In dealing with matters relating to the prosecution and progress of a war, we must accord great respect and consideration to the judgments of the military authorities who are on the scene and who have full knowledge of the military facts. The scope of their discretion must, as a matter of necessity and common sense, be wide. And their judgments ought not to be overruled lightly by those whose training and duties ill-equip them to deal intelligently with matters, so vital to the physical security of the nation.

At the same time, however, it is essential that there be definite limits to military discretion, especially where martial law has not been declared. Individuals must not be left impoverished of their constitutional rights on a plea of military necessity that has neither substance nor support. Thus, like other claims conflicting with the asserted constitutional rights of the individual, the military claim must subject itself to the judicial process. . . .

The judicial test of whether the Government, on a plea of military necessity, can validly deprive an individual of any of his constitutional rights is whether the deprivation is reasonably related to a public danger that is so "immediate, imminent, and impending" as not to admit of delay and not to permit the intervention of ordinary constitutional processes to alleviate the danger. Civilian Exclusion Order No. 34, banishing from a prescribed area of the Pacific Coast "all persons of Japanese ancestry, both alien and nonalien," clearly does not meet that test. Being an obvious racial discrimination, the order deprives all those within its scope of the equal protection of the laws as guaranteed by the Fifth Amendment. It further deprives these individuals of their constitutional rights to live and work where they will, to establish a home where they choose and to move about freely. In excommunicating them without benefit of hearings, this order also deprives them of all their constitutional rights to procedural due process. Yet no reasonable relation to an "immediate, imminent, and impending" public danger is evident to support this racial restriction which is one of the most sweeping and complete deprivations of constitutional rights in the history of this nation in the absence of martial law.

It must be conceded that the military and naval situation in the spring of 1942 was such as to generate a very real fear of invasion of the Pacific Coast, accompanied by fears of sabotage and espionage in that area. . . . In adjudging the military action taken in light of the then apparent dangers, we must not erect too high or too meticulous standards; it is necessary only that the action have some reasonable relation to the removal of the dangers of invasion, sabotage and espionage. But the exclusion, either temporarily or permanently, of all persons with Japanese blood in their veins has no such reasonable relation. And that relation is lacking because the exclusion order necessarily must rely for its reasonableness upon the assumption that *all* persons of Japanese ancestry may have a dangerous tendency to commit sabotage and espionage and to aid our Japanese enemy in other ways. It is difficult to believe that reason, logic or experience could be marshalled in support of such an assumption.

That this forced exclusion was the result in good measure of this erroneous assumption of racial guilt rather than bona fide military necessity is evidenced by the Commanding General's Final Report on the evacuation from the Pacific Coast area. In it he refers to all individuals of Japanese descent as "subversive," as belonging to "an enemy race" whose "racial strains are undiluted," and as constituting "over 112,000 potential enemies . . . at large today" along the Pacific Coast. In support of this blanket condemnation of all persons of Japanese descent, however, no reliable evidence is cited to show that such individuals were generally disloyal, or had generally so conducted themselves in this area as to constitute a special menace to defense installations or war industries, or had otherwise by their behavior furnished reasonable ground for their exclusion as a group.

Justification for the exclusion is sought, instead, mainly upon questionable racial and sociological grounds not within the realm of expert military judgment, supplemented by certain semi-military conclusions drawn from an unwarranted use of circumstantial evidence. Individuals of Japanese ancestry are condemned because they are said to be "a large, unassimilated, tightly knit racial group, bound to an enemy nation by strong ties of race, culture, custom and religion." They are claimed to be given to "emperor worshipping ceremonies" and to "dual citizenship." . . . It is intimated that many of these individuals deliberately resided "adjacent to strategic points," thus enabling them "to carry into execution a tremendous program of sabotage on a mass scale should any considerable number of them have been inclined to do so." The need for protective custody is also asserted. The report refers without identity to "numerous incidents of violence" as well as to other admittedly unverified or cumulative incidents. From this, plus certain other events not shown to have been connected with the Japanese Americans, it is concluded that the "situation was fraught with danger to the Japanese population itself" and that the general public "was ready to take matters into its own hands." Finally, it is intimated, though not directly charged or proved, that persons of Japanese ancestry were responsible for three minor isolated shellings and bombings of the Pacific Coast area, as well as for unidentified radio transmissions and night signalling.

The main reasons relied upon by those responsible for the forced evacuation, therefore, do not prove a reasonable relation between the group characteristics of Japanese Americans and the dangers of invasion, sabotage and espionage. The reasons appear, instead, to be largely an accumulation of much of the misinformation, half-truths and insinuations that for years have been directed against Japanese Americans by people with racial and economic prejudices—the same people who have been among the foremost advocates of the evacuation. A military judgment based upon such racial and sociological considerations is not entitled to the great weight ordinarily given the judgments based upon strictly military considerations. . . .

The military necessity which is essential to the validity of the evacuation order thus resolves itself into a few intimations that certain individuals actively aided the enemy, from which it is inferred that the entire group of Japanese Americans could not be trusted to be or remain loyal to the United States. No one denies, of course, that there were some disloyal persons of Japanese descent on the Pacific Coast who did all in their power to aid their ancestral land. Similar disloyal activities have been engaged in by many persons of German, Italian and even more pioneer stock in our country. But to infer that examples of individual disloyalty prove group disloyalty and justify discriminatory action against the entire group is to deny that under our system of law individual guilt is the sole basis for deprivation of rights. . . .

No adequate reason is given for the failure to treat these Japanese Americans on an individual basis by holding investigations and hearings to separate the loyal from the disloyal, as was done in the case of persons of German and Italian ancestry. It is asserted merely that the loyalties of this group "were unknown and time was of the essence." Yet nearly four months elapsed after Pearl Harbor before the first exclusion order was issued; nearly eight months went by until the last order was issued; and the last of these "subversive" persons was not actually removed until almost eleven months had elapsed. Leisure and deliberation seem to have been more of the essence than speed. And the fact that conditions were not such as to warrant a declaration of martial law adds strength to the belief that the factors of time and military necessity were not as urgent as they have been represented to be.

. . . Nor is there any denial of the fact that not one person of Japanese ancestry was accused or convicted of espionage or sabotage after Pearl Harbor while they were still free, a fact which is some evidence of the loyalty of the vast majority of these individuals and of the effectiveness of the established methods of combatting these evils. It seems incredible that under these circumstances it would have been impossible to hold loyalty hearings for the mere 112,000 persons involved—or at least for the 70,000 American citizens—especially when a large part of this number represented children and elderly men and women. . . .

I dissent, therefore, from this legalization of racism. . . .

Justice Jackson, dissenting.

. . . [T]he "law" which this prisoner is convicted of disregarding is not found in an act of Congress, but in a military order. . . . And it is said that if the military commander had reasonable military grounds for promulgating the orders, they are constitutional and become law, and the Court is required to enforce them. There are several reasons why I cannot subscribe to this doctrine.

It would be impracticable and dangerous idealism to expect or insist that each specific military command in an area of probable operations will conform to conventional tests of constitutionality. When an area is so beset that it must be put under military control at all, the paramount consideration is that its measures be successful, rather than legal. The armed services must protect a society, not merely its Constitution. . . . No court can require such a commander in such circumstances to act as a reasonable man; he may be unreasonably cautious and exacting. Perhaps he should be. But a commander in temporarily focusing the life of a community on defense is carrying out a military program; he is not making law in the sense the courts know the term. He issues orders, and they may have a certain authority as military commands, although they may be very bad as constitutional law.

But if we cannot confine military expedients by the Constitution, neither would I distort the Constitution to approve all that the military may deem expedient. That is what the Court appears to be doing, whether consciously or not. I cannot say, from any evidence before me, that the orders of General DeWitt were not reasonably expedient military precautions, nor could I say that they were. But even if they were permissible military procedures, I deny that it follows that they are constitutional. If, as the Court holds, it does follow, then we may as well say that any military order will be constitutional and have done with it. . . .

In the very nature of things military decisions are not susceptible of intelligent judicial appraisal. They do not pretend to rest on evidence, but are made on information that often would not be admissible and on assumptions that could not be proved. Information in support of an order could not be disclosed to courts without danger that it would reach the enemy. Neither can courts act on communications made in confidence. Hence courts can never have any real alternative to accepting the mere declaration of the authority that issued the order that it was reasonably necessary from a military viewpoint.

Much is said of the danger to liberty from the Army program for deporting and detaining these citizens of Japanese extraction. But a judicial construction of the due process clause that will sustain this order is a far more subtle blow to liberty than the promulgation of the order itself. A military order, however unconstitutional, is not apt to last longer than the military emergency. Even during that period a succeeding commander may revoke it all. But once a judicial opinion rationalizes such an order to show that it conforms to the Constitution, or rather rationalizes the Constitution to show that the Constitution sanctions such an order, the Court for all time has validated the principle of racial discrimination in criminal procedure and of transplanting American citizens. The principle then lies about like a loaded weapon ready for the hand of any authority that can bring forward a plausible claim of an urgent need. Every repetition imbeds that principle more deeply in our law and thinking and expands it to new purposes. All who observe the work of courts are familiar with what Judge Cardozo described as "the tendency of a principle to expand itself to the limit of its logic." A military commander may overstep the bounds of constitutionality, and it is an incident. But if we review and approve, that passing incident becomes the doctrine of the Constitution. There it has a generative power of its own, and all that it creates will be in its own image. . . .

I should hold that a civil court cannot be made to enforce an order which violates constitutional limitations even if it is a reasonable exercise of military authority. The courts can exercise only the judicial power, can apply only law, and must abide by the Constitution, or they cease to be civil courts and become instruments of military policy.

Of course the existence of a military power resting on force, so vagrant, so centralized, so necessarily heedless of the individual, is an inherent threat to liberty. But I would not lead people to rely on this Court for a review that seems to me wholly delusive. The military reasonableness of these orders can only be determined by military superiors. If the people ever let command of the war power fall into irresponsible and unscrupulous hands, the courts wield no power equal to its restraint. The chief restraint upon those who command the physical forces of the country, in the future as in the past, must be their responsibility to the political judgments of their contemporaries and to the moral judgments of history.

My duties as justice as I see them do not require me to make a military judgment as to whether General DeWitt's evacuation and detention program was a reasonable military necessity. I do not suggest that the courts should have attempted to interfere with the Army in carrying out its task. But I do not think they may be asked to execute a military expedient that has no place in law under the Constitution. I would reverse the judgment and discharge the prisoner.

51

Abraham Lincoln

On the Suspension of the Writ of Habeas Corpus (1863)

Hon Erastus Corning and others*

Gentlemen Your letter of May 19th. inclosing the resolutions of a public meeting held at Albany, New York on the 16th of the same month, was
received several days ago.

The resolutions, as I understand them, are resolvable into two
propositions—first, the expression of a purpose to sustain the cause of

From *The Collected Works of Abraham Lincoln*, Vol. VI, Rutgers University Press,
1953.

---

*On June 30, Corning and others replied: ". . . We have carefully considered the
grounds on which your pretensions to more than legal authority are claimed to rest;
and if we do not misinterpret the misty and clouded forms of expression in which
those pretensions are set forth, your meaning is that while the rights of the citizen
are protected by the Constitution in time of peace, they are suspended or lost in
time of war, or when invasion or rebellion exist. You do not, like many others in
whose minds, reason and love of regulated liberty seem to be overthrown by the
excitements of the hour, attempt to base this conclusion upon a supposed military
necessity existing outside of and transcending the Constitution, a military necessity
behind which the Constitution itself disappears in a total eclipse. We do not find this
gigantic and monstrous heresy put forth in your plea for absolute power, but we do
find another equally subversive of liberty and law, and quite as certainly tending to
the establishment of despotism. Your claim to have found not outside, but within the
Constitution, a principle or germ of arbitrary power, which in time of war expands at
once into an absolute sovereignty, wielded by one man; so that liberty perished, or
is dependent on his will, his discretion or his caprice. This extraordinary doctrine,
you claim to derive wholly from that clause of the Constitution, which, in case of
invasion or rebellion, permits the writ of habeas corpus to be suspended. Upon this
ground your whole argument is based.

"You must permit us, to say to you with all due respect, but with the earnest-
ness demanded by the occasion, that the American people will never acquiese in
this doctrine. . . ." The Robert Todd Lincoln Collection of the Papers of Abraham
Lincoln, Library of Congress.

the Union, to secure peace through victory, and to support the administration in every constitutional, and lawful measure to suppress the rebellion; and secondly, a declaration of censure upon the administration for supposed unconstitutional action such as the making of military arrests.

And, from the two propositions a third is deduced, which is, that the gentlemen composing the meeting are resolved on doing their part to maintain our common government and country, despite the folly or wickedness, as they may conceive, of any administration. This position is eminently patriotic, and as such, I thank the meeting, and congratulate the nation for it. My own purpose is the same; so that the meeting and myself have a common object, and can have no difference, except in the choice of means or measures, for effecting that object.

And here I ought to close this paper, and would close it, if there were no apprehension that more injurious consequences, than any merely personal to myself, might follow the censures systematically cast upon me for doing what, in my view of duty, I could not forbear. The resolutions promise to support me in every constitutional and lawful measure to suppress the rebellion; and I have not knowingly employed, nor shall knowingly employ, any other. But the meeting, by their resolutions, assert and argue, that certain military arrests and proceedings following them for which I am ultimately responsible, are unconstitutional. I think they are not. The resolutions quote from the constitution, the definition of treason; and also the limiting safeguards and guarantees therein provided for the citizen, on trials for treason, and on his being held to answer for capital or otherwise infamous crimes, and, in criminal prosecutions, his right to a speedy and public trial by an impartial jury. They proceed to resolve "That these safeguards of the rights of the citizen against the pretentions of arbitrary power, were intended more *especially* for his protection in times of civil commotion." And, apparantly, to demonstrate the proposition, the resolutions proceed "They were secured substantially to the English people, *after* years of protracted civil war, and were adopted into our constitution at the *close* of the revolution." Would not the demonstration have been better, if it could have been truly said that these safe-guards had been adopted, and applied *during* the civil wars and *during* our revolution, instead of *after* the one, and at the *close* of the other. I too am devotedly for them *after* civil war, and *before* civil war, and at all times "except when, in cases of Rebellion or Invasion, the public Safety may require" their suspension. The resolutions proceed to tell us that these safeguards "have stood the test of seventy-six years of trial, under our republican system, under circumstances which show that while they constitute the foundation of all free government, they are the elements of the enduring stability of the Republic." No one denies that they have so stood the test up to the beginning of the present rebellion if we except a certain matter at New Orleans hereafter to be mentioned; nor does anyone question that they will stand the same test much longer after the rebellion closes. But these provisions of the constitution have no application to the case we have in hand, because the arrests complained of were not made for treason—that is, not for *the* treason defined in the constitution, and upon the conviction of which, the punishment is death—; nor yet were they made to hold persons to answer for any capital, or otherwise infamous crimes; nor were the proceedings following, in any constitutional or legal sense, "criminal prosecutions." The arrests were made on totally different grounds, and the proceedings following, accorded with the grounds of the arrests. Let us consider the real case with which we are dealing, and apply to it the parts of the constitution plainly made for such cases.

Prior to my installation here it had been inculcated that any State had a lawful right to secede from the national Union; and that it would be expedient to exercise the right, whenever the devotees of the doctrine should fail to elect a President to their own liking. I was elected contrary to their liking; and accordingly, so far as it was legally possible, they had taken seven states out of the Union, had seized many of the United States' Forts, and had fired upon the United States' Flag, all before I was inaugurated; and, of course, before I had done any official act whatever. The rebellion, thus began, soon ran into the present civil war; and, in certain respects, it began on very unequal terms between the parties. The insurgents had been preparing for it more than thirty years, while the government had taken no steps to resist them. The former had carefully considered all the means which could be turned to their account. It undoubtedly was a well pondered reliance with them that in their own unrestricted effort to destroy Union, constitution, and law, all together, the government would, in great degree, be restrained by the same constitution and law, from arresting their progress. Their sympathizers pervaded all departments of the government, and nearly all communities of the people. From this material, under cover of "Liberty of speech" "Liberty of the press" and *"Habeas corpus"* they hoped to keep on foot amongst us a most efficient corps of spies, informers, suppliers, and aiders and abettors of their cause in a thousand ways. They knew that in times such as they were inaugurating, by the constitution itself, the "Habeas corpus" might be suspended; but they also knew they had friends who would make a question as to *who* was to suspend it; meanwhile their spies and others might remain at large to help on their cause. Or if, as has happened, the executive should suspend the writ, without ruinous waste of time, instances of arresting innocent persons might occur, as are always likely to occur in such cases; and then a clamor could be raised in regard to this, which might be, at least, of some service to the insurgent cause. It needed no very keen perception to discover this part of the enemies' programme, so soon as by open hostilities their machinery was fairly put in motion. Yet, thoroughly imbued with a reverence for the guaranteed rights of individuals, I was slow to adopt the strong measures, which by degrees I have been forced to regard as being within the exceptions of the constitution, and as indispensable to the public Safety. Nothing is better known to history than that courts of justice are utterly incompetent to such cases. Civil courts are organized chiefly for trials of individuals, or, at most, a few individuals acting in concert; and this in quiet times, and on charges of crimes well defined in the law. Even in times of peace, bands of horse-thieves and robbers frequently grow too numerous and powerful for the ordinary courts of justice. But what comparison, in numbers, have such bands ever borne to the insurgent sympathizers even in many of the loyal states? Again, a jury too frequently have at least one member, more ready to hang the panel than to hang the traitor. And yet again, he who dissuades one man from volunteering, or induces one soldier to desert, weakens the Union cause as much as he who kills a union soldier in battle. Yet this dissuasion, or inducement, may be so conducted as to be no defined crime of which any civil court would take cognizance.

Ours is a case of Rebellion—so called by the resolutions before me—in fact, a clear, flagrant, and gigantic case of Rebellion; and the provision of the constitution that "The privilege of the writ of Habeas Corpus shall not be suspended, unless when in cases of Rebellion or Invasion, the public Safety may require it" is *the* provision which specially applies to our present case. This provision plainly attests the understanding of those who made the constitution that ordinary courts of justice are inadequate to "cases of Rebellion"—attests their purpose that in such cases, men may be held in custody whom the courts acting on ordinary rules, would discharge. Habeas Corpus does not discharge men who are proved to be guilty of defined crime; and its suspension is allowed by the constitution on purpose that, men may be arrested and held, who cannot be proved to be guilty of defined crime, "when, in cases of Rebellion or Invasion the public Safety may require it." This is precisely our present case—a case of Rebellion, wherein the public Safety does require the suspension. Indeed, arrests by process of courts, and arrests in cases of rebellion, do not proceed altogether upon the same basis. The former is directed at the small percentage of ordinary and continuous perpetration of crime; while the latter is directed at sudden and extensive uprisings against the government, which, at most, will succeed or fail, in no great length of time. In the latter case, arrests are made, not so much for what has been done, as for what probably would be done. The latter is more for the preventive, and less for the vindictive, than the former. In such cases the purposes of men are much more easily understood, than in cases of ordinary crime. The man who stands by and says nothing, when the peril of his government is discussed, cannot be misunderstood. If not hindered, he is sure to help the enemy. Much more, if he talks ambiguously—talks for his country with "buts" and "ifs" and "ands." Of how little value the constitutional provision I have quoted will be rendered, if arrests shall never be made until defined crimes shall have been committed, may be illustrated by a few notable examples. Gen. John C. Breckenridge, Gen. Robert E. Lee, Gen. Joseph E. Johnston, Gen. John B. Magruder, Gen. William B. Preston, Gen. Simon B. Buckner, and Commodore [Franklin] Buchanan, now occupying the very highest places in the rebel war service, were all within the power of the government since the rebellion began, and were nearly as well known to be traitors then as now. Unquestionably if we had seized and held them, the insurgent cause would be much weaker. But no one of them had then committed any crime defined in the law. Every one of them if arrested would have been discharged on Habeas Corpus, were the writ allowed to operate. In view of these and similar cases, I think the time not unlikely to come when I shall be blamed for having made too few arrests rather than too many.

By the third resolution the meeting indicate their opinion that military arrests may be constitutional in localities where rebellion actually exists; but that such arrests are unconstitutional in localities where rebellion, or insurrection, does not actually exist. They insist that such arrests shall not be made "outside of the lines of necessary military occupation, and the scenes of insurrection." Inasmuch, however, as the constitution itself makes no such distinction, I am unable to believe that there is any such constitutional distinction. I concede that the class of arrests complained of, can be constitutional only when, in cases of Rebellion or Invasion, the public Safety may require them; and I insist that in such cases, they are constitutional *wherever* the public safety does require them—as well in places to which they may prevent the rebellion extending, as in those where it may be already prevailing—as well where they may restrain mischievous interference with the raising and supplying of armies, to suppress the rebellion, as where the rebellion may actually be—as well where they may restrain the enticing men out of the army, as where they would prevent mutiny in the army—equally constitutional at all places where they will conduce to the public Safety, as against the dangers of Rebellion or Invasion.

Take the particular case mentioned by the meeting. They assert in substance that Mr. Vallandigham was by a military commander, seized and tried "for no other reason than words addressed to a public meeting, in criticism of the course of the administration, and in condemnation of the military orders of that general." Now, if there be no mistake about this—if this assertion is the truth and the whole truth—if there was no other reason for the arrest, then I concede that the arrest was wrong. But the arrest, as I understand, was made for a very different reason. Mr. Vallandigham avows his hostility to the war on the part of the Union; and his arrest was made because he was laboring, with some effect, to prevent the raising of troops, to encourage desertions from the army, and to leave the rebellion without an adequate military force to suppress it. He was not arrested because he was damaging the political prospects of the administration, or the personal interests of the commanding general; but because he was damaging the army, upon the existence, and vigor of which, the life of the nation depends. He was warring upon the military; and this gave the military constitutional jurisdiction to lay hands upon him. If Mr. Vallandigham was not damaging the military power of the country, then his arrest was made on mistake of fact, which I would be glad to correct, on reasonably satisfactory evidence.

I understand the meeting, whose resolutions I am considering, to be in favor of suppressing the rebellion by military force—by armies. Long experience has shown that armies cannot be maintained unless desertion shall be punished by the severe penalty of death. The case requires, and the law and the constitution, sanction this punishment. Must I shoot a simple-minded soldier boy who deserts, while I must not touch a hair of a wiley agitator who induces him to desert? This is none the less injurious when effected by getting a father, or brother, or friend, into a public meeting, and there working upon his feelings, till he is persuaded to write the soldier boy, that he is fighting in a bad cause, for a wicked administration of a contemptible government, too weak to arrest and punish him if he shall desert. I think that in such a case, to silence the agitator, and save the boy, is not only constitutional, but, withal, a great mercy.

If I be wrong on this question of constitutional power, my error lies in believing that certain proceedings are constitutional when, in cases of rebellion or Invasion, the public Safety requires them, which would not be constitutional when, in absence of rebellion or invasion, the public Safety does not require them—in other words, that the constitution is not in its application in all respects the same, in cases of Rebellion or invasion, involving the public Safety, as it is in times of profound peace and public security. The constitution itself makes the distinction; and I can no more be persuaded that the government can constitutionally take no strong measure in time of rebellion, because it can be shown that the same could not be lawfully taken in time of peace, than I can be persuaded that a particular drug is not good medicine for a sick man, because it can be shown to not be good food for a well one. Nor am I able to appreciate the danger, apprehended by the meeting, that the American people will, by means of military arrests during the rebellion, lose the right of public discussion, the liberty of speech and the press, the law of evidence, trial by jury, and Habeas corpus, throughout the indefinite peaceful future which I trust lies before them, any more than I am able to believe that a man could contract so strong an appetite for emetics during temporary illness, as to persist in feeding upon them through the remainder of his healthful life.

In giving the resolutions that earnest consideration which you request of me, I cannot overlook the fact that the meeting speak as "Democrats." Nor can I, with full respect for their known intelligence, and the fairly presumed deliberation with which they prepared their resolutions, be permitted to suppose that this occurred by accident, or in any way other than that they preferred to designate themselves "democrats" rather than "American citizens." In this time of national peril I would have preferred to meet you upon a level one step higher than any party platform; because I am sure that from such more elevated position, we could do better battle for the country we all love, than we possibly can from those lower ones, where from the force of habit, the prejudices of the past, and selfish hopes of the future, we are sure to expend much of our ingenuity and strength, in finding fault with, and aiming blows at each other. But since you have denied me this, I will yet be thankful, for the country's sake, that not all democrats have done so. He on whose discretionary judgment Mr. Vallandigham was arrested and tried, is a democrat, having no old party affinity with me; and the judge who rejected the constitutional view expressed in these resolutions, by refusing to discharge Mr. V. on Habeas Corpus, is a democrat of better days than these, having received his judicial mantle at the hands of President Jackson. And still more, of all those democrats who are nobly exposing their lives and shedding their blood on the battle-field, I have learned that many approve the course taken with Mr. V. while I have not heard of a single one condemning it. I can not assert that there are none such. . . .

52

Clinton v. Jones (1997)

Justice Stevens delivered the opinion of the Court.

This case raises a constitutional and a prudential question concerning the Office of the President of the United States. Respondent, a private citizen, seeks to recover damages from the current occupant of that office based on actions allegedly taken before his term began. The President submits that in all but the most exceptional cases the Constitution requires federal courts to defer such litigation until his term ends and that, in any event, respect for the office warrants such a stay. Despite the force of the arguments supporting the President's submissions, we conclude that they must be rejected.

. . . Petitioner's principal submission—that "in all but the most exceptional cases," the Constitution affords the President temporary immunity

From *Clinton v. Jones*, 520 U.S. 681 (1997).

from civil damages litigation arising out of events that occurred before he took office—cannot be sustained on the basis of precedent.

Only three sitting Presidents have been defendants in civil litigation involving their actions prior to taking office. Complaints against Theodore Roosevelt and Harry Truman had been dismissed before they took office; the dismissals were affirmed after their respective inaugurations. Two companion cases arising out of an automobile accident were filed against John F. Kennedy in 1960 during the Presidential campaign. After taking office, he unsuccessfully argued that his status as Commander in Chief gave him a right to a stay under the Soldiers' and Sailors' Civil Relief Act of 1940. The motion for a stay was denied by the District Court, and the matter was settled out of court. Thus, none of those cases sheds any light on the constitutional issue before us.

The principal rationale for affording certain public servants immunity from suits for money damages arising out of their official acts is inapplicable to unofficial conduct. In cases involving prosecutors, legislators, and judges we have repeatedly explained that the immunity serves the public interest in enabling such officials to perform their designated functions effectively without fear that a particular decision may give rise to personal liability. We explained in *Ferri v. Ackerman* (1979):

> "As public servants, the prosecutor and the judge represent the interest of society as a whole. The conduct of their official duties may adversely affect a wide variety of different individuals, each of whom may be a potential source of future controversy. The societal interest in providing such public officials with the maximum ability to deal fearlessly and impartially with the public at large has long been recognized as an acceptable justification for official immunity. The point of immunity for such officials is to forestall an atmosphere of intimidation that would conflict with their resolve to perform their designated functions in a principled fashion."

That rationale provided the principal basis for our holding that a former President of the United States was "entitled to absolute immunity from damages liability predicated on his official acts." . . .

This reasoning provides no support for an immunity for *unofficial* conduct. As we explained in *Fitzgerald*, "the sphere of protected action must be related closely to the immunity's justifying purposes." Because of the President's broad responsibilities, we recognized in that case an immunity from damages claims arising out of official acts extending to the "outer perimeter of his authority." But we have never suggested that the President, or any other official, has an immunity that extends beyond the scope of any action taken in an official capacity. . . .

Moreover, when defining the scope of an immunity for acts clearly taken within an official capacity, we have applied a functional approach. "Frequently our decisions have held that an official's absolute immunity should extend only to acts in performance of particular functions of his office." Hence, for example, a judge's absolute immunity does not extend to actions performed in a purely administrative capacity. As our opinions have made clear, immunities are grounded in "the nature of the function performed, not the identity of the actor who performed it." . . .

Petitioner's effort to construct an immunity from suit for unofficial acts grounded purely in the identity of his office is unsupported by precedent.

. . . Respondent, in turn, has called our attention to conflicting historical evidence. Speaking in favor of the Constitution's adoption at the Pennsylvania Convention, James Wilson—who had participated in the Philadelphia Convention at which the document was drafted—explained that, although the President "is placed [on] high," "not a single privilege is annexed to his character; far from being above the laws, he is amenable to them in his private character as a citizen, and in his public character by impeachment." This description is consistent with both the doctrine of presidential immunity as set forth in *Fitzgerald*, and rejection of the immunity claim in this case. With respect to acts taken in his "public character"—that is official acts—the President may be disciplined principally by impeachment, not by private lawsuits for damages. But he is otherwise subject to the laws for his purely private acts.

. . . Petitioner's strongest argument supporting his immunity claim is based on the text and structure of the Constitution. He does not contend that the occupant of the Office of the President is "above the law," in the sense that his conduct is entirely immune from judicial scrutiny. The President argues merely for a postponement of the judicial proceedings that will determine whether he violated any law. His argument is grounded in the character of the office that was created by Article II of the Constitution, and relies on separation of powers principles that have structured our constitutional arrangement since the founding.

As a starting premise, petitioner contends that he occupies a unique office with powers and responsibilities so vast and important that the public interest demands that he devote his undivided time and attention to his public duties. He submits that—given the nature of the office—the doctrine of separation of powers places limits on the authority of the Federal Judiciary to interfere with the Executive Branch that would be transgressed by allowing this action to proceed.

We have no dispute with the initial premise of the argument. Former presidents, from George Washington to George Bush, have consistently endorsed petitioner's characterization of the office. . . . In 1967, the Twenty-fifth Amendment to the Constitution was adopted to ensure continuity in the performance of the powers and duties of the office; one of the sponsors of that Amendment stressed the importance of providing that "at all times" there be a President "who has complete control and will be able to perform" those duties. . . . We have, in short, long recognized the "unique position in the constitutional scheme" that this office occupies. Thus, while we suspect that even in our modern era there remains some truth to Chief Justice Marshall's suggestion that the duties of the Presidency are not entirely "unremitting," we accept the initial premise of the Executive's argument.

It does not follow, however, that separation of powers principles would be violated by allowing this action to proceed. The doctrine of separation of powers is concerned with the allocation of official power among the three co-equal branches of our Government. . . .

. . . Of course the lines between the powers of the three branches are not always neatly defined. But in this case there is no suggestion that the Federal Judiciary is being asked to perform any function that might in some way be described as "executive." Respondent is merely asking the courts to exercise their core Article III jurisdiction to decide cases and controversies. Whatever the outcome of this case, there is no possibility that the decision will curtail the scope of the official powers of the Executive Branch. The litigation of questions that relate entirely to the unofficial conduct of the individual who happens to be the President poses no perceptible risk of misallocation of either judicial power or executive power.

Rather than arguing that the decision of the case will produce either an aggrandizement of judicial power or a narrowing of executive power, petitioner contends that—as a by-product of an otherwise traditional exercise of judicial power—burdens will be placed on the President that will hamper the performance of his official duties. We have recognized that "[e]ven when a branch does not arrogate power to itself . . . the separation-of-powers doctrine requires that a branch not impair another in the performance of its constitutional duties." As a factual matter, petitioner contends that this particular case—as well as the potential additional litigation that an affirmance of the Court of Appeals judgment might spawn—may impose an unacceptable burden on the President's time and energy, and thereby impair the effective performance of his office.

Petitioner's predictive judgment finds little support in either history or the relatively narrow compass of the issues raised in this particular case. As we have already noted, in the more than 200-year history of the Republic, only three sitting Presidents have been subjected to suits for their private actions. If the past is any indicator, it seems unlikely that a deluge of such litigation will ever engulf the Presidency. As for the case at hand, if properly managed by the District Court, it appears to us highly unlikely to occupy any substantial amount of petitioner's time.

Of greater significance, petitioner errs by presuming that interactions between the Judicial Branch and the Executive, even quite burdensome interactions, necessarily rise to the level of constitutionally forbidden impairment of the Executive's ability to perform its constitutionally mandated functions. . . . The fact that a federal court's exercise of its traditional Article III jurisdiction may significantly burden the time and attention of the Chief Executive is not sufficient to establish a violation of the Constitution. . . .

. . . In sum, "[i]t is settled law that the separation-of-powers doctrine does not bar every exercise of jurisdiction over the President of the United States." *Fitzgerald*. If the Judiciary may severely burden the Executive Branch by reviewing the legality of the President's official conduct, and if it may direct appropriate process to the President himself, it must follow that the federal courts have power to determine the legality of his unofficial conduct. The burden on the President's time and energy that is a mere by-product of such review surely cannot be considered as onerous as the direct burden imposed by judicial review and the occasional invalidation of his official actions. We therefore hold that the doctrine of separation of powers does not require federal courts to stay all private actions against the President until he leaves office.

. . . [W]e are persuaded that it was an abuse of discretion for the District Court to defer the trial until after the President leaves office. Such a lengthy and categorical stay takes no account whatever of the respondent's interest in bringing the case to trial. The complaint was filed within the statutory limitations period—albeit near the end of that period—and delaying trial would increase the danger of prejudice resulting from the loss of evidence, including the inability of witnesses to recall specific facts, or the possible death of a party. . . .

We add a final comment on two matters that are discussed at length in the briefs: the risk that our decision will generate a large volume of politically motivated harassing and frivolous litigation, and the danger that national security concerns might prevent the President from explaining a legitimate need for a continuance.

We are not persuaded that either of these risks is serious. Most frivolous and vexatious litigation is terminated at the pleading stage or on summary judgment, with little if any personal involvement by the defendant. Moreover, the availability of sanctions provides a significant deterrent to litigation directed at the President in his unofficial capacity for purposes of political gain or harassment. History indicates that the likelihood that a significant number of such cases will be filed is remote. Although scheduling problems may arise, there is no reason to assume that the District Courts will be either unable to accommodate the President's needs or unfaithful to the tradition—especially in matters involving national security—of giving "the utmost deference to Presidential responsibilities." Several Presidents, including petitioner, have given testimony without jeopardizing the Nation's security. In short, we have confidence in the ability of our federal judges to deal with both of these concerns.

The Federal District Court has jurisdiction to decide this case. Like every other citizen who properly invokes that jurisdiction, respondent has a right to an orderly disposition of her claims. Accordingly, the judgment of the Court of Appeals is affirmed.

53

Jordan T. Cash

Sovereign Immunity, Executive Privilege, and Congressional Investigatory Authority in the Trump Era (2019)

Listening to mainstream public discourse, one gets the impression that the Trump presidency has consisted of little more than unprecedented constitutional crises, corruption, and executive usurpation. This impression gains substance by the fact that Trump and his administration have been the focus of numerous investigations, including by Congress and Special Counsel Robert Mueller. For his part, Trump has not been reluctant to utilize his presidential authority to push back on these investigations and defend himself.

This chapter aims to put some of these issues into historical and constitutional context by reviewing three distinctive areas: sovereign immunity as it applies to the presidency; executive privilege; and congressional investigatory authority. These areas all touch on a central question of American politics: how do we ensure the president is able to effectively administer the law, but also ensure he does not break the law? The Constitution addresses this question through its structure of separation of powers. As we shall see, there are legitimate reasons for the president to possess sovereign immunity and executive privilege, but those powers are not unlimited, and both Congress and the judiciary are positioned to limit those powers, albeit in different ways. The precise boundaries of these limits, however, are difficult to define, as the Constitution allows for a significant amount of contestation between the branches. By placing the Trump presidency within a larger constitutional context, we will be able to better evaluate the current issues facing Trump and think about how the constitutional dialogue between the branches balances executive effectiveness and accountability.

I will begin by reviewing the constitutional basis and historical development of sovereign immunity, executive privilege, and congressional investigations up to the beginning of Trump's administration in 2017. I will then discuss each of these issues in the context of the Trump administration and how they relate to the constitutional separation of powers.

SOVEREIGN IMMUNITY

As a basic legal principle, sovereign immunity is simply the idea that the government cannot be sued without its consent. In the United States, this principle has most often been brought up within the context of federalism, in disputes over whether states possess sovereign immunity. Yet sovereign immunity also applies to other governmental actors, including the president.

Presidential sovereign immunity may arise on two different levels. The first regards civil suits—whether the president can be sued for civil damages while in office—and the second concerns criminal indictments—whether a president can be arrested while in office.

In the last forty years, the Supreme Court has ruled on the president's civil liability twice. First, in *Nixon v. Fitzgerald* (1982), the Court held that the president has absolute immunity from civil suits when acting in an official capacity. Because the president is uniquely involved with a wide variety of issues of the highest national importance, he requires a more robust immunity than the qualified immunity provided to other government officials. This argument was refined fifteen years later in *Clinton v. Jones* (1997). There the Court held that while the president has immunity for official actions taken while in office, he is not immune from civil litigation for unofficial acts done before he was president.

Presidential criminality is a bit more complicated. The Supreme Court has not ruled on it, but in 1973 the Office of Legal Counsel (OLC)—an office within the Justice Department—issued a memorandum concluding that the president could not be indicted or criminally prosecuted while in office. This immunity applies only to the president; all other officers, including the vice president, may be indicted and prosecuted while in office. The memorandum argued that the unique position of the president required him to be exempt from criminal indictment and prosecution during his term as a criminal trial might prevent the president from performing official duties that no other government officer may discharge. Additionally, as the president is the chief executive officer, indicting a president effectively puts him in the position of prosecuting himself. Impeachment was instituted partially to resolve such an awkward situation, allowing potentially criminal presidents to be removed from office, at which point they can be prosecuted. Overall, the president's constitutional position and responsibilities give him strong claims of sovereign immunity from both civil litigation and criminal prosecution.

EXECUTIVE PRIVILEGE

At its core, executive privilege is the idea that the president may withhold information from the public and Congress. While simple in theory, its use has been criticized. Opponents of executive privilege argue that it is not listed in the Constitution and grants too much unchecked power to the executive, risking misuse and potentially unbalancing the constitutional system. Because Congress is the branch that makes laws—and in the Senate's case ratifies treaties and confirms appointments—it must be able to get information from the executive branch to legislative effectively, and executive privilege may interfere with those functions. Similarly, executive privilege may prevent citizens from being informed about what their government is doing. Despite these objections, nearly every president, from Washington to Trump, has invoked executive privilege at some point.

In 1974 the Supreme Court finally weighed in on executive privilege in the case *United States v. Nixon*. In determining whether President Nixon could withhold tapes of conversations related to the Watergate scandal, a unanimous Court determined that while executive privilege was a legitimate constitutional power of the presidency, it was not absolute. Chief Justice Warren Burger contended that executive privilege was necessary for two reasons. First, because there are cases when it is in the national interest for information to be withheld from the public, particularly when the issue concerns diplomacy or national security. Second, and more fundamentally, the secrecy provided by executive privilege is necessary to preserve the integrity of the advice presidents receive and the decision-making process within the executive branch. While Burger established the constitutional legitimacy of executive privilege, he also made it clear that executive privilege was not unlimited. In this case, Nixon's claims of executive privilege did not outweigh the Watergate burglars' claims for due process, as the tapes were vital to their criminal cases, thus the president had to turn over the tapes.

Since Nixon, other presidents have had their use of executive privilege restrained by the other branches. For example, Bill Clinton's use of executive privilege to prevent senior aides from testifying about his relationship with White House intern Monica Lewinsky was overturned by a federal court. Similarly, Barack Obama had his claim of executive privilege concerning documents related to the "Fast and Furious" gunwalking scandal struck down. Congress also cited Obama's Attorney General Eric Holder—who oversaw the operation—with contempt of Congress for not turning over the documents. Thus even while executive privilege is recognized as a legitimate power, the other branches have acted to limit it.

CONGRESSIONAL INVESTIGATORY AUTHORITY

While executive privilege allows the president to withhold information from Congress and the public, Congress has its own legitimate constitutional authority to investigate the executive branch. Such authority goes back to the Founding, as Congress launched its first investigation during the Washington administration. Congress' power to launch investigations was given firm constitutional grounding in the 1927 Supreme Court case *McGrain v. Daugherty*, which asserted that Congress' investigatory powers, including the ability to issue subpoenas and compel testimony, were a necessary corollary to its legislative function. This holding was reiterated in 1957's *Watkins v. United States* in which the Court noted that Congress' investigatory authority gave it power both to gather information useful to the legislative process and to oversee the administration's execution of the laws. On this constitutional basis, Congress has often been involved in investigating executive misconduct and the possibility of illegal activities by the president or his subordinates.

Yet such investigations always risk becoming bound up with partisan politics, particularly if Congress and the presidency are controlled by different parties. When there is divided government, Congress might become overeager to use its investigatory authority on a president. Conversely, when Congress and the presidency are held by the same party, Congress may not use its investigatory powers and instead seek to protect the president. There is also a risk of politicized investigations within the executive branch. Congress attempted to address this problem after Watergate with the passage of the Ethics in Government Act of 1978, which codified and institutionalized the role of a special prosecutor, making this office independent of the normal Justice Department hierarchy and of the president himself.

Yet special prosecutors—later called independent counsels and today referred to as special counsels—raise separation of powers problems. This became particularly evident in the Supreme Court case *Morrison v. Olson* (1988). While the Court determined that the independent counsel was constitutional, Justice Antonin Scalia issued a blistering dissent arguing that because prosecution was an inherently executive power it could not be separated from the president. Nonetheless, since that decision there have been numerous independent and special counsel investigations, the most prominent being Independent Counsel Kenneth Starr's investigation into Bill and Hillary Clinton's real estate investments that eventually led to Clinton's impeachment in 1998. Yet the fact that independent counsels cannot indict presidents—per the OLC memo—and are essentially limited to reporting to Congress whether the evidence meets the standard for indictment highlights the office's strange position in the constitutional system.

IMMUNITY, PRIVILEGE, AND INVESTIGATIONS IN THE TRUMP ERA

Each of these issues, sovereign immunity, executive privilege, and congressional investigations, particularly with special counsels, have arisen during the first two years of the Trump presidency. With sovereign immunity, both civil immunity and immunity from indictment have been brought up. The civil immunity question arises out of a lawsuit filed against Trump by Summer Zervos, a former contestant on Trump's reality television show *The Apprentice*. During the 2016 presidential campaign, Zervos accused

Trump of sexually harassing her in 2007. Trump responded by accusing Zervos of lying for political purposes. In January 2017, Zervos filed a lawsuit against Trump, accusing the president-elect of defamation.

On the surface, this case looks quite similar to *Clinton v. Jones*; a president is being sued for conduct from before he was president. One major difference, however, is that Zervos filed her lawsuit in New York state court, whereas *Clinton* was decided in federal court. Trump's lawyers tried to turn that to their advantage, arguing that the Constitution's supremacy clause— which makes the Constitution and national laws supreme over state constitutions and laws—meant that the president could not be subject to civil litigation at the state level. Unfortunately for Trump, the New York appellate court disagreed, asserting that the precedent of *Clinton* applied and that the president does not have sovereign immunity from state-level civil cases for conduct from before he was president. Trump has appealed the decision, and if it proceeds to the Supreme Court, the Court's decision could further clarify and limit the president's claims of sovereign immunity for civil cases at both the federal and state levels.

Trump has also come under scrutiny for potential criminal behavior. Most famously, Special Counsel Robert Mueller conducted a two-year investigation into whether the Trump campaign conspired with Russia during the 2016 presidential election. Mueller ultimately concluded there was not sufficient evidence that the Trump campaign was involved in a Russian conspiracy. That did not end the investigation, however, as Mueller also looked into whether Trump had obstructed justice. While the report did not definitively conclude that Trump had not obstructed justice, Mueller prefaced his investigation by citing the 1973 OLC memo on the impermissibility of indicted a sitting president. In his testimony before Congress, Mueller also asserted that, because of the OLC memo, he and his team did not even calculate whether Trump's actions amounted to obstruction of justice. Under this standard, even if Mueller had found conclusive evidence of obstruction of justice or conspiracy, he would not have sought the president's indictment until after he was no longer in office. Because Mueller's report did not consider whether the president's actions amounted to obstruction of justice, he effectively left it to Congress and the people to decide if Trump should stay in office, as Congress could impeach and remove the president and the people could vote him out of office in the next election. Once out of office, the immunity described by the OLC no longer applies and Trump could be prosecuted by the new president. Mueller, therefore, in not coming to a conclusion on whether Trump should be indicted, indicates that when it comes to presidents, political punishments like impeachment or electoral defeat must necessarily precede the legal process of prosecution.

The other major criminal investigation concerning Trump revolves around alleged campaign finance violations. This case is being pursued by the U.S. Attorney for the Southern District of New York, an office of the Justice Department with a noted independent streak. Yet even that office must get approval for indictments from the Justice Department hierarchy, indicating that the OLC memo would likely restrict any attempts to indict the president while he is in office if any criminal activity is uncovered.

These investigations have been the primary context for Trump's use of executive privilege. He asserted executive privilege to prevent the release of the unredacted Mueller report and its underlying material and to prevent former White House officials from testifying before Congress. The latter instance highlights Trump and the Justice Department's argument that executive privilege extends to executive branch officials possessing testimonial immunity so they do not have to testify before Congress. This concept is not an innovation of the Trump administration but was raised in an OLC opinion issued during the Obama administration, arguing that just as the president possesses absolute immunity from being compelled to testify before Congress, being a co-equal branch of government, so do his immediate advisors. As of August 2019, the Supreme Court has not addressed this particular outgrowth of executive privilege. The only court that has addressed this question is the District Court for the District of Columbia in the 2008 case *Committee on Judiciary v. Miers*. There, the court determined that presidential advisors did not have such immunity. The OLC, however, respectfully disagreed. Unsurprisingly, the Trump administration agrees with the OLC and has claimed testimonial immunity for several former advisors, and even considered invoking executive privilege for his former campaign manager Corey Lewandowski, despite the fact that Lewandowski never served as a White House official and thus falls outside the scope of the OLC opinion.

Of course, these actions are largely in reaction to the investigations begun by Congress. These investigations are fairly wide-ranging, covering not only the alleged Russia conspiracy but also questions about abuses of White House security clearances, adding a citizenship question to the census—which also solicited an executive privilege claim from Trump—inquiries into corruption and obstruction of justice, and Trump's personal financial and tax records. While Trump has pushed back on some of these investigations with executive privilege, Congress, particularly the Democratic House, has been able to exercise its investigatory authority quite forcefully. The House held both Attorney General William Barr and Commerce Secretary Wilbur Ross in contempt for not turning over documents related to the census citizenship question. As with Eric Holder who was also held in contempt, these contempt votes nevertheless have not had much of an effect in actually limiting the president or forcing Ross or Barr to comply with congressional demands. Beyond these contempt citations, House Democrats filed a lawsuit to obtain the materials from Mueller's grand jury report, insisting the materials are needed to determine whether the House should pursue impeachment. They also filed a lawsuit seeking Trump's tax returns. Such actions, especially when considered alongside Trump's use of executive immunity, are indicative of the conflict between the branches and the willingness of both the president and Congress to aggressively use the powers at their disposal.

The relevance of sovereign immunity, executive privilege, and congressional investigations leads us to consider normative questions about the extent to which these principles and powers should be applied or exercised, particularly as they lay at the intersection of the rule of law, separation of powers, and public administration. Sovereign immunity, in its division between civil and criminal and between official actions and unofficial actions, seems relatively well-balanced. In civil matters, the courts have ruled that the president's official conduct receives immunity, recognizing the discretion needed in administering the law. Unofficial conduct, particularly from before the president is inaugurated, does not have such leeway. Thus, it appears proper for the defamation lawsuit against Trump to proceed as he was a private person when the comments were made and he should not receive the privileges of office for official conduct.

Criminal immunity, however, does seem to offend Americans' natural sense of equality and the notion that no one is above the law. Yet to allow the criminal indictment of a sitting president would raise several other difficult problems. Constitutionally, the president is unique. He alone is vested with executive power and his office is vested with constitutional responsibilities that only he can perform, including signing bills into law and appointing administrators, diplomats, and judges. There is also the issue of presidential pardons. If the president was indicted, what would stop him from simply pardoning himself, a possibility Trump himself has raised? Sovereign immunity avoids that complication, and the complication of the president effectively prosecuting himself, by not allowing the individual with both prosecutorial and pardon power to be a criminal defendant. Thus, even while it may seem like an affront to our notion of the rule of law, presidential immunity from indictment serves a constitutional purpose.

We also should not forget that the Constitution provides two methods by which to strip the president of his immunity. The first is to impeach and remove him from office. If the issue was presidential criminality, that would likely create bipartisan support for impeachment, as happened with Nixon and Clinton. Of course, if the charges are minimal, or viewed as driven by political partisanship, it could hinder the removal component of impeachment, as also happened with Clinton. Even if there is no impeachment, the electoral process provides an opportunity for the public to remove a president from office. If there was clear evidence the president had broken the law, it seems likely that he would be challenged at the primary level, and even more likely he would be defeated in the general election. Even if the president is in his second term and not eligible for reelection, he can be criminally indicted after leaving office. All this to say that executive immunity is always temporary.

A similar dynamic is at play with executive privilege and congressional investigations. Both are needed for the president and Congress to exercise their respective constitutional responsibilities. But is there a point when executive privilege goes too far, or when congressional investigations are no longer simply for oversight or legislation, but to score political points? To the first question, the Supreme Court has affirmed there are cases when executive privilege goes too far, as we saw with Nixon, Clinton, and Obama. For Trump, it seems likely that his use of executive privilege will be challenged in court, particularly on the issue of testimonial immunity for presidential advisors. Certainly, if he extends it to individuals who have not been presidential advisors, like Lewandowski, that would go beyond the limits of executive privilege. To the more specific question of testimonial immunity, it does logically follow from executive privilege, yet it does not appear to be as absolute as the Trump administration might like, particularly given the *Miers* decision. It is likely, therefore, that the applicability of testimonial immunity, like executive privilege itself, would depend on the individual and the subject matter. It may also depend on how Congress approaches the testimony. A closed executive session would be less likely to elicit a claim of testimonial immunity from the president than a public committee hearing. Similarly, a court would be less likely to uphold a claim of testimonial immunity if the testimony was given in executive session where there is confidentiality. Thus, some of Trump's invocations of executive privilege, such as redacting the Mueller report and withholding census documents, can be supported with legitimate legal or administrative reasoning. Other uses, such as asserting testimonial immunity, may be supported by legitimate arguments but also push the limits of the president's authority. As of August 2019, they remain in a legal grey area.

As to congressional investigations for aiding Congress in legislating, Congress clearly has the constitutional authority. The point at which they might go too far, hindering the president in fulfilling his constitutional duty to "take Care that the Laws be faithfully executed" or using congressional resources that might be used elsewhere, is difficult to determine. It is unlikely the courts will step in on Congress' investigatory actions or on the allocation of congressional resources: the first is probably a nonjusticiable political question that the legislative and executive branches must resolve, and the second, a matter of congressional discretion. In either case, it might be left to the public to determine if Congress' actions are acceptable, either rewarding the members of Congress involved with reelection or punishing them with electoral defeat. For the moment, the investigations' efficacy is more a matter of politics and prudence than strict constitutionality.

Placing all these issues within the larger context of American constitutional history allows us to see that the legal issues raised during the Trump administration are not unique but are similar to past events in presidential history. It also allows us to see that there is a measure of ambiguity in these questions, and that is because the Constitution, with its separation of powers framework, creates room for contestation between the branches. Each branch has its own institutional characteristics and pressures that it must respond to: Congress needs information to legislate and exercise proper oversight, the president needs secrecy and immunity to effectively administer the law, and the Court needs independence to uphold the law against the political branches. Such pressures push against each other and force us to consider the nuances of these questions and how the Constitution simultaneously balances each branch's institutional pressures and characteristics to allow for an efficient government under the rule of law.

54

Frederick Douglass

Oration in Memory of Abraham Lincoln (1876)

. . . We stand today at the national center to perform something like a national act—an act which is to go into history; and we are here where every pulsation of the national heart can be heard, felt, and reciprocated. A thousand wires, fed with thought and winged with lightning, put us in instantaneous communication with the loyal and true men all over this country.

Few facts could better illustrate the vast and wonderful change which has taken place in our condition as a people than the fact of our assembling here for the purpose we have today. Harmless, beautiful, proper, and praiseworthy as this demonstration is, I cannot forget that no such demonstration would have been tolerated here twenty years ago. The spirit of slavery and barbarism, which still lingers to blight and destroy in some dark and distant parts of our country, would have made our assembling here the signal and

From "Oration in Memory of Abraham Lincoln," delivered at the Unveiling of the Freedmen's Monument in Memory of Abraham Lincoln, in Lincoln Park, Washington, D.C., April 14, 1876.

excuse for opening upon us all the flood-gates of wrath and violence. That we are here in peace today is a compliment and a credit to American civilization, and a prophecy of still greater national enlightenment and progress in the future. I refer to the past not in malice, for this is no day for malice; but simply to place more distinctly in front the gratifying and glorious change which has come both to our white fellow-citizens and ourselves, and to congratulate all upon the contrast between now and then; the new dispensation of freedom with its thousand blessings to both races, and the old dispensation of slavery with its ten thousand evils to both races—white and black. . . .

[W]e are here to express, as best we may, by appropriate forms and ceremonies, our grateful sense of the vast, high, and preëminent services rendered to ourselves, to our race, to our country, and to the whole world by Abraham Lincoln.

The sentiment that brings us here to-day is one of the noblest that can stir and thrill the human heart. It has crowned and made glorious the high places of all civilized nations with the grandest and most enduring works of art, designed to illustrate the characters and perpetuate the memories of great public men. It is the sentiment which from year to year adorns with fragrant and beautiful flowers the graves of our loyal, brave, and patriotic soldiers who fell in defence of the Union and liberty. It is the sentiment of gratitude and appreciation. . . .

For the first time in the history of our people, and in the history of the whole American people, we join in this high worship, and march conspicuously in the line of this time-honored custom. First things are always interesting, and this is one of our first things. It is the first time that, in this form and manner, we have sought to do honor to an American great man, however deserving and illustrious. I commend the fact to notice; let it be told in every part of the Republic; let men of all parties and opinions hear it; let those who despise us, not less than those who respect us, know that now and here, in the spirit of liberty, loyalty, and gratitude, let it be known everywhere, and by everybody who takes an interest in human progress and in the amelioration of the condition of mankind, that . . . we, the colored people, newly emancipated and rejoicing in our blood-bought freedom, near the close of the first century in the life of this Republic, have now and here unveiled, set apart, and dedicated a monument of enduring granite and bronze, in every line, feature, and figure of which the men of this generation may read, and those of aftercoming generations may read, something of the exalted character and great works of Abraham Lincoln, the first martyr President of the United States.

Fellow-citizens, in what we have said and done today, and in what we may say and do hereafter, we disclaim everything like arrogance and assumption. We claim for ourselves no superior devotion to the character, history, and memory of the illustrious name whose monument we have here dedicated today. We fully comprehend the relation of Abraham Lincoln both to our-selves and to the white people of the United States. Truth is proper and beau-tiful at all times and in all places, and it is never more proper and beautiful in any case than when speaking of a great public man whose example is likely to be commended for honor and imitation long after his departure to the solemn shades, the silent continents of eternity. It must be admitted, truth compels me to admit, even here in the presence of the monument we have erected to his memory, Abraham Lincoln was not, in the fullest sense of the word, either our man or our model. In his interests, in his associations, in his habits of thought, and in his prejudices, he was a white man.

He was preëminently the white man's President, entirely devoted to the welfare of white men. He was ready and willing at any time during the first years of his administration to deny, postpone, and sacrifice the rights of humanity in the colored people to promote the welfare of the white people of this country. In all his education and feeling he was an American of the Americans. He came into the Presidential chair upon one principle alone, namely, opposition to the extension of slavery. His arguments in furtherance of this policy had their motive and mainspring in his patriotic devotion to the interests of his own race. To protect, defend, and perpetuate slavery in the states where it existed Abraham Lincoln was not less ready than any other President to draw the sword of the nation. He was ready to execute all the supposed guarantees of the United States Constitution in favor of the slave system anywhere inside the slave states. He was willing to pursue, recapture, and send back the fugitive slave to his master, and to suppress a slave rising for liberty, though his guilty master were already in arms against the Government. The race to which we belong were not the special objects of his consideration. Knowing this, I concede to you, my white fellow-citizens, a preëminence in this worship at once full and supreme. First, midst, and last, you and yours were the objects of his deepest affection and his most earnest solicitude. You are the children of Abraham Lincoln. We are at best only his step-children; children by adoption, children by forces of circum-stances and necessity. . . .

Fellow-citizens, ours is no new-born zeal and devotion—merely a thing of this moment. The name of Abraham Lincoln was near and dear to our hearts in the darkest and most perilous hours of the Republic. We were no more ashamed of him when shrouded in clouds of darkness, of doubt, and defeat than when we saw him crowned with victory, honor, and glory. Our faith in him was often taxed and strained to the uttermost, but it never failed. When he tarried long in the mountain; when he strangely told us that we were the cause of the war; when he still more strangely told us that we were to leave the land in which we were born; when he refused to employ our arms in defence of the Union; when, after accepting our services as colored soldiers, he refused to retaliate our murder and torture as colored prisoners; when he told us he would save the Union if he could with slavery; when he revoked the Proclamation of Emancipation of General Fremont; when he refused to remove the popular commander of the Army of the Potomac, in the days of its inaction and defeat, who was more zealous in his efforts to protect slavery than to suppress rebellion; when we saw all this, and more, we were at times grieved, stunned, and greatly bewildered; but our hearts believed while they ached and bled. Nor was this, even at that time, a blind and unreasoning superstition. Despite the mist and haze that surrounded him; despite the tumult, the hurry, and confusion of the hour, we were able to take a comprehensive view of Abraham Lincoln, and to make reasonable allowance for the circumstances of his position. We saw him, measured him, and estimated him; not by stray utterances to injudicious and tedious delegations, who often tried his patience; not by isolated facts torn from their connection; not by any partial and imperfect glimpses, caught at inopportune moments; but by a broad survey, in the light of the stern logic of great events, and in view of that divinity which shapes our ends, rough hew them how we will, we came to the conclusion that the hour and the man of our redemption had somehow met in the person of Abraham Lincoln. It mattered little to us what language he might employ on special occasions; it mattered little to us, when we fully knew him, whether he was swift or slow in his movements; it was enough for us that Abraham Lincoln was at the head of a great movement, and was in living and earnest sympathy with that movement, which, in the nature of things, must go on until slavery should be utterly and forever abolished in the United States.

When, therefore, it shall be asked what we have to do with the memory of Abraham Lincoln, or what Abraham Lincoln had to do with us, the answer is ready, full, and complete. Though he loved Caesar less than Rome, though the Union was more to him than our freedom or our future, under his wise and beneficent rule we saw ourselves gradually lifted from the depths of slavery to the heights of liberty and manhood; under his wise and beneficent rule, and by measures approved and vigorously pressed by him, we saw that the handwriting of ages, in the form of prejudice and proscription, was rapidly fading away from the face of our whole country; under his rule, and in due time, about as soon after all as the country could tolerate the strange spectacle, we saw our brave sons and brothers laying off the rags of bondage, and being clothed all over in the blue uniforms of the soldiers of the United States; under his rule we saw two hundred thousand of our dark and dusky people responding to the call of Abraham Lincoln, and with muskets on their shoulders, and eagles on their buttons, timing their high footsteps to liberty and union under the national flag; under his rule we saw the independence of the black republic of Haiti, the special object of slaveholding aversion and horror, fully recognized, and her minister, a colored gentleman, duly received here in the city of Washington; under his rule we saw the internal slave-trade, which so long disgraced the nation, abolished, and slavery abolished in the District of Columbia; under his rule we saw for the first time the law enforced against the foreign slave trade, and the first slave-trader hanged like any other pirate or murderer; under his rule, assisted by the greatest captain of our age, and his inspiration, we saw the Confederate States, based upon the idea that our race must be slaves, and slaves forever, battered to pieces and scattered to the four winds; under his rule, and in the fullness of time, we saw Abraham Lincoln, after giving the slaveholders three months' grace in which to save their hateful slave system, penning the immortal paper, which, though special in its language, was general in its principles and effect, making slavery forever impossible in the United States. Though we waited long, we saw all this and more. . . .

I have said that President Lincoln was a white man, and shared the prejudices common to his countrymen towards the colored race. Looking back to his times and to the condition of his country, we are compelled to admit that this unfriendly feeling on his part may be safely set down as one element of his wonderful success in organizing the loyal American people for the tremendous conflict before them, and bringing them safely through that conflict. His great mission was to accomplish two things: first, to save his country from dismemberment and ruin; and, second, to free his country from the great crime of slavery. To do one or the other, or both, he must have the earnest sympathy and the powerful coöperation of his loyal fellow-countrymen. Without this primary and essential condition to success his efforts must have been vain and utterly fruitless. Had he put the abolition of slavery before the salvation of the Union, he would have inevitably driven from him a powerful class of the American people and rendered resistance to rebellion impossible. Viewed from the genuine abolition ground, Mr. Lincoln seemed tardy, cold, dull, and indifferent; but measuring him by the sentiment of his country, a sentiment he was bound as a statesman to consult, he was swift, zealous, radical, and determined.

Though Mr. Lincoln shared the prejudices of his white fellow-countrymen against the Negro, it is hardly necessary to say that in his heart of hearts he loathed and hated slavery. . . . The man who could say, "Fondly do we hope, fervently do we pray, that this mighty scourge of war shall soon pass away, yet if God wills it continue till all the wealth piled by two hundred years of bondage shall have been wasted, and each drop of blood drawn by the lash shall have been paid for by one drawn by the sword, the judgments of the Lord are true and righteous altogether," gives all needed proof of his feeling on the subject of slavery. He was willing, while the South was loyal, that it should have its pound of flesh, because he thought that it was so nominated in the bond; but farther than this no earthly power could make him go.

Fellow-citizens, whatever else in this world may be partial, unjust, and uncertain, time, time! is impartial, just, and certain in its action. In the realm of mind, as well as in the realm of matter, it is a great worker, and often works wonders. The honest and comprehensive statesman, clearly discerning the needs of his country, and earnestly endeavoring to do his whole duty, though covered and blistered with reproaches, may safely leave his course to the silent judgment of time. Few great public men have ever been the victims of fiercer denunciation than Abraham Lincoln was during his administration. He was often wounded in the house of his friends. Reproaches came thick and fast upon him from within and from without, and from opposite quarters. He was assailed by Abolitionists; he was assailed by slaveholders; he was assailed by the men who were for peace at any price; he was assailed by those who were for a more vigorous prosecution of the war; he was assailed for not making the war an abolition war; and he was bitterly assailed for making the war an abolition war.

But now behold the change: the judgment of the present hour is, that taking him for all in all, measuring the tremendous magnitude of the work before him, considering the necessary means to ends, and surveying the end from the beginning, infinite wisdom has seldom sent any man into the world better fitted for his mission than Abraham Lincoln. His birth, his training, and his natural endowments, both mental and physical, were strongly in his favor. Born and reared among the lowly, a stranger to wealth and luxury, compelled to grapple single-handed with the flintiest hardships of life, from tender youth to sturdy manhood, he grew strong in the manly and heroic qualities demanded by the great mission to which he was called by the votes of his countrymen. The hard condition of his early life, which would have depressed and broken down weaker men, only gave greater life, vigor, and buoyancy to the heroic spirit of Abraham Lincoln. He was ready for any kind and any quality of work. . . .

All day long he could split heavy rails in the woods, and half the night long he could study his English Grammar by the uncertain flare and glare of the light made by a pine-knot. He was at home on the land with his axe, with his maul, with gluts, and his wedges; and he was equally at home on water, with his oars, with his poles, with his planks, and with his boat-hooks. And whether in his flat-boat on the Mississippi River, or at the fireside of his frontier cabin, he was a man of work. A son of toil himself, he was linked in brotherly sympathy with the sons of toil in every loyal part of the Republic. This very fact gave him tremendous power with the American people, and materially contributed not only to selecting him to the Presidency, but in sustaining his administration of the Government.

Upon his inauguration as President of the United States, an office, even when assumed under the most favorable conditions, fitted to tax and strain the largest abilities, Abraham Lincoln was met by a tremendous crisis. He was called upon not merely to administer the Government, but to decide, in the face of terrible odds, the fate of the Republic.

A formidable rebellion rose in his path before him; the Union was already practically dissolved; his country was torn and rent asunder at the center. Hostile armies were already organized against the Republic, armed with the munitions of war which the Republic had provided for its own defence. The tremendous question for him to decide was whether his country should survive the crisis and flourish, or be dismembered and perish. His predecessor in office had already decided the question in favor of national dismemberment, by denying to it the right of self-defence and self-preservation—a right which belongs to the meanest insect.

Happily for the country, happily for you and for me, the judgment of James Buchanan, the patrician, was not the judgment of Abraham Lincoln, the plebeian. He brought his strong common sense, sharpened in the school of adversity, to bear upon the question. He did not hesitate, he did not doubt, he did not falter; but at once resolved that at whatever peril, at whatever cost, the union of the States should be preserved. . . . The trust that Abraham Lincoln had in himself and in the people was surprising and grand, but it was also enlightened and well founded. He knew the American people better than they knew themselves, and his truth was based upon this knowledge.

Fellow-citizens, the fourteenth day of April, 1865, of which this is the eleventh anniversary, is now and will ever remain a memorable day in the annals of this Republic. It was on the evening of this day, while a fierce and sanguinary rebellion was in the last stages of its desolating power; while its armies were broken and scattered before the invincible armies of Grant and Sherman; while a great nation, torn and rent by war, was already beginning to raise to the skies loud anthems of joy at the dawn of peace, it was startled, amazed, and overwhelmed by the crowning crime of slavery . . . the assassination of Abraham Lincoln. It was a new crime, a pure act of malice. No purpose of the rebellion was to be served by it. It was the simple gratification of a hell-black spirit of revenge. But it has done good after all. It has filled the country with a deeper abhorrence of slavery and a deeper love for the great liberator.

Had Abraham Lincoln died from any of the numerous ills to which flesh is heir; had he reached that good old age of which his vigorous constitution and his temperate habits gave promise; had he been permitted to see the end of his great work; had the solemn curtain of death come down but gradually—we should still have been smitten with a heavy grief, and treasured his name lovingly. But dying as he did die, by the red hand of violence, killed, assassinated, taken off without warning, not because of personal hate—for no man who knew Abraham Lincoln could hate him—but because of his fidelity to union and liberty, he is doubly dear to us, and his memory will be precious forever.

Fellow-citizens, I end, as I began, with congratulations. We have done a good work for our race today. In doing honor to the memory of our friend and liberator, we have been doing highest honors to ourselves and those who come after us; we have been fastening ourselves to a name and fame imperishable and immortal; we have also been defending ourselves from a blighting scandal. When now it shall be said that the colored man is soulless, that he has no appreciation of benefits or benefactors; when the foul reproach of ingratitude is hurled at us, and it is attempted to scourge us beyond the range of human brotherhood, we may calmly point to the monument we have this day erected to the memory of Abraham Lincoln.

Chapter V

The Judiciary

In *The Federalist*, Alexander Hamilton argues that the Supreme Court's power of review follows from the concept of a limited constitution. Because there are limits to governmental activity, acts that exceed those limits are void, and therefore cannot be applied in particular cases by the Court. As a result, judicial review establishes not judicial supremacy, but constitutional supremacy. The particular function of the court is thus to protect the rule of law by maintaining the limits the Constitution imposes on government. Although the Constitution establishes the rule of law, there must be discretion for those who enact and administer the laws, or for the strictly political or elected branches of government. It is frequently difficult to draw the line between the discretion necessary for governing and the arbitrary exercise of power. When defending the Constitution, the Court must often draw that line, deciding what matters are justiciable, and can be resolved by the Court, and what matters are political, and must be left up to the judgment of the political branches and the American people. In making that decision the Court itself exercises discretion. But although the members of the political branches—the president and members of Congress—are accountable to the voters, the members of the judiciary are independent, holding office during good behavior. Hamilton argues that it is safe to give the judiciary such independence, since—holding neither the power of the purse nor the power of the sword—it is the weakest of the three branches. The power of a judge is "merely judgment;" judges are able to declare laws unconstitutional only when a case is brought before them and they depend on the executive to enforce their decisions.

The Anti-Federalist writer Brutus is not persuaded by Hamilton's argument. He believes that the Court has the potential to become the most dangerous branch of government, since it is empowered "to decide upon the meaning of the constitution" and judges in effect serve life terms. If, as in Britain, courts lacked power to definitively override the acts of the legislature, there would be less danger. But life tenure combined with the power of judicial review holds the potential for the exercise of unrestrained arbitrary power. If judges misinterpret the Constitution, neither the legislature nor the executive can overrule them. How, Brutus asks, can unelected judges be safely permitted to interpret the Constitution, particularly since "[t] here is no power above them that can correct their errors or control their decisions"?

Both Thomas Jefferson and Abraham Lincoln later expressed distrust of an arbitrary and powerful Court. Jefferson went so far as to deny that the Court possessed the power of judicial review. Each branch of government, Jefferson believed, must interpret the Constitution insofar as it applies to itself. He admits that "contradictory decisions" could arise under his scheme, but he relies on "the prudence of public functionaries, and the authority of public opinion" to "produce accommodation." In the absence of enlightened public opinion and statesmanship, Jefferson's version of separation of powers would almost certainly lead to great confusion about the meaning of the law and tremendous conflict between the three branches of government. Lincoln, like Jefferson, recognizes the danger of judicial review, but his position is more prudent. He argues that American citizens must abide by the Supreme Court's notorious decision in *Dred Scott v. Sandford* (which held that former slaves and the descendants of slaves could never be American citizens), but also insists that the specific decision applied only to the case at hand and should not be treated as a precedent. Thus, Lincoln believes that even an incorrect Supreme Court opinion must be obeyed in a specific case, but denies erroneous decisions more extensive influence.

In *Marbury v. Madison*, the Court declares that a statute enacted by Congress is unconstitutional. Chief Justice John Marshall, writing for the Court, explains why the Constitution implies that the Court has the power to strike down unconstitutional laws, famously declaring "It is emphatically the province and duty of the judicial department to say what the law is." Paradoxically, Marshall argues, Congress went beyond its powers when it enacted the Judiciary Act of 1789 and enlarged the powers of the Supreme Court. Thus, even as he asserted the power of judicial review, Marshall also declared that the Court's own powers were limited by the Constitution.

Matthew S. Brogdon therefore argues that Marshall's landmark *Marbury* opinion presents only a partial defense of judicial power. Although Marshall defends the right of judicial review, he at the same time grants Congress a great deal of discretion over the appellate jurisdiction of the Court. According to Marshall's argument, Congress would have unlimited power to restrict appellate jurisdiction. Brogdon claims that this view is inconsistent with the logic of Article III and would undermine the creation of the extensive system of lower federal courts necessary for a competent national judiciary. Through an examination of Federalist writings Brogdon shows that there is an earlier strain of Federalist thought that finds an extensive system of lower courts to be essential to the creation of a truly independent national government.

Marbury remains the preeminent argument for judicial review as a necessary element of limited constitutional government. In *Eakin v. Raub*, Justice John Bannister Gibson of the Pennsylvania Supreme Court argues that *Marbury* was incorrect, insisting that an unconstitutional act of the legislature should not be struck down by the courts. Where, he asks, does this power of judicial review come from, since it is not explicitly enumerated in the Constitution? Does not judicial review imply judicial supremacy, since a court may reverse a legislative act, while the legislature is powerless to overturn the decision of a court? Gibson believes that, instead of permitting judicial review and risking judicial supremacy, the people themselves, well instructed in the "first principles" of government, should hold the legislature responsible and force it to obey the Constitution.

Gibson may go too far in his rejection of judicial review, yet he is surely correct to warn that the courts, just like the other branches of government, may abuse their powers. In *Cooper v. Aaron*, the Supreme Court presented a novel argument for judicial supremacy. Although the Court relies on Marshall's assertion that it is the judiciary's duty "to say what the law is," it goes beyond Marshall's argument, insisting that the Supreme Court's "interpretation" of the Constitution "is the supreme law of the land." As the Court reasoned, since the Constitution is the supreme law of the land and the Supreme Court is the final interpreter of that law, "the federal judiciary is supreme in the exposition of the law of the Constitution." If Marshall believed the Court had a duty to interpret the supreme law and explain what it means, the *Cooper* Court argues that its own *interpretations* of the Constitution—that is, its opinions and precedents—*are themselves* the supreme law.

In contrast to the decision in *Cooper v. Aaron*, which asserts the powers of the federal judiciary without seriously considering limits to those powers, the Court's decision in *United States v. Nixon* acknowledges boundaries to judicial power and recognizes the legitimate claims of a coordinate branch of government. Chief Justice Warren Burger's opinion recognizes that the judiciary operates within a system of separation of powers and shows respect for the legitimate autonomy and authority of the executive branch. Thus, when considering whether President Richard Nixon could be required to turn over recordings of confidential conversations to a trial court, Burger acknowledges that each branch of government "must initially" interpret its own powers; as the officer who wields executive power under the Constitution, it is the president, rather than the Supreme Court, who must first interpret the extent of his own power. Despite this, Burger also insists that the Court must weigh in on separation of powers disputes, particularly when the rights of individual citizens are at stake. Thus, even though the Court rejects Nixon's absolute claim of executive privilege, it does recognize the constitutional importance of executive privilege. Ultimately, the Court weighs the president's interest in confidential communication with his officials against both the interest of the Watergate defendants in obtaining a fair trial and the interest of the trial court in carrying out its judicial duties.

As in *United States v. Nixon*, the majority of the Court in *American Legion v. American Humanist Association* recognizes that the federal courts have limited powers: they lack the authority to settle every constitutional question or to eliminate every perceived wrong. The case addresses a First Amendment challenge to the "Peace Cross," a World War I memorial located on property owned by the state of Maryland and maintained at government expense. The American Humanist Association claims that the government's involvement constitutes an infringement of the First Amendment's establishment clause. In his majority opinion, Justice Samuel Alito stresses the limits of judicial competence, pointing out that the Court has no way of knowing why the cross was originally erected in 1925. Does it reflect a religious purpose and an endorsement of Christianity, or does it primarily commemorate the dead? Similarly, concurrences by Justices Brett Kavanagh and Neil Gorsuch emphasize judicial modesty. Kavanaugh points out that even if the Supreme Court cannot order the removal of the cross, offended citizens can still seek a remedy through the regular political process. Gorsuch, for his part, argues that the Court cannot provide a remedy for hurt feelings. The Court can redress actual legal injuries done to individuals, but, in his view, simply being offended by the presence of the cross does not rise to the level of an injury to a constitutionally protected right. Thus, Alito, Kavanaugh, and Gorsuch each provide principles by which they impose principled limits on their own constitutional power as members of the federal judiciary.

In the next two selections we find a classical argument for liberal activism in a speech by Justice William J. Brennan, Jr., and a classic originalist call for restraint put forth by Judge Robert Bork. Brennan claims that the Court must look beyond the text of the Constitution and the intention of its framers in order to deal with problems that arise in the modern world. The Court was established in order to protect the rights of individuals, and especially of minorities. But in fulfilling its duties, Brennan claims the Court need not rely on any specific statutory or constitutional language. Instead, it should look to broader constitutional goals; the Constitution, he insists, embodies the nation's "aspirations to social justice, brotherhood, and human dignity." As a result, Brennan rejects originalism, which he believes "turn[s] a blind eye to social progress" by limiting these national aspirations to "the values of 1789."

In contrast, Judge Robert Bork argues that the doctrine of judicial activism is merely a convenient way to rationalize judicial overreach, a way of permitting judges to impose their own personal policy preferences on the Constitution and the nation. Bork believes that if the Constitution is to protect the rights of the people in the long run, the text of the document and the intention of its framers must provide the boundaries within which judicial interpretation takes place. If the Constitution fails to settle an issue, it is up to the political branches of government to fill in the gaps through legislation or constitutional amendment. In this way, Bork suggests, the Constitution can actually be updated in light of new aspirations and social progress—but it must be updated by a choice of elected, democratically responsible politicians, not by unelected judges.

Like Brennan, Jefferson fears that the framers of a Constitution may not be able to anticipate the changing needs of the nation. But unlike Brennan, Jefferson acknowledges that his position ultimately calls into question the possibility of an enduring constitutional system. To Jefferson's mind, an unchanging written Constitution is unjust, insofar as it allows the men who created the Constitution—now dead—to bind future generations and control or limit the choices they may make. Thus, he believes each generation must create its own Constitution. In response, Madison argued that generations are linked by the fact that later ones are beneficiaries of earlier ones, and to that extent obliged to follow their prescriptions. Since Madison was replying to Jefferson's objection to a "perpetual constitution," he must have had in mind his own generation's work of founding and the endurance of his own handiwork as the link among the individuals who were to live under the Constitution. Furthermore, creating a new government every generation, Madison argued, would destroy the people's natural prejudices in favor of their traditional government. As he put it in *Federalist 49*, frequent appeals to the people—allowing each generation to reinvent the fundamental principles of government—would "deprive the government of that veneration that time bestows on everything."

55

Alexander Hamilton

The Role of the Supreme Court (1788)

. . . As to the tenure by which the judges are to hold their places: this chiefly concerns their duration in office; the provisions for their support; the precautions for their responsibility.

According to the plan of the convention, all judges who may be appointed by the United States are to hold their offices *during good behavior*. The standard of good behavior for the continuance in office of the judicial magistracy, is certainly one of the most valuable of the modern improvements in the practice of government. In a monarchy it is an excellent barrier to the despotism of the prince; in a republic it is a no less excellent barrier to the encroachments and oppressions of the representative body. And it is the best expedient which can be devised in any government, to secure a steady, upright, and impartial administration of the laws.

Whoever attentively considers the different departments of power must perceive, that, in a government in which they are separated from each other, the judiciary, from the nature of its functions, will always be the least dangerous to the political rights of the Constitution; because it will be least in a capacity to annoy or injure them. The Executive not only dispenses the honors, but holds the sword of the community. The legislature not only commands the purse, but prescribes the rules by which the duties and rights of every citizen are to be regulated. The judiciary, on the contrary, has no influence over either the sword or the purse; no direction either of the strength or of the wealth of the society; and can take no active resolution whatever. It may truly be said to have neither FORCE nor WILL, but merely judgment; and must ultimately depend upon the aid of the executive arm even for the efficacy of its judgments.

This simple view of the matter suggests several important consequences. It proves incontestably, that the judiciary is beyond comparison the weakest of the three departments of power; that it can never attack with success either of the other two; and that all possible care is requisite to enable it to defend itself against their attacks. It equally proves, that though individual oppression may now and then proceed from the courts of justice, the general liberty of the people can never be endangered from that quarter; I mean so long as the judiciary remains truly distinct from both the legislature and the

From Federalist 78, in *The Federalist.*

Executive. For I agree, that "there is no liberty, if the power of judging be not separated from the legislative and executive powers." And it proves, in the last place, that as liberty can have nothing to fear from the judiciary alone, but would have every thing to fear from its union with either of the other departments; that as all the effects of such a union must ensue from a dependence of the former on the latter, notwithstanding a nominal and apparent separation; that as, from the natural feebleness of the judiciary, it is in continual jeopardy of being overpowered, awed, or influenced by its coordinate branches; and that as nothing can contribute so much to its firmness and independence as permanency in office, this quality may therefore be justly regarded as an indispensable ingredient in its constitution, and, in a great measure, as the citadel of the public justice and the public security.

The complete independence of the courts of justice is peculiarly essential in a limited Constitution. By a limited Constitution, I understand one which contains certain specified exceptions to the legislative authority; such, for instance, as that it shall pass no bills of attainder, no *ex-post-facto* laws, and the like. Limitations of this kind can be preserved in practice no other way than through the medium of courts of justice, whose duty it must be to declare all acts contrary to the manifest tenor of the Constitution void. Without this, all the reservations of particular rights or privileges would amount to nothing.

Some perplexity respecting the rights of the courts to pronounce legislative acts void, because contrary to the constitution, has arisen from an imagination that the doctrine would imply a superiority of the judiciary to the legislative power. It is urged that the authority which can declare the acts of another void, must necessarily be superior to the one whose acts may be declared void. As this doctrine is of great importance in all the American constitutions, a brief discussion of the ground on which it rests cannot be unacceptable.

There is no position which depends on clearer principles, than that every act of a delegated authority, contrary to the tenor of the commission under which it is exercised, is void. No legislative act, therefore, contrary to the Constitution, can be valid. To deny this, would be to affirm, that the deputy is greater than his principal; that the servant is above his master; that the representatives of the people are superior to the people themselves; that men acting by virtue of powers, may do not only what their powers do not authorize, but what they forbid.

If it be said that the legislative body are themselves the constitutional judges of their own powers, and that the construction they put upon them is conclusive upon the other departments, it may be answered, that this cannot be the natural presumption, where it is not to be collected from any particular provisions in the Constitution. It is not otherwise to be supposed, that the Constitution could intend to enable the representatives of the people to substitute their *will* to that of their constituents. It is far more rational to suppose, that the courts were designed to be an intermediate body between the people and the legislature, in order, among other things, to keep the latter within the limits assigned to their authority. The interpretation of the laws is the proper and peculiar province of the courts. A constitution is, in fact, and must be regarded by the judges, as a fundamental law. It therefore belongs to them to ascertain its meaning, as well as the meaning of any particular act proceeding from the legislative body. If there should happen to be an irreconcilable variance between the two, that which has the superior obligation and validity ought, of course, to be preferred; or, in other words, the Constitution ought to be preferred to the statute, the intention of the people to the intention of their agents.

Nor does this conclusion by any means suppose a superiority of the judicial to the legislative power. It only supposes that the power of the people is superior to both; and that where the will of the legislature, declared in its statutes, stands in opposition to that of the people, declared in the Constitution, the judges ought to be governed by the latter rather than the former. They ought to regulate their decisions by the fundamental laws, rather than by those which are not fundamental.

This exercise of judicial discretion, in determining between two contradictory laws, is exemplified in a familiar instance. It not uncommonly happens, that there are two statutes existing at one time, clashing in whole or in part with each other, and neither of them containing any repealing clause or expression. In such a case, it is the province of the courts to liquidate and fix their meaning and operation. So far as they can, by any fair construction, be reconciled to each other, reason and law conspire to dictate that this should be done; where this is impracticable, it becomes a matter of necessity to give effect to one, in exclusion of the other. The rule which has obtained in the courts for determining their relative validity is, that the last in order of time shall be preferred to the first. . . . [The Courts] thought it reasonable, that between the interfering acts of an *equal* authority, that which was the last indication of its will should have the preference.

But in regard to the interfering acts of a superior and subordinate authority, of an original and derivative power, the nature and reason of the thing indicate the converse of that rule as proper to be followed. They teach us that the prior act of a superior ought to be preferred to the subsequent act of an inferior and subordinate authority; and that accordingly, whenever a particular statute contravenes the Constitution, it will be the duty of the judicial tribunals to adhere to the latter and disregard the former.

It can be of no weight to say that the courts, on the pretence of a repugnancy, may substitute their own pleasure to the constitutional intentions of the legislature. This might as well happen in the case of two contradictory statutes; or it might as well happen in every adjudication upon any single statute. The courts must declare the sense of the law; and if they should be disposed to exercise WILL instead of JUDGMENT, the consequence would equally be the substitution of their pleasure to that of the legislative body. The observation, if it prove any thing, would prove that there ought to be no judges distinct from that body.

If, then, the courts of justice are to be considered as the bulwarks of a limited Constitution against legislative encroachments, this consideration will afford a strong argument for the permanent tenure of judicial offices since nothing will contribute so much as this to that independent spirit in the judges which must be essential to the faithful performance of so arduous a duty.

This independence of the judges is equally requisite to guard the Constitution and the rights of individuals from the effects of those ill humors, which the arts of designing men, or the influence of particular conjunctures, sometimes disseminate among the people themselves, and which, though they speedily give place to better information, and more deliberate reflection, have a tendency, in the meantime, to occasion dangerous innovations in the government, and serious oppressions of the minor party in the community. Though I trust the friends of the proposed Constitution will never concur with its enemies, in questioning that fundamental principle of republican government, which admits the right of the people to alter or abolish the established Constitution, whenever they find it inconsistent with their happiness, yet it is not to be inferred from this principle, that the representatives of the people, whenever a momentary inclination happens to lay hold of a majority of their constituents, incompatible with the provisions in the existing Constitution, would, on that account, be justifiable in a violation of those provisions; or that the courts would be under a greater obligation to connive at infractions in this shape, than when they had proceeded wholly from the cabals of the representative body. Until the people have, by some solemn and authoritative act, annulled or changed the established form, it is binding upon themselves collectively, as well as individually; and no presumption, or even knowledge, of their sentiments, can warrant their representatives in a departure from it, prior to such an act. But it is easy to see, that it would require an uncommon portion of fortitude in the judges to do their duty as faithful guardians of the Constitution, where legislative invasions of it had been instigated by the major voice of the community.

But it is not with a view to infractions of the Constitution only, that the independence of the judges may be an essential safeguard against the effects of occasional ill humors in the society. These sometimes extend no farther than to the injury of the private rights of particular classes of citizens, by unjust and partial laws. Here also the firmness of the judicial magistracy is of vast importance in mitigating the severity and confining the operation of such laws. It not only serves to moderate the immediate mischiefs of those which may have been passed but it operates as a check upon the legislative body in passing them; who, perceiving that obstacles to the success of iniquitous intention are to be expected from the scruples of the courts, are in a manner compelled, by the very motives of the injustice they meditate, to qualify their attempts. . . .

Periodical appointments, however regulated, or by whomsoever made, would, in some way or other, be fatal to [the judges'] necessary independence. . . .

There is yet a further and a weightier reason for the permanency of the judicial offices, which is deducible from the nature of the qualifications they require. It has been frequently remarked, with great propriety, that a voluminous code of laws is one of the inconveniences necessarily connected with the advantages of a free government. To avoid an arbitrary discretion in the courts, it is indispensable that they should be bound down by strict rules and precedents, which serve to define and point out their duty in every particular case that comes before them; and it will readily be conceived from the variety of controversies which grow out of the folly and wickedness of mankind, that the records of those precedents must unavoidably swell to a very considerable bulk, and must demand long and laborious study to acquire a competent knowledge of them. Hence it is, that there can be but few men in the society who will have sufficient skill in the laws to qualify them for the stations of judges. And making the proper deductions for the ordinary depravity of human nature, the number must be still smaller of those who unite the requisite integrity with the requisite knowledge. These considerations apprise us, that the government can have no great option between fit character; and that a temporary duration in office, which would naturally discourage such characters from quitting a lucrative line of practice to accept a seat on the bench, would have a tendency to throw the administration of justice into hands less able, and less well qualified, to conduct it with utility and dignity.

56

Brutus

The Problem of Judicial Review (1787)

. . . [T]he supreme court under this constitution [will] be exalted above all other power in the government, and subject to no controul. . . . I question whether the world ever saw, in any period of it, a court of justice invested with such immense powers, and yet placed in a situation so little responsible.

From Brutus XV, *New York Journal*, March 20, 1787.

Certain it is, that in England, and in the several states, where we have been taught to believe, the courts of law are put upon the most prudent establishment, they are on a very different footing.

The judges in England, it is true, hold their offices during their good behaviour, but then their determinations are subject to correction by the house of lords; and their power is by no means so extensive as that of the proposed supreme court of the union.—I believe they in no instance assume the authority to set aside an act of parliament under the idea that it is inconsistent with their constitution. They consider themselves bound to decide according to the existing laws of the land, and never undertake to controul them by adjudging that they are inconsistent with the constitution— much less are they vested with the power of giving an *equitable* construction to the constitution.

The judges in England are under the controul of the legislature, for they are bound to determine according to the laws passed by them. But the judges under this constitution will controul the legislature, for the supreme court are authorised in the last resort, to determine what is the extent of the powers of the Congress; they are to give the constitution an explanation, and there is no power above them to set aside their judgment. The framers of this constitution appear to have followed that of the British, in rendering the judges independent, by granting them their offices during good behaviour, without following the constitution of England, in instituting a tribunal in which their errors may be corrected; and without adverting to this, that the judicial under this system have a power which is above the legislative, and which indeed transcends any power before given to a judicial by any free government under heaven.

I do not object to the judges holding their commissions during good behaviour. I suppose it a proper provision provided they were made properly responsible. But I say, this system has followed the English government in this, while it has departed from almost every other principle of their jurisprudence, under the idea, of rendering the judges independent; which, in the British constitution, means no more than that they hold their places during good behaviour, and have fixed salaries, they have made the judges *independent*, in the fullest sense of the word. There is no power above them, to controul any of their decisions. There is no authority that can remove them, and they cannot be controuled by the laws of the legislature. In short, they are independent of the people, of the legislature, and of every power under heaven. Men placed in this situation will generally soon feel themselves independent of heaven itself. Before I proceed to illustrate the truth of these assertions, I beg liberty to make one remark—Though in my opinion the judges ought to hold their offices during good behaviour, yet I think it is clear, that the reasons in favour of this establishment of the judges in England, do by no means apply to this country.

The great reason assigned, why the judges in Britain ought to be commissioned during good behaviour, is this, that they may be placed in a situation, not to be influenced by the crown, to give such decisions, as would tend to increase its powers and prerogatives. While the judges held their places at the will and pleasure of the king, on whom they depended not only for their offices, but also for their salaries, they were subject to every undue influence. If the crown wished to carry a favorite point, to accomplish which the aid of the courts of law was necessary, the pleasure of the king would be signified to the judges. And it required the spirit of a martyr, for the judges to determine contrary to the king's will.—They were absolutely dependent upon him both for their offices and livings. The king, holding his office during life, and transmitting it to his posterity as an inheritance, has much stronger inducements to increase the prerogatives of his office than those who hold their offices for stated periods, or even for life. Hence the English nation gained a great point, in favour of liberty. When they obtained the appointment of the judges, during good behaviour, they got from the crown a concession, which deprived it of one of the most powerful engines with which it might enlarge the boundaries of the royal prerogative and encroach on the liberties of the people. But these reasons do not apply to this country, we have no hereditary monarch; those who appoint the judges do not hold their offices for life, nor do they descend to their children. The same arguments, therefore, which will conclude in favor of the tenor of the judge's offices for good behaviour, lose a considerable part of their weight when applied to the state and condition of America. But much less can it be shown, that the nature of our government requires that the courts should be placed beyond all account more independent, so much so as to be above controul.

I have said that the judges under this system will be *independent* in the strict sense of the word: To prove this I will show—That there is no power above them that can controul their decisions, or correct their errors. There is no authority that can remove them from office for any errors or want of capacity, or lower their salaries, and in many cases their power is superior to that of the legislature.

1st. There is no power above them that can correct their errors or controul their decisions—The adjudications of this court are final and irreversible, for there is no court above them to which appeals can lie, either in error or on the merits. In this respect it differs from the courts in England, for there the house of lords is the highest court, to whom appeals, in error, are carried from the highest of the courts of law.

2d. They cannot be removed from office or suffer a dimunition of their salaries, for any error in judgement or want of capacity.

It is expressly declared by the constitution,—"That they shall at stated times receive a compensation for their services which shall not be diminished during their continuance in office."

The only clause in the constitution which provides for the removal of the judges from office, is that which declares, that "the president, vice-president, and all civil officers of the United States, shall be removed from office, on impeachment for, and conviction of treason, bribery, or other high crimes and misdemeanors." By this paragraph, civil officers, in which the judges are included, are removable only for crimes. Treason and bribery are named, and the rest are included under the general terms of high crimes and misdemeanors.—Errors in judgement, or want of capacity to discharge the duties of the office, can never be supposed to be included in these words, *high crimes and misdemeanors*. A man may mistake a case in giving judgment, or manifest that he is incompetent to the discharge of the duties of a judge, and yet give no evidence of corruption or want of integrity. To support the charge, it will be necessary to give in evidence some facts that will shew, that the judges committed the error from wicked and corrupt motives.

3d. The power of this court is in many cases superior to that of the legislature. I have shewed, in a former paper, that this court will be authorised to decide upon the meaning of the constitution, and that, not only according to the natural and ob[vious] meaning of the words, but also according to the spirit and intention of it. In the exercise of this power they will not be subordinate to, but above the legislature. For all the departments of this government will receive their powers, so far as they are expressed in the constitution, from the people immediately, who are the source of power. The legislature can only exercise such powers as are given them by the constitution, they cannot assume any of the rights annexed to the judicial, for this plain reason, that the same authority which vested the legislature with their powers, vested the judicial with theirs—both are derived from the same source, both therefore are equally valid, and the judicial hold their powers independently of the legislature, as the legislature do of the judicial.—The supreme court then have a right, independent of the legislature, to give a construction to the constitution and every part of it, and there is no power provided in this system to correct their construction or do it away. If, therefore, the legislature pass any laws, inconsistent with the sense the judges put upon the constitution, they will declare it void; and therefore in this respect their power is superior to that of the legislature. . . .

57

Thomas Jefferson

Against Judicial Review (1815)

The . . . question, whether the judges are invested with exclusive authority to decide on the constitutionality of a law, has been heretofore a subject of consideration with me in the exercise of official duties. Certainly there is not a word in the constitution which has given that power to them more than to the executive or legislative branches. Questions of property, of character and of crime being ascribed to the judges, through a definite course of legal proceeding, laws involving such questions belong, of course, to them; and as they decide on them ultimately and without appeal, they of course decide *for themselves*. The constitutional validity of the law or laws again prescribing executive action, and to be administered by that branch ultimately and without appeal, the executive must decide for *themselves* also, whether, under the constitution, they are valid or not. So also as to laws governing the proceedings of the legislature, that body must judge *for itself* the constitutionality of the law, and equally without appeal or control from its coordinate branches. And, in general, that branch which is to act ultimately, and without appeal, on any law, is the rightful expositor of the validity of the law, uncontrolled by the opinions of the other co-ordinate authorities. It may be said that contradictory decisions may arise in such case, and produce inconvenience. This is possible, and is a necessary failing in all human proceedings. Yet the prudence of the public functionaries, and authority of public opinion, will generally produce accommodation. Such an instance of difference occurred between the judges of England (in the time of Lord Holt) and the House of Commons, but the prudence of those bodies prevented inconvenience from it. So in the cases of Duane and of William Smith of South Carolina, whose characters of citizenship stood precisely on the same ground, the judges in a question of meum and tuum which came before them, decided that Duane was not a citizen; and in a question of membership, the House of Representatives, under the same words of the same provision, adjudged

From *The Writings of Thomas Jefferson*, Vol. IX, G. P. Putnam's Sons, 1898.

William Smith to be a citizen. Yet no inconvenience has ensued from these contradictory decisions. This is what I believe myself to be sound. But there is another opinion entertained by some men of such judgment and information as to lessen my confidence in my own. That is, that the legislature alone is the exclusive expounder of the sense of the constitution, in every part of it whatever. And they allege in its support, that this branch has authority to impeach and punish a member of either of the others acting contrary to its declaration of the sense of the constitution. It may indeed be answered, that an act may still be valid although the party is punished for it, right or wrong. However, this opinion which ascribes exclusive exposition to the legislature, merits respect for its safety, there being in the body of the nation a control over them, which, if expressed by rejection on the subsequent exercise of their elective franchise, enlists public opinion against their exposition, and encourages a judge or executive on a future occasion to adhere to their former opinion. Between these two doctrines, every one has a right to choose, and I know of no third meriting any respect. . . .

58

Abraham Lincoln

The Authority of the Supreme Court (1857)

. . . And now as to the *Dred Scott* decision. That decision declares two propositions—first, that a negro cannot sue in the U.S. Courts; and secondly, that Congress cannot prohibit slavery in the Territories. It was made by a divided court—dividing differently on the different points. Judge Douglas does not discuss the merits of the decision; and, in that respect, I shall follow his example, believing I could no more improve on McLean and Curtis, than he could on Taney.

He denounces all who question the correctness of that decision, as offering violent resistance to it. But who resists it? Who has, in spite of the decision, declared Dred Scott free, and resisted the authority of his master over him?

From Speech at Springfield, Illinois, June 26, 1857, in *The Collected Works of Abraham Lincoln*, Vol. II, Rutgers University Press, 1953.

Judicial decisions have two uses—first, to absolutely determine the case decided, and secondly, to indicate to the public how other similar cases will be decided when they arise. For the latter use, they are called "precedents" and "authorities."

We believe, as much as Judge Douglas, (perhaps more) in obedience to, and respect for the judicial department of government. We think its decisions on Constitutional questions, when fully settled, should control, not only the particular cases decided, but the general policy of the country, subject to be disturbed only by amendments of the Constitution as provided in that instrument itself. More than this would be revolution. But we think the *Dred Scott* decision is erroneous. We know the court that made it, has often over-ruled its own decisions, and we shall do what we can to have it to over-rule this. We offer no *resistance* to it.

Judicial decisions are of greater or less authority as precedents, according to circumstances. That this should be so, accords both with common sense, and the customary understanding of the legal profession.

If this important decision had been made by the unanimous concurrence of the judges, and without any apparent partisan bias, and in accordance with legal public expectation, and with the steady practice of the departments throughout our history, and had been in no part, based on assumed historical facts which are not really true; or, if wanting in some of these, it had been before the court more than once, and had there been affirmed and re-affirmed through a course of years, it then might be, perhaps would be, factious, nay, even revolutionary, to not acquiesce in it as a precedent.

But when, as it is true we find it wanting in all these claims to the public confidence, it is not resistance, it is not factious, it is not even disrespectful, to treat it as not having yet quite established a settled doctrine for the country— But Judge Douglas considers this view awful. Hear him:

"The courts are the tribunals prescribed by the Constitution and created by the authority of the people to determine, expound and enforce the law. Hence, whoever resists the final decision of the highest judicial tribunal, aims a deadly blow to our whole Republican system of government—a blow, which if successful would place all our rights and liberties at the mercy of passion, anarchy and violence. I repeat, therefore, that if resistance to the decisions of the Supreme Court of the United States, in a matter like the points decided in the *Dred Scott* case, clearly within their jurisdiction as defined by the Constitution, shall be forced upon the country as a political issue, it will become a distinct and naked issue between the friends and the enemies of the Constitution—the friends and the enemies of the supremacy of the laws."

Why this same Supreme court once decided a national bank to be constitutional; but Gen. Jackson, as President of the United States, disregarded the decision, and vetoed a bill for a re-charter, partly on constitutional ground, declaring that each public functionary must support the Constitution, *"as he understands it."* But hear the General's own words. Here they are, taken from his veto message:

"It is maintained by the advocates of the bank, that its constitutionality, in all its features, ought to be considered as settled by precedent, and by the decision of the Supreme Court. To this conclusion I cannot assent. Mere precedent is a dangerous source of authority, and should not be regarded as deciding questions of constitutional power, except where the acquiescence of the people and the States can be considered as well settled. So far from this being the case on this subject, an argument against the bank might be based on precedent. One Congress in 1791, decided in favor of a bank; another in 1811, decided against it. One Congress in 1815 decided against a bank; another in 1816 decided in its favor. Prior to the present Congress, therefore, the precedents drawn from that source were equal. If we resort to the States, the expressions of legislative, judicial and executive opinions against the bank have been probably to those in its favor as four to one. There is nothing in precedent, therefore, which if its authority were admitted, ought to weigh in favor of the act before me."

I drop the quotations merely to remark that all there ever was, in the way of precedent up to the *Dred Scott* decision, on the points therein decided, had been against that decision. But hear Gen. Jackson further—

"If the opinion of the Supreme court covered the whole ground of this act, it ought not to control the co-ordinate authorities of this Government. The Congress, the executive and the court, must each for itself be guided by its own opinion of the Constitution. Each public officer, who takes an oath to support the Constitution, swears that he will support it as he understands it, and not as it is understood by others." . . .

59

Marbury v. Madison (1803)

Chief Justice Marshall delivered the opinion of the Court.

At the last term on the affidavits then read and filed with the clerk, a rule was granted in this case, requiring the secretary of state to show cause

From *Marbury v. Madison*, 1 Cranch 137 (1803).

why a mandamus should not issue, directing him to deliver to William Marbury his commission as a justice of the peace for the county of Washington in the District of Columbia.

No cause has been shown, and the present motion is for a mandamus. The peculiar delicacy of this case, the novelty of some of its circumstances, and the real difficulty attending the points which occur in it, require a complete exposition of the principles on which the opinion to be given by the court is founded.

In the order in which the court has viewed this subject the following questions have been considered and decided.

1st. Has the applicant a right to the commission he demands?

2d. If he has a right, and that right has been violated, do the laws of his country afford him a remedy?

3d. If they do afford him a remedy, is it a mandamus issuing from this court?

The first object of inquiry is,

1st. Has the applicant a right to the commission he demands?

[The Court's discussion showing Marbury's right to the commission is omitted.]

Mr. Marbury, then, since his commission was signed by the President, and sealed by the Secretary of State, was appointed; and as the law creating the office, gave the officer a right to hold for five years, independent of the executive, the appointment was not revocable, but vested in the officer legal rights, which are protected by the laws of his country.

To withhold his commission, therefore, is an act deemed by the court not warranted by law, but violative of a vested legal right.

This brings us to the second inquiry; which is,

2d. If he has a right, and that right has been violated, do the laws of his country afford him a remedy? The very essence of civil liberty certainly consists in the right of every individual to claim the protection of the laws, whenever he receives an injury. One of the first duties of government is to afford that protection. . . .

The government of the United States has been emphatically termed a government of laws, and not of men. It will certainly cease to deserve this high appellation, if the laws furnish no remedy for the violation of a vested legal right. . . .

[T]he question, whether the legality of an act of the head of a department be examinable in a court of justice or not, must always depend on the nature of that act. . . .

By the constitution of the United States, the President is invested with certain important political powers, in the exercise of which he is to use his own discretion, and is accountable only to his country in his political character and to his own conscience. To aid him in the performance of these duties, he is authorized to appoint certain officers, who act by his authority, and in conformity with his orders.

In such cases, their acts are his acts; and whatever opinion may be entertained of the manner in which executive discretion may be used, still there exists, and can exist, no power to control that discretion. The subjects are political. They respect the nation, not individual rights, and being intrusted to the executive, the decision of the executive is conclusive. . . .

But when the legislature proceeds to impose on that officer other duties; when he is directed peremptorily to perform certain acts; when the rights of individuals are dependent on the performance of those acts; he is so far the officer of the law; is amenable to the laws for his conduct; and cannot at his discretion sport away the vested rights of others.

The conclusion from this reasoning is, that where the heads of departments are the political or confidential agents of the executive, merely to execute the will of the President, or rather to act in cases in which the executive possesses a constitutional or legal discretion, nothing can be more perfectly clear than that their acts are only politically examinable. But where a specific duty is assigned by law, and individual rights depend upon the performance of that duty, it seems equally clear that the individual who considers himself injured, has a right to resort to the laws of his country for a remedy. . . .

It is, then, the opinion of the Court,

1st. That by signing the commission of Mr. Marbury, the President of the United States appointed him a justice of peace for the county of Washington, in the District of Columbia; and that the seal of the United States, affixed thereto by the Secretary of State, is conclusive testimony of the verity of the signature, and of the completion of the appointment; and that the appointment conferred on him a legal right to the office for the space of five years.

2d. That, having this legal title to the office, he has a consequent right to the commission; a refusal to deliver which is a plain violation of that right, for which the laws of his country afford him a remedy.

It remains to be inquired whether,

3d. He is entitled to the remedy for which he applies. This depends on, 1st. The nature of the writ applied for; and, 2d. The power of this court.

1st. The nature of the writ. . . .

This writ, if awarded, would be directed to an officer of government, and its mandate to him would be, to use the words of Blackstone, "to do a particular thing therein specified, which appertains to his office and duty, and which the court has previously determined, or at least supposes, to be consonant to right and justice." Or, in the words of Lord Mansfield, the applicant, in this case, has a right to execute an office of public concern, and is kept out of possession of that right.

These circumstances certainly concur in this case.

Still, to render the mandamus a proper remedy, the officer to whom it is to be directed, must be one to whom, on legal principles, such writ may be directed; and the person applying for it must be without any other specific and legal remedy.

1st. With respect to the officer to whom it would be directed. The intimate political relation subsisting between the President of the United States and the heads of departments, necessarily renders any legal investigation of the acts of one of those high officers peculiarly irksome, as well as delicate; and excites some hesitation with respect to the propriety of entering into such investigation. . . .

But, if [our inquiry] be not such a question; if, so far from being an intrusion into the secrets of the cabinet, it respects a paper which, according to law, is upon record, and to a copy of which the law gives a right, on the payment of ten cents; if it be no intermeddling with a subject over which the executive can be considered as having exercised any control; what is there in the exalted station of the officer, which shall bar a citizen from asserting, in a court of justice, his legal rights, or shall forbid a court to listen to the claim, or to issue a mandamus directing the performance of a duty, not depending on executive discretion, but on particular acts of congress, and the general principles of law?

If one of the heads of departments commits any illegal act, under colour of his office, by which an individual sustains an injury, it cannot be pretended that his office alone exempts him from being sued in the ordinary mode of proceeding, and being compelled to obey the judgment of the law. How, then, can his office exempt him from this particular mode of deciding on the legality of his conduct if the case be such a case as would, were any other individual the party complained of, authorize the process?

. . . [W]here he is directed by law to do a certain act affecting the absolute rights of individuals, in the performance of which he is not placed under the particular direction of the President, and the performance of which the President cannot lawfully forbid, and therefore is never presumed to have forbidden; as for example to record a commission, or a patent for land, which has received all the legal solemnities; or to give a copy of such record; in such cases, it is not perceived on what ground the courts of the country are further excused from the duty of giving judgment that right be done to an injured individual, than if the same services were to be performed by a person not the head of a department. . . .

This, then, is a plain case for a mandamus, either to deliver the commission, or a copy of it from the record; and it only remains to be inquired,

Whether it can issue from this court.

The act to establish the judicial courts of the United States authorizes the Supreme Court "to issue writs of mandamus in cases warranted by the principles and usages of law, to any courts appointed, or persons holding office, under the authority of the United States."

The Secretary of State, being a person holding an office under the authority of the United States, is precisely within the letter of the description, and if this court is not authorized to issue a writ of mandamus to such an officer, it must be because the law is unconstitutional, and therefore absolutely incapable of conferring the authority, and assigning the duties which its words purport to confer and assign.

The constitution vests the whole judicial power of the United States in one Supreme Court, and such inferior courts as congress shall, from time to time, ordain and establish. This power is expressly extended to all cases arising under the laws of the United States; and, consequently, in some form, may be exercised over the present case; because the right claimed is given by a law of the United States.

In the distribution of this power it is declared that "the Supreme Court shall have original jurisdiction in all cases affecting ambassadors, other public ministers and consuls, and those in which a state shall be a party. In all other cases, the Supreme Court shall have appellate jurisdiction."

It has been insisted, at the bar, that as the original grant of jurisdiction, to the Supreme and inferior courts, is general, and the clause, assigning original jurisdiction to the Supreme Court, contains no negative or restrictive words, the power remains to the legislature, to assign original jurisdiction to that court in other cases than those specified in the article which has been recited; provided those cases belong to the judicial power of the United States.

. . . [We reject this argument.] If congress remains at liberty to give this court appellate jurisdiction, where the constitution has declared their jurisdiction shall be original; and original jurisdiction where the constitution has declared it shall be appellate; the distribution of jurisdiction, made in the constitution, is form without substance. . . .

It is the essential criterion of appellate jurisdiction, that it revises and corrects the proceedings in a cause already instituted, and does not create that cause. Although, therefore, a mandamus may be directed to courts, yet to issue such a writ to an officer for the delivery of a paper, is in effect the same as to sustain an original action for that paper, and, therefore, seems not to belong to appellate but to original jurisdiction. . . .

The authority, therefore, given to the Supreme Court, by the act establishing the judicial courts of the United States, to issue writs of mandamus to public officers, appears not to be warranted by the constitution; and it becomes necessary to inquire whether a jurisdiction so conferred can be exercised. . . .

The government of the United States is [a government of limited powers]. The powers of the legislature are defined and limited; and that those limits may not be mistaken, or forgotten, the constitution is written. To what purpose are powers limited, and to what purpose is that limitation committed to writing, if these limits may, at any time, be passed by those intended to be restrained? . . . It is a proposition too plain to be contested, that the constitution controls any legislative act repugnant to it; or, that the legislature may alter the constitution by an ordinary act. . . .

If an act of the legislature, repugnant to the constitution, is void, does it, notwithstanding its invalidity, bind the courts, and oblige them to give it effect? Or, in other words, though it be not law, does it constitute a rule as operative as if it was a law? This would be to overthrow in fact what was established in theory; and would seem, at first view, an absurdity too gross to be insisted on. It shall, however, receive a more attentive consideration.

It is emphatically the province and duty of the judicial department to say what the law is. Those who apply the rule to particular cases, must of necessity expound and interpret that rule. If two laws conflict with each other, the courts must decide on the operation of each.

So if a law be in opposition to the constitution; if both the law and the constitution apply to a particular case, so that the court must either decide that case conformably to the law, disregarding the constitution; or conformably to the constitution, disregarding the law; the court must determine which of these conflicting rules governs the case. This is of the very essence of judicial duty.

If, then, the courts are to regard the constitution, and the constitution is superior to any ordinary act of the legislature, the constitution, and not such ordinary act, must govern the case to which they both apply. . . .

The judicial power of the United States is extended to all cases arising under the constitution.

Could it be the intention of those who gave this power, to say that in using it the constitution should not be looked into? That a case arising under the constitution should be decided without examining the instrument under which it arises?

This is too extravagant to be maintained.

In some cases, then, the constitution must be looked into by the judges. . . .

Why otherwise does [the Constitution] direct the judges to take an oath to support it? This oath certainly applies in an especial manner, to their conduct in their official character. How immoral to impose it on them, if they were to be used as the instruments, and the knowing instruments, for violating what they swear to support! . . .

It is also not entirely unworthy of observation, that in declaring what shall be the supreme law of the land, the constitution itself is first mentioned; and not the laws of the United States generally, but those only which shall be made in pursuance of the constitution, have that rank.

Thus, the particular phraseology of the constitution of the United States confirms and strengthens the principle, supposed to be essential to all written constitutions, that a law repugnant to the constitution is void; and that courts, as well as other departments, are bound by that instrument. . . .

60

Matthew S. Brogdon

Federalist Constitutionalism and Judicial Independence (2013)

When we speak of judicial independence, we tend to mean the independence of the individual judge, not of the judiciary as an institution. Thus we tend to emphasize, as did Publius in *Federalist 78*, the personal privileges of life tenure and irreducible salary and the power, which these privileges undergird, to disregard unconstitutional laws. But early Federalists conceived of judicial independence on a larger scale as the independence of the federal judiciary as a coequal and coextensive branch of the federal government. And for this sort of institutional independence something more than life tenure and judicial review is necessary. In particular, they emphasized an extensive system of inferior federal courts as an essential component of the constitutional order and promoted the role of the Supreme Court as a guarantor of compliance with constitutional limits and uniform administration of federal law. The following essay explores this Federalist view of the judiciary and in so doing provides a window onto their often-neglected understanding of the constitutional system of separated powers and federalism.

Before proceeding further, it is important to note that the early Federalist view discussed below is not entirely consonant with the jurisprudence of John Marshall, the great chief justice who did so much to defend federal supremacy and judicial review during his long tenure on the Supreme Court. Though Marshall is often—and for good reason—treated as the juridical representative of Federalist constitutionalism, his decisions evince a more modest understanding of the judiciary's independence from legislative control than that espoused by many of his Federalist predecessors on the Court and in the First Congress. In particular, Marshall admitted a broad scope for congressional control of federal judicial structure and jurisdiction, including the power to strip the Supreme Court of appellate jurisdiction. As we will see, this was inconsistent with the broader Federalist argument for an independent judiciary. The Federalists who drafted Article III in the Convention and secured the creation of federal trial courts in the First Congress refused to admit any such subordination of the judiciary to the legislature.

Courtesy of Matthew S. Brogdon.

Inferior Federal Courts and Direct Enforcement

In the view of early Federalists, an essential means of carrying the Constitution into effect was an extensive system of inferior federal trial courts capable of facilitating the direct enforcement of federal law on individuals. The fundamental defect in the Articles of Confederation had been the absence of independent executive and judicial institutions capable of administering federal law. Without the means of direct enforcement, Congress was forced to rely on states to carry federal policy into effect, an arrangement that proved unworkable. Thus, the most important work of the Framers was not the extension of federal legislative power to new objects like interstate commerce, necessary as that may have been, but the creation of executive and judicial institutions. In sum, the central object of the convention was to render the federal government independent of the states. As Madison explained to his fellow Framers in Philadelphia, "A government without a proper executive [and] judiciary would be the mere trunk of a body, without arms or legs to act or move." Reliance on state officers for the performance of federal functions was among the relics of the confederation left lying on the cutting room floor in the convention.

However, when the First Congress convened in 1789 and set about the work of giving effect to the Constitution, Anti-Federalists seeking to limit the growth of federal power and minimize the effects of their defeat in the ratification debates resisted the creation of inferior federal courts. They sought instead to rely on the existing state judiciaries for the administration of federal law, with an appeal to the Supreme Court for the correction of errors. This proposed reliance on state judges would in effect diminish the independence of the federal government and it therefore evoked a powerful defense of the new constitutional order from Federalists.

The two brightest expositors of the Federalist view in the First Congress proved to be Fisher Ames and James Madison, who met the challenge from the Anti-Federalists in the House. Using the language of Article III to great effect, they argued that state judges were constitutionally prohibited from exercising certain portions of federal jurisdiction and that Congress was therefore constitutionally obligated to create a system of inferior courts sufficiently extensive to decide these exclusively federal cases. Their exposition of Article III is worth taking time to explore, both because it won the day in the fight over the Judiciary Act of 1789 and because it directly challenged the Anti-Federalist contention, still prevalent today, that Congress may constitutionally decline to create inferior federal courts altogether.

The first section of Article III declares, "The judicial Power of the United States shall be vested in one supreme Court, and in such inferior Courts as the Congress may from time to time ordain and establish." Madison and Ames, among others, argued that this investiture of power in the federal courts—like Article II's similar investiture of executive power in the president—was exclusive. To declare that the judicial power of the

Union "shall be vested" in federal courts is to deny that same power to any other institution, state or federal. By vesting federal judicial power in federal judges alone and federal executive power in the president alone the Constitution simultaneously secured the separation of powers within the federal government and excluded the states from any share in the administration of federal law. In the midst of the House debate, Ames chided the Anti-Federalists for trying to "hire out" federal judicial power and observed that Congress might just as well "assign over our legislative . . . power" to the states since "it would not be more strange to get the laws made for this body, than after their passage to get them interpreted and executed by those whom we do not appoint, and cannot control." Congress could no more empower state judges to exercise federal jurisdiction than it could authorize state legislatures to make federal law.

Madison further elaborated the constitutional problems with reliance on state judges, drawing out the extended implications of the Federalists' exclusive reading of the Vesting Clause. Investing federal judicial power in state judges would require them to become federal judges within the meaning of Article III and would therefore require that they be appointed to office by the president, confirmed by the Senate, and enjoy the constitutional protections of life tenure and irreducible salary. Madison's observation revealed an unintended result of the Anti-Federalists' effort to rely on state officials for the performance of federal functions. The Anti-Federalists were seeking a means of preserving state autonomy from federal encroachment. But ironically, they would be making the state judges subordinate agents of federal power. Instead of being displaced by new federal trial courts, the state judiciaries would be coopted by federal authorities. Thus, reliance on state judges would arguably undermine state autonomy in a profound way. Interestingly, Madison's insight is confirmed by the history of federal expansion in the twentieth century, where the most intrusive innovations in federal policy— such as Johnson's Great Society programs—have relied on state administration as a substitute for direct federal enforcement.

Anti-Federalists objected to this exclusive construction of the Vesting Clauses on the ground that the Constitution elsewhere explicitly authorized the administration of federal law in state courts. The Supremacy Clause of Article VI declared, "This Constitution, and the Laws of the United States . . . shall be the supreme Law of the Land; and the Judges in every State shall be bound thereby, any Thing in the Constitution or Laws of any State to the Contrary notwithstanding." Here, the Anti-Federalists argued, was an explicit duty laid on state judges to exercise federal jurisdiction. But as Ames pointed out in reply, this argument failed to appreciate the precise nature of the duty embodied in the Supremacy Clause. Article VI did not authorize state judges to try federal cases, that is, cases "arising under" a federal law. It merely required that they give effect to any federal law that might apply to a case before them in their capacity as state judges. If, for example, a state bankruptcy law sought to relieve a debtor of his obligations, and the debtor sued in state court under the state law to cancel his debt, the aggrieved creditor could ask the state judge to disregard the state bankruptcy law and reinstate the debt under the Contracts Clause of the federal Constitution, which prohibits state laws "impairing the obligation of contracts." In this situation the state judge would derive jurisdiction to decide the case from the state bankruptcy law and yet be under an obligation to give effect to applicable federal law. Thus, to put it in the terms Ames employed, federal law would function as a "rule of decision" in the state courts but not as a "source of jurisdiction." By this line of reasoning, Ames reconciled the Supremacy Clause to the Federalists' exclusive reading of the Vesting Clause of Article III. And the Anti-Federalists failed to offer any compelling response to it.

Of course, the Vesting Clause of Article III did not, by itself, compel Congress to create inferior federal courts. Indeed, its use of the permissive phrase "may from time to time ordain and establish" seemed to suggest a measure of legislative discretion in the matter. The Vesting Clause merely deprived the state courts of jurisdiction in federal cases. But when combined with Article III's command that the "judicial Power shall extend to all Cases . . . arising under this Constitution, the Laws of the United States, and Treaties made . . . under their Authority" it furnished ample ground for the argument that Congress was under a constitutional obligation to create a certain number of inferior federal courts. Ames and Madison took the words "shall extend" to be mandatory. Federal jurisdiction must comprehend "all Cases arising under" the Constitution, laws, and treaties of the United States; the state judges are deprived by the Vesting Clause of jurisdiction over those same cases; therefore, Congress must provide a sufficient number of federal trial courts to decide them. And since Article III also provided that federal criminal trials "shall be held in the State where the . . . Crimes shall have been committed," there had to be at least one federal trial court in each state, which is the arrangement eventually adopted by Congress in the Judiciary Act of 1789. According to Ames and Madison, Congress could not, consistently with the Constitution, do less than this.

Modern scholars and jurists have generally rejected Ames and Madison's mandatory construction of Article III on the ground that it conflicts with the intent of the Framers. Ironically, the episode at the Constitutional Convention on which these critics of the Federalist view espoused by Madison in the First Congress rely most heavily is the so-called Madisonian Compromise. When the Virginia Plan was presented to the Convention at the outset of its deliberations, its language referred to the existence of both a supreme court and an unspecified number of inferior courts. Some delegates objected strenuously, advocating that Congress continue its reliance on state courts and confine the judicial power of the Union to a supreme court alone. When debate over the issue threatened to stall the proceedings, Madison and fellow Federalist James Wilson suggested that the passage be deleted and Congress be empowered to create inferior courts, observing that there was a difference between allowing for their creation by Congress and creating them outright in the Constitution. Scholars critical of the mandatory reading of Article III insist that this compromise should be an authoritative guide to our construction of the Constitution. But two considerations weigh heavily against their argument. First, the compromise took place shortly after the start of the convention when the great bulk of Article III was yet to be written. So it is conceivable that the language subsequently added—such as the Vesting Clause and the jurisdictional menu—may have superseded the compromise. Second, Madison, who brokered the original compromise, evidently did not think it binding since he disregards it altogether in the First Congress and instead construes the plain language of Article III as he finds it.

The Supreme Court and Uniformity

Though the establishment of a system of federal courts pervading the Union was the first priority of early Federalists, they also grasped the Supreme Court's essential role in securing uniformity in the administration of federal law and compliance with the Constitution in state and federal courts. In order to perform these crucial functions, the Supreme Court needed the authority to hear appeals from the decisions of state and federal courts alike.

Given the central role that the Supreme Court would eventually come to play in the legitimation and expansion of federal power, it is somewhat surprising to note that Federalists in the First Congress spent little time arguing for an increase of the Court's powers. Indeed, in comparison with their rhetorical effort on behalf of the expansion of inferior courts, their statements in the debate on the Judiciary Act of 1789 regarding the nation's highest tribunal are quite sparse. Federalists tended to assume rather than argue for the centrality of the Supreme Court. And they did so for a very simple reason. The Anti-Federalists were in surprisingly vehement agreement with them. As we saw in our discussion of the debate over inferior courts, when Anti-Federalists proposed alternatives to the Federalist judiciary in the Convention and the First Congress, they invariably emphasized the Supreme Court's role maintaining uniformity and constitutional limits. Federalists need not fear relying on state courts, Anti-Federalists reassured them, for state decisions in federal matters could be appealed to the Supreme Court. Indeed, the Supremacy Clause—the oft-cited constitutional warrant for appealing the decisions of a state court to the Supreme Court—owes its existence to incipient Anti-Federalists in the Constitutional Convention. The authors of the New Jersey Plan proposed the Supremacy Clause, which eventually found its way into Article VI of the Constitution, as a means of keeping states compliant with federal law. This was intended as a substitute for the more robust system of inferior federal courts that the Virginia Plan and its proponents had sought. In light of the Anti-Federalists' earnest assent to this view of the Supreme Court, Federalists initially took the power for granted.

Despite this general agreement between Federalists and Anti-Federalists on the necessity of the Supreme Court as a superintendent of uniformity and arbiter of constitutional disputes, the First Congress erected major institutional impediments to the Court's effective performance of these functions. And just a little experience working within the system created by the Judiciary Act of 1789 moved Federalist justices to argue strenuously for the centrality of their appellate role overseeing state courts and inferior federal courts.

What irked the justices and their Federalist allies most was the onerous task of riding circuit. Under the judiciary act, the justices were obligated to visit each state twice a year to hold circuit courts, which were responsible for trying most federal crimes and hearing appeals from the district trial courts. While circuit riding had the benefit of providing interaction between the justices and the people of the states, it also required as much as half the year to complete, especially for the unfortunate justices tasked with riding the Southern Circuit. More importantly, circuit riding left little time for the justices to see to their growing responsibilities at the Supreme Court. The justices wasted no time making known their objections to the system. As Chief Justice Jay, writing on behalf of the Court, explained in a letter to the president, the justices' dual role as judges of the supreme and circuit courts left them in the questionable position of hearing appeals from their own decisions and seemed to confound the Constitution's distinction between supreme and inferior court judges. And the justices were not alone in their complaint that circuit riding was undermining the Court's efficient performance of its duties. When Congress asked Attorney General Edmund Randolph to recommend reforms in the judicial system, he proposed that the number of inferior court judges be increased and the justices relieved of circuit duties. Among other things, he presciently argued that making the Court "stationary" would "promote uniformity" in the federal judiciary by permitting the justices more time to issue written opinions that could be published—as they now are in the U.S. Reports—and distributed to the bench and bar throughout the country. But Randolph's proposal was fruitless, as were the repeated attempts of Federalists in Congress to abolish circuit riding in the 1790s.

The circuit riding system's drain on the justices' attention was rendered all the more onerous by Congress's insistence on controlling the Supreme Court's docket. Instead of allowing the Court to decide which cases it would hear—something the Court now does on its own with little legislative interference—Congress established general rules to identify important cases and gave litigants a right of appeal. This left the Court with little discretion in the composition of its caseload and no means of controlling the number of cases appearing on its docket. This system was logistically untenable in the long term. The rapid growth of federal legislation steadily increased the flow of litigation into the Supreme Court, while westward expansion added to the burden of riding circuit and further diminished the justices' time for attending to the Court's affairs. The justices were squeezed between circuit riding and a swelling docket.

Congress's manipulation of the Court's appellate docket was also constitutionally suspect. Congress was in effect claiming authority not only to force the Supreme Court to hear certain cases as a matter of mandatory jurisdiction, but also to preclude the Court from hearing cases within its constitutionally vested jurisdiction. While the Judiciary Act of 1789 was still pending before Congress, Randolph, who played a key role drafting Article III on the committee of detail at the convention, wrote to Madison questioning Congress's effort to circumscribe federal jurisdiction. "Will the courts be bound by any definition of authority, which the constitution does not in their opinion warrant?" The justices quickly showed a spark of the defiance Randolph expected from them. In 1790, Supreme Court Justices James Wilson and John Rutledge—who had served on the committee of detail with Randolph and helped refine the language of Article III—issued a writ of certiorari to the Superior Court of North Carolina to move a case pending before that court, which was the highest tribunal in the state, into the federal circuit court. While the judiciary act had provided for the removal of some state cases into the federal courts, this particular case did not fit the description. Without explicit authorization from Congress, the justices simply assumed that such a power was inherent in the constitutional order and vested in them by Article III itself. There was nothing to prevent the extension of this logic to permit the removal of any case from inferior federal courts as well as from state courts into the Supreme Court. Six years later, in the case of *Wiscart v. D'Auchey*, Wilson would move in this very direction, sharpening his objection to congressional circumscription of Supreme Court jurisdiction. "Even, indeed, if a positive restriction [on the Supreme Court's appellate jurisdiction] existed by law, it would, in my judgment, be superseded by the superior authority of the constitutional provision" vesting the judicial power in a Supreme Court. Thus we find the key authors of Article III—Wilson, Randolph, and Rutledge—defending the jurisdictional reach of the Supreme Court from congressional tinkering.

Significantly, their position contradicts the orthodox interpretation of Article III, which condones the authority of Congress to strip the Supreme Court of appellate jurisdiction at will. The supposed source of Congress's authority to excise the Supreme Court's appellate jurisdiction is the Exceptions Clause of Article III. After setting out a list of cases and controversies to which "the judicial power shall extend" Article III distributes these cases between the original and appellate jurisdiction of the Supreme Court.

> In all Cases affecting Ambassadors, other public Ministers and Consuls, and those in which a State shall be a Party, the Supreme Court shall have original Jurisdiction. In all other Cases before mentioned, the Supreme Court shall have appellate Jurisdiction, both as to law and fact, with such Exceptions and under such Regulations as the Congress shall make. (Article III, Section 2)

The dispute over this provision hinges on what it means for Congress to make "exceptions" to the appellate jurisdiction of the Court. The ortho-dox reading of this passage holds that, by making an exception to its appel-late jurisdiction, Congress may remove a case entirely from the Court's jurisdictional reach. Critics of the orthodox interpretation argue that the clause simply authorizes Congress to make exceptions to the Court's appel-late jurisdiction by adding cases to the Court's original jurisdiction. Or, as one recent study phrases it, Congress has power to alter the "form" of the Court's jurisdiction, not "confiscate" it altogether. When read in isolation the language is arguably amenable to either interpretation. But when read in the context of the hierarchical language the Constitution consistently uses to describe the federal judicial system and in light of the development of the Exceptions Clause in the Federal Convention, the weight of the evidence shifts against the orthodox interpretation.

Constitutional provisions, especially those that may admit of more than one plausible interpretation, must be understood as part of a larger whole and thus interpreted by reference to the entire document. A legislative power to confiscate the appellate jurisdiction of the Supreme Court is in substantial tension with the other constitutional provisions relating to the judiciary. The Constitution carefully and consistently describes the judicial branch in hierarchical terms. In Article I, Section 8, from which Congress derives its power to create inferior courts, the text is careful to specify that they "shall have power . . . to constitute Tribunals *inferior to the supreme Court*" [empha-sis added]. The Vesting Clause of Article III merely acknowledges this power, and carefully maintains the judicial hierarchy, when it vests the judicial power of the Union "in *one supreme Court*, and in such inferior Courts as Congress may from time to time ordain and establish" [emphasis added]. Only two kinds of federal courts may therefore exist: one Supreme Court and an unspecified number of inferior courts. It is difficult to see how a court may remain inferior to the Supreme Court unless the Supreme Court may review its decisions. No other means exists by which to maintain the judicial hierarchy and preserve uniformity in the administration of federal law and the construction of the Constitution. The Court does not possess a power to remove or discipline the judges of inferior courts, for all judges are to hold their offices during good behavior subject only to impeachment. Without the review power, the Court is supreme in name only and its justices are left to console themselves with the grandeur of a mere title. The supremacy of the Supreme Court, an institutional principle upon which the text is so carefully insistent, is contingent upon its authority to review lower court decisions through its appellate jurisdiction or decide cases first and finally under its original jurisdiction. If, therefore, the Exceptions Clause is amenable to an alternative construction more consistent with the judicial hierarchy, we must take it seriously.

The development of Article III in the Federal Convention adds considerable weight to the position that the Exceptions Clause merely grants Congress the power to relocate cases from the appellate to the original jurisdiction of the Court. The clause originated in a draft written by Randolph for his colleagues on the committee of detail. "But this supreme jurisdiction shall be appellate only, except in those instances, in which the legislature shall make it original[.]" Like the eventual provision in Article III, Randolph's draft made the Court's jurisdiction appellate by default and then permitted Congress to make "except[ions]" by moving cases from the appellate to the original jurisdiction of the Court. This would allow Congress to expedite the settlement of cases—such as suits involving the states or foreign emissaries as parties—in which a drawn-out series of appeals might disrupt the stability of the Union or foreign relations. Rutledge and Wilson subsequently introduced a number of refinements to Randolph's original provision—none of which altered the nature of the power granted to Congress—rendering the clause reported by the committee and ultimately adopted by the convention. When Randolph, Wilson, and Rutledge later contended that Congress may not strip the Court of jurisdiction, they were merely giving voice to the original intention of the Exceptions Clause as it developed in the Convention, which ironically empowered Congress to expedite a decision in the Supreme Court, not prevent it altogether. This was a qualitatively different power more consistent with the hierarchical structure of the federal judiciary and the integrity of federal jurisdiction.

The even deeper irony surrounding the interpretation of the Exceptions Clause is that defenders of Congress's jurisdiction stripping power rely most heavily for the authority of their position on John Marshall, the greatest Federalist jurist ever to occupy the bench. As a delegate to the Virginia ratifying convention in 1788, a young Marshall sought to allay Anti-Federalist concerns over the vast powers of the judiciary by noting that, should the Supreme Court make a nuisance of itself, the Constitution authorized Congress to excise cases from its appellate jurisdiction. Fifteen years later, Marshall's opinion in *Marbury v. Madison* would clothe this construction of Article III in the authoritative garb of precedent. The *Marbury* opinion is of course most notable for its defense of judicial review as the logical corollary of a written constitution. But the substantive holding in the case—that the

Supreme Court could not issue a writ of mandamus commanding Secretary of State Madison to deliver Marbury's commission as a justice of the peace— required Marshall to construe the provision of Article III distributing the jurisdiction of the Supreme Court. The Court could not issue the writ that Marbury requested because the original jurisdiction of the Supreme Court was constitutionally fixed and did not include the power to issue writs of mandamus to executive officers. The provision of the Judiciary Act of 1789 conferring original jurisdiction on the Court to issue the writ was therefore an unconstitutional legislative alteration of the Court's original jurisdiction. This much is readily apparent in Marshall's opinion. Less obvious upon a first reading, however, is that this interpretation of Article III forced Marshall to acknowledge Congress's jurisdiction stripping authority. If Congress was unable to add cases to the original jurisdiction of the Supreme Court, then its constitutional power to make "exceptions" to the Court's appellate jurisdiction necessarily authorized Congress to place cases beyond the Court's reach. Consistent with this reading of the text, Congress might eliminate the appellate jurisdiction of the Court altogether. Coupled with the Anti-Federalist claim, discussed above, that Congress may decline to create inferior federal courts, this power would permit Congress to whittle down the federal judiciary to the original jurisdiction of the Supreme Court and leave all other federal judicial functions to be performed by the states. This amounts to a claim that Congress may, without violating the Constitution, eviscerate the judicial branch.

FEDERALISTS AND THE MODERN JUDICIARY

Though the Federalist construction of Article III has never won widespread acceptance, it has proved remarkably foresighted in its description of the eventual institutional shape of the federal judiciary. Federal law is now administered almost entirely in a system of district trial courts and circuit courts of appeal, none of which rely on circuit riding justices. The Supreme Court meanwhile is free to focus its attention on a relatively small number of important cases of its own choosing. Not since it finally relinquished control of the appellate docket in 1925 has Congress made a plausible attempt to control the flow of cases into the Court. In its essential outlines, this is the judicial institution Federalists sought to establish throughout the 1790s, and which they understood the Constitution to require.

This observation is no mere historical curiosity. Recovering the Federalist understanding of the judicial power, and of the constitutional system of separated powers generally, furnishes an important corrective to a number of prevalent misconceptions. First, it calls into question the prevailing originalist hostility toward judicial independence. Because they give too much weight to the Anti-Federalist—and later Jeffersonian—account of the constitutional order, originalists tend to see the late blooming of the federal judiciary in the twentieth century as a progressive innovation and thus at odds with the constitutional order. In their earnest desire to confine judicial discretion to the text of the Constitution and its original design—a laudable goal in itself—originalists have ironically neglected the weighty textual and historical bases for judicial independence. Second, it rebuts the contention of progressives and living constitutionalists that the Framers' Constitution is ill equipped to meet the demands of modern administration. When Justice Brennan insisted on the necessity of a living constitution in his 1984 Georgetown speech, he was appealing to a progressive tradition that sees the Constitution as anachronistic both in its conception of human liberty and in its institutional design. According to this tradition, the insistence on separated powers and federalism are as much an impediment to progress as the Contracts Clause. More recently, Justice Ginsburg gave voice to the same progressive view when she cited the constitutions of South Africa and Canada as better guides for framing a government in the twenty-first century than America's "rather old" Constitution. The superiority of the South African example in particular she attributed to its independent judiciary. The implication would seem to be that the bench she herself occupies derives its remarkably extensive independence from some source other than the Constitution. But if the Federalists are to be our guide, Article III, despite its vintage, embodies a substantially independent and presciently modern judicial institution.

Placing the modern judiciary in the light of the Federalist construction of Article III therefore helps us restore the constitutional foundation of the judicial power. This is essential to preserving the constitutional order. *Federalist 51* admonished the makers of constitutions that the "great security" against the concentration of power "consists in giving to those who administer each department the necessary constitutional means and personal motives to resist the encroachments of the others. Ambition must be made to counteract ambition. The interests of the man must be connected with the constitutional rights of the place." So long as judges understand the Constitution to be the fount and foundation of their independence and power, they will have a personal interest in preserving the Constitution. If, however, the judges continue to exercise power disconnected from its constitutional source, if they understand the fount of their power to be a progressive displacement of the original constitutional order, then a great motive in favor of fidelity to the Constitution is lost. It may be counterintuitive, but an effective defense of the relevance and puissance of the Framers' Constitution against its progressive critics must demonstrate not just how the Constitution limits judicial discretion—the predominant aim of originalist scholarship—but also how it creates and protects judicial independence, not merely of the judge but of the judiciary.

More fundamentally, the Federalists remind us that the Constitution's first concern was to empower the federal government and render it independent of the states. And by construing the Vesting Clauses as exclusive and self-executing grants of power to the executive and judicial branches, they remind us of the centrality of separated powers in the constitutional order. The executive and judiciary are not merely "separate branches sharing powers" but are separate branches wielding different types of powers, in the exercise of which they may each claim a measure of supremacy and independence from what the Framers disdainfully termed the legislative vortex.

61

Eakin v. Raub (1825)

Justice Gibson, dissenting.

. . . I am aware, that a right [of the courts] to declare all unconstitutional acts void . . . is generally held as a professional dogma; but, I apprehend rather as a matter of faith than of reason. . . . But I may premise, that it is not a little remarkable, that although the right in question has all along been claimed by the judiciary, no judge has ventured to discuss it, except Chief Justice Marshall, (in *Marbury v. Madison*) and if the argument of a jurist so distinguished for the strength of his ratiocinative powers to be found inconclusive, it may fairly be set down to the weakness of the position which he attempts to defend. . . .

The constitution and the right of the legislature to pass the act, may be in collision. But is that a legitimate subject for judicial determination? If it be, the judiciary must be a peculiar organ, to revise the proceedings of the legislature, and to correct its mistakes; and in what part of the constitution are we to look for this proud pre-eminence? Viewing the matter in the opposite direction, what would be thought of an act of assembly in which it should be declared that the Supreme Court had, in a particular case, put a wrong construction on the constitution of the United States, and that

From *Eakin v. Raub*, 12 Sergeant & Rawle 330 (Pa. 1825).

the judgment should therefore be reversed? It would doubtless be thought a usurpation of judicial power. But it is by no means clear, that to declare a law void which has been enacted according to the forms prescribed in the constitution, is not a usurpation of legislative power. It is an act of sovereignty; and sovereignty and legislative power are said by Sir William Blackstone to be convertible terms. It is the business of the judiciary to interpret the laws, not scan the authority of the lawgiver. . . .

Now, as the judiciary is not expressly constituted for that purpose, it must derive whatever authority of the sort it may possess, from the reasonableness and fitness of the thing. But, in theory, all the organs of the government are of equal capacity; or, if not equal, each must be supposed to have superior capacity only for those things which peculiarly belong to it; and, as legislation peculiarly involves the consideration of those limitations which are put on the law-making power, and the interpretation of the laws when made, involves only the construction of the laws themselves, it follows that the construction of the constitution in this particular belongs to the legislature, which ought therefore to be taken to have superior capacity to judge of the constitutionality of its own acts. But suppose all to be of equal capacity in every respect, why should one exercise a controlling power over the rest? That the judiciary is of superior rank, has never been pretended, although it has been said to be co-ordinate. . . .

It may be alleged, that no such power is claimed, and that the judiciary does no positive act, but merely refuses to be instrumental in giving effect to an unconstitutional law. This is nothing more than a repetition in a different form of the argument,—that an unconstitutional law is ipso facto void; for a refusal to act under the law, must be founded on a right in each branch to judge of the acts of all the others, before it is bound to exercise its functions to give those acts effect. No such right is recognised in the different branches of the national government, except the judiciary, (and that, too, on account of the peculiar provisions of the constitution). . . .

Every one knows how seldom men think exactly alike on ordinary subjects; and a government constructed on the principle of assent by all its parts, would be inadequate to the most simple operations. The notion of a complication of counter checks has been carried to an extent in theory, of which the framers of the constitution never dreamt. When the entire sovereignty was separated into its elementary parts, and distributed to the appropriate branches, all things incident to the exercise of its powers were committed to each branch exclusively. The negative which each part of the legislature may exercise, in regard to the acts of the other, was thought sufficient to prevent material infractions of the restraints which were put on the power of the whole; for, had it been intended to interpose the judiciary as an additional barrier, the matter would surely not have been left in doubt. The judges would not have been left to stand on the insecure and ever shifting ground of public opinion as to constructive powers: they would have been placed on the impregnable ground of an express grant. They would not have been compelled to resort to the debates in the convention, or the opinion that was generally entertained at the time. . . .

The power is said to be restricted to cases that are free from doubt or difficulty. But the abstract existence of a power cannot depend on the clearness or obscurity of the case in which it is to be exercised; for that is a consideration that cannot present itself, before the question of the existence of the power shall have been determined; and, if its existence be conceded, no considerations of policy arising from the obscurity of the particular case, ought to influence the exercise of it. The judge would have no discretion; but the party submitting the question of constitutionality would have an interest in the decision of it, which could not be postponed to motives of deference for the opinion of the legislature. His rights would depend not on the greatness of the supposed discrepancy with the constitution, but on the existence of any discrepancy at all; and the judge would therefore be bound to decide this question, like every other in respect to which he may be unable to arrive at a perfectly satisfactory conclusion. But he would evade the question instead of deciding it, were he to refuse to decide in accordance with the inclination of his mind. To say, therefore, that the power is to be exercised but in perfectly clear cases, is to betray a doubt of the propriety of exercising it at all. . . .

But what I have in view in this inquiry, is the supposed right of the judiciary, to interfere, in cases where the constitution is to be carried into effect through the instrumentality of the legislature, and where that organ must necessarily first decide on the constitutionality of its own act. The oath to support the constitution is not peculiar to the judges, but is taken indiscriminately by every officer of the government, and is designed rather as a test of the political principles of the man, than to bind the officer in the discharge of his duty: otherwise it were difficult to determine what operation it is to have in the case of a recorder of deeds, for instance, who, in the execution of his office, has nothing to do with the constitution. But granting it to relate to the official conduct of the judge, as well as every other officer, and not to his political principles, still it must be understood in reference to supporting the constitution, only as far as that may be involved in his official duty; and, consequently, if his official duty does not comprehend an inquiry into the authority of the legislature, neither does his oath. . . .

But do not the judges do a positive act in violation of the constitution, when they give effect to an unconstitutional law? Not if the law has been passed according to the forms established in the constitution. The fallacy of the question is, in supposing that the judiciary adopts the acts of the legislature as its own; whereas the enactment of a law and the interpretation of it are not concurrent acts, and as the judiciary is not required to concur in the enactment, neither is it in the breach of the constitution which may be the consequence of the enactment. The fault is imputable to the legislature, and on it the responsibility exclusively rests. . . .

But it has been said, that this construction would deprive the citizen of the advantages which are peculiar to a written constitution, by at once declaring the power of the legislature, in practice, to be illimitable. I ask, what are those advantages? The principles of a written constitution are more fixed and certain, and more apparent to the apprehension of the people, than principles which depend on tradition and the vague comprehension of the individuals who compose the nation, and who cannot all be expected to receive the same impressions or entertain the same notions on any given subject. But there is no magic or inherent power in parchment and ink, to command respect and protect principles from violation. In the business of government, a recurrence to first principles answers the end of an observation at sea with a view to correct the dead reckoning; and, for this purpose, a written constitution is an instrument of inestimable value.

It is of inestimable value, also, in rendering its principles familiar to the mass of the people; for, after all, there is no effectual guard against legislative usurpation but public opinion, the force of which, in this country, is inconceivably great. Happily this is proved, by experience, to be a sufficient guard against palpable infractions. The constitution of this state has withstood the shocks of strong party excitement for thirty years, during which no act of the legislature has been declared unconstitutional, although the judiciary has constantly asserted a right to do so in clear cases. But it would be absurd to say, that this remarkable observance of the constitution has been produced, not by the responsibility of the legislature to the people, but by an apprehension of control by the judiciary. Once let public opinion be so corrupt as to sanction every misconstruction of the constitution and abuse of power which the temptation of the moment may dictate, and the party which may happen to be predominant, will laugh at the puny efforts of a dependent power to arrest it in its course.

For these reasons, I am of opinion that it rests with the people, in whom full and absolute sovereign power resides to correct abuses in legislation, by instructing their representatives to repeal the obnoxious act. What is wanting to plenary power in the government, is reserved by the people for their own immediate use; and to redress an infringement of their rights in this respect, would seem to be an accessory of the power thus reserved.

It might, perhaps, have been better to vest the power in the judiciary; as it might be expected that its habits of deliberation, and the aid derived from the arguments of counsel, would more frequently lead to accurate conclusions. On the other hand, the judiciary is not infallible; and an error by it would admit of no remedy but a more distinct expression of the public will, through the extraordinary medium of a convention; whereas, an error by the legislature admits of a remedy by an exertion of the same will, in the ordinary exercise of the right of suffrage,—a mode better calculated to attain the end, without popular excitement.

It may be said, the people would probably not notice an error of their representatives. But they would as probably do so, as notice an error of the judiciary; and, beside, it is a postulate in the theory of our government, and the very basis of the superstructure, that the people are wise, virtuous, and competent to manage their own affairs: and if they are not so, in fact, still every question of this sort must be determined according to the principles of the constitution, as it came from the hands of its framers, and the existence of a defect which was not foreseen, would not justify those who administer the government, in applying a corrective in practice, which can be provided only by a convention. . . .

62

Cooper v. Aaron (1958)

Unanimous opinion of the Court.

As this case reaches us, it raises questions of the highest importance to the maintenance of our federal system of government. It necessarily involves a claim by the Governor and Legislature of a State that there is no duty on state officials to obey federal court orders resting on this Court's considered interpretation of the United States Constitution. Specifically, it involves actions by the Governor and Legislature of Arkansas upon the premise that they are not bound by our holding in *Brown v. Board of Education.* That holding was that the Fourteenth Amendment forbids States to use their governmental powers to bar children on racial grounds from attending schools where there is state participation through any arrangement, management, funds or property. We are urged to uphold a suspension of the Little Rock School Board's plan to do away with segregated public schools in Little Rock until state laws and efforts to upset and nullify our holding in *Brown v. Board of Education* have been further challenged and tested in the courts. We reject these contentions. . . .

The following are the facts and circumstances so far as necessary to show how the legal questions are presented.

From *Cooper v. Aaron,* 358 U.S. 1 (1958).

On May 17, 1954, this Court decided that enforced racial segregation in the public schools of a State is a denial of the equal protection of the laws enjoined by the Fourteenth Amendment. *Brown v. Board of Education.* . . . [In 1955,] the Court recognized that good faith compliance with the principles declared in *Brown* might, in some situations, "call for elimination of a variety of obstacles in making the transition to school systems operated in accordance with the constitutional principles set forth in our May 17, 1954, decision.". . .

. . . The District Courts were directed to require "a prompt and reasonable start toward full compliance," and to take such action as was necessary to bring about the end of racial segregation in the public schools "with all deliberate speed." Of course, in many locations, obedience to the duty of desegregation would require the immediate general admission of Negro children, otherwise qualified as students for their appropriate classes at particular schools. On the other hand, a District Court, after analysis of the relevant factors (which, of course, excludes hostility to racial desegregation), might conclude that justification existed for not requiring the present non-segregated admission of all qualified Negro children. In such circumstances, however, the Court should scrutinize the program of the school authorities to make sure that they had developed arrangements pointed toward the earliest practicable completion of desegregation, and had taken appropriate steps to put their program into effective operation. It was made plain that delay in any guise in order to deny the constitutional rights of Negro children could not be countenanced. . . .

On May 20, 1954, three days after the first *Brown* opinion, the Little Rock District School Board adopted, and on May 23, 1954, made public, a statement of policy entitled "Supreme Court Decision—Segregation in Public Schools." In this statement, the Board recognized that

> "It is our responsibility to comply with Federal Constitutional Requirements, and we intend to do so when the Supreme Court of the United States outlines the method to be followed."

Thereafter, the Board undertook studies of the administrative problems confronting the transition to a desegregated public school system at Little Rock. It instructed the Superintendent of Schools to prepare a plan for desegregation, and approved such a plan on May 24, 1955. . . . It was contemplated that desegregation at the high school level would commence in the fall of 1957, and the expectation was that complete desegregation of the school system would be accomplished by 1963. . . .

While the School Board was thus going forward with its preparation for desegregating the Little Rock school system, other state authorities, in contrast, were actively pursuing a program designed to perpetuate in Arkansas the system of racial segregation which this Court had held violated the Fourteenth

Amendment. First came, in November, 1956, an amendment to the State Constitution flatly commanding the Arkansas General Assembly to oppose "in every Constitutional manner the Unconstitutional desegregation decisions of May 17, 1954, and May 31, 1955, of the United States Supreme Court," and, through the initiative, a pupil assignment law. Pursuant to this state constitutional command, a law relieving school children from compulsory attendance at racially mixed schools, and a law establishing a State Sovereignty Commission, were enacted by the General Assembly in February, 1957. . . .

On September 2, 1957, the day before these Negro students were to enter Central High, the school authorities were met with drastic opposing action on the part of the Governor of Arkansas, who dispatched units of the Arkansas National Guard to the Central High School grounds and placed the school "off limits" to colored students. As found by the District Court in subsequent proceedings, the Governor's action had not been requested by the school authorities, and was entirely unheralded. . . .

The Governor's action caused the School Board to request the Negro students on September 2 not to attend the high school "until the legal dilemma was solved." The next day, September 3, 1957, the Board petitioned the District Court for instructions, and the court, after a hearing, found that the Board's request of the Negro students to stay away from the high school had been made because of the stationing of the military guards by the state authorities. The court determined that this was not a reason for departing from the approved plan, and ordered the School Board and Superintendent to proceed with it.

On the morning of the next day, September 4, 1957, the Negro children attempted to enter the high school, but, as the District Court later found, units of the Arkansas National Guard, "acting pursuant to the Governor's order, stood shoulder to shoulder at the school grounds and thereby forcibly prevented the 9 Negro students . . . from entering," as they continued to do every school day during the following three weeks. . . .

. . . [Shortly thereafter, the United States Attorney for the Eastern District of Arkansas] and the Attorney General of the United States . . . entered the proceedings and filed a petition on behalf of the United States, as *amicus curiae*, to enjoin the Governor of Arkansas and officers of the Arkansas National Guard from further attempts to prevent [desegregation]. . . . After hearings on the petition, the District Court found that the School Board's plan had been obstructed by the Governor through the use of National Guard troops, and granted a preliminary injunction on September 20, 1957, enjoining the Governor and the officers of the Guard from preventing the attendance of Negro children at Central High School, and from otherwise obstructing or interfering with the orders of the court in connection with the plan. The National Guard was then withdrawn from the school.

The next school day was Monday, September 23, 1957. The Negro children entered the high school that morning under the protection of the Little

Rock Police Department and members of the Arkansas State Police. But the officers caused the children to be removed from the school during the morning because they had difficulty controlling a large and demonstrating crowd which had gathered at the high school. On September 25, however, the President of the United States dispatched federal troops to Central High School, and admission of the Negro students to the school was thereby effected. Regular army troops continued at the high school until November 27, 1957. They were then replaced by federalized National Guardsmen who remained throughout the balance of the school year. Eight of the Negro students remained in attendance at the school throughout the school year.

We come now to the aspect of the proceedings presently before us. On February 20, 1958, the School Board and the Superintendent of Schools filed a petition in the District Court seeking a postponement of their program for desegregation. Their position, in essence, was that, because of extreme public hostility, which they stated had been engendered largely by the official attitudes and actions of the Governor and the Legislature, the maintenance of a sound educational program at Central High School, with the Negro students in attendance, would be impossible. The Board therefore proposed that the Negro students already admitted to the school be withdrawn and sent to segregated schools, and that all further steps to carry out the Board's desegregation program be postponed for a period later suggested by the Board to be two and one-half years.

After a hearing, the District Court granted the relief requested by the Board. . . .

The District Court's judgment was dated June 20, 1958. The Negro respondents appealed to the Court of Appeals for the Eighth Circuit. . . . The Court of Appeals . . . reversed the District Court. . . .

In affirming the judgment of the Court of Appeals which reversed the District Court, we have accepted without reservation the position of the School Board, the Superintendent of Schools, and their counsel that they displayed entire good faith in the conduct of these proceedings and in dealing with the unfortunate and distressing sequence of events which has been outlined. We likewise have accepted the findings of the District Court as to the conditions at Central High School during the 1957–1958 school year, and also the findings that the educational progress of all the students, white and colored, of that school has suffered, and will continue to suffer if the conditions which prevailed last year are permitted to continue.

The significance of these findings, however, is to be considered in light of the fact, indisputably revealed by the record before us, that the conditions they depict are directly traceable to the actions of legislators and executive officials of the State of Arkansas, taken in their official capacities, which reflect their own determination to resist this Court's decision in the *Brown* case and which have brought about violent resistance to that decision in Arkansas. In its petition for certiorari filed in this Court, the School Board itself describes the situation in this language:

> "The legislative, executive, and judicial departments of the state government opposed the desegregation of Little Rock schools by enacting laws, calling out troops, making statements villifying federal law and federal courts, and failing to utilize state law enforcement agencies and judicial processes to maintain public peace."

One may well sympathize with the position of the Board in the face of the frustrating conditions which have confronted it, but, regardless of the Board's good faith, the actions of the other state agencies responsible for those conditions compel us to reject the Board's legal position. . . .

The constitutional rights of respondents are not to be sacrificed or yielded to the violence and disorder which have followed upon the actions of the Governor and Legislature. . . .

The controlling legal principles are plain. The command of the Fourteenth Amendment is that no "State" shall deny to any person within its jurisdiction the equal protection of the laws. . . .

. . . [T]he prohibitions of the Fourteenth Amendment extend to all action of the State denying equal protection of the laws; whatever the agency of the State taking the action. In short, the constitutional rights of children not to be discriminated against in school admission on grounds of race or color declared by this Court in the *Brown* case can neither be nullified openly and directly by state legislators or state executive or judicial officers nor nullified indirectly by them through evasive schemes for segregation whether attempted "ingeniously or ingenuously."

What has been said, in the light of the facts developed, is enough to dispose of the case. However, we should answer the premise of the actions of the Governor and Legislature that they are not bound by our holding in the *Brown* case. It is necessary only to recall some basic constitutional propositions which are settled doctrine.

Article VI of the Constitution makes the Constitution the "supreme Law of the Land." In 1803, Chief Justice Marshall, speaking for a unanimous Court, referring to the Constitution as "the fundamental and paramount law of the nation," declared in the notable case of *Marbury v. Madison* that "It is emphatically the province and duty of the judicial department to say what the law is." This decision declared the basic principle that the federal judiciary is supreme in the exposition of the law of the Constitution, and that principle has ever since been respected by this Court and the Country as a permanent and indispensable feature of our constitutional system. It follows that the interpretation of the Fourteenth Amendment enunciated by this Court in the *Brown* case is the supreme law of the land, and Art. VI of the Constitution makes it of binding effect on the States "any Thing in the Constitution or Laws of any State to the Contrary notwithstanding." Every state legislator and executive and judicial officer is solemnly committed by oath taken pursuant to Art. VI, cl. 3 "to support this Constitution." Chief Justice Taney, speaking for a unanimous Court in 1859, said that this requirement reflected the framers'

> "anxiety to preserve it [the Constitution] in full force, in all its powers, and to guard against resistance to or evasion of its authority, on the part of a State. . . ."

No state legislator or executive or judicial officer can war against the Constitution without violating his undertaking to support it. Chief Justice Marshall spoke for a unanimous Court in saying that:

> "If the legislatures of the several states may at will, annul the judgments of the courts of the United States, and destroy the rights acquired under those judgments, the constitution itself becomes a solemn mockery. . . ."

A Governor who asserts a power to nullify a federal court order is similarly restrained. If he had such power, said Chief Justice Hughes, in 1932, also for a unanimous Court,

> "it is manifest that the fiat of a state Governor, and not the Constitution of the United States, would be the supreme law of the land; that the restrictions of the Federal Constitution upon the exercise of state power would be but impotent phrases. . . ."

It is, of course, quite true that the responsibility for public education is primarily the concern of the States, but it is equally true that such responsibilities, like all other state activity, must be exercised consistently with federal constitutional requirements as they apply to state action. The Constitution created a government dedicated to equal justice under law. The Fourteenth Amendment embodied and emphasized that ideal. State support of segregated schools through any arrangement, management, funds, or property cannot be squared with the Amendment's command that no State shall deny to any person within its jurisdiction the equal protection of the laws. The right of a student not to be segregated on racial grounds in schools so maintained is indeed so fundamental and pervasive that it is embraced in the concept of due process of law. The basic decision in *Brown* was unanimously reached by this Court only after the case had been briefed and twice argued and the issues had been given the most serious consideration. Since the first *Brown* opinion, three new Justices have come to the Court. They are at one with the Justices still on the Court who participated in that basic decision as to its correctness, and that decision is now unanimously reaffirmed. The principles announced in that decision and the obedience of the States to them, according to the command of the Constitution, are indispensable for the protection of the freedoms guaranteed by our fundamental charter for all of us. Our constitutional ideal of equal justice under law is thus made a living truth.

63

United States v. Nixon (1974)

Mr. Chief Justice Burger delivered the opinion of the Court.

On March 1, 1974, a grand jury of the United States District Court for the District of Columbia returned an indictment charging seven named individuals with various offenses, including conspiracy to defraud the United States and to obstruct justice. Although he was not designated as such in the indictment, the grand jury named the President, among others, as an unindicted coconspirator. On April 18, 1974, upon motion of the Special Prosecutor, a subpoena *duces tecum* was issued . . . to the President. . . . This subpoena required the production, in advance of the September 9 trial date, of certain tapes, memoranda, papers, transcripts or other writings relating to certain precisely identified meetings between the President and others. The Special Prosecutor was able to fix the time, place and persons present at these discussions because the White House daily logs and appointment records had been delivered to him. On April 30, the President publicly released edited transcripts of 43 conversations; portions of 20 conversations subject to subpoena in the present case were included. On May 1, 1974, the President's counsel filed a "special appearance" and a motion to quash the subpoena. . . . This motion was accompanied by a formal claim of privilege. . . .

In the District Court, the President's counsel argued that the court lacked jurisdiction to issue the subpoena because the matter was an intra-branch dispute between a subordinate and superior officer of the Executive Branch and hence not subject to judicial resolution. That argument has been renewed in this Court with emphasis on the contention that the dispute does not present a "case" or "controversy" which can be adjudicated in the federal courts. The President's counsel argues that the federal courts should not intrude into areas committed to the other branches of Government. He views the present dispute as essentially a "jurisdictional" dispute within the Executive Branch which he analogizes to a dispute between two congressional committees. Since the Executive Branch has exclusive authority and absolute discretion to decide whether to prosecute a case, it is contended that a President's decision is final in determining what evidence is to be used in a given criminal case. . . .

Our starting point is the nature of the proceeding for which the evidence is sought—here a pending criminal prosecution. It is a judicial

From *United States v. Nixon*, 418 U.S. 683 (1974).

proceeding in a federal court alleging violation of federal laws and is brought in the name of the United States as sovereign. Under the authority of Article II, §2, Congress has vested in the Attorney General the power to conduct the criminal litigation of the United States Government. It has also vested in him the power to appoint subordinate officers to assist him in the discharge of his duties. Acting pursuant to those statutes, the Attorney General has delegated the authority to represent the United States in these particular matters to a Special Prosecutor with unique authority and tenure. The regulation gives the Special Prosecutor explicit power to contest the invocation of executive privilege in the process of seeking evidence deemed relevant to the performance of these specially delegated duties. . . .

So long as this regulation remains in force the Executive Branch is bound by it, and indeed the United States as the sovereign composed of the three branches is bound to respect and to enforce it. . . .

Here at issue is the production or nonproduction of specified evidence deemed by the Special Prosecutor to be relevant and admissible in a pending criminal case. It is sought by one official of the Government within the scope of his express authority; it is resisted by the Chief Executive on the ground of his duty to preserve the confidentiality of the communications of the President. Whatever the correct answer on the merits, these issues are "of a type which are traditionally justiciable." . . .

[W]e turn to the claim that the subpoena should be quashed because it demands "confidential conversations between a President and his close advisors that it would be inconsistent with the public interest to produce." The first contention is a broad claim that the separation of powers doctrine precludes judicial review of a President's claim of privilege. The second contention is that if he does not prevail on the claim of absolute privilege, the court should hold as a matter of constitutional law that the privilege prevails over the subpoena *duces tecum*.

In the performance of assigned constitutional duties each branch of the Government must initially interpret the Constitution, and the interpretation of its powers by any branch is due great respect from the others. The President's counsel, as we have noted, reads the Constitution as providing an absolute privilege of confidentiality for all presidential communications. Many decisions of this Court, however, have unequivocally reaffirmed the holding of *Marbury v. Madison*, that "it is emphatically the province and duty of the judicial department to say what the law is."

No holding of the Court has defined the scope of judicial power specifically relating to the enforcement of a subpoena for confidential presidential communications for use in a criminal prosecution, but other exercises of powers by the Executive Branch and the Legislative Branch have been found invalid as in conflict with the Constitution. In a series of cases, the Court interpreted the explicit immunity conferred by express provisions of the Constitution on Members of the House and Senate by the Speech or Debate Clause, U.S. Const. Art. 1, §6. . . .

Our system of government "requires that federal courts on occasion interpret the Constitution in a manner at variance with the construction given the document by another branch." *Powell v. McCormack*. And in *Baker v. Carr*, the Court stated:

> "[D]eciding whether a matter has in any measure been committed by the Constitution to another branch of government, or whether the action of that branch exceeds whatever authority has been committed, is itself a delicate exercise in constitutional interpretation, and is a responsibility of this Court as ultimate interpreter of the Constitution."

Notwithstanding the deference each branch must accord the others, the "judicial power of the United States" vested in the federal courts by Art. III, § 1 of the Constitution can no more be shared with the Executive Branch than the Chief Executive, for example, can share with the Judiciary the veto power, or the Congress share with the Judiciary the power to override a presidential veto. Any other conclusion would be contrary to the basic concept of separation of powers and the checks and balances that flow from the scheme of a tripartite government. . . .

In support of his claim of absolute privilege, the President's counsel urges two grounds one of which is common to all governments and one of which is peculiar to our system of separation of powers. The first ground is the valid need for protection of communications between high government officials and those who advise and assist them in the performance of their manifold duties; the importance of this confidentiality is too plain to require further discussion. Human experience teaches that those who expect public dissemination of their remarks may well temper candor with a concern for appearances and for their own interests to the detriment of the decision-making process. Whatever the nature of the privilege of confidentiality of presidential communications in the exercise of Art. II powers the privilege can be said to derive from the supremacy of each branch within its own assigned area of constitutional duties. Certain powers and privileges flow from the nature of enumerated powers; the protection of the confidentiality of presidential communications has similar constitutional underpinnings.

The second ground asserted by the President's counsel in support of the claim of absolute privilege rests on the doctrine of separation of powers. Here it is argued that the independence of the Executive Branch within its own sphere insulates a president from a judicial subpoena in an ongoing criminal prosecution, and thereby protects confidential presidential communications.

However, neither the doctrine of separation of powers, nor the need for confidentiality of high level communications, without more, can sustain an absolute, unqualified presidential privilege of immunity from judicial process under all circumstances. The President's need for complete candor and objectivity from advisers calls for great deference from the courts. However, when the privilege depends solely on the broad, undifferentiated claim of public interest in the confidentiality of such conversations, a confrontation with other values arises. Absent a claim of need to protect military, diplomatic or sensitive national security secrets, we find it difficult to accept the argument that even the very important interest in confidentiality of presidential communications is significantly diminished by production of such material for *in camera* inspection with all the protection that a district court will be obliged to provide.

The impediment that an absolute, unqualified privilege would place in the way of the primary constitutional duty of the Judicial Branch to do justice in criminal prosecutions would plainly conflict with the function of the courts under Art. III. In designing the structure of our Government and dividing and allocating the sovereign power among three coequal branches, the Framers of the Constitution sought to provide a comprehensive system, but the separate powers were not intended to operate with absolute independence. . . . To read the Art. II powers of the President as providing an absolute privilege as against a subpoena essential to enforcement of criminal statutes on no more than a generalized claim of the public interest in confidentiality of nonmilitary and nondiplomatic discussions would upset the constitutional balance of "a workable government" and gravely impair the role of the courts under Art. III.

Since we conclude that the legitimate needs of the judicial process may outweigh presidential privilege, it is necessary to resolve those competing interests in a manner that preserves the essential functions of each branch. The right and indeed the duty to resolve that question does not free the judiciary from according high respect to the representations made on behalf of the President.

. . . A President and those who assist him must be free to explore alternatives in the process of shaping policies and making decisions and to do so in a way many would be unwilling to express except privately. These are the considerations justifying a presumptive privilege for presidential communications. The privilege is fundamental to the operation of government and inextricably rooted in the separation of powers under the Constitution. In *Nixon v. Sirica*, the Court of Appeals held that such presidential communications are "presumptively privileged," and this position is accepted by both parties in the present litigation. We agree with Mr. Chief Justice Marshall's observation, therefore, that "in no case of this kind would a court be required to proceed against the President as against an ordinary individual." *United States v. Burr.*

But this presumptive privilege must be considered in light of our historic commitment to the rule of law. This is nowhere more profoundly manifest than in our view that "the twofold aim [of criminal justice] is that guilt shall not escape or innocence suffer." *Berger v. United States.* We have elected to employ an adversary system of criminal justice in which the parties contest all issues before a court of law. The need to develop all relevant facts in the adversary system is both fundamental and comprehensive. The ends of criminal justice would be defeated if judgments were to be founded on a partial or speculative presentation of the facts. The very integrity of the judicial system and public confidence in the system depend on full disclosure of all the facts, within the framework of the rules of evidence. To ensure that justice is done, it is imperative to the function of courts that compulsory process be available for the production of evidence needed either by the prosecution or by the defense.

Only recently the Court restated the ancient proposition of law, albeit in the context of a grand jury inquiry rather than a trial, "'that the public . . . has a right to every man's evidence' except for those persons protected by a constitutional, common law, or statutory privilege." The privileges referred to by the Court are designed to protect weighty and legitimate competing interests. Thus, the Fifth Amendment to the Constitution provides that no man "shall be compelled in any criminal case to be a witness against himself." And, generally, an attorney or a priest may not be required to disclose what has been revealed in professional confidence. These and other interests are recognized in law by privileges against forced disclosure. . . .

In this case the President challenges a subpoena served on him as a third party requiring the production of materials for use in a criminal prosecution on the claim that he has a privilege against disclosure of confidential communications. He does not place his claim of privilege on the ground they are military or diplomatic secrets. As to these areas of Art. II duties the courts have traditionally shown the utmost deference to presidential responsibilities. . . . In *United States v. Reynolds,* dealing with a claimant's demand for evidence in a damage case against the Government the Court said:

> "It may be possible to satisfy the court, from all the circumstances of the case, that there is a reasonable danger that compulsion of the evidence will expose military matters which, in the interest of national security, should not be divulged. When this is the case, the occasion for the privilege is appropriate, and the court should not jeopardize the security which the privilege is meant to protect by insisting upon an examination of the evidence, even by the judge alone, in chambers."

No case of the Court, however, has extended this high degree of deference to a President's generalized interest in confidentiality. . . .

The right to the production of all evidence at a criminal trial similarly has constitutional dimensions. The Sixth Amendment explicitly confers upon every defendant in a criminal trial the right "to be confronted with the witnesses against him" and "to have compulsory process for obtaining witnesses in his favor." Moreover, the Fifth Amendment also guarantees that no person shall be deprived of liberty without due process of law. It is the manifest duty of the courts to vindicate those guarantees and to accomplish that it is essential that all relevant and admissible evidence be produced.

In this case we must weigh the importance of the general privilege of confidentiality of presidential communications in performance of his responsibilities against the inroads of such a privilege on the fair administration of criminal justice.* The interest in preserving confidentiality is weighty indeed and entitled to great respect. However we cannot conclude that advisers will be moved to temper the candor of their remarks by the infrequent occasions of disclosure because of the possibility that such conversations will be called for in the context of a criminal prosecution.

On the other hand, the allowance of the privilege to withhold evidence that is demonstrably relevant in a criminal trial would cut deeply into the guarantee of due process of law and gravely impair the basic function of the courts. A President's acknowledged need for confidentiality in the communications of his office is general in nature, whereas the constitutional need for production of relevant evidence in a criminal proceeding is specific and central to the fair adjudication of a particular criminal case in the administration of justice. Without access to specific facts a criminal prosecution may be totally frustrated. The President's broad interest in confidentiality of communications will not be vitiated by disclosure of a limited number of conversations preliminarily shown to have some bearing on the pending criminal cases.

We conclude that when the ground for asserting privilege as to subpoenaed materials sought for use in a criminal trial is based only on the generalized interest in confidentiality, it cannot prevail over the fundamental demands of due process of law in the fair administration of criminal justice. The generalized assertion of privilege must yield to the demonstrated, specific need for evidence in a pending criminal trial. . . .

---

*We are not here concerned with the balance between the President's generalized interest in confidentiality and the need for relevant evidence in civil litigation, nor with that between the confidentiality interest and congressional demands for information, nor with the President's interest in preserving state secrets. We address only the conflict between the President's assertion of a generalized privilege of confidentiality against the constitutional need for relevant evidence in criminal trials.

64

American Legion v. American Humanist Association (2019)

Justice Alito delivered the opinion of the Court.

Since 1925, the Bladensburg Peace Cross (Cross) has stood as a tribute to 49 area soldiers who gave their lives in the First World War. Eighty-nine years after the dedication of the Cross, respondents filed this lawsuit, claiming that they are offended by the sight of the memorial on public land and that its presence there and the expenditure of public funds to maintain it violate the Establishment Clause of the First Amendment. To remedy this violation, they asked a federal court to order the relocation or demolition of the Cross or at least the removal of its arms. The Court of Appeals for the Fourth Circuit agreed that the memorial is unconstitutional and remanded for a determination of the proper remedy. We now reverse. . . .

The cross came into widespread use as a symbol of Christianity by the fourth century, and it retains that meaning today. But there are many contexts in which the symbol has also taken on a secular meaning. Indeed, there are instances in which its message is now almost entirely secular. . . .

The image used in the Bladensburg memorial—a plain Latin cross—also took on new meaning after World War I. "During and immediately after the war, the army marked soldiers' graves with temporary wooden crosses or Stars of David"—a departure from the prior practice of marking graves in American military cemeteries with uniform rectangular slabs. The vast majority of these grave markers consisted of crosses, and thus when Americans saw photographs of these cemeteries, what struck them were rows and rows of plain white crosses. As a result, the image of a simple white cross "developed into a 'central symbol'" of the conflict.

After the 1918 armistice, the War Department announced plans to replace the wooden crosses and Stars of David with uniform marble slabs like those previously used in American military cemeteries. But the public outcry against that proposal was swift and fierce. Many organizations, including the American War Mothers, a nonsectarian group founded in 1917, urged the Department to retain the design of the temporary markers. . . . A Member of Congress likewise introduced a resolution noting that "these wooden

From *American Legion v. American Humanist Association*, 588 U.S.___(2019).

symbols have, during and since the World War, been regarded as emblematic of the great sacrifices which that war entailed . . . and have become peculiarly and inseparably associated in the thought of surviving relatives and comrades and of the Nation with these World War graves." This national debate and its outcome confirmed the cross's widespread resonance as a symbol of sacrifice in the war.

Recognition of the cross's symbolism extended to local communities across the country. In late 1918, residents of Prince George's County, Maryland, formed a committee for the purpose of erecting a memorial for the county's fallen soldiers. Among the committee's members were the mothers of 10 deceased soldiers. The committee decided that the memorial should be a cross. . . .

. . . By 1922, however, the committee had run out of funds, and progress on the Cross had stalled. The local post of the American Legion took over the project, and the monument was finished in 1925.

The completed monument is a 32-foot tall Latin cross that sits on a large pedestal. . . . The pedestal also features a 9- by 2.5-foot bronze plaque explaining that the monument is "Dedicated to the heroes of Prince George's County, Maryland who lost their lives in the Great War for the liberty of the world." The plaque lists the names of 49 local men . . . who died in the war. . . .

As the area around the Cross developed, the monument came to be at the center of a busy intersection. In 1961, the Maryland-National Capital Park and Planning Commission (Commission) acquired the Cross and the land on which it sits in order to preserve the monument and address traffic-safety concerns. The American Legion reserved the right to continue using the memorial to host a variety of ceremonies, including events in memory of departed veterans. Over the next five decades, the Commission spent approximately $117,000 to maintain and preserve the monument. . . .

In 2012, nearly 90 years after the Cross was dedicated and more than 50 years after the Commission acquired it, the American Humanist Association (AHA) lodged a complaint with the Commission. The complaint alleged that the Cross's presence on public land and the Commission's maintenance of the memorial violate the Establishment Clause of the First Amendment. The AHA, along with three residents of Washington, D. C., and Maryland, also sued the Commission. . . . The AHA sought declaratory and injunctive relief requiring "removal or demolition of the Cross, or removal of the arms from the Cross to form a non-religious slab or obelisk." The American Legion intervened to defend the Cross.

The District Court granted summary judgment for the Commission and the American Legion. The Cross, the District Court held, satisfies . . . the three-pronged test announced in *Lemon v. Kurtzman*. . . . Under the *Lemon* test, a court must ask whether a challenged government action

(1) has a secular purpose; (2) has a "principal or primary effect" that "neither advances nor inhibits religion"; and (3) does not foster "an excessive government entanglement with religion". Applying that test, the District Court determined that the Commission had secular purposes for acquiring and maintaining the Cross—namely, to commemorate World War I and to ensure traffic safety. The court also found that a reasonable observer aware of the Cross's history, setting, and secular elements "would not view the Monument as having the effect of impermissibly endorsing religion." Nor, according to the court, did the Commission's maintenance of the memorial create the kind of "continued and repeated government involvement with religion" that would constitute an excessive entanglement. . . .

A divided panel of the Court of Appeals for the Fourth Circuit reversed. The majority relied primarily on the *Lemon* test. . . . While recognizing that the Commission acted for a secular purpose, the court held that the Bladensburg Cross failed *Lemon's* "effects" prong because a reasonable observer would view the Commission's ownership and maintenance of the monument as an endorsement of Christianity. The court emphasized the cross's "inherent religious meaning" as the "preeminent symbol of Christianity.". . . [Moreover,] the court concluded, the Commission had become excessively entangled with religion by keeping a display that "aggrandizes the Latin cross" and by spending more than *de minimis* public funds to maintain it. . . .

The Establishment Clause of the First Amendment provides that "Congress shall make no law respecting an establishment of religion." While the concept of a formally established church is straightforward, pinning down the meaning of a "law respecting an establishment of religion" has proved to be a vexing problem. . . . [In 1971] *Lemon* ambitiously attempted to distill from the Court's existing case law a test that would bring order and predictability to Establishment Clause decisionmaking. . . .

. . . [But a]s Establishment Clause cases involving a great array of laws and practices came to the Court, it became more and more apparent that the *Lemon* test could not resolve them. . . .

For at least four reasons, the *Lemon* test presents particularly daunting problems. . . . Together, these considerations counsel against efforts to evaluate such cases under *Lemon* and toward application of a presumption of constitutionality for longstanding monuments, symbols, and practices. . . .

First, these cases often concern monuments, symbols, or practices that were first established long ago, and in such cases, identifying their original purpose or purposes may be especially difficult. In *Salazar* v. *Buono*, for example, we dealt with a cross that a small group of World War I veterans had put up at a remote spot in the Mojave Desert more than seven decades earlier. The record contained virtually no direct evidence regarding the specific motivations of these men. . . .

Without better evidence about the purpose of the monument, different Justices drew different inferences. The plurality thought that this particular cross was meant "to commemorate American servicemen who had died in World War I" and was not intended "to promote a Christian message." The dissent, by contrast, "presume[d]" that the cross's purpose "was a Christian one. . . ." The truth is that 70 years after the fact, there was no way to be certain about the motivations of the men who were responsible for the creation of the monument. . . .

Second, as time goes by, the purposes associated with an established monument, symbol, or practice often multiply. Take the example of Ten Commandments monuments, the subject we addressed in *Van Orden* [*v. Perry*] and *McCreary County* v. *American Civil Liberties Union of Ky.* For believing Jews and Christians, the Ten Commandments are the word of God handed down to Moses on Mount Sinai, but the image of the Ten Commandments has also been used to convey other meanings. They have historical significance as one of the foundations of our legal system, and for largely that reason, they are depicted in the marble frieze in our courtroom and in other prominent public buildings in our Nation's capital. In *Van Orden* and *McCreary*, no Member of the Court thought that these depictions are unconstitutional.

Just as depictions of the Ten Commandments in these public buildings were intended to serve secular purposes, the litigation in *Van Orden* and *McCreary* showed that secular motivations played a part in the proliferation of Ten Commandments monuments in the 1950s. In 1946, Minnesota Judge E. J. Ruegemer proposed that the Ten Commandments be widely disseminated as a way of combating juvenile delinquency. With this prompting, the Fraternal Order of the Eagles began distributing paper copies of the Ten Commandments to churches, school groups, courts, and government offices. The Eagles, "while interested in the religious aspect of the Ten Commandments, sought to highlight the Commandments' role in shaping civic morality." At the same time, Cecil B. DeMille was filming The Ten Commandments. He learned of Judge Ruegemer's campaign, and the two collaborated, deciding that the Commandments should be carved on stone tablets and that DeMille would make arrangements with the Eagles to help pay for them, thus simultaneously promoting his film and public awareness of the Decalogue. Not only did DeMille and Judge Ruegemer have different purposes, but the motivations of those who accepted the monuments and those responsible for maintaining them may also have differed. . . .

Third, just as the purpose for maintaining a monument, symbol, or practice may evolve, "[t]he 'message' conveyed . . . may change over time." Consider, for example, the message of the Statue of Liberty, which began as a monument to the solidarity and friendship between France and the United

States and only decades later came to be seen "as a beacon welcoming immigrants to a land of freedom."

With sufficient time, religiously expressive monuments, symbols, and practices can become embedded features of a community's landscape and identity. The community may come to value them without necessarily embracing their religious roots. . . .

In the same way, consider the many cities and towns across the United States that bear religious names. Religion undoubtedly motivated those who named Bethlehem, Pennsylvania; Las Cruces, New Mexico; Providence, Rhode Island; Corpus Christi, Texas; Nephi, Utah, and the countless other places in our country with names that are rooted in religion. Yet few would argue that this history requires that these names be erased from the map. Or take a motto like Arizona's, *"Ditat Deus"* ("God enriches"), which was adopted in 1864, or a flag like Maryland's, which has included two crosses since 1904. Familiarity itself can become a reason for preservation.

Fourth, when time's passage imbues a religiously expressive monument, symbol, or practice with this kind of familiarity and historical significance, removing it may no longer appear neutral, especially to the local community for which it has taken on particular meaning. A government that roams the land, tearing down monuments with religious symbolism and scrubbing away any reference to the divine will strike many as aggressively hostile to religion. . . .

These four considerations show that retaining established, religiously expressive monuments, symbols, and practices is quite different from erecting or adopting new ones. The passage of time gives rise to a strong presumption of constitutionality.

The role of the cross in World War I memorials is illustrative of each of the four preceding considerations. Immediately following the war, "[c]ommunities across America built memorials to commemorate those who had served the nation in the struggle to make the world safe for democracy." Although not all of these communities included a cross in their memorials, the cross had become a symbol closely linked to the war. . . . The solemn image of endless rows of white crosses became inextricably linked with and symbolic of the ultimate price paid by 116,000 soldiers. And this relationship between the cross and the war undoubtedly influenced the design of the many war memorials that sprang up across the Nation.

This is not to say that the cross's association with the war was the sole or dominant motivation for the inclusion of the symbol in every World War I memorial that features it. But today, it is all but impossible to tell whether that was so. The passage of time means that testimony from those actually involved in the decisionmaking process is generally unavailable, and attempting to uncover their motivations invites rampant speculation. And no matter what the original purposes for the erection of a monument, a community may wish to preserve it for very different reasons, such as the historic preservation and traffic-safety concerns the Commission has pressed here. . . .

Finally, as World War I monuments have endured through the years and become a familiar part of the physical and cultural landscape, requiring their removal would not be viewed by many as a neutral act. And an alteration like the one entertained by the Fourth Circuit—amputating the arms of the Cross—would be seen by many as profoundly disrespectful. . . .

. . . [W]e conclude that the Bladensburg Cross does not violate the Establishment Clause.

As we have explained, the Bladensburg Cross carries special significance in commemorating World War I. . . . That the cross originated as a Christian symbol and retains that meaning in many contexts does not change the fact that the symbol took on an added secular meaning when used in World War I memorials.

Not only did the Bladensburg Cross begin with this meaning, but with the passage of time, it has acquired historical importance. It reminds the people of Bladensburg and surrounding areas of the deeds of their predecessors and of the sacrifices they made in a war fought in the name of democracy. . . . The memorial represents what the relatives, friends, and neighbors of the fallen soldiers felt at the time and how they chose to express their sentiments. And the monument has acquired additional layers of historical meaning in subsequent years. The Cross now stands among memorials to veterans of later wars. It has become part of the community. . . .

Finally, it is surely relevant that the monument commemorates the death of particular individuals. It is natural and appropriate for those seeking to honor the deceased to invoke the symbols that signify what death meant for those who are memorialized. In some circumstances, the exclusion of any such recognition would make a memorial incomplete. This well explains why Holocaust memorials invariably include Stars of David or other symbols of Judaism. . . . And this is why the memorial for soldiers from the Bladensburg community features the cross. . . .

We reverse the judgment of the Court of Appeals for the Fourth Circuit and remand the cases for further proceedings.

It is so ordered.

Justice Kavanaugh, concurring.

. . . The Bladensburg Cross commemorates soldiers who gave their lives for America in World War I. I agree with the Court that the Bladensburg Cross is constitutional. At the same time, I have deep respect for the plaintiffs' sincere objections to seeing the cross on public land. . . .

The conclusion that the cross does not violate the Establishment Clause does not necessarily mean that those who object to it have no other recourse. The Court's ruling *allows* the State to maintain the cross on public land. The Court's ruling does not *require* the State to maintain the cross on public land. The Maryland Legislature could enact new laws requiring removal of the cross or transfer of the land. The Maryland Governor or other state or local executive officers may have authority to do so under current Maryland law. And if not, the legislature could enact new laws to authorize such executive action. The Maryland Constitution, as interpreted by the Maryland Court of Appeals, may speak to this question. And if not, the people of Maryland can amend the State Constitution.

Those alternative avenues of relief illustrate a fundamental feature of our constitutional structure: This Court is not the *only* guardian of individual rights in America. . . . Other federal, state, and local government entities generally possess authority to safeguard individual rights above and beyond the rights secured by the U. S. Constitution. . . .

Justice Gorsuch, with whom Justice Thomas joins, concurring in the judgment.

The American Humanist Association wants a federal court to order the destruction of a 94 year-old war memorial because its members are offended. Today, the Court explains that the plaintiffs are not entitled to demand the destruction of longstanding monuments, and I find much of its opinion compelling. In my judgment, however, it follows from the Court's analysis that suits like this one should be dismissed for lack of standing. . . .

The Association claims that its members "regularly" come into "unwelcome direct contact" with a World War I memorial cross in Bladensburg, Maryland "while driving in the area." And this, the Association suggests, is enough to allow it to insist on a federal judicial decree ordering the memorial's removal. . . .

This "offended observer" theory of standing has no basis in law. Federal courts may decide only those cases and controversies that the Constitution and Congress have authorized them to hear. And to establish standing to sue consistent with the Constitution, a plaintiff must show: (1) injury-in-fact, (2) causation, and (3) redressability. The injury-in-fact test requires a plaintiff to prove "an invasion of a legally protected interest which is (a) concrete and particularized . . . and (b) actual or imminent, not conjectural or hypothetical."

Unsurprisingly, this Court has already rejected the notion that offense alone qualifies as a "concrete and particularized" injury sufficient to confer standing. . . . Imagine if a bystander disturbed by a police stop tried to sue under the Fourth Amendment. . . . Or envision a religious group upset about the application of the death penalty trying to sue to stop it. Does anyone doubt those cases would be rapidly dispatched for lack of standing? . . . .

. . . If individuals and groups could invoke the authority of a federal court to forbid what they dislike for no more reason than they dislike it, we would risk exceeding the judiciary's limited constitutional mandate and infringing on powers committed to other branches of government. Courts would start to look more like legislatures, responding to social pressures rather than remedying concrete harms, in the process supplanting the right of the people and their elected representatives to govern themselves.

Proceeding on these principles, this Court has held offense alone insufficient to convey standing in analogous—and arguably more sympathetic—circumstances. Take *Allen* v. *Wright*, where the parents of African-American schoolchildren sued to compel the Internal Revenue Service to deny tax-exempt status to schools that discriminated on the basis of race. . . . [T]his Court refused to entertain the case, reasoning that standing extends "only to those persons who are personally denied equal treatment by the challenged discriminatory conduct." Now put the teachings there alongside the Association's standing theory here and you get this utterly unjustifiable result: An African-American offended by a Confederate flag atop a state capitol would lack standing to sue under the Equal Protection Clause, but an atheist who is offended by the cross on the same flag could sue under the Establishment Clause. Who really thinks *that* could be the law? . . . .

In a large and diverse country, offense can be easily found. Really, most every governmental action probably offends *somebody*. No doubt, too, that offense can be sincere, sometimes well taken, even wise. But recourse for disagreement and offense does not lie in federal litigation. Instead, in a society that holds among its most cherished ambitions mutual respect, tolerance, self-rule, and democratic responsibility, an "offended viewer" may "avert his eyes, " or pursue a political solution. Today's decision represents a welcome step toward restoring this Court's recognition of these truths, and I respectfully concur in the judgment.

Justice Ginsburg, with whom Justice Sotomayor joins, dissenting.

An immense Latin cross stands on a traffic island at the center of a busy three-way intersection in Bladensburg, Maryland. "[M]onumental, clear, and bold" by day, the cross looms even larger illuminated against the night-time sky. . . . Both the Peace Cross and the traffic island are owned and maintained by the Maryland-National Capital Park and Planning Commission, an agency of the State of Maryland.

Decades ago, this Court recognized that the Establishment Clause of the First Amendment to the Constitution demands governmental neutrality among religious faiths, and between religion and nonreligion. Numerous times since, the Court has reaffirmed the Constitution's commitment to neutrality. Today the Court erodes that neutrality commitment, diminishing precedent designed to preserve individual liberty and civic harmony in favor of a "presumption of constitutionality for longstanding monuments, symbols, and practices.". . .

The Latin cross is the foremost symbol of the Christian faith, embodying the "central theological claim of Christianity: that the son of God died on the cross, that he rose from the dead, and that his death and resurrection offer the possibility of eternal life." Precisely because the cross symbolizes these sectarian beliefs, it is a common marker for the graves of Christian soldiers. For the same reason, using the cross as a war memorial does not transform it into a secular symbol, as the Courts of Appeals have uniformly recognized. Just as a Star of David is not suitable to honor Christians who died serving their country, so a cross is not suitable to honor those of other faiths who died defending their nation. Soldiers of all faiths "are united by their love of country, but they are not united by the cross."

By maintaining the Peace Cross on a public highway, the Commission elevates Christianity over other faiths, and religion over nonreligion. Memorializing the service of American soldiers is an "admirable and unquestionably secular" objective. But the Commission does not serve that objective by displaying a symbol that bears "a starkly sectarian message.". . .

65

William J. Brennan, Jr.

Constitutional Interpretation (1985)

. . . [T]he text I have chosen for exploration is the amended Constitution of the United States, which, of course, entrenches the Bill of Rights and the Civil War amendments, and draws sustenance from the bedrock principles of another great text, the Magna Carta. So fashioned, the Constitution embodies the aspiration to social justice, brotherhood, and human dignity that brought this nation into being. The Declaration of Independence, the Constitution and the Bill of Rights solemnly committed the United States

From "Address to the Text and Teaching Symposium," Georgetown University, October 12, 1985, Washington, D.C.

to be a country where the dignity and rights of all persons were equal before all authority. In all candor we must concede that part of this egalitarianism in America has been more pretension than realized fact. But we are an aspiring people, a people with faith in progress. Our amended Constitution is the lodestar for our aspirations. Like every text worth reading, it is not crystalline. The phrasing is broad and the limitations of its provisions are not clearly marked. Its majestic generalities and ennobling pronouncements are both luminous and obscure. This ambiguity of course calls forth interpretation, the interaction of reader and text. The encounter with the constitutional text has been, in many senses, my life's work.

My approach to this text may differ from the approach of other participants in this symposium to their texts. Yet such differences may themselves stimulate reflection about what it is we do when we "interpret" a text. Thus I will attempt to elucidate my approach to the text as well as my substantive interpretation.

Perhaps the foremost difference is the fact that my encounters with the constitutional text are not purely or even primarily introspective; the Constitution cannot be for me simply a contemplative haven for private moral reflection. My relation to this great text is inescapably public. That is not to say that my reading of the text is not a personal reading, only that the personal reading perforce occurs in a public context, and is open to critical scrutiny from all quarters.

The Constitution is fundamentally a public text—the monumental charter of a government and a people—and a Justice of the Supreme Court must apply it to resolve public controversies. For, from our beginning, a most important consequence of the constitutionally created separation of powers has been the American habit, extraordinary to other democracies, of casting social, economic, philosophical and political questions in the form of lawsuits, in an attempt to secure ultimate resolution by the Supreme Court. In this way, important aspects of the most fundamental issues confronting our democracy may finally arrive in the Supreme Court for judicial determination. Not infrequently, these are the issues upon which contemporary society is most deeply divided. They arouse our deepest emotions. The main burden of my twenty-nine terms on the Supreme Court has thus been to wrestle with the Constitution in this heightened public context, to draw meaning from the text in order to resolve public controversies.

Two other aspects of my relation to this text warrant mention. First, constitutional interpretation for a federal judge is, for the most part, obligatory. When litigants approach the bar of court to adjudicate a constitutional dispute, they may justifiably demand an answer. Judges cannot avoid a definitive interpretation because they feel unable to, or would prefer not to, penetrate to the full meaning of the Constitution's provisions. Unlike literary critics, judges cannot merely savor the tensions or revel in the ambiguities inhering in the text—judges must resolve them.

Second, consequences flow from a Justice's interpretation in a direct and immediate way. A judicial decision respecting the incompatibility of Jim Crow with a constitutional guarantee of equality is not simply a contemplative exercise in defining the shape of a just society. It is an order—supported by the full coercive power of the State—that the present society change in a fundamental aspect. Under such circumstances the process of deciding can be a lonely, troubling experience for fallible human beings conscious that their best may not be adequate to the challenge. We Justices are certainly aware that we are not final because we are infallible; we know that we are infallible only because we are final. One does not forget how much may depend on the decision. More than the litigants may be affected. The course of vital social, economic and political currents may be directed.

These three defining characteristics of my relation to the constitutional text—its public nature, obligatory character, and consequentialist aspect cannot help but influence the way I read that text. When Justices interpret the Constitution they speak for their community, not for themselves alone. The act of interpretation must be undertaken with full consciousness that it is, in a very real sense, the community's interpretation that is sought. Justices are not platonic guardians appointed to wield authority to their personal moral predilections. Precisely because coercive force must attend any judicial decision to countermand the will of a contemporary majority, the Justices must render constitutional interpretations that are received as legitimate. The source of legitimacy is, of course, a wellspring of controversy in legal and political circles. At the core of the debate is what the late Yale Law School Professor Alexander Bickel labeled "the counter-majoritarian difficulty." Our commitment to self-governance in a representative democracy must be reconciled with vesting in electorally unaccountable Justices the power to invalidate the expressed desires of representative bodies on the ground of inconsistency with higher law. Because judicial power resides in the authority to give meaning to the Constitution, the debate is really a debate about how to read the text, about constraints on what is legitimate interpretation.

There are those who find legitimacy in fidelity to what they call "the intentions of the Framers." In its most doctrinaire incarnation, this view demands that Justices discern exactly what the Framers thought about the question under consideration and simply follow that intention in resolving the case before them. It is a view that feigns self-effacing deference to the specific judgments of those who forged our original social compact. But in truth it is little more than arrogance cloaked as humility. It is arrogant to pretend that from our vantage we can gauge accurately the intent of the Framers on application of principle to specific, contemporary questions. All too often, sources of potential enlightment such as records of the ratification debates provide sparse or ambiguous evidence of the original intention. Typically, all that can be gleaned is that the Framers themselves did not agree about the application or meaning of particular constitutional provisions, and hid their differences in cloaks of generality. Indeed, it is far from clear whose intention is relevant—that of the drafters, the congressional disputants, or the ratifiers in the states—or even whether the idea of an original intention is a coherent way of thinking about a jointly drafted document drawing its authority from a general assent of the states. And apart from the problematic nature of the sources, our distance of two centuries cannot but work as a prism refracting all we perceive. One cannot help but speculate that the chorus of lamentations calling for interpretation faithful to "original intention"—and proposing nullification of interpretations that fail this quick litmus test—must inevitably come from persons who have no familiarity with the historical record.

Perhaps most importantly, while proponents of this facile historicism justify it as a depoliticization of the judiciary, the political underpinnings of such a choice should not escape notice. A position that upholds constitutional claims only if they were within the specific contemplation of the Framers in effect establishes a presumption of resolving textual ambiguities against the claim of constitutional right. It is far from clear what justifies such a presumption against claims of right. Nothing intrinsic in the nature of interpretation—if there is such a thing as the "nature" of interpretation—commands such a passive approach to ambiguity. This is a choice no less political than any other; it expresses antipathy to claims of the minority rights against the majority. Those who would restrict claims of right to the values of 1789 specifically articulated in the Constitution turn a blind eye to social progress and eschew adaptation of overarching principles to changes of social circumstance.

Another, perhaps more sophisticated, response to the potential power of judicial interpretation stresses democratic theory: because ours is a government of the people's elected representatives, substantive value choices should by and large be left to them. This view emphasizes not the transcendant historical authority of the Framers but the predominant contemporary authority of the elected branches of government. Yet it has similar consequences for the nature of proper judicial interpretation. Faith in the majoritarian process counsels restraint. Even under more expansive formulations of this approach, judicial review is appropriate only to the extent of ensuring that our democratic process functions smoothly. Thus, for example, we would protect freedom of speech merely to ensure that the people are heard by their representatives, rather than as a separate, substantive value. When, by contrast, society tosses up to the Supreme Court a dispute that would require invalidation of a legislature's substantive policy choice, the Court generally would stay its hand because the Constitution was meant as a plan of government and not as an embodiment of fundamental substantive values.

The view that all matters of substantive policy should be resolved through the majoritarian process has appeal under some circumstances, but I think it ultimately will not do. Unabashed enshrinement of majority will would permit the imposition of a social caste system or wholesale confiscation of property so long as a majority of the authorized legislative body, fairly elected, approved. Our Constitution could not abide such a situation. It is the very purpose of a Constitution—and particularly of the Bill of Rights—to declare certain values transcendent, beyond the reach of temporary political majorities. The majoritarian process cannot be expected to rectify claims of minority right that arise as a response to the outcomes of that very majoritarian process. . . .

Faith in democracy is one thing, blind faith quite another. Those who drafted our Constitution understood the difference. One cannot read the text without admitting that it embodies substantive value choices; it places certain values beyond the power of any legislature. Obvious are the separation of powers; the privilege of the Writ of Habeas Corpus; prohibition of Bills of Attainder and *ex post facto* laws; prohibition of cruel and unusual punishments; the requirement of just compensation for official taking of property; the prohibition of laws tending to establish religion or enjoining the free exercise of religion; and, since the Civil War, the banishment of slavery and official race discrimination. With respect to at least such principles, we simply have not constituted ourselves as strict utilitarians. While the Constitution may be amended, such amendments require an immense effort by the People as a whole.

To remain faithful to the content of the Constitution, therefore, an approach to interpreting the text must account for the existence of these substantive value choices, and must accept the ambiguity inherent in the effort to apply them to modern circumstances. The Framers discerned fundamental principles through struggles against particular malefactions of the Crown; the struggle shapes the particular contours of the articulated principles. But our acceptance of the fundamental principles has not and should not bind us to those precise, at times anachronistic, contours. Successive generations of Americans have continued to respect these fundamental choices and adopt them as their own guide to evaluating quite different historical practices. Each generation has the choice to overrule or add to the fundamental principles enunciated by the Framers; the Constitution can be amended or it can be ignored. Yet with respect to its fundamental principles, the text has suffered neither fate. Thus, if I may borrow the words of an esteemed predecessor, Justice Robert Jackson, the burden of judicial interpretation is to translate "the majestic generalities of the Bill of Rights, conceived as part of the pattern of liberal government in the eighteenth century, into concrete restraints on officials dealing with the problems of the twentieth century." *Board of Education v. Barnette,* [319 U.S. 624, 639 (1943)].

We current justices read the Constitution in the only way that we can: as Twentieth Century Americans. We look to the history of the time of framing and to the intervening history of interpretation. But the ultimate question must be, what do the words of the text mean in our time? For the genius of the Constitution rests not in any static meaning it might have had in a world that is dead and gone, but in the adaptability of its great principles to cope with current problems and current needs. What the constitutional fundamentals meant to the wisdom of other times cannot be their measure to the vision of our time. Similarly, what those fundamentals mean for us, our descendants will learn, cannot be the measure to the vision of their time. This realization is not, I assure you, a novel one of my own creation. Permit me to quote from one of the opinions of our Court, *Weems v. United States,* [217 U.S. 349] written nearly a century ago:

> Time works changes, brings into existence new conditions and purposes. Therefore, a principle to be vital must be capable of wider application than the mischief which gave it birth. This is peculiarly true of constitutions. They are not ephemeral enactments, designed to meet passing occasions. They are, to use the words of Chief Justice John Marshall, 'designed to approach immortality as nearly as human institutions can approach it.' The future is their care and provision for events of good and bad tendencies of which no prophesy can be made. In the application of a constitution, therefore, our contemplation cannot be only of what has been, but of what may be.

Interpretation must account for the transformative purpose of the text. Our Constitution was not intended to preserve a preexisting society but to make a new one, to put in place new principles that the prior political community had not sufficiently recognized. Thus, for example, when we interpret the Civil War Amendments to the charter—abolishing slavery, guaranteeing blacks equality under law, and guaranteeing blacks the right to vote—we must remember that those who put them in place had no desire to enshrine the status quo. Their goal was to make over their world, to eliminate all vestige of slave caste.

Having discussed at some length how I, as a Supreme Court Justice, interact with this text, I think it time to turn to the fruits of this discourse. For the Constitution is a sublime oration on the dignity of man, a bold commitment by a people to the ideal of libertarian dignity protected through law. Some reflection is perhaps required before this can be seen.

The Constitution on its face is, in large measure, a structuring text, a blueprint for government. And when the text is not prescribing the form of government it is limiting the powers of that government. The original document, before addition of any of the amendments, does not speak primarily of the rights of man, but of the abilities and disabilities of government. When one reflects upon the text's preoccupation with the scope of government as well as its shape, however, one comes to understand that what this text is about is the relationship of the individual and the state. The text marks the metes and bounds of official authority and individual autonomy. When one studies the boundary that the text marks out, one gets a sense of the vision of the individual embodied in the Constitution.

As augmented by the Bill of Rights and the Civil War amendments, this text is a sparkling vision of the supremacy of the human dignity of every individual. This vision is reflected in the very choice of democratic self-governance: the supreme value of a democracy is the presumed worth of each individual. And this vision manifests itself most dramatically in the specific prohibitions of the Bill of Rights, a term which I henceforth will apply to describe not only the original first eight amendments, but the Civil War amendments as well. It is a vision that has guided us as a people throughout our history, although the precise rules by which we have protected fundamental human dignity have been transformed over time in response to both transformations of social condition and evolution of our concepts of human dignity.

Until the end of the nineteenth century, freedom and dignity in our country found meaningful protection in the institution of real property. In a society still largely agricultural, a piece of land provided men not just with sustenance but with the means of economic independence, a necessary precondition of political independence and expression. Not surprisingly, property relationships formed the heart of litigation and of legal practice, and lawyers and judges tended to think stable property relationships the highest aim of the law.

But the days when common law property relationships dominated litigation and legal practice are past. To a growing extent economic existence now depends on less certain relationships with government—licenses, employment, contracts, subsidies, unemployment benefits, tax exemptions, welfare and the like. Government participation in the economic existence of individuals is pervasive and deep. Administrative matters and other dealings with government are at the epicenter of the exploding law. We turn to government and to the law for controls which would never have been expected or tolerated before this century, when a man's answer to economic oppression or difficulty was to move two hundred miles west. Now hundreds of thousands of Americans live entire lives without any real prospect of the dignity and autonomy that ownership of real property could confer. Protection of the human dignity of such citizens requires a much modified view of the proper relationship of individual and state.

In general, problems of the relationship of the citizen with government have multiplied and thus have engendered some of the most important constitutional issues of the day. As government acts ever more deeply upon those areas of our lives once marked "private," there is an even greater need to see that individual rights are not curtailed or cheapened in the interest of what may temporarily appear to be the "public good." And as government continues in its role of provider for so many of our disadvantaged citizens, there is an even greater need to ensure that government act with integrity and consistency in its dealings with these citizens. To put this another way, the possibilities for collision between government activity and individual rights will increase as the power and authority of government itself expands, and this growth, in turn, heightens the need for constant vigilance at the collision points. If our free society is to endure, those who govern must recognize human dignity and accept the enforcement of constitutional limitations on their power conceived by the Framers to be necessary to preserve that dignity and the air of freedom which is our proudest heritage. Such recognition will not come from a technical understanding of the organs of government, or the new forms of wealth they administer. It requires something different, something deeper—a personal confrontation with the wellsprings of our society. . . .

I do not mean to suggest that we have in the last quarter century achieved a comprehensive definition of the constitutional ideal of human dignity. We are still striving toward that goal, and doubtless it will be an eternal quest. For if the interaction of this Justice and the constitutional text over the years confirms any single proposition, it is that the demands of human dignity will never cease to evolve. . . .

66

Robert H. Bork

Testimony before the Senate Judiciary Committee (1987)

Judge Bork: I want to begin by thanking the President for placing my name in nomination for this most important position. . . .

As you have said, quite correctly, Mr. Chairman, and as others have said here today, this is in large measure a discussion of judicial philosophy, and I want to make a few remarks at the outset on that subject of central interest.

That is, my understanding of how a judge should go about his or her work. That may also be described as my philosophy of the role of a judge in a constitutional democracy.

From Hearings Before the Committee on the Judiciary, United States Senate, 100th Congress First Session, Sept. 15, 1987, Senate No. J-100-4.

The judge's authority derives entirely from the fact that he is applying the law and not his personal values. That is why the American public accepts the decisions of its courts, accepts even decisions that nullify the laws a majority of the electorate or of their representatives voted for.

The judge, to deserve that trust and that authority, must be every bit as governed by law as is the Congress, the President, the State Governors and legislatures, and the American people. No one, including a judge, can be above the law. Only in that way will justice be done and the freedom of Americans assured.

How should a judge go about finding the law? The only legitimate way, in my opinion, is by attempting to discern what those who made the law intended. The intentions of the lawmakers govern whether the lawmakers are the Congress of the United States enacting a statute or whether they are those who ratified our Constitution and its various Amendments.

Where the words are precise and the facts simple, that is a relatively easy task. Where the words are general, as is the case with some of the most profound protections of our liberties—in the Bill of Rights and in the Civil War Amendments—the task is far more complex. It is to find the principle or value that was intended to be protected and to see that it is protected.

As I wrote in an opinion for our court, the judge's responsibility "is to discern how the framers' values, defined in the context of the world they knew, apply in the world we know."

If a judge abandons intention as his guide, there is no law available to him and he begins to legislate a social agenda for the American people. That goes well beyond his legitimate power.

He or she then diminishes liberty instead of enhancing it. That is why I agree with Judge Learned Hand, one of the great jurists in our history, when he wrote that the judge's "authority and his immunity depend upon the assumption that he speaks with the mouths of others: the momentum of his utterances must be greater than any which his personal reputation and character can command if it is to do the work assigned to it—if it is to stand against the passionate resentments arising out of the interests he must frustrate." To state that another way, the judge must speak with the authority of the past and yet accommodate that past to the present.

The past, however, includes not only the intentions of those who first made the law, it also includes those past judges who interpreted it and applied it in prior cases. That is why a judge must have great respect for precedent. It is one thing as a legal theorist to criticize the reasoning of a prior decision, even to criticize it severely, as I have done. It is another and more serious thing altogether for a judge to ignore or overturn a prior decision. That requires much careful thought.

Times come, of course, when even a venerable precedent can and should be overruled. The primary example of a proper overruling is *Brown v. Board of Education*, the case which outlawed racial segregation accomplished by government action. *Brown* overturned the rule of separate but equal laid down 58 years before in *Plessy v. Ferguson*. Yet *Brown*, delivered with the authority of a unanimous Court, was clearly correct and represents perhaps the greatest moral achievement of our constitutional law.

Nevertheless, overruling should be done sparingly and cautiously. Respect for precedent is a part of the great tradition of our law, just as is fidelity to the intent of those who ratified the Constitution and enacted our statutes. That does not mean that constitutional law is static. It will evolve as judges modify doctrine to meet new circumstances and new technologies. Thus, today we apply the first amendment's guarantee of the freedom of the press to radio and television, and we apply to electronic surveillance the fourth amendment's guarantee of privacy for the individual against unreasonable searches of his or her home.

I can put the matter no better than I did in an opinion on my present court. Speaking of the judge's duty, I wrote: "The important thing, the ultimate consideration, is the constitutional freedom that is given into our keeping. A judge who refuses to see new threats to an established constitutional value and hence provides a crabbed interpretation that robs a provision of its full, fair and reasonable meaning, fails in his judicial duty. That duty, I repeat, is to ensure that the powers and freedoms the framers specified are made effective in today's circumstances."

But I should add to that passage that when a judge goes beyond this and reads entirely new values into the Constitution, values the framers and the ratifiers did not put there, he deprives the people of their liberty. That liberty, which the Constitution clearly envisions, is the liberty of the people to set their own social agenda through the processes of democracy.

Conservative judges frustrated that process in the mid-1930's by using the concept they had invented, the 14th amendment's supposed guarantee of a liberty of contract, to strike down laws designed to protect workers and labor unions. That was wrong then and it would be wrong now.

My philosophy of judging, Mr. Chairman, as you pointed out, is neither liberal nor conservative. It is simply a philosophy of judging which gives the Constitution a full and fair interpretation but, where the Constitution is silent, leaves the policy struggles to the Congress, the President, the legislatures and executives of the 50 States, and to the American people.

I welcome this opportunity to come before the committee and answer whatever questions the members may have. I am quite willing to discuss with you my judicial philosophy and the approach I take to deciding cases. I cannot, of course, commit myself as to how I might vote on any particular case and I know you would not wish me to do that. . . .

67

Thomas Jefferson and James Madison

Exchange on the Binding
of Generations (1789–1790)

THOMAS JEFFERSON TO JAMES MADISON

Paris September 6, 1789.

Dear Sir

I sit down to write to you without knowing by what occasion I shall send my letter. I do it because a subject comes into my head which I would wish to develop a little more than is practicable in the hurry of the moment of making up general dispatches.

The question whether one generation of men has a right to bind another, seems never to have been stated either on this or our side of the water. Yet it is a question of such consequences as not only to merit decision, but place also, among the fundamental principles of every government. The course of reflection in which we are immersed here on the elementary principles of society has presented this question to my mind; and that no such obligation can be so transmitted I think very capable of proof.—I set out on this ground, which I suppose to be self evident, 'that the earth belongs in usufruct to the living': that the dead have neither powers nor rights over it. The portion occupied by any individual ceases to be his when himself ceases to be, and reverts to the society. If the society has formed no rules for the appropriation of its lands in severality, it will be taken by the first occupants. These will generally be the wife and children of the decedent. If they have formed rules of appropriation, those rules may give it to the wife and children, or to some one of them, or to the legatee of the deceased. So they may give it to his creditor. But the child, the legatee, or creditor takes it, not by any natural right, but by a law of the society of which they are members, and to which they are subject. Then no man can, by natural right, oblige the lands he occupied, or the persons who succeed him in that occupation, to the payment of debts contracted by him. For if he could, he might, during his own life, eat up the usufruct of the lands for several generations to come, and then the lands would belong to the dead, and not to the living, which would be the reverse of our principle.

From *The Papers of Thomas Jefferson*, Vol. 15, Vol. 16, Princeton University Press, 1969.

What is true of every member of the society individually, is true of them all collectively, since the rights of the whole can be no more than the sum of the rights of the individuals.—To keep our ideas clear when applying them to a multitude, let us suppose a whole generation of men to be born on the same day, to attain mature age on the same day, and to die on the same day, leaving a succeeding generation in the moment of attaining their mature age all together. Let the ripe age be supposed of 21 years, and their period of life 34 years more, that being the average term given by the bills of mortality to persons who have already attained 21 years of age. Each successive generation would, in this way, come on, and go off the stage at a fixed moment, as individuals do now. Then I say the earth belongs to each of these generations, during its course, fully, and in their own right. The 2d. generation receives it clear of the debts and incumberances of the 1st. the 3d of the 2d. and so on. For if the 1st. could charge it with a debt, then the earth would belong to the dead and not the living generation. Then no generation can contract debts greater than may be paid during the course of its own existence. . . .—But a material difference must be noted between the succession of an individual, and that of a whole generation. Individuals are parts only of a society, subject to the laws of the whole. These laws may appropriate the portion of land occupied by a decendent to his creditor rather than to any other, or to his child on condition he satisfies the creditor. But when a whole generation, that is, the whole society dies, as in the case we have supposed, and another generation or society succeeds, this forms a whole, and there is no superior who can give their territory to a third society, who may have lent money to their predecessors beyond their faculties of paying.

What is true of a generation all arriving to self-government on the same day, and dying all on the same day, is true of those in a constant course of decay and renewal, with this only difference. A generation coming in and going out entire, as in the first case, would have a right in the 1st. year of their self-dominion to contract a debt for 33. years, in the 10th. for 24. in the 20th. for 14. in the 30th. for 4. whereas generations, changing daily by daily deaths and births, have one constant term, beginning at the date of their contract, and ending when a majority of those of full age at that date shall be dead. The length of that term may be estimated from the tables of mortality, corrected by the circumstances of climate, occupation &c. peculiar to the country of the contractors. Take, for instance, the table of M. de Buffon wherein he states 23,994 deaths, and the ages at which they happened. Suppose a society in which 23,994 persons are born every year, and live to the ages stated in this table. The conditions of that society will be as follows. 1st. It will consist constantly of 617,703. persons of all ages. 2ly. Of those living at any one instant of time, one half will be dead in 24 years 8 months. 3dly. 10,675 will arrive every year at the age of 21 years complete. 4ly. It will constantly have 348,417 persons of all ages above 21 years. 5ly. And the half of those of 21 years and upwards living at any one instant of time will be dead in 18 years 8 months, or say 19 years as the nearest integral number. Then 19 years is the term beyond which neither the representatives of a nation, nor even the whole nation itself assembled, can validly extend a debt. . . .

I suppose that the received opinion, that the public debts of one generation devolve on the next, has been suggested by our seeing habitually in private life that he who succeeds to lands is required to pay the debts of his ancestor or testator: without considering that this requisition is municipal only, not moral; flowing from the will of the society, which has found it convenient to appropriate lands, become vacant by the death of their occupant, on the condition of a payment of his debts: but that between society and society, or generation and generation, there is no municipal obligation, no umpire but the law of nature. We seem not to have perceived that, by the law of nature, one generation is to another as one independent nation to another.

The interest of the national debt of France being in fact but a two thousandth part of its rent roll, the payment of it is practicable enough: and so becomes a question merely of honor, or of expediency. But with respect to future debts, would it not be wise and just for that nation to declare, in the constitution they are forming, that neither the legislature, nor the nation itself, can validly contract more debt than they may pay within their own age, or within the term of 19 years? And that all future contracts will be deemed void as to what shall remain unpaid at the end of 19 years from their date? This would put the tenders, and the borrowers also, on their guard. By reducing too the faculty of borrowing within its natural limits, it would bridle the spirit of war, to which too free a course has been procured by the inattention of money-lenders to this law of nature, that succeeding generations are not responsible for the preceding.

On similar ground it may be proved that no society can make a perpetual constitution, or even a perpetual law. The earth belongs always to the living generation. They may manage it then, and what proceeds from it, as they please, during their usufruct. They are masters too of their own persons, and consequently may govern them as they please. But persons and property make the sum of the objects of government. The constitution and the laws of their predecessors extinguished then in their natural course with those who gave them being. This could preserve that being till it ceased to be itself, and no longer. Every constitution then, and every law, naturally expires at the end of 19 years. If it be enforced longer, it is an act of force, and not of right.—It may be said that the succeeding generation exercising in fact the power of repeal, this leaves them as free as if the constitution or law had been expressly limited to 19 years only. In the first place, this objection admits the right, in proposing an equivalent. But the power of repeal is not an equivalent. It might be indeed if every form of government were so perfectly contrived that the will of the majority could always be obtained fairly and without impediment. But this is true of no form. The people cannot assemble themselves. Their representation is unequal and vicious. Various checks are opposed to every legislative proposition. Factions get possession of the public councils. Bribery corrupts them. Personal interests lead them astray from the general interests of their constituents: and other impediments arise so as to prove to every practical man that a law of limited duration is much more manageable than one which needs a repeal. . . .

Turn this subject in your mind, my dear Sir, and particularly as to the power of contracting debts; and develop it with that perspicuity and cogent logic so peculiarly yours. Your station in the councils of our country gives you an opportunity of producing it to public consideration, of forcing it into discussion. At first blush it may be rallied, as a theoretical speculation: but examination will prove it to be solid and salutary. It would furnish matter for a fine preamble to our first law for appropriating the public revenue; and it will exclude at the threshold of our new government the contagious and ruinous errors of this quarter of the globe, which have armed despots with means, not sanctioned by nature, for binding in chains their fellow men. We have already given in example one effectual check to the Dog of war by transferring the power of letting him loose from the Executive to the Legislative body, from those who are to spend to those who are to pay. I should be pleased to see this second obstacle held out by us also in the first instance. No nation can make a declaration against the validity of long-contracted debts so disinterestedly as we, since we do not owe a shilling which may not be paid with ease, principal and interest, within the time of our own lives.—Establish the principle also in the new law to be passed for protecting copyrights and new inventions, by securing the exclusive right for 19 instead of 14 years. Besides familiarizing us to this term, it will be an instance the more of our taking reason for our guide, instead of English precedent, the habit of which fetters us with all the political heresies of a nation equally remarkable for its early excitement from some errors, and long slumbering under others. . . .

JAMES MADISON TO THOMAS JEFFERSON

New York Feb. 4, 1790

Dear Sir

Your favor of Jan. 9 enclosing one of Sept. last did not get to hand till a few days ago. The idea which the latter evolves is a great one; and suggests many interesting reflections to legislators; particularly when contracting and providing for public debts. Whether it can be received in the extent to which your reasonings carry it, is a question which I ought to turn more in my thoughts than I have yet been able to do, before I should be justified in making up a full opinion on it. My first thoughts lead me to view the doctrine as not in all respects, compatible with the course of human affairs. I will endeavor to sketch the grounds of my skepticism.

> "As the Earth belongs to the living, not to the dead, a living generation can bind itself only: in every Society the will of the majority binds the whole: according to the laws of mortality, a majority of those ripe for the exercise of their will do not live beyond the term of 19 years: to this term then is limited the validity of every act of the Society; nor can any act be continued beyond this term without an *express* declaration of the public will."

This I understand to be the outline of the argument.

The acts of a political society may be divided into three classes.

1. The fundamental constitution of the government.
2. Laws involving some stipulation, which renders them irrevocable at the will of the legislature.
3. Laws involving no such irrevocable quality.

1. However applicable in theory the doctrine may be to a Constitution, it seems liable in practice to some weighty objections.

Would not a government ceasing of necessity at the end of a given term, unless prolonged by some constitutional act, previous to its expiration, be too subject to the casualty and consequences of an interregnum?

Would not a government so often revised become too mutable and novel to retain that share of prejudice in its favor which is a salutary aid to the most rational government?

Would not such a periodical revision engender pernicious factions that might not otherwise come into existence; and agitate the public mind more frequently and more violently than might be expedient?

2. In the second class of acts involving stipulations, must not exceptions at least to the doctrine, be admitted?

If the earth be the gift of *nature* to the living, their title can extend to the earth in its *natural* state only. The *improvements* made by the dead form a debt against the living who take the benefit of them. This debt cannot be otherwise discharged than by a proportionate obedience to the will of the authors of the improvements.

But a case less liable to be controverted may perhaps be stated. Debts may be incurred with a direct view to the interest of the unborn as well as of the living: Such are debts for repelling a conquest, the evils of which descend through many generations. Debts may even be incurred principally for the benefit of posterity: Such perhaps is the debt incurred by the U. States. In these instances the debts might not be dischargeable within the term of 19 years.

There seems then to be some foundation in the nature of things; in the relation which one generation bears to another, for the *descent* of obligations from one to another. Equity may require it. Mutual good may be promoted by it. And all that seems indispensable in stating the account between the dead and the living, is to see that the debits against the latter do not exceed the advances made by the former. Few of the incumbrances entailed on nations by their predecessors would bear a liquidation even on this principle.

3. Objections to the doctrine, as applied to the third class of acts must be merely practical. But in that view alone they appear to be material.

Unless such temporary laws should be kept in force by acts regularly anticipating their expiration, all the rights depending on positive laws, that is most of the rights of property would become absolutely defunct, and the most violent struggles ensue between the parties interested in reviving and those interested in reforming the antecedent state of property. Nor does it seem improbable that such an event might be suffered to take place. The checks and difficulties opposed to the passage of laws which render the power of repeal inferior to an opportunity to reject as a security against oppression, would here render the latter an insecure provision against anarchy. Add to this that the very possibility of an event so hazardous to the rights of property could not but depreciate its value; that the approach of the crisis would increase the effect; that the frequent return of periods superceding all the obligations depending on antecedent laws and usages, must by weakening the sense of them, co-operate with motives to licenciousness already too powerful; and that the general uncertainty and vicisitudes of such a state of things would, on one side, discourage every useful effort of steady industry pursued under the sanction of existing laws, and on the other, give an immediate advantage to the more sagacious over the less sagacious part of the society.

I can find no relief from such embarrassments, but in the received doctrine that a *tacit* assent may be given to established governments and laws, and that this assent is to be inferred from the omission of an express revocation. It seems more practicable to remedy by well constituted governments, the pestilent operation of this doctrine, in the unlimited sense in which it is at present received than it is to find a remedy for the evils necessarily springing from an unlimited admission of the contrary doctrine.

Is it not doubtful whether it be possible to exclude wholly the idea of an implied or tacit assent, without subverting the very foundation of civil society?

On what principle is it that the voice of the majority binds the minority? It does not result I conceive from a law of nature but from compact founded on utility. A greater proportion might be required by the fundamental constitution of society, if under any particular circumstances it were judged eligible. Prior therefore to the establishment of this principle, unanimity was necessary; and rigid theory, accordingly presupposes the assent of every individual to the rule, which subjects the minority to the will of the majority. If this assent cannot be given tacitly, or be not implied where no positive evidence forbids, no person born in society, could on attaining ripe age, be bound by any acts, of the majority, and either a unanimous renewal of every law would be necessary, as often as a new member should be added to the society, or the express consent of every new member be obtained to the rule by which the majority decides for the whole.

If these observations be not misapplied, it follows that a limitation of the validity of all acts to the computed life of the generation establishing them, is in some cases not required by theory, and in others not consistent with practice. They are not meant however to impeach either the utility of the principle as applied to the cases you have particularly in view, or the general importance of it in the eye of the philosophical legislator. On the contrary it would give me singular pleasure to see it first announced to the world in a law of the U. States, and always kept in view as a salutary restraint on living generations from unjust and unnecessary burdens on their successors. This is a pleasure however which I have no hope of enjoying. The spirit of philosophical legislation has not prevailed at all in some parts of America, and is by no means the fashion of this part, or of the present representative body. The evils suffered or feared from weakness in government and licenciousness in the people, have turned the attention more towards the means of strengthening the powers of the former, than of narrowing their extent in the minds of the latter. Besides this it is so much easier to descry the little difficulties immediately incident to every great plan, than to comprehend its general and remote benefits, that further light must be added to the councils of our country before many truths which are seen through the medium of philosophy, become visible to the naked eye of the ordinary politician.

68

James Madison

Federalist 49 (1788)

The author of the *Notes on the State of Virginia*, quoted in the last paper, has subjoined to that valuable work the draught of a constitution, which had been prepared in order to be laid before a convention expected to be called in 1783, by the legislature, for the establishment of a constitution for that commonwealth. . . . One of the precautions which he proposes, and on which he appears ultimately to rely as a palladium to the weaker

From *The Federalist*.

departments of power against the invasions of the stronger, is perhaps altogether his own. . . .

His proposition is "that whenever any two of the three branches of government shall concur in opinion, each by the voices of two thirds of their whole number, that a convention is necessary for altering the Constitution, *or correcting breaches of it,* a convention shall be called for the purpose."

As the people are the only legitimate fountain of power, and it is from them that the constitutional charter, under which the several branches of government hold their power, is derived, it seems strictly consonant to the republican theory to recur to the same original authority, not only whenever it may be necessary to enlarge, diminish, or new-model the powers of government, but also whenever any one of the departments may commit encroachments on the chartered authorities of the others. The several departments being perfectly coordinate by the terms of their common commission, neither of them, it is evident, can pretend to an exclusive or superior right of settling the boundaries between their respective powers; and how are the encroachments of the stronger to be prevented, or the wrongs of the weaker to be redressed, without an appeal to the people themselves, who, as the grantors of the commission, can alone declare its true meaning, and enforce its observance? . . .

In the next place, it may be considered as an objection inherent in the principle that as every appeal to the people would carry an implication of some defect in the government, frequent appeals would, in great measure, deprive the government of that veneration which time bestows on everything, and without which perhaps the wisest and freest governments would not possess the requisite stability. If it be true that all governments rest on opinion, it is no less true that the strength of opinion in each individual, and its practical influence on his conduct, depend much on the number which he supposes to have entertained the same opinion. The reason of man, like man himself, is timid and cautious when left alone, and acquires firmness and confidence in proportion to the number with which it is associated. When the examples which fortify opinion are ancient as well as numerous, they are known to have a double effect. In a nation of philosophers, this consideration ought to be disregarded. A reverence for the laws would be sufficiently inculcated by the voice of an enlightened reason. But a nation of philosophers is as little to be expected as the philosophical race of kings wished for by Plato. And in every other nation, the most rational government will not find it a superfluous advantage to have the prejudices of the community on its side.

The danger of disturbing the public tranquillity by interesting too strongly the public passions is a still more serious objection against a frequent reference of constitutional questions to the decision of the whole society. Notwithstanding the success which has attended the revisions of our established forms of government and which does so much honor to the virtue and intelligence of the people of America, it must be confessed that the experiments are of too ticklish a nature to be unnecessarily multiplied. We are to recollect that all the existing constitutions were formed in the midst of a danger which repressed the passions most unfriendly to order and concord; of an enthusiastic confidence of the people in their patriotic leaders, which stifled the ordinary diversity of opinions on great national questions; of a universal ardor for new and opposite forms, produced by a universal resentment and indignation against the ancient government; and whilst no spirit of party connected with the changes to be made, or the abuses to be reformed, could mingle its leaven in the operation. The future situations in which we must expect to be usually placed do not present any equivalent security against the danger which is apprehended.

But the greatest objection of all is that the decisions which would probably result from such appeals would not answer the purpose of maintaining the constitutional equilibrium of the government. We have seen that the tendency of republican governments is to an aggrandizement of the legislative at the expense of the other departments. The appeals to the people, therefore, would usually be made by the executive and judiciary departments. But whether made by one side or the other, would each side enjoy equal advantages on the trial? Let us view their different situations. The members of the executive and judiciary departments are few in number, and can be personally known to a small part only of the people. The latter, by the mode of their appointment, as well as by the nature and permanency of it, are too far removed from the people to share much in their prepossessions. The former are generally the objects of jealousy and their administration is always liable to be discolored and rendered unpopular. The members of the legislative department, on the other hand, are numerous. They are distributed and dwell among the people at large. Their connections of blood, of friendship, and of acquaintance embrace a great proportion of the most influential part of the society. The nature of their public trust implies a personal influence among the people, and that they are more immediately the confidential guardians of the rights and liberties of the people. With these advantages it can hardly be supposed that the adverse party would have an equal chance for a favorable issue.

But the legislative party would not only be able to plead their cause most successfully with the people. They would probably be constituted themselves the judges. The same influence which had gained them an election into the legislature would gain them a seat in the convention. . . .

Chapter VI

Politics and Economics

How much government regulation of the economy is desirable? What is the proper relationship between politics and economics? Conservatives typically support some version of *laissez-faire* capitalism, while liberals usually advocate some version of the welfare state. Milton Friedman argues for minimal interference in the economy, on the ground that economic freedom is both itself an important component of freedom and the condition for political freedom. For Friedman, economic power should be independent of political power in order to check political power; socialism, by destroying economic liberty, destroys a protector of political freedom. Furthermore, a market economy can coordinate the activities of large numbers of individuals without resorting to coercion: each person seeks to promote his own interest by voluntarily entering into relations with others. Rational self-interest, rather than government regulation, is both the safest and most beneficial guide for economic decision making. As a result, he believes government should be primarily an umpire of economic activity.

Friedman's views stand in sharp contrast to the arguments for the welfare state set forward by Franklin D. Roosevelt, Lyndon Baines Johnson, and many liberals today. According to FDR, the rights contained in the Declaration of Independence must be redefined as social conditions change. By adding to the traditional freedoms of religion and speech the new freedoms—the freedom from fear and the freedom from want—FDR gives to politics a new aim: making men happy by contenting them with their lot. In contrast to the free market society Friedman defends, which depends on rational self-interest and the individual's desire to acquire, FDR's vision offers an alternative. Cooperation, he believes, will replace competition in a future where the individual advances along a road on which thousands of others also advance, overcoming self-interest and practicing "reciprocal self-denial" for the sake of the common advantage. FDR says that America's modern task involves distributing and administering, rather than producing, wealth. However, it is not entirely clear in his thought whether it is the success or the failure of the free market that dictates this redefinition of political goals. He argues that we must end competition because our western frontiers have closed and opportunity for advancement no longer exists. Yet he also speaks of the enjoyment of the fruits of scientific progress and an ever rising standard of living as one of the basic things we can now expect government to provide.

In his famous commencement address at the University of Michigan, President Johnson lays out the blueprint for the "Great Society," a program he hoped would rival FDR's New Deal. For Johnson, the United States should shift its focus from mere production of goods—since concern for "soulless wealth" is a mark of the "rich society" and the "powerful society," but not the "Great Society"—and emphasize instead the enrichment and elevation of American political life. By a renewal of America's cities, a new concern for nature, and improved education, the Great Society will strive for social uplift; it will seek to promote knowledge, ensure leisure time for its citizens, and increase their desire for and appreciation of beauty and community. Ultimately, LBJ presents an image of endless progress and continuous elevation, rejecting the idea that the Great Society may be a "resting place" and insisting instead that it constantly beckons the country toward a higher destiny. This will occur, seemingly, not only through government programs to improve its cities, but through government programs to improve its citizens: the government must play a role in helping its people establish their priorities, encouraging and educating them to value nature, beauty, and community. What role should government play in promoting progress? At what point does government involvement in aiding its citizens as they pursue happiness become government redefinition of what it means to be happy? On the other hand, can a community exist if its members fundamentally disagree about what it means to be happy and can reach no consensus on the goals of their common life as fellow citizens?

The 2019 Green New Deal Resolution, sponsored by New York Congresswoman Alexandria Ocasio-Cortez, builds on the legacies of FDR and LBJ and promises a twenty-first century version of their vision. Although the resolution specifically responds to concerns about global warming, its solution is economic: it demands the United States work toward "reducing emissions through economic transformation." Indeed, Ms. Ocasio-Cortez's chief of staff stated "The interesting thing about the Green New Deal is it wasn't originally a climate thing at all. . . . [W]e really think of it as a how-do-you-change-the-entire-economy thing." Thus, the Green New Deal resolution proposes policies aimed not only at protecting the environment, but at ending or ameliorating "systemic racial, regional, social, environmental, and economic injustices" and "repairing historic oppression" of racial minorities, immigrants, the poor, and women. The Green New Deal seems to agree with FDR's insistence that we should focus less on producing wealth than on distributing and administering it; moreover, it seems to be in line with LBJ's efforts to recreate society and his focus on nature. Nevertheless, insofar as it attempts to correct perceived systemic prejudices and emphasizes the need to offer special protections for the economic interests of disadvantaged groups, the Green New Deal Resolution seems to focus a great deal on increasing the material prosperity of specific groups within the community. As a result, we must ask, does the resolution prioritize benefits for specific groups rather than general self-sacrifice for the good of the whole community? Does it stress wealth at the expense of beauty, leisure, and social uplift? Is the proposed Green New Deal an outgrowth and completion of the New Deal and the Great Society, or does it abandon the principles of these earlier programs?

In contrast to these liberal visions of increased government involvement in the economy, Ronald Reagan insisted that the government should play less of a role in promoting economic growth and regulating industry. For Reagan, government programs have been deleterious: they have created an unsustainable national debt, produced rampant inflation, and driven the rising cost of consumer goods. Where FDR, LBJ, and Ocasio-Cortez argue that government control of the economy is necessary for individual freedom and happiness, Reagan argues that the government has rejected restraint, involved itself in virtually every aspect of private life, and undermined the American Dream. Government initiatives, he believes, have not helped the average citizen; instead, they have subsumed individual initiative, harmed economic growth, and threatened personal freedom. A desire to promote freedom and equality through government programs, he warns, may ultimately threaten the rights of the average American.

In the early 19th century, Alexis de Tocqueville expressed the fear that in democracies the people would gradually give up their independence in exchange for the security offered by a powerful national government. Such a state would be a "soft despotism" in which men become passive, their basic needs taken care of by a benevolent government on whom they would eventually become completely dependent. Tocqueville thus shares with Reagan the fear that the quest for equal prosperity, to be attained through government regulation, might sacrifice individual dignity and freedom.

A consideration of earlier views on the relationship between government and economics helps to place contemporary economic debates in a broader perspective. Thomas Jefferson's argument in favor of farming and against manufacturing decries the desire for excess and emphasizes the nobility of the farmer's self-sufficiency. He opposes the promotion of manufactures because of the effect such work has on men—subservience, venality, and the stifling of virtue. Artisans, he fears, are not fit citizens of a republic but may easily become the tools of a despot. In contrast, as seen in his "Report on Manufactures," Alexander Hamilton is one of the greatest proponents of a commercial republic. Hamilton favors significant government regulation of the economy and argues Congress is empowered to promote industry and production by the general welfare clause of the Constitution. The constitutionality of much New Deal legislation is also derived from this clause. Although Hamilton thus shares with FDR a concept of active government, he focuses on the creation of wealth, and even hopes for national "opulence," whereas FDR emphasizes self-sacrifice and "the sufficiency of life." FDR may seem to share more with Jefferson's moderate goals than Hamilton's desire for a "plethora of riches." Yet Jefferson differentiates himself from FDR insofar as he, like Hamilton, sees economics as a way of promoting independence. For Jefferson, farming promotes independence and self-reliance for individuals; for Hamilton, manufactures promotes the independence and self-sufficiency of the nation. Thus, in both Jefferson and Hamilton, we can see an emphasis on independence and pride that is missing in FDR's thought.

Moreover, while Jefferson and Hamilton disagree about economics, they both agree that economic policy will directly contribute to creating a certain type of republic and a particular type of citizens. For both men, as a result, economic policy is intrinsically tied up with the character of the regime and its citizens. Such considerations are absent in both FDR and Friedman. While Friedman does make freedom his end, he does not adequately consider the political conditions and ends of economic freedom. For both FDR and Friedman, politics is in the service of economics: for Friedman, government regulates the acquisition of material benefits, and for FDR, government itself is the dispenser of these benefits. Their subordination of the public to the private stems from a denial that there are standards of right and wrong accepted by the entire community. Friedman, for example, argues that we should not coerce someone we see making a mistake, for, after all, he may be right and we might be wrong. Similarly, FDR cannot maintain that men have any rights in common, such as the natural rights referred to in the Declaration: since statesmen must redefine human rights as the social conditions change, there are at best only different rights for different social conditions.

In 2005, the Supreme Court called for a reconsideration of the constitutional constraints on public regulation of private property. According to the Fifth Amendment, "private property [shall not] be taken for public use without just compensation." In *Kelo v. New London*, however, Justice John Paul Steven's majority opinion allows the government broad discretion in determining what constitutes a public use or public purpose. He argues that the City of New London had every right to force homeowners to sell their property to the city, which will in turn sell that property to private developers, since these developers would increase the value of that property and promote economic growth. For Stevens, the Fifth Amendment does not place significant restrictions on the government's ability to take private property, so long as it pays for what it takes. Thus, he believes the Constitution allows the government to take private property from one individual and give it to another individual or corporation, if the government's goal is to promote progress. Justice Sandra Day O'Connor, however, contends that the majority opinion undermines important Constitutional protections of private property. For O'Connor, the Fifth Amendment demands not only just compensation when property is taken, but also requires that property be taken only if it is for a genuinely "public use." Under the majority's ruling, she argues, the words "public use" have been all but removed from the Constitution, thereby allowing the government to transfer property between its citizens.

The Court also weighed in on the constitutionality of the "Patient Protection and Affordable Care Act of 2010," a law which raised new questions about the extent and limits of the power of the federal government to regulate economic choices. *National Federation of Independent Business v. Sebelius* addressed the constitutionality of the "individual mandate," a provision of the law that required individuals to either purchase health insurance or make a "shared responsibility payment" to the government. Five members of the Court, including Chief Justice John Roberts, agreed that the mandate could not be justified under Congress' power to regulate interstate commerce. Nonetheless, the Court ultimately upheld the mandate, arguing that Congress had power to impose the "shared responsibility payment" under its tax power. In contrast, four conservative justices argue that the individual mandate cannot be upheld as a regulation of interstate commerce or as an exercise of tax power. Since the mandate requires individuals to purchase insurance, it creates commerce rather than regulating it, and since the purpose of a tax is to create revenue, a "shared responsibility payment" intended to encourage individuals to purchase insurance must be seen as a fine rather than a tax.

Adam M. Carrington maintains that the divisions on the Court in *Kelo* and *Sebelius* reflect an ongoing tension within the constitutional system between the need for government to protect liberty and the need for restraints on government power to prevent tyranny. Carrington shows that each perspective has its source in the Constitution, and argues that at its best the Court would recognize this healthy tension inherent in the Constitution.

69

Milton Friedman

Capitalism and Freedom (1962)

In a much quoted passage in his inaugural address, President Kennedy said, "Ask not what your country can do for you—ask what you can do for your country." It is a striking sign of the temper of our times that the controversy about this passage centered on its origin and not on its content. Neither half of the statement expresses a relation between the citizen and his government that is worthy of the ideals of free men in a free society. The paternalistic "what your country can do for you" implies that government is the patron, the citizen the ward, a view that is at odds with the free man's belief in his own responsibility for his own destiny. The organismic, "what you can do for your country" implies that government is the master or the deity, the citizen, the servant or the votary. To the free man, the country is the collection of individuals who compose it, not something over and above them. . . . He recognizes no national purpose except as it is the consensus of the purposes for which the citizens severally strive.

The free man will ask neither what his country can do for him nor what he can do for his country. He will ask rather "What can I and my compatriots do through government" to help us discharge our individual responsibilities, to achieve our several goals and purposes, and above all, to protect our freedom? . . . Government is necessary to preserve our freedom, it is an instrument through which we can exercise our freedom; yet by concentrating power in political hands, it is also a threat to freedom. . . .

How can we benefit from the promise of government while avoiding the threat to freedom? . . .

First, the scope of government must be limited. Its major function must be to protect our freedom both from the enemies outside our gates and from our fellow-citizens: to preserve law and order, to enforce private contracts, to foster competitive markets. Beyond this major function, government may enable us at times to accomplish jointly what we would find it more difficult or expensive to accomplish severally. However, any such use of government is fraught with danger. We should not and cannot avoid using government in this way. But there should be a clear and large balance of advantages before we do. By relying primarily on voluntary co-operation and private enterprise, in both economic and other activities, we can insure that the private sector is a check on the powers of the governmental sector and an effective protection of freedom of speech, of religion, and of thought.

The second broad principle is that government power must be dispersed. If government is to exercise power, better in the county than in the state, better in the state than in Washington. If I do not like what my local community does, be it in sewage disposal, or zoning, or schools, I can move to another local community, and though few may take this step, the mere possibility acts as a check. If I do not like what my state does, I can move to another. If I do not like what Washington imposes, I have few alternatives in this world of jealous nations. . . .

The preservation of freedom is the protective reason for limiting and decentralizing governmental power. But there is also a constructive reason. The great advances of civilization, whether in architecture or painting, in science or literature, in industry or agriculture, have never come from centralized government. . . .

Government can never duplicate the variety and diversity of individual action. At any moment in time, by imposing uniform standards in housing, or nutrition, or clothing, government could undoubtedly improve the level of living of many individuals; by imposing uniform standards in schooling, road construction, or sanitation, central government could undoubtedly improve the level of performance in many local areas and perhaps even on the average of all communities. But in the process, government would replace progress by stagnation, it would substitute uniform mediocrity for the variety essential for that experimentation which can bring tomorrow's laggards above today's mean. . . .

As it developed in the late eighteenth and early nineteenth centuries, the intellectual movement that went under the name of liberalism emphasized freedom as the ultimate goal and the individual as the ultimate entity in the society. It supported laissez faire at home as a means of reducing the role of the state in economic affairs and thereby enlarging the role of the individual. . . .

Beginning in the late nineteenth century, and especially after 1930 in the United States, the term liberalism came to be associated with a very different emphasis, particularly in economic policy. It came to be associated with a readiness to rely primarily on the state rather than on private voluntary arrangements to achieve objectives regarded as desirable. The catchwords became welfare and equality rather than freedom. The nineteenth-century liberal regarded an extension of freedom as the most effective way to promote welfare and equality; the twentieth-century liberal regards welfare and equality as either prerequisites of or alternatives to freedom. In the name of welfare and equality, the twentieth-century liberal has come to favor a revival of the very policies of state intervention and paternalism against which classical liberalism fought. . . .

⌒⌒⌒ ✕ ⌒⌒⌒

It is widely believed that politics and economics are separate and largely unconnected; that individual freedom is a political problem and material welfare an economic problem; and that any kind of political arrangements can be combined with any kind of economic arrangements. The chief contemporary manifestation of this idea is the advocacy of "democratic socialism" by many who condemn out of hand the restrictions on individual freedom imposed by "totalitarian socialism" in Russia, and who are persuaded that it is possible for a country to adopt the essential features of Russian economic arrangements and yet to ensure individual freedom through political arrangements. The thesis of this chapter is that such a view is a delusion. . . .

Economic arrangements play a dual role in the promotion of a free society. On the one hand, freedom in economic arrangements is itself a component of freedom broadly understood, so economic freedom is an end in itself. In the second place, economic freedom is also an indispensable means toward the achievement of political freedom.

The first of these roles of economic freedom needs special emphasis because intellectuals in particular have a strong bias against regarding this aspect of freedom as important. They tend to express contempt for what they regard as material aspects of life. . . .

A citizen of the United States who under the laws of various states is not free to follow the occupation of his own choosing unless he can get a license for it, is likewise being deprived of an essential part of his freedom. So is the man who would like to exchange some of his goods with, say, a Swiss for a watch but is prevented from doing so by a quota. So also is the Californian who was thrown into jail for selling Alka Seltzer at a price below that set by the manufacturer under so-called "fair trade" laws. So also is the farmer who cannot grow the amount of wheat he wants. And so on. Clearly, economic freedom, in and of itself, is an extremely important part of total freedom.

Viewed as a means to the end of political freedom, economic arrangements are important because of their effect on the concentration or dispersion of power. The kind of economic organization that provides economic freedom directly, namely, competitive capitalism, also promotes political freedom because it separates economic power from political power and in this way enables the one to offset the other. . . .

What are the logical links between economic and political freedom? In discussing these questions we shall consider first the market as a direct component of freedom, and then the indirect relation between market arrangements and political freedom. A by-product will be an outline of the ideal economic arrangements for a free society.

As liberals, we take freedom of the individual, or perhaps the family, as our ultimate goal in judging social arrangements. Freedom as a value in this sense has to do with the interrelations among people. . . . [I]n a society freedom has nothing to say about what an individual does with his freedom; it is not an all-embracing ethic. Indeed, a major aim of the liberal is to leave the ethical problem for the individual to wrestle with. The "really" important ethical problems are those that face an individual in a free society—what he should do with his freedom. . . .

The basic problem of social organization is how to co-ordinate the economic activities of large numbers of people. . . .

Literally millions of people are involved in providing one another with their daily bread, let alone with their yearly automobiles. The challenge to the believer in liberty is to reconcile this widespread interdependence with individual freedom.

Fundamentally, there are only two ways of coordinating the economic activities of millions. One is central direction involving the use of coercion—the technique of the army and of the modern totalitarian state. The other is voluntary co-operation of individuals—the technique of the market place.

The possibility of co-ordination through voluntary co-operation rests on the elementary—yet frequently denied—proposition that both parties to an economic transaction benefit from it, *provided the transaction is bilaterally voluntary and informed.*

Exchange can therefore bring about co-ordination without coercion. A working model of a society organized through voluntary exchange is a *free private enterprise exchange economy*—what we have been calling competitive capitalism. . . .

[I]n the complex enterprise and money-exchange economy, cooperation is strictly individual and voluntary *provided:* (a) that enterprises are private, so that the ultimate contracting parties are individuals and (b) that individuals are effectively free to enter or not to enter into any particular exchange, so that every transaction is strictly voluntary. . . .

So long as effective freedom of exchange is maintained, the central feature of the market organization of economic activity is that it prevents one person from interfering with another in respect of most of his activities. The consumer is protected from coercion by the seller because of the presence of other sellers with whom he can deal. The seller is protected from coercion by the consumer because of other consumers to whom he can sell. The employee is protected from coercion by the employer because of other employers for whom he can work, and so on. And the market does this impersonally and without centralized authority. . . .

The existence of a free market does not of course eliminate the need for government. On the contrary, government is essential both as a forum for determining the "rules of the game" and as an umpire to interpret and enforce the rules decided on. What the market does is to reduce greatly the range of issues that must be decided through political means, and thereby to minimize the extent to which government need participate directly in the game. The characteristic feature of action through political channels is that it tends to require or enforce substantial conformity. The great advantage of the market, on the other hand, is that it permits wide diversity. It is, in political terms, a system of proportional representation. Each man can vote, as it were, for the color of tie he wants and get it; he does not have to see what color the majority wants and then, if he is in the minority, submit.

It is this feature of the market that we refer to when we say that the market provides economic freedom. But this characteristic also has implications that go far beyond the narrowly economic. Political freedom means the absence of coercion of a man by his fellow men. . . . By removing the organization of economic activity from the control of political authority, the market eliminates this source of coercive power. It enables economic strength to be a check to political power rather than a reinforcement. . . .

One feature of a free society is surely the freedom of individuals to advocate and propagandize openly for a radical change in the structure of the society—so long as the advocacy is restricted to persuasion and does not include force or other forms of coercion. It is a mark of the political freedom of a capitalist society that men can openly advocate and work for socialism. Equally, political freedom in a socialist society would require that men be free to advocate the introduction of capitalism. How could the freedom to advocate capitalism be preserved and protected in a socialist society?

In order for men to advocate anything, they must in the first place be able to earn a living. This already raises a problem in a socialist society, since all jobs are under the direct control of political authorities. . . .

For advocacy of capitalism to mean anything, the proponents must be able to finance their cause—to hold public meetings, publish pamphlets, buy radio time, issue newspapers and magazines, and so on. How could they raise the funds? There might and probably would be men in the socialist society with large incomes, perhaps even large capital sums in the form of government bonds and the like, but these would of necessity be high public officials. . . .

The only recourse for funds would be to raise small amounts from a large number of minor officials. But this is no real answer. To tap these sources, many people would already have to be persuaded, and our whole problem is how to initiate and finance a campaign to do so. Radical movements in capitalist societies have never been financed this way. They have typically been supported by a few wealthy individuals who have become persuaded. . . . This is a role of inequality of wealth in preserving political freedom that is seldom noted—the role of the patron. . . .

[I]ndeed, it is not even necessary to persuade people or financial institutions with available funds of the soundness of the ideas to be propagated. It is only necessary to persuade them that the propagation can be financially successful; that the newspaper or magazine or book or other venture will be profitable. . . .

But we are not yet through. In a free market society, it is enough to have the funds. The suppliers of paper are as willing to sell it to the *Daily Worker* as to the *Wall Street Journal*. In a socialist society, it would not be enough to have the funds. The hypothetical supporter of capitalism would have to persuade a government factory making paper to sell to him, the government printing press to print his pamphlets, a government post office to distribute them among the people, a government agency to rent him a hall in which to talk, and so on. . . .

By contrast, it is clear how a free market capitalist society fosters freedom.

A striking practical example of these abstract principles is the experience of Winston Churchill. From 1933 to the outbreak of World War II, Churchill was not permitted to talk over the British radio, which was, of course, a government monopoly administered by the British Broadcasting Corporation. Here was a leading citizen of his country, a Member of Parliament, a former cabinet minister, a man who was desperately trying by every device possible to persuade his countrymen to take steps to ward off the menace of Hitler's Germany. He was not permitted to talk over the radio to the British people because the BBC was a government monopoly and his position was too "controversial." . . .

Another example of the role of the market in preserving political freedom, was revealed in our experience with McCarthyism. Entirely aside from the substantive issues involved, and the merits of the charges made, what protection did individuals, and in particular government employees, have against irresponsible accusations and probings into matters that it went against their conscience to reveal? Their appeal to the Fifth Amendment would have been a hollow mockery without an alternative to government employment.

Their fundamental protection was the existence of a private-market economy in which they could earn a living. . . .

The "social security" program is one of those things on which the tyranny of the status quo is beginning to work its magic. Despite the controversy that surrounded its inception, it has come to be so much taken for granted that its desirability is hardly questioned any longer. Yet it involves a large-scale invasion into the personal lives of a large fraction of the nation without, so far as I can see, any justification that is at all persuasive, not only on liberal principles, but on almost any other. I propose to examine the biggest phase of it, that which involves payments to the aged.

As an operational matter, the program known as old age and survivor's insurance (OASI) consists of a special tax imposed on payrolls, plus payments to persons who have reached a specified age, of amounts determined by the age at which payments begin, family status, and prior earning record.

As an analytical matter, OASI consists of three separable elements:

1. The requirement that a wide class of persons must purchase specified annuities, i.e., compulsory provision for old age.
2. The requirement that the annuity must be purchased from the government; i.e., nationalization of the provision of these annuities.
3. A scheme for redistributing income, insofar as the value of the annuities to which people are entitled when they enter the system is not equal to the taxes they will pay.

Clearly, there is no necessity for these elements to be combined. . . .

Let us therefore consider each of these elements in turn to see how far, if at all, each can be justified. It will facilitate our analysis, I believe, if we consider them in reverse order.

1. Income redistribution. The present OASI program involves two major kinds of redistribution; from some OASI beneficiaries to others; from the general taxpayer to OASI beneficiaries.

The first kind of redistribution is primarily from those who entered the system relatively young, to those who entered it at an advanced age. The latter are receiving, and will for some time be receiving, a greater amount as benefits than the taxes they paid could have purchased. Under present tax and benefit schedules, on the other hand, those who entered the system at a young age will receive decidedly less.

I do not see any grounds—liberal or other—on which this particular redistribution can be defended. . . .

The second kind of redistribution arises because the system is not likely to be fully self-financing. During the period when many were covered and paying taxes, and few had qualified for benefits, the system appeared to be self-financing and indeed to be having a surplus. But this appearance depends on neglecting the obligation being accumulated with respect to the persons paying the tax. It is doubtful that the taxes paid have sufficed to finance the accumulated obligation. . . .

[Could] a subsidy from the general taxpayer . . . be justified if it is required[?] I see no grounds on which such a subsidy can be justified. We may wish to help poor people. Is there any justification for helping people whether they are poor or not because they happen to be a certain age? Is this not an entirely arbitrary redistribution?

The only argument I have ever come across to justify the redistribution involved in OASI is one that I regard as thoroughly immoral despite its wide use. This argument is that OASI redistribution on the average helps low-income people more than high-income people despite a large arbitrary element; that it would be better to do this redistribution more efficiently; but that the community will not vote for the redistribution directly though it will vote for it as part of a social security package. In essence, what this argument says is that the community can be fooled into voting for a measure that it opposes by presenting the measure in a false guise. . . .

2. *Nationalization of the provision of required annuities.* Suppose we avoid redistribution by requiring each person to pay for the annuity he gets, in the sense of course, that the premium suffices to cover the present value of the annuity, account being taken both of mortality and interest returns. What justification is there then for requiring him to purchase it from a governmental concern? If redistribution is to be accomplished, clearly the taxing power of the government must be used. But if redistribution is to be no part of the program . . . why not permit individuals who wish to do so to purchase their annuities from private concerns? . . .

Possible economies of scale are no argument for nationalizing the provision of annuities. If they are present, and the government sets up a concern to sell annuity contracts, it may be able to undersell competitors by virtue of its size. In that case, it will get the business without compulsion. If it cannot undersell them, then presumably economies of scale are not present or are not sufficient to overcome other diseconomies of governmental operation. . . .

3. *Compulsory Purchase of Annuities.* . . . One possible justification for such compulsion is strictly paternalistic. People could if they wished decide to do individually what the law requires them to do as a group. But they are separately short-sighted and improvident. "We" know better than "they" that it is in their own good to provide for their old age to a greater extent than they would voluntarily; we cannot persuade them individually; but we can persuade 51 per cent or more to compel all to do what is in their own good. This paternalism is for responsible people, hence does not even have the excuse of concern for children or madmen.

This position is internally consistent and logical. A thorough-going paternalist who holds it cannot be dissuaded by being shown that he is making a mistake in logic. He is our opponent on grounds of principle, not simply a well-meaning but misguided friend. Basically, he believes in dictatorship, benevolent and maybe majoritarian, but dictatorship none the less.

Those of us who believe in freedom must believe also in the freedom of individuals to make their own mistakes. If a man knowingly prefers to live for today, to use his resources for current enjoyment, deliberately choosing a penurious old age, by what right do we prevent him from doing so? We may argue with him, seek to persuade him that he is wrong, but are we entitled to use coercion to prevent him from doing what he chooses to do? Is there not always the possibility that he is right and that we are wrong? Humility is the distinguishing virtue of the believer in freedom; arrogance, of the paternalist. . . .

A possible justification on liberal principles for compulsory purchase of annuities is that the improvident will not suffer the consequence of their own action but will impose costs on others. We shall not, it is said, be willing to see the indigent aged suffer in dire poverty. We shall assist them by private and public charity. Hence the man who does not provide for his old age will become a public charge. Compelling him to buy an annuity is justified not for his own good but for the good of the rest of us. . . .

The belief that a large fraction of the community would become public charges if not compelled to purchase annuities owed its plausibility, at the time OASI was enacted, to the Great Depression. . . . This experience was unprecedented and has not been repeated since. It did not arise because people were improvident and failed to provide for their old age. . . .

Private arrangements for the care of the aged have altered greatly over time. Children were at one time the major means whereby people provided for their own old age. As the community became more affluent, the mores changed. The responsibilities imposed on children to care for their parents declined and more and more people came to make provision for old age in the form of accumulating property or acquiring private pension rights. More recently, the development of pension plans over and above OASI has accelerated. Indeed, some students believe that a continuation of present trends points to a society in which a large fraction of the public scrimps in their productive years to provide themselves with a higher standard of life in old age than they ever enjoyed in the prime of life. Some of us may think such a trend perverse, but if it reflects the tastes of the community, so be it.

Compulsory purchase of annuities has therefore imposed large costs for little gain. It has deprived all of us of control over a sizable fraction of our income, requiring us to devote it to a particular purpose, purchase of a retirement annuity, in a particular way, by buying it from a government concern. It has inhibited competition in the sale of annuities and the development of retirement arrangements. It has given birth to a large bureaucracy that shows tendencies of growing by what it feeds on, of extending its scope from one area of our life to another. And all this, to avoid the danger that a few people might become charges on the public. . . .

70

Franklin Delano Roosevelt

The New Goals of Politics (1932, 1935, 1941)

. . . The issue of Government has always been whether individual men and women will have to serve some system of Government or economics, or whether a system of Government and economics exists to serve individual men and women. . . .

A glance at the situation today only too clearly indicates that equality of opportunity as we have known it no longer exists. Our industrial plant is built; the problem just now is whether under existing conditions it is not overbuilt. Our last frontier has long since been reached, and there is practically no more free land. . . .

Just as freedom to farm has ceased, so also the opportunity in business has narrowed. It still is true that men can start small enterprises, trusting to native shrewdness and ability to keep abreast of competitors; but area after area has been preempted altogether by the great corporations, and even in the fields which still have no great concerns, the small man starts under a handicap. . . . If the process of concentration goes on at the same rate, at the end of another century we shall have all American industry controlled by a dozen corporations, and run by perhaps a hundred men. But plainly, we are steering a steady course toward economic oligarchy, if we are not there already.

Clearly, all this calls for a reappraisal of values. A mere builder of more industrial plants, a creator of more railroad systems, an organizer of more corporations, is as likely to be a danger as a help. The day of the great promoter or the financial Titan, to whom we granted anything if only he would build, or develop, is over. Our task now is not discovery or exploitation of

From Roosevelt, "The Commonwealth Club Address" (Sept., 1932), in *The Public Papers and Addresses of Franklin D. Roosevelt,* Vol. 1, Random House, 1938; "Address to the Young Democratic Clubs of America" (Aug., 1935), in *The Public Papers and Addresses of Franklin D. Roosevelt,* Vol. IV, 1938; "The Four Freedoms Speech" (1941), in *Development of United States Foreign Policy: Addresses and Messages of Franklin D. Roosevelt* (77th Cong., 2d sess.; Senate Doc. No. 188, Serial No. 10676 [Washington, 1942]).

natural resources, or necessarily producing more goods. It is the soberer, less dramatic business of administering resources and plants already in hand, of seeking to reestablish foreign markets for our surplus production, of meeting the problem of underconsumption, of adjusting production to consumption, of distributing wealth and products more equitably, of adapting existing economic organizations to the service of the people. The day of enlightened administration has come. . . .

As I see it, the task of Government in its relation to business is to assist the development of an economic declaration of rights, an economic constitutional order. This is the common task of statesman and business man. It is the minimum requirement of a more permanently safe order of things.

Happily, the times indicate that to create such an order not only is the proper policy of Government, but it is the only line of safety for our economic structures as well. We know, now, that these economic units cannot exist unless prosperity is uniform, that is, unless purchasing power is well distributed throughout every group in the nation. That is why even the most selfish of corporations for its own interest would be glad to see wages restored and unemployment ended and to bring the Western farmer back to his accustomed level of prosperity and to assure a permanent safety to both groups. That is why some enlightened industries themselves endeavor to limit the freedom of action of each man and business group within the industry in the common interest of all; why business men everywhere are asking a form of organization which will bring the scheme of things into balance, even though it may in some measure qualify the freedom of action of individual units within the business. . . .

We have now to apply the earlier concepts of American Government to the conditions of today.

The Declaration of Independence discusses the problem of Government in terms of a contract. Government is a relation of give and take, a contract, perforce, if we would follow the thinking out of which it grew. Under such a contract rulers were accorded power, and the people consented to that power on consideration that they be accorded certain rights. The task of statesmanship has always been the redefinition of these rights in terms of a changing and growing social order. New conditions impose new requirements upon Government and those who conduct Government.

I held, for example, in proceedings before me as Governor, the purpose of which was the removal of the Sheriff of New York, that under modern conditions it was not enough for a public official merely to evade the legal terms of official wrongdoing. He owed a positive duty as well. I said in substance that if he had acquired large sums of money, he was when accused required to explain the sources of such wealth. To that extent this wealth was colored with a public interest. I said that in financial matters, public servants should, even beyond private citizens, be held to a stern and uncompromising rectitude.

I feel that we are coming to a view through the drift of our legislation and our public thinking in the past quarter century that private economic power is, to enlarge an old phrase, a public trust as well. I hold that continued enjoyment of that power by any individual or group must depend upon the fulfillment of that trust. The men who have reached the summit of American business life know this best; happily, many of these urge the binding quality of this greater social contract.

The terms of that contract are as old as the Republic, and as new as the new economic order.

Every man has a right to life; and this means that he has also the right to make a comfortable living. He may by sloth or crime decline to exercise that right; but it may not be denied him. We have no actual famine or dearth; our industrial and agricultural mechanism can produce enough and to spare. Our Government formal and informal, political and economic, owes to everyone an avenue to possess himself of a portion of that plenty sufficient for his needs, through his own work.

Every man has a right to his own property; which means a right to be assured, to the fullest extent attainable, in the safety of his savings. By no other means can men carry the burdens of those parts of life which, in the nature of things, afford no chance of labor; childhood, sickness, old age. In all thought of property, this right is paramount; all other property rights must yield to it. If, in accord with this principle, we must restrict the operations of the speculator, the manipulator, even the financier, I believe we must accept the restriction as needful, not to hamper individualism but to protect it.

These two requirements must be satisfied, in the main, by individuals who claim and hold control of the great industrial and financial combinations which dominate so large a part of our industrial life. They have undertaken to be, not business men, but princes of property. I am not prepared to say that the system which produces them is wrong. I am very clear that they must fearlessly and competently assume the responsibility which goes with the power. . . .

[T]he responsible heads of finance and industry instead of acting each for himself, must work together to achieve the common end. They must, where necessary, sacrifice this or that private advantage; and in reciprocal self-denial must seek a general advantage. It is here that formal Government—political Government, if you choose—comes in. Whenever in the pursuit of this objective the lone wolf, the unethical competitor, the reckless promoter, the Ishmael or Insull whose hand is against every man's, declines to join in achieving an end recognized as being for the public welfare, and threatens to drag the industry back to a state of anarchy, the Government may properly be asked to apply restraint. . . .

I say from my heart that no man of my generation has any business to address youth unless he comes to that task not in a spirt of exultation, but in a spirit of humilty. I cannot expect you of a newer generation to believe me, of an older generation, if I do not frankly acknowledge that had the generation that brought you into the world been wiser and more provident and more unselfish, you would have been saved from needless difficult problems and needless pain and suffering. We may not have failed you in good intentions but we have certainly not been adequate in results. Your task, therefore, is not only to maintain the best in your heritage, but to labor to lift from the shoulders of the American people some of the burdens that the mistakes of a past generation have placed there. . . .

The severity of the recent depression, toward which we had been heading for a whole generation, has taught us that no economic or social class in the community is so richly endowed and so independent of the general community that it can safeguard its own security, let alone assure security for the general community.

The very objectives of young people have changed. In the older days a great financial fortune was too often the goal. To rule through wealth, or through the power of wealth, fired our imagination. This was the dream of the golden ladder—each individual for himself.

It is my firm belief that the newer generation of America has a different dream. You place emphasis on sufficiency of life, rather than on a plethora of riches. You think of the security for yourself and your family that will give you good health, good food, good education, good working conditions, and the opportunity for normal recreation and occasional travel. Your advancement, you hope, is along a broad highway on which thousands of your fellow men and women are advancing with you.

You and I know that this modern economic world of ours is governed by rules and regulations vastly more complex than those laid down in the days of Adam Smith or John Stuart Mill. They faced simpler mechanical processes and social needs. It is worth remembering, for example, that the business corporation, as we know it, did not exist in the days of Washington and Hamilton and Jefferson. Private businesses then were conducted solely by individuals or by partnerships in which every member was immediately and wholly responsible for success or failure. Facts are relentless. We must adjust our ideas to the facts of today. . . .

In 1911, twenty-four years ago, when I was first a member of the New York State Legislature, a number of the younger members of the Legislature worked against these old conditions and called for laws governing factory inspection, for workmen's compensation and for the limitation of work for women and children to fifty-four hours, with one day's rest in seven. Those of us who joined in this movement in the Legislature were called reformers, socialists, and wild men. We were opposed by many of the same organizations and the same individuals who are now crying aloud about the socialism involved in social security legislation, in bank deposit insurance, in farm credit, in the saving of homes, in the protection of investors and the regulation of public utilities. The reforms, however, for which we were condemned twenty-four years ago are taken today as a matter of course. And so, I believe, will be regarded the reforms that now cause such concern to the reactionaries of 1935. We come to an understanding of these new ways of protecting people because our knowledge enlarges and our capacity for organized action increases. People have learned that they can carry their burdens effectively only by cooperation. We have found out how to conquer the ravages of diseases that years ago were regarded as unavoidable and inevitable. We must learn that many other social ills can be cured.

Let me emphasize that serious as have been the errors of unrestrained individualism, I do not believe in abandoning the system of individual enterprise. The freedom and opportunity that have characterized American development in the past can be maintained if we recognize the fact that the individual system of our day calls for the collaboration of all of us to provide, at the least, security for all of us. Those words "freedom" and "opportunity" do not mean a license to climb upwards by pushing other people down.

Any paternalistic system which tries to provide for security for everyone from above only calls for an impossible task and a regimentation utterly uncongenial to the spirit of our people. But Government cooperation to help make the system of free enterprise work, to provide that minimum security without which the competitive system cannot function, to restrain the kind of individual action which in the past has been harmful to the community—that kind of governmental cooperation is entirely consistent with the best tradition of America. . . .

More than ever, we cherish the elective form of democratic government, but progress under it can easily be retarded by disagreements that relate to method and to detail rather than to the broad objectives upon which we are agreed. It is as if all of us were united in the pursuit of a common goal, but that each and every one of us were marching along a separate road of our own. If we insist on choosing different roads, most of us will not reach our common destination. . . .

Therefore, to the American youth of all parties I submit a message of confidence—Unite and Challenge! Rules are not necessarily sacred; principles are. The methods of the old order are not, as some would have you believe, above the challenge of youth. . . .

~~~~~

. . . [T]here is nothing mysterious about the foundations of a healthy and strong democracy. The basic things expected by our people of their political and economic systems are simple. They are:

Equality of opportunity for youth and for others.

Jobs for those who can work.

Security for those who need it.

The ending of special privilege for the few.

The preservation of civil liberties for all.

The enjoyment of the fruits of scientific progress in a wider and constantly rising standard of living.

These are the simple, basic things that must never be lost sight of in the turmoil and unbelievable complexity of our modern world. The inner and abiding strength of our economic and political systems is dependent upon the degree to which they fulfill these expectations.

Many subjects connected with our social economy call for immediate improvement.

As examples:

We should bring more citizens under the coverage of old-age pensions and unemployment insurance.

We should widen the opportunities for adequate medical care.

We should plan a better system by which persons deserving or needing gainful employment may obtain it.

I have called for personal sacrifice. I am assured of the willingness of almost all Americans to respond to that call.

A part of the sacrifice means the payment of more money in taxes. . . .

In the future days, which we seek to make secure, we look forward to a world founded upon four essential human freedoms.

The first is freedom of speech and expression—everywhere in the world.

The second is freedom of every person to worship God in his own way—everywhere in the world.

The third is freedom from want—which, translated into world terms, means economic understandings which will secure to every nation a healthy peacetime life for its inhabitants—everywhere in the world.

The fourth is freedom from fear—which, translated into world terms, means a world-wide reduction of armaments to such a point and in such a thorough fashion that no nation will be in a position to commit an act of physical aggression against any neighbor—anywhere in the world.

That is no vision of a distant millennium. It is a definite basis for a kind of world attainable in our own time and generation. That kind of world is the very antithesis of the so-called new order of tyranny which the dictators seek to create with the crash of a bomb.

To that new order we oppose the greater conception—the moral order. A good society is able to face schemes of world domination and foreign revolutions alike without fear.

Since the beginning of our American history, we have been engaged in change—in a perpetual peaceful revolution—a revolution which goes on steadily, quietly adjusting itself to changing conditions—without the concentration camp or the quick-lime in the ditch. The world order which we seek is the cooperation of free countries, working together in a friendly, civilized society.

This nation has placed its destiny in the hands and heads and hearts of its millions of free men and women; and its faith in freedom under the guidance of God. Freedom means the supremacy of human rights everywhere. Our support goes to those who struggle to gain those rights or keep them. Our strength is our unity of purpose.

To that high concept there can be no end save victory.

71

Lyndon B. Johnson

The "Great Society" (1964)

President Hatcher, Governor Romney, Senators McNamara and Hart, Congressmen Meader and Staebler, and other members of the fine Michigan delegation, members of the graduating class, my fellow Americans:

It is a great pleasure to be here today. This university has been coeducational since 1870, but I do not believe it was on the basis of your accomplishments that a Detroit high school girl said, "In choosing a college, you first have to decide whether you want a coeducational school or an educational school."

Well, we can find both here at Michigan, although perhaps at different hours.

I came out here today very anxious to meet the Michigan student whose father told a friend of mine that his son's education had been a real value. It stopped his mother from bragging about him.

I have come today from the turmoil of your Capital to the tranquility of your campus to speak about the future of your country.

The purpose of protecting the life of our Nation and preserving the liberty of our citizens is to pursue the happiness of our people. Our success in that pursuit is the test of our success as a Nation.

For a century we labored to settle and to subdue a continent. For half a century we called upon unbounded invention and untiring industry to create an order of plenty for all of our people.

The challenge of the next half century is whether we have the wisdom to use that wealth to enrich and elevate our national life, and to advance the quality of our American civilization.

Your imagination, your initiative, and your indignation will determine whether we build a society where progress is the servant of our needs, or a society where old values and new visions are buried under unbridled growth. For in your time we have the opportunity to move not only toward the rich society and the powerful society, but upward to the Great Society.

The Great Society rests on abundance and liberty for all. It demands an end to poverty and racial injustice, to which we are totally committed in our time. But that is just the beginning.

The Great Society is a place where every child can find knowledge to enrich his mind and to enlarge his talents. It is a place where leisure is a welcome chance to build and reflect, not a feared cause of boredom and restlessness. It is a place where the city of man serves not only the needs of the body and the demands of commerce but the desire for beauty and the hunger for community.

It is a place where man can renew contact with nature. It is a place which honors creation for its own sake and for what it adds to the understanding of the race. It is a place where men are more concerned with the quality of their goals than the quantity of their goods.

But most of all, the Great Society is not a safe harbor, a resting place, a final objective, a finished work. It is a challenge constantly renewed, beckoning us toward a destiny where the meaning of our lives matches the marvelous products of our labor.

So I want to talk to you today about three places where we begin to build the Great Society—in our cities, in our countryside, and in our classrooms.

Many of you will live to see the day, perhaps 50 years from now, when there will be 400 million Americans—four-fifths of them in urban areas. In the remainder of this century urban population will double, city land will double, and we will have to build homes, highways, and facilities equal to all those built since this country was first settled. So in the next 40 years we must re-build the entire urban United States.

Aristotle said: "Men come together in cities in order to live, but they remain together in order to live the good life." It is harder and harder to live the good life in American cities today.

The catalog of ills is long: there is the decay of the centers and the despoiling of the suburbs. There is not enough housing for our people or transportation for our traffic. Open land is vanishing and old landmarks are violated.

Worst of all expansion is eroding the precious and time honored values of community with neighbors and communion with nature.

The loss of these values breeds loneliness and boredom and indifference.

Our society will never be great until our cities are great. Today the frontier of imagination and innovation is inside those cities and not beyond their borders.

New experiments are already going on. It will be the task of your generation to make the American city a place where future generations will come, not only to live but to live the good life.

I understand that if I stayed here tonight I would see that Michigan students are really doing their best to live the good life.

This is the place where the Peace Corps was started. It is inspiring to see how all of you, while you are in this country, are trying so hard to live at the level of the people.

A second place where we begin to build the Great Society is in our countryside. We have always prided ourselves on being not only America the strong and America the free, but America the beautiful. Today that beauty is in danger. The water we drink, the food we eat, the very air that we breathe, are threatened with pollution. Our parks are overcrowded, our seashores overburdened. Green fields and dense forests are disappearing.

A few years ago we were greatly concerned about the "Ugly American." Today we must act to prevent an ugly America.

For once the battle is lost, once our natural splendor is destroyed, it can never be recaptured. And once man can no longer walk with beauty or wonder at nature his spirit will wither and his sustenance be wasted.

A third place to build the Great Society is in the classrooms of America. There your children's lives will be shaped. Our society will not be great until every young mind is set free to scan the farthest reaches of thought and imagination. We are still far from that goal.

Today, 8 million adult Americans, more than the entire population of Michigan, have not finished 5 years of school. Nearly 20 million have not finished 8 years of school. Nearly 54 million—more than one quarter of all America—have not even finished high school.

Each year more than 100,000 high school graduates, with proved ability, do not enter college because they cannot afford it. And if we cannot educate today's youth, what will we do in 1970 when elementary school enrollment will be 5 million greater than 1960? And high school enrollment will rise by 5 million. College enrollment will increase by more than 3 million.

In many places, classrooms are overcrowded and curricula are outdated. Most of our qualified teachers are underpaid, and many of our paid teachers are unqualified. So we must give every child a place to sit and a teacher to learn from. Poverty must not be a bar to learning, and learning must offer an escape from poverty.

But more classrooms and more teachers are not enough. We must seek an educational system which grows in excellence as it grows in size. This means better training for our teachers. It means preparing youth to enjoy their hours of leisure as well as their hours of labor. It means exploring new techniques of teaching, to find new ways to stimulate the love of learning and the capacity for creation.

These are three of the central issues of the Great Society. While our Government has many programs directed at those issues, I do not pretend that we have the full answer to those problems.

But I do promise this: We are going to assemble the best thought and the broadest knowledge from all over the world to find those answers for America. I intend to establish working groups to prepare a series of White House conferences and meetings—on the cities, on natural beauty, on the quality of education, and on other emerging challenges. And from these meetings and from this inspiration and from these studies we will begin to set our course toward the Great Society.

The solution to these problems does not rest on a massive program in Washington, nor can it rely solely on the strained resources of local authority. They require us to create new concepts of cooperation, a creative federalism, between the National Capital and the leaders of local communities.

Woodrow Wilson once wrote: "Every man sent out from his university should be a man of his Nation as well as a man of his time."

Within your lifetime powerful forces, already loosed, will take us toward a way of life beyond the realm of our experience, almost beyond the bounds of our imagination.

For better or for worse, your generation has been appointed by history to deal with those problems and to lead America toward a new age. You have the chance never before afforded to any people in any age. You can help build a society where the demands of morality, and the needs of the spirit, can be realized in the life of the Nation.

So, will you join in the battle to give every citizen the full equality which God enjoins and the law requires, whatever his belief, or race, or the color of his skin?

Will you join in the battle to give every citizen an escape from the crushing weight of poverty?

Will you join in the battle to make it possible for all nations to live in enduring peace—as neighbors and not as mortal enemies?

Will you join in the battle to build the Great Society, to prove that our material progress is only the foundation on which we will build a richer life of mind and spirit?

There are those timid souls who say this battle cannot be won; that we are condemned to a soulless wealth. I do not agree. We have the power to shape the civilization that we want. But we need your will, your labor, your hearts, if we are to build that kind of society.

Those who came to this land sought to build more than just a new country. They sought a new world. So I have come here today to your campus to say that you can make their vision our reality. So let us from this moment begin our work so that in the future men will look back and say: It was then, after a long and weary way, that man turned the exploits of his genius to the full enrichment of his life.

Thank you. Good-bye.

72

The Green New Deal (2019)

Ms. Ocasio-Cortez . . . submitted the following resolution; which was referred to the Committee on Energy and Commerce, and in addition to the Committees on Science, Space, and Technology, Education and Labor, Transportation and Infrastructure, Agriculture, Natural Resources, Foreign Affairs, Financial Services, the Judiciary, Ways and Means, and Oversight and Reform, for a period to be subsequently determined by the Speaker, in each case for consideration of such provisions as fall within the jurisdiction of the committee concerned

RESOLUTION

Recognizing the duty of the Federal Government to create a Green New Deal.

Whereas the October 2018 report entitled "Special Report on Global Warming of 1.5 °C" by the Intergovernmental Panel on Climate Change and the November 2018 Fourth National Climate Assessment report found that—

(1) human activity is the dominant cause of observed climate change over the past century;

(2) a changing climate is causing sea levels to rise and an increase in wildfires, severe storms, droughts, and other extreme weather events that threaten human life, healthy communities, and critical infrastructure;

(3) global warming at or above 2 degrees Celsius beyond preindustrialized levels will cause—

   (A) mass migration from the regions most affected by climate change;

   (B) more than $500,000,000,000 in lost annual economic output in the United States by the year 2100;

   (C) wildfires that, by 2050, will annually burn at least twice as much forest area in the western United States than was typically burned by wildfires in the years preceding 2019;

From H. Res. 109, 116th Cong., 1st Sess. 2019.

(D) a loss of more than 99 percent of all coral reefs on Earth;

(E) more than 350,000,000 more people to be exposed globally to deadly heat stress by 2050; and

(F) a risk of damage to $1,000,000,000,000 of public infrastructure and coastal real estate in the United States; and

(4) global temperatures must be kept below 1.5 degrees Celsius above preindustrialized levels to avoid the most severe impacts of a changing climate, which will require—

(A) global reductions in greenhouse gas emissions from human sources of 40 to 60 percent from 2010 levels by 2030; and

(B) net-zero global emissions by 2050;

Whereas, because the United States has historically been responsible for a disproportionate amount of greenhouse gas emissions, having emitted 20 percent of global greenhouse gas emissions through 2014, and has a high technological capacity, the United States must take a leading role in reducing emissions through economic transformation;

Whereas the United States is currently experiencing several related crises, with—

(1) life expectancy declining while basic needs, such as clean air, clean water, healthy food, and adequate health care, housing, transportation, and education, are inaccessible to a significant portion of the United States population;

(2) a 4-decade trend of wage stagnation, deindustrialization, and antilabor policies that has led to—

(A) hourly wages overall stagnating since the 1970s despite increased worker productivity;

(B) the third-worst level of socioeconomic mobility in the developed world before the Great Recession;

(C) the erosion of the earning and bargaining power of workers in the United States; and

(D) inadequate resources for public sector workers to confront the challenges of climate change at local, State, and Federal levels; and

(3) the greatest income inequality since the 1920s, with—

(A) the top 1 percent of earners accruing 91 percent of gains in the first few years of economic recovery after the Great Recession;

(B) a large racial wealth divide amounting to a difference of 20 times more wealth between the average white family and the average black family; and

(C) a gender earnings gap that results in women earning approximately 80 percent as much as men, at the median;

Whereas climate change, pollution, and environmental destruction have exacerbated systemic racial, regional, social, environmental, and economic injustices (referred to in this preamble as "systemic injustices") by disproportionately affecting indigenous peoples, communities of color, migrant communities, deindustrialized communities, depopulated rural communities, the poor, low-income workers, women, the elderly, the unhoused, people with disabilities, and youth (referred to in this preamble as "frontline and vulnerable communities");

Whereas, climate change constitutes a direct threat to the national security of the United States—

(1) by impacting the economic, environmental, and social stability of countries and communities around the world; and

(2) by acting as a threat multiplier;

Whereas the Federal Government-led mobilizations during World War II and the New Deal created the greatest middle class that the United States has ever seen, but many members of frontline and vulnerable communities were excluded from many of the economic and societal benefits of those mobilizations; and

Whereas the House of Representatives recognizes that a new national, social, industrial, and economic mobilization on a scale not seen since World War II and the New Deal era is a historic opportunity—

(1) to create millions of good, high-wage jobs in the United States;

(2) to provide unprecedented levels of prosperity and economic security for all people of the United States; and

(3) to counteract systemic injustices: Now, therefore, be it

Resolved, That it is the sense of the House of Representatives that—

(1) it is the duty of the Federal Government to create a Green New Deal—

(A) to achieve net-zero greenhouse gas emissions through a fair and just transition for all communities and workers;

(B) to create millions of good, high-wage jobs and ensure prosperity and economic security for all people of the United States;

(C) to invest in the infrastructure and industry of the United States to sustainably meet the challenges of the 21st century;

(D) to secure for all people of the United States for generations to come—

(i) clean air and water;

(ii) climate and community resiliency;

(iii) healthy food;

(iv) access to nature; and

(v) a sustainable environment; and

(E) to promote justice and equity by stopping current, preventing future, and repairing historic oppression of indigenous peoples, communities of color, migrant communities, deindustrialized communities, depopulated rural communities, the poor, low-income workers, women, the elderly, the unhoused, people with disabilities, and youth (referred to in this resolution as "frontline and vulnerable communities");

(2) the goals described in subparagraphs (A) through (E) of paragraph (1) (referred to in this resolution as the "Green New Deal goals") should be accomplished through a 10-year national mobilization (referred to in this resolution as the "Green New Deal mobilization") that will require the following goals and projects—

(A) building resiliency against climate change-related disasters, such as extreme weather, including by leveraging funding and providing investments for community-defined projects and strategies;

(B) repairing and upgrading the infrastructure in the United States, including—

(i) by eliminating pollution and greenhouse gas emissions as much as technologically feasible;

(ii) by guaranteeing universal access to clean water;

(iii) by reducing the risks posed by climate impacts; and

(iv) by ensuring that any infrastructure bill considered by Congress addresses climate change;

(C) meeting 100 percent of the power demand in the United States through clean, renewable, and zero-emission energy sources, including—

(i) by dramatically expanding and upgrading renewable power sources; and

(ii) by deploying new capacity;

(D) building or upgrading to energy-efficient, distributed, and "smart" power grids, and ensuring affordable access to electricity;

(E) upgrading all existing buildings in the United States and building new buildings to achieve maximum energy efficiency, water efficiency, safety, affordability, comfort, and durability, including through electrification;

(F) spurring massive growth in clean manufacturing in the United States and removing pollution and greenhouse gas emissions from manufacturing and industry as much as is technologically feasible, including by expanding renewable energy manufacturing and investing in existing manufacturing and industry;

(G) working collaboratively with farmers and ranchers in the United States to remove pollution and greenhouse gas emissions from the agricultural sector as much as is technologically feasible, including—

    (i) by supporting family farming;

    (ii) by investing in sustainable farming and land use practices that increase soil health; and

    (iii) by building a more sustainable food system that ensures universal access to healthy food;

(H) overhauling transportation systems in the United States to remove pollution and greenhouse gas emissions from the transportation sector as much as is technologically feasible, including through investment in—

    (i) zero-emission vehicle infrastructure and manufacturing;

    (ii) clean, affordable, and accessible public transit; and

    (iii) high-speed rail;

(I) mitigating and managing the long-term adverse health, economic, and other effects of pollution and climate change, including by providing funding for community-defined projects and strategies;

(J) removing greenhouse gases from the atmosphere and reducing pollution by restoring natural ecosystems through proven low-tech solutions that increase soil carbon storage, such as land preservation and afforestation;

(K) restoring and protecting threatened, endangered, and fragile ecosystems through locally appropriate and science-based projects that enhance biodiversity and support climate resiliency;

(L) cleaning up existing hazardous waste and abandoned sites, ensuring economic development and sustainability on those sites;

(M) identifying other emission and pollution sources and creating solutions to remove them; and

(N) promoting the international exchange of technology, expertise, products, funding, and services, with the aim of making the United States the international leader on climate action, and to help other countries achieve a Green New Deal;

(3) a Green New Deal must be developed through transparent and inclusive consultation, collaboration, and partnership with frontline and vulnerable communities, labor unions, worker cooperatives, civil society groups, academia, and businesses; and

(4) to achieve the Green New Deal goals and mobilization, a Green New Deal will require the following goals and projects—

(A) providing and leveraging, in a way that ensures that the public receives appropriate ownership stakes and returns on investment, adequate capital (including through community grants, public banks, and other public financing), technical expertise, supporting policies, and other forms of assistance to communities, organizations, Federal, State, and local government agencies, and businesses working on the Green New Deal mobilization;

(B) ensuring that the Federal Government takes into account the complete environmental and social costs and impacts of emissions through—

(i) existing laws;

(ii) new policies and programs; and

(iii) ensuring that frontline and vulnerable communities shall not be adversely affected;

(C) providing resources, training, and high-quality education, including higher education, to all people of the United States, with a focus on frontline and vulnerable communities, so that all people of the United States may be full and equal participants in the Green New Deal mobilization;

(D) making public investments in the research and development of new clean and renewable energy technologies and industries;

(E) directing investments to spur economic development, deepen and diversify industry and business in local and regional economies, and build wealth and community ownership, while prioritizing high-quality job creation and economic, social, and environmental benefits in frontline and vulnerable communities, and deindustrialized communities, that may otherwise struggle with the transition away from greenhouse gas intensive industries;

(F) ensuring the use of democratic and participatory processes that are inclusive of and led by frontline and vulnerable communities and workers to plan, implement, and administer the Green New Deal mobilization at the local level;

(G) ensuring that the Green New Deal mobilization creates high-quality union jobs that pay prevailing wages, hires local workers, offers training and advancement opportunities, and guarantees wage and benefit parity for workers affected by the transition;

(H) guaranteeing a job with a family-sustaining wage, adequate family and medical leave, paid vacations, and retirement security to all people of the United States;

(I) strengthening and protecting the right of all workers to organize, unionize, and collectively bargain free of coercion, intimidation, and harassment;

(J) strengthening and enforcing labor, workplace health and safety, antidiscrimination, and wage and hour standards across all employers, industries, and sectors;

(K) enacting and enforcing trade rules, procurement standards, and border adjustments with strong labor and environmental protections—

   (i) to stop the transfer of jobs and pollution overseas; and

   (ii) to grow domestic manufacturing in the United States;

(L) ensuring that public lands, waters, and oceans are protected and that eminent domain is not abused;

(M) obtaining the free, prior, and informed consent of indigenous peoples for all decisions that affect indigenous peoples and their traditional territories, honoring all treaties and agreements with indigenous peoples, and protecting and enforcing the sovereignty and land rights of indigenous peoples;

(N) ensuring a commercial environment where every businessperson is free from unfair competition and domination by domestic or international monopolies; and

(O) providing all people of the United States with—

   (i) high-quality health care;

   (ii) affordable, safe, and adequate housing;

   (iii) economic security; and

   (iv) clean water, clean air, healthy and affordable food, and access to nature.

73

Ronald Reagan

Address to the Nation on the Economy (1981)

Good evening.

I'm speaking to you tonight to give you a report on the state of our Nation's economy. I regret to say that we're in the worst economic mess since the Great Depression.

A few days ago I was presented with a report I'd asked for, a comprehensive audit, if you will, of our economic condition. You won't like it. I didn't like it. But we have to face the truth and then go to work to turn things around. And make no mistake about it, we can turn them around.

I'm not going to subject you to the jumble of charts, figures, and economic jargon of that audit, but rather will try to explain where we are, how we got there, and how we can get back. First, however, let me just give a few "attention getters" from the audit.

The Federal budget is out of control, and we face runaway deficits of almost $80 billion for this budget year that ends September 30th. That deficit is larger than the entire Federal budget in 1957, and so is the almost $80 billion we will pay in interest this year on the national debt.

Twenty years ago, in 1960, our Federal Government payroll was less than $13 billion. Today it is 75 billion. During these 20 years our population has only increased by 23.3 percent. The Federal budget has gone up 528 percent.

Now, we've just had two years of back-to-back double-digit inflation—13.3 percent in 1979, 12.4 percent last year. The last time this happened was in World War I.

In 1960 mortgage interest rates averaged about 6 percent. They're 2½ times as high now, 15.4 percent.

The percentage of your earnings the Federal Government took in taxes in 1960 has almost doubled.

And finally there are 7 million Americans caught up in the personal indignity and human tragedy of unemployment. If they stood in a line, allowing three feet for each person, the line would reach from the coast of Maine to California.

Well, so much for the audit itself. Let me try to put this in personal terms. Here is a dollar such as you earned, spent, or saved in 1960. And here is a quarter, a dime, and a penny—36 cents. That's what this 1960 dollar is worth today. And if the present world inflation rate should continue three more years, that dollar of 1960 will be worth a quarter. What initiative is there to save? And if we don't save we're short of the investment capital needed for business and industry expansion. Workers in Japan and West Germany save several times the percentage of their income than Americans do.

What's happened to that American dream of owning a home? Only 10 years ago a family could buy a home, and the monthly payment averaged little more than a quarter—27 cents out of each dollar earned. Today, it takes 42 cents out of every dollar of income. So, fewer than 1 out of 11 families can afford to buy their first new home.

Regulations adopted by government with the best of intentions have added $666 to the cost of an automobile. It is estimated that altogether regulations of every kind, on shopkeepers, farmers, and major industries, add $100 billion or more to the cost of the goods and services we buy. And then another 20 billion is spent by government handling the paperwork created by those regulations.

I'm sure you're getting the idea that the audit presented to me found government policies of the last few decades responsible for our economic troubles. We forgot or just overlooked the fact that government—any government—has a built-in tendency to grow. Now, we all had a hand in looking to government for benefits as if government had some source of revenue other than our earnings. Many if not most of the things we thought of or that government offered to us seemed attractive.

In the years following the Second World War it was easy, for a while at least, to overlook the price tag. Our income more than doubled in the 25 years after the war. We increased our take-home pay in those 25 years by more than we had amassed in all the preceding 150 years put together. Yes, there was some inflation, 1 or 1½ percent a year. That didn't bother us. But if we look back at those golden years, we recall that even then voices had been raised, warning that inflation, like radioactivity, was cumulative and that once started it could get out of control.

Some government programs seemed so worthwhile that borrowing to fund them didn't bother us. By 1960 our national debt stood at $284 billion. Congress in 1971 decided to put a ceiling of 400 billion on our ability to borrow. Today the debt is 934 billion. So-called temporary increases or extensions in the debt ceiling have been allowed 21 times in these 10 years, and now I've been forced to ask for another increase in the debt ceiling or the government will be unable to function past the middle of February—and I've only been here 16 days. Before we reach the day when we can reduce the debt ceiling, we may in spite of our best efforts see a national debt in excess of a trillion dollars. Now, this is a figure that's literally beyond our comprehension.

We know now that inflation results from all that deficit spending. Government has only two ways of getting money other than raising taxes. It can go into the money market and borrow, competing with its own citizens and driving up interest rates, which it has done, or it can print money, and it's done that. Both methods are inflationary. . . .

Now, one way out would be to raise taxes so that government need not borrow or print money. But in all these years of government growth, we've reached, indeed surpassed, the limit of our people's tolerance or ability to bear an increase in the tax burden. Prior to World War II, taxes were such that on the average we only had to work just a little over one month each year to pay our total Federal, State, and local tax bill. Today we have to work four months to pay that bill.

Some say shift the tax burden to business and industry, but business doesn't pay taxes. Oh, don't get the wrong idea. Business is being taxed, so much so that we're being priced out of the world market. But business must pass its costs of operations—and that includes taxes—on to the customer in the price of the product. Only people pay taxes, all the taxes. Government just uses business in a kind of sneaky way to help collect the taxes. They're hidden in the price; we aren't aware of how much tax we actually pay.

Today this once great industrial giant of ours has the lowest rate of gain in productivity of virtually all the industrial nations with whom we must compete in the world market. We can't even hold our own market here in America against foreign automobiles, steel, and a number of other products. Japanese production of automobiles is almost twice as great per worker as it is in America. Japanese steelworkers outproduce their American counterparts by about 25 percent.

Now, this isn't because they're better workers. I'll match the American working man or woman against anyone in the world. But we have to give them the tools and equipment that workers in the other industrial nations have.

We invented the assembly line and mass production, but punitive tax policies and excessive and unnecessary regulations plus government borrowing have stifled our ability to update plant and equipment. When capital investment is made, it's too often for some unproductive alterations demanded by government to meet various of its regulations. Excessive taxation of individuals has robbed us of incentive and made overtime unprofitable. . . .

All of you who are working know that even with cost-of-living pay raises, you can't keep up with inflation. In our progressive tax system, as you increase the number of dollars you earn, you find yourself moved up into higher tax brackets, paying a higher tax rate just for trying to hold your own. The result? Your standard of living is going down.

Over the past decades we've talked of curtailing government spending so that we can then lower the tax burden. Sometimes we've even taken a run at doing that. But there were always those who told us that taxes couldn't be cut until spending was reduced. Well, you know, we can lecture our children about extravagance until we run out of voice and breath. Or we can cure their extravagance by simply reducing their allowance.

It's time to recognize that we've come to a turning point. We're threatened with an economic calamity of tremendous proportions, and the old business-as-usual treatment can't save us. Together, we must chart a different course.

We must increase productivity. That means making it possible for industry to modernize and make use of the technology which we ourselves invented. That means putting Americans back to work. And that means above all bringing government spending back within government revenues, which is the only way, together with increased productivity, that we can reduce and, yes, eliminate inflation.

In the past we've tried to fight inflation one year and then, with unemployment increased, turn the next year to fighting unemployment with more deficit spending as a pump primer. So, again, up goes inflation. It hasn't worked. We don't have to choose between inflation and unemployment— they go hand in hand. It's time to try something different, and that's what we're going to do.

I've already placed a freeze on hiring replacements for those who retire or leave government service. I've ordered a cut in government travel, the number of consultants to the government, and the buying of office equipment and other items. I've put a freeze on pending regulations and set up a task force under Vice President Bush to review regulations with an eye toward getting rid of as many as possible. I have decontrolled oil, which should result in more domestic production and less dependence on foreign oil. And I'm eliminating that ineffective Council on Wage and Price Stability.

But it will take more, much more. And we must realize there is no quick fix. At the same time, however, we cannot delay in implementing an economic program aimed at both reducing tax rates to stimulate productivity and reducing the growth in government spending to reduce unemployment and inflation.

On February 18th, I will present in detail an economic program to Congress embodying the features I've just stated. It will propose budget cuts in virtually every department of government. It is my belief that these actual budget cuts will only be part of the savings. As our Cabinet Secretaries take charge of their departments, they will search out areas of waste, extravagance, and costly overhead which could yield additional and substantial reductions.

Now, at the same time we're doing this, we must go forward with a tax relief package. I shall ask for a 10-percent reduction across the board in personal income tax rates for each of the next three years. Proposals will also be submitted for accelerated depreciation allowances for business to provide necessary capital so as to create jobs.

Now, here again, in saying this, I know that language, as I said earlier, can get in the way of a clear understanding of what our program is intended to do. Budget cuts can sound as if we're going to reduce total government spending to a lower level than was spent the year before. Well, this is not the case. The budgets will increase as our population increases, and each year we'll see spending increases to match that growth. Government revenues will increase as the economy grows, but the burden will be lighter for each individual, because the economic base will have been expanded by reason of the reduced rates.

Now, let me show you a chart that I've had drawn to illustrate how this can be.

Here you see two trend lines. The bottom line shows the increase in tax revenues. The red line on top is the increase in government spending. Both lines turn upward, reflecting the giant tax increase already built into the system for this year 1981, and the increases in spending built into the '81 and '82 budgets and on into the future. As you can see, the spending line rises at a steeper slant than the revenue line. And that gap between those lines illustrates the increasing deficits we've been running, including this year's $80 billion deficit.

Now, in the second chart, the lines represent the positive effects when Congress accepts our economic program. Both lines continue to rise, allowing for necessary growth, but the gap narrows as spending cuts continue over the next few years until finally the two lines come together, meaning a balanced budget.

I am confident that my administration can achieve that. At that point tax revenues, in spite of rate reductions, will be increasing faster than spending, which means we can look forward to further reductions in the tax rates. . . .

Our spending cuts will not be at the expense of the truly needy. We will, however, seek to eliminate benefits to those who are not really qualified by reason of need. . . .

Our basic system is sound. We can, with compassion, continue to meet our responsibility to those who, through no fault of their own, need our help. We can meet fully the other legitimate responsibilities of government. We cannot continue any longer our wasteful ways at the expense of the workers of this land or of our children.

Since 1960 our government has spent $5.1 trillion. Our debt has grown by 648 billion. Prices have exploded by 178 percent. How much better off are we for all that? Well, we all know we're very much worse off. When we measure how harshly these years of inflation, lower productivity, and uncontrolled government growth have affected our lives, we know we must act and act now. We must not be timid. We will restore the freedom of all men and women to excel and to create. We will unleash the energy and genius of the American people, traits which have never failed us. . . .

We can create the incentives which take advantage of the genius of our economic system—a system, as Walter Lippmann observed more than 40 years ago, which for the first time in history gave men "a way of producing wealth in which the good fortune of others multiplied their own."

Our aim is to increase our national wealth so all will have more, not just redistribute what we already have which is just a sharing of scarcity. We can begin to reward hard work and risk-taking, by forcing this Government to live within its means. . . .

We can leave our children with an unrepayable massive debt and a shattered economy, or we can leave them liberty in a land where every individual has the opportunity to be whatever God intended us to be. All it takes is a little common sense and recognition of our own ability. Together we can forge a new beginning for America.

Thank you, and good night.

74

Alexis de Tocqueville

Soft Despotism (1840)

The principle of equality, which makes men independent of each other, gives them a habit and a taste for following in their private actions no other guide but their own will. This complete independence, which they constantly enjoy toward their equals and in the intercourse of private life, tends to make them look upon all authority with a jealous eye and speedily suggests to them the notion and the love of political freedom. Men living at such times have a natural bias towards free institutions. Take any one of them at a venture and search if you can his most deep-seated instincts, and you will find that, of all governments, he will soonest conceive and most highly value that government whose head he has himself elected and whose administration he may control.

From *Democracy in America* by Alexis de Tocqueville, translated by Henry Reeve, 1862, with minor changes.

Of all the political effects produced by the equality of conditions, this love of independence is the first to strike the observing and to alarm the timid; nor can it be said that their alarm is wholly misplaced, for anarchy has a more formidable aspect in democratic countries than elsewhere. . . .

I am, however, persuaded that anarchy is not the principal evil that democratic ages have to fear, but the least. For the principle of equality begets two tendencies: the one leads men straight to independence and may suddenly drive them into anarchy; the other conducts them by a longer, more secret, but more certain road to servitude. Nations readily discern the former tendency and are prepared to resist it; they are led away by the latter, without perceiving its drift; hence it is peculiarly important to point it out.

For myself, I am so far from urging as a reproach to the principle of equality that it renders men intractable, that this very circumstance principally calls forth my approbation. I admire to see how it deposits in the mind and heart of man that dim conception and instinctive love of political independence, thus preparing the remedy for the ill which it engenders. It is on this very account that I am attached to it.

The notion of secondary powers placed between the sovereign and his subjects occurred naturally to the imagination of aristocratic nations, because those communities contained individuals or families raised above the common level and apparently destined to command by their birth, their education, and their wealth. This same notion is naturally wanting in the minds of men in democratic ages, for converse reasons; it can only be introduced artificially, it can only be kept there with difficulty. . . . Moreover, in politics as well as in philosophy and in religion the intellect of democratic nations is peculiarly open to simple and general notions. Complicated systems are repugnant to it, and its favorite conception is that of a great nation composed of citizens all resembling the same pattern and all governed by a single power.

The very next notion to that of a sole and central power which presents itself to the minds of men in the ages of equality is the notion of uniformity of legislation. As every man sees that he differs but little from those about him, he cannot understand why a rule that is applicable to one man should not be equally applicable to all others. Hence the slightest privileges are repugnant to his reason; the faintest dissimilarities in the political institutions of the same people offend him, and uniformity of legislation appears to him to be the first condition of good government. . . .

As the conditions of men become equal among a people, individuals seem of less importance and society of greater dimensions; or rather every citizen, being assimilated to all the rest, is lost in the crowd, and nothing stands conspicuous but the great and imposing image of the people at large. . . .

As the men who inhabit democratic countries have no superiors, no inferiors, and no habitual or necessary partners in their undertakings, they readily fall back upon themselves and consider themselves as beings apart.

I had occasion to point this out at considerable length in treating of individualism. Hence such men can never, without an effort, tear themselves from their private affairs to engage in public business. . . .

I have also had occasion to show how the increasing love of well-being and the fluctuating character of property cause democratic nations to dread all violent disturbance. The love of public tranquillity is frequently the only passion which these nations retain. . . .

As in ages of equality no man is compelled to lend his assistance to his fellow men, and none has any right to expect much support from them, everyone is at once independent and powerless. These two conditions, which must never be either separately considered or confounded together, inspire the citizen of a democratic country with very contrary propensities. His independence fills him with self-reliance and pride among his equals; his debility makes him feel from time to time the want of some outward assistance, which he cannot expect from any of them, because they are all impotent and unsympathizing. In this predicament he naturally turns his eyes to that imposing power which alone rises above the level of universal depression. . . .

My object is to remark that all these various rights which have been successively wrested, in our time, from classes, corporations, and individuals have not served to raise new secondary powers on a more democratic basis, but have uniformly been concentrated in the hands of the sovereign. Everywhere the state acquires more and more direct control over the humblest members of the community and a more exclusive power of governing each of them in his smallest concerns.

Almost all the charitable establishments of Europe were formerly in the hands of private persons or of corporations; they are now almost all dependent on the supreme government, and in many countries are actually administered by that power. The state almost exclusively undertakes to supply bread to the hungry, assistance and shelter to the sick, work to the idle, and to act as the sole reliever of all kinds of misery.

Education, as well as charity, has become in most countries at the present day a national concern. The state receives, and often takes, the child from the arms of the mother to hand it over to official agents; the state undertakes to train the heart and to instruct the mind of each generation. Uniformity prevails in the courses of public instruction as in everything else; diversity as well as freedom is disappearing day by day. . . .

There exists among the modern nations of Europe one great cause, independent of all those which have already been pointed out, which perpetually contributes to extend the agency or to strengthen the prerogative of the supreme power, though it has not been sufficiently attended to: I mean the growth of manufactures, which is fostered by the progress of social equality. Manufacturers generally collect a multitude of men on the same spot, among whom new and complex relations spring up. These men are exposed by their calling to great and sudden alternations of plenty and want, during which public tranquillity is endangered. It may also happen that these employments sacrifice the health and even the life of those who gain by them or of those who live by them. Thus the manufacturing classes require more regulation, superintendence, and restraint than the other classes of society, and it is natural that the powers of government should increase in the same proportion as those classes. . . .

As a nation becomes more engaged in manufactures, the want of roads, canals, harbors, and other works of a semi-public nature, which facilitate the acquisition of wealth, is more strongly felt; and as a nation becomes more democratic, private individuals are less able, and the state more able, to execute works of such magnitude. I do not hesitate to assert that the manifest tendency of all governments at the present time is to take upon themselves alone the execution of these undertakings, by which means they daily hold in closer dependence the population which they govern.

On the other hand, in proportion as the power of a state increases and its necessities are augmented, the state consumption of manufactured produce is always growing larger; and these commodities are generally made in the arsenals or establishments of the government. Thus in every kingdom the ruler becomes the principal manufacturer: he collects and retains in his service a vast number of engineers, architects, mechanics, and handicraftsmen.

Not only is he the principal manufacturer, but he tends more and more to become the chief, or rather the master, of all other manufacturers. As private persons become powerless by becoming more equal, they can effect nothing in manufactures without combination; but the government naturally seeks to place these combinations under its own control.

It must be admitted that these collective beings, which are called combinations, are stronger and more formidable than a private individual can ever be, and that they have less of the responsibility for their own actions; whence it seems reasonable that they should not be allowed to retain so great an independence of the supreme government as might be conceded to a private individual. . . .

[T]he incessant increase of the prerogative of the supreme government [becomes] more centralized, more adventurous, more absolute, more extensive, [and] the people perpetually falling under the control of the public administration [are] led insensibly to surrender to it some further portion of their individual independence, till the very men who from time to time upset a throne and trample on a race of kings bend more and more obsequiously to the slightest dictate of a clerk. . . .

I seek to trace the novel features under which despotism may appear in the world. The first thing that strikes the observation is an innumerable multitude of men, all equal and alike, incessantly endeavoring to procure the petty and paltry pleasures with which they glut their lives. Each of them, living apart, is as a stranger to the fate of all the rest; his children and his private friends constitute to him the whole of mankind. As for the rest of his fellow citizens, he is close to them, but he sees them not; he touches them, but he feels them not; he exists but in himself and for himself alone; and if his kin-dred still remain to him, he may be said at any rate to have lost his country.

Above this race of men stands an immense and tutelary power, which takes upon itself alone to secure their gratifications and to watch over their fate. That power is absolute, minute, regular, provident, and mild. It would be like the authority of a parent if, like that authority, its object was to prepare men for manhood; but it seeks, on the contrary, to keep them in perpetual childhood: it is well content that the people should rejoice, provided they think of nothing but rejoicing. For their happiness such a government will-ingly labors, but it chooses to be the sole agent and the only arbiter of that happiness; it provides for their security, foresees and supplies their necessities, facilitates their pleasures, manages their principal concerns, directs their indus-try, regulates the descent of property, and subdivides their inheritances: what remains, but to spare them all the care of thinking and all the trouble of living?

Thus it every day renders the exercise of the free agency of man less useful and less frequent; it circumscribes the will within a narrower range and gradually robs a man of all the uses of himself. The principle of equality has prepared men for these things; it has predisposed men to endure them and often to look on them as benefits.

After having thus successively taken each member of the community in its powerful grasp and fashioned him at will, the supreme power then extends its arm over the whole community. It covers the surface of society with a network of small complicated rules, minute and uniform, through which the most original minds and the most energetic characters cannot penetrate, to rise above the crowd. The will of man is not shattered, but softened, bent, and guided; men are seldom forced by it to act, but they are constantly restrained from acting. Such a power does not destroy, but it prevents existence; it does not tyrannize, but it compresses, enervates, extinguishes, and stupefies a peo-ple, till each nation is reduced to being nothing better than a flock of timid and industrious animals, of which the government is the shepherd.

I have always thought that servitude of the regular, quiet, and gentle kind which I have just described might be combined more easily than is commonly believed with some of the outward forms of freedom, and that it might even establish itself under the wing of the sovereignty of the people.

Our contemporaries are constantly excited by two conflicting passions: they want to be led, and they wish to remain free. As they cannot destroy either the one or the other of these contrary propensities, they strive to satisfy them both at once. They devise a sole, tutelary, and all-powerful form of government, but elected by the people. They combine the principle of centralization and that of popular sovereignty; this gives them a respite: they console themselves for being in tutelage by the reflection that they have chosen their own guardians. Every man allows himself to be put in leading-strings, because he sees that it is not a person or a class of persons, but the people at large who hold the end of his chain.

By this system the people shake off their state of dependence just long enough to select their master and then relapse into it again. A great many persons at the present day are quite contented with this sort of compromise between administrative despotism and the sovereignty of the people; and they think they have done enough for the protection of individual freedom when they have surrendered it to the power of the nation at large. This does not satisfy me: the nature of him I am to obey signifies less to me than the fact of extorted obedience. . . .

It is in vain to summon a people who have been rendered so dependent on the central power to choose from time to time the representatives of that power; this rare and brief exercise of their free choice, however important it may be, will not prevent them from gradually losing the faculties of thinking, feeling, and acting for themselves, and thus gradually falling below the level of humanity. . . .

75

Thomas Jefferson

Against Manufacturing (1787)

. . . The political economists of Europe have established it as a principle, that every State should endeavor to manufacture for itself; and this principle, like many others, we transfer to America, without calculating the difference of circumstance which should often produce a difference of result. In Europe the lands are either cultivated, or locked up against the cultivator. Manu-facture must therefore be resorted to of necessity not of choice, to support the surplus of their people. But we have an immensity of land courting the industry of the husbandman. Is it best then that all our citizens should be employed in its improvement, or that one half should be called off from that to exercise manufactures and handicraft arts for the other? Those who labor in the earth are the chosen people of God, if ever He had a chosen people, whose breasts He has made His peculiar deposit for substantial and genuine virtue. It is the focus in which he keeps alive that sacred fire, which otherwise might escape from the face of the earth. Corruption of morals in

From Jefferson, "Query XIX," in *Notes on the State of Virginia*, London, 1787.

the mass of cultivators is a phenomenon of which no age nor nation has furnished an example. It is the mark set on those, who, not looking up to heaven, to their own soil and industry, as does the husbandman, for their subsistence, depend for it on casualties and caprice of customers. Dependence begets subservience and venality, suffocates the germ of virtue, and prepares fit tools for the designs of ambition. This, the natural progress and consequence of the arts, has sometimes perhaps been retarded by accidental circumstances; but, generally speaking, the proportion which the aggregate of the other classes of citizens bears in any State to that of its husbandmen, is the proportion of its unsound to its healthy parts, and is a good enough barometer whereby to measure its degree of corruption. While we have land to labor then, let us never wish to see our citizens occupied at a workbench, or twirling a distaff. Carpenters, masons, smiths, are wanting in husbandry; but, for the general operations of manufacture, let our workshops remain in Europe. It is better to carry provisions and materials to workmen there, than bring them to the provisions and materials, and with them their manners and principles. The loss by the transportation of commodities across the Atlantic will be made up in happiness and permanence of government. The mobs of great cities add just so much to the support of pure government, as sores do to the strength of the human body. It is the manners and spirit of a people which preserve a republic in vigor. A degeneracy in these is a canker which soon eats to the heart of its laws and constitution.

76

Alexander Hamilton

Report on Manufactures (1791)

. . . It ought readily to be conceded that the cultivation of the earth—as the primary and most certain source of national supply—as the immediate and chief source of subsistence to man—as the principal source of those materials which constitute the nutriment of other kinds of labor—as including a state most favourable to the freedom and independence of the

From Hamilton, *Report on Manufactures*, in *Reports of the Secretary of the Treasury of the United States*, Vol. I (Washington, 1837).

human mind—one, perhaps, most conducive to the multiplication of the human species—has *intrinsically a strong claim to pre-eminence over every other kind of industry.*

But, that it has a title to anything like an exclusive predilection, in any country, ought to be admitted with great caution. . . .

It has been maintained that agriculture is, not only, the most productive, but the only productive, species of industry. . . .

To this it has been answered. . . .

"That the annual produce of the land and labour of a country can only be increased in two ways—by some improvement in the *productive powers* of the useful labour, which actually exists within it, or by some increase in the quantity of such labour: That with regard to the first, the labor of artificers being capable of greater subdivision and simplicity of operation than that of cultivators, it is susceptible, in a proportionably greater degree, of improvement in its *productive powers,* whether to be derived from an accession of skill, or from the application of ingenious machinery; in which particular, therefore, the labor employed in the culture of land can pretend to no advantage over that engaged in manufactures. . . ."

. . . But while the *exclusive* productiveness of agricultural labour has been thus denied and refuted, the superiority of its productiveness has been conceded without hesitation. . . .

One of the arguments made use of in support of the idea may be pronounced both quaint and superficial—It amounts to this—That in the productions of the soil, nature co-operates with man; and that the effect of their joint labour must be greater than that of the labour of man alone.

This however, is far from being a necessary inference. It is very conceivable, that the labor of man alone, laid out upon a work requiring great skill and art to bring it to perfection, may be more productive, *in value*, than the labour of nature and man combined, when directed towards more simple operations and objects: And when it is recollected to what an extent the agency of nature, in the application of the mechanical powers, is made auxiliary to the prosecution of manufactures, the suggestion, which has been noticed, loses even the appearance of plausibility.

It might also be observed, with a contrary view, that the labor employed in agriculture is in a great measure periodical and occasional, depending on seasons, liable to various and long intermissions; while that occupied in many manufactures is constant and regular, extending through the year, embracing in some instances night as well as day. It is also probable, that there are among the cultivators of land, more examples of remissness, than among artificers. The farmer, from the peculiar fertility of his land, or some other favorable circumstance, may frequently obtain a livelihood, even with a considerable degree of carelessness in the mode of cultivation; but the artisan can with difficulty effect the same object, without exerting himself pretty equally with all those who are engaged in the same pursuit. And if it may likewise be assumed as a fact, that manufactures open a wider field to exertions of ingenuity than agriculture, it would not be a strained conjecture, that the labour employed in the former, being at once more *constant*, more uniform and more ingenious, than that which is employed in the latter, will be found, at the same time more productive. . . .

It is now proper to proceed a step further, and to enumerate the principal circumstances, from which it may be inferred—that manufacturing establishments not only occasion a positive augmentation of the produce and revenue of the society, but that they contribute essentially to rendering them greater than they could possibly be, without such establishments. These circumstances are—

1. The division of labour.
2. An extension of the use of machinery.
3. Additional employment to classes of the community not ordinarily engaged in the business.
4. The promoting of emigration from foreign countries.
5. The furnishing greater scope for the diversity of talents and dispositions which discriminate men from each other.
6. The affording a more ample and various field for enterprize.
7. The creating in some instances a new, and securing in all, a more certain and steady demand for the surplus produce of the soil.

Each of these circumstances has a considerable influence upon the total mass of industrious effort in a community: Together, they add to it a degree of energy and effect, which are not easily conceived. . . .

It has justly been observed, that there is a scarcely any thing of greater moment in the economy of a nation than the proper division of labour. The separation of occupations causes each to be carried to a much greater perfection, than it could possibly acquire, if they were blended. This arises principally from three circumstances—

1st. The greater skill and dexterity naturally resulting from a constant and undivided application to a single object. It is evident, that these properties must increase, in proportion to the separation and simplification of objects and the steadiness of the attention devoted to each; and must be less in proportion to the complication of objects, and the number among which the attention is distracted.

2nd. The economy of time, by avoiding the loss of it, incident to a frequent transition from one operation to another of a different nature. This depends on various circumstanes—the transition itself—the orderly disposition of the implements, machines and materials employed in the operation to be relinquished—the preparatory steps to the commencement of a new one—the interruption of the impulse, which the mind of the workman acquires, from being engaged in a particular operation—the distractions, hesitations and reluctances, which attend the passage from one kind of business to another.

3rd. An extension of the use of machinery. A man occupied on a single object will have it more in his power, and will be more naturally led to exert his imagination in devising methods to facilitate and abridge labour, than if he were perplexed by a variety of independent and dissimilar operations. . . .

The employment of Machinery forms an item of great importance in the general mass of national industry. 'Tis an artificial force brought in aid of the natural force of man; and, to all the purposes of labour, is an increase of hands; an accession of strength, *unencumbered too by the expense of maintaining the laborer*. May it not therefore be fairly inferred, that those occupations, which give greatest scope to the use of this auxiliary, contribute most to the general Stock of industrious effort, and, in consequence, to the general product of industry? . . .

[A] domestic market is greatly to be preferred to a foreign one; because it is the nature of things, far more to be relied upon. . . .

[T]he multiplication of manufactories not only furnishes a market for those articles which have been accustomed to be produced in abundance in a country, but it likewise creates a demand for such as were either unknown or produced in inconsiderable quantities. The bowels as well as the surface of the earth are ransacked for articles which were before neglected. Animals, plants and minerals acquire a utility and a value which were before unexplored. . . .

If the system of perfect liberty to industry and commerce were the prevailing system of nations, the arguments which dissuade a country, in the predicament of the United States, from the zealous pursuit of manufactures, would doubtless have great force. . . . In such a state of things, each country would have the full benefit of its peculiar advantages to compensate for its deficiencies or disadvantages. . . .

But the system which has been mentioned, is far from characterising the general policy of nations. The prevalent one has been regulated by an opposite spirit. The consequence of it is, that the United States are to a certain extent in the situation of a country precluded from foreign commerce. They can indeed, without difficulty obtain from abroad the manufactured supplies, of which they are in want; but they experience numerous and very injurious impediments to the emission and vent of their own commodities. . . .

In such a position of things, the United States cannot exchange with Europe on equal terms; and the want of reciprocity would render them the victim of a system which should induce them to confine their views to agriculture, and refrain from manufactures. A constant and increasing necessity, on their part, for the commodities of Europe, and only a partial and occasional demand for their own, in return, could not but expose them to a state of impoverishment, compared with the opulence to which their political and natural advantages authorise them to aspire. . . .

The conversion of their waste into cultivated lands is certainly a point of great moment in the political calculations of the United States. . . .

But it does, by no means, follow, that the progress of new settlements would be retarded by the extension of manufactures. The desire of being an independent proprietor of land is founded on such strong principles in the human breast, that where the opportunity of becoming so is as great as it is in the United States, the proportion will be small of those, whose situations would otherwise lead to it, who would be diverted from it towards manufactures. . . .

The remaining objections to a particular encouragement of manufacturers in the United States now require to be examined.

One of these turns on the proposition, that industry, if left to itself, will naturally find its way to the most useful and profitable employment: whence it is inferred that manufactures without the aid of government will grow up as soon and as fast, as the natural state of things and the interest of the community may require.

Against the solidity of this hypothesis, in the full latitude of the terms, very cogent reasons may be offered. These have relation to—the strong influence of habit and the spirit of imitation—the fear of want of success in untried enterprises—the intrinsic difficulties incident to first essays towards a competition with those who have previously attained to perfection in the business to be attempted—the bounties premiums and other artificial encouragements, with which foreign nations second the exertions of their own citizens in the branches, in which they are to be rivalled.

Experience teaches, that men are often so much governed by what they are accustomed to see and practise, that the simplest and most obvious improvements, in the most ordinary occupations, are adopted with hesitation, reluctance, and by slow gradations. The spontaneous transition to new pursuits, in a community long habituated to different ones, may be expected to be attended with proportionably greater difficulty. When former occupations ceased to yield a profit adequate to the subsistence of their followers, or when there was an absolute deficiency of employment in them, owing to the superabundance of hands, changes would ensue; but these changes would be likely to be more tardy than might consist with the interest either of individuals or of the society. In many cases they would not happen, while a bare support could be insured by an adherence to ancient courses; though a resort to a more profitable employment might be practicable. To produce the desirable changes as early as may be expedient, may therefore require the incitement and patronage of government. . . .

Not only the wealth, but the independence and security of a country, appear to be materially connected with the prosperity of manufactures. Every nation, with a view to those great objects, ought to endeavour to possess within itself all the essentials of national supply. These comprise the means of *subsistence, habitation, clothing,* and *defence.*

The possession of these is necessary to the perfection of the body politic; to the safety as well as to the welfare of the society; the want of either is the want of an important organ of political life and motion; and in the various crises which await a state, it must severely feel the effects of any such deficiency. The extreme embarrassments of the United States during the late war, from an incapacity of supplying themselves, are still matter of keen recollection: A future war might be expected again to exemplify the mischiefs and dangers of a situation to which that incapacity is still in too great a degree applicable, unless changed by timely and vigorous exertion. To effect this change, as fast as shall be prudent, merits all the attention and all the Zeal of our Public Councils; 'tis the next great work to be accomplished. . . .

Among the political means for promoting manufactures that Hamilton discusses are duties on foreign articles competing with domestic ones, prohibitions of competing articles, pecuniary bounties for new enterprises, premiums, exempting materials of manufacture from duties, encouraging new inventions and discoveries, and facilitating transportation of commodities. In discussing objections to bounties, Hamilton wrote:

It is a species of encouragement more positive and direct than any other, and for that very reason, has a more immediate tendency to stimulate and uphold new enterprises, increasing the chances of profit, and diminishing the risks of loss, in the first attempts. . . .

A question has been made concerning the constitutional right of the government of the United States to apply this species of encouragement, but there is certainly no good foundation for such a question. The National Legislature has express authority "To lay and collect taxes, duties, imposts, and excises, to pay the debts, and provide for the *common defence* and *general welfare*" with no other qualifications than that "all duties, imposts, and excises shall be *uniform* throughout the United States and that no capitation or other direct tax shall be laid unless in proportion to numbers ascertained by a census or enumeration taken on the principles prescribed in the Constitution," and that "no tax or duty shall be laid on articles exported from any State."

These three qualifications excepted the power to *raise money* is plenary and *indefinite,* and the objects to which it may be *appropriated* are no less comprehensive than the payment of the public debts, and the providing for the common defence and *general welfare.* The terms "*general welfare*" were doubtless intended to signify more than was expressed or imported in those which preceded; otherwise, numerous exigencies incident to the affairs of a nation would have been left without a provision. The phrase is as comprehensive as any that could have been used; because it was not fit that the constitutional authority of the Union to appropriate its revenues should have been restricted within narrower limits than the "General Welfare" and because this necessarily embraces a vast variety of particulars, which are susceptible neither of specification or of definition.

It is therefore of necessity left to the discretion of the National Legislature, to pronounce upon the objects, which concern the general welfare, and for which under that description, an appropriation of money is requisite and proper. And there seems to be no room for a doubt that whatever concerns the general interest of *learning*, of *agriculture*, of *manufactures*, and of *commerce*, are within the sphere of the national councils, *as far as regards an application of money*. . . .

77

Kelo v. New London (2005)

Justice Stevens delivered the opinion of the Court.

In 2000, the city of New London approved a development plan that, in the words of the Supreme Court of Connecticut, was "projected to create in excess of 1,000 jobs, to increase tax and other revenues, and to revitalize an economically distressed city, including its downtown and waterfront areas." In assembling the land needed for this project, the city's development agent has purchased property from willing sellers and proposes to use the power of eminent domain to acquire the remainder of the property from unwilling owners in exchange for just compensation. The question presented is whether the city's proposed disposition of this property qualifies as a "public use" within the meaning of the Takings Clause of the Fifth Amendment to the Constitution.

The city of New London (hereinafter City) sits at the junction of the Thames River and the Long Island Sound in southeastern Connecticut. Decades of economic decline led a state agency in 1990 to designate the City a "distressed municipality." . . . In 1998, the City's unemployment rate was nearly double that of the State, and its population of just under 24,000 residents was at its lowest since 1920.

These conditions prompted state and local officials to target New London, and particularly its Fort Trumbull area, for economic revitalization. To

From *Kelo v. New London*, 545 U.S. 469 (2005).

this end, respondent New London Development Corporation (NLDC), a private nonprofit entity established some years earlier to assist the City in planning economic development, was reactivated. In January 1998, the State authorized a $5.35 million bond issue to support the NLDC's planning activities and a $10 million bond issue toward the creation of a Fort Trumbull State Park. In February, the pharmaceutical company Pfizer Inc. announced that it would build a $300 million research facility on a site immediately adjacent to Fort Trumbull; local planners hoped that Pfizer would draw new business to the area, thereby serving as a catalyst to the area's rejuvenation. . . . Upon obtaining state-level approval, the NLDC finalized an integrated development plan focused on 90 acres of the Fort Trumbull area. . . .

The NLDC intended the development plan to capitalize on the arrival of the Pfizer facility and the new commerce it was expected to attract. In addition to creating jobs, generating tax revenue, and helping to "build momentum for the revitalization of downtown New London," the plan was also designed to make the City more attractive and to create leisure and recreational opportunities on the waterfront and in the park.

The city council approved the plan in January 2000, and designated the NLDC as its development agent in charge of implementation. The city council also authorized the NLDC to purchase property or to acquire property by exercising eminent domain in the City's name. The NLDC successfully negotiated the purchase of most of the real estate in the 90-acre area, but its negotiations with petitioners failed. As a consequence, in November 2000, the NLDC initiated the condemnation proceedings that gave rise to this case.

Petitioner Susette Kelo has lived in the Fort Trumbull area since 1997. She has made extensive improvements to her house, which she prizes for its water view. Petitioner Wilhelmina Dery was born in her Fort Trumbull house in 1918 and has lived there her entire life. Her husband Charles (also a petitioner) has lived in the house since they married some 60 years ago. In all, the nine petitioners own 15 properties in Fort Trumbull. . . . Ten of the parcels are occupied by the owner or a family member; the other five are held as investment properties. There is no allegation that any of these properties is blighted or otherwise in poor condition; rather, they were condemned only because they happen to be located in the development area.

. . . [T]he Supreme Court of Connecticut . . . held, over a dissent, that all of the City's proposed takings were valid. It began by upholding the lower court's determination that the takings were authorized by chapter 132, the State's municipal development statute. That statute expresses a legislative determination that the taking of land, even developed land, as part of an economic development project is a "public use" and in the "public interest." Next, relying on cases such as *Hawaii Housing Authority v. Midkiff* (1984) and *Berman v. Parker* (1954), the court held that such economic development qualified as a valid public use under both the Federal and State Constitutions. . . .

We granted certiorari to determine whether a city's decision to take property for the purpose of economic development satisfies the "public use" requirement of the Fifth Amendment.

Two polar propositions are perfectly clear. On the one hand, it has long been accepted that the sovereign may not take the property of A for the sole purpose of transferring it to another private party B, even though A is paid just compensation. On the other hand, it is equally clear that a State may transfer property from one private party to another if future "use by the public" is the purpose of the taking; the condemnation of land for a railroad with common-carrier duties is a familiar example. Neither of these propositions, however, determines the disposition of this case.

As for the first proposition, the City would no doubt be forbidden from taking petitioners' land for the purpose of conferring a private benefit on a particular private party. Nor would the City be allowed to take property under the mere pretext of a public purpose, when its actual purpose was to bestow a private benefit. The takings before us, however, would be executed pursuant to a "carefully considered" development plan. The trial judge and all the members of the Supreme Court of Connecticut agreed that there was no evidence of an illegitimate purpose in this case. Therefore, as was true of the statute challenged in *Midkiff*, the City's development plan was not adopted "to benefit a particular class of identifiable individuals."

On the other hand, this is not a case in which the City is planning to open the condemned land—at least not in its entirety—to use by the general public. Nor will the private lessees of the land in any sense be required to operate like common carriers, making their services available to all comers. But although such a projected use would be sufficient to satisfy the public use requirement, this "Court long ago rejected any literal requirement that condemned property be put into use for the general public." Indeed, while many state courts in the mid-19th century endorsed "use by the public" as the proper definition of public use, that narrow view steadily eroded over time. Not only was the "use by the public" test difficult to administer (*e.g.*, what proportion of the public need have access to the property? at what price?), but it proved to be impractical given the diverse and always evolving needs of society. Accordingly, when this Court began applying the Fifth Amendment to the States at the close of the 19th century, it embraced the broader and more natural interpretation of public use as "public purpose." . . .

The disposition of this case therefore turns on the question whether the City's development plan serves a "public purpose." Without exception, our cases have defined that concept broadly, reflecting our longstanding policy of deference to legislative judgments in this field.

In *Berman v. Parker*, this Court upheld a redevelopment plan targeting a blighted area of Washington, D. C., in which most of the housing for the area's 5,000 inhabitants was beyond repair. Under the plan, the area would be condemned and part of it utilized for the construction of streets, schools, and other public facilities. The remainder of the land would be leased or sold to private parties for the purpose of redevelopment, including the construction of low-cost housing.

The owner of a department store located in the area challenged the condemnation, pointing out that his store was not itself blighted and arguing that the creation of a "better balanced, more attractive community" was not a valid public use. Writing for a unanimous Court, Justice Douglas refused to evaluate this claim in isolation, deferring instead to the legislative and agency judgment that the area "must be planned as a whole" for the plan to be successful. The Court explained that "community redevelopment programs need not, by force of the Constitution, be on a piecemeal basis—lot by lot, building by building." The public use underlying the taking was unequivocally affirmed:

> "We do not sit to determine whether a particular housing project is or is not desirable. The concept of the public welfare is broad and inclusive. . . . The values it represents are spiritual as well as physical, aesthetic as well as monetary. It is within the power of the legislature to determine that the community should be beautiful as well as healthy, spacious as well as clean, well-balanced as well as carefully patrolled. In the present case, the Congress and its authorized agencies have made determinations that take into account a wide variety of values. It is not for us to reappraise them. If those who govern the District of Columbia decide that the Nation's Capital should be beautiful as well as sanitary, there is nothing in the Fifth Amendment that stands in the way."

In *Hawaii Housing Authority v. Midkiff*, the Court considered a Hawaii statute whereby fee title was taken from lessors and transferred to lessees (for just compensation) in order to reduce the concentration of land ownership. We unanimously upheld the statute and rejected the Ninth Circuit's view that it was "a naked attempt on the part of the state of Hawaii to take the property of A and transfer it to B solely for B's private use and benefit." Reaffirming *Berman's* deferential approach to legislative judgments in this field, we concluded that the State's purpose of eliminating the "social and economic evils of a land oligopoly" qualified as a valid public use. Our opinion also rejected the contention that the mere fact that the State immediately transferred the properties to private individuals upon condemnation somehow diminished the public character of the taking. "[I]t is only the taking's purpose, and not its mechanics," we explained, that matters in determining public use. . . .

Viewed as a whole, our jurisprudence has recognized that the needs of society have varied between different parts of the Nation, just as they have evolved over time in response to changed circumstances. Our earliest cases in particular embodied a strong theme of federalism, emphasizing the "great respect" that we owe to state legislatures and state courts in discerning local public needs. For more than a century, our public use jurisprudence has wisely eschewed rigid formulas and intrusive scrutiny in favor of affording legislatures broad latitude in determining what public needs justify the use of the takings power.

Those who govern the City were not confronted with the need to remove blight in the Fort Trumbull area, but their determination that the area was sufficiently distressed to justify a program of economic rejuvenation is entitled to our deference. The City has carefully formulated an economic development plan that it believes will provide appreciable benefits to the community, including—but by no means limited to—new jobs and increased tax revenue. . . . Given the comprehensive character of the plan, the thorough deliberation that preceded its adoption, and the limited scope of our review, it is appropriate for us, as it was in *Berman,* to resolve the challenges of the individual owners, not on a piecemeal basis, but rather in light of the entire plan. Because that plan unquestionably serves a public purpose, the takings challenged here satisfy the public use requirement of the Fifth Amendment.

To avoid this result, petitioners urge us to adopt a new bright-line rule that economic development does not qualify as a public use. Putting aside the unpersuasive suggestion that the City's plan will provide only purely economic benefits, neither precedent nor logic supports petitioners' proposal. Promoting economic development is a traditional and long accepted function of government. There is, moreover, no principled way of distinguishing economic development from the other public purposes that we have recognized. In our cases upholding takings that facilitated agriculture and mining, for example, we emphasized the importance of those industries to the welfare of the States in question, in *Berman,* we endorsed the purpose of transforming a blighted area into a "well-balanced" community through redevelopment, in *Midkiff,* we upheld the interest in breaking up a land oligopoly that "created artificial deterrents to the normal functioning of the State's residential land market". . . . It would be incongruous to hold that the City's interest in the economic benefits to be derived from the development of the Fort Trumbull area has less of a public character than any of those other interests. Clearly, there is no basis for exempting economic development from our traditionally broad understanding of public purpose.

Petitioners contend that using eminent domain for economic development impermissibly blurs the boundary between public and private takings. Again, our cases foreclose this objection. Quite simply, the government's pursuit of a public purpose will often benefit individual private parties. For example, in *Midkiff,* the forced transfer of property conferred a direct and significant benefit on those lessees who were previously unable to purchase their homes. . . . We cannot say that public ownership is the sole method of promoting the public purposes of community redevelopment projects.

It is further argued that without a bright-line rule nothing would stop a city from transferring citizen A's property to citizen B for the sole reason that citizen B will put the property to a more productive use and thus pay more taxes. Such a one-to-one transfer of property, executed outside the confines of an integrated development plan, is not presented in this case. While such an unusual exercise of government power would certainly raise a suspicion that a private purpose was afoot, the hypothetical cases posited by petitioners can be confronted if and when they arise. They do not warrant the crafting of an artificial restriction on the concept of public use.

Alternatively, petitioners maintain that for takings of this kind we should require a "reasonable certainty" that the expected public benefits will actually accrue. Such a rule, however, would represent an even greater departure from our precedent. "When the legislature's purpose is legitimate and its means are not irrational, our cases make clear that empirical debates over the wisdom of takings–no less than debates over the wisdom of other kinds of socioeconomic legislation–are not to be carried out in the federal courts." . . .

In affirming the City's authority to take petitioners' properties, we do not minimize the hardship that condemnations may entail, notwithstanding the payment of just compensation. We emphasize that nothing in our opinion precludes any State from placing further restrictions on its exercise of the takings power. Indeed, many States already impose "public use" requirements that are stricter than the federal baseline. . . . As the submissions of the parties and their *amici* make clear, the necessity and wisdom of using eminent domain to promote economic development are certainly matters of legitimate public debate. This Court's authority, however, extends only to determining whether the City's proposed condemnations are for a "public use" within the meaning of the Fifth Amendment to the Federal Constitution. Because over a century of our case law interpreting that provision dictates an affirmative answer to that question, we may not grant petitioners the relief that they seek.

The judgment of the Supreme Court of Connecticut is affirmed.

Justice O'Connor, with whom The Chief Justice, Justice Scalia, and Justice Thomas join, dissenting.

Over two centuries ago, just after the Bill of Rights was ratified, Justice Chase wrote:

> "An act of the Legislature (for I cannot call it a law) contrary to the great first principles of the social compact, cannot be considered a rightful exercise of legislative authority. . . . A few instances will suffice to explain what I mean. . . . [A] law that takes property from A. and gives it to B: It is against all reason and justice, for a people to entrust a Legislature with such powers; and, therefore, it cannot be presumed that they have done it." *Calder v. Bull* (1798).

Today the Court abandons this long-held, basic limitation on government power. Under the banner of economic development, all private property is now vulnerable to being taken and transferred to another private owner, so long as it might be upgraded–*i.e.*, given to an owner who will use it in a way that the legislature deems more beneficial to the public–in the process. To reason, as the Court does, that the incidental public benefits resulting from the subsequent ordinary use of private property render economic development takings "for public use" is to wash out any distinction between private and public use of property–and thereby effectively to delete the words "for public use" from the Takings Clause of the Fifth Amendment. Accordingly I respectfully dissent. . . .

To save their homes, petitioners sued New London and the NLDC, to whom New London has delegated eminent domain power. . . . They claim that the NLDC's proposed use for their confiscated property is not a "public" one for purposes of the Fifth Amendment. While the government may take their homes to build a road or a railroad or to eliminate a property use that harms the public, say petitioners, it cannot take their property for the private use of other owners simply because the new owners may make more productive use of the property.

The Fifth Amendment to the Constitution, made applicable to the States by the Fourteenth Amendment, provides that "private property [shall not] be taken for public use, without just compensation." When interpreting the Constitution, we begin with the unremarkable presumption that every word in the document has independent meaning, "that no word was unnecessarily used, or needlessly added." In keeping with that presumption, we have read the Fifth Amendment's language to impose two distinct conditions on the exercise of eminent domain: "the taking must be for a 'public use' and 'just compensation' must be paid to the owner." . . .

While the Takings Clause presupposes that government can take private property without the owner's consent, the just compensation requirement spreads the cost of condemnations and thus "prevents the public from loading upon one individual more than his just share of the burdens of government." The public use requirement, in turn, imposes a more basic limitation, circumscribing the very scope of the eminent domain power: Government may compel an individual to forfeit her property for the *public's* use, but not for the benefit of another private person. This requirement promotes fairness as well as security.

Where is the line between "public" and "private" property use? . . .

Our cases have generally identified three categories of takings that comply with the public use requirement, though it is in the nature of things that the boundaries between these categories are not always firm. Two are relatively straightforward and uncontroversial. First, the sovereign may transfer private property to public ownership–such as for a road, a hospital, or a military base.

Second, the sovereign may transfer private property to private parties, often common carriers, who make the property available for the public's use–such as with a railroad, a public utility, or a stadium. But "public ownership" and "use-by-the-public" are sometimes too constricting and impractical ways to define the scope of the Public Use Clause. Thus we have allowed that, in certain circumstances and to meet certain exigencies, takings that serve a public purpose also satisfy the Constitution even if the property is destined for subsequent private use.

This case returns us for the first time in over 20 years to the hard question of when a purportedly "public purpose" taking meets the public use requirement. It presents an issue of first impression: Are economic development takings constitutional? I would hold that they are not. We are guided by two precedents about the taking of real property by eminent domain. In *Berman*, we upheld takings within a blighted neighborhood of Washington, D. C. The neighborhood had so deteriorated that, for example, 64.3% of its dwellings were beyond repair. It had become burdened with "overcrowding of dwellings," "lack of adequate streets and alleys," and "lack of light and air." Congress had determined that the neighborhood had become "injurious to the public health, safety, morals, and welfare" and that it was necessary to "eliminat[e] all such injurious conditions by employing all means necessary and appropriate for the purpose," including eminent domain. Mr. Berman's department store was not itself blighted. Having approved of Congress' decision to eliminate the harm to the public emanating from the blighted neighborhood, however, we did not second-guess its decision to treat the neighborhood as a whole rather than lot-by-lot.

In *Midkiff*, we upheld a land condemnation scheme in Hawaii whereby title in real property was taken from lessors and transferred to lessees. At that time, the State and Federal Governments owned nearly 49% of the State's land, and another 47% was in the hands of only 72 private landowners. Concentration of land ownership was so dramatic that on the State's most urbanized island, Oahu, 22 landowners owned 72.5% of the fee simple titles. The Hawaii Legislature had concluded that the oligopoly in land ownership was "skewing the State's residential fee simple market, inflating land prices, and injuring the public tranquility and welfare," and therefore enacted a condemnation scheme for redistributing title.

In those decisions, we emphasized the importance of deferring to legislative judgments about public purpose. . . .

Yet for all the emphasis on deference, *Berman* and *Midkiff* hewed to a bedrock principle without which our public use jurisprudence would collapse: "A purely private taking could not withstand the scrutiny of the public use requirement; it would serve no legitimate purpose of government and would thus be void." . . .

The Court's holdings in *Berman* and *Midkiff* were true to the principle underlying the Public Use Clause. In both those cases, the extraordinary, precondemnation use of the targeted property inflicted affirmative harm on society–in *Berman* through blight resulting from extreme poverty and in *Midkiff* through oligopoly resulting from extreme wealth. And in both cases, the relevant legislative body had found that eliminating the existing property use was necessary to remedy the harm. Thus a public purpose was realized when the harmful use was eliminated. Because each taking *directly* achieved a public benefit, it did not matter that the property was turned over to private use. Here, in contrast, New London does not claim that Susette Kelo's and Wilhelmina Dery's well-maintained homes are the source of any social harm. . . .

In moving away from our decisions sanctioning the condemnation of harmful property use, the Court today significantly expands the meaning of public use. It holds that the sovereign may take private property currently put to ordinary private use, and give it over for new, ordinary private use, so long as the new use is predicted to generate some secondary benefit for the public–such as increased tax revenue, more jobs, maybe even aesthetic pleasure. . . .

Any property may now be taken for the benefit of another private party, but the fallout from this decision will not be random. The beneficiaries are likely to be those citizens with disproportionate influence and power in the political process, including large corporations and development firms. As for the victims, the government now has license to transfer property from those with fewer resources to those with more. The Founders cannot have intended this perverse result. "[T]hat alone is a *just* government," wrote James Madison, "which *impartially* secures to every man, whatever is his *own*."

78

National Federation of Independent Business v. Sebelius (2012)

Chief Justice Roberts announced the judgment of the Court and delivered the opinion of the Court . . . .

Today we resolve constitutional challenges to two provisions of the Patient Protection and Affordable Care Act of 2010: the individual mandate, which requires individuals to purchase a health insurance policy providing a minimum level of coverage; and the Medicaid expansion, which

From *National Federation of Independent Business v. Sebelius*, 567 U.S. 519 (2012).

gives funds to the States on the condition that they provide specified health care to all citizens whose income falls below a certain threshold. . . .

In our federal system, the National Government possesses only limited powers; the States and the people retain the remainder. . . . In this case we must again determine whether the Constitution grants Congress powers it now asserts, but which many States and individuals believe it does not possess. . . .

This case concerns two powers that the Constitution does grant the Federal Government, but which must be read carefully to avoid creating a general federal authority akin to the police power. The Constitution authorizes Congress to "regulate Commerce with foreign Nations, and among the several States, and with the Indian Tribes." Art. I, §8, cl. 3. . . .

Congress may also "lay and collect Taxes, Duties, Imposts and Excises, to pay the Debts and provide for the common Defence and general Welfare of the United States." U.S. Const., Art. I, §8, cl. 1. Put simply, Congress may tax and spend. . . .

Our permissive reading of these powers is explained in part by a general reticence to invalidate the acts of the Nation's elected leaders. "Proper respect for a co-ordinate branch of the government" requires that we strike down an Act of Congress only if "the lack of constitutional authority to pass [the] act in question is clearly demonstrated." . . .

The questions before us must be considered against the background of these basic principles.

In 2010, Congress enacted the Patient Protection and Affordable Care Act. The Act aims to increase the number of Americans covered by health insurance and decrease the cost of health care. . . . The individual mandate requires most Americans to maintain "minimum essential" health insurance coverage. . . .

Beginning in 2014, those who do not comply with the mandate must make a "[s]hared responsibility payment" to the Federal Government. . . .

The Government advances two theories for the proposition that Congress had constitutional authority to enact the individual mandate. First, the Government argues that Congress had the power to enact the mandate under the Commerce Clause. . . . Second, the Government argues that if the commerce power does not support the mandate, we should nonetheless uphold it as an exercise of Congress's power to tax. . . .

The Government contends that the individual mandate is within Congress's power because the failure to purchase insurance "has a substantial and deleterious effect on interstate commerce." . . . The path of our Commerce Clause decisions has not always run smooth, but it is now well established that Congress has broad authority under the Clause. We have recognized, for example, that "[t]he power of Congress over interstate commerce is not confined to the regulation of commerce among the states," but extends to activities that "have a substantial effect on interstate commerce." Congress's power, moreover, is not limited to regulation of an activity that by itself substantially affects interstate commerce, but also extends to activities that do so only when aggregated with similar activities of others. . . .

The Constitution grants Congress the power to "*regulate* Commerce." Art. I, §8, cl. 3 (emphasis added). The power to *regulate* commerce presupposes the existence of commercial activity to be regulated. . . .

Our precedent also reflects this understanding. As expansive as our cases construing the scope of the commerce power have been, they all have one thing in common: They uniformly describe the power as reaching "activity." . . .

The individual mandate, however, does not regulate existing commercial activity. It instead compels individuals to become active in commerce by purchasing a product, on the ground that their failure to do so affects interstate commerce. Construing the Commerce Clause to permit Congress to regulate individuals precisely because they are doing nothing would open a new and potentially vast domain to congressional authority. Every day individuals do not do an infinite number of things. In some cases they decide not to do something; in others they simply fail to do it. Allowing Congress to justify federal regulation by pointing to the effect of inaction on commerce would bring countless decisions an individual could potentially make within the scope of federal regulation, and—under the Government's theory—empower Congress to make those decisions for him. . . .

. . . Accepting the Government's theory would give Congress the same license to regulate what we do not do, fundamentally changing the relation between the citizen and the Federal Government. . . .

The Government sees things differently. It argues that because sickness and injury are unpredictable but unavoidable, "the uninsured as a class are active in the market for health care, which they regularly seek and obtain." . . .

The proposition that Congress may dictate the conduct of an individual today because of prophesied future activity finds no support in our precedent. We have said that Congress can anticipate the *effects* on commerce of an economic activity. But we have never permitted Congress to anticipate that activity itself in order to regulate individuals not currently engaged in commerce. . . .

Everyone will likely participate in the markets for food, clothing, transportation, shelter, or energy; that does not authorize Congress to direct them to purchase particular products in those or other markets today. The Commerce Clause is not a general license to regulate an individual from cradle to grave, simply because he will predictably engage in particular transactions. Any police power to regulate individuals as such, as opposed to their activities, remains vested in the States. . . .

That is not the end of the matter. Because the Commerce Clause does not support the individual mandate, it is necessary to turn to the

Government's second argument: that the mandate may be upheld as within Congress's enumerated power to "lay and collect Taxes." Art. I, §8, cl. 1.

The Government's tax power argument asks us to view the statute differently than we did in considering its commerce power theory. . . . [T]he Government asks us to read the mandate not as ordering individuals to buy insurance, but rather as imposing a tax on those who do not buy that product. . . .

The exaction the Affordable Care Act imposes on those without health insurance looks like a tax in many respects. The "[s]hared responsibility payment," as the statute entitles it, is paid into the Treasury by "taxpayer[s]" when they file their tax returns. It does not apply to individuals who do not pay federal income taxes because their household income is less than the filing threshold in the Internal Revenue Code. For taxpayers who do owe the payment, its amount is determined by such familiar factors as taxable income, number of dependents, and joint filing status. The requirement to pay is found in the Internal Revenue Code and enforced by the IRS, which . . . must assess and collect it "in the same manner as taxes." This process yields the essential feature of any tax: it produces at least some revenue for the Government. . . .

It is of course true that the Act describes the payment as a "penalty," not a "tax." But . . . it does not determine whether the payment may be viewed as an exercise of Congress's taxing power. . . .

In distinguishing penalties from taxes, this Court has explained that "if the concept of penalty means anything, it means punishment for an unlawful act or omission." . . . While the individual mandate clearly aims to induce the purchase of health insurance, it need not be read to declare that failing to do so is unlawful. Neither the Act nor any other law attaches negative legal consequences to not buying health insurance, beyond requiring a payment to the IRS. . . .

The Affordable Care Act's requirement that certain individuals pay a financial penalty for not obtaining health insurance may reasonably be characterized as a tax. Because the Constitution permits such a tax, it is not our role to forbid it, or to pass upon its wisdom or fairness. . . .

Justice Ginsburg, with whom Justice Sotomayor joins, and with whom Justice Breyer and Justice Kagan join . . . . concurring in the judgment in part, and dissenting in part.

I agree with The Chief Justice . . . that the minimum coverage provision is a proper exercise of Congress' taxing power. . . . Unlike The Chief Justice, however, I would hold, alternatively, that the Commerce Clause authorizes Congress to enact the minimum coverage provision. . . .

The Framers understood that the "general Interests of the Union" would change over time, in ways they could not anticipate. Accordingly, they recognized that the Constitution was of necessity a "great outlin[e]," not a detailed blueprint, see *McCulloch v. Maryland* (1819), and that its provisions included broad concepts, to be "explained by the context or by the facts of the case." Letter from James Madison to N. P. Trist (Dec. 1831). . . .

Consistent with the Framers' intent, we have repeatedly emphasized that Congress' authority under the Commerce Clause is dependent upon "practical" considerations, including "actual experience." . . .

Until today, this Court's pragmatic approach to judging whether Congress validly exercised its commerce power was guided by two familiar principles. First, Congress has the power to regulate economic activities "that substantially affect interstate commerce." This capacious power extends even to local activities that, viewed in the aggregate, have a substantial impact on interstate commerce. . . .

Second, we owe a large measure of respect to Congress when it frames and enacts economic and social legislation. . . . When appraising such legislation, we ask only (1) whether Congress had a "rational basis" for concluding that the regulated activity substantially affects interstate commerce, and (2) whether there is a "reasonable connection between the regulatory means selected and the asserted ends."

Straightforward application of these principles would require the Court to hold that the minimum coverage provision is proper Commerce Clause legislation. Beyond dispute, Congress had a rational basis for concluding that the uninsured, as a class, substantially affect interstate commerce. Those without insurance consume billions of dollars of health-care products and services each year. Those goods are produced, sold, and delivered largely by national and regional companies who routinely transact business across state lines. The uninsured also cross state lines to receive care. . . .

Not only do those without insurance consume a large amount of health care each year; critically, . . . their inability to pay for a significant portion of that consumption drives up market prices, foists costs on other consumers, and reduces market efficiency and stability. . . .

The minimum coverage provision, furthermore, bears a "reasonable connection" to Congress' goal of protecting the health-care market from the disruption caused by individuals who fail to obtain insurance. By requiring those who do not carry insurance to pay a toll, the minimum coverage provision gives individuals a strong incentive to insure. This incentive, Congress had good reason to believe, would reduce the number of uninsured and, correspondingly, mitigate the adverse impact the uninsured have on the national health-care market. . . .

Rather than evaluating the constitutionality of the minimum coverage provision in the manner established by our precedents, The Chief Justice relies on a newly minted constitutional doctrine. The commerce power does not, The Chief Justice announces, permit Congress to "compe[l] individuals to become active in commerce by purchasing a product." . . .

In concluding that the Commerce Clause does not permit Congress to regulate commercial "inactivity," and therefore does not allow Congress to adopt the practical solution it devised for the health-care problem, The Chief Justice views the Clause as a "technical legal conception," precisely what our case law tells us not to do. . . . This Court's former endeavors to impose categorical limits on the commerce power have not fared well. . . .

These line-drawing exercises were untenable, and the Court long ago abandoned them. . . . Failing to learn from this history, The Chief Justice plows ahead with his formalistic distinction between those who are "active in commerce" and those who are not. . . .

Underlying The Chief Justice's view that the Commerce Clause must be confined to the regulation of active participants in a commercial market is a fear that the commerce power would otherwise know no limits. . . . This concern is unfounded.

First, The Chief Justice could certainly uphold the individual mandate without giving Congress carte blanche to enact any and all purchase mandates. As several times noted, the unique attributes of the health-care market render everyone active in that market and give rise to a significant free-riding problem that does not occur in other markets. . . .

Other provisions of the Constitution also check congressional over-reaching. A mandate to purchase a particular product would be unconstitutional if, for example, the edict impermissibly abridged the freedom of speech, interfered with the free exercise of religion, or infringed on a liberty interest protected by the Due Process Clause. . . .

Ultimately, the Court upholds the individual mandate as a proper exercise of Congress' power to tax and spend "for the . . . general Welfare of the United States." I concur in that determination, which makes The Chief Justice's Commerce Clause essay all the more puzzling. Why should The Chief Justice strive so mightily to hem in Congress' capacity to meet the new problems arising constantly in our ever-developing modern economy? I find no satisfying response to that question in his opinion. . . .

Justice Scalia, Justice Kennedy, Justice Thomas, and Justice Alito, dissenting.

Congress has set out to remedy the problem that the best health care is beyond the reach of many Americans who cannot afford it. It can assuredly do that, by exercising the powers accorded to it under the Constitution. The question in this case, however, is whether the complex structures and provisions of the Patient Protection and Affordable Care Act (Affordable Care Act or ACA) go beyond those powers. We conclude that they do. . . .

In our view it must follow that the entire statute is inoperative.

THE INDIVIDUAL MANDATE

. . .We do not doubt that the buying and selling of health insurance con-tracts is commerce generally subject to federal regulation. But when Con-gress provides that (nearly) all citizens must buy an insurance contract, it goes beyond "adjust[ing] by rule or method," or "direct[ing] according to rule"; it directs the creation of commerce. . . .

. . . [The Government claims the Individual Mandate] is valid because it is actually a "regulat[ion of] activities having a substantial relation to interstate commerce, . . . i.e., . . . activities that substantially affect interstate commerce.". . .

The primary problem with this argument is that §5000A does not apply only to persons who purchase all, or most, or even any, of the health care services or goods that the mandated insurance covers. Indeed, the main objection many have to the Mandate is that they have no intention of pur-chasing most or even any of such goods or services and thus no need to buy insurance for those purchases. The Government responds that the health-care market involves "essentially universal participation." The principal difficulty with this response is that it is, in the only relevant sense, not true. It is true enough that everyone consumes "health care," if the term is taken to include the purchase of a bottle of aspirin. But the health care "market" that is the object of the Individual Mandate not only includes but principally consists of goods and services that the young people primarily affected by the Mandate *do not purchase*. . . . Such a definition of market participants is unprecedented, and were it to be a premise for the exercise of national power, it would have no principled limits. . . .

THE TAXING POWER

As far as [individual mandate] is concerned, we would stop there. Congress has attempted to regulate beyond the scope of its Commerce Clause authority, and [the mandate] is therefore invalid. The Government contends, however, . . . that "the minimum coverage provision is independently authorized by congress's taxing power." . . . The issue is not whether Congress had the power to frame the minimum-coverage provision as a tax, but whether it did so. . . ..

In this case, there is simply no way, "without doing violence to the fair meaning of the words used," to escape what Congress enacted: a mandate that individuals maintain minimum essential coverage, enforced by a penalty.

Our cases establish a clear line between a tax and a penalty: "[A] tax is an enforced contribution to provide for the support of government; a penalty . . . is an exaction imposed by statute as punishment for an unlawful act." . . . In a few cases, this Court has held that a "tax" imposed upon private conduct was so onerous as to be in effect a penalty. But we have never held—never—that a penalty imposed for violation of the law was so trivial as to be in effect a tax. . . .

So the question is, quite simply, whether the exaction here is imposed for violation of the law. It unquestionably is. The minimum-coverage provision . . . commands that every "applicable individual shall . . . . ensure that the individual . . . is covered under minimum essential coverage." And the immediately following provision states that, "[i]f . . . . an applicable individual . . . fails to meet the requirement of subsection (a) . . .there is hereby imposed . . . a penalty."

Quite separately, the fact that Congress (in its own words) "imposed . . . a penalty," for failure to buy insurance is alone sufficient to render that failure unlawful. It is one of the canons of interpretation that a statute that penalizes an act makes it unlawful. . . .

And the nail in the coffin is that the mandate and penalty are located in Title I of the Act, its operative core, rather than where a tax would be found—in Title IX, containing the Act's "Revenue Provisions." In sum, "the terms of [the] act rende[r] it unavoidable," that Congress imposed a regulatory penalty, not a tax. . . .

The Court today decides to save a statute Congress did not write. It rules that what the statute declares to be a requirement with a penalty is instead an option subject to a tax.

The Court regards its strained statutory interpretation as judicial modesty. It is not. It amounts instead to a vast judicial overreaching. It creates a debilitated, inoperable version of health-care regulation that Congress did not enact and the public does not expect. . . .

79

Adam M. Carrington

Regulation and Liberty (2013)

As James Madison reminds us in *Federalist 51:* "In framing a government which is to be administered by men over men, the great difficulty lies in this: you must first enable the government to control the governed; and in the next place oblige it to control itself." Nowhere do we see this need for balance more than in the economic realm. So much human interaction is entwined with the exchange of goods and services, government regulation of

Courtesy of Adam M. Carrington.

economics affects our daily lives, often significantly. Thus we see Madison's balancing act playing out. Too much regulation makes government a threat to liberty. Too little allows other entities—through discrimination, willful negligence, and other unjust practices—to oppress liberty.

The Court in particular is often asked to address this balance. In the so-called "Lochner Era," from the 1890s to 1937, the Court was criticized for tipping the balance too much toward liberty from government, striking down numerous economic statutes. Partially in reaction to this perception, the Court during the New Deal Era began upholding any and all economic laws placed before it. Regulation reigned. Individual liberty, so far as economic issues were concerned, was dependent upon the will of state and national majorities. In economics, the balance of *Federalist 51* received no judicial support.

This circumstance began to change again in the 1980s and 1990s. The Court began to insist on limits to regulation's reach. First, the Court asserted parameters to state regulation in the Fifth Amendment's Takings Clause, which forbids the government to take private property for public use without just compensation. Soon afterward they began to enforce limits on the reach of the commerce power to justify regulation by the national government.

These efforts, however, resulted in only a partial retreat from New Deal Era regulative carte blanche, as we see in two more recent cases. In *Kelo v. City of New London*, the Court's majority opinion returned to a very broad reading of public use doctrine under the Takings Clause. In *National Federation of Independent Business v. Sebelius*, while recognizing limits on the commerce power, the Court gave an expansive reading of the taxing power to uphold a major portion of the "Patient Affordable Care Act."

The facts surrounding the *Kelo* case are as follows. Reeling from the loss of industry and jobs, Connecticut and city officials sought to revitalize the City of New London's economic prospects. Following Pfizer Pharmaceuticals' announcement of a plan to build a new plant in New London, the city authorized a private group, the New London Development Corporation (NLDC) to purchase homes to develop the area near where the plant would operate. When area homeowners refused offers to purchase their homes the city granted NLDC the use of its power of eminent domain—the power to take the homes without the owners' consent. While many residents then agreed to sell, several refused. When eminent domain was invoked, these remaining owners sued.

The suit focused on the meaning of the Takings Clause. The clause says, "nor shall private property be taken for public use, without just compensation." This constitutional provision lays out the need for balance in economic regulation. Government provides certain services, such as roads, schools, and government offices, which may require the acquisition of private property. The Takings Clause recognizes that government has the power to compel the sale of property. The needs of the community must take precedence over the rights of private property in some circumstances. At the same time, however, the clause recognizes limits. Government cannot merely take property in any way it desires. It must provide "just compensation" for the property. Furthermore, private property receives protection through the phrase "public use." Government may not confiscate private property for any reason. It must take only for a public purpose.

Therefore, the clause states both why and how the government can take private property. It empowers government and restrains that power's exercise. The question in *Kelo* did not concern how. The owners received fair market value when forcibly removed. Instead, the question concerned why. Government may only take property "for public use." But what comprises public use?

Justice Stevens, writing for the majority, said the reasons for taking the property fit within the description of "public use." Fundamental to his argument was the movement in Court jurisprudence from a tightly defined notion of "public use" to a wider conception of "public purpose." "Public use" might be limited to mean only those goods or services that would be available for the use of the entire community, whereas a "public purpose" required only that the public would benefit in some way from the taking. In the case of New London, the new development "was 'projected to create in excess of 1,000 jobs, to increase tax and other revenues, and to revitalize an economically distressed city.' " Though the property would not be opened to the general population nor would the developments on the land be required to act as a common carrier, servicing all comers, it realized a "public purpose" in the promised economic benefits. If the city reasonably thought economic growth could result and help the distressed situation of New London, then the Court should exercise deference to its use of the Takings Clause.

Justice O'Connor's dissent notes, however, that the Majority opinion's reading threatens "to wash away any distinction between private and public use of property. . ." thereby also eliminating the liberty protections that distinction intended to establish. O'Connor admits that "takings that serve a public purpose also satisfy the Constitution even if the property is destined for private use," but she thinks that the majority in *Kelo* goes too far. She gives the examples of previous cases in which the takings were allowed by the Constitution because they involved property whose use had "inflicted affirmative harm on society." Only by removing the property from their owners could those harms be remedied. That the government later gave the property over to private use did not affect the legitimacy of its taking, for "each taking *directly* achieved a public benefit." This establishes a standard whereby curbing a present, ongoing harm must be the primary goal sought by the takings.

In the case of New London, the standard did not apply. The continued possession of the homes by their owners did not cause an affirmative harm to the community. The purpose of this taking was to replace innocuous use of property with what the city deemed a more lucrative, thus more publicly beneficial use. Nor were the proffered goods directly benefiting the public. Private owners would receive the direct benefits of using the land for purely private reasons. Only as a result of that purely private use would "some secondary benefit for the public" result. But O'Connor rightly says that "nearly any lawful use of real private property can be said to generate some incidental benefit to the public." To allow such takings makes all property subject to eminent domain for almost any reason. Thus, governments exercising eminent domain could take property from anyone at any time and give it to other private parties, so long as it made a plausible argument, subject to the deference of the Court, that doing so could possibly result in some incidental public good. Under such rules, no private property was safe.

The story did not end well. The Pfizer plant never came. No development occurred. In light of *Kelo* many states heightened their own protections for private property. State supreme courts also added state precedents to bolster individual liberty. At the same time, the Supreme Court has done little in subsequent cases either to cement or undermine the decision's reasoning. The matter, therefore, seems far from settled.

The second case, *National Federation of Independent Business v. Sabelius* (known as the Health Care case), dealt with the constitutionality of the "Patient Affordable Care Act," passed in 2010. The law mandated that individuals purchase health insurance or face a financial penalty. (The law also expanded Medicaid coverage, provided subsidies for the purchase of health insurance, required insurance companies to cover patients with preexisting conditions, and added a host of other regulations, but our focus will be on the individual mandate provision.) The question before the Court on this issue was whether Congress had the power under the Commerce Clause to require the purchase of health insurance or whether such a requirement was an infringement on the liberty of the individual.

Although the Court ultimately upheld the constitutionality of the mandate, the implications of the decision for the balance between government regulation and individual liberty are difficult to discern. Five justices said the law was constitutional, but only four (Breyer, Ginsberg, Kagan, and Sotamayor) claimed it to be a legitimate exercise of national power under the Commerce Clause. Five justices (Roberts, Alito, Kennedy, Scalia, and Thomas) argued that the Commerce Clause could not be stretched to cover the individual mandate. But Justice Roberts joined with the Court's more liberal wing to uphold the act by citing the taxing power as its constitutional justification.

In defending the law on the basis of the Commerce Clause, Justice Ginsberg held the law constitutional in that the national government regulates a national, and thus interstate, health care market. Like previous legislation regarding Social Security and Medicare, the law seeks "the economic and social welfare" of the nation. The Justice notes that many problems exist within the health care market. The high costs of care and of insurance on that care puts great strain on individual and family finances. Many must forego care or insurance which they cannot afford. Others, due to certain preexisting conditions, cannot even get health insurance or must do so at much higher costs. Furthermore, those who receive health care service in emergency rooms cause providers to pass the costs on to those who can and do pay. Ginsberg claims that the Health Care bill seeks to "remedy an economic and social problem" arising from those without health insurance. Because the problem is both economic and social, Ginsberg points to the need for government regulation of the sort Madison had envisioned in *Federalist 51*. People are being hurt financially, physically, and emotionally by the current state of health care. This puts at risk their health, even their lives, as well as their economic well-being.

Justice Ginsberg attempts to identify some limits on the government's power, claiming that it is only because of the unique problems presented by the health care market that national regulation is legitimate. But her reasoning subverts her intention. The uniqueness of the health care market, she claims, rests in the fact that nearly everyone will consume health care at some point. Yet the broad categories of "food, clothing, transportation, shelter, or energy" among others would fall under this same heading. One would be hard-pressed to find particular activities, or inactivities, which do not fall within at least one of them. And as the universality of health care supported the regulation of more particular, less universal services, so these broad categories could do the same. The list of activities or in-activities which such regulation could not reach would become small, if it even exists.

Ginsberg's other efforts to provide limits to government regulation are also inadequate. For example, she observes that political resistance to legislation may also check unwanted regulation. The democratic process is certainly a key feature of any popular government. But based on her own record in cases like *U.S. v. Virginia* and *Lawrence v. Texas*, in which she supported the Court's action upholding the rights of individuals, she likely would agree the democratic process does not always protect minority rights. Accordingly, Ginsberg adds that any law that infringed on free speech or exercise, or the Due Process Clause would be void. Her argument assumes from the outset an all-powerful government limited only by the specific exceptions set forth in the Constitution, and particularly in the Bill of Rights. Yet the Constitution does not merely limit powers, it also bestows them. Ginsberg's reasoning separates the origin of the government's powers from the Constitution itself in a way that misunderstands the character of our limited government.

Justice Ginsberg attacks the "line-drawing exercises" on Commerce Clause questions in past jurisprudence, noting "the difficulty courts (and

Congress) would encounter in distinguishing statutes, for example, that regulate 'activity' from those that regulate 'inactivity.' " Instead of drawing such lines, she says that "'practical' considerations, including 'actual' experience" should rule. The line-drawing to which she objects, however, involves the very sort of complex distinctions that Courts in particular are called upon to make. Drawing broad, bright lines reduces complexity, but, Ginsberg in the face of complexity, draws no line at all. All is deference to regulation.

Although Roberts found in favor of the individual mandate, he objected to relying on the Commerce Clause to do so. Like O'Connor's interpretation of the Takings Clause in her *Kelo* dissent, Roberts's arguments against the Court's use of the Commerce Clause in the Health Care case seek to balance government regulation and individual liberty. He affirms expansive precedents, such as *Wickard v. Filburn*, which allowed interstate commercial regulations to reach deeply into purely local economic activity. At the same time, some distinctions must be made to assure some realm for the states and thereby, according to Roberts's logic, better protection of liberty. The Chief Justice draws that distinction between activity and inactivity. Congress has the power to regulate commerce. Roberts states that "[t]he power to *regulate* commerce presupposes the existence of commercial activity to be regulated." Regulation does not create. It only prescribes and proscribes the manner in which some existing entity may be used. In the individual mandate, however, the government does not regulate existing activity. Congress instead creates it in order to regulate it. Individuals are told first to participate in the health insurance market and then how that participation may be conducted. It thus gives the national government power to dictate both "what we do" as well as "what we do not." A person is either acting or not acting. If both commission and omission may be addressed by legislation, then nothing would lie beyond national governmental reach.

Problems exist with Roberts's argument. The activity/inactivity distinction certainly carves out some room for liberty. But does it truly balance this claim with that of regulation? One would hope some form of liberty was protected within activity, not merely the choice to abstain from it. Liberty is for doing as well as refraining. Furthermore, Roberts's view of federalism leaves open the possibility that states, as opposed to the national government, exercise a "general license to regulate an individual from cradle to grave." One wonders whether his view of states as more accountable and thus less susceptible to infringing on rights is accurate. It certainly conflicts with certain notable statements of Madison. The Founder famously argued in *Federalist 10* for a national government being more protective of minority rights due to its size while elsewhere attacking states for their persistent infringements on rights.

In the end, the Chief Justice Roberts joined the four justices who held the Health Care law's individual mandate constitutional. But instead of appealing to the commerce power, Roberts argued that the law was an exercise of Congress's power to tax. Ginsberg's broad interpretation of the Commerce Clause thus does not have the backing of a majority of the Court. The case thus leaves open whether the Commerce Clause will remain the main vehicle through which the national government justifies economic regulation. As limits continue to be placed on its extent, the government instead could look to the taxing power to justify regulation. But the taxing power presents similar questions. Government must collect revenues in order to fulfill its ends. But is this power without limit? The answer must be no. If liberty is to exist from and by regulation, then some distinctions exist. Unlike the Commerce Clause, however, the limits of Congress' power to tax and spend has not been thoroughly tested in recent decades. Its exact contours will be a matter for future definition. Roberts's opinion begins this process on bad footing, giving wide latitude to regulation in the form of taxation. Where the next decade of debate goes may hinge on how this issue is adjudicated, both on the Court and in the political branches. Here, as in Fifth Amendment issues, the balance of regulation and individual liberty is at stake.

In conclusion, determining where regulation protects and where it infringes on liberty is no easy task. Each case involves competing claims of the community as represented by the government and the individual. The mean may shift in one direction or another depending on the facts surrounding a particular regulation. Certain times and circumstances will call for greater regulation. Others will move the needle toward individual liberty. No bright line will make the choice for us. Nor will the absence of lines. Adjudicating these tasks requires judgment. Thus Americans should not be lured by the purity and clarity of simple liberty from government. Nor should we seek a solution to our problems merely in government regulation. Madison famously observed that "If men were angels, no government would be necessary. If angels were to govern men, neither external nor internal controls on government would be necessary." We should strive to find the balance struck in *Federalist 51*—that true liberty calls on us to recognize our nonangelic status as both governors and governed.

Chapter VII

Foreign Policy and the American Regime

What is America's role in the world? What goals does it seek through its foreign policy? The United States has never proposed a single, permanent answer to these questions; instead, its foreign policy presents us with a complex and varied set of arguments and themes. Alexander Hamilton, in *Federalist 11*, argues that the United States should pursue its own national interest through active and independent commerce and a strong navy. Ultimately, he promises that the United States will rise to "a dangerous greatness" and be able to "dictate the terms of the connection between the old and the new world." Is Hamilton correct that the United States' highest foreign policy priority should be the national interest? Does Hamilton acknowledge any moral principles, or is his devotion to the nation based on mere calculation and interest?

If Alexander Hamilton stresses the interests of his own nation, James Monroe presents a somewhat broader vision, for he argues that both the United States and the "free and independent" republics of South America share a common desire to be free from European control. Thus, should a European colonial power, whose political system is "essentially different" from a republican regime, seek to recolonize a now-free South American state, its actions would endanger the United States' "peace and happiness." According to the Monroe Doctrine, America has a particular common interest with other free governments in the western hemisphere. Notably, however, Monroe does not insist that the United States has any significant interest in common with free governments in other parts of the world; for example, although he hopes for Greek independence, he also acknowledges that America will not interfere in European affairs and will treat with a "government de facto," whether it is autocratic or free. Does the United States share a special interest only with nations that are both in our region of the world and free? Or should Monroe's principles be expanded to embrace all free governments?

In contrast to both Hamilton and Monroe, who emphasize the importance of considering America's national interest, Woodrow Wilson strives to transcend nationalism in favor of universal ideas about morality, arguing that America's foreign policy serves the good of all humanity. In his 1917 war message, Wilson asserts that the United States must go to war against Imperial Germany. Yet the United States should declare war not because Germany has harmed the United States by sinking her shipping, but because Germany's use of unrestricted submarine warfare marks a declaration of war against "law and humanity" itself. Thus, Wilson's call for American involvement in World War I is predicated on his belief that the United States must stand for universal principles of right and support a universal good. Ultimately, Wilson argues that it is democratic governments alone that can promote the good of humankind, whereas autocratic governments promote simply the good of the ruling class. Thus, America should promote the creation of "a concert of free peoples" who will come together and work to "make the world itself . . . free." Wilson, in the end, hopes that national interests ("selfish ends") can be set aside in favor of the universal interest of mankind.

As Stephen Sims argues, these statesmen show us the complications and contradictions within our nation's historical approaches to international relations, but their divergent arguments should also lead us to recognize that the very complexity of American foreign policy is responsible for its success. At the beginning of the republic's life, Hamilton's vision of the importance of power in international relations allowed the nation to rise from colonial status to independence and, eventually, greatness. This development continued under Monroe, whose recognition of the importance of geography permitted us to see our own interests with clarity while also acknowledging limits to our principles. In the early twentieth century, the United States attained a substantial degree of power and influence. This stature, which owed its existence in large part to Hamilton and Monroe, allowed the United States to play a decisive role on the world stage under Wilson's leadership. Thus, if Hamilton and Monroe may seem to deemphasize morality and principle in favor of the national interest, Wilson's moral vision could be proposed by a great power only because of the apparently narrow visions of his predecessors.

Moving from broad principles to institutional concerns, the debates between Hamilton (Pacificus and Americanus) and James Madison (Helvidius) help us to consider the constitutional authority of Congress and the president in international affairs. Hamilton claims a central role for the president in the conduct of American foreign policy. He explains that whether in war making, treaty-making, or the reception of ambassadors, the Constitution requires that the president act as the spokesman of the nation in its relations with other nations. In his Helvidius letters, Madison rejects Hamilton's reading of the Constitution, insisting that the president must be understood as a mere executor. He contends that in foreign affairs as in domestic affairs Congress makes policy and the president merely executes that policy. According to Madison, Hamilton's principles would undermine republican government and turn the American president into a British monarch.

Addressing more recent international challenges, James Pontuso describes the "end of history" thesis. At the end of the Cold War, an idea emerged that history had ended, or come to a sort of completion. Liberal democracy appeared triumphant and ascendant; with the fall of the Soviet Union, there seemed to be no major alternative to the western way of life. Democratic governments and global free trade were, it was hoped, the inevitable wave of the future, promising peace, prosperity, and material comfort. Yet if history has ended because the great powers no longer seem bent on conflict, new threats have emerged to challenge the liberal order. Terrorism—particularly the attacks of September 11—demonstrates that even the world's largest superpower can be humbled by a small group of determined fanatics. The material prosperity promised by liberal democracies has not fully satisfied human longings, since it has not always led to greater equality and it does not of itself provide for man's deepest needs. Finally, the very fact of globalization, which has made free trade and immigration easier, has resulted in increased ethnic conflict, cultural and religious differences, and nationalism. As Pontuso concludes, these contemporary challenges refute the idea that an era of peaceful coexistence and material well-being is just around the corner.

More recently, President Donald J. Trump's speech to the United Nations explained his administration's approach to foreign policy. Interestingly, although Trump is famous for promoting a nationalist vision and promising to "Make America Great Again," his speech suggests that he sees a certain unity between the good of the United States and the good of the entire world. As he argues, "We are standing up for America. . . . And we are also standing up for the world." In fact, Trump seems to present a mixed vision, which draws on aspects of both Hamilton and Wilson's thought, while also explicitly citing the Monroe Doctrine. Thus, Trump agrees with Hamilton's focus on the national interest, stressing the importance of "fair and reciprocal" trade (rather than simply free trade), protecting American manufacturing jobs, and controlling immigration into the country. At the same time, Trump seems to be influenced by Wilson's moral vision when he sees a role for the United States in addressing terrorism in the Middle East, seeking an end to a civil war in Yemen, and amelioration for a refugee crisis in Jordan. Trump both "reject[s] the ideology of globalism" and argues that his administration's "principled realism" will permit the country to promote its own national interest even while playing a global role.

Whatever one thinks of the Trump Administration's approach to foreign policy, his speech invites us to ask whether America's foreign policy can promote the national interest even while recognizing moral duties. Joseph Cropsey suggests that morality and self-interest need not be in irremediable conflict. In considering the role of morality in foreign policy, he presents the arguments for two predominant and extreme foreign policy perspectives: one states that we have a duty to other nations, while the other advocates a crude and calculating self-interest. Finding that both the morality of selfless duty and a self-interest that abstracts from virtue are inadequate guides to action, Cropsey offers a synthesis of these two positions that meets the demands of both morality and survival. This synthesis is a self-regarding morality based on nobility and honor rather than on altruism. Unfortunately, Cropsey argues, the American regime vacillates between the two extremes that he criticizes. It is therefore not likely to adopt a self-regarding morality of honor, but perhaps a healthy self-regard may bring us within sight of the morality of honor.

80

Alexander Hamilton

Federalist 11 (1787)

To the People of the State of New York:

THE importance of the Union, in a commercial light, is one of those points about which there is least room to entertain a difference of opinion, and which has, in fact, commanded the most general assent of men who have any acquaintance with the subject. This applies as well to our inter-course with foreign countries as with each other.

There are appearances to authorize a supposition that the adventurous spirit, which distinguishes the commercial character of America, has already excited uneasy sensations in several of the maritime powers of Europe. They seem to be apprehensive of our too great interference in that carrying trade, which is the support of their navigation and the foundation of their naval strength. Those of them which have colonies in America look forward to what this country is capable of becoming, with painful solicitude. They foresee the dangers that may threaten their American dominions from the neighborhood of States, which have all the dispositions, and would possess all the means, requisite to the creation of a powerful marine. Impressions of this kind will naturally indicate the policy of fostering divisions among us, and of depriving us, as far as possible, of an ACTIVE COMMERCE in our own bottoms. This would answer the threefold purpose of preventing our interference in their navigation, of monopolizing the profits of our trade, and of clipping the wings by which we might soar to a dangerous greatness. Did not prudence forbid the detail, it would not be difficult to trace, by facts, the workings of this policy to the cabinets of ministers.

If we continue united, we may counteract a policy so unfriendly to our prosperity in a variety of ways. By prohibitory regulations, extending, at the same time, throughout the States, we may oblige foreign countries to bid against each other, for the privileges of our markets. This assertion will not appear chimerical to those who are able to appreciate the importance of the markets of three millions of people—increasing in rapid progression, for the

From *The Federalist*.

most part exclusively addicted to agriculture, and likely from local circum-stances to remain so—to any manufacturing nation; and the immense differ-ence there would be to the trade and navigation of such a nation, between a direct communication in its own ships, and an indirect conveyance of its products and returns, to and from America, in the ships of another country. Suppose, for instance, we had a government in America, capable of exclud-ing Great Britain (with whom we have at present no treaty of commerce) from all our ports; what would be the probable operation of this step upon her politics? Would it not enable us to negotiate, with the fairest prospect of success, for commercial privileges of the most valuable and extensive kind, in the dominions of that kingdom? . . . .

A mature consideration of the objects suggested by these questions will justify a belief that the real disadvantages to Britain from such a state of things, conspiring with the pre-possessions of a great part of the nation in favor of the American trade, and with the importunities of the West India islands, would produce a relaxation in her present system, and would let us into the enjoyment of privileges in the markets of those islands elsewhere, from which our trade would derive the most substantial benefits. Such a point gained from the British government, and which could not be expected without an equivalent in exemptions and immunities in our markets, would be likely to have a correspondent effect on the conduct of other nations, who would not be inclined to see themselves altogether supplanted in our trade.

A further resource for influencing the conduct of European nations toward us, in this respect, would arise from the establishment of a federal navy. There can be no doubt that the continuance of the Union under an efficient government would put it in our power, at a period not very distant, to create a navy which, if it could not vie with those of the great maritime powers, would at least be of respectable weight if thrown into the scale of either of two contending parties. This would be more peculiarly the case in relation to operations in the West Indies. A few ships of the line, sent opportunely to the reinforcement of either side, would often be sufficient to decide the fate of a campaign, on the event of which interests of the greatest magnitude were suspended. Our position is, in this respect, a most command-ing one. And if to this consideration we add that of the usefulness of supplies from this country, in the prosecution of military operations in the West Indies, it will readily be perceived that a situation so favorable would enable us to bargain with great advantage for commercial privileges. A price would be set not only upon our friendship, but upon our neutrality. By a steady adherence to the Union we may hope, erelong, to become the arbiter of Europe in America, and to be able to incline the balance of European com-petitions in this part of the world as our interest may dictate. . . .

Under a vigorous national government, the natural strength and resources of the country, directed to a common interest, would baffle all the combinations of European jealousy to restrain our growth. This situation would even take away the motive to such combinations, by inducing an impracticability of success. An active commerce, an extensive navigation, and a flourishing marine would then be the offspring of moral and physical necessity. We might defy the little arts of the little politicians to control or vary the irresistible and unchangeable course of nature. . . .

There are rights of great moment to the trade of America which are rights of the Union—I allude to the fisheries, to the navigation of the Western lakes, and to that of the Mississippi. The dissolution of the Confederacy would give room for delicate questions concerning the future existence of these rights; which the interest of more powerful partners would hardly fail to solve to our disadvantage. The disposition of Spain with regard to the Mississippi needs no comment. France and Britain are concerned with us in the fisheries, and view them as of the utmost moment to their navigation. They, of course, would hardly remain long indifferent to that decided mastery, of which experience has shown us to be possessed in this valuable branch of traffic, and by which we are able to undersell those nations in their own markets. What more natural than that they should be disposed to exclude from the lists such dangerous competitors?

This branch of trade ought not to be considered as a partial benefit. All the navigating States may, in different degrees, advantageously participate in it, and under circumstances of a greater extension of mercantile capital, would not be unlikely to do it. As a nursery of seamen, it now is, or when time shall have more nearly assimilated the principles of navigation in the several States, will become, a universal resource. To the establishment of a navy, it must be indispensable. . . .

There are other points of view in which this subject might be placed, of a striking and animating kind. But they would lead us too far into the regions of futurity, and would involve topics not proper for a newspaper discussion. I shall briefly observe, that our situation invites and our interests prompt us to aim at an ascendant in the system of American affairs. The world may politically, as well as geographically, be divided into four parts, each having a distinct set of interests. Unhappily for the other three, Europe, by her arms and by her negotiations, by force and by fraud, has, in different degrees, extended her dominion over them all. Africa, Asia, and America, have successively felt her domination. The superiority she has long maintained has tempted her to plume herself as the Mistress of the World, and to consider the rest of mankind as created for her benefit. Men admired as profound philosophers have, in direct terms, attributed to her inhabitants a physical superiority, and have gravely asserted that all animals, and with them the human species, degenerate in America—that even dogs cease to bark after having breathed awhile in our atmosphere. Facts have too long supported these arrogant pretensions of the Europeans. It belongs to us to vindicate the

honor of the human race, and to teach that assuming brother, moderation. Union will enable us to do it. Disunion will add another victim to his triumphs. Let Americans disdain to be the instruments of European greatness! Let the thirteen States, bound together in a strict and indissoluble Union, concur in erecting one great American system, superior to the control of all transatlantic force or influence, and able to dictate the terms of the connection between the old and the new world!
PUBLIUS

81

James Monroe

The Monroe Doctrine (1823)

Fellow-Citizens of the Senate and House of Representatives:

Many important subjects will claim your attention during the present session. . . .

At the proposal of the Russian Imperial Government, made through the minister of the Emperor residing here, a full power and instructions have been transmitted to the minister of the United States at St. Petersburg to arrange by amicable negotiation the respective rights and interests of the two nations on the North West coast of this continent. A similar proposal had been made by His Imperial Majesty to the Government of Great Britain, which has likewise been acceded to. The Government of the United States has been desirous by this friendly proceeding of manifesting the great value which they have invariably attached to the friendship of the Emperor and their solicitude to cultivate the best understanding with his Government. In the discussions to which this interest has given rise and in the arrangements by which they may terminate the occasion has been judged proper for asserting, as a principle in which the rights and interests of the United States are involved, that the American continents, by the free and independent condition which they have assumed and maintain, are henceforth not to be considered as subjects for future colonization by any European powers. . . .

At the commencement of the recent war between France and Spain it was declared by the French Government that it would grant no commissions to privateers, and that neither the commerce of Spain herself nor of neutral nations should be molested by the naval force of France, except in the breach of a lawful blockade. This declaration, which appears to have been faithfully carried into effect, concurring with principles proclaimed and cherished by the United States from the first establishment of their independence, suggested the hope that the time had arrived when the proposal for adopting it as a permanent and invariable rule in all future maritime wars might meet the favorable consideration of the great European powers. Instructions have accordingly been given to our ministers with France, Russia, and Great Britain to make those proposals to their respective Governments, and when the friends of humanity reflect on the essential amelioration to the condition of the human race which would result from the abolition of private war on the sea and on the great facility by which it might be accomplished, requiring only the consent of a few sovereigns, an earnest hope is indulged that these overtures will meet with an attention animated by the spirit in which they were made, and that they will ultimately be successful. . . .

A strong hope has been long entertained, founded on the heroic struggle of the Greeks, that they would succeed in their contest and resume their equal station among the nations of the earth. It is believed that the whole civilized world take a deep interest in their welfare. Although no power has declared in their favor, yet none according to our information, has taken part against them. Their cause and their name have protected them from dangers which might ere this have overwhelmed any other people. The ordinary calculations of interest and of acquisition with a view to aggrandizement, which mingles so much in the transactions of nations, seem to have had no effect in regard to them. From the facts which have come to our knowledge there is good cause to believe that their enemy has lost forever all dominion over them; that Greece will become again an independent nation. That she may obtain that rank is the object of our most ardent wishes.

It was stated at the commencement of the last session that a great effort was then making in Spain and Portugal to improve the condition of the people of those countries, and that it appeared to be conducted with extraordinary moderation. It need scarcely be remarked that the result has been so far very different from what was then anticipated. Of events in that quarter of the globe, with which we have so much intercourse and from which we derive our origin, we have always been anxious and interested spectators.

The citizens of the United States cherish sentiments the most friendly in favor of the liberty and happiness of their fellow men on that side of the Atlantic. In the wars of the European powers in matters relating to themselves we have never taken any part, nor does it comport with our policy so to do.

It is only when our rights are invaded or seriously menaced that we resent injuries or make preparation for our defense. With the movements in this hemisphere we are of necessity more immediately connected, and by causes which must be obvious to all enlightened and impartial observers.

The political system of the allied powers is essentially different in this respect from that of America. This difference proceeds from that which exists in their respective Governments; and to the defense of our own, which has been achieved by the loss of so much blood and treasure, and matured by the wisdom of their most enlightened citizens, and under which we have enjoyed unexampled felicity, this whole nation is devoted.

We owe it, therefore, to candor and to the amicable relations existing between the United States and those powers to declare that we should consider any attempt on their part to extend their system to any portion of this hemisphere as dangerous to our peace and safety. With the existing colonies or dependencies of any European power we have not interfered and shall not interfere, but with the Governments who have declared their independence and maintained it, and whose independence we have, on great consideration and on just principles, acknowledged, we could not view any interposition for the purpose of oppressing them, or controlling in any other manner their destiny, by any European power in any other light than as the manifestation of an unfriendly disposition toward the United States.

In the war between those new Governments and Spain we declared our neutrality at the time of their recognition, and to this we have adhered, and shall continue to adhere, provided no change shall occur which, in the judgment of the competent authorities of this Government, shall make a corresponding change on the part of the United States indispensable to their security.

The late events in Spain and Portugal show that Europe is still unsettled. Of this important fact no stronger proof can be adduced than that the allied powers should have thought it proper, on any principle satisfactory to themselves, to have interposed by force in the internal concerns of Spain. To what extent such interposition may be carried, on the same principle, is a question in which all independent powers whose governments differ from theirs are interested, even those most remote, and surely none more so than the United States.

Our policy in regard to Europe, which was adopted at an early stage of the wars which have so long agitated that quarter of the globe, nevertheless remains the same, which is, not to interfere in the internal concerns of any of its powers; to consider the government de facto as the legitimate government for us; to cultivate friendly relations with it, and to preserve those relations by a frank, firm, and manly policy, meeting in all instances the just claims of every power, submitting to injuries from none.

But in regard to those continents circumstances are eminently and conspicuously different. It is impossible that the allied powers should extend their political system to any portion of either continent without endangering our peace and happiness; nor can anyone believe that our southern brethren, if left to themselves, would adopt it of their own accord. It is equally impossible, therefore, that we should behold such interposition in any form with indifference. If we look to the comparative strength and resources of Spain and those new Governments, and their distance from each other, it must be obvious that she can never subdue them. It is still the true policy of the United States to leave the parties to themselves, in the hope that other powers will pursue the same course. . . .

82

Woodrow Wilson

War Message (1917)

I have called the Congress into extraordinary session because there are serious, very serious, choices of policy to be made, and made immediately, which it was neither right nor constitutionally permissible that I should assume the responsibility of making.

On the third of February last I officially laid before you the extraordinary announcement of the Imperial German Government that on and after the first day of February it was its purpose to put aside all restraints of law or of humanity and use its submarines to sink every vessel that sought to approach either the ports of Great Britain and Ireland or the western coasts of Europe or any of the ports controlled by the enemies of Germany within the Mediterranean. That had seemed to be the object of the German submarine warfare earlier in the war, but since April of last year the Imperial Government had somewhat restrained the commanders of its undersea craft in conformity with its promise then given to us that passenger boats should not be sunk and that due warning would be given to all other vessels which its submarines might seek to destroy when no resistance was offered or escape attempted, and care taken that their crews were given at least a fair chance to save their lives in their open boats. The precautions taken were meager and haphazard enough, as was proved in distressing instance after instance in the progress of the cruel and unmanly business, but a certain degree of restraint was observed. The new policy has swept every restriction aside. Vessels of every kind, whatever their flag, their character, their cargo, their destination, their errand, have been ruthlessly sent to the bottom: without warning and without thought of help or mercy for those on board, the vessels of friendly neutrals along with those of belligerents. Even hospital ships and ships carrying relief to the sorely bereaved and stricken people of Belgium, though the latter were provided with safe conduct through the proscribed areas by the German Government itself and were distinguished by unmistakable marks of identity, have been sunk with the same reckless lack of compassion or of principle. I was for a little while unable to believe that such things would in fact be done by any government that had hitherto subscribed to the humane practices of civilized nations. International law had its origin in the attempt to set up some law which would be respected and observed upon the seas, where no nation had right of dominion and where lay the free highways of the world. This minimum of right the German Government has swept aside under the plea of retaliation and necessity and because it had no weapons which it could use at sea except these which it is impossible to employ as it is employing them without throwing to the winds all scruples of humanity or of respect for the understandings that were supposed to underlie the intercourse of the world. I am not now thinking of the loss of property involved, immense and serious as that is, but only of the wanton and wholesale destruction of the lives of noncombatants, men, women, and children, engaged in pursuits which have always, even in the darkest periods of modern history, been deemed innocent and legitimate. Property can be paid for; the lives of peaceful and innocent people cannot be. The present German submarine warfare against commerce is a warfare against mankind.

It is a war against all nations. American ships have been sunk, American lives taken, in ways which it has stirred us very deeply to learn of, but the ships and people of other neutral and friendly nations have been sunk and overwhelmed in the waters in the same way. There has been no discrimination. The challenge is to all mankind. Each nation must decide for itself how it will meet it. The choice we make for ourselves must be made with a moderation of counsel and a temperateness of judgment befitting our character and our motives as a nation. We must put excited feeling away. Our motive will not be revenge or the victorious assertion of the physical might of the nation, but only the vindication of right, of human right, of which we are only a single champion.

When I addressed the Congress on the twenty-sixth of February last I thought that it would suffice to assert our neutral rights with arms, our right to use the seas against unlawful interference, our right to keep our people safe against unlawful violence. But armed neutrality, it now appears, is impracticable. . . . The German Government denies the right of neutrals to use arms at all within the areas of the sea which it has proscribed, even in the defense of rights which no modern publicist has ever before questioned their right to defend. . . . Armed neutrality is ineffectual enough at best; in such circumstances and in the face of such pretensions it is worse than ineffectual: it is likely only to produce what it was meant to prevent;

it is practically certain to draw us into the war without either the rights or the effectiveness of belligerents. There is one choice we cannot make, we are incapable of making: we will not choose the path of submission and suffer the most sacred rights of our Nation and our people to be ignored or violated. The wrongs against which we now array ourselves are no common wrongs; they cut to the very roots of human life.

With a profound sense of the solemn and even tragical character of the step I am taking and of the grave responsibilities which it involves, but in unhesitating obedience to what I deem my constitutional duty, I advise that the Congress declare the recent course of the Imperial German Government to be in fact nothing less than war against the government and people of the United States; that it formally accept the status of belligerent which has thus been thrust upon it, and that it take immediate steps not only to put the country in a more thorough state of defense but also to exert all its power and employ all its resources to bring the Government of the German Empire to terms and end the war.

What this will involve is clear. It will involve the utmost practicable cooperation in counsel and action with the governments now at war with Germany, and, as incident to that, the extension to those governments of the most liberal financial credit, in order that our resources may so far as possible be added to theirs. It will involve the organization and mobilization of all the material resources of the country to supply the materials of war and serve the incidental needs of the Nation in the most abundant and yet the most economical and efficient way possible. It will involve the immediate full equipment of the navy in all respects but particularly in supplying it with the best means of dealing with the enemy's submarines. It will involve the immediate addition to the armed forces of the United States already provided for by law in case of war at least five hundred thousand men, who should, in my opinion, be chosen upon the principle of universal liability to service, and also the authorization of subsequent additional increments of equal force so soon as they may be needed and can be handled in training. It will involve also, of course, the granting of adequate credits to the Government, sustained, I hope, so far as they can equitably be sustained by the present generation, by well conceived taxation. I say sustained so far as may be equitable by taxation because it seems to me that it would be most unwise to base the credits which will now be necessary entirely on money borrowed. It is our duty, I most respectfully urge, to protect our people so far as we may against the very serious hardships and evils which would be likely to arise out of the inflation which would be produced by vast loans.

In carrying out the measures by which these things are to be accomplished we should keep constantly in mind the wisdom of interfering as little as possible in our own preparation and in the equipment of our own military forces with the duty—for it will be a very practical duty—of supplying the nations already at war with Germany with the materials which they can obtain only from us or by our assistance. They are in the field and we should help them in every way to be effective there. . . .

While we do these things, these deeply momentous things, let us be very clear, and make very clear to all the world what our motives and our objects are. . . . Our object . . . is to vindicate the principles of peace and justice in the life of the world as against selfish and autocratic power and to set up amongst the really free and self governed peoples of the world such a concert of purpose and of action as will henceforth insure the observance of those principles Neutrality is no longer feasible or desirable where the peace of the world is involved and the freedom of its peoples, and the menace to that peace and freedom lies in the existence of autocratic governments backed by organized force which is controlled wholly by their will, not by the will of their people. We have seen the last of neutrality in such circumstances. We are at the beginning of an age in which it will be insisted that the same standards of conduct and of responsibility for wrong done shall be observed among nations and their governments that are observed among the individual citizens of civilized states.

We have no quarrel with the German people. We have no feeling towards them but one of sympathy and friendship. It was not upon their impulse that their government acted in entering this war. It was not with their previous knowledge or approval. It was a war determined upon as wars used to be determined upon in the old, unhappy days when peoples were nowhere consulted by their rulers and wars were provoked and waged in the interest of dynasties or of little groups of ambitious men who were accustomed to use their fellow men as pawns and tools.

Self-governed nations do not fill their neighbor states with spies or set the course of intrigue to bring about some critical posture of affairs which will give them an opportunity to strike and make conquest. Such designs can be successfully worked out only under cover and where no one has the right to ask questions. Cunningly contrived plans of deception or aggression, carried, it may be, from generation to generation, can be worked out and kept from the light only within the privacy of courts or behind the carefully guarded confidences of a narrow and privileged class. They are happily impossible where public opinion commands and insists upon full information concerning all the nation's affairs.

A steadfast concert for peace can never be maintained except by a partnership of democratic nations. No autocratic government could be trusted to keep faith within it or observe its covenants. It must be a league of honor, a partnership of opinion. Intrigue would eat its vitals away; the plottings of inner circles who could plan what they would and render account to no one would be a corruption seated at its very heart. Only free peoples can hold their purpose and their honor steady to a common end and prefer the interests of mankind to any narrow interest of their own. . . .

One of the things that has served to convince us that the Prussian, autocracy was not and could never be our friend is that from the very outset of the present war it has filled our unsuspecting communities and even our offices of government with spies and set criminal intrigues everywhere afoot against our national unity of counsel, our peace Within and without, our industries and our commerce. Indeed it is now evident that its spies were here even before the war began; and it is unhappily not a matter of conjecture but a fact proved in our courts of justice that the intrigues which have more than once come perilously near to disturbing the peace and dislocating the industries of the country have been carried on at the instigation, with the support, and even under the personal direction of official agents of the Imperial Government accredited to the Government of the United States. Even in checking these things and trying to extirpate them we have sought to put the most generous interpretation possible upon them because we knew that their source lay, not in any hostile feeling or purpose of the German people towards us (who were, no doubt, as ignorant of them as we ourselves were), but only in the selfish designs of a Government that did what it pleased and told its people nothing. But they have played their part in serving to convince us at last that that Government entertains no real friendship for us and means to act against our peace and security at its convenience. That it means to stir up enemies against us at our very doors the intercepted note to the German Minister at Mexico City is eloquent evidence.

We are accepting this challenge of hostile purpose because we know that in such a Government, following such methods, we can never have a friend; and that in the presence of its organized power, always lying in wait to accomplish we know not what purpose, there can be no assured security for the democratic Governments of the world. We are now about to accept gauge of battle with this natural foe to liberty and shall, if necessary, spend the whole force of the nation to check and nullify its pretensions and its power. We are glad, now that we see the facts with no veil of false pretense about them to fight thus for the ultimate peace of the world and for the liberation of its peoples, the German peoples included: for the rights of nations great and small and the privilege of men everywhere to choose their way of life and of obedience. The world must be made safe for democracy. Its peace must be planted upon the tested foundations of political liberty. We have no selfish ends to serve.

We desire no conquest, no dominion. We seek no indemnities for ourselves, no material compensation for the sacrifices we shall freely make. We are but one of the champions of the rights of mankind. We shall be satisfied when those rights have been made as secure as the faith and the freedom of nations can make them. Just because we fight without rancor and without selfish object, seeking nothing for ourselves but what we shall wish to share with all free peoples, we shall, I feel confident, conduct our operations as belligerents without passion and ourselves observe with proud punctilio the principles of right and of fair play we profess to be fighting for. . . .

It will be all the easier for us to conduct ourselves as belligerents in a high spirit of right and fairness because we act without animus, not in enmity towards a people or with the desire to bring any injury or disadvantage upon them, but only in armed opposition to an irresponsible government which has thrown aside all considerations of humanity and of right and is running amuck. We are, let me say again, the sincere friends of the German people, and shall desire nothing so much as the early reestablishment of intimate relations of mutual advantage between us,—however hard it may be for them, for the time being, to believe that this is spoken from our hearts. We have borne with their present Government through all these bitter months because of that friendship,—exercising a patience and forbearance which would otherwise have been impossible. . . .

It is a distressing and oppressive duty, Gentlemen of the Congress, which I have performed in thus addressing you. There are, it may be many months of fiery trial and sacrifice ahead of us. It is a fearful thing to lead this great peaceful people into war, into the most terrible and disastrous of all wars, civilization itself seeming to be in the balance.

But the right is more precious than peace, and we shall fight for the things which we have always carried nearest our hearts,—for democracy, for the right of those who submit to authority to have a voice in their own Governments, for the rights and liberties of small nations, for a universal dominion of right by such a concert of free peoples as shall bring peace and safety to all nations and make the world itself at last free. To such a task we can dedicate our lives and our fortunes, every thing that we are and everything that we have, with the pride of those who know that the day has come when America is privileged to spend her blood and her might for the principles that gave her birth and happiness and the peace which she has treasured. God helping her, she can do no other.

83

Stephen P. Sims

The Principles and Purposes of American Foreign Policy (2019)

The United States' foreign policy helped a fledgling republic become the greatest player in global great power politics. American foreign policy is therefore a matter of concern for the whole world, and, all too often, an object of its contempt. American foreign policy is judged too imperialistic by some and not imperialistic enough by others, too isolationist by some and too globalist by others, too idealistic by some and too vicious by others. The contradictory criticisms of American foreign policy reveal certain truths about its character: it is complex and cannot be reduced to a singular interest. This complexity causes the widespread misunderstanding of American diplomacy. It is also the cause of its success. I will illustrate this point by reflecting on the principles and purposes of foreign policy according to Woodrow Wilson, Alexander Hamilton, and James Monroe.

Woodrow Wilson's approach to American foreign policy is perhaps the most well-known and well-represented in American politics today. For this reason, we will begin with Wilson. His approach to American foreign policy marries the use of military power with a moral clarity based in the superiority of democracy as a way of life, human rights as a more important consideration than state sovereignty, and the multilateralism of international institutions as inherently morally superior to unilateral foreign policy. One can find each of these themes in Wilson's war message to Congress in 1917.

The justification for the declaration of war against Germany was its use of unrestricted submarine warfare. By attacking American shipping, Germany violated American sovereign rights and its declaration of neutrality. International law primarily protects the sovereign rights of nations, including the sovereign right of neutrality. Germany was consequently in violation of international law, and thus the United States was within its rights to declare war. In this respect, Wilson's request for Congress to declare war against the German Empire was well within the normal course of foreign policy.

But Wilson saw the American entry into World War I in larger and more significant terms rather than as another example of the ordinary course of international affairs. The German regime, in approving unrestricted submarine warfare, made itself the enemy of all nations, indeed the human species. Therefore, the American declaration of war on Germany was not a vindication of American rights alone, but the rights of humanity as a whole. But the notion that one can fight a war on behalf of humanity as a whole is strange; are not the Germans human? How, then, did Wilson claim to fight on behalf of humanity rather than a mere portion of it, even if a rather large portion? Wilson did so by distinguishing the German people from the German state: In championing the rights of humanity, the United States was the friend and champion of the German people and the enemy of their true enemy, their own government. Wilson separated the German people from their own government because the German government was autocratic and thus ruled with a will that was not the general will of the German people, but rather the particular wills of the Kaiser and the few that ruled with him.

Wilson's criticism of German foreign policy was radical: It was, he believed, no accident that the Kaiser's regime had an immoral foreign policy. It is the very nature of nondemocratic regimes to be guided by immoral maxims of conduct. Nondemocratic regimes are not governed by the will of the people; as such, nondemocratic regimes, by definition, are governed by the partial particular will of the regime rather than the general will of all. But a particular will is oriented toward a particular interest rather than the general interest; it is selfish and immoral. Thus, a government that is not founded on the general will must be immoral in itself, and its policies will necessarily be immoral as well. Wilson's conclusion is that the policy of nondemocratic regimes is of necessity unjust; conversely, the policy of genuine democracies will be, by definition, just. Wilson was thus justified in making the argument that not only the policy, but even the very existence of nondemocratic regimes is immoral and an affront to the rights of humanity. It follows then that the United States' enemies, the German Empire and the Austro-Hungarian Empire, were essentially unjust. Wilson, representing a democratic regime, represented the interests of the German people better than their own state and thus benefited the German people by declaring war upon their rulers.

If only democratic regimes are capable of pursuing selflessness, it is just and good to work toward a future world of democratic states. The ideal society of states will exist, then, when there is a world of democracies interacting selflessly with each other, every state cooperating with others, each thinking only of the common interest of the world. It follows that democracy promotion abroad is both useful and just. This is the meaning of Wilson's claim that "peace can never be maintained except by a partnership of democratic nations." A diplomatic community that seeks stability and order in the society of states, without reference to the type of regime, is insufficiently just to guarantee future peace. Consequently, any future international organization designed to guarantee future peace must be made up of those who have a "partnership in opinion" that would allow them to aim steadily at "a common end and prefer the interests of mankind to any narrow interest of their own." It is this future world of democratic regimes, cooperating toward a righteous peace, that Wilson sees as the purpose of American foreign policy. As he puts it, "The world must be made safe for democracy. Its peace must be planted upon the tested foundations of political liberty. We have no selfish ends to serve." The goals of the state should be the same as those of the individual citizen: selfless devotion to the common good, in this case an international common good. Hence, Wilson asserts that "[W]e are at the beginning of an age in which it will be insisted that the same standards of conduct and of responsibility for wrong done shall be observed among nations and their governments that are observed among the individual citizens of civilized states." There would be no difference in how we morally evaluate the conduct of individuals and states. Just as we expect individuals to sacrifice nobly on behalf of the common good, so too nations must sacrifice.

Traditionally, a nation is not held to the standards of individual morality in its conduct among other nations. This is because a nation is not an individual but rather a community of citizens; the task of the ruler of the community is to care directly for the common good of the community, whereas most citizens in their ordinary lives are concerned with their own affairs and are only remotely concerned with the common good. Morality is usually evaluated in terms of a political community in which the moral life is lived out. Wilson obviates the traditional evaluations of political morality by comparing the nation to a citizen. It, like the citizen, will be mostly concerned with its own affairs but its moral standards are set by a greater community to which it belongs, and not the community of citizens that make it up. The individuals within the nation become mere individuals without the traditional distinction of being a community of citizens. Hence, the role of the community as adjudicator of moral evaluation is transferred to a community that transcends the national community. The only community that can plausibly replace the national community is the community of humanity. Hence, traditional sovereign rights, vested in the nation as a community of citizens will be transferred to a community of nations, or, more precisely, a great community of humanity. That community of humanity, represented by democratically elected individuals like Wilson himself, will exercise the traditional rights of sovereignty and will legislate for the society of states. The partnership of democratic nations will become something like a democratic assembly of the world, all ruling all.

Effecting this transformation will be the end of American foreign policy as such. American foreign policy will end because the necessary consequence of this great transformation is the depoliticization of human beings; they would be "global citizens," which is to say not citizens at all in the original and ordinary meaning of the word. Since everyone is an apolitical "individual," there would be no particular or common tie of one person to another beyond the common bond of humanity and its moral laws. In such circumstances, "foreign" policy would be replaced with mere "policy" since the ancient and most fundamental distinction of citizen and foreigner would be erased. To the degree that this radical, perhaps even unnatural, transformation of the human condition has occurred, we see the victory of Wilson's vision.

If Wilson thought that foreign policy should be guided by the wellbeing of the human community, Alexander Hamilton thought it should be guided by the national interest of keeping and maintaining power. Hamilton was a strong advocate for the new Constitution of the United States to replace the Articles of Confederacy. In that advocacy, he emphasized the importance of a vigorous national government that had the capacity to care for the common good of the entirety of the United States, especially protecting and nourishing a vibrant commercial economy.

Human beings are meant for virtue and justice but all too often prefer what is pleasant or expedient. The human appetite for pleasure and expediency must be constrained, especially in the case of rulers. Because justice and virtue should reign, the power of the ruler must be constrained lest it be oppressive. In thinking about the relation of the American republic to other nations, Hamilton saw the same problem of human appetite and the need to constrain it. Whereas a constitutional order may constrain ambition through counteracting ambition, in the international realm power counteracts power, and thus a balance of power is requisite for any sort of decent international order.

For Hamilton, the chief source of American power is political unity under the Constitution. An example of the utmost importance of political unity can be found in Hamilton's discussion of how the United States should approach international trade. A unified and effective national government could regulate the commercial relationship of the United States with European powers, preventing those powers from dividing the individual American states from each other and weakening the whole republic. In so doing, the American people would gain the capacity to engage in "active commerce," that is, setting the terms of its international commerce. The American people have an interest in setting the terms of its international commerce so that they are not taken advantage of by foreign powers, especially the British Empire. This could entail even denying British ships entry in American ports unless they agreed to a trading relationship more favorable to the United States.

From this perspective, the economic component of foreign policy is simply one more aspect to the competition between states, and, as such, Hamilton considers it in terms of advantage and interest. Whatever the pacific tendencies of international commerce in the long run, in the immediate horizon commerce is not necessarily beneficent. American political relations with Great Britain would determine its economic relations, i.e. as a junior partner, if not a rival, to be stymied rather than increased. Thus, even a global "market" does not evince a natural tendency toward a common interest, but rather the interests of those who are powerful; if a common interest is possible, it is possible through political judgment and action. American solidarity and forceful diplomacy that is made possible through political unity could change those relations. If free trade is the ideal condition of international commerce, deliberate choice, not spontaneity, creates the conditions for free trade.

Diplomacy must be coupled with the means to resist and project force if the American ports need to close to foreign shipping. Naval power was a prerequisite to the United States becoming a full-fledged commercial republic; economic and military power are inseparable. In fact, naval power could not only defend the commerce of the United States, but also further its trade relationship with other nations. Such a navy, "if it could not vie with those of the great maritime powers, would at least be of respectable weight if thrown into the scale of either of two contending parties." If the United States Navy were unable to dictate the terms of American commercialism as a great power, it should be able to affect the balance of power in such a way as to promote American interests. Of course, the creation of an effective American navy depended on establishing American political unity through a genuine constitution. From Hamilton's perspective, the Constitution was a necessary safeguard against foreign predation.

If Hamilton's view of international relations is depressing, it comes from a moral conviction that human nature is flawed. The human heart is more mysterious than intelligible, and while we may think we understand ourselves, we rarely do, let alone others. Often we believe that we are acting for justice and truth, when we are in fact aiming at vengeance or honor. This modicum of self-knowledge suggests caution in our political activity, for all too often we conflate our private interest with the common good. But the difficulty in understanding, to say nothing of effecting, the common good in a single republic should make manifest the problem of understanding and effecting the common good of a "community" of nations. Indeed, it is not apparent that such a common good even exists.

Underlying Hamilton's view of foreign policy is the vital distinction of the individual citizen and the republic to which he belongs. The republic is not the same sort of thing as the citizen because it is the common possession of all the citizens. As a common possession, its good is a common good, shared by all the citizens. The purpose of government, indeed the very government that Hamilton was trying to bring into being, is to secure the common good of the people. As such, a policy that secures the common good of the American republic—protecting its sovereignty and sources of power—is not selfishness but a manifestation of the nature and virtue of republics.

The republic is a moral whole, and the status of the individuals within it changes inasmuch as they are citizens who participate in the common life of the republic. A ruler that sacrifices the well-being of his own citizens for the sake of "humanity"—a community greater than the republic—is a bad ruler. Hence, Hamilton argued against assisting the French in 1793 even though this would appear to be both ungrateful for French assistance in the War of Independence, and even unjust in the lack of reciprocity. The safety of the nation was threatened too much to assist erstwhile allies. This understanding of the political community and its moral obligations, one that emphasizes the solidarity of fellow citizens and the duties to secure the well-being of each other and the republic as a whole, claims to better supply the human need for virtue than is possible in social arrangements that devalue citizenship. But when one ascends to the level of international relations, the necessary expression of this republican solidarity is the frank and morally required assertion of national sovereignty and the means necessary to maintain that sovereignty.

To sacrifice the sovereignty or vital interests of the republic undermines the solidarity that makes constitutional orders functional. As such, an office holder who undermines this solidarity for the sake of a more depoliticized globalism make the most fundamental of moral and political errors. Armed with this complex truth of the human condition, the "realist" tradition of American foreign policy, as represented by Hamilton, is far from morally immature. It is a competing view of the purpose of American politics, indeed the purpose of politics as such, and the consequent human conduct that we praise.

As the fifth president of the United States, James Monroe oversaw some of the greatest accomplishments in American foreign policy and, with the help of the equally skilled John Quincy Adams, his Secretary of State, formulated its greatest principle, the Monroe Doctrine. According to the Doctrine, the United States will eschew interference in European affairs and in the affairs of their colonies, but at the same time consider any colonial expansion or interference in the New World as an act of aggression against the United States. On one hand, the Doctrine established the apparently limited interest of the United States in the affairs of the Eastern Hemisphere, or the Old World. As such, it serves as a limiting principle on American foreign policy and helps define which interests are truly vital and which are not. On the other hand, the Doctrine affirms American vital interests in the Western Hemisphere, especially in ensuring the presence of the Old World remains limited and ineffectual.

The Monroe Doctrine showed how inventive foreign policy can effectively secure the national interest. At first glance, it seems to establish the isolation of the United States: it remains aloof from European disputes while keeping Europe out of American concerns. This fits with a Hamiltonian policy of a strong navy to protect the commercial interests of the American republic. But even as the Doctrine shelters the United States from the great power competition of the Eastern Hemisphere, it does so only by effectively guaranteeing the integrity of South America. Thus the Doctrine is also a statement of American hegemony, protecting the freedom of the New World from the predations of the Old. Even if American policy toward the southern continent has at times bordered on imperialism, there can be no doubt that the security, even the existence, of South American nations depended on keeping European nations out. Monroe's foreign policy shows how the United States can guarantee its own common good, ensuring an atmosphere of republican freedom at home, while understanding that its good is wrapped up in the freedom of the entire hemisphere. The national interest and the common interest of the region coincided at this point. This example shows how expedience might be guaranteed through a nobler vision.

When the doctrine was formulated, Great Britain was the preponderant naval power. While the United States could protect itself, it certainly could not protect the entirety of the Western Hemisphere. Hence the Monroe Declaration relied on the cooperation of the British Navy, which in turn meant a coincidence of goals for the United States and Great Britain. Traditional British foreign policy aimed at maintaining the balance of power in Europe in order to ensure no other power could rival her maritime empire. The interest of the United States was similar, but expressed in a different way: Europe must remain divided against itself. Consequently, since the formulation of the Monroe Doctrine, the United States has never taken up arms against their English speaking cousins, but rather always took their side against others: first the Germans, and then the Soviets.

In establishing the United States as a sort of protector of the New World, Monroe accomplished many things at once. Perhaps most importantly, Monroe laid the foundation for an American preponderance of power in the Western Hemisphere, as well as a diplomacy and a navy that maintains that preponderance. He did this by declaring the Western Hemisphere a separate area of concern, a distinct society of states from the European society. In making this distinction, Monroe made it clear that the young republic's interests were global. This is a continuation of Hamilton's concern with protecting and extending the sovereignty of the United States. In order to protect that sovereignty, the United States could not allow for a great power competition and constant preparation for war to take place in a land of new-born freedom. Likewise, by officially declaring American noninterference in European affairs, the United States protected itself from being drawn into that competition itself. We can see, then, how the Monroe Doctrine laid the foundation and established the permanent contours of American foreign policy: a preference for limited action in the Old World, while sheltering the United States from any potential rival great power influence in its own geographical region. The guarantee of peace near the United States was the necessary condition for the enormous growth of the American republic in terms of population, territory, and economic capacity, which of course was the cornerstone of the global reach of the United States today. Through the prudent limitation of Monroe and the broadly Hamiltonian approach of American foreign policy, the United States was able to extend its protection to Europe against Soviet imperialism when that step became necessary for the global balance of power.

The Monroe Doctrine is a preeminent example of American political judgment. It shows that the United States has an interest in promoting a certain kind of international order based on keeping the great powers of the Eastern Hemisphere out of the Western Hemisphere. If the United States has sought isolation, it did so with an active diplomacy. When achieving isolation from European great power conflicts, it did so by claiming authority in its region of the world. But even as the United States asserts its active role in ordering international affairs, it does so through limiting its interests and role in the world. The limiting principle for Monroe is mostly geographic: The affairs of nations near the United States are very much its concern, while the affairs of the Old World are not. To the degree that the United States will have a policy toward Europe and Asia, it is promoting a balance of power that will make it impossible for a rival to endanger the United States at home. While preferring republican governments to nonrepublican, Monroe clearly excludes the domestic affairs of states outside the Western hemisphere as an object of American foreign policy. Indeed, Monroe insisted that the proper diplomatic partner is "the government de facto;" regardless of the character of the regime; diplomacy and cooperation cannot wait for the morally perfect regime. Thus, Monroe shows the way for an active American foreign policy that avoids the draw of Wilson's universalism. Through political judgment, it sees what is possible in the context of necessary limits.

The thinking and rhetoric of Hamilton, Monroe, and Wilson show that American foreign policy has a complexity as old as the republic itself. Indeed, it is this complex tradition of American foreign policy that is partly responsible for the current geopolitical order. Hamilton's republicanism, appreciation for the significance of power in international relations, emphasis on fostering American commercialism, and building an international order that is favorable to that commercialism are the lodestars by which the United States rose up from being mere colonies to being a great power. Monroe's keen awareness of the importance of geography in determining the possibilities and limits of foreign policy and forthright articulation of American interests allowed the New World to escape the great power struggles of Europe and develop in relative peace and prosperity. This prepared the way for the rise of the United States as a decisive factor in shifting the European balance of power under the leadership of Wilson, while at the same time articulating a moral vision that claimed to transcend the narrow interests of great power politics as usual.

Given the decisive importance of American foreign policy for the world in the 20th century, it is perhaps no surprise that we observe the marks of these presidents on the contemporary international order. For example, we see the influence of Wilson in the formation of the European Union, international law, and international institutions. In his time, he sought to prove to the royal houses of Europe that democracy is the superior regime. Europe appears to have learned this lesson; it is entirely democratic and has divested itself of its imperial holdings. The EU purports to provide institutional checks on the abuse of political power within member states. The entire premise of the EU is replacing great power competition with full cooperation of every European state. All of these developments in the European system bear out the moral vision of Wilson.

When we consider the broader horizon of the global state system, Wilson's idealism fades. This is most evident in the case of the United Nations. Often billed as a more effective version of the failed League of Nations, the primary purpose of the UN is to uphold international peace. The way in which the UN accomplishes this goal is through the Security Council, and the requirement for unanimity among the permanent members. The provision for unanimity means that the UN is in effect unable to move against any one of the permanent members' interests. Since all use of UN-sanctioned force must go through the Security Council, all questions of using force to deal with threats to peace must be answered in such a way that does not threaten the interests of any permanent members. This means that while the UN claims to stand for human rights and the rule of law, it is in effect guided by the national interests of the few. While this fact is deplorable to many politicians, citizens, and scholars, it does have the salutary effect of reducing the likelihood of violence between the great powers, particularly the United States, Russia, and China. It recognizes, and to a degree constitutionalizes, the peculiar role of great powers and their interests as necessary for geopolitical stability. In doing so, the UN and the hence the global system reflects the wisdom of Hamilton rather than the ideals of Wilson.

This does not mean that there is no protection for those states who are not blessed with Security Council permanent membership. The Charter explicitly recognizes the inherent right to self-defense for any state. But few states are so powerful as to need no allies, and so the Charter also permits the establishment of military alliances formed on a regional basis to secure the integrity of states on a local level. These elements of the UN Charter tacitly suggest that, whatever the pretensions of the UN itself, states had better rely on their own resources to defend themselves. Hence the establishment of the North Atlantic Treaty Organization (NATO), defined in theory by geographical necessity and similarity of regime type. This alliance exists for the protection of constitutional democracies in North America and Western Europe; its charter is conservative rather than universalizing. Furthermore, NATO reflects the permanent American interest in promoting a balance of power in Europe and Asia; after the Second World War, this meant an active American presence in Europe itself. As such, one can see how NATO illustrates the capacity of states to maintain an active and cooperative foreign policy based upon geographic and political common interests while avoiding the limitless universalization of "a world safe for democracy." In this prudent recognition of possibilities and limits of diplomacy, we see the legacy of Monroe.

Studying the sources of American foreign policy helps make clear how the United States arrived to its position of preponderant power, and, in doing so, helps make intelligible our current international order. Appreciating the complexity and internal tensions of the principles and purposes of American foreign policy makes the world in which we live—a world of injustice and power, rendered into a tolerable order of peace and prosperity.

84

Alexander Hamilton

Selections from Pacificus and Americanus (1793–1794)

When war broke out between the British and the French, Washington issued a proclamation declaring the neutrality of the United States in the conflict. Hamilton, perceiving the growth of opposition to the president's policy, published a defense of the proclamation under the pseudonyms "Pacificus" and "Americanus."

The objections which have been raised against the Proclamation of Neutrality lately issued by the President have been urged in a spirit of acrimony and invective, which demonstrates, that more was in view than merely a free discussion of an important public measure; that the discussion covers a

From Hamilton, "Pacificus I–IV" and "Americanus I–II," *The Papers of Alexander Hamilton*, Vol. XV and XVI, Columbia University Press, 1969.

design of weakening the confidence of the People in the author of the measure . . . . This Reflection . . . endeavours by proper explanations to place it in a just light. Such explanations at least cannot but be satisfactory to those who may not have leisure or opportunity for pursuing themselves an investigation of the subject, and who may wish to perceive that the policy of the Government is not inconsistent with its obligations or its honor.

The [first of the] objections [is] that the proclamation was without authority. . . .

The inquiry then is—what department of the Government of the UStates is the proper one to make a declaration of Neutrality in the cases in which the engagements of the Nation permit and its interests require such a declaration.

A correct and well informed mind will discern at once that it can belong neither to the Legislative nor Judicial Department and of course must belong to the Executive.

The Legislative Department is not the *organ* of intercourse between the UStates and foreign Nations. It is charged neither with *making* nor *interpreting* Treaties. It is therefore not naturally that Organ of the Government which is to pronounce the existing condition of the Nation, with regard to foreign Powers, or to admonish the Citizens of their obligations and duties as founded upon that condition of things. Still less is it charged with enforcing the execution and observance of these obligations and those duties.

It is equally obvious that the act in question is foreign to the Judiciary Department of the Government. The province of that Department is to decide litigations in particular cases. It is indeed charged with the interpretation of treaties; but it exercises this function only in the litigated cases; that is where contending parties bring before it a specific controversy. It has no concern with pronouncing upon the external political relations of Treaties between Government and Government. This position is too plain to need being insisted upon.

It must then of necessity belong to the Executive Department to exercise the function in Question—when a proper case for the exercise of it occurs.

It appears to be connected with that department in various capacities, as the *organ* of intercourse between the Nation and foreign Nations—as the interpreter of the National Treaties in those cases in which the Judiciary is not competent, that is in the cases between Government and Government—as that Power, which is charged with the Execution of the Laws, of which Treaties form a part—as that Power which is charged with the command and application of the Public Force. . . .

The second Article of the Constitution of the UStates, section 1st, establishes this general Proposition, That "The EXECUTIVE POWER shall be vested in a President of the United States of America." . . .

The general doctrine then of our constitution is, that the Executive Power of the Nation is vested in the President; subject only to the *exceptions* and *qualifications* which are expressed in the instrument.

Two of these [exceptions are] the participation of the Senate in the appointment of Officers and the making of Treaties. A third remains to be mentioned the right of the Legislature "to declare war and grant letters of marque and reprisal."

. . . [H]owever true it may be, that the right of the Legislature to declare war includes the right of judging whether the Nation be under obligations to make War or not—it will not follow that the Executive is in any case excluded from a similar right of Judgment, in the execution of its own functions.

If the Legislature have a right to make war on the one hand—it is on the other the duty of the Executive to preserve Peace till war is declared; and in fulfilling that duty, it must necessarily possess a right of judging what is the nature of the obligations which the treaties of the Country impose on the Government; and when in pursuance of this right it has concluded that there is nothing in them inconsistent with a *state* of neutrality, it becomes both its province and its duty to enforce the laws incident to that state of the Nation. The Executive is charged with the execution of all laws, the laws of Nations as well as the Municipal law, which recognises and adopts those laws. It is consequently bound, by faithfully executing the laws of neutrality, when that is the state of the Nation, to avoid giving a cause of war to foreign Powers. . . .

Those who object to the proclamation will readily admit that it is the right and duty of the Executive to judge of, or to interpret, those articles of our treaties which give to France particular privileges, in order to the enforcement of those privileges: But the necessary consequence of this is, that the Executive must judge what are the proper bounds of those privileges—what rights are given to other nations by our treaties with them—what rights the law of Nature and Nations gives and our treaties permit, in respect to those Nations with whom we have no treaties; in fine what are the reciprocal rights and obligations of the United States & of all & each of the powers at War.

The right of the Executive to receive ambassadors and other public Ministers may serve to illustrate the relative duties of the Executive and Legislative Departments. This right includes that of judging, in the case of a Revolution of Government in a foreign Country, whether the new rulers are competent organs of the National Will and ought to be recognised or not: And where a treaty antecedently exists between the UStates and such nation that right involves the power of giving operation or not to such treaty. For until the new Government is *acknowleged*, the treaties between the nations, as far at least as regards *public* rights, are of course suspended.

This power of determining virtually in the case supposed upon the operation of national Treaties as a consequence, of the power to receive ambassadors and other public Ministers, is an important instance of the right of the Executive to decide the obligations of the Nation with regard to foreign Nations. To apply it to the case of France, if there had been a Treaty of alliance *offensive* and defensive between the UStates and that Country, the unqualified acknowlegement of the new Government would have put the UStates in a condition to become an associate in the War in which France was engaged—and would have laid the Legislature under an obligation, if required, and there was otherwise no valid excuse, of exercising its power of declaring war.

This serves as an example of the right of the Executive, in certain cases, to determine the condition of the Nation, though it may consequentially affect the proper or improper exercise of the Power of the Legislature to declare war. The Executive indeed cannot control the exercise of that power—further than by the exercise of its general right of objecting to all acts of the Legislature; liable to being overruled by two thirds of both houses of Congress. The Legislature is free to perform its own duties according to its own sense of them—though the Executive in the exercise of its constitutional powers, may establish an antecedent state of things which ought to weigh in the legislative decisions. From the division of the Executive Power there results . . . a *concurrent* authority . . . .

Hence in the case stated, though treaties can only be made by the President and Senate, their activity may be continued or suspended by the President alone. . . .

It deserves to be remarked, that as the participation of the senate in the making of Treaties and the power of the Legislature to declare war are exceptions out of the general "Executive Power" vested in the President, they are to be construed strictly—and ought to be extended no further than is essential to their execution.

While therefore the Legislature can alone declare war, can alone actually transfer the nation from a state of Peace to a state of War—it belongs to the "Executive Power," to do whatever else the laws of Nations cooperating with the Treaties of the Country enjoin, in the intercourse of the UStates with foreign Powers.

In this distribution of powers the wisdom of our constitution is manifested. It is the province and duty of the Executive to preserve to the Nation the blessings of peace. The Legislature alone can interrupt those blessings, by placing the Nation in a state of War. . . .

. . . [The] objection to the Proclamation [of Neutrality] namely that it is inconsistent with the Treaties between the United States and France will now be examined. . . .

The Alliance between the United States and France is a Defensive *Alliance*. In the Caption of it it is denominated a "Treaty of Alliance eventual and *defensive*." . . .

[I]n determining the *legal* and *positive* obligations of the UStates the only point of inquiry is—whether the War was *in fact* begun by France or by her enemies. . . . [I]n a *defensive* alliance, when *war is made upon* one of the allies, the other is bound to fulfil the conditions stipulated on its part, without inquiry whether the war is rightfully begun or not—as on the other hand when war is begun by one of the allies the other is exempted from the obligation of assisting; however just the commencement of it may have been. . . .

[T]hough the manifest injustice of the war has been affirmed by some, to be a good cause for not executing the formal obligations of a treaty, I have no where found it maintained, that the justice of a war is a consideration, which can *oblige* a nation to do what its formal obligations do not require; as in the case of a *defensive* alliance, to furnish the succours stipulated, though the formal obligation did not exist, by reason of the ally having begun the war, instead of being the party attacked.

But if this were not the true doctrine, an impartial examination would prove, that with respect to some of the powers, France is not blameless in the circumstances, which preceded and led to the war with those powers; that if she received, she also gave cause of offense, and that the justice of the War on her side is, in those cases, not a little problematical. . . .

[France] gave a general and just cause of alarm to Nations, by that Decree of the 19th. of November 1792 whereby the Convention, in the name of the French Nation, declare that they will grant *fraternity* and *assistance* to every People who *wish* to recover their liberty and charge the Executive Power to send the necessary orders to *the Generals* to give assistance to such people, and to *defend those citizens who may have been or who may be vexed for the cause of liberty;* which decree was ordered to be printed *in all languages.*

When a Nation has actually come to a resolution to throw off a yoke, under which it may have groaned, and to assert its liberties—it is justifiable and meritorious in another nation to afford assistance to the one which has been oppressed & is *in the act* of liberating itself; but it is not warrantable for any Nation *beforehand* to hold out a general invitation to insurrection and revolution, by promising to assist *every people* who may *wish* to recover their liberty and to defend *those citizens,* of every country, *who may have been or who may be vexed for the cause of liberty;* still less to commit to the *Generals* of its armies the discretionary power of judging when the Citizens of a foreign Country have been vexed for the cause of Liberty by their own government. . . .

Such a conduct as that indicated by this Decree has a natural tendency to disturb the tranquillity of nations, to excite fermentation and revolt every where; and therefore justified neutral powers, who were in a situation to be affected by it in taking measures to repress the spirit by which it had been dictated.

But the principle of this Decree received a more particular application to Great Britain by some subsequent circumstances.

Among the proofs of this are two answers, which were given by the President of the National Convention at a public sitting on the 28th. of November. . . .

"Nature and *principles* draw *towards us* England Scotland and Ireland. Let the cries of friendship resound through the two *REPUBLICS*." "Principles are waging war against Tyranny, which will fall under the blows of philosophy. *Royalty in Europe is either destroyed or on the point of perishing*, on the ruins of feudality; and the *Declaration of Rights placed by the side of thrones is a devouring fire which will consume them. WORTHY Republicans*."

Declarations of this sort cannot but be considered as a direct application of the principle of the Decree to Great Britain; as an open patronage of a Revolution in that Country; a conduct which proceeding from the head of the body that governed France in the presence and on behalf of that body was unquestionably an offense and injury to the Nation to which it related.

The decree of the 15 of November is another cause of offence to all the Governments of Europe. By That Decree "*The French Nation declares,* that it will *treat as enemies the people,* who *refusing* or *renouncing* liberty and equality *are desirous* of preserving their *Prince* and *privileged castes*—or of *entering into an accomodation* with them &c." This decree was little short of a declaration of War against all Nations, having *princes* and *privileged classes*. . . .

Whatever partiality may be entertained for the general object of the French Revolution, it is impossible for any well informed or soberminded man not to condemn the proceedings which have been stated; as repugnant to the general rights of Nations, to the true principles of liberty, to the freedom of opinion of mankind; & not to acknowledge as a consequence of this, that the justice of the war on the part of France, with regard to some of the powers with which she is engaged, is from those causes questionable enough to free the UStates from all embarrassment on that score; if it be at all incumbent upon them to go into the inquiry.

The policy of a defensive alliance is so essentially distinct from that of an offensive one, that it is every way important not to confound their effects. The first kind has in view the prudent object of mutual defence, when either of the allies is involuntarily forced into a war by the attack by some third power. The latter kind subjects the peace of each ally to the will of the other, and obliges each to partake in the wars of policy & interest, as well as in those of safety and defence, of the other. . . .

It is known that we are wholly destitute of naval force. France, with all the great maritime Powers united against her, is unable to supply this deficiency. She can not afford us that species of cooperation, which is necessary to render our efforts useful to her and to prevent our experiencing the entire destruction of our Trade and the most calamitous inconveniences in other respects. . . .

There would be no proportion between the mischiefs and perils, to which the UStates would expose themselves by embarking in the War, and the benefit *which the nature of their stipulation aims at securing* to France, or that, which it would be in their power actually to render her, by becoming a party.

. . . All contracts are to receive a reasonable construction. Self preservation is the first duty of a Nation; and though in the performance of stipulations relating to war, good faith requires that the *ordinary hazards* of war should be fairly encountered, because they are directly contemplated by such stipulations, yet it does not require that *extraordinary* and *extreme* hazards should be run; especially where the object, for which they are to be run, is only a *partial* and *particular* interest of the ally, for whom they are to to be run.

As in the present instance good faith does not require, that the UStates should put in jeopardy their essential interests, perhaps their very existence . . .

[Another] objection to the Proclamation is, that it is inconsistent with the gratitude due to France, for the services rendered us in our own Revolution. . . .

[I]t may not be without use to indulge some reflections on this very favourite topic of gratitude to France; since it is at this shrine we are continually invited to sacrifice the true interests of the Country; as if "*All for love and the world well lost*" were a fundamental maxim in politics.

Faith and Justice between nations are virtues of a nature sacred and unequivocal. They cannot be too strongly inculcated nor too highly respected. Their obligations are definite and positive their utility unquestionable. . . .

But the same cannot be said of gratitude. . . .

The basis of gratitude, is a benefit received or intended, which there was no right to claim, originating in a regard to the interest or advantage of the party, on whom the benefit is or is meant to be conferred. If a service is rendered from views *chiefly* relative to the immediate interest of the party, who renders it, and is productive of reciprocal advantages, there seems scarcely in such a case to be an adequate basis for a sentiment like that of gratitude. . . .

Between individuals, occasion is not unfrequently given to the exercise of gratitude. Instances of conferring benefits, from kind and benevolent dispositions or feelings towards the person benefitted, without any other interest on the part of the person, who confers the benefit, than the pleasure of doing a good action, occur every day among individuals. But among nations they perhaps never occur. It may be affirmed as a general principle, that the predominant motive of good offices from one nation to another is the interest or advantage of the Nations, which performs them.

Indeed the rule of morality is in this respect not exactly the same between Nations as between individuals. The duty of making its own welfare the guide of its actions is much stronger upon the former than upon the latter; in proportion to the greater magnitude and importance of national compared with individual happiness, to the greater permanency of the effects of national than of individual conduct. Existing Millions and for the most part future generations are concerned in the present measures of a government: While the consequences of the private actions of an individual, for the most part, terminate with himself or are circumscribed within a narrow compass.

Whence it follows, that an individual may on numerous occasions meritoriously indulge the emotions of generosity and benevolence; not only without an eye to, but even at the expence of his own interest. But a Nation can rarely be justified in pursuing a similar course; and when it does so ought to confine itself within much stricter bounds. Good offices, which are indifferent to the Interest of a Nation performing them, or which are compensated by the existence or expectation of some reasonable equivalent or which produce an essential good to the nation, to which they are rendered, without real detriment to the affairs of the nation rendering them, prescribe the limits of national generosity or benevolence.

It is not meant here to advocate a policy absolutely selfish or interested in nations; but to show that a policy regulated by their own interest, as far as justice and good faith permit, is, and ought to be their prevailing policy: and that either to ascribe to them a different principle of action, or to deduce from the supposition of it arguments for a self-denying and self-sacrificing gratitude on the part of a Nation, which may have received from another good offices, is to misconceive or mistake what usually are and ought to be the springs of National Conduct. . . .

An examination into the question how far *regard to the cause of Liberty* ought to induce the United States to take part with France in the present war, is rendered necessary by the efforts which [some] are making to establish an opinion that it ought to have that effect. . . .

[W]e are told that our own Liberty is at stake upon the event of the war against France—that if she falls we shall be the next victim. The combined powers, it is said, will never forgive in us the origination of those principles which were the germs of the French Revolution. They will endeavour to eradicate them from the world.

If this suggestion were ever so well founded, it would perhaps be a sufficient answer to it to say, that our interference is not likely to alter the case—that it could only serve prematurely to exhaust our strength.

But other answers more conclusive present themselves. . . .

There are too great errors in our reasoning upon this subject. One is that the combined Powers will certainly attribute to us the same principles which they deem so exceptionable in France; the other, that our principles are in fact the same.

If left to themselves, they will all except one naturally see in us a people who originally resorted to a Revolution in Government as a refuge from encroachment on rights and privileges *antecedently* enjoyed—not as a people who from choice have sought a radical and entire change in the established Government, in pursuit of new privileges and rights carried to an extreme, not reconciliable perhaps with any form of regular Government. They will see in us a people who have a due respect for property and personal security—who in the midst of our revolution abstained with exemplary moderation from everything violent or sanguinary instituting governments adequate to the protection of persons and property; who since the completion of our revolution have in a very short period, from mere reasoning and reflection, without tumult or bloodshed adopted a form of general Government calculated as well as the nature of things would permit—to remedy antecedent defects—to give strength and security to the Nation—to rest the foundations of Liberty on the basis of Justice Order and Law—who at all times have been content to govern ourselves; unmeddling in the Governments or Affairs of other Nations: in fine, they will see in us sincere Republicans but decided enemies to licentiousness and anarchy—sincere republicans but decided friends to the freedom of opinion, to the order and tranquility of all Mankind. They will not see in us a people whose best passions have been misled and whose best qualities have been perverted from their true aim by headlong fanatical or designing leaders to the perpetration of acts from which humanity shrinks—to the commission of outrages, over which the eye of reason weeps—to the profession and practice of principles which tend to shake the foundations of morality—to dissolve the social bands—to disturb the peace of mankind—to substitute confusion [for] order, anarchy [for] Government.

Such at least is the light in which the Reason or the passions of the Powers confederated against France lead them to view her principles and conduct. And it is to be lamented that so much cause has been given for their opinions. If on our part, we give no incitement to their passions, facts too prominent and too decisive to be combated will forbid their reason to bestow the same character upon us.

It is therefore matter of real regret that there should be an effort on our part to level the distinctions, which discriminate our case from that of France—to confound the two cases in the view of foreign powers—and to hazard our own principles, by persuading ourselves of a similitude which does not exist. . . .

But let us not corrupt ourselves by false comparisons or glosses—nor shut our eyes to the true nature of transactions which ought to grieve and warn us—not rashly mingle our destiny in the consequences of the errors and extravagances of another nation.

85

James Madison

Selections from Helvidius (1793)

Jefferson, who served as the Secretary of State, when President Washington issued a Proclamation of Neutrality in the war between France and England, objected to the Proclamation and favored commitment to the French. Unwilling to criticize the president while serving in the cabinet, Jefferson recruited Madison, then a member of the House of Representatives, to answer Hamilton, which he did under the pseudonym "Helvidius." In our selection Madison argues against Hamilton's understanding of the powers of the Executive to issue the Proclamation.

Several pieces with the signature of Pacificus were lately published . . . .

In these disguises they have appeared to claim the attention I propose to bestow on them; with a view to shew, from the publication itself, that under colour of vindicating an important public act, of a chief magistrate, who enjoys the confidence and love of his country, principles are advanced which strike at the vitals of its constitution, as well as at its honor and true interest. . . .

If we consult for a moment, the nature and operation of the two powers to declare war and make treaties, it will be impossible not to see that they can never fall within a proper definition of executive powers. The natural province of the executive magistrate is to execute laws, as that of the legislature is to make laws. All his acts therefore, properly executive, must presuppose the existence of the laws to be executed. A treaty is not an execution of laws: it does not pre-suppose the existence of laws. It is, on the contrary, to have itself the force of a *law*, and to be carried into *execution*, like all *other laws*, by the *executive magistrate*. To say then that the power of making treaties which are confessedly laws, belongs naturally to the department which is to execute laws, is to say, that the executive department naturally includes a legislative power. In theory, this is an absurdity—in practice a tyranny.

The power to declare war is subject to similar reasoning. A declaration that there shall be war, is not an execution of laws: it does not suppose preexisting laws to be executed: it is not in any respect, an act merely executive. It is, on the contrary, one of the most deliberative acts that can

From *The Papers of James Madison*, Vol. XV, University Press of Virginia, 1985.

be performed; and when performed, has the effect of *repealing* all the *laws* operating in a state of peace, so far as they are inconsistent with a state of war: and of *enacting* as *a rule for the executive*, a *new code* adapted to the relation between the society and its foreign enemy. In like manner a conclusion of peace *annuls* all the *laws* peculiar to a state of war, and *revives* the general laws incident to a state of peace. . . .

From this view of the subject it must be evident, that although the executive may be a convenient organ of preliminary communications with foreign governments, on the subjects of treaty or war; and the proper agent for carrying into execution the final determinations of the competent authority; yet it can have no pretensions from the nature of the powers in question compared with the nature of the executive trust, to that essential agency which gives validity to such determinations.

It must be further evident that, if these powers be not in their nature purely legislative, they partake so much more of that, than of any other quality, that under a constitution leaving them to result to their most natural department, the legislature would be without a rival in it. . . .

In the general distribution of powers, we find that of declaring war expressly vested in the Congress, where every other legislative power is declared to be vested, and without any other qualification than what is common to every other legislative act. The constitutional idea of this power would seem then clearly to be, that it is of a legislative and not an executive nature.

This conclusion becomes irresistible, when it is recollected, that the constitution cannot be supposed to have placed either any power legislative in its nature, entirely among executive powers, or any power executive in its nature, entirely among legislative powers, without charging the constitution, with that kind of intermixture and consolidation of different powers, which would violate a fundamental principle in the organization of free governments. If it were not unnecessary to enlarge on this topic here, it could be shown, that the constitution was originally vindicated, and has been constantly expounded, with a disavowal of any such intermixture.

The power of treaties is vested jointly in the President and in the Senate, which is a branch of the legislature. From this arrangement merely, there can be no inference that would necessarily exclude the power from the executive class: since the senate is joined with the President in another power, that of appointing to offices, which as far as relate to executive offices at least, is considered as of an executive nature. Yet on the other hand, there are sufficient indications that the power of treaties is regarded by the constitution as materially different from mere executive power, and as having more affinity to the legislative than to the executive character.

One circumstance indicating this, is the constitutional regulation under which the senate give their consent in the case of treaties. In all other cases the consent of the body is expressed by a majority of voices. In this particular case, a concurrence of two thirds at least is made necessary, as a substitute or compensation for the other branch of the legislature, which on certain occasions, could not be conveniently a party to the transaction.

But the conclusive circumstance is, that treaties when formed according to the constitutional mode, are confessedly to have the force and operation of *laws*, and are to be a rule for the courts in controversies between man and man, as much as any *other laws*. They are even emphatically declared by the constitution to be "the supreme law of the land."

Whence then can the writer [Pacificus] have borrowed [this doctrine of executive power]? . . .

The power of making treaties and the power of declaring war, are *royal prerogatives* in the *British government,* and are accordingly treated as Executive prerogatives by *British commentators.*

86

James Pontuso

1989: It Was Too Soon to Celebrate (2019)

1989 was an extraordinary year. It was so astonishing that almost no one predicted and few could believe what happened. Suddenly, one of the most monumental struggles in history ended. Communism collapsed and the Cold War, which had begun in 1945, was over. The United States and its allies were triumphant, and the future seemed full of opportunities for peace and prosperity.

1989 was also the year that a then little-known academic and policy advisor, Francis Fukuyama, became famous for proclaiming "the end of history." The idea touched a nerve; it was discussed widely in the popular press and in academic circles. But from the beginning, the concept was controversial, partly because people were confused about what the end of history meant.

The end of history does not mean that time has stopped or that nothing will ever happen again; not end as in "it's all over," but end as "it's reached its culmination, where it wants to go." Fukuyama maintained that since the

Contributed by James Pontuso. © Kendall Hunt Publishing Company time of the American Revolution, liberal democracies (governments, such as America's, that protect individual rights and decide issues by consent of the governed) have triumphed over all their enemies. They defeated monarchy and autocracy during World War I, Fascism during World War II, and Communism during the Cold War. Fukuyama hypothesized that the ideas of liberal democracy have become almost universally accepted as the proper way to organize political communities. Those nations that have not adopted the institutions of liberal democracy would eventually do so because ideas precede actions. At the end of history there would no longer be revolutionary movements based on new philosophic doctrines to challenge the status quo. Once people establish liberal democracy, they won't want to change to another form of government. No epoch-shattering upheavals as occurred during the American, French, and Bolshevik Revolutions would mark the future.

Fukuyama viewed the end of the Cold War as a seminal event because Marxist Communism was a genuine alternative to the liberal democratic way of life. For almost fifty years, the struggle between the Communist nations of the East and the liberal democracies of the West was fought out on the world stage. The conflict was dubbed the Cold War since neither side wanted a direct military confrontation that might begin a nuclear exchange—a war far too hot for everybody. When Communism disintegrated in 1989, it marked the end of the contest between East and West. Not only was Eastern Europe liberated, but people all over the world broke free from the yoke of Communism.

We might ask in hindsight why a political and social system that failed so miserably came to dominate the politics of most of the 20th century. The answer is found in the theories of Karl Marx, who maintained that although workers in liberal democracies are "free" to vote and to sell their labor to the highest bidder, they are reduced to subsistence wages. This "iron law," as he called it, is true because of the intense competition inherent in capitalism.

In order to keep up with their rivals, corporations are compelled to produce goods rapidly and efficiently, and at the same time to keep prices low by reducing the cost of production. To attain these goals, owners must introduce ever-more complex machines and simultaneously decrease wages. Thus, laborers—the most numerous class—become alienated from their toil and, indeed, from their very existence. They are made to work at tedious jobs, on assembly lines with advanced machinery, for meager wages, the absolute minimum expenditure needed to maintain them as functioning units of production. Any fulfillment is lost in such labor since the workers have control over neither the finished product nor the means by which goods are created. For workers, political freedom results in slavery and degradation.

Marx theorized that capitalism's very efficiency would eventually cause its downfall. It would produce such a glut of goods that consumption would fall behind production, resulting in massive layoffs and, finally, economic collapse (as almost occurred during the Great Depression of the 1930s). The inequity of a system in which the owners enjoy all the luxuries of life but do no labor, and the workers labor but live in poverty would eventually become obvious. The people would seize the means of production and transform the social arrangement so that all would share equally in its bounty. The inexorable movement of history made it inevitable that a new era of equality, liberty, and universal brotherhood would arrive.

Marx's vision was appealing because it promised equality, liberation, and community. Some people were so enchanted by the promise of such a future that they devoted their lives to Communism. Little worked out as Marx predicted. The very idealism of Marx's philosophy led people to believe that society could be thoroughly reformed. When Communists came to power in the Soviet Union in 1918, they worked tirelessly to transform the human condition.

But most Russians could not measure up to this perfect image; they were more often concerned with their own interests than with the triumph of Communism. In an effort to make reality conform to theory, the Communist Party employed the most uncompromising forms of control, and when people *still* failed to meet expectations, Communists became vicious. Despite the tightly controlled media in Communist countries, stories of ruthlessness and savagery filtered to the West from émigrés who had escaped.

The most important account of Soviet terror was written by the Russian dissident Aleksandr Solzhenitsyn in his massive work, *The Gulag Archipelago*. The tales were almost too horrific to be believed. Millions had been executed for political offenses. Even more had been sent to forced labor camps where many died from overwork. People were imprisoned for being born into the wrong social class (bourgeois) or for opposing the government in any way. Under Soviet leader Joseph Stalin, a person could be jailed for, among other things, "anti-Soviet thought" or for being a "wife or child of an enemy of the people."

For many years, Communist rulers denied these allegations, and people in the West, although wary, thought them exaggerated. However, secret police files made public since the collapse of Communism show that many of the seemingly most far-fetched anecdotes were true.

An overwhelming majority of Americans believed that no matter how humane Communism's aims, its principles were unworkable. Human beings are not equal in ability or determination. The attempt to make all people equal means denying liberty to some, normally the talented. In practice, Marx's promise to make people equal resulted in denying equality of opportunity to everyone.

Critics of Marx also maintained that total liberation is not feasible. Human beings need some form of government to restrain their baser instincts. By its very nature, government means restrictions on people's liberty. Even universal community is unrealistic; in all of recorded history people have chosen to live in distinct political communities. In the United States, a strong consensus was formed in opposition to the Soviet Union, and indeed, to Communist governments throughout the world. The American public was correct in its appraisal, for wherever Communism was implemented, totalitarian governments arose.

The key to understanding the end of history, Fukuyama maintained, is that people want to improve their material condition. The basis of economic progress is free trade, open communication, and the unfettered flow of information and technology. Societies that pursue closed, inward-looking policies cannot satisfy the aspirations of their people. Free nations have superior economies. Governments not dedicated to protecting economic liberty will eventually fall.

Moreover, since liberal democracies rest on the consent of the governed, citizens in those societies are "recognized" as full and equal members of the community. Their views must be heard by political leaders before policies can be adopted. Free and fair elections support what most everyone wants: peace, security, and prosperity.

Economists seem to agree with Fukuyama, although they do not like the idea of the end of history. Instead, they gave the phenomenon of globalization an even more paradoxical explanation; they insist that the world is flat. But they don't *really* think the world is flat; they mean that there is now a global market. Goods, services, news, technology, and ideas move freely from one part of the globe to another, as if the world *were* flat. Everyone gains from this exchange because people concentrate on what they do well.

Worldwide commerce is not possible unless certain values are shared, most importantly, protection of property rights. Would you trade with someone who stole your money? In places that do not or cannot protect property rights, the world is still round, for although people truck, barter, and exchange—as they always have done—there is little long-term incentive to save and invest. Violence and brutality interfere with the hope for gain, and people in unstable areas are often poor.

People in the flat regions of the planet, however, put aside long-standing religious, ethnic, and cultural hatreds to pursue rational self-interest. They look to the future instead of the past. They know that business cannot thrive amid war, hostility, and distrust. Flat-worlders seek peace, security, and prosperity. It turns out that the world is flattest where liberal democracy reigns.

For Fukuyama, the victory of liberal democracy is a good thing, except that life might become boring. He wonders what people will do with themselves during an era of universal peace and prosperity. Will they pursue only bodily pleasures, or expend themselves in mindless distractions such as peering at their cell phones for most of the day? There may be nothing to inspire

people, no excitement, no desire for distinction, no need for noble or coura-
geous sacrifice. The serious question that Fukuyama raises is whether life will
be satisfying if the magnificent enterprises people have so valued in the past
are no longer required.

At the end of the Cold War, America became the world's predominant
power, a situation that created difficulties for American policy-makers.
The United States was so dominant that it was often blamed for its behavior whether it acted or not. For instance, when President Bush (the elder)
refused to intervene to restore an elected government in Haiti, the United
States was accused of supporting a military dictatorship. But when President
Clinton sent marines to Haiti to halt civil unrest, the United States was
criticized for meddling in the affairs of a weaker neighbor. President Clinton
was blamed for not acting to end the bloodshed during Rwanda's civil wars,
but when he sent American peace-keeping forces into the Balkans, he was
reproached for making America the "policeman of the world."

The terrorist attacks of September 11, 2001, were a turning point for
American foreign policy. President George W. Bush ordered American
troops into Afghanistan, from where the assaults against the World Trade
Center and Pentagon had been hatched. The war in Afghanistan became
the longest in America history. In 2003, the United States military invaded
Iraq, where Bush claimed dictator Saddam Hussein concealed weapons of
mass destruction. Bush mistakenly believed that removing the tyrant would
clear the way for a liberal democracy in Iraq. Instead, a long and gruesome
ethnic war ensued.

Many people maintain that America's wars in the Middle East indicate
that Bush's policies were a failure, and that Fukuyama was premature in proclaiming the end of history. Life has hardly been tranquil since the end of
the Cold War. Liberal democracies have fulfilled their promise of producing
a better material life for most people—they are now the richest societies in
human history. This modern miracle of affluence has been less successful
explaining the meaning of life.

Liberal democracies are founded on truth discovered by the scientific
method, not on the precepts understood by faith. They are secular and have,
for the most part, scrupulously avoided spiritual matters. But, since human
beings are finite creatures who can imagine the infinite, it is natural that
they have questions involving life and death and the purpose of existence.
Because of lingering doubts about the meaning of our lives—issues that liberal democracies have not addressed—religious movements (which do offer
answers to spiritual perplexities) continue to flourish.

Most especially, Islamic fundamentalism challenges the West's scientific
mode of thought and secular way of life. Since most Islamic-majority nations
have no separation of religion and state, they have been rarely successful at
founding or maintaining liberal democracies.

Other on-going sources of discord in the world are tribalism, sectarianism, ethnic tensions, and nationalism. Why is nationalism likely to remain a disruptive force in international relations?

"There are certain social principles in human nature," Alexander Hamilton stated, "from which we may draw the most solid conclusions with respect to the conduct of individuals, and of communities. We love our families, more than we love our neighbors: We love our neighbors, more than our countrymen in general. The human affections, like solar heat, lose their intensity, as they depart the center."

This "love of one's own," as it might be called, is more than mere narrow-minded bigotry. In fact, it counteracts personal selfishness and attracts people into political communities. As such, it can be a source of civic responsibility and dedication to one's friends and countrymen. But caring for one's own means one must exclude outsiders, since the extent to which human affections can be stretched is not infinite. (This process explains why sporting events are more fun to watch when rooting for a home team.) Other people, too, form themselves into communities, and because the interests of these groups are sometimes at odds, clashes erupt.

It is exactly because of these conflicts that some citizens are able to show their commitment to the community. They seek "recognition" from their fellow citizens and are even willing to risk their own safety to protect their family, country, or way of life (and, of course, to attain prestige for themselves in the process). Indeed, there seems to be an element of the human soul that longs to transcend the physical part of our being, and it is this urge that makes us discipline and suppress our bodily desires to achieve something extraordinary. This impulse motivates people to imperil themselves to attain honor.

But there is also a darker side to this passion. Those under its influence, often not constrained by laws or morality, strike out at others either from the pleasure of defeating a rival or from the sheer exhilaration of trammeling social norms.

During the years of the Cold War, ethnic and national rivalries were kept at bay by the intense ideological struggle that gripped the world, and by the discipline that the superpowers enforced on their allies. People on both sides of the Iron Curtain put aside their parochial distrust of each other in order to combat a more threatening enemy.

As Abraham Lincoln argued, a common opponent can be a powerful motive for unity. During the first fifty years of American nationhood, he explained, "the jealousy, envy, and avarice, incident to our nature, and so common to a state of peace, prosperity and conscious strength, were, for the time, in a great measure smothered and rendered inactive; while the deep rooted principle of *hate*, and the powerful motive of *revenge*, instead of being turned against each other, were directed exclusively against the British nation."

Today, when the Cold War is over and the fear of the common enemy is gone, the spirit of "hatred" and "revenge" within the former political blocs is likely to predominate.

Harvard Professor Samuel Huntington countered the end of history thesis by maintaining that cultural and religious differences would become the source of conflict in the post-Cold War era. He reasoned that Fukuyama may have been correct to assert that the foreseeable future would lack ideological conflicts such as between democracy and Marxism. But he predicted that other struggles among cultures or religions would cause international disharmony. Rather than an end of history, Huntington foresaw a clash of civilizations.

There is evidence that Fukuyama's hopes for a harmonious world were premature, or perhaps impossible. He was correct to suppose that globalization would bring prosperity on a scale unseen in times past. International competition has reduced the price of almost every commodity and service. However, free-market forces have transformed the economic landscape profoundly. While the cost of goods and services has decreased, wages have not grown, making people feel as if their careers have stagnated. Moreover, companies have moved to parts of the world where labor costs, tax burdens, and regulations are modest. Whole industries have been uprooted, and some have disappeared entirely. Technology has changed the way people live. The shopping mall, once a center of commerce, is being replaced by online businesses.

While many Americans admit that the free-market system is dynamic, many believe that it is unfair. Leaders in the Democratic Party have responded to the public's anxiety by echoing Marx's criticisms of capitalism and advocating programs that promote social justice, a term that implies moving to a socialist economy.

The economic success of the Western nations has not been uniform internationally or domestically. Some people in less developed areas of the globe see the accomplishments of the West not as an achievement, but rather as exploitation. In many places, inequality has spawned an underlying sense of grievance.

Lack of opportunity in the West has created fertile ground for recruiting terrorists. Radical groups rarely employ economic arguments when enlisting followers, but they do appeal to a sense of victimization, claiming that the Western way of life has not treated all people equally or fairly.

Terrorism has become a world-wide phenomenon. It has many roots, but it seems to be best organized by groups devoted to Islam. Whatever its sources, terrorism has sown doubt and anxiety among citizens in liberal democracies. The Internet and 24-hour news channels have prompted paranoia and fear. Scenes of devastation and carnage are almost instantaneously reported from and viewed all over the world.

Huntington could be right. In some places, clashes between ethnic and religious groups are all too prevalent. It might be a mistake to call it a clash of "civilizations," however. Most people really do want the same things in life: peace, security, personal autonomy, dignity, and prosperity. There are perhaps 2% or at most 3% of the people who would rather fight than switch. They have guns, rockets, and bombs with which they hope to destroy any semblance of rationality or sensible judgment. Sadly, it is not only numbers but also intensity that counts in political life. Opponents of liberal democracy and economic advancement seem doggedly attached to past slights and injustices; they are all-too-fond of spheres. There is grounds for thinking both Fukuyama and Huntington are right.

Ironically, the economic success of Western nations has attracted immigrants from less prosperous and unstable parts of the world seeking opportunity and security. Millions of people have entered Europe from the Middle East and Africa trying to escape the chaos and uncertainty of their homelands. Many immigrants from Latin and Central America have entered the United States seeking better lives.

The combination of economic uncertainty, immigration, and scenes of terrorism has significantly influenced voters in democratic countries. Populist-nationalist leaders, who distrust multinational organizations, disparage international trade, and oppose immigration, have been elected to office. Hungarian Prime Minister Viktor Orban called the movement "illiberal democracy," meaning that citizens will still vote and have rights, but leaders will look out for their own people first. Voters in many democratic countries have responded to calls to protect the homeland. The most glaring example is Brexit, the referendum that resulted in the United Kingdom leaving the European Union.

President Donald Trump proclaimed that international trade has brought "carnage" to America's workers. He has disparaged traditional alliances, pulled back from international agreements, and placed tariffs on many goods produced outside the United States. His "America first" policies have reshaped both foreign and domestic policy. It is not clear whether Trump's agenda will succeed or whether his successors will return to more globalist strategies. But one thing is clear 30 years after 1989: it was too soon to celebrate.

87

Donald Trump

Speech to the United Nations (2018)

Madam President, Mr. Secretary-General, world leaders, ambassadors, and distinguished delegates:

One year ago, I stood before you for the first time in this grand hall. I addressed the threats facing our world, and I presented a vision to achieve a brighter future for all of humanity.

Today, I stand before the United Nations General Assembly to share the extraordinary progress we've made. . . .

We have passed the biggest tax cuts and reforms in American history. We've started the construction of a major border wall, and we have greatly strengthened border security.

We have secured record funding for our military—$700 billion this year, and $716 billion next year. Our military will soon be more powerful than it has ever been before.

In other words, the United States is stronger, safer, and a richer country than it was when I assumed office less than two years ago.

We are standing up for America and for the American people. And we are also standing up for the world.

This is great news for our citizens and for peace-loving people everywhere. We believe that when nations respect the rights of their neighbors, and defend the interests of their people, they can better work together to secure the blessings of safety, prosperity, and peace.

Each of us here today is the emissary of a distinct culture, a rich history, and a people bound together by ties of memory, tradition, and the values that make our homelands like nowhere else on Earth.

That is why America will always choose independence and cooperation over global governance, control, and domination.

I honor the right of every nation in this room to pursue its own customs, beliefs, and traditions. The United States will not tell you how to live or work or worship.

From Remarks by President Trump to the 73rd Session of the United Nations General Assembly, September 25, 2018.

We only ask that you honor our sovereignty in return.

From Warsaw to Brussels, to Tokyo to Singapore, it has been my highest honor to represent the United States abroad. I have forged close relationships and friendships and strong partnerships with the leaders of many nations in this room, and our approach has already yielded incredible change.

With support from many countries here today, we have engaged with North Korea to replace the specter of conflict with a bold and new push for peace.

In June, I traveled to Singapore to meet face to face with North Korea's leader, Chairman Kim Jong Un.

We had highly productive conversations and meetings, and we agreed that it was in both countries' interest to pursue the denuclearization of the Korean Peninsula. Since that meeting, we have already seen a number of encouraging measures that few could have imagined only a short time ago.

The missiles and rockets are no longer flying in every direction. Nuclear testing has stopped. Some military facilities are already being dismantled. Our hostages have been released. And as promised, the remains of our fallen heroes are being returned home to lay at rest in American soil.

I would like to thank Chairman Kim for his courage and for the steps he has taken, though much work remains to be done. The sanctions will stay in place until denuclearization occurs. . . .

In the Middle East, our new approach is also yielding great strides and very historic change.

Following my trip to Saudi Arabia last year, the Gulf countries opened a new center to target terrorist financing. They are enforcing new sanctions, working with us to identify and track terrorist networks, and taking more responsibility for fighting terrorism and extremism in their own region.

The UAE, Saudi Arabia, and Qatar have pledged billions of dollars to aid the people of Syria and Yemen. And they are pursuing multiple avenues to ending Yemen's horrible, horrific civil war.

Ultimately, it is up to the nations of the region to decide what kind of future they want for themselves and their children.

For that reason, the United States is working with the Gulf Cooperation Council, Jordan, and Egypt to establish a regional strategic alliance so that Middle Eastern nations can advance prosperity, stability, and security across their home region.

Thanks to the United States military and our partnership with many of your nations, I am pleased to report that the bloodthirsty killers known as ISIS have been driven out from the territory they once held in Iraq and Syria. We will continue to work with friends and allies to deny radical Islamic terrorists any funding, territory or support, or any means of infiltrating our borders.

The ongoing tragedy in Syria is heartbreaking. Our shared goals must be the de-escalation of military conflict, along with a political solution that honors the will of the Syrian people. In this vein, we urge the United Nations-led peace process be reinvigorated. But, rest assured, the United States will respond if chemical weapons are deployed by the Assad regime.

I commend the people of Jordan and other neighboring countries for hosting refugees from this very brutal civil war.

As we see in Jordan, the most compassionate policy is to place refugees as close to their homes as possible to ease their eventual return to be part of the rebuilding process. This approach also stretches finite resources to help far more people, increasing the impact of every dollar spent.

Every solution to the humanitarian crisis in Syria must also include a strategy to address the brutal regime that has fueled and financed it: the corrupt dictatorship in Iran.

Iran's leaders sow chaos, death, and destruction. They do not respect their neighbors or borders, or the sovereign rights of nations. Instead, Iran's leaders plunder the nation's resources to enrich themselves and to spread mayhem across the Middle East and far beyond.

The Iranian people are rightly outraged that their leaders have embezzled billions of dollars from Iran's treasury, seized valuable portions of the economy, and looted the people's religious endowments, all to line their own pockets and send their proxies to wage war.

Iran's neighbors have paid a heavy toll for the [regime's] agenda of aggression and expansion. That is why so many countries in the Middle East strongly supported my decision to withdraw the United States from the horrible 2015 Iran Nuclear Deal and re-impose nuclear sanctions.

The Iran deal was a windfall for Iran's leaders. In the years since the deal was reached, Iran's military budget grew nearly 40 percent. The dictatorship used the funds to build nuclear-capable missiles, increase internal repression, finance terrorism, and fund havoc and slaughter in Syria and Yemen.

The United States has launched a campaign of economic pressure to deny the regime the funds it needs to advance its bloody agenda. Last month, we began re-imposing hard-hitting nuclear sanctions that had been lifted under the Iran deal. Additional sanctions will resume November 5th, and more will follow. And we're working with countries that import Iranian crude oil to cut their purchases substantially.

We cannot allow the world's leading sponsor of terrorism to possess the planet's most dangerous weapons. We cannot allow a regime that chants "Death to America," and that threatens Israel with annihilation, to possess the means to deliver a nuclear warhead to any city on Earth. Just can't do it.

We ask all nations to isolate Iran's regime as long as its aggression continues. And we ask all nations to support Iran's people as they struggle to reclaim their religious and righteous destiny. . . .

America's policy of principled realism means we will not be held hostage to old dogmas, discredited ideologies, and so-called experts who have been proven wrong over the years, time and time again. This is true not only in matters of peace, but in matters of prosperity.

We believe that trade must be fair and reciprocal. The United States will not be taken advantage of any longer.

For decades, the United States opened its economy—the largest, by far, on Earth—with few conditions. We allowed foreign goods from all over the world to flow freely across our borders.

Yet, other countries did not grant us fair and reciprocal access to their markets in return. Even worse, some countries abused their openness to dump their products, subsidize their goods, target our industries, and manipulate their currencies to gain unfair advantage over our country. As a result, our trade deficit ballooned to nearly $800 billion a year.

For this reason, we are systematically renegotiating broken and bad trade deals.

Last month, we announced a groundbreaking U.S.-Mexico trade agreement. And just yesterday, I stood with President Moon to announce the successful completion of the brand new U.S.-Korea trade deal. And this is just the beginning.

Many nations in this hall will agree that the world trading system is in dire need of change. For example, countries were admitted to the World Trade Organization that violate every single principle on which the organization is based. While the United States and many other nations play by the rules, these countries use government-run industrial planning and state-owned enterprises to rig the system in their favor. They engage in relentless product dumping, forced technology transfer, and the theft of intellectual property.

The United States lost over 3 million manufacturing jobs, nearly a quarter of all steel jobs, and 60,000 factories after China joined the WTO. And we have racked up $13 trillion in trade deficits over the last two decades.

But those days are over. We will no longer tolerate such abuse. We will not allow our workers to be victimized, our companies to be cheated, and our wealth to be plundered and transferred. America will never apologize for protecting its citizens.

The United States has just announced tariffs on another $200 billion in Chinese-made goods for a total, so far, of $250 billion. I have great respect and affection for my friend, President Xi, but I have made clear our trade imbalance is just not acceptable. China's market distortions and the way they deal cannot be tolerated.

As my administration has demonstrated, America will always act in our national interest.

I spoke before this body last year and warned that the U.N. Human Rights Council had become a grave embarrassment to this institution, shielding egregious human rights abusers while bashing America and its many friends.

Our Ambassador to the United Nations, Nikki Haley, laid out a clear agenda for reform, but despite reported and repeated warnings, no action at all was taken.

So the United States took the only responsible course: We withdrew from the Human Rights Council, and we will not return until real reform is enacted.

For similar reasons, the United States will provide no support in recognition to the International Criminal Court. As far as America is concerned, the ICC has no jurisdiction, no legitimacy, and no authority. The ICC claims near-universal jurisdiction over the citizens of every country, violating all principles of justice, fairness, and due process. We will never surrender America's sovereignty to an unelected, unaccountable, global bureaucracy.

America is governed by Americans. We reject the ideology of globalism, and we embrace the doctrine of patriotism.

Around the world, responsible nations must defend against threats to sovereignty not just from global governance, but also from other, new forms of coercion and domination.

In America, we believe strongly in energy security for ourselves and for our allies. We have become the largest energy producer anywhere on the face of the Earth.

The United States stands ready to export our abundant, affordable supply of oil, clean coal, and natural gas. . . .

Reliance on a single foreign supplier can leave a nation vulnerable to extortion and intimidation. That is why we congratulate European states, such as Poland, for leading the construction of a Baltic pipeline so that nations are not dependent on Russia to meet their energy needs. Germany will become totally dependent on Russian energy if it does not immediately change course.

Here in the Western Hemisphere, we are committed to maintaining our independence from the encroachment of expansionist foreign powers.

It has been the formal policy of our country since President Monroe that we reject the interference of foreign nations in this hemisphere and in our own affairs. The United States has recently strengthened our laws to better screen foreign investments in our country for national security threats, and we welcome cooperation with countries in this region and around the world that wish to do the same. You need to do it for your own protection.

The United States is also working with partners in Latin America to confront threats to sovereignty from uncontrolled migration. Tolerance for human struggling and human smuggling and trafficking is not humane. It's a horrible thing that's going on, at levels that nobody has ever seen before. It's very, very cruel.

Illegal immigration funds criminal networks, ruthless gangs, and the flow of deadly drugs. Illegal immigration exploits vulnerable populations, hurts hardworking citizens, and has produced a vicious cycle of crime, violence, and poverty. Only by upholding national borders, destroying criminal gangs, can we break this cycle and establish a real foundation for prosperity.

We recognize the right of every nation in this room to set its own immigration policy in accordance with its national interests, just as we ask other countries to respect our own right to do the same—which we are doing. That is one reason the United States will not participate in the new Global Compact on Migration. Migration should not be governed by an international body unaccountable to our own citizens.

Ultimately, the only long-term solution to the migration crisis is to help people build more hopeful futures in their home countries. Make their countries great again.

Currently, we are witnessing a human tragedy, as an example, in Venezuela. More than 2 million people have fled the anguish inflicted by the socialist Maduro regime and its Cuban sponsors.

Not long ago, Venezuela was one of the richest countries on Earth. Today, socialism has bankrupted the oil-rich nation and driven its people into abject poverty.

Virtually everywhere socialism or communism has been tried, it has produced suffering, corruption, and decay. Socialism's thirst for power leads to expansion, incursion, and oppression. All nations of the world should resist socialism and the misery that it brings to everyone.

In that spirit, we ask the nations gathered here to join us in calling for the restoration of democracy in Venezuela. Today, we are announcing additional sanctions against the repressive regime, targeting Maduro's inner circle and close advisors.

We are grateful for all the work the United Nations does around the world to help people build better lives for themselves and their families.

The United States is the world's largest giver in the world, by far, of foreign aid. But few give anything to us. That is why we are taking a hard look at U.S. foreign assistance. That will be headed up by Secretary of State Mike Pompeo. We will examine what is working, what is not working, and whether the countries who receive our dollars and our protection also have our interests at heart.

Moving forward, we are only going to give foreign aid to those who respect us and, frankly, are our friends. And we expect other countries to pay their fair share for the cost of their defense.

The United States is committed to making the United Nations more effective and accountable. I have said many times that the United Nations has unlimited potential. As part of our reform effort, I have told our negotiators that the United States will not pay more than 25 percent of the U.N.

peacekeeping budget. This will encourage other countries to step up, get involved, and also share in this very large burden.

And we are working to shift more of our funding from assessed contributions to voluntary so that we can target American resources to the programs with the best record of success.

Only when each of us does our part and contributes our share can we realize the U.N.'s highest aspirations. We must pursue peace without fear, hope without despair, and security without apology.

Looking around this hall where so much history has transpired, we think of the many before us who have come here to address the challenges of their nations and of their times. And our thoughts turn to the same question that ran through all their speeches and resolutions, through every word and every hope. It is the question of what kind of world will we leave for our children and what kind of nations they will inherit.

The dreams that fill this hall today are as diverse as the people who have stood at this podium, and as varied as the countries represented right here in this body are. It really is something. It really is great, great history. . . .

Many countries are pursuing their own unique visions, building their own hopeful futures, and chasing their own wonderful dreams of destiny, of legacy, and of a home.

The whole world is richer, humanity is better, because of this beautiful constellation of nations, each very special, each very unique, and each shining brightly in its part of the world.

In each one, we see awesome promise of a people bound together by a shared past and working toward a common future.

As for Americans, we know what kind of future we want for ourselves. We know what kind of a nation America must always be.

In America, we believe in the majesty of freedom and the dignity of the individual. We believe in self-government and the rule of law. And we prize the culture that sustains our liberty—a culture built on strong families, deep faith, and fierce independence. We celebrate our heroes, we treasure our traditions, and above all, we love our country.

Inside everyone in this great chamber today, and everyone listening all around the globe, there is the heart of a patriot that feels the same powerful love for your nation, the same intense loyalty to your homeland.

The passion that burns in the hearts of patriots and the souls of nations has inspired reform and revolution, sacrifice and selflessness, scientific breakthroughs, and magnificent works of art.

Our task is not to erase it, but to embrace it. To build with it. To draw on its ancient wisdom. And to find within it the will to make our nations greater, our regions safer, and the world better.

To unleash this incredible potential in our people, we must defend the foundations that make it all possible. Sovereign and independent nations are the only vehicle where freedom has ever survived, democracy has ever endured, or peace has ever prospered. And so we must protect our sovereignty and our cherished independence above all.

When we do, we will find new avenues for cooperation unfolding before us. We will find new passion for peacemaking rising within us. We will find new purpose, new resolve, and new spirit flourishing all around us, and making this a more beautiful world in which to live.

So together, let us choose a future of patriotism, prosperity, and pride. Let us choose peace and freedom over domination and defeat. And let us come here to this place to stand for our people and their nations, forever strong, forever sovereign, forever just, and forever thankful for the grace and the goodness and the glory of God.

Thank you. God bless you. And God bless the nations of the world. . . .

88

Joseph Cropsey

The Moral Basis of International Action (1961)

The power of nations to inflict pain, destruction, and death in warfare has been brought to such a peak that men feel themselves compelled as never before to find means for preventing that power from being used. The instruments of mutilation and devastation are tremendous and their action comprehensive to such a degree that their employment would produce effects that shock the mind, for they reach perhaps to the impairment of the human race as a whole. It is by no means easy to obtain agreement as to the essence of moral offense in general; but it is transcendently easy to obtain agreement that it would be monstrous, and if monstrous then immoral, for men to burn up the moiety of mankind and to denature the loins of those who survive. . . .

From Cropsey, "The Moral Basis of International Action," in *America Armed*, ed. Robert A. Goldwin, Rand McNally College Publishing Company, 1961. Reprinted by permission of the Public Affairs Conference Center, Kenyon College, Gambier, Ohio.

It therefore appears that each nation is by duty bound to practice a voluntary restraint, to limit its own action and power of action in the interest of some good which is not its obvious, immediate self-benefit. For the sake of fulfilling a duty to the rest of mankind, each nation should to some extent deprive itself of the means to supremacy or even of defense. As we reflect on this duty, we notice how well it corresponds with what appears as the notion of morality at large. Morality is a standard of conduct which guides men to recognize and show concern for others, and to act out of some larger motive than the convenience, safety and well-being of themselves.

The demand of morality may be said to be in the direction of deliberate self-incapacitation. So far as this is true, morality is in apparent conflict with policy, or in other words with calculation in the interest of the actor. This is admitted both by the friends of morality, who see it as moderating the brutal egotism of life, and by the cynics, who see it as the delusion by which the strong are seduced to abstain from benefiting from their strength. . . .

[T]he two moral extremes, the one of absolute duty to all men as men and the other of simple calculation in the interest of the agent, [present] these difficulties: either the moral action of the one party exposes him to ruin at the hands of an immoral antagonist (with the consequence that morality leads invariably to the triumph of evil); or the possibility of moral discrimination disappears entirely, leaving as the only criterion of action the submoral criterion of success in survival. In either case, what begins as morality ends as immorality.

With this behind us, we can set down the requirements of a moral ground for international action, military and other. And if it turns out that no moral system can without self-contradiction meet these requirements, then we may conclude that morality is irrelevant to the conduct of nations, and all is just in hate and lust. The requirements for such a moral order are these: (1) That a nation be able to abide by the rules of right conduct without harm to itself even if every other nation in the world ignore or violate them. (2) That notwithstanding the full compatibility of the moral order with survival and victory, the rule of morality not simply dissolve into the right of the stronger, that is, the criterion of success.

Beginning again, we recur to the simplest and most generally admitted notion as to the meaning of morality: morality is self-restraint. Hitherto, we have taken self-restraint to mean a voluntary holding back either from violating an abstract precept of duty or from injuring others. The implicit supposition has been that the overriding problem to which morality addresses itself is how to define the duties or rights of men, the extreme solutions to the problem being either duty apart from calculation or calculation apart from duty. But there is no need for morality to mean either the one or the other so exclusively. This becomes clear to us when we consult the normal human understanding of what conduct deserves blame and what deserves praise.

We blame people who deceive, defraud, plunder, attack, and murder; but curiously we also blame those who are vacillating, miserly, gluttonous, lewd, or craven, although it is not possible to say, for example, "gluttonous toward others." These latter defects are not primarily the sources of injury to other men. They are rather flaws of weakness, for example, the weakness of being unrestrainedly fond of some external good, or of being incapable of exercising that amount of self-control that enables a man to come to a conclusion or to suppress cruel, effete, or otherwise disgusting passions. We might note at the same time that a man overcome with the sense of duty, who plunged incontinently, that is, unrestrainedly into every situation where good needed to be done, would come under deserved censure as a dangerous meddler, especially if the only good accomplished was the salving of his conscience. There is a path between morality in the service of preservation and morality in the service of duty, abstractly considered; and that path is the one indicated by the general understanding of mankind. It follows the rule that self-restraint is not confined to the agent's acts against others but touches his character more comprehensively. . . .

Morality . . . is not intelligible as an abstract or formal principle but only as the sum of concrete characteristics, the possession of which enables the agent to deserve praise and respect. Morality without virtues is vanity.

What are those praiseworthy characteristics, and what does any of this have to do with the international action of the United States? The answer to the first will be tantamount to the answer to the second. Neither a nation nor a man can avoid shame if it is craven, heedless, self-indulgent, wanton in ease, irresolute in deliberation, wastrel in pleasure, squeamish in contest, faint in adversity. Virtue is etymologically related to manliness; but the relation is evidently more than etymological. . . .

I believe that if we test this rule of morality, which rises more or less directly out of common human experience, we will find that it meets the two conditions laid down earlier as being indispensable if the moral criterion is to be applicable to the nation's action. We are at no disadvantage if all the world but us behave brutally, foolishly, aggressively, deceitfully, and in every other way immorally. Prudence and decency demand of us that we make every effort to withstand every attempt that can be made against us; to do less would be contemptible and thus immoral. To do as much would be to work toward safety through morality. It goes without saying that morality so conceived utterly excludes those avoidable deeds of massive violence that can be defended only on the premise that success justifies everything. Certainly success is not the touchstone of morality as naturally understood, and it is not sensible to infer righteousness from survival, nor vice from failure. It is indeed possible to be respectable in defeat and contemptible in victory; but it is not possible to be respectable in defeat if defeat is the result of sloth, decadence, or a failure of nerve.

By this view, war and therefore the preparation for war are, in themselves, neither morally good nor morally bad, any more than homicide is morally good or bad. The homicide of a police officer upon a fleeing criminal is morally good, the homicide of a fleeing criminal upon a police officer morally bad. War is dreadful, and the preparation for it painful; but a theory that defines the painful as the immoral is nothing but hedonism or an encouragement to hedonism, no matter what appeals it may make to sentiment, conscience, or a show of rights. War is bad but it is not bad in the way that a supine indifference to disgrace and slavery are bad, for the latter comes from moral corruption and the former only from a fearful necessity that some men cannot, because of the vice of others, avoid.

War is bad because pain and death are bad, and death worse than pain. But we must reflect on the order of things, and recognize the difference between the death of men and the death of nations. Individuals die, but those remaining make up the loss. Cities are reduced to material chaos, but in an amazingly short time the destruction is repaired. The resurrection of a regime, however, is a thing rarely seen. The Constitution subverted, liberty disappears, and the human flotsam remaining suffer the ultimate demoralization, which is not death but subjection to the unlimited will of a master. Those who would investigate war and peace as part of the moral problem may never stray out of sight of the fact that the necessary condition for all morality is freedom, and the condition for freedom is the absolute integrity of the body politic—guaranteed by the power and willingness to make war.

It is evident that morality can retain its connection with self-restraint without collapsing into self-incapacitation. On the contrary, the demands of morality, seen in their relation to freedom and honor, are more energizing than they are paralyzing. Then the question arises whether there is anything at all that could contribute to the greatness and safety of the nation for which a justification could not be found by appealing to honor. The answer to this is surely No if the appeal to honor is a specious pretext, and as surely Yes if the appeal to honor is itself honorable. But assuming for the moment that the appeal to honor is not hypocritical, what sort of act would a nation be compelled to deny itself for purely moral reasons, contrary to its urgent interest? Is there something dishonorable, for example, in espionage? In deceitful counterintelligence? In the apprehension of a rebel by means of a ruse? In the subversion of a foreign government with which we are not at war? Not one of these questions can be answered except with knowledge of concrete circumstances. The most relevant circumstance is the character of the nation doing the deed in question, and the character of the men or nation to which it is done. . . .

Those who raise the question, Who shall judge? do so, very often, in the belief that it is self-evidently absurd for us to be judge of our own morality. In truth it is no less, and perhaps far more absurd to hope that a reliable judgment on our morality will be brought by a poll of the nations, many of which are moved by animosity and envy, and more by ignorance. . . . The teaching of morality may be reduced to this: we must do everything that needs to be done to insure the survival of ourselves, our friends, and our free principles, indulging neither ourselves nor others, avoiding sentimentality no less than brutality, and mindful that if we weakly hang back, we will ignominiously hang alone. Those who desire to see this wisdom reduced to a punched-tape program must await their translation to another, better universe; likewise those who wish to see it purged of all severity.

It will surely be objected that to imperil the human race on the point of honor is to inflate Quixotism from an eccentricity to a calamity. We must therefore try to keep separate in our minds these two principles of action: the one, that it is wrong and dishonorable weakly to submit to domination; and the second, quite different, that what deserves to be defended should be defended, and what deserves to be resisted should be resisted, but that it is not sober to make a virtue out of defense and resistance regardless of the worth of things to be defended and resisted. In other words, the appeal to honor alone is defective, and must be perfected by a showing that honor is aroused in a good cause; otherwise it is suspected of being a euphemism for truculence or ferocious obstinacy. Do we have any reason for believing that the sovietization of the world is an evil commensurate with the peril created by opposing it? that it is the menace to dignity and freedom it was earlier said to be? To answer this question fully would require a full statement of the character of communism; here we can provide only the barest intimation.

Marxism begins with materialism and ends with the homogeneity of mankind. Marxist materialism differs from traditional materialism in attaching fundamental importance to the process of production, that is, to self-preservation by means of "technology," primitive or complex. The problem of preservation is primarily a technological, not a political problem for Marx. Indeed the complete solution of the problem of preservation is radically non-political: when the means of production are commonly owned and production is made a wholly social process, politics, or ruling and being ruled, will cease among men. The aspiration of communism is a total solution of the economic problem by means that would reduce all mankind to a single classless, that is, homogeneous mass: a huge herd of sheep safely grazing. Human distinction is the source of the human problem, and therefore distinction must be terminated. The "heroes" will be "heroes of the shovel" and "heros of the loom": heroes of social production. This could be called the ultimate vulgarization of humanity, or the final indignity. We see it foreshadowed in the substitution of the shoe for the gavel in council, and the hairy chest for the clean collar in diplomacy. Because dignity is inseparable from distinction, the resistance to sovietization was said to be in the interest of human dignity.

What of freedom? Communism aims at life without the state, or without formal government. . . . The formlessness of the herd without distinction exposes it perpetually to the highest concentration of irresponsible authority—wielded for the noble end of administration, all other problems having vanished. More simply, a flock demands a shepherd.

The bias of Marxism toward matter and in opposition to form bears fruit in an unprecedented threat to human dignity and freedom. Honorable resistance to sovietization is thus more than merely honorable.

Readers may be pardoned for failing to see in the Soviet Union now a population of grazing sheep. Far from a fat and torpid flock, they are an active, patriotic, spirited community, exhilarated by their hard-won achievements, conscious of greatness and lusting for its gratifications. That they are all these things is a vindication, not a contradiction of what was said above: finding their revolution confronted by hindrances, they compel themselves to rise to formidable heights of exertion. They are in the irrational condition of heroically laboring to destroy the possibility of any future heroic labor, while congratulating themselves on their own heroism. It is not the self-contradiction but the menace in their doings that is our present concern, and how we must respond to it.

We are in the position of respecting and praising the sense of honor, and of discerning it well-developed in our enemy. We will prove his right to rule us if we do not prevent him from exercising it; and we can maintain our right to be free only by being in a position to exercise it. In plain language, to his irresistible force we must oppose an immovable obstacle. . . .

There is not one iota of preponderance on the side of the view that the activator of the great force will choose to dash it against an absolute resistance. But if he entertains any reasonable doubt that our response will be absolute and remorseless, he will have less reason to keep the peace. This means that at a certain moment we must harden ourselves to look at the beauties of peace and prepare to see in their stead a contaminated chaos peopled with human carrion. If we cannot stand this thought, we are not ready to fight and will therefore be compelled to do so—or to truckle and prostrate ourselves.

On one condition would the sacrifice of ruin not be excessive: if we triumphed and the enemy were in the end destroyed. It is absurd to say that there are no victors in war. The one who survives in freedom is the victor; the one who must humble himself and surrender his ways and institutions at the dictate of his enemy is vanquished. . . .

Perhaps it will be said that there can be no victory where there are no survivors. . . . Then there must not be a next war. To argue so is plausible, but . . . inconclusive, for the argument tells us nothing about the form in which the cost of avoiding war must be paid. It might be that we pay for peace by abject surrender. That is unthinkable. It is unthinkable because the argument in favor of doing so is based upon the premise that, morally and politically, nothing matters—nothing, that is, except survival. The proper name for this position is not philanthropic morality but nihilism without intestines. The fortified species of nihilism also argues that nothing matters—except success. We have lost contact with the human spirit if we can no longer sense the repulsiveness of nihilism and the depravity of it in its emasculated form. If nothing matters, then human life does not matter. (Who would mourn it?) If anything matters, it is the decency of life and the possible self-respect of men. Still, where there is life there is hope for some amendment of any evil. We agree, and recommend the thought to our enemy; it deserves his consideration no less than ours. In brief, there is one cost of avoiding war which is more than we can afford: subhuman self-abasement.

Then we must pay for peace by making such a preparation for war that apprehensions for the safety of mankind will for once begin to influence the calculations of the enemy. If he is beyond or beneath a care for man's preservation, he is the manifest enemy of the race, fit to be hedged in or destroyed, certainly requiring to be diligently guarded against. If he is capable of such a care, then we need not, as truly we ought not assume the whole burden of providence. . . .

We seem to have concluded that the dictate of morality coincides with the interest of men and nations whose purposes are compatible with freedom and high-mindedness. This conclusion was the one intended.

In the course of our attempt to clarify the moral basis of international action, we have been led to take up two extreme but not unrepresentative examples of moral doctrine and a third which avoids the extremes. To simplify, the three could be said to turn, respectively, on Duty, Rights, and Honor. The conclusion has been that the first two are, for the purposes of guiding international action, imperfect, and the third is to be preferred. Supposing this for the moment to be true, of what practical value is the conclusion? Is it possible for a nation simply to adopt the moral principle of its choice for application to its international business? There is reason to doubt that this can be done with complete ease or freedom. The reason is that each nation is given its character by the elaborate set of moral judgments already embodied in its system of laws and practices. Implicit in the laws and customs is a notion of what action is just, what is proper and decent, what is worthy of esteem—in brief, of morality. . . . If all our notions of tolerable conduct are fashioned by one system of judgments, can we act externally on another?

The problem is made especially severe by the kinship that exists between our general moral outlook as a community and the two moral dispensations described above as the "extremes." When we go back to the Declaration of Independence, for example, we read of man's inalienable rights—which are the same natural rights that we noticed earlier in the discussion—all derivative from the natural right of all men to self-preservation. The Declaration enumerates the inalienable rights to life, liberty, and the pursuit of happiness; the Constitution speaks of life, liberty, and property. The replacement made by the Constitution is not of the nature of a revision but a clarification: the rights to life, liberty, and property are inseparably connected with happiness, in our moral and political understanding as a nation. It is only when each man is guaranteed in his person that his property is secure, and only when he is safeguarded in his property that his person is inviolate. Our political system makes provision for translating those natural rights into a meaningful ground of civil life by wedding the institutions of capitalism to those of constitutional government. Political freedom is possible on various bases; in the Western world it exists on the foundation of certain economic institutions, and the concurrence of capitalism and modern democracy is by no means a coincidence. Liberty and prosperity, the aims of our order, are provided for at one and the same time by a principle that authorizes the individuals to act in their own behalf under the protection of a government to whose rule they give their consent so long as it defends them in their freedom to act in their own behalf. The essence of acting in one's own behalf is calculation. This is the basis for the remark made at the head of this paragraph, to the effect that deep in our own moral and political foundations there is a kinship with the extreme moral principle named after "Rights," leading to undiluted calculation.

But the assertion was also made that as a nation we have an affinity for the opposite moral extreme as well, the one called by the name of "absolute Duty." Long ago, the reduction of morality to the rules of calculation was seen to be open to various objections. One line of objection was to the effect that when morality collapses into mere calculation, patriotism or love of the common good tends to languish or to disappear. This view when broadened or exaggerated becomes the criticism that, under the reign of private calculation or institutionalized egotism, care for the absolute worth or dignity of man as man vanishes, and life deteriorates accordingly in the moral respect. Those who hold this view feel a need to oppose "human rights" to "property rights." The objection on behalf of patriotism or civic virtue found a certain expression in the yearning for republican, agrarian simplicity often voiced in our earlier history. The criticism on behalf of man as man is more characteristic of the reforming or Liberal tendency as it now is among us. What began as solicitude for a sort of virtue that can become patriotism has been replaced by a solicitude for humanity or Society, a care that need not eventuate in patriotism.

Thus our moral life as a nation vibrates between the poles of calculation and a radicalized alternative to it, the former polarizing on Property, the latter on hostility to it and on radical, undiscriminating Equality. The former is at the heart of our national conservatism, the latter epitomizes contemporary Liberalism. Neither . . . pays heed above all to honor, the sober mean somewhere between calculation and duty.

There is indeed a lack of perfect congruity between our ruling moral predilections and the preferred moral basis of international action. But if we must act on the strength of what we are rather than what we might wish to be, there is little doubt as to the course we ought to follow. One of the two poles of our moral world stands as an encouragement to men to love their theory of homogeneous mankind more than they love their country and their countrymen, where the demands of the two come in competition. The other pole, grounded on the perhaps low but surely solid principle of calculation, is not out of contact with the intermediate moral ground of decent self-regard or honor. Husbanding our strength, gathering our allies, and preparing to avoid the supreme disaster of servility and disgrace, we at least avoid the imprudence of opposing armed brutality with impotent dogma. . . . Under the circumstances, we may allow ourselves to be led by calculation where perhaps we cannot be taught to soar by honor.

We began by thinking of man's duty to mankind. Reflecting on morality in its connection with the deeds of nations, we could not avoid the themes of honor and nobility, or more largely of human excellence. Human excellence, as it finds its expression among the masses of men ranked in their nations, is called civilization. Whatever reminds us of civilization reminds us at the same time of our duty to civilization, which means in practice to civilized men. What begins as a reflection on duty to man ends, under the influence of a glimpse at human superiority, as a reflection on duty to civilized man and to civilized nations. The way to discharge our duty to civilization is to sustain it where it exists before trying to inspire it where it never has been. Upon this point, remote from doctrinairism, the morality of calculation and the morality of honor come within sight of one another. The resulting gain in strategic competence brings them within earshot of one another. We must not despair if they never join hands.

Chapter VIII

Liberty and Equality

The two dominant principles of the American regime are liberty and equality. But what do they mean? Are they unqualified goods or do they require limitation? Are they mutually reinforcing, or are they at odds with one another? When the Supreme Court interprets and applies the Bill of Rights and the Fourteenth Amendment, it explores the meaning of these two principles.

The First Amendment to the Constitution clearly states that "Congress shall make no law respecting an establishment of religion, or prohibiting the free exercise thereof; or abridging the freedom of speech . . . ." Thus any restrictions on the freedom of speech or the free exercise of religion are immediately suspect under our constitutional system. In spite of the explicit and seemingly unambiguous character of these prohibitions, government does in fact regulate both speech and religious activity. Shouting "fire!" in a crowded theater is not held to be constitutionally protected speech, nor are all forms of religious practice protected against government regulation. Three contemporary cases demonstrate the difficulty of determining where to draw the line between the power of government to regulate in the name of the health, safety, and morals of the community and the liberty of individuals to express themselves and worship as they choose.

The first case in our readings, *United States v. Stevens*, involves the constitutionality of a statute that criminalized the creation, sale, or possession of certain depictions of animal cruelty. The law arose from Congress' desire to ban "crush videos," films in which small animals are crushed under the heel of a woman's shoe; however, in *Stevens*, the defendant was charged with the creation and distribution of dog fighting videos. Does the government have a legitimate interest in regulating such videos or does the First Amendment protect such "speech" (understood broadly as expressive conduct)? The majority claims that this particular regulation is overly broad and might prohibit speech that deserves protection under the First Amendment. However, the lone dissenter, Justice Samuel Alito, argues that depictions of animal cruelty do not rise to the level of protected speech, and that the statute as applied is not in conflict with the Constitution. How should we approach the issue of determining what sort of speech is worthy of protection and what kinds of speech deserve little or no protection against government regulation?

Whereas the Court has been willing to grant freedom of speech very broad protections, it has often interpreted the free exercise clause in a way that allows the government to regulate or prohibit certain religious practices. In *Oregon v. Smith* the Court upholds the right of a state to deny unemployment insurance to two individuals who were fired from their jobs for illegally using peyote during a religious ritual. Writing for the majority, Justice Antonin Scalia argues that the First Amendment does not render invalid "a neutral, generally applicable law," even if that law may hinder some religious practices. Justice Sandra Day O'Connor agrees that in this case the state interest in regulating drug use outweighs the free exercise rights of the individual, but she argues that Justice Scalia gives too much latitude to government regulation. She contends that the First Amendment requires that the Court must always take into account both the government's interest in regulation and the effect of any regulation on the rights explicitly protected by the Constitution. If the First Amendment does not limit the powers the government might otherwise legitimately exercise, it becomes meaningless.

In *Burwell v. Hobby Lobby*, the Supreme Court decided a dispute between the Green family, which owns Hobby Lobby, and the Department of Health and Human Services (HHS). Under HHS rules, Hobby Lobby was required to purchase health insurance plans for its employees; yet the company's owners insisted that they could not comply with the administrative regulations, because they had a conscientious objection to purchasing insurance that provided coverage for abortifacients. The Supreme Court sided with the Greens, but based its decision not on the First Amendment, but on the Religious Freedom Restoration Act (RFRA). Congress enacted RFRA in 1993 in an attempt to push back against the Court's holding in *Smith*. Whereas in *Smith*, the Court held that neutral and generally applicable laws did not violate the free exercise clause, RFRA asserts that even neutral and generally applicable laws may hinder the free exercise of religion. As a result, it requires the federal courts to strike down any federal law that "substantially burden[s] a person's free exercise of religion" unless the government can show first, that the law promotes "a compelling governmental interest" and second, that the law "is the least restrictive means of furthering" that interest. In his majority opinion, Justice Samuel Alito assumes that the government has a compelling interest in ensuring women are provided with contraceptive coverage, but insists that the HHS rule was not the least restrictive means for reaching that goal. However, Justice Ruth Bader Ginsburg's dissent argues that the Supreme Court has allowed businesses to ignore any government regulation "they judge incompatible with their sincerely held religious beliefs" and worries that the majority has failed adequately to consider the "disadvantages that religion-based opt-outs impose on" Hobby Lobby's employees.

Perhaps the most controversial issue concerning the definition and limits of liberty in recent years has been the issue of abortion.

Both the "pro-life" and the "pro-choice" camps consider themselves to be the defenders of individual rights. As suggested by the name each camp has chosen for itself, the dispute comes down to a disagreement over how to settle the competition between claims of a right to life and claims of a right to liberty (i.e. choice). Pro-lifers appeal to the rights of the unborn child while supporters of legalized abortion appeal to the right of a woman to control her own body. The Supreme Court has handed down two important cases that have determined how far a state may go in regulating or banning abortion. In both *Roe v. Wade* and *Planned Parenthood of Southeastern Pennsylvania v. Casey*, the Court has insisted that it must strike a balance between two extreme positions and has called on the nation as a whole to accept the compromise it proposes.

In *Roe v. Wade* (1973) Justice Harry Blackmun acknowledges the need to take into account both the mother's "right to privacy" and the state's "interests in safeguarding health, in maintaining medical standards, and in protecting potential life." His majority opinion nevertheless posits the "Trimester Framework," which severely restricts a state's right to regulate abortion. Under this framework, a state may not regulate abortion either to protect "potential life" or out of concern for medical safety in the first trimester of pregnancy. In the second trimester, the state may impose regulations in order to guarantee medical safety. Finally, at the point of viability (when a prematurely born infant could survive outside the womb; about 28 weeks of pregnancy in 1973), the state may regulate both to promote medical safety and out of concern for protecting "potential life." This structure is based upon Blackmun's understanding of the point in pregnancy when an abortion becomes more dangerous than childbirth and of the point of viability, when the Court recognizes that the potential for "meaningful human life" should allow a state to protect the child.

The opinion of the Court in *Roe* has led to confusion and controversy over the extent of permissible state regulation of abortion. In *Planned Parenthood v. Casey* (1992), the liberal wing of the Court, including Blackmun, argues that any restrictions on abortion must be subject to strict scrutiny. On the other side, Chief Justice William Rehnquist, alongside Justices Antonin Scalia, Clarence Thomas, and Byron White insist that *Roe* was wrongly decided and should be overturned. The plurality opinion, authored by Justices Sandra Day O'Connor, Anthony Kennedy, and David Souter, reaffirms what it calls the "central holding" of *Roe*, but also abandons the Trimester Framework and ultimately permits states greater leeway in regulating abortion. These three justices propose a new test, under which the state's legitimate interest in "potential life" allows it to regulate abortion prior to viability (between 23 and 24 weeks of pregnancy in 1992), so long as it does not impose an "undue burden" on a woman; after viability, the state may impose more substantial regulations and may even prohibit abortion, so long as its law has a life or health exception. The plurality are not willing to judge particular cases on the basis of an unqualified right of the mother or unquestioned deference to a state's concern for protecting life. Instead, they see a need for the Court to define both the extent of powers and the limits of rights in an effort to promote compromise. For them, the doctrine of individual rights does not require or even allow an absolutist interpretation. Is the Court correct in its insistence that both individual rights and state power to protect life must recognize certain limitations? Do constitutional principles require both the pro-life and pro-choice camps to abandon their adherence to absolute principles of life and choice?

In *Obergefell v. Hodges* the Supreme Court struck down all state prohibitions on same sex marriage. The Court relied primarily on the Fourteenth Amendment's due process clause, which prevents the government from depriving individuals of liberty without due process of law, but also referenced the equal protection clause, which prevents a state from denying an individual the equal protection of the law. Justice Kennedy's majority opinion argues that marriage is an important element of individual liberty and autonomy. Thus, he argues that although "limitation of marriage to opposite-sex couples may long have seemed natural and just" the Court should guarantee the right of homosexual couples to marry in order to protect their dignity. In contrast, Justice Alito's dissenting opinion insists that the Constitution does not force the states either to allow or prevent same sex marriage; instead, it leaves that decision to the representatives elected by the people of each state. In contrast to the majority, which posited that the decision to marry reflected an individual's dignity and autonomy, Alito argues that marriage must be understood as a social structure ordered toward procreation. Thus, we see that the majority and dissent reached differing conclusions in part because of how they understand marriage. Where Kennedy believes that a state ban on same sex marriage harms the dignity of the individual, Alito suggests that it is not appropriate to focus on individuals, because marriage has to do with more than one person: it involves two adults and the children they produce together.

In contrast to cases dealing with abortion and marriage, which typically emphasize the liberty protected by the Fourteenth Amendment, racial discrimination cases have been understood almost exclusively in terms of the Fourteenth Amendment's equal protection clause. In *Plessy v. Ferguson* the Court determined that the constitutional guarantee of "the equal protection of the laws" did not prevent state legislatures from instituting legal segregation. The only requirement was that separate accommodations be equal. (In practice, even this limited nod toward equality was largely ignored for many years, as many accommodations were separate, but unequal.) Thus, the Court ruled that equality had a very limited meaning. In his dissent in *Plessy v. Ferguson* Justice John Marshall Harlan argued that the Constitution and the laws should be color blind and that the Constitution's promise of equality should guarantee equality of opportunity. He would permit neither a color consciousness that justifies legal segregation nor a color consciousness that guarantees equality of result by instituting what is now sometimes called "benign discrimination."

It was not until 1954 and the decision in *Brown v. Board of Education* that the "separate but equal" doctrine was overturned. But the *Brown* decision raised new questions about the meaning of equality. Not only did the Court say that the state could not impose distinctions based on race, the Court also called into question the legitimacy of any policy that resulted in inequalities between the races. Segregation was wrong, according to the Court, because it produced feelings of inferiority and did irremediable damage to the hearts and minds of black children. But can the elimination of feelings of inferiority be the goal of the Court, or should the Court limit itself to preventing legally sanctioned inequalities? Or, in more familiar terms, is the goal of the Constitution equal opportunity or equal outcome?

Another argument against racial discrimination is found in *Bolling v. Sharpe*, a companion case to *Brown*, which challenged the constitutionality of school segregation in the District of Columbia. Because the District of Columbia is not a state, the equal protection clause of the Fourteenth Amendment does not apply to it. Thus, whereas in its other segregation cases the Court based its judgment on the principle of equality, in *Bolling* the Court relied on the principle of liberty contained in the due process clause of the Fifth Amendment. Chief Justice Earl Warren argued that policies based on racial discrimination are arbitrary and therefore an infringement of the liberty of individuals. Arbitrary government action is inconsistent with the constitutional guarantee that liberty cannot be denied without due process of law. Are the arguments of *Brown* and *Bolling* consistent with each other? Since the Fourteenth Amendment, like the Fifth Amendment, provides guarantees against a deprivation of liberty without due process of law, could the Court have relied solely on the principles of *Bolling* in deciding both cases?

The distinction raised by Justice Harlan, between equality of opportunity and equality of result, is a key component of the Court's decision in *Grutter v. Bollinger*. In *Grutter*, the Court ruled on the constitutionality of the University of Michigan Law School's use of race in admissions decisions. Under its affirmative action program, the state law school takes account of applicants' race in order to admit a diverse cohort of students. Justice O'Connor's majority opinion insists that although race-based classification should always be suspect, the school nevertheless has a compelling interest in admitting a diverse student body. Deferring to the school's judgment that its educational program will be strengthened if it encourages the expression of diverse viewpoints by admitting a "critical mass" of minority races, she upholds the admissions program against an equal protection challenge. The dissent argues, however, that her opinion ignores any constitutional principles that might limit affirmative action in the present or future. More troubling, from the dissenters' point of view, is the fact that they believe the school is using its program as a means of "careful race based planning," which violates basic American commitments to equal treatment regardless of race or ethnicity.

In line with this debate over equality of opportunity and equality of result, Eugene McCarthy argues that the goal of many current reforms is to guarantee equality itself. Limitations on campaign contributions, for example, are "attempts to equalize the non-voting influence on candidates." Further results of the emphasis on equality, he argues, would include such guarantees as a college diploma to all. He finds this "security of equalization" degrading to the human personality. Kurt Vonnegut depicts the horrors of an egalitarian society where outstanding individuals are handicapped in order that they be made equal to everybody else. The radical egalitarianism McCarthy and Vonnegut criticize has its counterpart in the belief in absolute freedom; a desire for equal results, like a desire for absolute freedom, stems from a leveling of distinctions between higher and lower.

Thomas Jefferson, in stark contrast, sees the importance of distinguishing between higher and lower and proposes a means of ameliorating the apparent tensions between freedom and equality. He defends equality as the condition for the emergence of a natural aristocracy. In free elections, citizens will elevate men of uncommon virtue and ability to public office. But a system of public education is necessary to prepare people to select the natural aristocracy and to prepare the natural aristocracy for its tasks. From the free schools in each community, the best students would be selected for further education at district schools, and the best selected from these to attend a university. Public education, like free elections, would separate the wheat from the chaff. Thus, Jefferson defends the freedom of the best and most talented citizens to rise, while also insisting that the government plays a role in promoting a certain level of equality among its citizens.

Tocqueville suggests reasons why Jefferson's scheme for education is not likely to be actualized in America. Equality, he says, produces men who envy excellence rather than men who wish to elevate the most excellent among them. Moreover, in equal social conditions, there is a universal competition for the goods of life; consequently, there is much ambition to rise without any hope of rising very far. Thus, he teaches that the emergence of a natural aristocracy is unlikely in the United States. The greatest danger for America, Tocqueville believes, comes from a failure to allow those who are naturally best and most talented to rise. The United States is threatened less by the potential boldness and tenacity of a natural aristocracy than from the mediocrity that may come about in the absence of a natural aristocracy. Therefore it would be beneficial, he concludes, if the community were from time to time exposed to matters of difficulty and danger "in order to raise ambition and give it a field of action." The freedom and equality of every citizen, he suggests, may only be sustained if they are defended by the free actions of very unequal statesmen.

89

United States v. Stevens (2010)

Justice Roberts delivered the opinion of the Court, [in which Justices Stevens, Scalia, Kennedy, Thomas, Ginsburg, Breyer, and Sotomayor joined].

Congress enacted 18 U. S. C. §48 to criminalize the commercial creation, sale, or possession of certain depictions of animal cruelty. The statute does not address underlying acts harmful to animals, but only portrayals of such conduct. The question presented is whether the prohibition in the statute is consistent with the freedom of speech guaranteed by the First Amendment.

Section 48 establishes a criminal penalty of up to five years in prison for anyone who knowingly "creates, sells, or possesses a depiction of animal cruelty," if done "for commercial gain" in interstate or foreign commerce. A depiction of "animal cruelty" is defined as one "in which a living animal is intentionally maimed, mutilated, tortured, wounded, or killed," if that conduct violates federal or state law where "the creation, sale, or possession takes place." In what is referred to as the "exceptions clause," the law exempts from prohibition any depiction "that has serious religious, political, scientific, educational, journalistic, historical, or artistic value."

The legislative background of §48 focused primarily on the interstate market for "crush videos." According to the House Committee Report on the bill, such videos feature the intentional torture and killing of helpless animals, including cats, dogs, monkeys, mice, and hamsters. Crush videos often depict women slowly crushing animals to death "with their bare feet or while wearing high heeled shoes," sometimes while "talking to the animals in a kind of dominatrix patter" over "[t]he cries and squeals of the animals, obviously in great pain." Apparently these depictions "appeal to persons with a very specific sexual fetish who find them sexually arousing or otherwise exciting." The acts depicted in crush videos are typically prohibited by the animal cruelty laws enacted by all 50 States and the District of Columbia. But crush videos rarely disclose the participants' identities, inhibiting prosecution of the underlying conduct.

From *United States v. Stevens*, 559 U.S. 460 (2010).

This case, however, involves an application of §48 to depictions of animal fighting. . . . Respondent Robert J. Stevens ran a business, "Dogs of Velvet and Steel," and an associated Web site, through which he sold videos of pit bulls engaging in dogfights and attacking other animals. Among these videos were Japan Pit Fights and Pick-A-Winna: A Pit Bull Documentary, which include contemporary footage of dogfights in Japan (where such conduct is allegedly legal) as well as footage of American dogfights from the 1960's and 1970's. A third video, Catch Dogs and Country Living, depicts the use of pit bulls to hunt wild boar, as well as a "gruesome" scene of a pit bull attacking a domestic farm pig. On the basis of these videos, Stevens was indicted on three counts of violating §48. . . .

The Government's primary submission is that §48 necessarily complies with the Constitution because the banned depictions of animal cruelty, as a class, are categorically unprotected by the First Amendment. We disagree.

The First Amendment provides that "Congress shall make no law . . . abridging the freedom of speech." "[A]s a general matter, the First Amendment means that government has no power to restrict expression because of its message, its ideas, its subject matter, or its content." Section 48 explicitly regulates expression based on content: The statute restricts "visual [and] auditory depiction[s]," such as photographs, videos, or sound recordings, depending on whether they depict conduct in which a living animal is intentionally harmed. As such, §48 is " 'presumptively invalid,' and the Government bears the burden to rebut that presumption."

"From 1791 to the present," however, the First Amendment has "permitted restrictions upon the content of speech in a few limited areas," and has never "include[d] a freedom to disregard these traditional limitations." These "historic and traditional categories long familiar to the bar"—including obscenity, defamation, fraud, incitement, and speech integral to criminal conduct—are "well-defined and narrowly limited classes of speech, the prevention and punishment of which have never been thought to raise any Constitutional problem."

The Government argues that "depictions of animal cruelty" should be added to the list. It contends that depictions of "illegal acts of animal cruelty" that are "made, sold, or possessed for commercial gain" necessarily "lack expressive value," and may accordingly "be regulated as *unprotected* speech." . . .

As the Government correctly notes, this Court has often described historically unprotected categories of speech as being "of such slight social value as a step to truth that any benefit that may be derived from them is clearly outweighed by the social interest in order and morality." In *New York v. Ferber* (1982), we noted that within these categories of unprotected speech, "the evil to be restricted so overwhelmingly outweighs the expressive interests, if any, at stake, that no process of case-by-case adjudication is required," because "the balance of competing interests is clearly struck." The Government derives its proposed test from these descriptions in our precedents.

But such descriptions are just that—descriptive. They do not set forth a test that may be applied as a general matter to permit the Government to imprison any speaker so long as his speech is deemed valueless or unnecessary, or so long as an ad hoc calculus of costs and benefits tilts in a statute's favor. . . .

Our decisions . . . cannot be taken as establishing a freewheeling authority to declare new categories of speech outside the scope of the First Amendment. Maybe there are some categories of speech that have been historically unprotected, but have not yet been specifically identified or discussed as such in our case law. But if so, there is no evidence that "depictions of animal cruelty" is among them. We need not foreclose the future recognition of such additional categories to reject the Government's highly manipulable balancing test as a means of identifying them.

Because we decline to carve out from the First Amendment any novel exception for §48, we review Stevens's First Amendment challenge under our existing doctrine. . . .

In the First Amendment context . . . this Court recognizes [that] a law may be invalidated as overbroad if "a substantial number of its applications are unconstitutional, judged in relation to the statute's plainly legitimate sweep." Stevens argues that §48 applies to common depictions of ordinary and lawful activities, and that these depictions constitute the vast majority of materials subject to the statute. The Government makes no effort to defend such a broad ban as constitutional. Instead, the Government's entire defense of §48 rests on interpreting the statute as narrowly limited to specific types of "extreme" material. As the parties have presented the issue, therefore, the constitutionality of §48 hinges on how broadly it is construed. It is to that question that we now turn. . . .

We read §48 to create a criminal prohibition of alarming breadth. To begin with, the text of the statute's ban on a "depiction of animal cruelty" nowhere requires that the depicted conduct be cruel. That text applies to "any . . . depiction" in which "a living animal is intentionally maimed, mutilated, tortured, wounded, or killed." §48(c)(1). "[M]aimed, mutilated, [and] tortured" convey cruelty, but "wounded" or "killed" do not suggest any such limitation. . . .

While not requiring cruelty, §48 does require that the depicted conduct be "illegal." But this requirement does not limit §48 along the lines the Government suggests. There are myriad federal and state laws concerning the proper treatment of animals, but many of them are not designed to guard against animal cruelty. Protections of endangered species, for example, restrict even the humane "wound[ing] or kill[ing]" of "living animal[s]."

Livestock regulations are often designed to protect the health of human beings, and hunting and fishing rules (seasons, licensure, bag limits, weight requirements) can be designed to raise revenue, preserve animal populations, or prevent accidents. The text of §48(c) draws no distinction based on the reason the intentional killing of an animal is made illegal, and includes, for example, the humane slaughter of a stolen cow. . . .

What is more, the application of §48 to depictions of illegal conduct extends to conduct that is illegal in only a single jurisdiction. Under subsection (c)(1), the depicted conduct need only be illegal in "the State in which the creation, sale, or possession takes place, regardless of whether the . . . wounding . . . or killing took place in [that] State." A depiction of entirely lawful conduct runs afoul of the ban if that depiction later finds its way into another State where the same conduct is unlawful. This provision greatly expands the scope of §48, because although there may be "a broad societal consensus" against cruelty to animals, there is substantial disagreement on what types of conduct are properly regarded as cruel. Both views about cruelty to animals and regulations having no connection to cruelty vary widely from place to place. . . .

Those seeking to comply with the law thus face a bewildering maze of regulations from at least 56 separate jurisdictions. . . . Missouri allows the "canned" hunting of ungulates held in captivity, but Montana restricts such hunting to certain bird species. The sharp-tailed grouse may be hunted in Idaho, but not in Washington.

The only thing standing between defendants who sell such depictions and five years in federal prison—other than the mercy of a prosecutor—is the statute's exceptions clause. Subsection (b) exempts from prohibition "any depiction that has serious religious, political, scientific, educational, journalistic, historical, or artistic value." The Government argues that this clause substantially narrows the statute's reach: News reports about animal cruelty have "journalistic" value; pictures of bullfights in Spain have "historical" value; and instructional hunting videos have "educational" value. Thus, the Government argues, §48 reaches only crush videos, depictions of animal fighting (other than Spanish bullfighting, and perhaps other depictions of "extreme acts of animal cruelty."

The Government's attempt to narrow the statutory ban, however, requires an unrealistically broad reading of the exceptions clause. . . .

When this legislation was enacted, the Executive Branch announced that it would interpret §48 as covering only depictions "of wanton cruelty to animals designed to appeal to a prurient interest in sex." See Statement by President William J. Clinton. No one suggests that the videos in this case fit that description. The Government's assurance that it will apply §48 far more restrictively than its language provides is pertinent only as an implicit acknowledgment of the potential constitutional problems with a more natural reading. . . .

Our construction of §48 decides the constitutional question; the Government makes no effort to defend the constitutionality of §48 as applied beyond crush videos and depictions of animal fighting. It argues that those particular depictions are intrinsically related to criminal conduct or are analogous to obscenity (if not themselves obscene), and that the ban on such speech is narrowly tailored to reinforce restrictions on the underlying conduct, prevent additional crime arising from the depictions, or safeguard public mores. But the Government nowhere attempts to extend these arguments to depictions of any other activities—depictions that are presumptively protected by the First Amendment but that remain subject to the criminal sanctions of §48.

Nor does the Government seriously contest that the presumptively impermissible applications of §48 (properly construed) far outnumber any permissible ones. However "growing" and "lucrative" the markets for crush videos and dogfighting depictions might be, they are dwarfed by the market for other depictions, such as hunting magazines and videos, that we have determined to be within the scope of §48. We therefore need not and do not decide whether a statute limited to crush videos or other depictions of extreme animal cruelty would be constitutional. We hold only that §48 is not so limited but is instead substantially overbroad, and therefore invalid under the First Amendment.

The judgment of the United States Court of Appeals for the Third Circuit is affirmed.

It is so ordered.

Justice Alito, dissenting.

The Court strikes down in its entirety a valuable statute, that was enacted not to suppress speech, but to prevent horrific acts of animal cruelty—in particular, the creation and commercial exploitation of "crush videos," a form of depraved entertainment that has no social value. The Court's approach, which has the practical effect of legalizing the sale of such videos and is thus likely to spur a resumption of their production, is unwarranted. Respondent was convicted under §48 for selling videos depicting dogfights. On appeal, he argued, among other things, that §48 is unconstitutional as applied to the facts of this case, and he highlighted features of those videos that might distinguish them from other dogfight videos brought to our attention. The Court of Appeals— incorrectly, in my view—declined to decide whether §48 is unconstitutional as applied to respondent's videos and instead reached out to hold that the statute is facially invalid. Today's decision does not endorse the Court of Appeals' reasoning, but it nevertheless strikes down §48 using what has been aptly termed the "strong medicine" of the overbreadth doctrine.

Instead of applying the doctrine of overbreadth, I would vacate the decision below and instruct the Court of Appeals on remand to decide whether the videos that respondent sold are constitutionally protected. If the question of overbreadth is to be decided, however, I do not think the present record supports the Court's conclusion that §48 bans a substantial quantity of protected speech. . . .

The overbreadth doctrine "strike[s] a balance between competing social costs." Specifically, the doctrine seeks to balance the "harmful effects" of "invalidating a law that in some of its applications is perfectly constitutional" against the possibility that "the threat of enforcement of an overbroad law [will] dete[r] people from engaging in constitutionally protected speech." "In order to maintain an appropriate balance, we have vigorously enforced the requirement that a statute's overbreadth be substantial, not only in an absolute sense, but also relative to the statute's plainly legitimate sweep." . . .

In holding that §48 violates the overbreadth rule, the Court declines to decide whether, as the Government maintains, §48 is constitutional as applied to two broad categories of depictions that exist in the real world: crush videos and depictions of deadly animal fights. Instead, the Court tacitly assumes for the sake of argument that §48 is valid as applied to these depictions, but the Court concludes that §48 reaches too much protected speech to survive. The Court relies primarily on depictions of hunters killing or wounding game and depictions of animals being slaughtered for food. I address the Court's examples below. . . .

The Court's interpretation is seriously flawed. "When a federal court is dealing with a federal statute challenged as overbroad, it should, of course, construe the statute to avoid constitutional problems, if the statute is subject to such a limiting construction." ("[T]o the extent the statutory text alone is unclear, our duty to avoid constitutional objections makes it especially appropriate to look beyond the text in order to ascertain the intent of its drafters").

Applying this canon, I would hold that §48 does not apply to depictions of hunting. . . .

I do not have the slightest doubt that Congress, in enacting §48, had no intention of restricting the creation, sale, or possession of depictions of hunting. . . .

Although the Court's overbreadth analysis rests primarily on the proposition that §48 substantially restricts the sale and possession of hunting depictions, the Court cites a few additional examples, including depictions of methods of slaughter and the docking of the tails of dairy cows. . . .

Such examples do not show that the statute is substantially overbroad, for two reasons. First, as explained above, §48 can reasonably be construed to apply only to depictions involving acts of animal cruelty as defined by applicable state or federal law, and anti-cruelty laws do not ban the sorts of acts depicted in the Court's hypotheticals. . . . Second, nothing in the record suggests that any one has ever created, sold, or possessed for sale a depiction of the slaughter of food animals or of the docking of the tails of dairy cows that would not easily qualify under the exception set out in §48(b). Depictions created to show proper methods of slaughter or tail-docking would presumably have serious "educational" value, and depictions created to focus attention on methods thought to be inhumane or otherwise objectionable would presumably have either serious "educational" or "journalistic" value or both. In short, the Court's examples of depictions involving the docking of tails and humane slaughter do not show that §48 suffers from any overbreadth, much less substantial overbreadth. . . .

As the Court of Appeals recognized, "the primary conduct that Congress sought to address through its passage [of §48] was the creation, sale, or possession of 'crush videos.' A sample crush video, which has been lodged with the Clerk, records the following event:

"[A] kitten, secured to the ground, watches and shrieks in pain as a woman thrusts her high-heeled shoe into its body, slams her heel into the kitten's eye socket and mouth loudly fracturing its skull, and stomps repeatedly on the animal's head. The kitten hemorrhages blood, screams blindly in pain, and is ultimately left dead in a moist pile of blood-soaked hair and bone."

It is undisputed that the conduct depicted in crush videos may constitutionally be prohibited. All 50 States and the District of Columbia have enacted statutes prohibiting animal cruelty. But before the enactment of §48, the underlying conduct depicted in crush videos was nearly impossible to prosecute. These videos, which "often appeal to persons with a very specific sexual fetish," were made in secret, generally without a live audience, and "the faces of the women inflicting the torture in the material often were not shown, nor could the location of the place where the cruelty was being inflicted or the date of the activity be ascertained from the depiction." Thus, law enforcement authorities often were not able to identify the parties responsible for the torture. . . .

In light of the practical problems thwarting the prosecution of the creators of crush videos under state animal cruelty laws, Congress concluded that the only effective way of stopping the underlying criminal conduct was to prohibit the commercial exploitation of the videos of that conduct. And Congress' strategy appears to have been vindicated. We are told that "[b]y 2007, sponsors of §48 declared the crush video industry dead. Even overseas Websites shut down in the wake of §48. Now, after the Third Circuit's decision [facially invalidating the statute], crush videos are already back online."

The First Amendment protects freedom of speech, but it most certainly does not protect violent criminal conduct, even if engaged in for expressive purposes. Crush videos present a highly unusual free speech issue because they are so closely linked with violent criminal conduct. . . .

The most relevant of our prior decisions is *Ferber*, which concerned child pornography. The Court there held that child pornography is not protected speech, and I believe that *Ferber*'s reasoning dictates a similar conclusion here.

In *Ferber*, an important factor—I would say the most important factor—was that child pornography involves the commission of a crime that inflicts severe personal injury to the "children who are made to engage in sexual conduct for commercial purposes." . . .

Second, *Ferber* emphasized the fact that these underlying crimes could not be effectively combated without targeting the distribution of child pornography. . . .

> "[T]here is no serious contention that the legislature was unjustified in believing that it is difficult, if not impossible, to halt the exploitation of children by pursuing only those who produce the photographs and movies. . . . The most expeditious if not the only practical method of law enforcement may be to dry up the market for this material by imposing severe criminal penalties on persons selling, advertising, or otherwise promoting the product."

Third, the *Ferber* Court noted that the value of child pornography "is exceedingly modest, if not de minimis," and that any such value was "overwhelmingly outweigh[ed]" by "the evil to be restricted."

All three of these characteristics are shared by §48, as applied to crush videos. . . .

In sum, §48 may validly be applied to at least two broad real-world categories of expression covered by the statute: crush videos and dogfighting videos. Thus, the statute has a substantial core of constitutionally permissible applications. Moreover, for the reasons set forth above, the record does not show that §48, properly interpreted, bans a substantial amount of protected speech in absolute terms. A fortiori, respondent has not met his burden of demonstrating that any impermissible applications of the statute are "substantial" in relation to its "plainly legitimate sweep." Accordingly, I would reject respondent's claim that §48 is facially unconstitutional under the overbreadth doctrine.

For these reasons, I respectfully dissent.

90

Employment Division, Department of Human Resources of Oregon v. Smith (1990)

Justice Scalia delivered the opinion of the Court.

This case requires us to decide whether the Free Exercise Clause of the First Amendment permits the State of Oregon to include religiously inspired peyote use within the reach of its general criminal prohibition on use of that drug, and thus permits the State to deny unemployment benefits to persons dismissed from their jobs because of such religiously inspired use.

Oregon law prohibits the knowing or intentional possession of . . . the drug peyote, a hallucinogen derived from the plant Lophophora williamsii Lemaire.

Respondents Alfred Smith and Galen Black were fired from their jobs with a private drug rehabilitation organization because they ingested peyote for sacramental purposes at a ceremony of the Native American Church, of which both are members. When respondents applied to petitioner Employment Division for unemployment compensation, they were determined to be ineligible for benefits because they had been discharged for work-related "misconduct". The Oregon Court of Appeals reversed that determination, holding that the denial of benefits violated respondents' free exercise rights under the First Amendment. . . .

Respondents' claim for relief rests on our decisions in *Sherbert v. Verner* [and subsequent cases], in which we held that a State could not condition the availability of unemployment insurance on an individual's willingness to forgo conduct required by his religion. [H]owever, the conduct at issue in those cases was not prohibited by law. We [hold] that distinction to be critical, for "if Oregon does prohibit the religious use of peyote, and if that prohibition is consistent with the Federal Constitution, there is no federal right to engage in that conduct in Oregon," and "the State is free to withhold unemployment compensation from respondents for engaging in work-related misconduct, despite its religious motivation." . . . Oregon does prohibit the religious use of peyote, [thus] we proceed to consider whether that prohibition is permissible under the Free Exercise Clause.

From *Employment Division, Department of Human Resources of Oregon v. Smith*, 494 U.S. 872 (1990).

The Free Exercise Clause of the First Amendment, which has been made applicable to the States by incorporation into the Fourteenth Amendment, provides that "Congress shall make no law respecting an establishment of religion, or *prohibiting the free exercise thereof . . . .*" The free exercise of religion means, first and foremost, the right to believe and profess whatever religious doctrine one desires. Thus, the First Amendment obviously excludes all "governmental regulation of religious beliefs as such." The government may not compel affirmation of religious belief, punish the expression of religious doctrines it believes to be false, impose special disabilities on the basis of religious views or religious status, or lend its power to one or the other side in controversies over religious authority or dogma.

But the "exercise of religion" often involves not only belief and profession but the performance of (or abstention from) physical acts: assembling with others for a worship service, participating in sacramental use of bread and wine, proselytizing, abstaining from certain foods or certain modes of transportation. It would be true, we think (though no case of ours has involved the point), that a state would be "prohibiting the free exercise [of religion]" if it sought to ban such acts or abstentions only when they are engaged in for religious reasons, or only because of the religious belief that they display. It would doubtless be unconstitutional, for example, to ban the casting of "statues that are to be used for worship purposes," or to prohibit bowing down before a golden calf.

Respondents in the present case, however, seek to carry the meaning of "prohibiting the free exercise [of religion]" one large step further. They contend that their religious motivation for using peyote places them beyond the reach of a criminal law that is not specifically directed at their religious practice, and that is concededly constitutional as applied to those who use the drug for other reasons. They assert, in other words, that "prohibiting the free exercise [of religion]" includes requiring any individual to observe a generally applicable law that requires (or forbids) the performance of an act that his religious belief forbids (or requires). As a textual matter, we do not think the words must be given that meaning. It is no more necessary to regard the collection of a general tax, for example, as "prohibiting the free exercise [of religion]" by those citizens who believe support of organized government to be sinful than it is to regard the same tax as "abridging the freedom . . . of the press" of those publishing companies that must pay the tax as a condition of staying in business. It is a permissible reading of the text, in the one case as in the other, to say that, if prohibiting the exercise of religion (or burdening the activity of printing) is not the object of the tax, but merely the incidental effect of a generally applicable and otherwise valid provision, the First Amendment has not been offended.

Our decisions reveal that the latter reading is the correct one. We have never held that an individual's religious beliefs excuse him from compliance with an otherwise valid law prohibiting conduct that the State is free to regulate. On the contrary, the record of more than a century of our free exercise jurisprudence contradicts that proposition. . . . We first had occasion to assert that principle in *Reynolds v. United States* (1879), where we rejected the claim that criminal laws against polygamy could not be constitutionally applied to those whose religion commanded the practice. "Laws," we said, "are made for the government of actions, and while they cannot interfere with mere religious belief and opinions, they may with practices. . . . Can a man excuse his practices to the contrary because of his religious belief? To permit this would be to make the professed doctrines of religious belief superior to the law of the land, and in effect to permit every citizen to become a law unto himself." Subsequent decisions have consistently held that the right of free exercise does not relieve an individual of the obligation to comply with a "valid and neutral law of general applicability on the ground that the law proscribes (or prescribes) conduct that his religion prescribes (or proscribes)." . . .

The only decisions in which we have held that the First Amendment bars application of a neutral, generally applicable law to religiously motivated action have involved not the Free Exercise Clause alone, but the Free Exercise Clause in conjunction with other constitutional protections, such as freedom of speech and of the press, or the right of parents, acknowledged in *Pierce v. Society of Sisters* (1925), to direct the education of their children. . . . The present case does not present such a hybrid situation, but a free exercise claim unconnected with any communicative activity or parental right. Respondents urge us to hold, quite simply, that when otherwise prohibitable conduct is accompanied by religious convictions, not only the convictions but the conduct itself must be free from governmental regulation. We have never held that, and decline to do so now. There being no contention that Oregon's drug law represents an attempt to regulate religious beliefs, the communication of religious beliefs, or the raising of one's children in those beliefs, the rule to which we have adhered ever since *Reynolds* plainly controls.

Respondents argue that, even though exemption from generally applicable criminal laws need not automatically be extended to religiously motivated actors, at least the claim for a religious exemption must be evaluated under the balancing test set forth in *Sherbert v. Verner* (1963). Under the *Sherbert* test, governmental actions that substantially burden a religious practice must be justified by a compelling governmental interest. Applying that test, we have, on three occasions, invalidated state unemployment compensation rules that conditioned the availability of benefits upon an applicant's willingness to work under conditions forbidden by his religion. We have never invalidated any governmental action on the basis of the *Sherbert* test except the denial of unemployment compensation. Although we have sometimes purported to apply the *Sherbert* test in contexts other than that, we have always found the test satisfied. In recent years we have abstained from applying the *Sherbert* test (outside the unemployment compensation field) at all. . . .

. . . We conclude today that the sounder approach, and the approach in accord with the vast majority of our precedents, is to hold the test inapplicable to such challenges. The government's ability to enforce generally applicable prohibitions of socially harmful conduct, like its ability to carry out other aspects of public policy, "cannot depend on measuring the effects of a governmental action on a religious objector's spiritual development." To make an individual's obligation to obey such a law contingent upon the law's coincidence with his religious beliefs, except where the State's interest is "compelling"—permitting him, by virtue of his beliefs, "to become a law unto himself," *Reynolds v. United States*—contradicts both constitutional tradition and common sense.

The "compelling government interest" requirement seems benign, because it is familiar from other fields. But using it as the standard that must be met before the government may accord different treatment on the basis of race or before the government may regulate the content of speech is not remotely comparable to using it for the purpose asserted here. What it produces in those other fields—equality of treatment, and an unrestricted flow of contending speech—are constitutional norms; what it would produce here—a private right to ignore generally applicable laws—is a constitutional anomaly. . . .

If the "compelling interest" test is to be applied at all . . . it must be applied across the board, to all actions thought to be religiously commanded. Moreover, if "compelling interest" really means what it says (and watering it down here would subvert its rigor in the other fields where it is applied), many laws will not meet the test. Any society adopting such a system would be courting anarchy, but that danger increases in direct proportion to the society's diversity of religious beliefs, and its determination to coerce or suppress none of them. Precisely because "we are a cosmopolitan nation made up of people of almost every conceivable religious preference," and precisely because we value and protect that religious divergence, we cannot afford the luxury of deeming *presumptively invalid*, as applied to the religious objector, every regulation of conduct that does not protect an interest of the highest order. The rule respondents favor would open the prospect of constitutionally required religious exemptions from civic obligations of almost every conceivable kind—ranging from compulsory military service, to the payment of taxes; to health and safety regulation such as manslaughter and child neglect laws, compulsory vaccination laws, drug laws, and traffic laws; to social welfare legislation such as minimum wage laws, child labor laws, animal cruelty laws, environmental protection laws, and laws providing for equality of opportunity for the races. The First Amendment's protection of religious liberty does not require this.

Values that are protected against government interference through enshrinement in the Bill of Rights are not thereby banished from the political process. Just as a society that believes in the negative protection accorded to the press by the First Amendment is likely to enact laws that affirmatively foster the dissemination of the printed word, so also a society that believes in the negative protection accorded to religious belief can be expected to be solicitous of that value in its legislation as well. It is therefore not surprising that a number of States have made an exception to their drug laws for sacramental peyote use. But to say that a nondiscriminatory religious practice exemption is permitted, or even that it is desirable, is not to say that it is constitutionally required, and that the appropriate occasions for its creation can be discerned by the courts. It may fairly be said that leaving accommodation to the political process will place at a relative disadvantage those religious practices that are not widely engaged in; but that unavoidable consequence of democratic government must be preferred to a system in which each conscience is a law unto itself or in which judges weigh the social importance of all laws against the centrality of all religious beliefs.

Because respondents' ingestion of peyote was prohibited under Oregon law, and because that prohibition is constitutional, Oregon may, consistent with the Free Exercise Clause, deny respondents unemployment compensation when their dismissal results from use of the drug. The decision of the Oregon Supreme Court is accordingly reversed.

Justice O'Connor, concurring in the judgment.

Although I agree with the result the Court reaches in this case, I cannot join its opinion. In my view, today's holding dramatically departs from well settled First Amendment jurisprudence, appears unnecessary to resolve the question presented, and is incompatible with our Nation's fundamental commitment to individual religious liberty. . . .

The Court today interprets the [Free Exercise] Clause to permit the government to prohibit, without justification, conduct mandated by an individual's religious beliefs, so long as that prohibition is generally applicable. But a law that prohibits certain conduct—conduct that happens to be an act of worship for someone—manifestly does prohibit that person's free exercise of his religion. . . .

The Court responds that generally applicable laws are "one large step" removed from laws aimed at specific religious practices. The First Amendment, however, does not distinguish between laws that are generally applicable and laws that target particular religious practices. Indeed, few States would be so naive as to enact a law directly prohibiting or burdening a religious practice as such. Our free exercise cases have all concerned generally applicable laws that had the effect of significantly burdening a religious practice. If the First Amendment is to have any vitality, it ought not be construed to cover only the extreme and hypothetical situation in which a State directly targets a religious practice. . . .

To say that a person's right to free exercise has been burdened, of course, does not mean that he has an absolute right to engage in the conduct. Under our established First Amendment jurisprudence, we have recognized that the freedom to act, unlike the freedom to believe, cannot be absolute. Instead, we have respected both the First Amendment's express textual mandate and the governmental interest in regulation of conduct by requiring the Government to justify any substantial burden on religiously motivated conduct by a compelling state interest and by means narrowly tailored to achieve that interest. The compelling interest test effectuates the First Amendment's command that religious liberty is an independent liberty, that it occupies a preferred position, and that the Court will not permit encroachments upon this liberty, whether direct or indirect, unless required by clear and compelling governmental interests "of the highest order." . . .

The Court attempts to support its narrow reading of the Clause by claiming that "[w]e have never held that an individual's religious beliefs excuse him from compliance with an otherwise valid law prohibiting conduct that the State IS free to regulate." But as the Court later notes, as it must, in cases such as *Cantwell* [*v. Connecticut*] and [*Wisconsin v.*] *Yoder*, we have in fact interpreted the Free Exercise Clause to forbid application of a generally applicable prohibition to religiously motivated conduct. Indeed, in *Yoder* we expressly rejected the interpretation the Court now adopts. . . .

The Court endeavors to escape from our decisions in *Cantwell* and *Yoder* by labeling them "hybrid" decisions, but there is no denying that both cases expressly relied on the Free Exercise Clause and that we have consistently regarded those cases as part of the mainstream of our free exercise jurisprudence. . . .

. . . Once it has been shown that a government regulation or criminal prohibition burdens the free exercise of religion, we have consistently asked the Government to demonstrate that unbending application of its regulation to the religious objector "is essential to accomplish an overriding governmental interest" or represents "the least restrictive means of achieving some compelling state interest." To me, the sounder approach—the approach more consistent with our role as judges to decide each case on its individual merits—is to apply this test in each case to determine whether the burden on the specific plaintiffs before us is constitutionally significant, and whether the particular criminal interest asserted by the State before us is compelling. Even if, as an empirical matter, a government's criminal laws might usually serve a compelling interest in health, safety, or public order, the First Amendment at least requires a case-by-case determination of the question, sensitive to the facts of each particular claim. Given the range of conduct that a State might legitimately make criminal, we cannot assume, merely because a law carries criminal sanctions and is generally applicable, that the First Amendment never requires the State to grant a limited exemption for religiously motivated conduct. . . .

Because the health effects caused by the use of controlled substances exist regardless of the motivation of the user, the use of such substances, even for religious purposes, violates the very purpose of the laws that prohibit them. Cf. *State v. Massey* (denying religious exemption to municipal ordinance prohibiting handling of poisonous reptiles). Moreover, in view of the societal interest in preventing trafficking in controlled substances, uniform application of the criminal prohibition at issue is essential to the effectiveness of Oregon's stated interest in preventing any possession of peyote. Cf. *Jacobson v. Massachusetts* (denying exemption from smallpox vaccination requirement).

For these reasons, I believe that granting a selective exemption in this case would seriously impair Oregon's compelling interest in prohibiting possession of peyote by its citizens. Under such circumstances, the Free Exercise Clause does not require the State to accommodate respondents' religiously motivated conduct I would therefore adhere to our established free exercise jurisprudence and hold that the State in this case has a compelling interest in regulating peyote use by its citizens, and that accommodating respondents' religiously motivated conduct "will unduly interfere with fulfillment of the governmental interest." Accordingly, I concur in the judgment of the Court.

91

Burwell v. Hobby Lobby (2014)

Justice Alito delivered the opinion of the Court.

We must decide in these cases whether the Religious Freedom Restoration Act of 1993 (RFRA) permits the United States Department of Health and Human Services (HHS) to demand that three closely held corporations provide health-insurance coverage for methods of contraception that violate the sincerely held religious beliefs of the companies' owners. We hold that the regulations that impose this obligation violate RFRA, which prohibits the Federal Government from taking any action that substantially burdens

From *Burwell v. Hobby Lobby Stores, Inc.*, 573 U.S.___(2014).

the exercise of religion unless that action constitutes the least restrictive means of serving a compelling government interest. . . .

Congress enacted RFRA in 1993 in order to provide very broad protection for religious liberty. RFRA's enactment came three years after this Court's decision in *Employment Div., Dept. of Human Resources of Ore. v. Smith* (1990), which largely repudiated the method of analyzing free-exercise claims that had been used in cases like *Sherbert v. Verner* (1963), and *Wisconsin v. Yoder* (1972). In determining whether challenged government actions violated the Free Exercise Clause of the First Amendment, those decisions used a balancing test that took into account whether the challenged action imposed a substantial burden on the practice of religion, and if it did, whether it was needed to serve a compelling government interest. . . .

In *Smith*, however, the Court rejected "the balancing test set forth in *Sherbert*." *Smith* concerned two members of the Native American Church who were fired for ingesting peyote for sacramental purposes. When they sought unemployment benefits, the State of Oregon rejected their claims on the ground that consumption of peyote was a crime. . . .

This Court . . . [disagreed with the state,] observing that use of the *Sherbert* test whenever a person objected on religious grounds to the enforcement of a generally applicable law "would open the prospect of constitutionally required religious exemptions from civic obligations of almost every conceivable kind." The Court therefore held that, under the First Amendment, "neutral, generally applicable laws may be applied to religious practices even when not supported by a compelling governmental interest." *City of Boerne v. Flores* (1997).

Congress responded to Smith by enacting RFRA. "[L]aws [that are] 'neutral' toward religion," Congress found, "may burden religious exercise as surely as laws intended to interfere with religious exercise." In order to ensure broad protection for religious liberty, RFRA provides that "Government shall not substantially burden a person's exercise of religion even if the burden results from a rule of general applicability." If the Government substantially burdens a person's exercise of religion, under the Act that person is entitled to an exemption from the rule unless the Government "demonstrates that application of the burden to the person—(1) is in furtherance of a compelling governmental interest; and (2) is the least restrictive means of furthering that compelling governmental interest.". . .

At issue in these cases are HHS regulations promulgated under the Patient Protection and Affordable Care Act of 2010 (ACA). ACA generally requires employers with 50 or more full-time employees to offer "a group health plan or group health insurance coverage" that provides "minimum essential coverage." Any covered employer that does not provide such coverage must pay a substantial price. Specifically, if a covered employer provides group health insurance but its plan fails to comply with ACA's group-health-plan requirements, the employer may be required to pay $100 per day for each affected "individual." And if the employer decides to stop providing health insurance altogether and at least one full-time employee enrolls in a health plan and qualifies for a subsidy on one of the government-run ACA exchanges, the employer must pay $2,000 per year for each of its full-time employees.

Unless an exception applies, ACA requires an employer's group health plan or group-health-insurance coverage to furnish "preventive care and screenings" for women without "any cost sharing requirements." Congress itself, however, did not specify what types of preventive care must be covered. Instead, Congress authorized the Health Resources and Services Administration (HRSA), a component of HHS, to make that important and sensitive decision. . . .

In August 2011 . . . the HRSA promulgated the Women's Preventive Services Guidelines. The Guidelines provide that nonexempt employers are generally required to provide "coverage, without cost sharing" for "[a]ll Food and Drug Administration [(FDA)] approved contraceptive methods, sterilization procedures, and patient education and counseling." Although many of the required, FDA-approved methods of contraception work by preventing the fertilization of an egg, four of those methods (those specifically at issue in these cases) may have the effect of preventing an already fertilized egg from developing any further by inhibiting its attachment to the uterus.

HHS also authorized the HRSA to establish exemptions from the contraceptive mandate for "religious employers." That category encompasses "churches, their integrated auxiliaries, and conventions or associations of churches," as well as "the exclusively religious activities of any religious order.". . .

In addition, HHS has effectively exempted certain religious nonprofit organizations, described under HHS regulations as "eligible organizations," from the contraceptive mandate. An "eligible organization" means a nonprofit organization that "holds itself out as a religious organization" and "opposes providing coverage for some or all of any contraceptive services required to be covered . . . on account of religious objections.". . .

In addition to these exemptions for religious organizations, ACA exempts a great many employers from most of its coverage requirements. Employers providing "grandfathered health plans"—those that existed prior to March 23, 2010, and that have not made specified changes after that date—need not comply with many of the Act's requirements, including the contraceptive mandate. And employers with fewer than 50 employees are not required to provide health insurance at all.

All told, the contraceptive mandate "presently does not apply to tens of millions of people." This is attributable, in large part, to grandfathered health plans: Over one-third of the 149 million nonelderly people in America with employer-sponsored health plans were enrolled in grandfathered plans in 2013. The count for employees working for firms that do not have to provide insurance at all because they employ fewer than 50 employees is 34 million workers. . . .

David and Barbara Green and their three children are Christians who own and operate two family businesses. Forty-five years ago, David Green started an arts-and-crafts store that has grown into a nationwide chain called Hobby Lobby. There are now 500 Hobby Lobby stores, and the company has more than 13,000 employees. Hobby Lobby is organized as a for-profit corporation under Oklahoma law. . . .

Though these two businesses have expanded over the years, they remain closely held, and David, Barbara, and their children retain exclusive control of both companies. David serves as the CEO of Hobby Lobby, and his three children serve as the president, vice president, and vice CEO.

Hobby Lobby's statement of purpose commits the Greens to "[h]onoring the Lord in all [they] do by operating the company in a manner consistent with Biblical principles." Each family member has signed a pledge to run the businesses in accordance with the family's religious beliefs and to use the family assets to support Christian ministries. In accordance with those commitments, Hobby Lobby and Mardel stores close on Sundays, even though the Greens calculate that they lose millions in sales annually by doing so. The businesses refuse to engage in profitable transactions that facilitate or promote alcohol use; they contribute profits to Christian missionaries and ministries; and they buy hundreds of full-page newspaper ads inviting people to "know Jesus as Lord and Savior."

. . . [T]he Greens believe that life begins at conception and that it would violate their religion to facilitate access to contraceptive drugs or devices that operate after that point. They specifically object to . . . four contraceptive methods . . . [but] they have no objection to the other 16 FDA-approved methods of birth control. Although their group-health-insurance plan predates the enactment of ACA, it is not a grandfathered plan because Hobby Lobby elected not to retain grandfathered status before the contraceptive mandate was proposed.

The Greens [and] Hobby Lobby . . . sued HHS and other federal agencies and officials to challenge the contraceptive mandate under RFRA and the Free Exercise Clause. . . .

RFRA prohibits the "Government [from] substantially burden[ing] a person's exercise of religion even if the burden results from a rule of general applicability" unless the Government "demonstrates that application of the burden to the person—(1) is in furtherance of a compelling governmental interest; and (2) is the least restrictive means of furthering that compelling governmental interest." The first question that we must address is whether this provision applies to regulations that govern the activities of for-profit corporations like Hobby Lobby. . . .

HHS contends that neither these companies nor their owners can even be heard under RFRA. According to HHS, the companies cannot sue because they seek to make a profit for their owners, and the owners cannot be heard because the regulations, at least as a formal matter, apply only to the companies and not to the owners as individuals. HHS's argument would have dramatic consequences.

Consider this Court's decision in *Braunfeld v. Brown* (1961). In that case, five Orthodox Jewish merchants who ran small retail businesses in Philadelphia challenged a Pennsylvania Sunday closing law as a violation of the Free Exercise Clause. Because of their faith, these merchants closed their shops on Saturday, and they argued that requiring them to remain shut on Sunday threatened them with financial ruin. The Court entertained their claim. . . . According to HHS, however, if these merchants chose to incorporate their businesses—without in any way changing the size or nature of their businesses—they would forfeit all RFRA (and free-exercise) rights. HHS would put these merchants to a difficult choice: either give up the right to seek judicial protection of their religious liberty or forgo the benefits, available to their competitors, of operating as corporations.

As we will show, [in enacting RFRA,] Congress provided protection for people like the . . . Greens by employing a familiar legal fiction: It included corporations within RFRA's definition of "persons." But it is important to keep in mind that the purpose of this fiction is to provide protection for human beings. A corporation is simply a form of organization used by human beings to achieve desired ends. An established body of law specifies the rights and obligations of the people (including shareholders, officers, and employees) who are associated with a corporation in one way or another. When rights, whether constitutional or statutory, are extended to corporations, the purpose is to protect the rights of these people. For example, extending Fourth Amendment protection to corporations protects the privacy interests of employees and others associated with the company. . . . [Similarly,] protecting the free-exercise rights of corporations like Hobby Lobby . . . protects the religious liberty of the humans who own and control those companies. . . .

. . . Corporations, "separate and apart from" the human beings who own, run, and are employed by them, cannot do anything at all.

As we noted above, RFRA applies to "a person's" exercise of religion, and RFRA itself does not define the term "person." We therefore look to the Dictionary Act, which we must consult "[i]n determining the meaning of any Act of Congress, unless the context indicates otherwise."

Under the Dictionary Act, "the wor[d] 'person' . . . include[s] corporations, companies, associations, firms, partnerships, societies, and joint stock companies, as well as individuals." Thus, unless there is something about the RFRA context that "indicates otherwise," the Dictionary Act provides a quick, clear, and affirmative answer to the question whether the companies involved in these cases may be heard.

We see nothing in RFRA that suggests a congressional intent to depart from the Dictionary Act definition, and HHS makes little effort to argue otherwise. We have entertained RFRA and free-exercise claims brought by nonprofit corporations, and HHS concedes that a nonprofit corporation can be a "person" within the meaning of RFRA.

This concession effectively dispatches any argument that the term "person" as used in RFRA does not reach the closely held corporations involved in these cases. . . . The term "person" sometimes encompasses artificial persons (as the Dictionary Act instructs), and it sometimes is limited to natural persons. But no conceivable definition of the term includes natural persons and nonprofit corporations, but not for-profit corporations.

The principal argument advanced by HHS . . . regarding RFRA protection for Hobby Lobby . . . focuses not on the statutory term "person," but on the phrase "exercise of religion." According to HHS and the dissent, these corporations are not protected by RFRA because they cannot exercise religion. Neither HHS nor the dissent, however, provides any persuasive explanation for this conclusion.

Is it because of the corporate form? The corporate form alone cannot provide the explanation because, as we have pointed out, HHS concedes that nonprofit corporations can be protected by RFRA. . . .

If the corporate form is not enough, what about the profit-making objective? In *Braunfeld*, we entertained the free-exercise claims of individuals who were attempting to make a profit as retail merchants, and the Court never even hinted that this objective precluded their claims. . . .

If, as *Braunfeld* recognized, a sole proprietorship that seeks to make a profit may assert a free-exercise claim, why can't Hobby Lobby . . . do the same?

Some lower court judges have suggested that RFRA does not protect for-profit corporations because the purpose of such corporations is simply to make money. This argument flies in the face of modern corporate law. . . . While it is certainly true that a central objective of for-profit corporations is to make money, modern corporate law does not require for-profit corporations to pursue profit at the expense of everything else, and many do not do so. . . . Many examples come readily to mind. So long as its owners agree, a for-profit corporation may take costly pollution-control and energy-conservation measures that go beyond what the law requires. A for-profit corporation that operates facilities in other countries may exceed the requirements of local law regarding working conditions and benefits.

If for-profit corporations may pursue such worthy objectives, there is no apparent reason why they may not further religious objectives as well. . . .

For all these reasons, we hold that a federal regulation's restriction on the activities of a for-profit closely held corporation must comply with RFRA.

Because RFRA applies in these cases, we must next ask whether the HHS contraceptive mandate "substantially burden[s]" the exercise of religion. We have little trouble concluding that it does.

As we have noted, the . . . Greens have a sincere religious belief that life begins at conception. They therefore object on religious grounds to providing health insurance that covers methods of birth control that, as HHS acknowledges may result in the destruction of an embryo. By requiring the . . . Greens and [Hobby Lobby] . . . to arrange for such coverage, the HHS mandate demands that they engage in conduct that seriously violates their religious beliefs.

If the . . . Greens . . . do not yield to this demand, the economic consequences will be severe. If the companies continue to offer group health plans that do not cover the contraceptives at issue, they will be taxed $100 per day for each affected individual. For Hobby Lobby, the bill could amount to $1.3 million per day or about $475 million per year. . . . These sums are surely substantial.

It is true that the plaintiffs could avoid these assessments by dropping insurance coverage altogether and thus forcing their employees to obtain health insurance on one of the exchanges established under ACA. But if at least one of their full-time employees were to qualify for a subsidy on one of the government-run exchanges, this course would also entail substantial economic consequences. [Hobby Lobby] . . . could face penalties of $2,000 per employee each year. These penalties would amount to roughly $26 million for Hobby Lobby. . . .

Although these totals are high, amici supporting HHS have suggested that the $2,000 per-employee penalty is actually less than the average cost of providing health insurance, and therefore, they claim, the companies could readily eliminate any substantial burden by forcing their employees to obtain insurance in the government exchanges. . . .

Even if we were to reach this argument, we would find it unpersuasive. As an initial matter, it entirely ignores the fact that the . . . Greens . . . have religious reasons for providing health-insurance coverage for their employees. Before the advent of ACA, they were not legally compelled to provide insurance, but they nevertheless did so—in part, no doubt, for conventional business reasons, but also in part because their religious beliefs govern their relations with their employees. . . .

In taking the position that the HHS mandate does not impose a substantial burden on the exercise of religion, HHS's main argument (echoed by the principal dissent) is basically that the connection between what the objecting parties must do (provide health-insurance coverage for four methods of contraception that may operate after the fertilization of an egg) and the end that they find to be morally wrong (destruction of an embryo) is simply too attenuated. HHS and the dissent note that providing the coverage would not itself result in the destruction of an embryo; that would occur only if an employee chose to take advantage of the coverage and to use one of the four methods at issue.

This argument dodges the question that RFRA presents (whether the HHS mandate imposes a substantial burden on the ability of the objecting parties to conduct business in accordance with their religious beliefs) and instead addresses a very different question that the federal courts have no business addressing (whether the religious belief asserted in a RFRA case is reasonable). The . . . Greens believe that providing the coverage demanded by the HHS regulations is connected to the destruction of an embryo in a way that is sufficient to make it immoral for them to provide the coverage. This belief implicates a difficult and important question of religion and moral philosophy, namely, the circumstances under which it is wrong for a person to perform an act that is innocent in itself but that has the effect of enabling or facilitating the commission of an immoral act by another. Arrogating the authority to provide a binding national answer to this religious and philosophical question, HHS and the principal dissent in effect tell the plaintiffs that their beliefs are flawed. For good reason, we have repeatedly refused to take such a step. . . .

Since the HHS contraceptive mandate imposes a substantial burden on the exercise of religion, we must move on and decide whether HHS has shown that the mandate both "(1) is in furtherance of a compelling governmental interest; and (2) is the least restrictive means of furthering that compelling governmental interest."

HHS asserts that the contraceptive mandate serves a variety of important interests, but many of these are couched in very broad terms, such as promoting "public health" and "gender equality.". . .

We find it unnecessary to adjudicate this issue. We will assume that the interest in guaranteeing cost-free access to the four challenged contraceptive methods is compelling within the meaning of RFRA, and we will proceed to consider the final prong of the RFRA test, i.e., whether HHS has shown that the contraceptive mandate is "the least restrictive means of furthering that compelling governmental interest."

The least-restrictive-means standard is exceptionally demanding, and it is not satisfied here. HHS has not shown that it lacks other means of achieving its desired goal without imposing a substantial burden on the exercise of religion by the objecting parties in these cases.

The most straightforward way of doing this would be for the Government to assume the cost of providing the four contraceptives at issue to any women who are unable to obtain them under their health-insurance policies due to their employers' religious objections. This would certainly be less restrictive of the plaintiffs' religious liberty, and HHS has not shown, this is not a viable alternative. . . .

In the end, however, we need not rely on the option of a new, government-funded program in order to conclude that the HHS regulations fail the least-restrictive-means test. HHS itself has demonstrated that it has at its disposal an approach that is less restrictive than requiring employers to fund contraceptive methods that violate their religious beliefs. As we explained above, HHS has already established an accommodation for nonprofit organizations with religious objections. Under that accommodation, the organization can self-certify that it opposes providing coverage for particular contraceptive services. If the organization makes such a certification, the organization's insurance issuer or third-party administrator must "[e]xpressly exclude contraceptive coverage from the group health insurance coverage provided in connection with the group health plan" and "[p]rovide separate payments for any contraceptive services required to be covered" without imposing "any cost-sharing requirements . . . on the eligible organization, the group health plan, or plan participants or beneficiaries."

We do not decide today whether an approach of this type complies with RFRA for purposes of all religious claims. At a minimum, however, it does not impinge on the plaintiffs' religious belief that providing insurance coverage for the contraceptives at issue here violates their religion, and it serves HHS's stated interests equally well. . . .

HHS . . . argue[s] that a ruling in favor of the objecting parties in these cases will lead to a flood of religious objections regarding a wide variety of medical procedures and drugs, such as vaccinations and blood transfusions, but HHS has made no effort to substantiate this prediction. HHS points to no evidence that insurance plans in existence prior to the enactment of ACA excluded coverage for such items. Nor has HHS provided evidence that any significant number of employers sought exemption, on religious grounds, from any of ACA's coverage requirements other than the contraceptive mandate.

It is HHS's apparent belief that no insurance-coverage mandate would violate RFRA—no matter how significantly it impinges on the religious liberties of employers—that would lead to intolerable consequences. Under HHS's view, RFRA would permit the Government to require all employers to provide coverage for any medical procedure allowed by law in the jurisdiction in question—for instance, third-trimester abortions or assisted suicide. The owners of many closely held corporations could not in good conscience provide such coverage, and thus HHS would effectively exclude these people from full participation in the economic life of the Nation. RFRA was enacted to prevent such an outcome.

In any event, our decision in these cases is concerned solely with the contraceptive mandate. Our decision should not be understood to hold that an insurance-coverage mandate must necessarily fall if it conflicts with an employer's religious beliefs. Other coverage requirements, such as immunizations, may be supported by different interests (for example, the need to combat the spread of infectious diseases) and may involve different arguments about the least restrictive means of providing them. . . .

The contraceptive mandate, as applied to closely held corporations, violates RFRA. Our decision on that statutory question makes it unnecessary to reach the First Amendment claim. . . .

Justice Ginsburg, with whom Justice Sotomayor, Justice Breyer and Justice Kagan join, dissenting.

In a decision of startling breadth, the Court holds that commercial enterprises, including corporations, along with partnerships and sole proprietorships, can opt out of any law (saving only tax laws) they judge incompatible with their sincerely held religious beliefs. Compelling governmental interests in uniform compliance with the law, and disadvantages that religion-based opt-outs impose on others, hold no sway, the Court decides, at least when there is a "less restrictive alternative." And such an alternative, the Court suggests, there always will be whenever, in lieu of tolling an enterprise claiming a religion-based exemption, the government, i.e., the general public, can pick up the tab.

The Court does not pretend that the First Amendment's Free Exercise Clause demands religion-based accommodations so extreme, for our decisions leave no doubt on that score. Instead, the Court holds that Congress, in the Religious Freedom Restoration Act of 1993 (RFRA), dictated the extraordinary religion-based exemptions today's decision endorses. In the Court's view, RFRA demands accommodation of a for-profit corporation's religious beliefs no matter the impact that accommodation may have on third parties who do not share the corporation owners' religious faith—in these cases, thousands of women employed by Hobby Lobby and Conestoga or dependents of persons those corporations employ. Persuaded that Congress enacted RFRA to serve a far less radical purpose, and mindful of the havoc the Court's judgment can introduce, I dissent. . . .

92

Roe v. Wade (1973)

Mr. Justice Blackmun delivered the opinion of the Court.

. . . Three reasons have been advanced to explain historically the enactment of criminal abortion laws in the 19th century and to justify their continued existence.

It has been argued occasionally that these laws were the product of a Victorian social concern to discourage illicit sexual conduct. Texas, however, does not advance this justification in the present case, and it appears that no court or commentator has taken the argument seriously. The appellants and amici contend, moreover, that this is not a proper state purpose at all and suggest that, if it were, the Texas statutes are overbroad in protecting it since the law fails to distinguish between married and unwed mothers.

A second reason is concerned with abortion as a medical procedure. When most criminal abortion laws were first enacted, the procedure was a hazardous one for the woman. . . .

Modern medical techniques have altered this situation. Appellants and various amici refer to medical data indicating that abortion in early pregnancy, this is, prior to the end of the first trimester, although not without its risk, is now relatively safe. Mortality rates for women undergoing early abortions, where the procedure is legal, appear to be as low as or lower than the rates for normal childbirth. Consequently, any interest of the State in protecting the woman from an inherently hazardous procedure, except when it would be equally dangerous for her to forgo it, has largely disappeared. Of course, important state interests in the area of health and medical standards do remain.

The State has a legitimate interest in seeing to it that abortion, like any other medical procedure, is performed under circumstances that insure maximum safety for the patient. This interest obviously extends at least to the performing physician and his staff, to the facilities involved, to the availability of aftercare, and to adequate provision for any complication or emergency that might arise. The prevalence of high mortality rates at illegal "abortion mills" strengthens, rather than weakens, the State's interest in regulating the conditions under which abortions are performed. Moreover, the risk to the woman increases as her pregnancy continues. Thus, the State retains a

From *Roe v. Wade*, 410 U.S. 113 (1973).

definite interest in protecting the woman's own health and safety when an abortion is proposed at a late stage of pregnancy.

The third reason is the State's interest—some phrase it in terms of duty—in protecting prenatal life. Some of the argument for this justification rests on the theory that a new human life is present from the moment of conception. The State's interest and general obligation to protect life then extends, it is argued, to prenatal life. Only when the life of the pregnant mother herself is at stake, balanced against the life she carries within her, should the interest of the embryo or fetus not prevail. Logically, of course, a legitimate state interest in this area need not stand or fall on acceptance of the belief that life begins at conception or at some other point prior to live birth. In assessing the State's interest, recognition may be given to the less rigid claim that as long as at least potential life is involved, the State may assert interests beyond the protection of the pregnant woman alone. . . .

The Constitution does not explicitly mention any right of privacy. In a line of decisions, however, going back perhaps as far as *Union Pacific R. Co. v. Botsford* (1891), the Court has recognized that a right of personal privacy, or a guarantee of certain areas or zones of privacy, does exist under the Constitution. In varying contexts, the Court or individual Justices have, indeed, found at least the roots of that right in the First Amendment, *Stanley v. Georgia* (1969); in the Fourth and Fifth Amendments, *Terry v. Ohio* (1968), *Katz v. United States* (1967), in the penumbras of the Bill of Rights, *Griswold v. Connecticut* (1965) . . .; in the Ninth Amendment, [*Griswold*] (Goldberg, J., concurring); or in the concept of liberty guaranteed by the first section of the Fourteenth Amendment, see *Meyer v. Nebraska* (1923). These decisions make it clear that only personal rights that can be deemed "fundamental" or "implicit in the concept of ordered liberty," *Palko v. Connecticut* (1937), are included in this guarantee of personal privacy. They also make it clear that the right has some extension to activities relating to marriage, *Loving v. Virginia* (1967); procreation, *Skinner v. Oklahoma* (1942); contraception, *Eisenstadt v. Baird* (1972) (White, J., concurring in result); family relationships, *Prince v. Massachusetts* (1944); and child rearing and education, *Pierce v. Society of Sisters* (1925). . . .

This right of privacy, whether it be founded in the Fourteenth Amendment's concept of personal liberty and restrictions upon state action, as we feel it is, or, as the District Court determined, in the Ninth Amendment's reservation of rights to the people, is broad enough to encompass a woman's decision whether or not to terminate her pregnancy. The detriment that the State would impose upon the pregnant woman by denying this choice altogether is apparent. Specific and direct harm medically diagnosable even in early pregnancy may be involved. Maternity, or additional offspring, may force upon the woman a distressful life and future. Psychological harm may be imminent. Mental and physical health may be taxed by child care. There is also the distress, for all concerned, associated with the unwanted child, and there is the problem of bringing a child into a family already unable, psychologically and otherwise, to care for it. In other cases, as in this one, the additional difficulties and continuing stigma of unwed motherhood may be involved. All these are factors the woman and her responsible physician necessarily will consider in consultation.

On the basis of elements such as these, appellant and some amici argue that the woman's right is absolute and that she is entitled to terminate her pregnancy at whatever time, in whatever way, and for whatever reason she alone chooses. With this we do not agree. Appellant's arguments that Texas either has no valid interest at all in regulating the abortion decision, or no interest strong enough to support any limitation upon the woman's sole determination, is unpersuasive. The Court's decisions recognizing a right of privacy also acknowledge that some state regulation in areas protected by that right is appropriate. As noted above, a State may properly assert important interests in safeguarding health, in maintaining medical standards, and in protecting potential life. At some point in pregnancy, these respective interests become sufficiently compelling to sustain regulation of the factors that govern the abortion decision. The privacy right involved, therefore, cannot be said to be absolute. In fact, it is not clear to us that the claim asserted by some amici that one has an unlimited right to do with one's body as one pleases bears a close relationship to the right of privacy previously articulated in the Court's decisions. The Court has refused to recognize an unlimited right of this kind in the past. *Jacobson v. Massachusetts* (1905) . . . (vaccination); *Buck v. Bell* (1927) . . . (sterilization).

We, therefore, conclude that the right of personal privacy includes the abortion decision, but that this right is not unqualified and must be considered against important state interests in regulation.

Where certain "fundamental rights" are involved, the Court has held that regulation limiting these rights may be justified only by a "compelling state interest," . . . and that legislative enactments must be narrowly drawn to express only the legitimate state interests at stake. . . .

The District Court held that the appellee failed to meet his burden of demonstrating that the Texas statute's infringement upon Roe's rights was necessary to support a compelling state interest. . . . Appellee argues that the State's determination to recognize and protect prenatal life from and after conception constitutes a compelling state interest. As noted above, we do not agree fully with either formulation.

A. The appellee and certain amici argue that the fetus is a "person" within the language and meaning of the Fourteenth Amendment. In support of this, they outline at length and in detail the well-known facts of fetal development. If this suggestion of personhood is established, the appellant's case, of course, collapses, for the fetus' right to life is then guaranteed specifically by the Amendment. The appellant conceded as much on reargument. On the other hand, the appellee conceded on reargument that no case could be cited that holds that a fetus is a person within the meaning of the Fourteenth Amendment.

The Constitution does not define "person" in so many words. Section 1 of the Fourteenth Amendment contains three references to "person." The first, in defining "citizens," speaks of "persons born or naturalized in the United States." The word also appears both in the Due Process Clause and in the Equal Protection Clause. "Person" is used in other places in the Constitution. . . . But in nearly all these instances, the use of the word is such that it has application only postnatally. None indicates, with any assurance, that it has any possible prenatal application.

All this, together with our observation, supra, that throughout the major portion of the 19th century prevailing legal abortion practices were far freer than they are today, persuades us that the word "person," as used in the Fourteenth Amendment, does not include the unborn. . . .

B. The pregnant woman cannot be isolated in her privacy. She carries an embryo and, later, a fetus, if one accepts the medical definitions of the developing young in the human uterus. . . . The situation therefore is inherently different from marital intimacy, or bedroom possession of obscene material, or marriage, or procreation, or education, with which *Eisenstadt, Griswold, Stanley, Loving, Skinner, Pierce,* and *Meyer* were respectively concerned. As we have intimated above, it is reasonable and appropriate for a State to decide that at some point in time another interest, that of health of the mother or that of potential human life, becomes significantly involved. The woman's privacy is no longer sole and any right of privacy she possesses must be measured accordingly.

Texas urges that, apart from the Fourteenth Amendment, life begins at conception and is present throughout pregnancy, and that, therefore, the State has a compelling interest in protecting that life from and after conception. We need not resolve the difficult question of when life begins. When those trained in the respective disciplines of medicine, philosophy, and theology are unable to arrive at any consensus, the judiciary, at this point in the development of man's knowledge, is not in a position to speculate as to the answer.

It should be sufficient to note briefly the wide divergence of thinking on this most sensitive and difficult question. . . .

In view of all this, we do not agree that, by adopting one theory of life, Texas may override the rights of the pregnant woman that are at stake. We repeat, however, that the State does have an important and legitimate interest in preserving and protecting the health of the pregnant woman, whether she be a resident of the State or a nonresident who seeks medical consultation and treatment there, and that it has still another important and legitimate interest in protecting the potentiality of human life. These interests are separate and distinct. Each grows in substantiality as the woman approaches term and, at a point during pregnancy, each becomes "compelling."

With respect to the State's important and legitimate interest in the health of the mother, the "compelling" point, in the light of present medical knowledge, is at approximately the end of the first trimester. This is so because of the now-established medical fact, referred to above . . . that until the end of the first trimester mortality in abortion may be less than mortality in normal childbirth. It follows that, from and after this point, a State may regulate the abortion procedure to the extent that the regulation reasonably relates to the preservation and protection of maternal health. Examples of permissible state regulation in this area are requirements as to the qualifications of the person who is to perform the abortion; as to the licensure of that person; as to the facility in which the procedure is to be performed, that is, whether it must be a hospital or may be a clinic or some other place of less-than-hospital status; as to the licensing of the facility; and the like.

This means, on the other hand, that, for the period of pregnancy prior to this "compelling" point, the attending physician, in consultation with his patient, is free to determine, without regulation by the State, that, in his medical judgment, the patient's pregnancy should be terminated. If that decision is reached, the judgment may be effectuated by an abortion free of interference by the State.

With respect to the State's important and legitimate interest in potential life, the "compelling" point is at viability. This is so because the fetus then presumably has the capability of meaningful life outside the mother's womb. State regulation protective of fetal life after viability thus has both logical and biological justifications. If the State is interested in protecting fetal life after viability, it may go so far as to proscribe abortion during that period, except when it is necessary to preserve the life or health of the mother.*

Measured against these standards, Art. 1196 of the Texas Penal Code, in restricting legal abortions to those "procured or attempted by medical advice for the purpose of saving the life of the mother," sweeps too broadly. The statute makes no distinction between abortions performed early in pregnancy and those performed later, and it limits to a single reason, "saving" the mother's life, the legal justification for the procedure. The statute, therefore, cannot survive the constitutional attack made upon it here. . . .

---

*In *Doe v. Bolton*, 410 U.S. 179 (1973), the companion case to Roe, the Court laid out specific criteria for considering the "health" exception to a state's power to proscribe abortion. ". . . [M]edical judgment may be exercised in the light of all factors—physical, emotional, psychological, familial, and the woman's age—relevant to the wellbeing of the patient. All these factors may relate to health. This allows the attending physician the room he needs to make his best medical judgment. And it is room that operates for the benefit, not the disadvantage, of the pregnant woman."

93

Planned Parenthood of Southeastern Pa. v. Casey (1992)

Justice O'Connor, Justice Kennedy, and Justice Souter announced the judg-ment of the Court and delivered the opinion of the Court.

Liberty finds no refuge in a jurisprudence of doubt. Yet 19 years after our holding that the Constitution protects a woman's right to terminate her pregnancy in its early stages, *Roe v. Wade*, that definition of liberty is still questioned. Joining the respondents as *amicus curiae*, the United States, as it has done in five other cases in the last decade, again asks us to overrule *Roe*.

At issue in these cases are five provisions of the Pennsylvania Abortion Control Act of 1982 as amended in 1988 and 1989. The Act requires that a woman seeking an abortion give her informed consent prior to the abortion procedure, and specifies that she be provided with certain information at least 24 hours before the abortion is performed. For a minor to obtain an abortion, the Act requires the informed consent of one of her parents, but provides for a judicial bypass option if the minor does not wish to or cannot obtain a parent's consent. Another provision of the Act requires that, unless certain exceptions apply, a married woman seeking an abortion must sign a statement indicating that she has notified her husband of her intended abortion. The Act exempts compliance with these three requirements in the event of a "medical emergency," which is defined in § 3203 of the Act. In addition to the above provisions regulating the performance of abortions, the Act imposes certain reporting requirements on facilities that provide abor-tion services.

. . . After considering the fundamental constitutional questions resolved by *Roe*, principles of institutional integrity, and the rule of *stare decisis*, we are led to conclude this: the essential holding of *Roe v. Wade* should be retained and once again reaffirmed.

It must be stated at the outset and with clarity that *Roe*'s essential holding, the holding we reaffirm, has three parts. First is a recognition of the right of the woman to choose to have an abortion before viability and to obtain it without undue interference from the State. Before viability, the State's interests are not strong enough to support a prohibition of

From *Planned Parenthood of Southeastern Pa. v. Casey*, 505 U.S. 833 (1992).

abortion or the imposition of a substantial obstacle to the woman's effect-ive right to elect the procedure. Second is a confirmation of the State's power to restrict abortions after fetal viability, if the law contains excep-tions for pregnancies which endanger a woman's life or health. And third is the principle that the State has legitimate interests from the outset of the pregnancy in protecting the health of the woman and the life of the fetus that may become a child. These principles do not contradict one another; and we adhere to each.

. . . Men and women of good conscience can disagree, and we suppose some always shall disagree, about the profound moral and spiritual impli-cations of terminating a pregnancy, even in its earliest stage. Some of us as individuals find abortion offensive to our most basic principles of morality, but that cannot control our decision. Our obligation is to define the liberty of all, not to mandate our own moral code. The underlying constitutional issue is whether the State can resolve these philosophic questions in such a definitive way that a woman lacks all choice in the matter, except perhaps in those rare circumstances in which the pregnancy is itself a danger to her own life or health, or is the result of rape or incest.

It is conventional constitutional doctrine that where reasonable people disagree the government can adopt one position or the other. That theorem, however, assumes a state of affairs in which the choice does not intrude upon a protected liberty. Thus, while some people might disagree about whether or not the flag should be saluted, or disagree about the proposition that it may not be defiled, we have ruled that a State may not compel or enforce one view or the other.

Our law affords constitutional protection to personal decisions relating to marriage, procreation, contraception, family relationships, child rearing, and education. Our cases recognize "the right of the *individual*, married or single, to be free from unwarranted governmental intrusion into matters so fundamentally affecting a person as the decision whether to bear or beget a child." Our precedents "have respected the private realm of family life which the state cannot enter." These matters, involving the most intimate and personal choices a person may make in a lifetime, choices central to personal dignity and autonomy, are central to the liberty protected by the Fourteenth Amendment. At the heart of liberty is the right to define one's own concept of existence, of meaning, of the universe, and of the mystery of human life. Beliefs about these matters could not define the attributes of personhood were they formed under compulsion of the State.

. . . While we appreciate the weight of the arguments made on behalf of the State in the case before us, arguments which in their ultimate for-mulation conclude that *Roe* should be overruled, the reservations any of us may have in reaffirming the central holding of *Roe* are outweighed by the explication of individual liberty we have given combined with the force of *stare decisis*. . . .

. . . We have seen how time has overtaken some of *Roe*'s factual assumptions: advances in maternal health care allow for abortions safe to the mother later in pregnancy than was true in 1973, and advances in neonatal care have advanced viability to a point somewhat earlier. But these facts go only to the scheme of time limits on the realization of competing interests, and the divergences from the factual premises of 1973 have no bearing on the validity of *Roe*'s central holding, that viability marks the earliest point at which the State's interest in fetal life is constitutionally adequate to justify a legislative ban on nontherapeutic abortions. The soundness or unsoundness of that constitutional judgment in no sense turns on whether viability occurs at approximately 28 weeks, as was usual at the time of *Roe*, at 23 to 24 weeks, as it sometimes does today, or at some moment even slightly earlier in pregnancy, as it may if fetal respiratory capacity can somehow be enhanced in the future. Whenever it may occur, the attainment of viability may continue to serve as the critical fact, just as it has done since *Roe* was decided; which is to say that no change in *Roe*'s factual underpinning has left its central holding obsolete, and none supports an argument for overruling it.

. . . The Court's duty in the present case is clear. In 1973, it confronted the already divisive issue of governmental power to limit personal choice to undergo abortion, for which it provided a new resolution based on the due process guaranteed by the Fourteenth Amendment. Whether or not a new social consensus is developing on that issue, its divisiveness is no less today than in 1973, and pressure to overrule the decision, like pressure to retain it, has grown only more intense. A decision to overrule *Roe*'s essential holding under the existing circumstances would address error, if error there was, at the cost of both profound and unnecessary damage to the Court's legitimacy, and to the Nation's commitment to the rule of law. It is therefore imperative to adhere to the essence of *Roe*'s original decision, and we do so today.

From what we have said so far it follows that it is a constitutional liberty of the woman to have some freedom to terminate her pregnancy. We conclude that the basic decision in *Roe* was based on a constitutional analysis which we cannot now repudiate. The woman's liberty is not so unlimited, however, that from the outset the State cannot show its concern for the life of the unborn, and at a later point in fetal development the State's interest in life has sufficient force so that the right of the woman to terminate the pregnancy can be restricted.

. . . We conclude the line should be drawn at viability, so that before that time the woman has a right to choose to terminate her pregnancy. We adhere to this principle for two reasons. First, as we have said, is the doctrine of *stare decisis*. Any judicial act of line drawing may seem somewhat arbitrary, but *Roe* was a reasoned statement, elaborated with great care. . . .

The second reason is that the concept of viability, as we noted in *Roe*, is the time at which there is a realistic possibility of maintaining and nourishing a life outside the womb, so that the independent existence of the second life can in reason and all fairness be the object of state protection that now overrides the rights of the woman. . . .

Yet it must be remembered that *Roe v. Wade* speaks with clarity in establishing not only the woman's liberty but also the State's "important and legitimate interest in potential life." That portion of the decision in *Roe* has been given too little acknowledgement and implementation by the Court in its subsequent cases. Those cases decided that any regulation touching upon the abortion decision must survive strict scrutiny, to be sustained only if drawn in narrow terms to further a compelling state interest. Not all of the cases decided under that formulation can be reconciled with the holding in *Roe* itself that the State has legitimate interests in the health of the woman and in protecting the potential life within her. In resolving this tension, we choose to rely upon *Roe*, as against the later cases.

Roe established a trimester framework to govern abortion regulations. Under this elaborate but rigid construct, almost no regulation at all is permitted during the first trimester of pregnancy; regulations designed to protect the woman's health, but not to further the State's interest in potential life, are permitted during the second trimester; and during the third trimester, when the fetus is viable, prohibitions are permitted provided the life or health of the mother is not at stake. . . .

The trimester framework no doubt was erected to ensure that the woman's right to choose not become so subordinate to the State's interest in promoting fetal life that her choice exists in theory but not in fact. We do not agree, however, that the trimester approach is necessary to accomplish this objective. A framework of this rigidity was unnecessary and in its later interpretation sometimes contradicted the State's permissible exercise of its powers.

Though the woman has a right to choose to terminate or continue her pregnancy before viability, it does not at all follow that the State is prohibited from taking steps to ensure that this choice is thoughtful and informed. Even in the earliest stages of pregnancy, the State may enact rules and regulations designed to encourage her to know that there are philosophic and social arguments of great weight that can be brought to bear in favor of continuing the pregnancy to full term and that there are procedures and institutions to allow adoption of unwanted children as well as a certain degree of state assistance if the mother chooses to raise the child herself. "[T]he Constitution does not forbid a State or city, pursuant to democratic processes, from expressing a preference for normal childbirth." It follows that States are free to enact laws to provide a reasonable framework for a woman to make a decision that has such profound and lasting meaning. This, too, we

find consistent with *Roe's* central premises, and indeed the inevitable consequence of our holding that the State has an interest in protecting the life of
the unborn.

We reject the trimester framework, which we do not consider to be
part of the essential holding of *Roe*. Measures aimed at ensuring that a
woman's choice contemplates the consequences for the fetus do not necessarily interfere with the right recognized in *Roe*, although those measures
have been found to be inconsistent with the rigid trimester framework
announced in that case. A logical reading of the central holding in *Roe*
itself, and a necessary reconciliation of the liberty of the woman and the
interest of the State in promoting prenatal life, require, in our view, that we
abandon the trimester framework as a rigid prohibition on all previability
regulation aimed at the protection of fetal life. The trimester framework
suffers from these basic flaws: in its formulation it misconceives the nature
of the pregnant woman's interest; and in practice it undervalues the State's
interest in potential life, as recognized in *Roe*. As our jurisprudence relating
to all liberties save perhaps abortion has recognized, not every law which
makes a right more difficult to exercise is, *ipso facto*, an infringement of that
right. An example clarifies the point. We have held that not every ballot
access limitation amounts to an infringement of the right to vote. Rather,
the States are granted substantial flexibility in establishing the framework
within which voters choose the candidates for whom they wish to vote.
The abortion right is similar. Numerous forms of state regulation might
have the incidental effect of increasing the cost or decreasing the availability of medical care, whether for abortion or any other medical procedure.
The fact that a law which serves a valid purpose, one not designed to strike
at the right itself, has the incidental effect of making it more difficult or
more expensive to procure an abortion cannot be enough to invalidate it.
Only where state regulation imposes an undue burden on a woman's ability
to make this decision does the power of the State reach into the heart of
the liberty protected by the Due Process Clause. . . .

Not all governmental intrusion is of necessity unwarranted; and that
brings us to the other basic flaw in the trimester framework: even in *Roe's*
terms, in practice it undervalues the State's interest in the potential life
within the woman.

Roe v. Wade was express in its recognition of the State's "important and
legitimate interest[s] in preserving and protecting the health of the pregnant
woman [and] in protecting the potentiality of human life." The trimester
framework, however, does not fulfill *Roe's* own promise that the State has an
interest in protecting fetal life or potential life. *Roe* began the contradiction
by using the trimester framework to forbid any regulation of abortion
designed to advance that interest before viability. Before viability, *Roe* and
subsequent cases treat all governmental attempts to influence a woman's

decision on behalf of the potential life within her as unwarranted. This treatment is, in our judgment, incompatible with the recognition that there is a substantial state interest in potential life throughout pregnancy.

The very notion that the State has a substantial interest in potential life leads to the conclusion that not all regulations must be deemed unwarranted. Not all burdens on the right to decide whether to terminate a pregnancy will be undue. In our view, the undue burden standard is the appropriate means of reconciling the State's interest with the woman's constitutionally protected liberty. . . .

A finding of an undue burden is a shorthand for the conclusion that a state regulation has the purpose or effect of placing a substantial obstacle in the path of a woman seeking an abortion of a nonviable fetus. A statute with this purpose is invalid because the means chosen by the State to further the interest in potential life must be calculated to inform the woman's free choice, not hinder it. And a statute which, while furthering the interest in potential life or some other valid state interest, has the effect of placing a substantial obstacle in the path of a woman's choice cannot be considered a permissible means of serving its legitimate ends. . . . In our considered judgment, an undue burden is an unconstitutional burden. . . .

Some guiding principles should emerge. What is at stake is the woman's right to make the ultimate decision, not a right to be insulated from all others in doing so. Regulations which do no more than create a structural mechanism by which the State, or the parent or guardian of a minor, may express profound respect for the life of the unborn are permitted, if they are not a substantial obstacle to the woman's exercise of the right to choose. Unless it has that effect on her right of choice, a state measure designed to persuade her to choose childbirth over abortion will be upheld if reasonably related to that goal. Regulations designed to foster the health of a woman seeking an abortion are valid if they do not constitute an undue burden. . . .

. . . The Court of Appeals applied what it believed to be the undue burden standard and upheld each of the provisions except for the husband notification requirement. We agree generally with this conclusion, but refine the undue burden analysis in accordance with the principles articulated above. We now consider the separate statutory sections at issue.

. . . Except in a medical emergency, the statute requires that at least 24 hours before performing an abortion a physician inform the woman of the nature of the procedure, the health risks of the abortion and of childbirth, and the "probable gestational age of the unborn child." The physician or a qualified nonphysician must inform the woman of the availability of printed materials published by the State describing the fetus and providing information about medical assistance for childbirth, information about child support from the father, and a list of agencies which provide adoption and other services as alternatives to abortion. An abortion may not be performed unless the woman certifies in writing that she has been informed of the availability of these printed materials and has been provided them if she chooses to view them.

Our prior decisions establish that as with any medical procedure, the State may require a woman to give her written informed consent to an abortion. . . .

. . . [With regard to the information that must be given to the woman, our prior decisions] recognize a substantial government interest justifying a requirement that a woman be apprised of the health risks of abortion and childbirth. It cannot be questioned that psychological well being is a facet of health. Nor can it be doubted that most women considering an abortion would deem the impact on the fetus relevant, if not dispositive, to the decision. In attempting to ensure that a woman apprehend the full consequences of her decision, the State furthers the legitimate purpose of reducing the risk that a woman may elect an abortion, only to discover later, with devastating psychological consequences, that her decision was not fully informed. If the information the State requires to be made available to the woman is truthful and not misleading, the requirement may be permissible.

. . . Whether the mandatory 24-hour waiting period is nonetheless invalid because in practice it is a substantial obstacle to a woman's choice to terminate her pregnancy is a closer question. The findings of fact by the District Court indicate that because of the distances many women must travel to reach an abortion provider, the practical effect will often be a delay of much more than a day because the waiting period requires that a woman seeking an abortion make at least two visits to the doctor. The District Court also found that in many instances this will increase the exposure of women seeking abortions to "the harassment and hostility of anti-abortion protestors demonstrating outside a clinic." As a result, the District Court found that for those women who have the fewest financial resources, those who must travel long distances, and those who have difficulty explaining their whereabouts to husbands, employers, or others, the 24-hour waiting period will be "particularly burdensome."

These findings are troubling in some respects, but they do not demonstrate that the waiting period constitutes an undue burden. We do not doubt that, as the District Court held, the waiting period has the effect of "increasing the cost and risk of delay of abortions," but the District Court did not conclude that the increased costs and potential delays amount to substantial obstacles. . . . [A]s we have stated, under the undue burden standard a State is permitted to enact persuasive measures which favor childbirth over abortion, even if those measures do not further a health interest. And while the waiting period does limit a physician's discretion, that is not, standing alone, a reason to invalidate it. In light of the construction given the statute's definition of medical emergency by the Court of Appeals, and the District Court's findings, we cannot say that the waiting period imposes a real health risk. . . .

Section 3209 of Pennsylvania's abortion law provides, except in cases of medical emergency, that no physician shall perform an abortion on a married woman without receiving a signed statement from the woman that she has notified her spouse that she is about to undergo an abortion. The woman has the option of providing an alternative signed statement certifying that her husband is not the man who impregnated her; that her husband could not be located; that the pregnancy is the result of spousal sexual assault which she has reported; or that the woman believes that notifying her husband will cause him or someone else to inflict bodily injury upon her. A physician who performs an abortion on a married woman without receiving the appropriate signed statement will have his or her license revoked, and is liable to the husband for damages. The District Court heard the testimony of numerous expert witnesses, and made detailed findings of fact regarding the effect of this statute. . . .

. . . The American Medical Association (AMA) has published a summary of the recent research in this field, which indicates that in an average 12-month period in this country, approximately two million women are the victims of severe assaults by their male partners. In a 1985 survey, women reported that nearly one of every eight husbands had assaulted their wives during the past year. The AMA views these figures as "marked underestimates," because the nature of these incidents discourages women from reporting them, and because surveys typically exclude the very poor, those who do not speak English well, and women who are homeless or in institutions or hospitals when the survey is conducted. According to the AMA, "[r]esearchers on family violence agree that the true incidence of partner violence is probably *double* the above estimates; or four million severely assaulted women per year. Studies suggest that from one fifth to one third of all women will be physically assaulted by a partner or ex partner during their lifetime." Thus on an average day in the United States, nearly 11,000 women are severely assaulted by their male partners. Many of these incidents involve sexual assault. In families where wife beating takes place, moreover, child abuse is often present as well . . .

. . . This information and the District Court's findings reinforce what common sense would suggest. In well functioning marriages, spouses discuss important intimate decisions such as whether to bear a child. But there are millions of women in this country who are the victims of regular physical and psychological abuse at the hands of their husbands. Should these women become pregnant, they may have very good reasons for not wishing to inform their husbands of their decision to obtain an abortion. Many may have justifiable fears of physical abuse, but may be no less fearful of the consequences of reporting prior abuse to the Commonwealth of Pennsylvania. Many may have a reasonable fear that notifying their husbands will provoke further instances of child abuse; these women are not exempt from § 3209's notification requirement. Many may fear devastating forms of psychological abuse from their husbands, including verbal harassment, threats of future violence, the destruction of possessions, physical confinement to the home, the withdrawal of financial support, or the disclosure of the abortion to family and friends. . . .

The spousal notification requirement is thus likely to prevent a significant number of women from obtaining an abortion. It does not merely make abortions a little more difficult or expensive to obtain; for many women, it will impose a substantial obstacle. . . .

. . . The unfortunate yet persisting conditions we document above will mean that in a large fraction of the cases in which § 3209 is relevant, it will operate as a substantial obstacle to a woman's choice to undergo an abortion. It is an undue burden, and therefore invalid.

. . . The husband's interest in the life of the child his wife is carrying does not permit the State to empower him with this troubling degree of authority over his wife. The contrary view leads to consequences reminiscent of the common law. A husband has no enforceable right to require a wife to advise him before she exercises her personal choices. . . .

. . . We next consider the parental consent provision. Except in a medical emergency, an unemancipated young woman under 18 may not obtain an abortion unless she and one of her parents (or guardian) provide informed consent as defined above. If neither a parent nor a guardian provides consent, a court may authorize the performance of an abortion upon a determination that the young woman is mature and capable of giving informed consent and has in fact given her informed consent, or that an abortion would be in her best interests. We have been over most of this ground before. Our cases establish, and we reaffirm today, that a State may require a minor seeking an abortion to obtain the consent of a parent or guardian, provided that there is an adequate judicial bypass procedure. Under these precedents, in our view, the one parent consent requirement and judicial bypass procedure are constitutional.

. . . Under the recordkeeping and reporting requirements of the statute, every facility which performs abortions is required to file a report stating its name and address as well as the name and address of any related entity, such as a controlling or subsidiary organization. In the case of state funded institutions, the information becomes public.

For each abortion performed, a report must be filed identifying: the physician (and the second physician where required); the facility; the referring physician or agency; the woman's age; the number of prior pregnancies and prior abortions she has had; gestational age; the type of abortion procedure; the date of the abortion; whether there were any pre-existing medical conditions which would complicate pregnancy; medical complications with the abortion; where applicable, the basis for the determination that the abortion was medically necessary; the weight of the aborted fetus; and whether the woman was married, and if so, whether notice was provided or the basis for the failure to give notice. Every abortion facility must also file quarterly reports showing the number of abortions performed broken down by trimester. In all events, the identity of each woman who has had an abortion remains confidential.

In *Danforth,* we held that recordkeeping and reporting provisions "that are reasonably directed to the preservation of maternal health and that properly respect a patient's confidentiality and privacy are permissible." We think that under this standard, all the provisions at issue here except that relating to spousal notice are constitutional. Although they do not relate to the State's interest in informing the woman's choice, they do relate to health. The collection of information with respect to actual patients is a vital element of medical research, and so it cannot be said that the requirements serve no purpose other than to make abortions more difficult. Nor do we find that the requirements impose a substantial obstacle to a woman's choice. . . .

The Constitution is a covenant running from the first generation of Americans to us and then to future generations. It is a coherent succession. Each generation must learn anew that the Constitution's written terms embody ideas and aspirations that must survive more ages than one. We accept our responsibility not to retreat from interpreting the full meaning of the covenant in light of all of our precedents. We invoke it once again to define the freedom guaranteed by the Constitution's own promise, the promise of liberty.

Justice Blackmun, concurring in part, concurring in the judgment in part, and dissenting in part.

. . . Today, no less than yesterday, the Constitution and decisions of this Court require that a State's abortion restrictions be subjected to the strictest of judicial scrutiny. Our precedents and the joint opinion's principles require us to subject all non *de minimis* abortion regulations to strict scrutiny. Under this standard, the Pennsylvania statute's provisions requiring content based counseling, a 24-hour delay, informed parental consent, and reporting of abortion related information must be invalidated. . . .

. . . Strict scrutiny of state limitations on reproductive choice still offers the most secure protection of the woman's right to make her own reproductive decisions, free from state coercion. No majority of this Court has ever agreed upon an alternative approach. The factual premises of the trimester framework have not been undermined, and the *Roe* framework is far more administrable, and far less manipulable, than the "undue burden" standard adopted by the joint opinion. . . .

In sum, *Roe's* requirement of strict scrutiny as implemented through a trimester framework should not be disturbed. No other approach has gained a majority, and no other is more protective of the woman's fundamental right. Lastly, no other approach properly accommodates the woman's constitutional right with the State's legitimate interests. . . .

Chief Justice Rehnquist, with whom Justice White, Justice Scalia, and Justice Thomas join, concurring in the judgment in part and dissenting in part.

The joint opinion, following its newly minted variation on *stare decisis*, retains the outer shell of *Roe v. Wade*, but beats a wholesale retreat from the substance of that case. We believe that *Roe* was wrongly decided, and that it can and should be overruled consistently with our traditional approach to *stare decisis* in constitutional cases. We would adopt the approach of the plurality in *Webster v. Reproductive Health Services*, and uphold the challenged provisions of the Pennsylvania statute in their entirety.

. . . The joint opinion of Justices O'Connor, Kennedy, and Souter cannot bring itself to say that *Roe* was correct as an original matter, but the authors are of the view that "the immediate question is not the soundness of *Roe*'s resolution of the issue, but the precedential force that must be accorded to its holding." Instead of claiming that *Roe* was correct as a matter of original constitutional interpretation, the opinion therefore contains an elaborate discussion of *stare decisis*. This discussion of the principle of *stare decisis* appears to be almost entirely dicta, because the joint opinion does not apply that principle in dealing with *Roe*. *Roe* decided that a woman had a fundamental right to an abortion. The joint opinion rejects that view. *Roe* decided that abortion regulations were to be subjected to "strict scrutiny" and could be justified only in the light of "compelling state interests." The joint opinion rejects that view. *Roe* analyzed abortion regulation under a rigid trimester framework, a framework which has guided this Court's decisionmaking for 19 years. The joint opinion rejects that framework.

Stare decisis is defined in Black's Law Dictionary as meaning "to abide by, or adhere to, decided cases." Whatever the "central holding" of *Roe* that is left after the joint opinion finishes dissecting it is surely not the result of that principle. While purporting to adhere to precedent, the joint opinion instead revises it. *Roe* continues to exist, but only in the way a storefront on a western movie set exists: a mere facade to give the illusion of reality. . . .

. . . Apparently realizing that conventional *stare decisis* principles do not support its position, the joint opinion advances a belief that retaining a portion of *Roe* is necessary to protect the "legitimacy" of this Court. Because the Court must take care to render decisions "grounded truly in principle," and not simply as political and social compromises, the joint opinion properly declares it to be this Court's duty to ignore the public criticism and protest that may arise as a result of a decision. . . .

But the joint opinion goes on to state that when the Court "resolve[s] the sort of intensely divisive controversy reflected in *Roe* and those rare, comparable cases," its decision is exempt from reconsideration under established principles of *stare decisis* in constitutional cases. This is so, the joint opinion contends, because in those "intensely divisive" cases the Court has "call[ed] the contending sides of a national controversy to end their national division by accepting a common mandate rooted in the Constitution," and must therefore take special care not to be perceived as "surrender[ing] to political pressure" and continued opposition. This is a truly novel principle, one which is contrary to both the Court's historical practice and to the Court's traditional willingness to tolerate criticism of its opinions. Under this principle, when the Court has ruled on a divisive issue, it is apparently prevented from overruling that decision for the sole reason that it was incorrect, *unless opposition to the original decision has died away*.

. . . We have stated above our belief that the Constitution does not subject state abortion regulations to heightened scrutiny. Accordingly, we think that the correct analysis is that set forth by the plurality opinion in *Webster*. A woman's interest in having an abortion is a form of liberty protected by the Due Process Clause, but States may regulate abortion procedures in ways rationally related to a legitimate state interest. . . .

94

Obergefell v. Hodges (2015)

Justice Kennedy delivered the opinion of the Court.

The Constitution promises liberty to all within its reach, a liberty that includes certain specific rights that allow persons, within a lawful realm, to define and express their identity. The petitioners in these cases seek to find that liberty by marrying someone of the same sex and having their marriages deemed lawful on the same terms and conditions as marriages between persons of the opposite sex.

These cases come from Michigan, Kentucky, Ohio, and Tennessee, States that define marriage as a union between one man and one woman. The petitioners are 14 same-sex couples and two men whose same-sex partners are deceased. The respondents are state officials responsible for enforcing the laws in question. The petitioners claim the respondents violate the Fourteenth Amendment by denying them the right to marry or to have their marriages, lawfully performed in another State, given full recognition. . . .

Before addressing the principles and precedents that govern these cases, it is appropriate to note the history of the subject now before the Court.

From *Obergefell v. Hodges*, 576 U.S.___(2015).

From their beginning to their most recent page, the annals of human history reveal the transcendent importance of marriage. The lifelong union of a man and a woman always has promised nobility and dignity to all persons, without regard to their station in life. Marriage is sacred to those who live by their religions and offers unique fulfillment to those who find meaning in the secular realm. Its dynamic allows two people to find a life that could not be found alone, for a marriage becomes greater than just the two persons. Rising from the most basic human needs, marriage is essential to our most profound hopes and aspirations. . . .

That history is the beginning of these cases. The respondents say it should be the end as well. . . . Marriage, in their view, is by its nature a gender-differentiated union of man and woman. This view long has been held and continues to be held in good faith by reasonable and sincere people here and throughout the world.

The petitioners acknowledge this history but contend that these cases cannot end there. . . . [Indeed,] it is the enduring importance of marriage that underlies the petitioners' contentions. This, they say, is their whole point. Far from seeking to devalue marriage, the petitioners seek it for themselves because of their respect and need for its privileges and responsibilities. And their immutable nature dictates that same-sex marriage is their only real path to this profound commitment. . . .

The ancient origins of marriage confirm its centrality, but it has not stood in isolation from developments in law and society. The history of marriage is one of both continuity and change. That institution even as confined to opposite-sex relations has evolved over time.

For example, marriage was once viewed as an arrangement by the couple's parents based on political, religious, and financial concerns; but by the time of the Nation's founding it was understood to be a voluntary contract between a man and a woman. As the role and status of women changed, the institution further evolved. Under the centuries-old doctrine of coverture, a married man and woman were treated by the State as a single, male-dominated legal entity. As women gained legal, political, and property rights, and as society began to understand that women have their own equal dignity, the law of coverture was abandoned. These and other developments in the institution of marriage over the past centuries were not mere superficial changes. Rather, they worked deep transformations in its structure, affecting aspects of marriage long viewed by many as essential. . . .

This Court first gave detailed consideration to the legal status of homosexuals in *Bowers v. Hardwick* (1986) . There it upheld the constitutionality of a Georgia law deemed to criminalize certain homosexual acts. . . . Then, in 2003, the Court overruled *Bowers*, holding that laws making same-sex intimacy a crime "demea[n] the lives of homosexual persons." *Lawrence v. Texas*. . . .

Under the Due Process Clause of the Fourteenth Amendment, no State shall "deprive any person of life, liberty, or property, without due process of law." The fundamental liberties protected by this Clause include most of the rights enumerated in the Bill of Rights. In addition these liberties extend to certain personal choices central to individual dignity and autonomy, including intimate choices that define personal identity and beliefs.

The identification and protection of fundamental rights is an enduring part of the judicial duty to interpret the Constitution. That responsibility, however, "has not been reduced to any formula." Rather, it requires courts to exercise reasoned judgment in identifying interests of the person so fundamental that the State must accord them its respect. That process is guided by many of the same considerations relevant to analysis of other constitutional provisions that set forth broad principles rather than specific requirements. History and tradition guide and discipline this inquiry but do not set its outer boundaries. That method respects our history and learns from it without allowing the past alone to rule the present.

The nature of injustice is that we may not always see it in our own times. The generations that wrote and ratified the Bill of Rights and the Fourteenth Amendment did not presume to know the extent of freedom in all of its dimensions, and so they entrusted to future generations a charter protecting the right of all persons to enjoy liberty as we learn its meaning. When new insight reveals discord between the Constitution's central protections and a received legal stricture, a claim to liberty must be addressed.

Applying these established tenets, the Court has long held the right to marry is protected by the Constitution. In *Loving v. Virginia* (1967), which invalidated bans on interracial unions, a unanimous Court held marriage is "one of the vital personal rights essential to the orderly pursuit of happiness by free men.". . .

It cannot be denied that [*Loving*] . . . presumed a relationship involving opposite-sex partners. The Court, like many institutions, has made assumptions defined by the world and time of which it is a part. . . .

. . . In defining the right to marry . . . [this Court's] cases have identified essential attributes of that right based in history, tradition, and other constitutional liberties inherent in this intimate bond. And in assessing whether the force and rationale of its cases apply to same-sex couples, the Court must respect the basic reasons why the right to marry has been long protected.

This analysis compels the conclusion that same-sex couples may exercise the right to marry. The four principles and traditions to be discussed demonstrate that the reasons marriage is fundamental under the Constitution apply with equal force to same-sex couples.

A first premise of the Court's relevant precedents is that the right to personal choice regarding marriage is inherent in the concept of individual autonomy. This abiding connection between marriage and liberty is why *Loving* invalidated interracial marriage bans under the Due Process Clause. Like choices concerning contraception, family relationships, procreation, and childrearing, all of which are protected by the Constitution, decisions concerning marriage are among the most intimate that an individual can make. Indeed, the Court has noted it would be contradictory "to recognize a right of privacy with respect to other matters of family life and not with respect to the decision to enter the relationship that is the foundation of the family in our society."

Choices about marriage shape an individual's destiny. . . .

The nature of marriage is that, through its enduring bond, two persons together can find other freedoms, such as expression, intimacy, and spirituality. This is true for all persons, whatever their sexual orientation. There is dignity in the bond between two men or two women who seek to marry and in their autonomy to make such profound choices.

A second principle in this Court's jurisprudence is that the right to marry is fundamental because it supports a two-person union unlike any other in its importance to the committed individuals. This point was central to *Griswold* v. *Connecticut*, which held the Constitution protects the right of married couples to use contraception. Suggesting that marriage is a right "older than the Bill of Rights," *Griswold* described marriage this way:

> "Marriage is a coming together for better or for worse, hopefully enduring, and intimate to the degree of being sacred. It is an association that promotes a way of life, not causes; a harmony in living, not political faiths; a bilateral loyalty, not commercial or social projects. Yet it is an association for as noble a purpose as any involved in our prior decisions."

. . . The right to marry thus dignifies couples who "wish to define themselves by their commitment to each other." *Windsor*. Marriage responds to the universal fear that a lonely person might call out only to find no one there. It offers the hope of companionship and understanding and assurance that while both still live there will be someone to care for the other. . . .

A third basis for protecting the right to marry is that it safeguards children and families and thus draws meaning from related rights of childrearing, procreation, and education. The Court has recognized these connections by describing the varied rights as a unified whole: "[T]he right to 'marry, establish a home and bring up children' is a central part of the liberty protected by the Due Process Clause." Under the laws of the several States, some of marriage's protections for children and families are material. But marriage also confers more profound benefits. By giving recognition and legal structure to their parents' relationship, marriage allows children "to understand the integrity and closeness of their own family and its concord with other families in their community and in their daily lives." Marriage also affords the permanency and stability important to children's best interests. . . .

That is not to say the right to marry is less meaningful for those who do not or cannot have children. An ability, desire, or promise to procreate is not and has not been a prerequisite for a valid marriage in any State. In light of precedent protecting the right of a married couple not to procreate, it cannot be said the Court or the States have conditioned the right to marry on the capacity or commitment to procreate. The constitutional marriage right has many aspects, of which childbearing is only one.

Fourth and finally, this Court's cases and the Nation's traditions make clear that marriage is a keystone of our social order. . . .

In *Maynard v. Hill* (1888), the Court . . . explain[ed] that marriage is "the foundation of the family and of society, without which there would be neither civilization nor progress." Marriage, the *Maynard* Court said, has long been "a great public institution, giving character to our whole civil polity." This idea has been reiterated even as the institution has evolved in substantial ways over time, superseding rules related to parental consent, gender, and race once thought by many to be essential. Marriage remains a building block of our national community.

For that reason, just as a couple vows to support each other, so does society pledge to support the couple, offering symbolic recognition and material benefits to protect and nourish the union. Indeed, while the States are in general free to vary the benefits they confer on all married couples, they have throughout our history made marriage the basis for an expanding list of governmental rights, benefits, and responsibilities. These aspects of marital status include: taxation; inheritance and property rights; rules of intestate succession; spousal privilege in the law of evidence; hospital access; medical decisionmaking authority; adoption rights; the rights and benefits of survivors; birth and death certificates; professional ethics rules; campaign finance restrictions; workers' compensation benefits; health insurance; and child custody, support, and visitation rules. Valid marriage under state law is also a significant status for over a thousand provisions of federal law. The States have contributed to the fundamental character of the marriage right by placing that institution at the center of so many facets of the legal and social order. . . .

The limitation of marriage to opposite-sex couples may long have seemed natural and just, but its inconsistency with the central meaning of the fundamental right to marry is now manifest. With that knowledge must come the recognition that laws excluding same-sex couples from the marriage right impose stigma and injury of the kind prohibited by our basic charter. . . .

The right to marry is fundamental as a matter of history and tradition, but rights come not from ancient sources alone. They rise, too, from a better informed understanding of how constitutional imperatives define a liberty that remains urgent in our own era. . . . Under the Constitution, same-sex couples seek in marriage the same legal treatment as opposite-sex couples, and it would disparage their choices and diminish their personhood to deny them this right.

The right of same-sex couples to marry that is part of the liberty promised by the Fourteenth Amendment is derived, too, from that Amendment's guarantee of the equal protection of the laws. The Due Process Clause and the Equal Protection Clause are connected in a profound way, though they set forth independent principles. Rights implicit in liberty and rights secured by equal protection may rest on different precepts and are not always coextensive, yet in some instances each may be instructive as to the meaning and reach of the other. In any particular case one Clause may be thought to capture the essence of the right in a more accurate and comprehensive way, even as the two Clauses may converge in the identification and definition of the right. This interrelation of the two principles furthers our understanding of what freedom is and must become.

The Court's cases touching upon the right to marry reflect this dynamic. In *Loving* the Court invalidated a prohibition on interracial marriage under both the Equal Protection Clause and the Due Process Clause. The Court first declared the prohibition invalid because of its unequal treatment of interracial couples. It stated: "There can be no doubt that restricting the freedom to marry solely because of racial classifications violates the central meaning of the Equal Protection Clause." With this link to equal protection the Court proceeded to hold the prohibition offended central precepts of liberty: "To deny this fundamental freedom on so unsupportable a basis as the racial classifications embodied in these statutes, classifications so directly subversive of the principle of equality at the heart of the Fourteenth Amendment, is surely to deprive all the State's citizens of liberty without due process of law." The reasons why marriage is a fundamental right became more clear and compelling from a full awareness and understanding of the hurt that resulted from laws barring interracial unions. . . .

This dynamic also applies to same-sex marriage. It is now clear that the challenged laws burden the liberty of same-sex couples, and it must be further acknowledged that they abridge central precepts of equality. Here the marriage laws enforced by the respondents are in essence unequal: same-sex couples are denied all the benefits afforded to opposite-sex couples and are barred from exercising a fundamental right. . . . And the Equal Protection Clause, like the Due Process Clause, prohibits this unjustified infringement of the fundamental right to marry.

These considerations lead to the conclusion that the right to marry is a fundamental right inherent in the liberty of the person, and under the Due Process and Equal Protection Clauses of the Fourteenth Amendment couples of the same-sex may not be deprived of that right and that liberty. The Court now holds that same-sex couples may exercise the fundamental right to marry. No longer may this liberty be denied to them. . . .

There may be an initial inclination in these cases to proceed with caution to await further legislation, litigation, and debate. The respondents warn there has been insufficient democratic discourse before deciding an issue so basic as the definition of marriage. . . .

Of course, the Constitution contemplates that democracy is the appropriate process for change, so long as that process does not abridge fundamental rights. . . . Indeed, it is most often through democracy that liberty is preserved and protected in our lives. . . .

[However, t]he dynamic of our constitutional system is that individuals need not await legislative action before asserting a fundamental right. . . . An individual can invoke a right to constitutional protection when he or she is harmed, even if the broader public disagrees and even if the legislature refuses to act. The idea of the Constitution "was to withdraw certain subjects from the vicissitudes of political controversy, to place them beyond the reach of majorities and officials and to establish them as legal principles to be applied by the courts.". . .

Finally, it must be emphasized that religions, and those who adhere to religious doctrines, may continue to advocate with utmost, sincere conviction that, by divine precepts, same-sex marriage should not be condoned. The First Amendment ensures that religious organizations and persons are given proper protection as they seek to teach the principles that are so fulfilling and so central to their lives and faiths, and to their own deep aspirations to continue the family structure they have long revered. The same is true of those who oppose same-sex marriage for other reasons. In turn, those who believe allowing same-sex marriage is proper or indeed essential, whether as a matter of religious conviction or secular belief, may engage those who disagree with their view in an open and searching debate. The Constitution, however, does not permit the State to bar same-sex couples from marriage on the same terms as accorded to couples of the opposite sex. . . .

The judgment of the Court of Appeals for the Sixth Circuit is reversed.

Justice Alito, with whom Justice Scalia and Justice Thomas join, dissenting.

Until the federal courts intervened, the American people were engaged in a debate about whether their States should recognize same-sex marriage. The question in these cases, however, is not what States *should* do about same-sex marriage but whether the Constitution answers that question for them. It does not. The Constitution leaves that question to be decided by the people of each State. . . .

To prevent five unelected Justices from imposing their personal vision of liberty upon the American people, the Court has held that "liberty" under the Due Process Clause should be understood to protect only those rights that are "deeply rooted in this Nation's history and tradition." And it is beyond dispute that the right to same-sex marriage is not among those rights. . . .

Attempting to circumvent the problem presented by the newness of the right found in these cases, the majority claims that the issue is the right to equal treatment. Noting that marriage is a fundamental right, the majority argues that a State has no valid reason for denying that right to same-sex couples. This reasoning is dependent upon a particular understanding of the purpose of civil marriage. Although the Court expresses the point in loftier terms, its argument is that the fundamental purpose of marriage is to promote the well-being of those who choose to marry. . . .

This understanding of marriage, which focuses almost entirely on the happiness of persons who choose to marry, is shared by many people today, but it is not the traditional one. For millennia, marriage was inextricably linked to the one thing that only an opposite-sex couple can do: procreate.

Adherents to different schools of philosophy use different terms to explain why society should formalize marriage and attach special benefits and obligations to persons who marry. Here, the States defending their adherence to the traditional understanding of marriage have explained their position using the pragmatic vocabulary that characterizes most American political discourse. Their basic argument is that States formalize and promote marriage, unlike other fulfilling human relationships, in order to encourage potentially procreative conduct to take place within a lasting unit that has long been thought to provide the best atmosphere for raising children. They thus argue that there are reasonable secular grounds for restricting marriage to opposite-sex couples.

If this traditional understanding of the purpose of marriage does not ring true to all ears today, that is probably because the tie between marriage and procreation has frayed. Today, for instance, more than 40% of all children in this country are born to unmarried women. This development undoubtedly is both a cause and a result of changes in our society's understanding of marriage.

While, for many, the attributes of marriage in 21st-century America have changed, those States that do not want to recognize same-sex marriage have not yet given up on the traditional understanding. They worry that by officially abandoning the older understanding, they may contribute to marriage's further decay. It is far beyond the outer reaches of this Court's authority to say that a State may not adhere to the understanding of marriage that has long prevailed. . . .

Today's decision usurps the constitutional right of the people to decide whether to keep or alter the traditional understanding of marriage. The decision will also have other important consequences.

It will be used to vilify Americans who are unwilling to assent to the new orthodoxy. In the course of its opinion, the majority compares traditional marriage laws to laws that denied equal treatment for African-Americans and women. The implications of this analogy will be exploited by those who are determined to stamp out every vestige of dissent.

Perhaps recognizing how its reasoning may be used, the majority attempts, toward the end of its opinion, to reassure those who oppose same-sex marriage that their rights of conscience will be protected. We will soon see whether this proves to be true. I assume that those who cling to old beliefs will be able to whisper their thoughts in the recesses of their homes, but if they repeat those views in public, they will risk being labeled as bigots and treated as such by governments, employers, and schools. . . .

95

Plessy v. Ferguson (1896)

Mr. Justice Brown delivered the opinion of the Court.

This case turns upon the constitutionality of an act of the General Assembly of the State of Louisiana, passed in 1890, providing for separate railway carriages for the white and colored races.

The first section of the statute enacts "that all railway companies carrying passengers in their coaches in this State, shall provide equal but separate accommodations for the white, and colored races, by providing two or more passenger coaches for each passenger train, or by dividing the passenger coaches by a partition so as to secure separate accommodations: *Provided,* That this section shall not be construed to apply to street railroads. No person or persons shall be permitted to occupy seats in coaches other than the ones assigned to them, on account of the race they belong to." . . .

The information filed in the criminal district court charged in substance that Plessy, being a passenger between two stations within the state of Louisiana, was assigned by officers of the company to the coach used by the race to which he belonged, but he insisted upon going into a coach used by the race to which he did not belong. Neither in the information nor plea was his particular race or color averred. . . .

The constitutionality of this act is attacked upon the ground that it conflicts . . . [with] the Fourteenth Amendment, which prohibits certain restrictive legislation on the part of the States. . . .

From *Plessy v. Ferguson*, 163 U.S. 537 (1896).

By the Fourteenth Amendment . . . the States are forbidden from making or enforcing any law which shall abridge the privileges or immunities of citizens of the United States, or shall deprive any person of life, liberty, or property without due process of law, or deny to any person within their jurisdiction the equal protection of the laws.

The object of the amendment was undoubtedly to enforce the absolute equality of the two races before the law, but in the nature of things it could not have been intended to abolish distinctions based upon color, or to enforce social as distinguished from political equality, or a commingling of the two races upon terms unsatisfactory to either. Laws permitting, and even requiring, their separation in places where they are liable to be brought into contact do not necessarily imply the inferiority of either race to the other, and have been generally, if not universally, recognized as within the competency of the state legislatures in the exercise of their police power. The most common instance of this is connected with the establishment of separate schools for white and colored children, which has been held to be a valid exercise of the legislative power even by courts of States where the political rights of the colored race have been longest and most earnestly enforced. . . .

The distinction between laws interfering with the political equality of the negro and those requiring the separation of the two races in schools, theaters, and railway carriages, has been frequently drawn by this court. Thus, in *Strauder v. West Virginia,* it was held that a law of West Virginia limiting to white male persons, twenty-one years of age and citizens of the state, the right to sit upon juries, was a discrimination which implied a legal inferiority in civil society. . . .

So far, then, as a conflict with the 14th Amendment is concerned, the case reduces itself to the question whether the statute of Louisiana is a reasonable regulation, and with respect to this there must necessarily be a large discretion on the part of the legislature. In determining the question of reasonableness it is at liberty to act with reference to the established usages, customs and traditions of the people, and with a view to the promotion of their comfort, and preservation of the public peace and good order. Gauged by this standard, we cannot say that a law which authorizes or even requires the separation of the two races in public conveyances is unreasonable, or more obnoxious to the 14th Amendment than the acts of Congress requiring separate schools for colored children in the District of Columbia, the constitutionality of which does not seem to have been questioned, or the corresponding acts of state legislatures.

We consider the underlying fallacy of the plaintiff's argument to consist in the assumption that the enforced separation of the two races stamps the colored race with a badge of inferiority. If this be so, it is not by reason of anything found in the act, but solely because the colored race chooses to put that construction upon it. The argument necessarily assumes that if as has been more than once the case, and is not unlikely to be so again, the colored race should become the dominant power in the state legislature, and should enact a law in precisely similar terms, it would thereby relegate the white race to an inferior position. We imagine that the white race, at least, would not acquiesce in this assumption. The argument also assumes that social prejudices may be overcome by legislation, and that equal rights cannot be secured to the negro except by an enforced commingling of the two races. We cannot accept this proposition. If the two races are to meet upon terms of social equality, it must be the result of natural affinities, a mutual appreciation of each other's merits and voluntary consent of individuals. As was said by the court of appeals of New York in *People v. Gallagher*, "this end can neither be accomplished nor promoted by laws which conflict with the general sentiment of the community upon whom they are designed to operate. When the government, therefore, has secured to each of its citizens equal rights before the law and equal opportunities for improvement and progress, it has accomplished the end for which it was organized and performed all of the functions respecting social advantages with which it is endowed." Legislation is powerless to eradicate racial instincts or to abolish distinctions based upon physical differences, and the attempt to do so can only result in accentuating the difficulties of the present situation. If the civil and political rights of both races be equal, one cannot be inferior to the other civilly or politically. If one race be inferior to the other socially, the Constitution of the United States cannot put them upon the same plane. . . .

Mr. Justice Harlan, dissenting.

. . . It was said in argument that the statute of Louisiana does not discriminate against either race, but prescribes a rule applicable alike to white and colored citizens. But this argument does not meet the difficulty. Every one knows that the statute in question had its origin in the purpose, not so much to exclude white persons from railroad cars occupied by blacks, as to exclude colored people from coaches occupied by or assigned to white persons. Railroad corporations of Louisiana did not make discrimination among whites in the matter of accommodation for travelers. The thing to accomplish was, under the guise of giving equal accommodation for whites and blacks, to compel the latter to keep to themselves while traveling in railroad passenger coaches. No one would be so wanting in candor as to assert the contrary. The fundamental objection, therefore, to the statute, is that it interferes with the personal freedom of citizens. . . .

The white race deems itself to be the dominant race in this country. And so it is, in prestige, in achievements, in education, in wealth, and in power. So, I doubt not, it will continue to be for all time, if it remains true to its great heritage, and holds fast to the principles of constitutional liberty. But in view of the constitution, in the eye of the law, there is in this country no superior, dominant, ruling class of citizens. There is no caste here. Our constitution is color-blind, and neither knows nor tolerates classes among citizens. In respect of civil rights, all citizens are equal before the law. The humblest is the peer of the most powerful. The law regards man as man, and takes no account of his surroundings or of his color when his civil rights as guaranteed by the supreme law of the land are involved. It is therefore to be regretted that this high tribunal, the final expositor of the fundamental law of the land, has reached the conclusion that it is competent for a state to regulate the enjoyment by citizens of their civil rights solely upon the basis of race. . . .

The arbitrary separation of citizens, on the basis of race, while they are on a public highway, is a badge of servitude wholly inconsistent with the civil freedom and the equality before the law established by the constitution. It cannot be justified upon any legal grounds.

If evils will result from the commingling of the two races upon public highways established for the benefit of all, they will be infinitely less than those that will surely come from state legislation regulating the enjoyment of civil rights upon the basis of race. We boast of the freedom enjoyed by our people above all other peoples. But it is difficult to reconcile that boast with a state of the law which, practically, puts the brand of servitude and degradation upon a large class of our fellow citizens,—our equals before the law. The thin disguise of "equal" accommodations for passengers in railroad coaches will not mislead anyone, nor atone for the wrong this day done. . . .

96

Brown v. Board of Education (1954)

Mr. Chief Justice Warren delivered the opinion of the Court.

These cases come to us from the States of Kansas, South Carolina, Virginia, and Delaware. They are premised on different facts and different local conditions, but a common legal question justifies their consideration together in this consolidated opinion.

In each of the cases, minors of the Negro race, through their legal representatives, seek the aid of the courts in obtaining admission to the public

From *Brown v. Board of Education*, 347 U.S. 483 (1954).

schools of their community on a nonsegregated basis. In each instance, they have been denied admission to schools attended by white children under laws requiring or permitting segregation according to race. This segregation was alleged to deprive the plaintiffs of the equal protection of the laws under the Fourteenth Amendment. . . .

In the first cases in this Court construing the Fourteenth Amendment, decided shortly after its adoption, the Court interpreted it as proscribing all state-imposed discriminations against the Negro race. The doctrine of "separate but equal" did not make its appearance in this Court until 1896 in the case of *Plessy v. Ferguson,* involving not education but transportation. American courts have since labored with the doctrine for over half a century. In this Court, there have been six cases involving the "separate but equal" doctrine in the field of public education. In *Cumming v. Board of Education of Richmond County,* and *Gong Lum v. Rice,* the validity of the doctrine itself was not challenged. In more recent cases, all on the graduate school level, inequality was found in that specific benefits enjoyed by white students were denied to Negro students of the same educational qualifications. In none of these cases was it necessary to reexamine the doctrine to grant relief to the Negro plaintiff. And in *Sweatt v. Painter* the Court expressly reserved decision on the question whether *Plessy v. Ferguson* should be held inapplicable to public education.

In approaching this problem, we cannot turn the clock back to 1868 when the Amendment was adopted, or even to 1896 when *Plessy v. Ferguson* was written. We must consider public education in the light of its full development and its present place in American life throughout the Nation. Only in this way can it be determined if segregation in public schools deprives these plaintiffs of the equal protection of the laws.

Today, education is perhaps the most important function of state and local governments. Compulsory school attendance laws and the great expenditures for education both demonstrate our recognition of the importance of education to our democratic society. It is required in the performance of our most basic public responsibilities, even service in the armed forces. It is the very foundation of good citizenship. Today it is a principal instrument in awakening the child to cultural values, in preparing him for later professional training, and in helping him to adjust normally to his environment. In these days, it is doubtful that any child may reasonably be expected to succeed in life if he is denied the opportunity of an education. Such an opportunity, where the state has undertaken to provide it, is a right which must be made available to all on equal terms.

We come then to the question presented: Does segregation of children in public schools solely on the basis of race, even though the physical facilities and other "tangible" factors may be equal, deprive the children of the minority group of equal educational opportunities? We believe that it does.

In *Sweatt v. Painter*, in finding that a segregated law school for Negroes could not provide them equal educational opportunities, this Court relied in large part on "those qualities which are incapable of objective measurement but which make for greatness in a law school." In *McLaurin v. Oklahoma State Regents*, the Court, in requiring that a Negro admitted to a white graduate school be treated like all other students, again resorted to intangible considerations: ". . . his ability to study, to engage in discussions and exchange views with other students, and, in general, to learn his profession." Such considerations apply with added force to children in grade and high schools. To separate them from others of similar age and qualifications solely because of their race generates a feeling of inferiority as to their status in the community that may affect their hearts and minds in a way unlikely ever to be undone. The effect of this separation on their educational opportunities was well stated by a finding in the Kansas case by a court which nevertheless felt compelled to rule against the Negro plaintiffs:

> "Segregation of white and colored children in public schools has a detrimental effect upon the colored children. The impact is greater when it has the sanction of the law; for the policy of separating the races is usually interpreted as denoting the inferiority of the negro group. A sense of inferiority affects the motivation of a child to learn. Segregation with the sanction of law, therefore, has a tendency to [retard] the educational and mental development of Negro children and to deprive them of some of the benefits they would receive in a racial[ly] integrated school system."

Whatever may have been the extent of psychological knowledge at the time of *Plessy v. Ferguson*, this finding is amply supported by modern authority.* Any language in *Plessy v. Ferguson* contrary to this finding is rejected.

We conclude that in the field of public education the doctrine of "separate but equal" has no place. Separate educational facilities are inherently unequal. Therefore, we hold that the plaintiffs and others similarly situated for whom the actions have been brought are, by reason of the segregation complained of, deprived of the equal protection of the laws guaranteed by the Fourteenth Amendment. . . .

---

*K. B. Clark, Effect of Prejudice and Discrimination on Personality Development (Mid-century White House Conference on Children and Youth, 1950); Witmer and Kotinsky, Personality in the Making (1952), c. VI; Deutscher and Chen, The Psychological Effects of Enforced Segregation: A Survey of Social Science Opinion, 26 J. Psychol. 259 (1948); Chein, What are the Psychological Effects of Segregation Under Conditions of Equal Facilities?, 3 Int. J. Opinion and Attitude Res. 229 (1949); Brameld, Educational Costs, in Discrimination and National Welfare (Maclver, ed. 1949), 44–48; Frazier, the Negro in the United States (1949), 674–681. And see generally Myrdal, An American Dilemma (1944).

97

Bolling v. Sharpe (1954)

Chief Justice Warren delivered the opinion of the Court.

This case challenges the validity of segregation in the public schools of the District of Columbia. The petitioners, minors of the Negro race, allege that such segregation deprives them of due process of law under the Fifth Amendment. They were refused admission to a public school attended by white children solely because of their race. . . .

We have this day held that the Equal Protection Clause of the Fourteenth Amendment prohibits the states from maintaining racially segregated public schools. The legal problem in the District of Columbia is somewhat different, however. The Fifth Amendment, which is applicable in the District of Columbia, does not contain an equal protection clause, as does the Fourteenth Amendment, which applies only to the states. But the concepts of equal protection and due process, both stemming from our American ideal of fairness, are not mutually exclusive. The "equal protection of the laws" is a more explicit safeguard of prohibited unfairness than "due process of law," and therefore we do not imply that the two are always interchangeable phrases. But, as this Court has recognized, discrimination may be so unjustifiable as to be violative of due process.

Classifications based solely upon race must be scrutinized with particular care, since they are contrary to our traditions, and hence constitutionally suspect. . . .

[I]n *Buchanan v. Warley* (1917), the Court held that a statute which limited the right of a property owner to convey his property to a person of another race was, as an unreasonable discrimination, a denial of due process of law.

Although the Court has not assumed to define "liberty" with any great precision, that term is not confined to mere freedom from bodily restraint. Liberty under law extends to the full range of conduct which the individual is free to pursue, and it cannot be restricted except for a proper governmental objective. Segregation in public education is not reasonably related to any

From *Bolling v. Sharpe*, 347 v.s. 497 (1954).

proper governmental objective, and thus it imposes on Negro children of the District of Columbia a burden that constitutes an arbitrary deprivation of their liberty in violation of the Due Process Clause.

In view of our decision that the Constitution prohibits the states from maintaining racially segregated public schools, it would be unthinkable that the same Constitution would impose a lesser duty on the Federal Government. We hold that racial segregation in the public schools of the District of Columbia is a denial of the due process of law guaranteed by the Fifth Amendment to the Constitution.

98

Grutter v. Bollinger (2003)

Justice O'Connor delivered the opinion of the Court.

This case requires us to decide whether the use of race as a factor in student admissions by the University of Michigan Law School is unlawful.

We last addressed the use of race in public higher education over 25 years ago. In the landmark *Bakke* case, we reviewed a racial set-aside program that reserved 16 out of 100 seats in a medical school class for members of certain minority groups. The decision produced six separate opinions, none of which commanded a majority of the Court. . . . The only holding for the Court in *Bakke* was that a "State has a substantial interest that legitimately may be served by a properly devised admissions program involving the competitive consideration of race and ethnic origin." Thus, we reversed that part of the lower court's judgment that enjoined the university "from any consideration of the race of any applicant."

Since this Court's splintered decision in *Bakke*, Justice Powell's opinion announcing the judgment of the Court has served as the touchstone for constitutional analysis of race-conscious admissions policies. Public and private universities across the Nation have modeled their own admissions programs on Justice Powell's views on permissible race-conscious policies.

Justice Powell began by stating that "[t]he guarantee of equal protection cannot mean one thing when applied to one individual and something else when applied to a person of another color. If both are not accorded the same

From *Grutter v. Bollinger*, 539 U.S. 306 (2003).

protection, then it is not equal." In Justice Powell's view, when governmental decisions "touch upon an individual's race or ethnic background, he is entitled to a judicial determination that the burden he is asked to bear on that basis is precisely tailored to serve a compelling governmental interest." Under this exacting standard, only one of the interests asserted by the university survived Justice Powell's scrutiny.

First, Justice Powell rejected an interest in "reducing the historic deficit of traditionally disfavored minorities in medical schools and in the medical profession "as an unlawful interest in racial balancing. Second, Justice Powell rejected an interest in remedying societal discrimination because such measures would risk placing unnecessary burdens on innocent third parties "who bear no responsibility for whatever harm the beneficiaries of the special admissions program are thought to have suffered." Third, Justice Powell rejected an interest in "increasing the number of physicians who will practice in communities currently underserved," concluding that even if such an interest could be compelling in some circumstances the program under review was not "geared to promote that goal."

Justice Powell approved the university's use of race to further only one interest: "the attainment of a diverse student body." . . .

We apply strict scrutiny to all racial classifications to "smoke out' illegitimate uses of race by assuring that [government] is pursuing a goal important enough to warrant use of a highly suspect tool."

Strict scrutiny is not "strict in theory, but fatal in fact." Although all governmental uses of race are subject to strict scrutiny, not all are invalidated by it. . . . When race-based action is necessary to further a compelling governmental interest, such action does not violate the constitutional guarantee of equal protection so long as the narrow-tailoring requirement is also satisfied. . . .

The Law School's educational judgment that such diversity is essential to its educational mission is one to which we defer. The Law School's assessment that diversity will, in fact, yield educational benefits is substantiated by respondents and their *amici*. Our scrutiny of the interest asserted by the Law School is no less strict for taking into account complex educational judgments in an area that lies primarily within the expertise of the university. Our holding today is in keeping with our tradition of giving a degree of deference to a university's academic decisions, within constitutionally prescribed limits.

We have long recognized that, given the important purpose of public education and the expansive freedoms of speech and thought associated with the university environment, universities occupy a special niche in our constitutional tradition. In announcing the principle of student body diversity as a compelling state interest, Justice Powell invoked our cases recognizing a constitutional dimension, grounded in the First Amendment, of

educational autonomy: "The freedom of a university to make its own judgment as to education includes the selection of its student body." From this
premise, Justice Powell reasoned that by claiming "the right to select those
students who will contribute the most to the 'robust exchange of ideas,' "
a university "seek[s] to achieve a goal that is of paramount importance in
the fulfillment of its mission." Our conclusion that the Law School has a
compelling interest in a diverse student body is informed by our view that
attaining a diverse student body is at the heart of the Law School's proper
institutional mission, and that "good faith" on the part of a university is
"presumed" absent "a showing to the contrary."

As part of its goal of "assembling a class that is both exceptionally academically qualified and broadly diverse," the Law School seeks to "enroll a
'critical mass' of minority students." The Law School's interest is not simply
"to assure within its student body some specified percentage of a particular
group merely because of its race or ethnic origin." That would amount to
outright racial balancing, which is patently unconstitutional. Rather, the
Law School's concept of critical mass is defined by reference to the educational benefits that diversity is designed to produce.

The Law School does not premise its need for critical mass on "any
belief that minority students always (or even consistently) express some
characteristic minority viewpoint on any issue." To the contrary, diminishing the force of such stereotypes is both a crucial part of the Law School's
mission, and one that it cannot accomplish with only token numbers of
minority students. Just as growing up in a particular region or having particular professional experiences is likely to affect an individual's views, so
too is one's own, unique experience of being a racial minority in a society,
like our own, in which race unfortunately still matters. The Law School has
determined, based on its experience and expertise, that a "critical mass" of
underrepresented minorities is necessary to further its compelling interest in
securing the educational benefits of a diverse student body.

Even in the limited circumstance when drawing racial distinctions is
permissible to further a compelling state interest, government is still "constrained in how it may pursue that end: [T]he means chosen to accomplish
the [government's] asserted purpose must be specifically and narrowly framed
to accomplish that purpose." The purpose of the narrow tailoring requirement is to ensure that "the means chosen 'fit' . . . th[e] compelling goal so
closely that there is little or no possibility that the motive for the classification was illegitimate racial prejudice or stereotype."

We find that the Law School's admissions program bears the hallmarks of
a narrowly tailored plan. As Justice Powell made clear in *Bakke*, truly individualized consideration demands that race be used in a flexible, nonmechanical
way. It follows from this mandate that universities cannot establish quotas for
members of certain racial groups or put members of those groups on separate

admissions tracks. Nor can universities insulate applicants who belong to certain racial or ethnic groups from the competition for admission. Universities can, however, consider race or ethnicity more flexibly as a "plus" factor in the context of individualized consideration of each and every applicant. . . .

Moreover, as Justice Kennedy concedes, between 1993 and 2000, the number of African-American, Latino, and Native-American students in each class at the Law School varied from 13.5 to 20.1 percent, a range inconsistent with a quota. . . .

That a race-conscious admissions program does not operate as a quota does not, by itself, satisfy the requirement of individualized consideration. When using race as a "plus" factor in university admissions, a university's admissions program must remain flexible enough to ensure that each applicant is evaluated as an individual and not in a way that makes an applicant's race or ethnicity the defining feature of his or her application.

What is more, the Law School actually gives substantial weight to diversity factors besides race. The Law School frequently accepts nonminority applicants with grades and test scores lower than underrepresented minority applicants (and other nonminority applicants) who are rejected. This shows that the Law School seriously weighs many other diversity factors besides race that can make a real and dispositive difference for nonminority applicants as well. By this flexible approach, the Law School sufficiently takes into account, in practice as well as in theory, a wide variety of characteristics besides race and ethnicity that contribute to a diverse student body. . . .

We agree with the Court of Appeals that the Law School sufficiently considered workable race-neutral alternatives. The District Court took the Law School to task for failing to consider race-neutral alternatives such as "using a lottery system" or "decreasing the emphasis for all applicants on undergraduate GPA and LSAT scores." But these alternatives would require a dramatic sacrifice of diversity, the academic quality of all admitted students, or both.

We acknowledge that "there are serious problems of justice connected with the idea of preference itself." . . . To be narrowly tailored, a race-conscious admissions program must not "unduly burden individuals who are not members of the favored racial and ethnic groups."

We are mindful, however, that "[a] core purpose of the Fourteenth Amendment was to do away with all governmentally imposed discrimination based on race." Accordingly, race-conscious admissions policies must be limited in time. This requirement reflects that racial classifications, however compelling their goals, are potentially so dangerous that they may be employed no more broadly than the interest demands. Enshrining a permanent justification for racial preferences would offend this fundamental equal protection principle. We see no reason to exempt race-conscious admissions programs from the requirement that all governmental use of race must have a logical end point. The Law School, too, concedes that all "race-conscious programs must have reasonable durational limits."

In the context of higher education, the durational requirement can be met by sunset provisions in race-conscious admissions policies and periodic reviews to determine whether racial preferences are still necessary to achieve student body diversity. Universities in California, Florida, and Washington State, where racial preferences in admissions are prohibited by state law, are currently engaged in experimenting with a wide variety of alternative approaches. Universities in other States can and should draw on the most promising aspects of these race-neutral alternatives as they develop.

The requirement that all race-conscious admissions programs have a termination point "assure[s] all citizens that the deviation from the norm of equal treatment of all racial and ethnic groups is a temporary matter, a measure taken in the service of the goal of equality itself.". . . .

We take the Law School at its word that it would "like nothing better than to find a race-neutral admissions formula" and will terminate its race-conscious admissions program as soon as practicable. It has been 25 years since Justice Powell first approved the use of race to further an interest in student body diversity in the context of public higher education. Since that time, the number of minority applicants with high grades and test scores has indeed increased. We expect that 25 years from now, the use of racial preferences will no longer be necessary to further the interest approved today.

Chief Justice Rehnquist, with whom Justice Scalia, Justice Kennedy, and Justice Thomas join, dissenting.

I agree with the Court that, "in the limited circumstance when drawing racial distinctions is permissible," the government must ensure that its means are narrowly tailored to achieve a compelling state interest. I do not believe, however, that the University of Michigan Law School's means are narrowly tailored to the interest it asserts. The Law School claims it must take the steps it does to achieve a " 'critical mass' " of underrepresented minority students. But its actual program bears no relation to this asserted goal. Stripped of its "critical mass" veil, the Law School's program is revealed as a naked effort to achieve racial balancing.

Before the Court's decision today, we consistently applied the same strict scrutiny analysis regardless of the government's purported reason for using race and regardless of the setting in which race was being used. . . .

Although the Court recites the language of our strict scrutiny analysis, its application of that review is unprecedented in its deference.

In practice, the Law School's program bears little or no relation to its asserted goal of achieving "critical mass.". . . From 1995 through 2000, the Law School admitted between 1,130 and 1,310 students. Of those, between 13 and 19 were Native American, between 91 and 108 were

African-Americans, and between 47 and 56 were Hispanic. If the Law School is admitting between 91 and 108 African-Americans in order to achieve "critical mass," thereby preventing African-American students from feeling "isolated or like spokespersons for their race," one would think that a number of the same order of magnitude would be necessary to accomplish the same purpose for Hispanics and Native Americans. Similarly, even if all of the Native American applicants admitted in a given year matriculate, which the record demonstrates is not at all the case, how can this possibly constitute a "critical mass" of Native Americans in a class of over 350 students? In order for this pattern of admission to be consistent with the Law School's explanation of "critical mass," one would have to believe that the objectives of "critical mass" offered by respondents are achieved with only half the number of Hispanics and one-sixth the number of Native Americans as compared to African-Americans. But respondents offer no race-specific reasons for such disparities. Instead, they simply emphasize the importance of achieving "critical mass," without any explanation of why that concept is applied differently among the three under-represented minority groups. . . .

But the correlation between the percentage of the Law School's pool of applicants who are members of the three minority groups and the percentage of the admitted applicants who are members of these same groups is far too precise to be dismissed as merely the result of the school paying "some attention to [the] numbers." . . . [F]rom 1995 through 2000 the percentage of admitted applicants who were members of these minority groups closely tracked the percentage of individuals in the school's applicant pool who were from the same groups.

The tight correlation between the percentage of applicants and admittees of a given race, therefore, must result from careful race based planning by the Law School. It suggests a formula for admission based on the aspirational assumption that all applicants are equally qualified academically, and therefore that the proportion of each group admitted should be the same as the proportion of that group in the applicant pool. . . .

I do not believe that the Constitution gives the Law School such free rein in the use of race. The Law School has offered no explanation for its actual admissions practices and, unexplained, we are bound to conclude that the Law School has managed its admissions program, not to achieve a "critical mass," but to extend offers of admission to members of selected minority groups in proportion to their statistical representation in the applicant pool. But this is precisely the type of racial balancing that the Court itself calls "patently unconstitutional."

The Court suggests a possible 25-year limitation on the Law School's current program. Respondents, on the other hand, remain more ambiguous, explaining that "the Law School of course recognizes that race-conscious programs must have reasonable durational limits, and the Sixth Circuit properly found such a limit in the Law School's resolve to cease considering race when genuine race-neutral alternatives become available." These discussions of a time limit are the vaguest of assurances. In truth, they permit the Law School's use of racial preferences on a seemingly permanent basis. Thus, an important component of strict scrutiny—that a program be limited in time—is casually subverted.

The Court, in an unprecedented display of deference under our strict scrutiny analysis, upholds the Law School's program despite its obvious flaws. We have said that when it comes to the use of race, the connection between the ends and the means used to attain them must be precise. But here the flaw is deeper than that; it is not merely a question of "fit" between ends and means. Here the means actually used are forbidden by the Equal Protection Clause of the Constitution.

99

Eugene J. McCarthy

A Note on the New Equality (1977)

. . . Alexis de Tocqueville, in *Democracy in America*, wrote of the powerful appeal and danger of the idea of equality in a democratic society. He wrote also of its potential for demagoguery. I would be less concerned about the rise to popularity of the word, and the idea, if I thought it the result of conscious intention to elicit political support—that is, if those who made the appeal knew that they were being demagogic. I fear, however, that the use of the word is not intentionally demagogic. It seems to approach the automatic "It is good" justification that George Orwell described as characterizing the world order of 1984.

In his inaugural address President Carter said: "We have already found a high degree of personal liberty, and we are now struggling to enhance equality of opportunity." One may well question the President's language. Liberty was a goal of the American Revolution. We have it in this country

Reprinted from *Commentary*, by permission; copyright 1977 by the American Jewish Committee.

not because we "found" it but rather as a result of our having declared it a political and social goal and then achieving it in some measure. As to the President's second point, that "we are now struggling to enhance equality of opportunity," such language does not clearly describe the concept of "equality" as it is applied today. Economic, educational, political, and cultural equality—and not equality of opportunity, "enhanced" or otherwise—is the goal in the new application.

Economic equality is in this new conception to be achieved primarily through equalizing income. Equalization of wealth—that is, of wealth already accumulated—may come later. Economic equality is not conceived as a base upon which differences may then build, but as an average. One state governor occasionally asks if it might be better if people doing unpleasant work were paid as much as or more than those whose work is culturally and physically preferable.

Political economists have developed the notion of a negative income tax as the basis for tax reform. Essentially the idea is this: that everyone should have enough income to pay taxes at the beginning or threshold rate, and that if one does not have enough income to reach that level, something should be done to make up for the deficiency. Where the idea came from, or how the taxable level of income was chosen as the absolute standard for relative judgments and adjustments, is not clear. It seems that the tax base is to be accepted as a first principle upon which we are to build. It is an axiom, rather like "I think, therefore I am." One could as well arbitrarily assert that everyone should, for the good of the commonwealth, pay $100 in income taxes, and then proceed through measures of redistribution to raise all incomes to the level at which everyone would have to pay $100 in taxes. . . .

The second area in which the new concept of equality is being applied is in politics and government. The principle of one-person-one-vote was formally recognized in a Supreme Court ruling affecting defined political jurisdictions. The court did not in its ruling extend the principle to relationships among jurisdictions. The ruling simply said that, within given units of government, each vote should be equal to every other vote. Thus, since the Constitution provides for direct election of the House of Representatives on the basis of population, the rule requires that each congressional district have roughly the same number of persons.

The Constitution also provides that each state, no matter what its size, shall have two Senators. Thus the citizen of a small state gets proportionally more of a vote than the resident of a large state. The Constitution further provides that the President shall be elected through the Electoral College, on a state-by-state basis, thus weighting the votes of smaller states favorably as against those cast in larger states. The drive now is to eliminate that weighting by abolishing the Electoral College and instituting direct popular election of the President. No proposal has yet been made to reduce senatorial representation to a strict population base.

The principle of equality is also applied through the Federal Election Campaign Act, which attempts to equalize the non-voting influence of citizens on candidates for political office. The present law limits the size of contributions to a political candidate in any one campaign to $1,000 per contributor. This is considered a transitional phase to a time when all campaigns will be publicly financed. The argument for the limitation is that the larger the contribution, the greater the influence a contributor has on the officeholder and the more time he gets to spend with the officeholder. Theoretically, with public financing, every taxpayer will have made an equal contribution and will be entitled to as much time with the officeholder as any other taxpayer. What time non-taxpayers will get has not yet been determined by the reformers. Despite the $1,000 limit on contributions in the last national elections, and the fact that the presidential campaigns were financed principally through federal grants, within a few days of the election President-elect Carter flew to St. Simon's Island, the domain of the Reynolds family, and President Ford went to Palm Springs—presumably to speak to the average citizens who dwell in those precincts.

It does not take much imagination to foresee a time when citizens might go to court, charging that they were discriminated against because their calls were not taken in presidential telethons and transmitted to the President for his attention. A full practical application of this principle would argue for an equal right to speak or otherwise communicate with all officeholders, even removing the personal screening of Walter Cronkite.

The objective of equalizing communications and influence on office-holders is also sought in efforts to control lobbyists. Proposals generally recommend more thorough regulation of lobbyists, limits on their expenditures, and public disclosure not only of expenditures but also of meetings and communications with officeholders.

It will not be surprising if someone suggests having lobbyists provided at government expense, so as to insulate them from the undue influence of their principals, in somewhat the same way that officeholders are to be insulated from their constituencies. Under this arrangement, anyone who had a case to make to the government would apply for a lobbyist who would be assigned from a pool in the way that public defenders are assigned by the courts. . . .

The new concept of equality is also applied in government and government-influenced employment practices, in what has been labeled the "quota system." The rationale of the quota system is that, since not every person can be hired, we should have within each employed group a representation or sampling of the total employable work force. Selection currently is on the basis of physiological characteristics of age, sex, and race. There are some obvious historical reasons as to why these standards are being tried. There are also some obvious difficulties in their application, especially if one attempts to extend the principle—as will surely be done—to other racial and ethnic groups, or to groups less easily defined in terms of psychological and cultural differences.

A similar drive to realize the new idea of equality has marked educational development in recent years. The standardized curriculum, quota admissions, open admissions, and free college education are all manifestations of this drive. Full application of the principle could lead to compulsory college education, with the level of education so reduced that all who enter do so with assurance of successful graduation. With no possible abandonment of hope at any point, they could look forward to something like the judgment of the Dodo after the caucus race in Alice in Wonderland. "*Everybody* has won, and *all* must have prizes."

What are the dangers in this drive to a newly conceived equality? I see a danger first in the inevitable weakening of those institutions that are expected to give form and direction to society, such as professional and educational institutions, and which have traditionally been treated as having an identity separate from politically-controlled areas of society.

I see it also as significantly affecting the individual's conception of his place in society. Most persons cannot stand either physical or cultural isolation, and will seek a base of some certainty in a community of persons and in a cultural complex. The cultural security of Americans traditionally has been found in a society of some tension, but a society in which a balance between individual freedom and liberty on the one side and the social good on the other could be achieved. The alternative now offered, the security of equalization, is depersonalizing. It is a deceptively angelistic conception of man in society. It is one which cannot be sustained. It will in all likelihood move persons in search of security, if not identity, to accept greater and greater socialization in politics, in economics, and in culture.

100

Kurt Vonnegut, Jr.

Harrison Bergeron (1961)

The year was 2081, and everybody was finally equal. They weren't only equal before God and the law. They were equal every which way. Nobody was smarter than anybody else. Nobody was better looking than anybody else. Nobody was stronger or quicker than anybody else. All this equality was due to the 211th, 212th, and 213th Amendments to the Constitution, and to the unceasing vigilance of agents of the United States Handicapper General.

Some things about living still weren't quite right, though. April, for instance, still drove people crazy by not being springtime. And it was in that clammy month that the H-G men took George and Hazel Bergeron's fourteen-year-old son, Harrison, away.

It was tragic, all right, but George and Hazel couldn't think about it very hard. Hazel had a perfectly average intelligence, which meant she couldn't think about anything except in short bursts. And George, while his intelligence was way above normal, had a little mental handicap radio in his ear. He was required by law to wear it at all times. It was tuned to a government transmitter. Every twenty seconds or so, the transmitter would send out some sharp noise to keep people like George from taking unfair advantage of their brains.

George and Hazel were watching television. There were tears on Hazel's cheeks, but she'd forgotten for the moment what they were about.

On the television screen were ballerinas.

A buzzer sounded in George's head. His thoughts fled in panic, like bandits from a burglar alarm.

"That was a real pretty dance, that dance they just did," said Hazel.

"Huh?" said George.

"That dance—it was nice," said Hazel.

"Yup," said George. He tried to think a little about the ballerinas. They weren't really very good—no better than anybody else would have been, anyway. They were burdened with sashweights and bags of birdshot, and their faces were masked, so that no one, seeing a free and graceful gesture or a pretty face, would feel like something the cat drug in. George was toying with the vague notion that maybe dancers shouldn't be handicapped. But he didn't get very far with it before another noise in his ear radio scattered his thoughts.

George winced. So did two out of the eight ballerinas.

Hazel saw him wince. Having no mental handicap herself, she had to ask George what the latest sound had been.

"Sounded like somebody hitting a milk bottle with a ball peen hammer," said George.

"I'd think it would be real interesting, hearing all the different sounds," said Hazel, a little envious. "All the things they think up."

"Um," said George.

"Only, if I was Handicapper General, you know what I would do?" said Hazel. Hazel, as a matter of fact, bore a strong resemblance to the Handicapper General, a woman named Diana Moon Glampers. "If I was Diana Moon Glampers," said Hazel, "I'd have chimes on Sunday—just chimes. Kind of in honor of religion."

"I could think, if it was just chimes," said George.

"Well—maybe make 'em real loud," said Hazel. "I think I'd make a good Handicapper General."

"Good as anybody else," said George.

"Who knows bett'n I do what normal is?" said Hazel.

"Right," said George. He began to think glimmeringly about his abnormal son who was now in jail, about Harrison, but a twenty-one-gun salute in his head stopped that.

"Boy!" said Hazel, "that was a doozy, wasn't it?"

It was such a doozy that George was white and trembling, and tears stood on the rims of his red eyes. Two of the eight ballerinas had collapsed to the studio floor, were holding their temples.

"All of a sudden you look so tired," said Hazel. "Why don't you stretch out on the sofa, so's you can rest your handicap bag on the pillows, honeybunch." She was referring to the forty-seven pounds of birdshot in a canvas bag, which was padlocked around George's neck. "Go on and rest the bag for a little while," she said. "I don't care if your're not equal to me for a while."

George weighed the bag with his hands. "I don't mind it," he said. "I don't notice it any more. It's just a part of me."

"You been so tired lately—kind of wore out," said Hazel. "If there was just some way we could make a little hole in the bottom of the bag, and just take out a few of them lead balls. Just a few."

"Two years in prison and two thousand dollars fine for every ball I took out, " said George. "I don't call that a bargain."

"If you could just take a few out when you came home from work," said Hazel. "I mean—you don't compete with anybody around here. You just set around."

"If l tried to get away with it," said George, "then other people'd get away with it—and pretty soon we'd be right back to the dark ages again, with everybody competing against everybody else. You wouldn't like that, would you?"

"I'd hate it," said Hazel.

"There you are," said George. "The minute people start cheating on laws, what do you think happens to society?"

If Hazel hadn't been able to come up with an answer to this question, George couldn't have supplied one. A siren was going off in his head. "Reckon it'd fall all apart," said Hazel.

"What would?" said George blankly.

"Society," said Hazel uncertainly. "Wasn't that what you just said?"

"Who knows?" said George.

The television program was suddenly interrupted for a news bulletin. It wasn't clear at first as to what the bulletin was about, since the announcer, like all announcers, had a serious speech impediment. For about half a minute, and in a state of high excitement, the announcer tried to say, "Ladies and gentlemen—"

He finally gave up, handed the bulletin to a ballerina to read.

"That's all right—" Hazel said of the announcer, "he tried. That's the big thing. He tried to do the best he could with what God gave him. He should get a nice raise for trying so hard. "

"Ladies and gentlemen—" said the ballerina, reading the bulletin. She must have been extraordinarily beautiful, because the mask she wore was hideous. And it was easy to see that she was the strongest and most graceful of all the dancers, for her handicap bags were as big as those worn by two-hundred-pound men.

And she had to apologize at once for her voice, which was a very unfair voice for a woman to use. Her voice was a warm, luminous, timeless melody. "Excuse me—" she said, and she began again, making her voice absolutely uncompetitive.

"Harrison Bergeron, age fourteen," she said in a grackle squawk, "has just escaped from jail, where he was held on suspicion of plotting to overthrow the government. He is a genius and an athlete, is underhandicapped, and should be regarded as extremely dangerous."

A police photograph of Harrison Bergeron was flashed on the screen upside down, then sideways, upside down again, then right side up. The picture showed the full length of Harrison against a background calibrated in feet and inches. He was exactly seven feet tall.

The rest of Harrison's appearance was Halloween and hardware. Nobody had ever born heavier handicaps. He had outgrown hindrances faster than the H-G men could think them up. Instead of a little ear radio for a mental handicap, he wore a tremendous pair of earphones, and spectacles with thick wavy lenses. The spectacles were intended to make him not only half blind, but to give him whanging headaches besides.

Scrap metal was hung all over him. Ordinarily, there was a certain symmetry, a military neatness to the handicaps issued to strong people, but Harrison looked like a walking junkyard. In the race of life, Harrison carried three hundred pounds.

And to offset his good looks, the H-G men required that he wear at all times a red rubber ball for a nose, keep his eyebrows shaved off, and cover his even white teeth with black caps at snaggle-tooth random.

"If you see this boy," said the ballerina, "do not—I repeat, do not—try to reason with him."

There was the shriek of a door being torn from its hinges.

Screams and barking cries of consternation came from the television set. The photograph of Harrison Bergeron on the screen jumped again and again, as though dancing to the tune of an earthquake.

George Bergeron correctly identified the earthquake, and well he might have—for many was the time his own home had danced to the same crashing tune. "My God—" said George, "that must be Harrison!"

The realization was blasted from his mind instantly by the sound of an automobile collision in his head.

When George could open his eyes again, the photograph of Harrison was gone. A living, breathing Harrison filled the screen.

Clanking, clownish, and huge, Harrison stood in the center of the studio. The knob of the uprooted studio door was still in his hand. Ballerinas, technicians, musicians, and announcers cowered on their knees before him, expecting to die.

"I am the Emperor!" cried Harrison. "Do you hear? I am the Emperor! Everybody must do what I say at once!" He stamped his foot and the studio shook.

"Even as I stand here—" he bellowed, "crippled, hobbled, sickened—I am a greater ruler than any man who ever lived! Now watch me become what I *can* become!"

Harrison tore the straps of his handicap harness like wet tissue paper, tore straps guaranteed to support five thousand pounds.

Harrison's scrap-iron handicaps crashed to the floor.

Harrison thrust his thumbs under the bar of the padlock that secured his head harness. The bar snapped like celery. Harrison smashed his headphones and spectacles against the wall.

He flung away his rubber-ball nose, revealed a man that would have awed Thor, the god of thunder.

"I shall now select my Empress!" he said, looking down on the cowering people. "Let the first woman who dares rise to her feet claim her mate and her throne!"

A moment passed, and then a ballerina arose, swaying like a willow.

Harrison plucked the mental handicap from her ear, snapped off her physical handicaps with marvelous delicacy. Last of all, he removed her mask.

She was blindingly beautiful.

"Now—" said Harrison, taking her hand, "shall we show the people the meaning of the word dance? Music!" he commanded.

The musicians scrambled back into their chairs, and Harrison stripped them of their handicaps, too. "Play your best," he told them, "and I'll make you barons and dukes and earls."

The music began. It was normal at first—cheap, silly, false. But Harrison snatched two musicians from their chairs, waved them like batons as he sang the music as he wanted it played. He slammed them back into their chairs.

The music began again and was much improved.

Harrison and his Empress merely listened to the music for a while listened gravely, as though synchronizing their heartbeats with it.

They shifted their weights to their toes.

Harrison placed his big hands on the girl's tiny waist, letting her sense the weightlessness that would soon be hers.

And then, in an explosion of joy and grace, into the air they sprang!

Not only were the laws of the land abandoned, but the law of gravity and the laws of motion as well.

They reeled, whirled, swiveled, flounced, capered, gamboled, and spun.

They leaped like deer on the moon.

The studio ceiling was thirty feet high, but each leap brought the dancers nearer to it.

It became their obvious intention to kiss the ceiling.

They kissed it.

And then, neutralizing gravity with love and pure will, they remained suspended in air inches below the ceiling, and they kissed each other for a long, long time.

It was then that Diana Moon Glampers, the Handicapper General, came into the studio with a double-barreled ten-gauge shotgun. She fired twice, and the Emperor and the Empress were dead before they hit the floor.

Diana Moon Glampers loaded the gun again. She aimed it at the musicians and told them they had ten seconds to get their handicaps back on.

It was then that the Bergerons' television tube burned out.

Hazel turned to comment about the blackout to George. But George had gone out into the kitchen for a can of beer.

George came back in with the beer, paused while a handicap signal shook him up. And then he sat down again. "You been crying?" he said to Hazel.

"Yup," she said.

"What about?" he said.

"I forget," she said. "Something real sad on television."

"What was it?" he said.

"It's all kind of mixed up in my mind," said Hazel.

"Forget sad things," said George.

"I always do," said Hazel.

"That's my girl," said George. He winced. There was the sound of a rivetting gun in his head.

"Gee—I could tell that one was a doozy," said Hazel.

"You can say that again," said George.

"Gee—" said Hazel, "I could tell that one was a doozy."

101

Thomas Jefferson

The Natural Aristocracy (1813)

JEFFERSON TO ADAMS

. . . For I agree with you that there is a natural aristocracy among men. The grounds of this are virtue and talents. Formerly bodily powers gave place among the aristoi. But since the invention of gunpowder has armed the weak as well as the strong with missile death, bodily strength, like

From *The Adams-Jefferson Letters*. Vol. 11, Lester J. Cappon, ed., University of North Carolina Press, 1959.

beauty, good humor, politeness and other accomplishments, has become but an auxiliary ground of distinction. There is also an artificial aristocracy founded on wealth and birth, without either virtue or talents; for with these it would belong to the first class. The natural aristocracy I consider as the most precious gift of nature for the instruction, the trusts, and government of society. And indeed it would have been inconsistent in creation to have formed man for the social state, and not to have provided virtue and wisdom enough to manage the concerns of the society. May we not even say that that form of government is the best which provides the most effectually for a pure selection of these natural aristoi into the offices of government? The artificial aristocracy is a mischievous ingredient in government, and provision should be made to prevent it's ascendancy. On the question, What is the best provision, you and I differ; but we differ as rational friends, using the free exercise of our own reason, and mutually indulging its errors. *You* think it best to put the Pseudo-aristoi into a separate chamber of legislation where they may be hindered from doing mischief by their coordinate branches, and where also they may be a protection to wealth against the Agrarian and plundering enterprises of the Majority of the people. I think that to give them power in order to prevent them from doing mischief, is arming them for it, and increasing instead of remedying the evil. For if the coordinate branches can arrest their action, so may they that of the coordinates. Mischief may be done negatively as well as positively. Of this a cabal in the Senate of the U.S. has furnished many proofs. Nor do I believe them necessary to protect the wealthy; because enough of these will find their way into every branch of the legislation to protect themselves. From 15 to 20 legislatures of our own, in action for 30 years past, have proved that no fears of an equalisation of property are to be apprehended from them.

I think the best remedy is exactly that provided by all our constitutions, to leave to the citizens the free election and separation of the aristoi from the pseudo-aristoi, of the wheat from the chaff. In general they will elect the real good and wise. In some instances, wealth may corrupt, and birth blind them; but not in sufficient degree to endanger the society.

It is probable that our difference of opinion may in some measure be produced by a difference of character in those among whom we live. From what I have seen of Massachusetts and Connecticut myself, and still more from what I have heard and the character given of the former by yourself, who know them so much better, there seems to be in these two states a traditionary reverence for certain families, which has rendered the offices of the government nearly hereditary in those families. I presume that from an early period of your history, members of these families happening to possess virtue and talents, have honestly exercised them for the good of the people, and by their services have endeared their names to them. . . .

At the first session of our legislature after the Declaration of Independence, we passed a law abolishing entails. And this was followed by one abolishing the privilege of Primogeniture, and dividing the lands of intestates equally among all their children, or other representatives. These laws, drawn by myself, laid the axe to the root of Pseudo-aristocracy. And had another which I prepared been adopted by the legislature, our work would have been complete. It was a Bill for more general diffusion of learning. This proposed to divide every county into wards of 5 or 6 miles square, like your townships; to establish in each ward a free school for reading, writing and common arithmetic; to provide for the annual selection of the best subjects from these schools who might receive at the public expense a higher degree of education at a district school; and from these district schools to select a certain number of the most promising subjects to be completed at an University, where all the useful sciences should be taught. Worth and genius would thus have been sought out from every condition of life, and completely prepared by education for defeating the competition of wealth and birth for public trusts.

My proposition had for a further object to impart to these wards those portions of self-government for which they are best qualified, by confiding to them the care of their poor, their roads, police, elections, the nomination of jurors, administration of justice in small cases, elementary exercises of militia, in short, to have made them little republics, with a Warden at the head of each, for all those concerns which, being under their eye, they would better manage than the larger republics of the county or state. A general call of ward-meetings by their Wardens on the same day thro' the state would at any time produce the genuine sense of the people on any required point, and would enable the state to act in mass, as your people have so often done, and with so much effect, by their town meetings. The law for religious freedom, which made a part of this system, having put down the aristocracy of the clergy, and restored to the citizen the freedom of the mind, and those of entails and descents nurturing an equality of condition among them, this on Education would have raised the mass of the people to the high ground of moral respectability necessary to their own safety, and to orderly government; and would have completed the great object of qualifying them to select the veritable aristoi, for the trusts of government, to the exclusion of the Pseudalists: and the same Theognis who has furnished the epigraphs of your two letters assures us that 'ουδεμιαν' πω Κυρν' αγαθοι πολιν ωλεσαν ανδρεσ ["Curnis, good men have never harmed any city"]'. Altho' this law has not yet been acted on but in a small and inefficient degree, it is still considered as before the legislature, with other bills of the revised code, not yet taken up, and I have great hope that some patriotic spirit will, at a favorable moment, call it up, and make it the key-stone of the arch of our government.

With respect to Aristocracy, we should further consider that, before the establishment of the American states, nothing was known to History but the Man of the old world, crowded within limits either small or over-charged, and steeped in the vices which that situation generates. A government adapted to such men would be one thing; but a very different one than for the Man of these states. Here every one may have land to labor for himself if he chuses; or, preferring the exercise of any other industry, may exact for it such compensation as not only to afford a comfortable subsistence, but wherewith to provide for a cessation from labor in old age. Every one, by his property, or by his satisfactory situation, is interested in the support of law and order. And such men may safely and advantageously reserve to themselves a wholesome control over their public affairs, and a degree of freedom, which in the hands of the Canaille of the cities of Europe, would be instantly perverted to the demolition and destruction of every thing public and private. The history of the last 25 years of France, and of the last 40 years in America, nay of it's last 200 years, proves the truth of both parts of this observation.

But even in Europe a change has sensibly taken place in the mind of Man. Science had liberated the ideas of those who read and reflect, and the American example had kindled feelings of right in the people. An insurrection has consequently begun, of science, talents and courage against rank and birth, which have fallen into contempt. It has failed in it's first effort, because the mobs of the cities, the instrument used for it's accomplishment, debased by ignorance, poverty and vice, could not be restrained to rational action. But the world will recover from the panic of this first catastrophe. Science is progressive, and talents and enterprize on the alert. Resort may be had to the people of the country, a more governable power from their principles and subordination; and rank, and birth, and tinsel-aristocracy will finally shrink into insignificance, even there. This however we have no right to meddle with. It suffices for us, if the moral and physical condition of our own citizens qualifies them to select the able and good for the direction of their government, with a recurrence of elections at such short periods as will enable them to displace an unfaithful servant before the mischief he meditates may be irremediable. . . .

102

Alexis de Tocqueville

Why So Many Ambitious Men and So Little Lofty Ambition Are to Be Found in the United States (1840)

The first thing that strikes a traveler in the United States is the innumerable multitude of those who seek to emerge from their original condition; and the second is the rarity of lofty ambition to be observed in the midst of the universally ambitious stir of society. No Americans are devoid of a yearning desire to rise, but hardly any appear to entertain hopes of great magnitude or to drive at very lofty aims. All are constantly seeking to acquire property, power, and reputation; few contemplate these things upon a great scale; and this is the more surprising as nothing is to be discerned in the manners or laws of America to limit desire or to prevent it from spreading its impulses in every direction. . . .

What chiefly diverts the men of democracies from lofty ambition is not the scantiness of their fortunes, but the vehemence of the exertions they daily make to improve them. They strain their faculties to the utmost to achieve paltry results, and this cannot fail speedily to limit their discernment and to circumscribe their powers. They might be much poorer and still be greater.

The small number of opulent citizens who are to be found amidst a democracy do not constitute an exception to this rule. A man who raises himself by degrees to wealth and power contracts, in the course of this protracted labor, habits of prudence and restraint which he cannot afterwards shake off. A man cannot enlarge his mind as he does his house. . . .

In a democratic society, as well as elsewhere, there is only a certain number of great fortunes to be made; and as the paths that lead to them are indiscriminately open to all, the progress of all must necessarily be slackened. As the candidates appear to be nearly alike, and as it is difficult to make a selection without infringing the principle of equality, which is the supreme law of democratic societies, the first idea which suggests itself is to make them

From *Democracy in America* by Alexis de Tocqueville, translated by Henry Reeve, 1862, with minor changes.

all advance at the same rate and submit to the same probation. . . . From hatred of privilege and from the embarrassment of choosing, all men are at last constrained, whatever may be their standard, to pass the same ordeal; all are indiscriminately subjected to a multitude of petty preliminary exercises, in which their youth is wasted and their imagination quenched, so that they despair of ever fully attaining what is held out to them; and when at length they are in a condition to perform any extraordinary acts, the taste for such things has forsaken them.

In China, where the equality of conditions is exceedingly great and very ancient, no man passes from one public office to another without undergoing a probationary trial. This probation occurs afresh at every stage of his career; and the notion is now so rooted in the manners of the people that I remember to have read a Chinese novel in which the hero, after numberless crosses, succeeds at length in touching the heart of his mistress by taking honors. A lofty ambition breathes with difficulty in such an atmosphere.

I confess that I apprehend much less for democratic society from the boldness that from the mediocrity of desires. What appears to me most to be dreaded is that in the midst of the small, incessant occupations of private life, ambition should lose its vigor and its greatness; that the passions of man should abate, but at the same time be lowered; so that the march of society should every day become more tranquil and less aspiring.

I think, then, that the leaders of modern society would be wrong to seek to lull the community by a state of too uniform and too peaceful happiness, and that it is well to expose it from time to time to matters of difficulty and danger in order to raise ambition and to give it a field of action.

Moralists are constantly complaining that the ruling vice of the present time is pride. This is true in one sense, for indeed everyone thinks that he is better than his neighbor or refuses to obey his superior; but it is extremely false in another, for the same man who cannot endure subordination or equality has so contemptible an opinion of himself that he thinks he is born only to indulge in vulgar pleasures. He willingly takes up with low desires without daring to embark on lofty enterprises, of which he scarcely dreams.

Thus, far from thinking that humility ought to be preached to our contemporaries, I would have endeavors made to give them a more enlarged idea of themselves and of their kind. Humility is unwholesome to them; what they most want is, in my opinion, pride. I would willingly exchange several of our small virtues for this one vice.

Appendix

The Constitution of the United States of America

We the People of the United States, in Order to form a more perfect Union, establish Justice, insure domestic Tranquillity, provide for the common defence, promote the general Welfare, and secure the Blessings of Liberty to ourselves and our Posterity, do ordain and establish this Constitution for the United States of America.

ARTICLE. I.

Section. 1. All legislative Powers herein granted shall be vested in a Congress of the United States, which shall consist of a Senate and House of Representatives.

Section. 2. The House of Representatives shall be composed of Members chosen every second Year by the People of the several States, and the Electors in each State shall have the Qualifications requisite for Electors of the most numerous Branch of the State Legislature.

No Person shall be a Representative who shall not have attained to the age of twenty-five Years, and been seven Years a Citizen of the United States, and who shall not, when elected, be an Inhabitant of that State in which he shall be chosen.

Representatives and direct Taxes shall be apportioned among the several States which may be included within this Union, according to their respective Numbers, which shall be determined by adding to the whole Number of free Persons, including those bound to Service for a Term of Years, and excluding Indians not taxed, three-fifths of all other Persons. The actual Enumeration shall be made within three Years after the first Meeting of the Congress of the United States, and within every subsequent Term of ten Years, in such Manner as they shall by Law direct. The Number of Representatives shall not exceed one for every thirty Thousand, but each State shall have at Least one Representative; and until such enumeration shall be made, the State of New Hampshire shall be entitled to chuse three, Massachusetts eight, Rhode-Island and Providence Plantations one, Connecticut five,

New York six, New Jersey four, Pennsylvania eight, Delaware one, Maryland six, Virginia ten, North Carolina five, South Carolina five, and Georgia three.

When vacancies happen in the Representation from any State, the Executive Authority thereof shall issue Writs of Election to fill such Vacancies.

The House of Representatives shall chuse their Speaker and other Officers; and shall have the sole Power of Impeachment.

Section. 3. The Senate of the United States shall be composed of two Senators from each State, chosen by the Legislature thereof, for six Years; and each Senator shall have one Vote.

Immediately after they shall be assembled in Consequence of the first Election, they shall be divided as equally as may be into three Classes. The Seats of the Senators of the first Class shall be vacated at the Expiration of the second Year, of the second Class at the Expiration of the fourth Year, and of the third Class at the Expiration of the sixth Year, so that one third may be chosen every second Year; and if Vacancies happen by Resignation, or otherwise, during the Recess of the Legislature of any State, the Executive thereof may make temporary Appointments until the next Meeting of the Legislature, which shall then fill such Vacancies.

No Person shall be a Senator who shall not have attained to the Age of thirty Years, and been nine Years a Citizen of the United States, and who shall not, when elected, be an Inhabitant of that State for which he shall be chosen.

The Vice President of the United States shall be President of the Senate, but shall have no Vote, unless they be equally divided.

The Senate shall chuse their other Officers, and also a President pro tempore, in the Absence of the Vice President, or when he shall exercise the Office of President of the United States.

The Senate shall have the sole Power to try all Impeachments. When sitting for that Purpose, they shall be on Oath or Affirmation. When the President of the United States is tried the Chief Justice shall preside: And no Person shall be convicted without the Concurrence of two thirds of the Members present.

Judgment in Cases of Impeachment shall not extend further than to removal from Office, and disqualification to hold and enjoy any Office of honor, Trust or Profit under the United States: but the Party convicted shall nevertheless be liable and subject to Indictment, Trial, Judgment and Punishment, according to Law.

Section. 4. The Times, Places and Manner of holding Elections for Senators and Representatives, shall be prescribed in each State by the Legislature thereof; but the Congress may at any time by Law make or alter such Regulations, except as to the Places of chusing Senators.

The Congress shall assemble at least once in every Year, and such Meeting shall be on the first Monday in December, unless they shall by Law appoint a different Day.

Section. 5. Each House shall be the Judge of the Elections, Returns and Qualifications of its own Members, and a Majority of each shall constitute a Quorum to do Business; but a smaller Number may adjourn from day to day, and may be authorized to compel the Attendance of absent Members, in such Manner, and under such Penalties as each House may provide.

Each House may determine the Rules of its Proceedings, punish its Members for disorderly Behaviour, and, with the Concurrence of two-thirds, expel a Member.

Each House shall keep a Journal of its Proceedings, and from time to time publish the same, excepting such Parts as may in their Judgment require Secrecy; and the Yeas and Nays of the Members of either House on any question shall, at the Desire of one-fifth of those Present, be entered on the Journal.

Neither House, during the Session of Congress, shall, without the Consent of the other, adjourn for more than three days, nor to any other Place than that in which the two Houses shall be sitting.

Section. 6. The Senators and Representatives shall receive a Compensation for their Services, to be ascertained by Law, and paid out of the Treasury of the United States. They shall in all Cases, except Treason, Felony and Breach of the Peace, be privileged from Arrest during their Attendance at the Session of their respective Houses, and in going to and returning from the same; and for any Speech or Debate in either House, they shall not be questioned in any other Place.

No Senator or Representative shall, during the Time for which he was elected, be appointed to any civil Office under the Authority of the United States, which shall have been created, or the Emoluments whereof shall have been encreased during such time; and no Person holding any Office under the United States, shall be a Member of either House during his Continuance in Office.

Section. 7. All Bills for raising Revenue shall originate in the House of Representatives; but the Senate may propose or concur with amendments as on other Bills.

Every Bill which shall have passed the House of Representatives and the Senate, shall, before it become a Law, be presented to the President of the United States; If he approve he shall sign it, but if not he shall return it, with his Objections to that House in which it shall have originated, who shall enter the Objections at large on their Journal, and proceed to reconsider it. If after such Reconsideration two thirds of that House shall agree to pass the Bill, it shall be sent, together with the Objections, to the other House, by which it shall likewise be reconsidered, and if approved by two thirds of that House, it shall become a Law. But in all such Cases the Votes of both Houses shall be determined by yeas and Nays, and the Names of the Persons voting for and against the Bill shall be entered on the Journal of each House respectively. If any Bill shall not be returned by the President within ten Days (Sunday excepted) after it shall have been presented to him, the Same shall be a Law, in like Manner as if he had signed it, unless the Congress by their Adjournment prevent its Return, in which Case it shall not be a Law.

Every Order, Resolution, or Vote to which the Concurrence of the Senate and House of Representatives may be necessary (except on a question of Adjournment) shall be presented to the President of the United States; and before the Same shall take Effect, shall be approved by him, or being disapproved by him, shall be repassed by two thirds of the Senate and House of Representatives, according to the Rules and Limitations prescribed in the Case of a Bill.

Section. 8. The Congress shall have Power To lay and collect Taxes, Duties, Imposts, and Excises, to pay the Debts and provide for the common Defence and general Welfare of the United States; but all Duties, Imposts and Excises shall be uniform throughout the United States;

To borrow Money on the credit of the United States;

To regulate Commerce with foreign Nations, and among the several States, and with the Indian Tribes;

To establish an uniform Rule of Naturalization, and uniform Laws on the subject of Bankruptcies throughout the United States;

To coin Money, regulate the Value thereof, and of foreign Coin, and fix the Standard of Weights and Measures;

To provide for the Punishment of counterfeiting the Securities and current Coin of the United States; To establish Post Offices and Post Roads;

To promote the Progress of Science and useful Arts, by securing for limited Times to Authors and Inventors the exclusive Right to their respective Writings and Discoveries;

To constitute Tribunals inferior to the supreme Court;

To define and punish Piracies and Felonies committed on the high Seas, and Offences against the Law of Nations;

To declare War, grant Letters of Marque and Reprisal, and make Rules concerning Captures on Land and Water;

To raise and support Armies, but no Appropriation of Money to that Use shall be for a longer Term than two Years;

To provide and maintain a Navy;

To make Rules for the Government and Regulation of the land and naval Forces;

To provide for calling forth the Militia to execute the Laws of the Union, suppress Insurrections and repel Invasions;

To provide for organizing, arming, and disciplining, the Militia, and for governing such Part of them as may be employed in the Service of the United States, reserving to the States respectively, the Appointment of the Officers, and the Authority of training the Militia according to the discipline prescribed by Congress;

To exercise exclusive Legislation in all Cases whatsoever, over such District (not exceeding ten Miles square) as may, by Cession of Particular States, and the Acceptance of Congress, become the Seat of the Government of the United States, and to exercise like Authority over all Places purchased by the Consent of the Legislature of the State in which the Same shall be, for the Erection of Forts, Magazines, Arsenals, dock-Yards, and other needful Buildings;—And

To make all Laws which shall be necessary and proper for carrying into Execution the foregoing Powers, and all other Powers vested by this Constitution in the Government of the United States, or in any Department or Officer thereof.

Section. 9. The Migration or Importation of such Persons as any of the States now existing shall think proper to admit, shall not be prohibited by the Congress prior to the Year one thousand eight hundred and eight, but a Tax or duty may be imposed on such Importation, not exceeding ten dollars for each Person.

The Privilege of the Writ of Habeas Corpus shall not be suspended, unless when in Cases of Rebellion or Invasion the public Safety may require it.

No Bill of Attainder or ex post facto Law shall be passed.

No Capitation, or other direct, Tax shall be laid, unless in Proportion to the Census of Enumeration herein before directed to be taken.

No Tax or Duty shall be laid on Articles exported from any State.

No Preference shall be given by any Regulation of Commerce or Revenue to the Ports of one State over those of another; nor shall Vessels bound to, or from, one State, be obliged to enter, clear or pay Duties in another.

No Money shall be drawn from the Treasury, but in Consequence of Appropriations made by Law; and a regular Statement and Account of the Receipts and Expenditures of all public Money shall be published from time to time.

No Title of Nobility shall be granted by the United States; And no Person holding any Office of Profit or Trust under them, shall, without the Consent of the Congress, accept of any present, Emolument, Office, or Title, of any kind whatever, from any King, Prince, or foreign State.

Section. 10. No State shall enter into any Treaty, Alliance, or Confederation; grant Letters of Marque and Reprisal; coin Money; emit Bills of Credit; make any Thing but gold and silver Coin a Tender in Payment of Debts; pass any Bill of Attainder, ex post facto Law, or Law impairing the Obligation of Contracts, or grant any Title of Nobility.

No State shall, without the Consent of the Congress, lay any Imposts or Duties on Imports or Exports, except what may be absolutely necessary for executing its inspection Laws; and the net Produce of all Duties and Imposts, laid by any State on Imports or Exports, shall be for the Use of the Treasury of the United States; and all such Laws shall be subject to the Revision and Controul of the Congress.

No State shall, without the Consent of Congress, lay any Duty of Tonnage, keep Troops, or Ships of War in time of Peace, enter into any Agreement or Compact with another State, or with a foreign Power, or engage in War, unless actually invaded, or in such imminent Danger as will not admit of delay.

Article. II.

Section. 1. The executive Power shall be vested in a President of the United States of America. He shall hold his Office during the Term of four Years, and, together with the Vice President, chosen for the same Term, be elected, as follows

Each State shall appoint, in such Manner as the Legislature thereof may direct, a Number of Electors, equal to the whole Number of Senators and Representatives to which the State may be entitled in the Congress: but no Senator or Representative, or Person holding an Office of Trust or Profit under the United States, shall be appointed an Elector.

The Electors shall meet in their respective States, and vote by Ballot for two Persons, of whom one at least shall not be an Inhabitant of the same State with themselves. And they shall make a List of all the Persons voted for, and of the Number of Votes for each; which List they shall sign and certify, and transmit sealed to the Seat of the Government of the United States, directed to the President of the Senate. The President of the Senate shall, in the Presence of the Senate and House of Representatives, open all the Certificates, and the Votes shall then be counted. The Person having the greatest Number of Votes shall be the President, if such Number be a Majority of the whole Number of Electors appointed; and if there be more than one who have such Majority, and have an equal Number of Votes, then the House of Representatives shall immediately chuse by Ballot one of them for President; and if no Person have a Majority, then from the five highest on the List the said House shall in like Manner chuse the President. But in chusing the President, the Votes shall be taken by States, the Representation from each State having one Vote; a quorum for this Purpose shall consist of a Member or Members from two thirds of the States, and a Majority of all the States shall be necessary to a Choice. In every Case, after the Choice of the President, the Person having the greatest Number of Votes of the Electors shall be the Vice President. But if there should remain two or more who have equal Votes, the Senate shall chose from them by Ballot the Vice President.

The Congress may determine the Time of chusing the Electors, and the Day on which they shall give their votes; which Day shall be the same throughout the United States.

No Person except a natural born Citizen, or a Citizen of the United States, at the time of the Adoption of this Constitution, shall be eligible to the Office of President; neither shall any person be eligible to that Office who shall not have attained to the Age of thirty five Years, and been fourteen Years a Resident within the United States.

In Case of the Removal of the President from Office, or of his Death, Resignation, or Inability to discharge the Powers and Duties of the said Office, the Same shall devolve on the Vice President, and the Congress may by Law provide for the Case of Removal, Death, Resignation or Inability, both of the President and Vice President, declaring what Officer shall then act as President, and such Officer shall act accordingly, until the Disability be removed, or a President shall be elected.

The President shall, at stated Times, receive for his Services, a Compensation, which shall neither be encreased nor diminished during the Period for which he shall have been elected, and he shall not receive within that Period any other Emolument from the United States, or any of them.

Before he enter on the Execution of his Office, he shall take the following Oath or Affirmation:—"I do solemnly swear (or affirm) that I will faithfully execute the Office of President of the United States, and will to the best of my Ability, preserve, protect and defend the Constitution of the United States."

Section. 2. The President shall be Commander in Chief of the Army and Navy of the United States, and of the Militia of the several States, when called into the actual Service of the United States; he may require the Opinion, in writing, of the principal Officer in each of the executive Departments, upon any Subject relating to the Duties of their respective Offices, and he shall have Power to grant Reprieves and Pardons for Offenses against the United States, except in Cases of Impeachment.

He shall have Power, by and with the Advice and Consent of the Senate, to make Treaties, provided two thirds of the Senators present concur; and he shall nominate, and by and with the Advice and Consent of the Senate, shall appoint Ambassadors, other public Ministers and Consuls, Judges of the supreme Court, and all other Officers of the United States, whose Appointments are not herein otherwise provided for, and which shall be established by Law; but the Congress may by Law vest the Appointment of such inferior Officers, as they think proper, in the President alone, in the Courts of Law, or in the Heads of Departments.

The President shall have Power to fill up all Vacancies that may happen during the Recess of the Senate, by granting Commissions which shall expire at the End of their next Session.

Section. 3. He shall from time to time give to the Congress Information of the State of the Union, and recommend to their Consideration such Measures as he shall judge necessary and expedient; he may, on extraordinary Occasions, convene both Houses, or either of them, and in Case of Disagreement between them, with Respect to the Time of Adjournment, he may adjourn them to such Time as he shall think proper; he shall receive Ambassadors and other public Ministers; he shall take Care that the Laws be faithfully executed, and shall Commission all the Officers of the United States.

Section. 4. The President, Vice President and all Civil Officers of the United States, shall be removed from Office on Impeachment for, and Conviction of, Treason, Bribery, or other high Crimes and Misdemeanors.

Article. III.

Section. 1. The judicial Power of the United States, shall be vested in one supreme Court, and in such inferior Courts as the Congress may from time to time ordain and establish. The Judges, both of the supreme and inferior Courts, shall hold their Offices during good Behaviour, and shall, at stated Times, receive for their Services, a Compensation, which shall not be diminished during their Continuance in Office.

Section. 2. The judicial Power shall extend to all Cases, in Law and Equity, arising under this Constitution, the Laws of the United States, and Treaties made, or which shall be made, under their Authority;—to all Cases affecting Ambassadors, other public Ministers and Consuls;—to all Cases of admiralty and maritime Jurisdiction;—to Controversies to which the United States shall be a Party;—to Controversies between two or more States;—between a State and Citizens of another State;—between Citizens of different States;—between Citizens of the same State claiming Lands under Grants of different States, and between a State, or the Citizens thereof, and foreign States, Citizens or Subjects.

In all Cases affecting Ambassadors, other public Ministers and Consuls, and those in which a State shall be Party, the supreme Court shall have original Jurisdiction. In all the other Cases before mentioned, the supreme Court shall have appellate Jurisdiction, both as to Law and Fact, with such Exceptions, and under such Regulations as the Congress shall make.

The Trial of all Crimes, except in Cases of Impeachment, shall be by Jury; and such Trial shall be held in the State where the said Crimes shall have been committed; but when not committed within any State, the Trial shall be at such Place or Places as the Congress may by Law have directed.

Section. 3. Treason against the United States, shall consist only in levying War against them, or in adhering to their Enemies, giving them Aid and Comfort. No Person shall be convicted of Treason unless on the Testimony of two Witnesses to the same overt Act, or on Confession in open Court. The Congress shall have Power to declare the Punishment of Treason, but no Attainder of Treason shall work Corruption of Blood, or Forfeiture except during the Life of the Person attainted.

Article. IV.

Section. 1. Full Faith and Credit shall be given in each State to the public Acts, Records, and judicial Proceedings of every other State. And the Congress may by general Laws prescribe the Manner in which such Acts, Records and Proceedings shall be proved, and the Effect thereof.

Section. 2. The Citizens of each State shall be entitled to all Privileges and Immunities of Citizens in the several States.

A Person charged in any State with Treason, Felony, or other Crime, who shall flee from Justice, and be found in another State, shall on Demand of the executive Authority of the State from which he fled, be delivered up, to be removed to the State having Jurisdiction of the Crime.

No Person held to Service or Labour in one State, under the Laws thereof, escaping into another, shall, in Consequence of any Law or Regulation therein, be discharged from such Service or Labour, but shall be delivered up on Claim of the Party to whom such Service or Labour may be due.

Section. 3. New States may be admitted by the Congress into this Union; but no new State shall be formed or erected within the Jurisdiction of any other State; nor any State be formed by the Junction of two or more States, or Parts of States, without the Consent of the Legislatures of the States concerned as well as of the Congress.

The Congress shall have Power to dispose of and make all needful Rules and Regulations respecting the Territory or other Property belonging to the United States; and nothing in this Constitution shall be so construed as to Prejudice any Claims of the United States, or of any particular State.

Section. 4. The United States shall guarantee to every State in this Union a Republican Form of Government, and shall protect each of them against Invasion; and on Application of the Legislature, or of the Executive (when the Legislature cannot be convened) against domestic Violence.

ARTICLE. V.

The Congress, whenever two thirds of both Houses shall deem it necessary, shall propose Amendments to this Constitution, or, on the Application of the Legislatures of two thirds of the several States, shall call a Convention for proposing Amendments, which, in either Case, shall be valid to all Intents and Purposes, as Part of this Constitution, when ratified by the Legislatures of three fourths of the several States, or by Conventions in three fourths thereof, as the one or the other Mode of Ratification may be proposed by the Congress; Provided that no Amendment which may be made prior to the Year One thousand eight hundred and eight shall in any Manner affect the first and fourth Clauses in the Ninth Section of the first Article; and that no State, without its Consent, shall be deprived of its equal Suffrage in the Senate.

ARTICLE. VI.

All Debts contracted and Engagements entered into, before the Adoption of this Constitution, shall be as valid against the United States under this Constitution, as under the Confederation.

This Constitution, and the Laws of the United States which shall be made in Pursuance thereof; and all Treaties made, or which shall be made, under the Authority of the United States, shall be the supreme Law of the Land; and the Judges in every State shall be bound thereby, any Thing in the Constitution or Laws of any State to the Contrary notwithstanding.

The Senators and Representatives before mentioned, and the Members of the several State Legislatures, and all executive and judicial Officers, both of the United States and of the several States, shall be bound by Oath or Affirmation, to support this Constitution; but no religious Test shall ever be required as a Qualification to any Office or public Trust under the United States.

ARTICLE. VII.

The Ratification of the Conventions of nine States, shall be sufficient for the Establishment of this Constitution between the States so ratifying the Same.

done in Convention by the Unanimous Consent of the States present the Seventeenth Day of September in the Year of our Lord one thousand seven hundred and Eighty seven and of the Independence of the United States of America the Twelfth In witness where of We have hereunto subscribed our Names, Go. Washington—President. and deputy from Virginia

AMENDMENTS TO THE CONSTITUTION

Amendment [I]*ᵛ

Congress shall make no law respecting an establishment of religion, or prohibiting the free exercise thereof; or abridging the freedom of speech, or of the press; or the right of the People peaceably to assemble, and to petition the Government for a redress of grievances.
[Ratified December 15, 1791]

Amendment [II]

A well regulated Militia, being necessary to the security of a free State, the right of the people to keep and bear Arms, shall not be infringed.
[Ratified December 15, 1791]

Amendment [III]

No Soldier shall, in time of peace be quartered in any house, without the consent of the Owner, nor in time of war, but in a manner to be prescribed by law.
[Ratified December 15, 1791]

ᵛ* Brackets enclosing an amendment number indicate that the number was not specifically assigned in the resolution proposing the amendment.
ᵛ

Amendment [IV]

The right of the people to be secure in their persons, houses, papers, and effects, against unreasonable searches and seizures, shall not be violated, and no Warrants shall issue, but upon probable cause, supported by Oath or affirmation, and particularly describing the place to be searched, and the persons or things to be seized.
[Ratified December 15, 1791]

Amendment [V]

No person shall be held to answer for a capital, or otherwise infamous crime, unless on a presentment or indictment of a Grand Jury, except in cases arising in the land or naval forces, or in the Militia, when in actual service in time of War or public danger; nor shall any person be subject for the same offence to be twice put in jeopardy of life or limb; nor shall be compelled in any criminal case to be a witness against himself, nor be deprived of life, liberty, or property, without due process of law; nor shall private property be taken for public use, without just compensation.
[Ratified December 15, 1791]

Amendment [VI]

In all criminal prosecutions, the accused shall enjoy the right to a speedy and public trial, by an impartial jury of the State and district wherein the crime shall have been committed, which district shall have been previously ascertained by law, and to be informed of the nature and cause of the accusation; to be confronted with the witnesses against him; to have compulsory process for obtaining witnesses in his favor, and to have the Assistance of Counsel for his defence.
[Ratified December 15, 1791]

Amendment [VII]

In Suits at common law, where the value in controversy shall exceed twenty dollars, the right of trial by jury shall be preserved, and no fact tried by a jury, shall be otherwise re-examined in any Court of the United States, than according to the rules of the common law.
[Ratified December 15, 1791]

Amendment [VIII]

Excessive bail shall not be required, nor excessive fines imposed, nor cruel and unusual punishments inflicted.
[Ratified December 15, 1791]

Amendment [IX]

The enumeration in the Constitution, of certain rights, shall not be construed to deny or disparage others retained by the people.
[Ratified December 15, 1791]

Amendment [X]

The powers not delegated to the United States by the Constitution, nor prohibited by it to the States, are reserved to the States respectively, or to the people.
[Ratified December 15, 1791]

Amendment [XI]

The Judicial power of the United States shall not be construed to extend to any suit in law or equity, commenced or prosecuted against one of the United States by Citizens of another State, or by Citizens or Subjects of any Foreign State.
[Ratified January 23, 1798]

Amendment [XII]

The Electors shall meet in their respective states and vote by ballot for President and Vice-President, one of whom, at least, shall not be an inhabitant of the same state with themselves; they shall name in their ballots the person voted for as President, and in distinct ballots the person voted for as Vice-President, and they shall make distinct lists of all persons voted for as President, and of all persons voted for as Vice-President, and of the number of votes for each, which lists they shall sign and certify, and transmit sealed to the seat of the government of the United States, directed to the President of the Senate;—The President of the Senate shall, in the presence of the Senate and House of Representatives, open all the certificates and the votes shall then be counted;—The person having the greatest number of votes for President, shall be the President, if such number be a majority of the whole number of Electors appointed; and if no person have such majority, then from the persons having the highest numbers not exceeding three on the list of those voted for as President, the House of Representatives shall choose immediately by ballot, the President. But in choosing the President, the votes shall be taken by states, the representation from each state having one vote; a quorum for this purpose shall consist of a member or members from two-thirds of the states, and a majority of all the states shall be necessary to a choice. And if the House of Representatives shall not choose a President whenever the right of choice shall devolve upon them, before the fourth day of March next following, then the Vice-President shall act as President, as in the case of the death or other constitutional disability of the President.—The

person having the greatest number of votes as Vice-President, shall be the Vice-President, if such number be a majority of the whole number of Electors appointed, and if no person have a majority, then from the two highest numbers on the list, the Senate shall choose the Vice-President; a quorum for the purpose shall consist of two-thirds of the whole number of Senators, and a majority of the whole number shall be necessary to a choice. But no person constitutionally ineligible to the office of President shall be eligible to that of Vice-President of the United States.
[Ratified June 15, 1804]

Amendment [XIII]

Section 1. Neither slavery nor involuntary servitude, except as a punishment for crime whereof the party shall have been duly convicted, shall exist within the United States, or any place subject to their jurisdiction.

Section 2. Congress shall have power to enforce this article by appropriate legislation.
[Ratified December 6, 1865]

Amendment [XIV]

Section 1. All persons born or naturalized in the United States and subject to the jurisdiction thereof, are citizens of the United States and of the State wherein they reside. No State shall make or enforce any law which shall abridge the privileges or immunities of citizens of the United States; nor shall any State deprive any person of life, liberty, or property, without due process of law; nor deny to any person within its jurisdiction the equal protection of the laws.

Section 2. Representatives shall be apportioned among the several States according to their respective numbers, counting the whole number of persons in each State, excluding Indians not taxed. But when the right to vote at any election for the choice of electors for President and Vice President of the United States, Representatives in Congress, the Executive and Judicial officers of a State, or the members of the Legislature thereof, is denied to any of the male inhabitants of such State, being twenty-one years of age, and citizens of the United States, or in any way abridged, except for participation in rebellion, or other crime, the basis of representation therein shall be reduced in the proportion which the number of such male citizens shall bear to the whole number of male citizens twenty-one years of age in such State.

Section 3. No person shall be a Senator or Representative in Congress, or elector of President and Vice President, or hold any office, civil or military, under the United States, or under any State, who, having previously taken an oath, as a member of Congress, or as an officer of the United States, or as a member of any State legislature, or as an executive or judicial officer of any State, to support the Constitution of the United States, shall have engaged in insurrection or rebellion against the same, or given aid or comfort to the enemies thereof. But Congress may by a vote of two-thirds of each House, remove such disability.

Section 4. The validity of the public debt of the United States, authorized by law, including debts incurred for payment of pensions and bounties for services in suppressing insurrection or rebellion, shall not be questioned. But neither the United States nor any State shall assume or pay any debt or obligation incurred in aid of insurrection or rebellion against the United States, or any claim for the loss or emancipation of any slave; but all such debts, obligations and claims shall be held illegal and void.

Section 5. The Congress shall have power to enforce, by appropriate legislation, the provisions of this article.
[Ratified July 9, 1868]

Amendment [XV]

Section 1. The right of citizens of the United States to vote shall not be denied or abridged by the United States or by any State on account of race, color, or previous condition of servitude.

Section 2. The Congress shall have power to enforce this article by appropriate legislation.
[Ratified February 2, 1870]

Amendment [XVI]

The Congress shall have power to lay and collect taxes on incomes, from whatever source derived, without apportionment among the several States, and without regard to any census or enumeration.
[Ratified February 3, 1913]

Amendment [XVII]

The Senate of the United States shall be composed of two Senators from each State, elected by the people thereof, for six years; and each Senator shall have one vote. The electors in each State shall have the qualifications requisite for electors of the most numerous branch of the State legislatures.

When vacancies happen in the representation of any State in the Senate, the executive authority of such State shall issue writs of election to fill such vacancies; *Provided*, That the legislature of any State may empower the executive thereof to make temporary appointments until the people fill the vacancies by election as the legislature may direct.

This amendment shall not be so construed as to affect the election or term of any Senator chosen before it becomes valid as part of the Constitution. [Ratified April 8, 1913]

Amendment [XVIII]

Section 1. After one year from the ratification of this article the manufacture, sale, or transportation of intoxicating liquors within, the importation thereof into, or the exportation thereof from the United States and all territory subject to the jurisdiction thereof for beverage purposes is hereby prohibited.

Section 2. The Congress and the several States shall have concurrent power to enforce this article by appropriate legislation.

Section 3. This article shall be inoperative unless it shall have been ratified as an amendment to the Constitution by the legislatures of the several States, as provided in the Constitution, within seven years from the date of the submission hereof to the States by the Congress. [Ratified January 16, 1919]

Amendment [XIX]

The right of citizens of the United States to vote shall not be denied or abridged by the United States or by any State on account of sex.

Congress shall have power to enforce this article by appropriate legislation. [Ratified August 18, 1920]

Amendment [XX]

Section 1. The terms of the President and Vice President shall end at noon on the 20th day of January, and the terms of Senators and Representatives at noon on the 3d day of January, of the years in which such terms would have ended if this article had not been ratified; and the terms of their successors shall then begin.

Section 2. The Congress shall assemble at least once in every year, and such meeting shall begin at noon on the 3d day of January, unless they shall by law appoint a different day.

Section 3. If, at the time fixed for the beginning of the term of the President, the President elect shall have died, the Vice President elect shall become President. If a President shall not have been chosen before the time fixed for the beginning of his term, or if the President elect shall have failed to qualify, then the Vice President elect shall act as President until a President shall have qualified; and the Congress may by law provide for the case wherein neither a President elect nor a Vice President elect shall have qualified, declaring who shall then act as President, or the manner in which one who is to act shall be selected, and such person shall act accordingly until a President or Vice President shall have qualified.

Section 4. The Congress may by law provide for the case of the death of any of the persons for whom the House of Representatives may choose a President whenever the right of choice shall have devolved upon them, and for the case of the death of any of the persons from whom the Senate may choose a Vice President whenever the right of choice shall have devolved upon them.

Section 5. Sections 1 and 2 shall take effect on the 15th day of October following the ratification of this article.

Section 6. This article shall be inoperative unless it shall have been ratified as an amendment to the Constitution by the legislatures of three-fourths of the several States within seven years from the date of its submission.
[Ratified January 23, 1933]

Amendment [XXI]

Section 1. The eighteenth article of amendment to the Constitution of the United States is hereby repealed.

Section 2. The transportation or importation into any State, Territory or possession of the United States for delivery or use therein of intoxicating liquors, in violation of the laws thereof, is hereby prohibited.

Section 3. This article shall be inoperative unless it shall have been ratified as an amendment to the Constitution by conventions in the several States, as provided in the Constitution, within seven years from the date of the submission thereof to the States by the Congress.
[Ratified December 5, 1933]

Amendment [XXII]

Section 1. No person shall be elected to the office of the President more than twice, and no person who has held the office of President, or acted as President, for more than two years of a term to which some other person was elected President shall be elected to the office of the President more than once. But this Article shall not apply to any person holding the office of President when this Article was proposed by the Congress, and shall not prevent any person who may be holding the office of President, or acting as President, during the term within which this Article becomes operative from holding the office of President or acting as President during the remainder of such term.

Section 2. This Article shall be inoperative unless it shall have been ratified as an amendment to the Constitution by the legislatures of threefourths of the several States within seven years from the date of its submission to the States by the Congress.
[Ratified March 1, 1951]

Amendment [XXIII]

Section 1. The District constituting the seat of Government of the United States shall appoint in such manner as the Congress may direct:

A number of electors of President and Vice President equal to the whole number of Senators and Representatives in Congress to which the District would be entitled if it were a State, but in no event more than the least populous State; they shall be in addition to those appointed by the States, but they shall be considered, for the purposes of the election of President and Vice President, to be electors appointed by a State; and they shall meet in the District and perform such duties as provided by the twelfth article of amendment.

Section 2. The Congress shall have power to enforce this article by appropriate legislation.
[Ratified April 3, 1961]

Amendment [XXIV]

Section. 1. The right of citizens of the United States to vote in any primary or other election for President or Vice President, for electors for President or Vice President, or for Senator or Representative in Congress, shall not be denied or abridged by the United States or any State by reason of failure to pay any poll tax or other tax.

Section 2. The Congress shall have power to enforce this article by appropriate legislation.
[Ratified January 23, 1964]

Amendment [XXV]

Section 1. In case of the removal of the President from office or his death or resignation, the Vice President shall become President.

Section 2. Whenever there is a vacancy in the office of the Vice President, the President shall nominate a Vice President who shall take office upon confirmation by a majority vote of both houses of Congress.

Section 3. Whenever the President transmits to the President pro tempore of the Senate and the Speaker of the House of Representatives his written declaration that he is unable to discharge the powers and duties of his office, and until he transmits to them a written declaration to the contrary, such powers and duties shall be discharged by the Vice President as Acting President.

Section 4. Whenever the Vice President and a majority of either the principal officers of the executive department or of such other body as Congress may by law provide, transmit to the President pro tempore of the Senate and the Speaker of the House of Representatives their written declaration that the President is unable to discharge the powers and duties of his office, the

Vice President shall immediately assume the powers and duties of the office as Acting President.

Thereafter, when the President transmits to the President pro tempore of the Senate and the Speaker of the House of Representatives his written declaration that no inability exists, he shall resume the powers and duties of his office unless the Vice President and a majority of either the principal officers of the executive department or of such other body as Congress may by law provide, transmit within four days to the President pro tempore of the Senate and the Speaker of the House of Representatives their written declaration that the President is unable to discharge the powers and duties of his office. Thereupon Congress shall decide the issue, assembling within 48 hours for that purpose if not in session. If the Congress, within 21 days after receipt of the latter written declaration, or, if Congress is not in session, within 21 days after Congress is required to assemble, determines that the President is unable to discharge the powers and duties of his office, the Vice President shall continue to discharge the same as Acting President; otherwise, the President shall resume the powers and duties of his office.
[Ratified February 11, 1967]

Amendment [XXVI]

Section 1. The right of citizens of the United States, who are 18 years of age or older, to vote shall not be denied or abridged by the United States or any state on account of age.

Section 2. The Congress shall have the power to enforce this article by appropriate legislation.
[Ratified July 5, 1971]

Amendment [XXVII]

No law, varying the compensation for the services of the Senators and Representatives, shall take effect, until an election of Representatives shall have intervened.
[Ratified May 5, 1992]

9 781792 406478